Good Gardens Guide 1992

GOOD
GARDENS
GUIDE 1992

*Over 1,000 of the best gardens
in Great Britain and Ireland*

EDITED BY GRAHAM ROSE AND PETER KING

VERMILION
LONDON

Published by Vermilion
an imprint of the Random Century Group
Random Century House 20 Vauxhall Bridge Road
London SW1V 2SA

First impression 1992

A catalogue record for this book may be found in the British
Library.

ISBN 0 09 175240 X

Managing Editor   Sarah Bailey
Proofreader   Lizzie Boyd
Disk Editor   Angie Hipkin
Designer   Gwyn Lewis
Cover design   Martin Hendry
Cover photograph of Wootton Place   Hugh Palmer
with thanks to Country Living Magazine

Typeset from authors' disks by Saxon Printing Limited, Derby

Printed and bound by The Bath Press, Avon

Contents

Acknowledgements

Our thanks to everyone who has helped with the preparation of the *Guide* – to owners, custodians, professional gardening staff, and many others. In particular, we thank our inspectors and those who advised them. Some of those who have given advice do not wish to be listed, and, although anonymous they have been every bit as valuable. We are also obliged to staff of The National Trust and The National Trust for Scotland for their cooperation. The names which follow include inspectors (but not all of them) and advisors: Rosie Atkins, Mrs David Barnes, Kerry Bate, Kathryn Bradley-Hole, Cecil Brown, Adam Caplin, Anne Chamberlain, Sarah Coles, Anne Collins, Beatrice Cowan, Simon Cramp, Jo and Rosie Currie, the late Michael Davis, Rosemary Dodgson, Daphne Dormer, Lady Edmonstone, Daphne Fisher, Michael and Freda Fisher, Lucy Gent, Alison Gregory, Elizabeth Hamilton, Steve Hipkin, Judith Hitchings, Hilary Hodgson, Jackie Hone, Sophie Hughes, Pam Hummer, Judith Jenkins, Vanessa Johnston, Rosemarie Johnstone, Jo Kenaghan, Jean Laughton, Charles Lyte, Janet Macnutt, Michael Mallett, Pat McCrostie, Deirdre McSharry, Lucinda Parry, John and Carol Pease, Victoria Petrie-Hay, Stephen Player, Lorna Ramsay, Christopher Rogers, George and Jane Scott, Gillian Sladen, Dr Gordon Smith, Vera Taggart, Sally Tamplin, Bill Tobias, Michael Tooley, Myra Wheeldon, Cynthia Wickham. The editors also express their appreciation of the dedicated assistance of Lizzie Boyd, Angie Hipkin and Wendy Turner.

Introduction

This is the third annual edition of the *Guide*, containing a considerable number of gardens which were not in the 1991 book, as well as deleting those that, for one reason or another, it was not appropriate to repeat. In all over 150 'new' gardens are listed this year.

All the gardens listed are open to the public and there is an emphasis on those which are open frequently or 'by appointment' over several months of the year. Some owners are only able or willing to open once or twice and certain gardens of this kind are included on merit; we hope that such owners may be encouraged to open more frequently if they can. The award of star rating to those gardens which our inspectors believe to be of particular interest continues this year, though there have been some changes from previous editions of the *Guide*, with a few gardens up-rated and others the reverse. Some 'new' gardens are given ★ rating on their début, but where gardens are open to the public for the first time we have felt it right to withhold ★ rating until they have been visited again next year.

We decided to compile this guide because, both of us being by trade and by inclination avid garden visitors, we were constantly put off by the necessity of consulting several books at once in order to obtain the basic information needed to find the gardens of our choice. Why couldn't the facts be collected into one book? Small enough to keep in the car and with just enough information to whet our appetite, we thought it should also give some indication of the various features to be found so that choices could be made between the many wonderful offerings available to the public on a given day.

The result is a guide which we know is subjective. It is a compilation of the work of a large number of inspectors, each with different gardening interests, each with his or her favourites in the areas on which they have concentrated. This subjectivity we believe to be a benefit and we hope that our inspectors' enthusiasm will convey itself to the reader in a way which the modest descriptions written by the garden-owners themselves often fail to achieve.

Far more gardens are open to the public in the affluent south than elsewhere, and we have therefore tried to strike a balance by making a particular effort to find good gardens in other parts of the country. The same considerations apply to London and our other large cities where live huge numbers of garden lovers without gardens of their own. They find it hard to satisfy their craving for the luxury of being able to have a green thought in a green shade and our inspectors have therefore tried to help them by including parks and other public spaces which may well not be gardens in the strictest sense of the word. For this reason and others, comparison of standards between one county and another are bound to be uneven.

We have not, in general, included gardens which appeared to our inspectors to require substantial improvement, although sometimes their grading or comments indicate that a garden might have been given a higher rating if, for instance, its maintenance could be improved. Conversely the absence of a garden from our lists does not by any means indicate that it is not praiseworthy, as exclusion might have happened for all kinds of other reasons, our ignorance being the most probable.

Graham Rose and *Peter King*, London 1992

The Garden Scene

Is it a sign of health or decay that while 450 gardens dropped out of the National Gardens Scheme openings in 1991, more than that number were added, and though some 50 or so have been deleted from the *Good Gardens'* list, over 150 new ones have been included? The answer is complicated. There are a number of reasons for owners to close gardens once open to the public. Houses are sold or owners become too ill to manage their gardens. When, like that noble plantsman John Codrington who died in 1991, they leave their gardens to others, must this mean the death, too, of their creation?

'Lost' gardens are often fine gardens. What will happen to Chastleton (up for sale), Abbey Leix in Ireland (probably for sale), Pusey (sold and being extensively refurbished) and dozens more? Like Sir Geoffrey Jellicoe's famous garden at Sutton Place, they may, after sale, be open to the public no longer. There is of course no public right to be able to view privately-owned gardens but it is a sad fact that so many disappear from view. Twenty years ago in his excellent little book *The English Garden*, Edward Hyams made a personal list of about 200 'notable' ones open to the public of which only half are now available. It is doubtful if 100 new 'notable' gardens have become available since 1970 to make up that loss.

In any event, the 'lost' properties are in many cases such a significant part of our garden heritage that it is highly regrettable that they are no longer available to the public at large, and even worse if they have become building sites or wildernesses. Gardens can be 'listed', but there is no system for giving them the financial assistance that is rightly meted out to historic houses. Fortunately, great gardens are often attached to heritage houses, and thus saved with them, but that system does not benefit memorable gardens which are part of less distinguished properties.

Enlightened patronage is required. The church, the crown and the nobility made sure in the past that their heritage was protected and enlarged. The delightful *nouveau riches* quickly followed with *largesse* which was often on an equal if not more generous scale. Today we must look to the state as patron, but alas too many of our political masters and mistresses are philistines. Amongst these is the Department of the Environment which has announced its intention of 'laying off' all 340 staff in the London royal parks and has dilly-dallied for more than a year about the appointment of a royal bailiff. The training school which provided new staff has been closed. The aim is to privatise the work and bring in extra cash by introducing 'commercial activities' into the parks. That ardent watchdog Marcus Binney describes the situation as 'serious' and calls for widespread and sustained debate.

Fortunately The National Trust can often step into the breach to protect the grander properties. Their combination of commercial activities and environ-mental development has so far been a sensitive one. For example, at Fountains Abbey and Studley Royal they have spent and are still to spend several millions with the result that this fine site drew over 300,000 visitors last year. How long The Trust will be able to continue investment on this scale is doubtful and already they have been accused of having more people fundraising in their offices than working in their gardens. Such criticisms are easy to make by contrasting the present position with that of 100 years ago when there were perhaps 25 gardeners working in the average Stately Home (though we have to remind ourselves that this was before the invention of labour-saving machinery).

We are told that there is a shortage of professionally-trained gardeners in Britain able and, or, willing to work on our finest properties. The position is so serious that the Historic Houses Association was forced to call a conference in 1991 to discuss the matter. Some might say that its 13,000 owner-members could probably make a start by paying their staff better, otherwise, come 1992, many of our brilliant professionals will probably find their way to European employment.

These high-class problems of the heritage garden may attract more attention – and visitors – than some of the smaller but equally fine gardens in Britain, but there are two important reasons why our minds should be focussed on the latter just as keenly. First, the 'average' garden in Britain has as much variety and interest as any elsewhere in the world and, despite the difficulty of attracting or affording professional help, the standard of plantsmanship and design has remained high. When these smaller, non-heritage gardens open to the public, visitors are often heard to comment on the contrast between their plant and shrub varieties and the boring standardisation of the offerings of commercial garden centres. Swapping plants and cuttings remains a national hobby. It is therefore important that everything be done to encourage the smaller garden and to discourage (what is all too common in the so-called 'front' garden) its replacement by low-maintenance concrete paving stones.

Young people, despite their notorious aversion to gardening, must be encouraged to enjoy gardens. One positive sign has been the setting up of a trust to turn the asphalt of school playgrounds into gardens. Playgrounds, if put end to end, would cover some 120,000 acres of Britain, an area the size of the New Forest. Already some 4,000 school authorities are said to be supporting this welcome initiative towards broadening juvenile interest in horticulture.

The second reason for directing attention towards the 'average' garden and away from the grand garden is that as a nation we simply are far too negative about the new and far too dedicated to the old. We must stop looking so determinedly backwards. By all means cherish our heritage but must we turn Great Britain into Great Museum? By their nature, the 'heritage' gardens are museum pieces and the efforts of owners and of The National Trust is primarily directed towards mummification, and there is nothing wrong with that. But reverence for the past must be matched by appreciation of the innovative. Some interesting stylistic ideas have been developed in relatively modest gardens though it is true that the great original designers like Sir Geoffrey Jellicoe have usually had the benefit of the patronage of the rich or the developer. Those who garden on a smaller scale must be encouraged to develop new ideas by experimenting with novel plantings and designing for the twenty-first century rather than the eighteenth. If this encouragement is not forthcoming, the average British garden could become a run-down museum exhibit and we shall have to look in the future to the Americans and Europeans for the innovative ideas which will shape the gardens of the centuries to come.

Two-starred Gardens ★★

BERKSHIRE
Folly Farm
The Old Rectory

BUCKINGHAMSHIRE
Ascott
Cliveden
The Manor House, Bledlow
Stowe Landscape Garden
Waddesdon Manor

CAMBRIDGESHIRE
Peckover House
University Botanic Garden

CHESHIRE
Tatton Park

CORNWALL
Caerhays Castle Garden
Trebah
Tresco Abbey
Trewithen

CUMBRIA
Holehird
Holker Hall
Levens Hall

DERBYSHIRE
Chatsworth

DEVON
Castle Drogo
Coleton Fishacre Garden
Knightshayes
Marwood Hill
Rosemoor Garden

DORSET
Abbotsbury Gardens
Cranborne Manor Gardens
Forde Abbey
Shute House

ESSEX
Saling Hall

GLOUCESTERSHIRE
Hidcote Manor Garden
Kiftsgate Court
Westbury Court Garden
Westonbirt Arboretum

HAMPSHIRE
Exbury Gardens
Mottisfont Abbey
The Sir Harold Hillier
    Garden and Arboretum

Ventnor Botanic Garden

HERTFORDSHIRE
Hatfield House

KENT
Belmont
Hever Castle
Sissinghurst Castle

LEICESTERSHIRE
Wartnaby Gardens

LONDON (Greater)
Chiswick House
Ham House
Hampton Court Palace
Royal Botanic Gardens
    (Kew)
Syon Park

MERSEYSIDE
Ness Gardens

NORFOLK
Blickling Hall

NORTHAMPTONSHIRE
Cottesbrooke Hall

OXFORDSHIRE
23 Beech Croft Road
Blenheim Palace
Greys Court
Oxford Botanic Garden
Rousham House

SHROPSHIRE
Hodnet Hall

SOMERSET
Greencombe

SUFFOLK
Helmingham Hall
Shrubland Hall
Somerleyton Hall

SURREY
Painshill Park
Royal Horticultural Society's
    Garden
The Savill Garden
The Valley Gardens

SUSSEX (East)
Great Dixter

SUSSEX (West)
Leonardslee Gardens

Nymans
Standen
Wakehurst Place Garden

WILTSHIRE
Iford Manor
Stourhead

YORKSHIRE (North)
Castle Howard
Studley Royal and Fountains
    Abbey

IRELAND
Annes Grove
Ardnamona
Birr Castle Desmesne
Butterstream
Castlewellan National
    Arboretum
Glenveagh Castle
Ilnacullin
Mount Congreve
Mount Stewart House,
    Garden and Temple of
    the Winds
National Botanic Gardens,
    Glasnevin
Rowallane
45 Sandford Road

SCOTLAND
Brodick Castle
Castle of Mey
Castle Kennedy and
    Lochinch Gardens
Crarae Glen Garden
Crathes Castle Garden
Culzean Castle
Drummond Castle
Inverewe Garden
Little Sparta
Logan Botanic Garden
Mellerstain
Pitmedden Garden
Royal Botanic Garden
Younger Botanic Garden

WALES
Bodnant Garden
Clyne Gardens
Dyffryn Botanic Garden
Newcastle House
Powis Castle

How to Use the Guide

The *Guide* is arranged by counties. Within each county the gardens are listed alphabetically by the normal name of the garden/house. The index at the end of the book can also be used to find a garden whose name only is known to the reader.

The county maps show numbers which refer to those given against each garden entry. For detailed information about how to reach gardens use the data given in the garden entry itself. The maps at the end of the *Guide* can be used to locate gardens in neighbouring counties which may be close enough to the named county to be visited at the same time.

The information given is believed to be correct at the time of going to press but changes do occur – properties sold or ownership varied and routes improved by motorway extensions etc. There may also be closures of over-visited properties, or limitations imposed on opening times. Prices of entry may be varied without notice.

Gardens in Great Britain which are open by courtesy of the owners for one of the many interested charities are included here where the gardens are of special interest even if, as on some occasions, they are open in this way on only one day in the year. However, many such gardens are also open at other specific times, such as for local charities or church restoration funds, and it is not generally possible to give dates for these locally-publicised openings. Readers should note that other nearby gardens, not listed in this guide for one reason or another, may well be open at similar times to those listed.

Readers are invited to advise the *Guide* of any gardens which in their opinion should be listed in future editions, and where possible arrangements will be made to review such suggestions.

It has not been possible for *Guide* inspectors to visit every garden which is open to the public at some time in the year, and certain gardens in the *Guide* may not have been visited for over twelve months. In general, inspections have been made on an anonymous basis to ensure objectivity. Readers who would like to add information about gardens listed are warmly invited to write to the *Guide* with their comments, all of which will be acknowledged, and may be used in future editions without attribution.

Detailed use of the *Guide*

Address This is the address given by the owner or some other reputable source.

Telephone Except where owners have specifically requested them to be excluded, telephone numbers to which enquiries may be directed are given for each property. To maintain the support and cooperation of private owners it is suggested that the telephone be used with discretion. Where visits are by appointment, the telephone can of course be used except where written application is specifically requested. Code numbers are given in brackets. In all cases where visits by parties are proposed, owners should be advised in advance and arrangements preferably confirmed in writing. For the Republic of Ireland phone 010353 followed by the code (Dublin is 1) followed by the subscriber's number.

Owners Names given are those available at the time of going to press. In the case of The National Trust, some properties may be the homes of tenants of the Trust. Some other gardens are owned or managed by other trusts.

Location This information has been supplied by inspectors and is aimed to be the best available to those travelling by car. The unreliability of train and bus services makes it unrewarding to include details, particularly as many garden visits are made on Sundays. However, a number of properties can be reached by public transport.

Access Times of access given are the best available at the moment of going to press, but some may have been changed subsequently. In the entries, the times given are inclusive – that is, an entry such as May to Sept means that the garden is open from May 1st to Sept 30th inclusive and 2 – 5pm also means that visits will be effective during that period, although some gardens may close to visitors beforehand and it is wise to arrive half an hour before closing time. Please note that many owners will open their gardens to visitors by appointment. They will often arrange to give a personally-conducted tour on these occasions.

Best season These are inspectors' suggestions though the garden concerned may well be highly attractive at other times and usually no garden will be open at a time when it does not merit a visit. The vagaries of climate prevent this information from being anything but a rough guide.

Entrance fees As far as is known, these are correct at times of going to press, but changes may be made without notice. Where there are variations, these will be upwards, but the amount of increase is usually small. Children are often charged at a lower rate, but are expected to be accompanied by an adult. Charges for parties are often at special rates. National Trust charges are explained in their literature with special concessions for members. Accompanied children are normally admitted by the Trust at half-price and this is why no specific charge for children is usually listed for Trust properties. Figures for the Republic of Ireland are given in punts (IR£) which is approximately equal to 85p.

Parking If there is no entry for parking this means no close convenient area available and visitors should allow time to find somewhere suitable.

Refreshments A guide only. Where TEAS is marked, this normally implies that the owners have arranged to serve a simple tea on the property, or near at hand, at reasonable prices during opening hours. An ☆ indicates that the inspector enjoyed a tea of particularly high quality. No entry means that no specific refreshment arrangements are known to the inspector.

Toilet facilities Specific facilities are marked. Where there is no entry there appears to be no specific toilets for visitors and enquiries will have to be directed to staff or owners.

Wheelchairs Inspectors have indicated where they believe a garden can reasonably be negotiated by someone in a wheelchair. No such entry means that the garden is probably unsuitable.

Dogs If dogs are allowed in a car park, or in the property on a lead, this is indicated. No entry means dogs not allowed.

Plants for sale This often means that the plants are grown on the property but this is not always the case as some owners now buy-in plants from a commercial source for re-sale. No entry means plants not normally for sale.

Shop This entry refers to special shops on the premises, such as National Trust shop selling souvenirs etc. No entry means no shop.

House open No entry means that the house is not normally open to the visiting public. Where houses are open, there is often an extra charge, usually indicated here, but again subject to change without notice.

Gardens of special distinction To help give the reader the opinion which inspectors and editors have formed about the status of certain gardens, some 80 properties have been marked with ★★ to indicate that in our opinion these are amongst the finest gardens in the world in terms of design and content. Many are of historic importance but some are of recent origin. Readers will appreciate that direct comparisons cannot be made between a vast estate like Chatsworth with its staff of professional gardeners and a tiny plantsman's garden at a terraced house, although that having been said both may be excellent of their kind. Those gardens which are of very high quality, though not perhaps as unique as the ★★ ones, are given a single ★. The latter gardens will be worth travelling a considerable distance to see, and sometimes the general ambiance of the property as a whole will make the visit especially rewarding. The bulk of the gardens in the *Guide* which are not given a mark of distinction have considerable merit and will be well worth visiting when in the region. Some of them will have distinctive features of design or plant content, noted in the description, which will justify making a special journey.

Northern Ireland:

The National Gardens Scheme does not extend into Northern Ireland, but the local Garden Committee of the National Trust organizes the opening of small private gardens during weekends in spring, summer and early autumn. A leaflet is printed giving times and directions and this may be obtained from the National Trust, Rowallane House, Saintfield, County Down BT24 7LH. (Please enclose a stamped, self-addressed envelope). On all occasions there is a charge for admission (£1.00 or 25p for children). National Trust membership is not valid for these gardens, and dogs are strictly *not* allowed in any of the gardens. The Northern Ireland Tourist Board does not provide any information about gardens in the province, but the Heritage Gardens Committee has issued a booklet describing some of the gardens and parks of outstanding historical importance (some of which are NOT open to the public). *Northern Gardens*, published by Ulster Horticultural Heritage Society, Belfast, is available for £1.50 (p&p included) by writing to Heritage Gardens Committee c/o Institute of Irish Studies, Queen's University, 8 Fitzwilliam Street, Belfast BT9 6AW.

Republic of Ireland:

There is no scheme operated in the Republic of Ireland similar to the National Gardens Scheme and Scottish Gardens Scheme in Britain or to the National Trust Scheme in Northern Ireland. The Irish Tourist Board does, however, issue annually a list of gardens open to the public; this may be obtained by writing to Mary Nash (Heritage), Bord Failte, Baggot Street Bridge, Dublin 2 (enclose an addressed envelope – and 40p (UK stamps) separately or 48p (Irish) stamps separately. This leaflet will give current admission times, entry fees, etc. for gardens in the Republic.

AVON

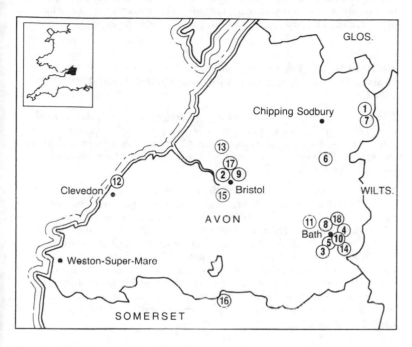

Two-starred gardens are ringed in bold.

BADMINTON ★   1
Chipping Sodbury, Avon.

The Duke and Duchess of Beaufort ✳ *5m E of Chipping Sodbury, B4040, N of M4 junction 18* ✳ *Parking* ✳ *Teas on open day* ✳ *Toilet facilities* ✳ *Suitable for wheelchairs* ✳ *Garden open by appointment and one day in June for charity, 2 – 6pm. Park open all year round but no cars* ✳ *Entrance on charity day: £1.50, OAP £1, children under 5 free*

These two private gardens have been designed in the last five years to the south and east sides of the house. Very cleverly planted, they manage to answer both the grandeur and the muddle of the house. Two conservatories on the east side are exuberant with all the best conservatory plants – large myrtle bushes in tubs and clambering cobaea. On the south side a series of enclosures or 'rooms' contain very successful mixed planting. Vistas running down and across the garden lead the eye through to an urn or doorway and glimpses of further excitement. Lilies burst out from the alchemillas and annual mallows. A cool 'room' contains only blue and white flowers. The furthest part is a heady mass of old-fashioned roses. Work is starting on the walled garden, further from the house, with huge warm brick walls and a monumental gateway. In response to the massive scale of this garden a large allée of laburnum, wisteria and lilac has been erected. The development of this garden should be exciting.

BRISTOL BOTANIC GARDEN 2
Bracken Hill, North Road, Leigh Woods, Bristol, Avon. Tel: (0272) 733682

*University of Bristol * Cross the Suspension Bridge from Clifton, turn first right (North Road) and go ¹/₄m up on the left * Parking * Partly suitable for wheelchairs * Become a Friend and get free plants and seeds. Otherwise plant sales will be held 12th July, 13th Sept, 2 – 5.30 * Open Mon – Fri except Bank Holidays, 9am – 5pm * Entrance: free*

The Botanic Garden moved to this site in 1959 and is very interesting for the keen plantsman. Collections of New Zealand cistus, sempervivums, campanulas. Everything is well labelled and agreeably set out. It aims to be educational, to represent most native trees and shrubs, and particularly the local flora peculiar to the Avon Gorge. Glasshouses contain ferns, orchids, bromeliads, epiphytic cacti, tender bulbs. The African stone plants are fascinating, small succulents resembling pebbles in shape and colour. There are also insectivorous plants and sensitive plants which move when touched. Altogether a fascinating place which needs a lot of support in these hard pressed times – it costs only £10 to become a member of the Association of Friends.

CITY OF BATH BOTANICAL GARDENS 3
Royal Victoria Park, Bath, Avon.

*City of Bath * In Royal Victoria Park * Best season: spring * Parking * Toilet facilities in Royal Victoria Park * Suitable for wheelchairs * Dogs on lead * Open daily, 9am – dusk, Sun, 10am – dusk * Entrance: free*

Located in the city's Royal Victoria Park the botanical gardens are a monument to Victorian taste, with splendid cedars and magnolias, a classical temple (actually 1924) and bridges over a stream and lily pond. Plants are labelled haphazardly and, as with yuccas and ornamental thistles, grow menacingly large in the humid atmosphere. The herbaceous border was replanted in 1990. Entered through a wrought iron gate the Botanic Gardens are a green refuge in the busy seven-acre park.

CLAVERTON MANOR 4
Claverton, Bath, Avon. Tel: (0225) 460503

*The American Museum * 2m SE of Bath off A36, signposted American Museum*

* Parking * Refreshments * Toilet facilities * Partly suitable for wheelchairs
* Herbs for sale * Shop * Museum and New Gallery open * Garden open
28th March to 1st Nov, daily except Mon (but open Bank Holiday Mons) 2 – 5pm,
Bank Holiday Sun and Mon, 11am – 5pm * Entrance: £1 (house and grounds
£4, OAP £3.25, children £2.50) (1991 prices)

The house, designed by Jeffrey Wyatville, and garden are set on the side of the
valley of the Avon in a stunning position with splendid views from the terrace.
Despite the storms of 1989 which brought down the cedar of Lebanon on the
main lawn, and many trees in the park, the grounds display good beech, ilex and
cedars and have been replanted. The rather stark high walls of the house and
the terrace support honeysuckle, clematis and old rose climbers, and fastigiate
yews make strong buttress shapes up the south-facing wall. The Colonial Herb
Garden is modest in size but the little herbarium is popular for seeds, herbs,
tussie-mussies and so on. The Mount Vernon garden, a re-creation of George
Washington's famous garden, with rampant old-fashioned roses, trained pear
trees and box and beech hedges, is surrounded by white palings. There is a
replica of the octagonal garden house used as a school room for Washington's
step-grandchildren. The seven-acre arboretum containing a very fine collection of exclusively native American trees and shrubs is believed to be the only
one of its kind.

CROWE HALL ★   5
Widcombe Hill, Bath, Avon. Tel: (0225) 310322

Mr John Barratt * Behind Bath Spa station off the A36 within walking distance
of station * Best seasons: late March and July * Parking on Widcombe Hill *
Teas * Partly suitable for wheelchairs * Dogs * Plants sometimes for sale *
Open 26th April, 7th June (approximate dates only), 2 – 6pm * Entrance: 70p,
children 30p

These gardens, which extend to 30 acres on the hillside above Widcombe, are
some of the most mysterious and beautiful in Bath. Through the gates there is
an intriguing view of a drive, portico and terrace, and once inside the grounds
few gardens in the area offer so many surprises and delights. As the owner says
'The garden is an island of classical simplicity surrounded by romantic
wilderness'. Around the Regency-style house are Italianate terraces, a pond,
grottos, tunnels, woods, glades, kitchen gardens and a long walk with a stone
statue facing a stunning view of Prior Park, a Palladian mansion, on the horizon.
Vistas and views are a feature of this steeply-banked garden where down one
walk you suddenly come on the roof of the fifteenth-century church of St
Thomas à Becket. The loss of 20 trees in recent storms is regarded as an
improvement by the owner because new vistas have opened up. Beyond the
recently restored grotto is a new meadow garden and an amusing garden
dedicated to Hercules, with a theatrically ferocious hero. Magnificent trees
include mulberries and nut. For its stunning setting in the meadows above and
facing away from Bath and for the romantic ambiance, Crowe Hall is an
experience not to be missed.

DYRHAM PARK ★   6
Nr Chippenham, Avon. Tel: (027582) 2501

The National Trust * 8m N of Bath, 12m E of Bristol on A46. Take M4 junction

18 in direction of Bath * *Parking on grass* * *Refreshments in Orangery and picnics in park* * *Toilet facilities* * *Suitable for wheelchairs on ground floor of house and terrace only. Park suitable but many inclines* * *Dogs in dog walking area on lead only* * *Park open all year (except 25th Dec), 12 noon – 5.30pm or dusk. House and garden open April to 1st Nov, daily except Thurs and Fri, 12 noon – 5.30pm (last admission 5pm)* * *Entrance: Park only £1.40 (house and garden £4.40)*

Only a tiny fragment of the London and Wise extensive 'Dutch' Garden shown in the view by Kip in 1712 survives. The terraces were all smoothed out in the early nineteenth century to form an 'English' landscape of now five mature Spanish chestnut, Lucombe oak, Red oak, Black walnut and ilex. Avenues of elms survived until the mid-1970s when they were wiped out by Dutch elm disease. They have since been replanted with limes. The cascade is still working and one can make out the form of the original garden and enjoy the terrace and the orangery which is almost certainly by Talman. It is the views towards Bristol and the elegance of the 'natural' landscape with the house tucked into the hillside that still make this an outstanding example of English landscape gardening. In all, 263 acres of ancient parkland.

ESSEX HOUSE ★   7
Badminton, Chipping Sodbury, Avon.

Mr and Mrs James Lees-Milne * *1m N of Acton Turville on B4040. M4 junction 18* * *Toilet facilities nearby* * *Partly suitable for wheelchairs* * *Open by written appointment only to the seriously-interested, May to Aug*

Mrs Lees-Milne is to give up having Open Days which she has done for over 20 years but says that she really enjoys showing people who are seriously interested around the garden. Those that are will be impressed. Although not large and dominated by a mammoth cedar of Lebanon which casts a swathe of dry shade across the garden one could spend longer and learn more than in any number of more showy plots. It demonstrates what intelligence in dealing with site, sureness of hand in planting, lightness of touch in design can achieve. This garden is broken up by surprises but always maintains a consistency of thought behind it. Climbers, bulbs, alliums, and annuals are woven throughout to reinforce the bones of the planting as the season progresses. The beds are full enough and the plants vigorous, everything is just in check but never too clipped or too manicured. This is a lesson to gardeners on how to achieve rampant growth and a sense of wealth (the back of the house is groaning with climbers like humulus) and yet fend off rank chaos. Clipped box and lollipop euonymus maintain order, while a garden bench is lost in a cloud of mallow or honeysuckle. There are a lot of old-fashioned roses but their short-comings are disguised by accompanying floribundas such as 'Cardinal Hume' which soldier on until November. And all this in a spot discovered by the present owner only a dozen years ago which many would have declared impossible to garden without a full-time gardener.

THE GEORGIAN GARDEN   8
Gravel Walk, Bath, Avon.

Bath Museums Service * *Enter garden by the Gravel Walk* * *Parking in*

Charlotte Street, 5 minutes walk across Victoria Park ✳ *Toilet facilities in Park*
✳ *Open May to Oct, Mon – Fri, 9am – 4.30pm* ✳ *Entrance: free*

Anyone interested in seeing how a Georgian town garden looked should not
miss the newly restored garden behind No 4 The Circus (but do not ring the
doorbell, please). Designed to be seen from the house, the garden plan is based
on excavations conducted by the Bath Archaeological Trust of the original
garden, laid out in the 1770s. Surprisingly simple, there is no grass but a bed of
yellow gravel edged with stone paving. Three flower beds are on a central axis.
Box-rimmed borders planted starkly with scented varieties of phlox, stock,
asters and a good deal of love-lies-bleeding. Honeysuckle clings to a central
white pole. An eyecatcher is a curious bench copied from an eighteenth-
century original. The planting sets out to show how a Georgian town garden
might have evolved between 1770 and 1836. It is a pity that an opportunity was
missed to confine the planting to the early period, and that many modern colour
derivatives of earlier plants have been used. All authentic according to the
Garden History Society.

GOLDNEY HALL 9
Lower Clifton Hill, Clifton, Bristol, Avon. Tel: (0272) 265698

University of Bristol ✳ *In centre of Bristol at top of Constitution Hill, Clifton* ✳
Teas on open days ✳ *Garden open two Suns in May (please telephone for details), 2
– 6pm. Grotto open by special appointment for those with a serious interest* ✳
Entrance: £1.50, OAP and children 75p

Although not large or notably planted this is historically an important garden
with much packed into it and a rare survival of a medium sized garden covering
nine acres. The grotto is astonishingly elaborate, water really gushes through it
and its walls are literally encrusted with shells and minerals. Its facade is a very
striking example of early but sophisticated Gothic. The grotto is now justly
famous but the entire garden (or what remains) is a thrilling discovery in the
middle of this busy once bombed city. It is full of surprises not least of which is
the small formal canal with orangery at its head. From the house one is lead
through the shadows of an allée of Irish yews to the dank grotto entrance.
Passing through the grotto and out by narrow labyrinthine passages, suddenly
there is a terrace, a broad airy walk with magnificent views over the old dock. At
the far end of this terrace is the Gothic gazebo and towering above the other
end is the castellated water tower which holds the water for the grotto. Garden
follies, parterre and herb garden.

HOLBURNE MUSEUM AND CRAFTS STUDY CENTRE 10
Bath, Avon. Tel: (0225) 466669

Trustees of the Museum ✳ *On A36 south junction of Great Pulteney Street* ✳
Best season: summer ✳ *Parking* ✳ *Refreshments: licensed teahouse in grounds* ✳
Toilet facilities in museum ✳ *Suitable for wheelchairs* ✳ *Dogs on lead* ✳ *Shop*
✳ *Museum open Mon – Sat, 11am – 5pm, Sun, 2.30 – 6pm. Closed mid-Dec to
mid-Feb and Mons from Nov to Easter* ✳ *Garden open all year* ✳ *Entrance: free*

AVON

The gardens provide a delightful complement to the Holburne Museum which houses an exceptional collection of decorative and fine art. Originally part of Sydney Gardens, little remains of the early fashionable eighteenth-century pleasure gardens modelled on Vauxhall Gardens. However, over the past two years a restoration programme has been under way using only plant material such as would have been found in the garden prior to 1800.

23 KELSTON ROAD 11
Bath, Avon.

Mr B. Williams ✳ *3m NW of Bath on A431 Bitton road* ✳ *Parking* ✳ *Teas* ✳ *Plants for sale* ✳ *Open 5th April, 12th July, 2 – 6pm and by written appointment* ✳ *Entrance: 75p, children 30p*

A fine terraced garden of particular interest to plantsmen. The garden was redesigned and planted out in 1982, and displays a wide variety of bulbs, herbaceous plants, roses and climbers, with lime-free beds containing specimen plants.

MANOR FARM, West Kington
(see Wiltshire)

THE MANOR HOUSE 12
Walton-in-Gordano, Clevedon, Bristol, Avon. Tel: (0272) 872067

Mr and Mrs S. Wills ✳ *2m NE of Clevedon on B3124. Entrance on N side of entry to village nearest Clevedon* ✳ *Parking. Coaches by appointment only* ✳ *Suitable for wheelchairs* ✳ *Plants for sale* ✳ *Open all year by appointment. Also Wed and Thurs, 8th April to 17th Sept, 10am – 4pm, and Suns and Mons, 20th April, 3rd, 4th, 24th, 25th May, 30th, 31st Aug, 2 – 6pm* ✳ *Entrance: £1, children under 14 free*

A most unusual plantsman's garden of about five acres which is basically only 15 years old although the owners have taken advantage of some plantings, mostly trees, which remain from the mid-eighteenth century onwards. The Wills have aimed mainly at an informal effect and they have planted ornamental trees, shrubs, herbaceous plants and bulbs to give colour and structure throughout the year. The colour in autumn is particularly remarkable. The new plantings to the south of the house, which include the White and Silver beds, retain something of the original layout but on the other side the owners have transformed the conventional sloping lawn and rose beds by including a sensitive mixture of plants many of which are unusual. There is one formal area, called the Pool Garden, with rectangular pools and fountains,and, at one end, the raised Asian bank planted with pink, blue and white colours. The yew hedges round the area are still at an early stage. Overall the Wills have achieved a remarkably attractive garden, the very opposite of what is usually meant by the description 'plantsman's'. Note too their emphasis on labour saving such as the gravel mulch in the White bed.

OLD DOWN HOUSE 13
Tockington, Bristol, Avon. Tel: (0454) 413605

Mr and Mrs Bernays ✳ *On B4461, 10m N of Bristol, 2m N of M4/M5 intersection. Take A38 towards Thornbury, turn left at Alveston on to B4061 and B4461 towards Aust and Severn Bridge* ✳ *Best seasons: spring and autumn* ✳ *Parking* ✳ *Refreshments* ✳ *Toilet facilities* ✳ *Suitable for wheelchairs* ✳ *Dogs on lead* ✳ *Plants for sale* ✳ *Farm shop* ✳ *Open 22nd March, 30th, 31st May, 28th June, 12th, 13th Sept, 2 – 6pm* ✳ *Entrance: £1, children free (1991 price)*

A Victorian estate on the escarpment overlooking the Severn, with extensive views over the Welsh hills. Small informal gardens on a five-acre site, at their best in the spring with carpets of wild flowers and cyclamen and when the large rock and water garden is in full colour. Fine trees, herbaceous borders and sweeping lawns. Exceptionally good specimens of weeping beech.

ORCHARD HOUSE 14
Claverton, Nr Bath, Avon.

Rear-Admiral and Mrs Hugh Tracy ✳ *3¹/₂m from Bath on A36, signposted to Claverton village, or follow signs to American Museum and proceed ¹/₂m down the hill* ✳ *Plants for sale. Small nursery, proceeds to charity* ✳ *Open every Wed in May, 3rd June, 1st, 8th July, 2 – 6pm and by appointment for groups of 15 or more* ✳ *Entrance: £1, children free*

On the edge of a pretty village and in the lea of an extended sixteenth-century Bath stone house this is an easy restful garden that slopes away in a series of lawns and effective rockeries. Begun as a retirement garden 25 years ago, the two and a half acres are planted with unusual species and trees for a planned and stunning foliage effect. Vistas and a secret water garden offer surprises and the vegetable garden is a treat. The garden has views into the Avon valley and Rear-Admiral Tracy has added a viewing mound which was a feature of medieval walled gardens. There are good alpines, two new tufa gardens and the glasshouses and nurseries are testimonials to Mrs Tracy's botanical expertise. The American Museum, Claverton Manor, is nearby – see entry.

THE RED LODGE 15
Park Row, Bristol, Avon. Tel: (0272) 211360

Bristol Corporation ✳ *Located in city centre* ✳ *House open* ✳ *Garden open June to Aug, Sat and Bank Holiday Mon, 10am – 1pm and 2 – 5pm* ✳ *Entrance free*

Good reconstruction of the seventeenth-century town garden of a merchant's house. Old varieties of fruit trees trained and espaliered. Trellis work recreated from seventeenth-century prints and similarly a knot garden. A sheet of plant names is available for 50p.

SHERBORNE GARDEN 16
Pear Tree House, Litton, Avon. Tel: (076121) 220

Mr and Mrs J. Southwell ✳ *15m S of Bristol, 7m N of Wells on B3114 ¹/₄m* *beyond Litton and Ye Olde Kings Arms * Best season: June/July * Field car park and picnic area * Refreshments: tea and coffee * Suitable for wheelchairs * Dogs on lead * Gallery open with exhibition of watercolours * Open 13th June to 7th Sept, Sat, Sun and Mon, also 19th, 20th April and 10th, 11th Oct, 11am – 6.30pm. Other days by appointment * Entrance: £1, children free*

A rather surreal garden that displays a very personal choice of species trees, grasses and water garden features in a three and a half-acre site reclaimed from farmland. The owner gardeners are compulsive tree people who since 1963 have planted hundreds of species and exotic trees expanding the original cottage garden and pond into a mini-arboretum. Having purchased the original house because of the charm of the mature pear trees, the long narrow site now boasts a pinetum, a larch wood, nut hedges, splendid hip hedges and the latest manifestation, a prickly wood that offers 136 varieties of holly. (A list is provided for real holly lovers.) Most trees and plants are clearly labelled. This garden is an interesting example of how natural pasture land may be tamed and surface water channelled into ponds. Worth a detour to read the signpost THE HOLLYWOOD – on-Avon, and to see the evocative watercolours of winter painter, John Southwell, shown in a small gallery.

VINE HOUSE ★ 17
Henbury, Bristol, Avon. Tel: (0272) 503573

*Professor and Mrs T.F. Hewer * 4m N of Bristol centre, in Henbury, next to Salutation pub * Best seasons: spring and autumn * Suitable for wheelchairs * Dogs on lead * Plants for sale * Open 19th, 20th April, 24th, 25th May, 2 – 7pm and by appointment all year * Entrance: £1, OAP and children 50p*

Two acres of garden developed by the present owners since 1946 which although within the city has the good fortune to back on to the woodland of the large Blaise estate landscaped by Repton. This is a particularly interesting garden because its designers started by reducing it to 'brown earth' and planning the positioning of the planting by using sticks 'surmounted by caps of white paper as though they were trees and shrubs'. The result, surprisingly, is in 'large part a wild garden' although the specimen trees are labelled and one could call this an arboretum and botanical collection. There is a glade with bulbs, cyclamen and other small plants and a pond and water garden. Collection of herbaceous and hybrid tree peonies.

WILLIAM HERSCHEL MUSEUM 18
19 New King Street, Bath, Avon. Tel: (0225) 311342

*Trustees of the Museum * On New King Street close to Queen's Square and Green Park Station * Best season: summer * Parking on street * Toilet facilities * Shop * Museum open * Garden open March to 1st Nov, daily, 2 – 5pm, Nov to Feb, Sat and Sun, 2 – 5pm * Entrance: £2, OAP and students £1.50, children 50p*

This museum is one of the smaller and more fascinating museums, from whose garden William Herschel discovered the planet Uranus in 1781. Over the years the garden has suffered from neglect, but recent replanting has now recreated a charming small town garden such as might well have existed in William Herschel's time.

TELEPHONE NUMBERS

Except where owners have specifically requested that they be excluded, telephone numbers to which enquiries may be directed are given for each property. To maintain the support and cooperation of private owners it is suggested that the telephone be used with discretion. Where visits are by appointment, the telephone can of course be used except where written application, particularly for parties, is specifically requested. Code numbers are given in brackets. For the Republic of Ireland phone 010353 followed by the code (Dublin is 1) followed by the subscriber's number. In all cases where visits by parties are proposed, owners should be advised in advance and arrangements preferably confirmed in writing.

BEDFORDSHIRE

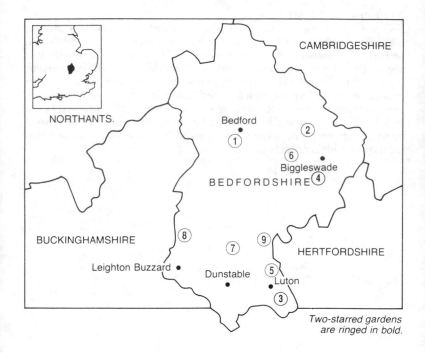

Two-starred gardens are ringed in bold.

EMBANKMENT GARDENS 1
The Embankment, Bedford, Bedfordshire. Tel: (0234) 267422

North Bedfordshire Borough Council ✳ *Russell Park, near the town centre* ✳
Parking ✳ *Suitable for wheelchairs* ✳ *Dogs* ✳ *Open all year* ✳ *Entrance: free*

A charming Victorian set piece, begun in 1890 by the Corporation and later incorporated with Russell Park, started in 1894. It runs along the banks of the River Ouse with swans and a wonderful vista to Mill Meadow with John J. Webster's delightful iron bridge. Pollarded acacias now replace the original willows which lined the bank. John Lund designed the layout which is formal with a statue and urns, and symmetrical beds of shaded pink geraniums, busy Lizzies and African marigolds. Balanced by miniature pampas grasses and yuccas. A tranquil and delightful spot. The 'Riverside Walks' leaflet includes Embankment Gardens and the Russell Park area.

THE LODGE 2
Sandy, Bedfordshire. Tel: (0767) 680551

Royal Society for the Protection of Birds ✱ *1m E of A1 off B1042 Sandy – Potton road* ✱ *Best season: spring* ✱ *Parking* ✱ *Toilet facilities* ✱ *Suitable for wheelchairs* ✱ *Shop* ✱ *Open daily, dawn to dusk* ✱ *Entrance: £1.50, OAP £1, children 50p*

The garden has many woodland walks and nature trails with extensive bird life and the rare Natterjack toad reintroduced and breeding happily. Nature trail and Nature Discovery Room. The Lodge was bought in 1934 by Sir Malcolm Stewart, who improved the garden and made a terraced fish pond on the south side. There is a Victorian terrace and fine trees in good lawns. Other features include a large weeping birch, Wellingtonias, azalea walks to a woodland heath, colchicums, acers, sweet chestnuts. A large bignonia on the house. A huge wisteria, camellias and many big mature conifers. Two small walled gardens with *Garrya elliptica*, old wisterias and many *Clematis tangutica*. A very well planted vista of old cedar trees. No peat used and organic principles reign supreme.

LUTON HOO ★ 3
Luton, Bedfordshire. Tel: (0582) 30909

The Wernher family ✱ *2m SE of Luton, entrance W off A6129. Enter by Park Street gates* ✱ *Best season: summer* ✱ *Parking* ✱ *Restaurant* ✱ *Toilet facilities* ✱ *Suitable for wheelchairs* ✱ *Plants for sale most spring and summer weekends* ✱ *House open* ✱ *Garden open 14th March to 18th Oct, daily except Mon, 12 noon – 6pm (last admission 5pm). Open Bank Holidays* ✱ *Entrance: £1.60, OAP £1.35, children 50p (house and garden £3.70, OAP £3.20, children £1.50) (1991 prices)*

The house stands magnificently in a landscape by 'Capability' Brown with an abundance of large cedars, oaks, ashes and other mature trees. On the south side of the house is the formal garden with a large herbaceous border, recently replanted, and two vast *Magnolia* x *soulangiana*. The lower terrace forms the rose garden in eight large beds edged with box and with a sheltering yew hedge. The walls of the terrace are covered in musk roses, *Garrya elliptica* and *Wisteria sinensis*. The rock garden, built early this century as a present for Lady Wernher from her husband, has small pools running through the centre with many water lilies. Some of the maples and dwarf conifers are the original planting, including *Juniperus horizontalis* and several different forms of *Acer palmatum*. There has been much new work with scree beds of *Iris reticulata*, sedum, lewisia, thymus etc. and peat walls with erica, abies, picea and pinus. Extensive replanting in the rock gardens with shrub roses.

SOUTHILL PARK 4
Biggleswade, Bedfordshire. Tel: (0462) 813272

Mr and Mrs S.C. Whitbread ✱ *5m SW of Biggleswade. On A600, turn N at Shefford for Southill and Old Warren* ✱ *Parking* ✱ *Teas may be available*

depending on renovation of House ✳ *Toilet facilities* ✳ *Suitable for wheelchairs*
✳ *Dogs on lead* ✳ *Plants for sale* ✳ *Open 7th June, 2 - 6pm* ✳ *Entrance: £1,*
children 50p

The main part of the garden lies on the south side of the house, where wide lawns flanked by choice rhododendrons reach down to a ha-ha. The nineteenth-century copies of classical statues which adorn this part of the garden came from John Cheere's yard in 1812 when Samuel Whitbread II paid £700 for them after much haggling. There are some wonderful mature trees including vast cedars, sweet chestnuts, old cherry trees and a huge copper beech which has been layered over a large area. A herbaceous border against an old wall is interestingly planted with passion flowers, clematis, piptanthus, and much else. The Victorian conservatory, recently renovated, displays fruiting bananas and pineapples, variegated rubber plants, roses and pink passion flowers. Not a plantsman's garden but with much of historic interest.

STOCKWOOD PARK 5
Stockwood Craft Museum, Farley Hill, Luton, Bedfordshire. Tel: (0582) 38714

Borough of Luton ✳ *From M1 take junction 10 to Luton. Take Farley Hill*
(Chapel Street) turn off the A505 Dunstable road out of Luton. Signposted from
A1081 old London road ✳ *Parking* ✳ *Refreshments: in Conservatory tea room at*
weekends ✳ *Toilet facilities* ✳ *Suitable for wheelchairs* ✳ *Shop* ✳ *Stockwood*
Craft Museum in stable block ✳ *Open April to Oct, Wed – Sat, 10am – 5pm, Sun*
and Bank Holidays, 10am – 6pm; Nov to March, Fri – Sun, 10am – 4pm ✳
Entrance: free

A series of period gardens have been laid out within the walled gardens of the old house – a Victorian garden, a cottage garden, a seventeenth-century knot garden – designed by Robert Burgoyne, Luton's gifted master gardener, ably assisted by Peter Ansell, the head gardener at Stockwood Park. In the park is a landscape garden with sculpture by Ian Hamilton-Finlay – the one artist to have given a convincing continuity to the landscape gardening tradition. His modern fragments of 'antique' buildings, partly buried, suggest the eighteeth-century ideal of a harmonious blend of planting, architecture and sculpture – arguably the greatest art form to have originated in Britain.

THE SWISS GARDEN 6
Old Warden, Biggleswade, Bedfordshire. Tel: (0234) 228330

Bedfordshire County Council ✳ *Take A1 to Biggleswade and follow signposts from*
A1 Biggleswade roundabout. Signposted on A600, Shefford – Bedford road ✳ *Best*
season: end May/June ✳ *Parking opposite Shuttleworth Collection* ✳
Refreshments at Aerodrome. Lakeside picnic area ✳ *Toilet facilities inc. disabled*
✳ *Suitable for wheelchairs (wheelchairs for loan)* ✳ *Dogs in woodland and picnic*
area only ✳ *Shop* ✳ *Open Easter to Oct, Wed–Sun and Bank Holiday Mons,*
1.30 – 6pm last admission 5.15pm). Guided tours available ✳ *Entrance: £1,*
OAP and children 50p. Special rates for parties.

This fascinating garden is said to have been created in 1830 by Lord Ongley of the East India Company for his Swiss mistress. It was closed for 40 years from

1939, then leased by Bedfordshire County Council and restored. It has wonderful trees; cedar of Lebanon, the largest Arolla pines in England, vast pieris 300 years old underplanted with *Helleborus orientalis* and a most unusual variegated sweet chestnut. Innumerable curly iron bridges cross over miniature canals made by a Mr Hart, blacksmith of Old Warden and uncle of Lady Emma Hamilton of Nelson fame, who was a nursery maid at nearby Ickwell Bury. Little Swiss period summer houses with sheets of bulbs in the spring underplanting azaleas, rhododendrons and spring-flowering shrubs. A grotto and fernery provide dramatic contrast between the gloom of the grotto and the dazzling light of the fernery. The garden is so haunted that the gardeners will only work in twos, it is rumoured, so single visitors beware.

TODDINGTON MANOR 7
Toddington, Bedfordshire. Tel: (05255) 2576

Sir Neville and Lady Bowman-Shaw * *1m NW of Toddington, 1m from M1 junction 12. First right in village, signed Milton Bryan* * *Parking* * *Teas* * *Suitable for wheelchairs* * *Plants for sale* * *Open 21st June, 2nd Aug, 12 noon – 6pm* * *Entrance: £1.50, children 50p*

The Bowman-Shaws moved here in 1979 to find a wilderness, since reclaimed and planted with spring bulbs, flowering trees and other plants which lend colour on into the summer. They also inherited some wonderful old trees, especially beeches and Wellingtonias. They themselves made the pleached lime walk along a lovely old paved path, now bordered with pink and grey. A series of grey stone walled gardens are fully planted and mature with a good mixture of shrubs and plants, vines, viburnums, davidia, crinums, tree peonies, and *Hydrangea villosa*. In general planting has been of old favourites, but there are some rare and tender specimens in the greenhouse. Round the doorways between the gardens and in the borders, large daturas (both *sanguinea* and the semi-double 'Knightii') strike an unusual and interesting note. A very large herb garden was planted in 1988.

WOBURN ABBEY 8
Woburn, Bedfordshire. Tel: (0525) 290666

The Marquis of Tavistock * *From M1 junction 13 follow signs* * *Parking* * *Restaurant* * *Toilet facilities* * *Shop* * *Pottery and Antiques Centre* * *Open Weekend only from 28th March to Oct, 10am – 4.45pm* * *Entrance: £5 per car inc. one passenger's entry to house. Pedestrians 50p*

While unimpressive as a garden in the sense that the word is most usually employed, a visit to the deer park at Woburn Abbey will be greatly enjoyed by anyone who is interested in the history of gardens because it was landscaped by Humphry Repton who considered it one of his finest achievements. A series of linked ponds is a feature of beautifully-graded slopes in the middle ground which is clad with magnificent oak and sweet chestnut trees. These frame a glorious vista along a broad avenue which appears to run to infinity. Gardening is not altogether ignored at Woburn – near the house is a private garden which can be glimpsed from a window at the sculpture gallery. There is a fine curved conservatory with some hale and hearty and very ancient camellias and a fascinating grotto which is integrated into the house. Behind the house are 40 acres of lawns studded with trees and shrubs, criss-crossed by pathways, one of which leads to an eye-catching classicial temple.

WREST PARK 9
Silsoe, Bedfordshire. Tel: (0525) 60152

English Heritage ✳ *¹/₂m E of Silsoe village off A6* ✳ *Parking* ✳ *Refreshments* ✳ *Toilet facilities* ✳ *Dogs on lead* ✳ *Shop* ✳ *House open* ✳ *Garden open April to Sept, Sat, Sun and Bank Holidays only, 10am – 6pm* ✳ *Entrance: £1.30, OAP 95p, children 5 – 15 65p (1991 prices)*

Wrest Park is one of the few places in England where it is possible to see an early eighteenth-century garden in the manner of Bridgeman. A very rigid and formal layout dominates the main axis of the grounds which feature an impressive canal; many subsidiary and frequently meandering cross-axis cut through thick blocks of natural and unrestrained woodland leading to statues and giant vases set in grassy glades. Later in the eighteenth century 'Capability' Brown worked at Wrest Park and made several alterations without destroying much of its earlier plan. He made a highly naturalistic artificial river to surround the grounds and loosened the planting at their perimeter. In the nineteenth century, when the house was rebuilt in the French style, it was fronted by Italianate terraces with parterres. Apart from the statuary the park contains several other interesting features. A Palladian building by the former bowling green is thought to be the work of Batty Langley and the spendid domed pavilion which terminates the vista down the long water was designed by Thomas Archer. An elegant orangery was built at the same period as the new house, and at some time in the late-eighteenth century a pleasing rustic folly was built to incorporate a bath house. Two deep mixed borders separated by a wide turf alley have recently been refurbished and should look well for much of the summer if the rabbits can be kept at bay while the new plants are becoming established.

BERKSHIRE

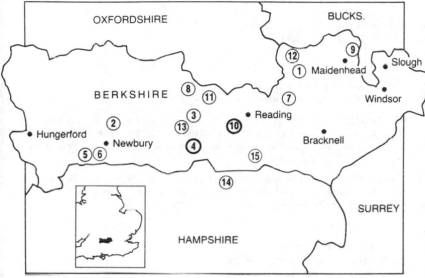

Two-starred gardens are ringed in bold.

BEAR ASH
1
Hare Hatch, Nr Reading, Berkshire. Tel: (0734) 402639

Lord and Lady Remnant ✻ 2m E of Wargrave, ¹/₂m N of A4 at Hare Hatch ✻ Teas ✻ Toilet facilities ✻ Plants for sale ✻ Open 14th June, 2 – 6pm ✻ Entrance: £1, children free

A delightful and immaculately-kept two-acre garden with a pleasant view over parkland. Silver and gold sundial border. Shrubs, old-fashioned roses, swimming pool garden, Pandora's secret garden and a small vineyard. In 1991, work began on a lake in the park which can be viewed from the garden.

CHIEVELEY MANOR
2
Newbury, Berkshire. Tel: (0635248) 208

Mr and Mrs C.J. Spence ✻ ¹/₂m from M4 in Chieveley village, Manor Lane by church ✻ Parking in field near house ✻ Teas ✻ Toilet facilities ✻ Suitable for wheelchairs ✳ *Plants for sale* ✳ *Open 12th July, 2 – 6pm* ✳ *Entrance: £1, children free*

Medium sized garden, including walled garden, swimming pool garden, herbaceous borders, shrubs and roses. Very well-maintained with new planting by owners.

CLIVEDEN
(see Buckinghamshire)

ENGLEFIELD HOUSE ★   3
Theale, Reading, Berkshire. Tel: (0734) 302221

Mr and Mrs W.R. Benyon ✳ *Entrance is on A340, near Theale* ✳ *Teas and Toilet facilities on Sun openings only* ✳ *Suitable for wheelchairs* ✳ *Plants for sale* ✳ *Open every Mon, 10am – dusk, and 12th April, 12th July, 2 – 6pm* ✳ *Entrance: £1.50, children free*

A beautiful garden with a spectacular view. Deer park. Seven acres of woodland with interesting trees and shrubs. Stream and water garden. Terrace with borders, all excellently maintained.

FOLLY FARM ★★   4
Sulhamstead, Nr Reading, Berkshire.

7m SW of Reading. 2m W of junction 12 on M4. Turn left at road marked Sulhamstead at Mulligan's Fish Restaurant 1m after Theale roundabout; entrance ³/₄m on right through a brown gate ✳ *Best season: spring/summer* ✳ *Parking* ✳ *Teas on charity open days* ✳ *Toilet facilities* ✳ *Partly suitable for wheelchairs* ✳ *Plants for sale on open days when available* ✳ *Open 12th April, 25th May, 28th June, 2 – 6pm. Individual or group applications in writing* ✳ *Entrance: £1, children free. Individuals or parties at other times £2 per person*

A sublime example of the Lutyens and Jekyll partnership in its vintage years before World War I. The intimate relationship of house and garden personifies Lutyens' genius for design and craftmanship. A complex arrangement of spaces and courts is linked by herringbone-patterned brick paths, enhancing the vernacular origins of an attractive Edwardian country house. The gardens retain much of their original character, although planting has also been chosen to suit the taste of the present owners. The formal sunken rose garden surrounded by a high yew hedge is particularly notable for its masterful design on several levels. Other features include formal entrance court, barn court, Dutch-inspired canal garden, flower parterre and tank cloister. This is one of the country's most important twentieth-century gardens.

FOXGROVE FARM   5
Enborne, Newbury, Berkshire. Tel: (0635) 40554

Miss Audrey Vockins ✳ *Enborne is 2¹/₂m SW of Newbury. From A343 turn right* *at The Gun Inn for 1¹/2m, then right down Wheatlands Lane and right at T-junction * Teas on open days * Suitable for wheelchairs * Plants for sale * Open by appointment Feb and March. Nursery open daily * Entrance: 60p, children free*

This small garden adjoins a nursery run by the Vockins family. They specialize in bulbs especially specie snowdrops, also primroses, auriculas, alpines, and small herbaceous plants. The apple tree which fell to the gales has made way for an enlarged peat bed where a flourishing *Tropaeolum speciosum* (nasturtium) is doing so well that 'it is becoming a bit of a menace'.

HAZELBY HOUSE 6
North End, Nr Newbury, Berkshire. Tel: (0635) 253162

*Mr and Mrs M.J. Lane Fox * 6m SW of Newbury. Turn right off A343 to Ball Hill. The garden is about ¹/4m beyond Ball Hill on Kintbury road * Parking * Teas * Suitable for wheelchairs * Plants for sale * Open 28th June, 2 – 6.30pm or by written appointment only * Entrance: £1.50, children 75p (1991 prices)*

Sissinghurst-inspired five-acre garden with excellent plantings of shrubs and herbaceous perennials created by the present owners over the last generation. Trees lost in the gales have been replaced by azaleas, rhododendrons and other shrubs. Adjoining the small lake is a newly created water garden, surrounded by woodland.

HOLLINGTON HERB GARDEN
(see Hampshire)

HURST LODGE 7
Broadcommon Road, Hurst, Berkshire.

*Mr and Mrs A. Peck * On A321 Twyford – Wokingham road * Parking * Teas * Suitable for wheelchairs * Dogs on lead * Plants for sale * Open 10th May, 23rd Aug, 2 – 5.30pm * Entrance: £1, children 20p*

This old five-acre garden was developed by Lady Ingram who died in 1989. Her placing of trees and shrubs to give sensitive colour combinations makes for attractive views. The displays of flowers, bulbs, magnolias, hydrangeas, camellias and rhododendrons give a pleasing year-round effect. The most notable features of the garden are the fine trees, old yews, copper beeches and scarlet oaks, a huge old oak and a Scots pine. New walks have been opened up and borders developed and extended during the year. Large kitchen garden. Lawns and a play area with several pieces of children's outdoor equipment make the garden inviting for young children, and overall there is an atmosphere conducive to a pleasant family day out.

LITTLE BOWDEN 8
Pangbourne, Berkshire. Tel: (0734) 842210

*Mr and Mrs Geoffrey Verey * 1¹/2m W of Pangbourne on the Pangbourne –*

Yattendon road ✳ *Best season: mid-May, late June/early July* ✳ *Parking: small groups in front of house. Open days parking in field* ✳ *Teas on open days* ✳ *Toilet facilities* ✳ *Suitable for wheelchairs* ✳ *Dogs on lead* ✳ *Plants for sale* ✳ *Open for charity 24th May, 5th July and by appointment, 2.30 – 6pm* ✳ *Entrance: £1*

Much of this three-acre semi-formal garden and three acres of woodland garden has been developed by the Vereys since 1949. But a glade with specimen trees and borders was developed by Percy Cane early this century. In May the canopy of the cherry wood is so thick with blossom, from far off it looks like snow; underfoot there is a carpet of bluebells below flowering shrubs, especially magnolias, azaleas, camellias. In July the herbaceous border along the whole length of the house is at its best, as are two other mixed borders of roses, shrubs and herbaceous plants; disaster struck the bed of *Cardiocrinum giganteum*, burying the corms, but Mrs Verey hopes to rescue these over the next couple of years. In October the visitor should look out for the weeping lime. The terrace garden with original 1920s Italian olive jars and paved sunken garden with white flowers adjoins the house; also in the paved area is a pond with water lilies, surrounded with plantings of roses and lilies. A silver plant border leads to a swimming pool area which is landscaped and sheltered by yew hedges and walls bearing roses, ceanothus and clematis.

ODNEY CLUB 9
Cookham, Berkshire.

John Lewis Partnership ✳ *Off A4094 near Cookham Bridge* ✳ *Parking in grounds* ✳ *Teas* ✳ *Toilet facilities* ✳ *Suitable for wheelchairs* ✳ *Dogs on lead* ✳ *Plants for sale as available* ✳ *Open 12th April, 2 – 6pm* ✳ *Entrance: £1, children 25p*

Although only open one day this is a huge 120-acre site along the Thames and makes a long afternoon visit. Well-cared for and continuously developing. A favourite with Stanley Spencer who visited often to paint the magnolia which featured in his work. There is a magnificent wisteria walk, specimen trees, herbaceous borders, small side gardens, and terraces with spring bedding plants.

THE OLD RECTORY ★★ 10
Burghfield, Reading, Berkshire.

Mr and Mrs R.R. Merton ✳ *5m SW of Reading. Turn S off A4 to Burghfield village and right after Hatch Gate Inn* ✳ *Parking* ✳ *Suitable for wheelchairs* ✳ *Plants for sale inc. unusual plants* ✳ *Open last Wed in each month Feb to Oct, 11am – 4pm and by appointment in writing* ✳ *Entrance: 50p, children 30p*

This garden has achieved wide renown and its maturity and the amazing generosity of plants skillfully planted are remarkable in a site started from scratch in 1950. Mrs Merton, described by herself as 'a green-fingered lunatic', has collected plants from all over the world notably some rare items from Japan and China. The terrace has a fine display most of the year, the herbaceous border and beds are impressive with collections of hellebores, pinks, violas, paeonies, snowdrops, old roses and many others. In the spring there are drifts of daffodils and rather rare cowslips and so many other plants to see that it is well worth making a visit month by month if you live within reasonable range. There is something here for every type of gardener most of the year. The Mertons propagate everything so sales on open days are fascinating, and there is a 'mini-market' of stalls by other plantsmen.

OLD RECTORY COTTAGE ★   11
Tidmarsh, Pangbourne, Berkshire. Tel: (0734) 843241

Mr and Mrs A.W.A. Baker ✻ *¹/₂m S of Pangbourne towards Tidmarsh. Turn E down narrow lane* ✻ *Parking* ✻ *Plants for sale* ✻ *Open by appointment for individual members of the RHS Lily Group, Alpine Garden Society and Hardy Plant Society and garden societies and 1st March, 12th April, 3rd May, 7th June, 12th July, 2 – 6pm* ✻ *Entrance: 75p, children free*

Although this is not a large garden it is full of rare and exciting plants, many of them collected by the owner. It has a very dry area, with early spring bulbs, a wild garden round a small lake. Lilies, roses, unusual shrubs and climbers. It is worth visiting on each of the open days as there is always something new to stimulate the interest of a keen gardener. In addition there are Carolina ducks, ornamental pheasants, white doves and Arab horses. Quite rightly this garden has had much media coverage.

THE SAVILL GARDEN
(see Surrey)

SCOTLANDS   12
Cockpole Green, Berkshire. Tel: (0628) 822648

Mr M. and the Hon. Mrs Payne ✻ *Halfway between Wargrave and Henley. At top of Remenham Hill on A423 take turning to Cockpole Green* ✻ *Parking in paddock* ✻ *Teas* ✻ *Suitable for wheelchairs* ✻ *Dogs on lead* ✻ *Open 16th, 17th May, 4th Oct, 2 – 6pm* ✻ *Entrance: £1, children free*

Well-planned and planted watergarden created by Mrs Payne from a mere trickle. Astilbes, hostas, ferns, primulas, gunneras and many more moisture-loving plants look very comfortable even after unusually dry summers. There is hardly a space to be seen at the water's edge and in the surrounding shrub, fuchsia and ground cover borders even in October; a Humphry Repton style rustic summer house marks the merging of landscaped water garden with natural woodland. Mown grass paths lead past the water garden through the woodland, around the pond, past the waterfall and back up towards the house. On the other side of the drive and nearest the house is the formal garden, terrace awash with crevice plants, paved pool garden where a lead statue of a drummer boy holds court, among planted stone tubs, herbaceous borders and kitchen, herb and flowers-for-cutting garden. The gazebo is a new and successful addition.

ST MARY'S FARM ★   13
Beenham, Nr Reading, Berkshire.

Charles and Mary Keen ✳ *2m N of A4, halfway between Reading and Newbury* ✳ *Open on written application only, enclosing SAE* ✳ *Entrance: £1*

This eighteenth-century parsonage with fine trees and views has been given a wonderful uplift by the imaginative design and planting of the Keens. They have not been afraid of experimenting with bright colours, and the kitchen garden path flanked by pear trees holding hands, underplanted with brightly-coloured flowers is very striking. There is plenty to see and the herbaceous border is particularly glorious.

STRATFIELD SAYE HOUSE   14
Reading, Berkshire. Tel: (0252) 882882

The Duke of Wellington ✳ *1m W of A33, halfway between Reading and Basingstoke. Turn off at Wellington Arms Hotel* ✳ *Parking* ✳ *Refreshments* ✳ *Toilet facilities* ✳ *Suitable for wheelchairs* ✳ *Shop* ✳ *House open. Wellington Country Park, 3m from house caters for many tastes, and can be visited on combined entry ticket with house and gardens* ✳ *Gardens open daily except Fri, May to last Sun in Sept, 11.30am – 4pm* ✳ *Entrance: £3.50, children £1.85. Special rates for parties of 20 or more*

Horticulture and history are inextricably linked, from Pleasure Gardens laid out in the seventeenth century for the first owners with thousands of fine trees including many varieties of oaks, maples and walnuts to the 155 year-old *Quercus cerris* or Turkey oak under which the first duke's horse Copenhagen is buried; from *Sequoiadendron giganteum*, also known as Wellingtonia after the first duke, to the avenue of plane trees planted in 1972. In the pleasure gardens around 300 trees were victims of the gales and storms, among them the famous liquidambar and *Nyssa sylvatica*, but the damage has been cleared and new plantings are in hand. Fresh arrivals also in the wildfowl sanctuary which leads on from the small lake formed by a widening of the River Loddon. The walled gardens and American garden were designed for the first duke who also placed the traditional Victorian summer house in the Pleasure Gardens. A large walled garden for vegetables and fruit is laid out in the Victorian manner, and contains a camellia house (possibly built by Paxton whose boss, the Duke of Devonshire, was a chum of the Iron Duke) from where a substantial herbaceous border leads down the centre to the Rose Garden which was replanted in 1972. Here all the roses have been chosen for their scent and new varieties are added every year. Additions also in the American garden designed for the first duke by his head gardener. This still retains many of the original plants introduced from North America with the emphasis on azaleas, rhododendrons and kalmias but now contains plants from all over the world selected to give year round interest.

SWALLOWFIELD PARK   15
Reading, Berkshire. Tel: (0734) 883815

Country Houses Association Ltd ✳ *5m S between Reading and Wokingham on*

A33 under M4; 2m then left to Swallowfield village. Entrance by the village hall ∗
Limited parking in small courtyard in front of house ∗ *Toilet facilities* ∗ *Suitable for wheelchairs* ∗ *Dogs on lead* ∗ *Open May to Sept, Wed and Thurs, 2 – 5pm*
∗ *Entrance: £1.50, children 50p*

The diarist John Evelyn called seventeenth-century Swallowfield 'a worthy house' and is said to have planted the row of yew trees (not the ancient yew hedge); Charles Dickens buried his dog Bumble in the garden, and in the hot dry summer of 1989 BBC TV transformed the existing walled garden into a formal period garden of early nineteenth-century design. The gardens round the house, which is now divided into private apartments, are taken care of by the residents.

CUTTINGS

Readers may wish to be reminded that the taking of cuttings without the owner's permission can lead to embarrassment and, if it continues on a large scale, may cause the owners to close their gardens to the public. This has to be seen in the context of an increasing number of thefts from gardens. At Nymans, the famous Sussex garden, thefts have reached such a level that the gardener will not now plant out any shrub until it is semi-mature and of such a size that its theft would be very difficult. Other owners have reported the theft of artifacts as well as plants.

BUCKINGHAMSHIRE

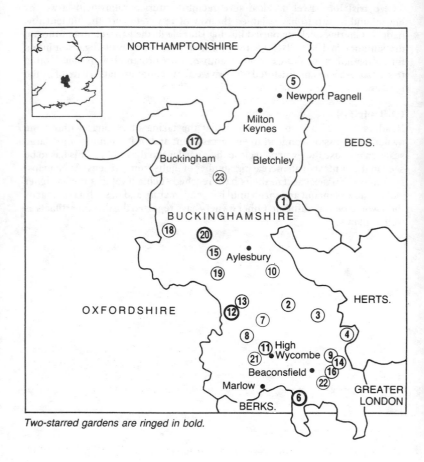

Two-starred gardens are ringed in bold.

ASCOTT ★★   1
Wing, Buckinghamshire. Tel: (0296) 688242

The National Trust ✻ ¹/₂m E of Wing, 2m SW of Leighton Buzzard on S of A418 ✻ Best season: spring/summer ✻ Parking 220 yards from house ✻ Toilet facilities ✻ Partly suitable for wheelchairs ✻ Dogs in car park only ✻ House and garden open 14th April to 17th May, and Sept: Tues – Sun, 2 – 6pm (last admission 5pm); also Bank Holiday Mons during period but closed Tues 21st April and 5th May ✻ Garden only open 20th May to 31st Aug: every Wed and last Sun in month; also Bank Holiday Mons, and for charity 12th April, 7th June, 2 – 6pm, (last admision 5pm) ✳ *Entrance: £2.50, children £1.25 (house and garden £4, children £2)*

Thirty acres of Victorian gardening at its very best, laid out with the aid of James Veitch and Sons of Chelsea. Formidable collection of mature trees of all shapes and colours set in rolling lawns. Fascinating topiary includes evergreen sundial with yew gnomon and inscription: 'Light and shade by turn but love always' in golden yew. Wide lawns slope away to magnificent views across the Vale of Aylesbury glimpsed between towering cedars. Formal gardens include the Madeira Walk with sheltered flower borders and the bedded-out Dutch garden. Two stately fountains were created by Story – one a large group in bronze, the other a slender composition in marble. Rock garden and fernery. Interesting all year, spring gardens feature massed carpets of bulbs.

BLOSSOMS   2
Cobblers Hill, Nr Great Missenden, Buckinghamshire. Tel: (02406) 3140

Dr and Mrs Frank Hytten ✳ *From Great Missenden follow Rignall Road towards Butlers Cross. Turn into Kings Lane and up to top of Cobblers Hill. At T-junction see yellow stone marker in hedgerow. Turn right. After 50 yards turn right at Blossoms sign* ✳ *Best season: spring and early summer* ✳ *Limited parking* ✳ *Teas* ✳ *Toilet facilities* ✳ *Suitable for wheelchairs* ✳ *Plants for sale* ✳ *Open by appointment only* ✳ *Entrance: £1*

A five-acre garden, including one acre of woodland, mainly created by the owners since 1975. Spring-flowering bulbs, shrubs and trees followed by bluebells. There are new rock and cutting gardens, with plans for an extended herbaceous border. Collections of eucalyptus and acers and many other specimen trees, including *Euodia hupehensis* and a magnificent ivy-leaved beech. Interesting features include a small lake with island where it is hoped mallard will make a home, and sculpture by the owner and friends; two other water gardens and a paved well garden with sundial linked by woodland paths.

CAMPDEN COTTAGE   3
51 Clifton Road, Chesham Bois, Buckinghamshire. Tel: (0494) 726818

Mrs P. Liechti ✳ *On A416 between Amersham and Chesham. Turn into Clifton Road by Catholic Church (opposite primary school). Close to traffic lights at a pedestrian crossing* ✳ *Parking in road, but on open days in school car park by arrangement* ✳ *Refreshments in Old Amersham* ✳ *Toilet facilities in Amersham on the Hill and Old Amersham* ✳ *Unusual plants for sale* ✳ *Open by appointment for parties (but no coaches) and 16th Feb (if winter mild), 15th March, 12th April, 10th May, 14th June, 19th July, 16th Aug, 6th Sept, 2 – 6pm* ✳ *Entrance: £1, accompanied children free*

A generation ago the owner described herself as 'never having given gardening a thought', and started to 'tidy' the neglected garden while builders took over the house. Straight lines have given way to a design adapted to take advantage of a magnificent weeping ash and the original network of stone paths has become a large York stone terrace surrounding the house. The owner's speciality is rare and unusual plants – when asked to point out those of interest in early September for a TV programme Mrs Liechti counted more than 400. She is also skilled in interesting associations of colour, shape and foliage. Mrs Leichti has created a new formal area with yew hedge, walled border and extended lawns. Worth visiting month by month to keep up with developments.

CHENIES MANOR HOUSE ★ 4
Chenies, Nr Amersham, Buckinghamshire. Tel: (049476) 2888

Lt. Col. and Mrs MacLeod Matthews ✳ *Off A404 between Amersham and Rickmansworth. If approaching via M25, take junction 18* ✳ *Best season: summer* ✳ *Parking* ✳ *Teas* ✳ *Toilet facilities* ✳ *Suitable for wheelchairs* ✳ *Herbs for sale* ✳ *Shop* ✳ *House open. Extra charge* ✳ *Garden open April to Oct, Wed, Thurs and 25th May and 31st Aug, 2 – 5pm* ✳ *Entrance: £1.50, children 75p*

The owners have created several extremely fine linked gardens in keeping with their fifteenth/sixteenth-century brick manor house. The gardens are highly decorative and maintained to the highest standards. Planted for a long season of colour and using many old-fashioned roses and cottage plants, there is always something to enjoy here. Formal topiary in the 'white' garden, collections of medicinal and poisonous plants in a 'physic' garden, an historic turf maze and a highly productive kitchen garden. On her visits here, Queen Elizabeth I had a favourite tree and the Elizabeth Oak is named after her. In 1991 '*The Sunday Times Maze*' was planted in yew hedging with a layout based on the geometric figure, the icosahedron.

CHICHELEY HALL 5
Chicheley, Newport Pagnell, Buckinghamshire. Tel: (023065) 252

Trustees of the Hon Nicholas Beatty and Mrs John Nutting ✳ *On A422 between Bedford and Newport Pagnell, 3m from M1 junction 14* ✳ *Parking* ✳ *Teas* ✳ *Toilet facilities* ✳ *Suitable for wheelchairs* ✳ *Shop* ✳ *House open* ✳ *Garden open 19th April, 31st May, Sun and Bank Holiday Mon, 2.30 – 5.30pm* ✳ *Entrance: £3, children £1.50. Parties special rates*

One of the best and least altered Georgian houses in the country is surrounded by an elegant park with fine avenues and views. Mature trees include oaks, cedars and limes. C-shaped canal lake attributed to London and Wise in 1709. Formal avenues (lime and laburnum) recently planted near the house.

CLIVEDEN ★★ 6
Taplow, Maidenhead, Berkshire. Tel: (0628) 605069

The National Trust ✳ *2m N of Taplow* ✳ *Parking* ✳ *Refreshments: light lunches, coffee, teas, in Conservatory Restaurant* ✳ *Toilet facilities* ✳ *Partly suitable for wheelchairs* ✳ *Dogs in specified woodlands only, not in gardens* ✳

Shop ✳ *House open April to Oct, Thurs and Sun, 3 – 6pm (last admission 5.30pm)* ✳ *Gardens open March to Oct, daily, 11am – 6pm and Nov to Dec, 11am – 4pm. Closed Jan and Feb* ✳ *Entrance: £3 (house £1 extra. Timed ticket)*

A famous house built in 1666 by the Duke of Buckingham in the grand manner overlooking the Thames which flows at the foot of a steep slope below. The present house and terrace designed by Sir Charles Barry incorporates a famous balustrade brought by the 1st Viscount Astor from the Villa Borghese in Rome in the 1890s. The water garden, rose garden and herbaceous borders are attractive in spring, summer and autumn respectively. The formal gardens below the house and the Long Garden, fountains, temples and statuary are pleasing throughout the year. Amongst famous designers who have worked on the grounds are John Fleming (the parterre) Leoni (The Octagon Temple) Bridgeman (walks and the amphitheatre) and Jellicoe (rose garden). Part of the house is a luxury hotel, and there is an Open Air Theatre Festival in summer.

GRACEFIELD 7
Lacey Green, Nr Bradenham, Buckinghamshire.

Mr and Mrs B. Wicks ✳ *Take A4010 High Wycombe – Aylesbury road. In Bradenham turn right by Red Lion inn towards Walters Ash. Turn left at T-junction to Lacey Green. Brick and flint house is beyond the church facing Kiln Lane* ✳ *Best season: May to Sept* ✳ *Parking at village hall* ✳ *Teas on open day* ✳ *Suitable for wheelchairs* ✳ *Dogs on lead* ✳ *Plants for sale if available* ✳ *Open 25th May, 2 – 6pm. Parties by written arrangement* ✳ *Entrance: £1, children free*

A steeply-terraced water garden is a fine feature in this one and a half-acre garden. Plants for the flower arranger; new designs for paved terraces, statuary and trough gardens; collections of clematis and shrub roses; specimen trees include a special malus – 'Marshal Oyama' giving fantastic jelly. The owner is a self-confessed plantaholic and has thoughtfully named many specimens in her unusual collection.

GREAT BARFIELD 8
Bradenham, High Wycombe, Buckinghamshire.

Mr Richard Nutt ✳ *4m NW of High Wycombe. From A4010 at the Red Lion turn into village. At bottom of village green turn right and walk down 'no through road'* ✳ *Best season: spring and summer* ✳ *Parking on village green* ✳ *Teas* ✳ *Suitable for wheelchairs* ✳ *Plants for sale Feb and April only* ✳ *Open 23rd Feb, 2 – 5pm, 20th April, 12th July, 2 – 6pm* ✳ *Entrance: £1, children under 16 free*

A plant connoisseur's garden of one and a half acres with new flower beds in preparation for the latest acquisitions. Designed by the owner for interest over a long season, this starts in February with snowdrops, hellebores and spring bulbs. The position and choice of plants and trees in the island beds combine with the axis of the garden in relation to the house to show to great advantage the many varieties of trees, shrubs and climbing plants. There are generous plantings of roses, lilies, bulbs and herbaceous plants.

HAREWOOD 9
Harewood Road, Chalfont St Giles, Buckinghamshire. Tel: (049476) 3553

Mr and Mrs J. Heywood ✳ From A404 Amersham – Rickmansworth road, at miniroundabout in Little Chalfont turn S down Cokes Lane. Harewood Road is 200 yards on left ✳ Best season: spring to autumn ✳ Parking on street ✳ Teas ✳ Toilet facilities for disabled ¹/₄m away ✳ Suitable for wheelchairs once beyond gravel driveway ✳ Plants for sale ✳ Open by appointment and 3rd May, 2 – 5.30pm ✳ Entrance: £1, children 25p

This one-acre garden has been developed over the last decade but specimen trees planted a century ago and mature yew and box hedges give it a sense of privacy and enclosure. Many unusual roses and clematis. Interesting hardy plants have been chosen for foliage effect and climbers trained into neighbouring shrubs and trees. Other features include a pool garden with statuary and a superb trellis-supported white wisteria. The condition throughout is very good all year round. Extensive plant list available. Woody plants are labelled.

HERON PATH HOUSE 10
Chapel Lane, Wendover, Buckinghamshire.

Mr and Mrs Bryan C. Smith ✳ ¹/₂m S of Wendover on A413. House at bottom of Chapel Lane ✳ Parking ✳ Teas ✳ Toilet facilities ✳ Suitable for wheelchairs ✳ Plants for sale ✳ Open 30th, 31st Aug, 2 – 6pm ✳ Entrance: £1.50, children 50p

Immaculate two and a half-acre garden designed to make the most of the sharply-rising site. Walled terraces; a water garden intriguingly incorporated into the terraces and crossing one of the paths. Faultless lawns. Shrubs and herbaceous plants, together with generous bedding of geraniums, begonias and fuchsias near the house. Rockery. Orchard at highest point and furthest away from the house. A front border with retaining wall is currently being developed adjoining the perimeter stream.

HUGHENDEN MANOR ★ 11
High Wycombe, Buckinghamshire. Tel: (0494) 532580

The National Trust ✳ 1¹/₂m N of High Wycombe on A4128 ✳ Parking ✳ Toilet facilities inc. disabled ✳ Suitable for wheelchairs ✳ National Trust shop ✳ House open ✳ Garden open March, Sat and Sun only, 2 – 6pm, April to Oct, Wed – Sat, 2 – 6pm, Sun and Bank Holiday Mon, 12 noon – 6pm (last admission 5.30pm). Closed Good Fri ✳ Entrance: £3. Party rates on application

High-Victorian garden created by Mrs Disraeli in 1860s and recently restored. Particularly pleasing is the human scale of house and gardens set in picturesque, unspoilt landscape. Woodland walks amongst ancient beeches and yews. Unusual chimaera shrub *Laburnocytisus adamii* produces yellow and mauve laburnum flowers and mauve sprays of *Cytisus purpureus* in late spring/early summer.

THE MANOR HOUSE ★★ 12
Bledlow, Buckinghamshire.

The Lord and Lady Carrington ＊ ¹/₂m from B4009 in middle of Bledlow village ＊ Best season: spring – autumn ＊ Parking at farm next door ＊ Teas served on June open day for charity ＊ Partly suitable for wheelchairs ＊ Open by written appointment, May to Sept and 3rd May, 20th, 21st June, 2 – 6pm ＊ Entrance: £1.50, children free. Lyde Garden open free every day

With the help of landscape architect Robert Adams, Lord and Lady Carrington have created an elegant English garden of exceptionally high standard. Visit the highly productive and colourful walled vegetable garden, with York stone paths and central gazebo. Formal gardens are enclosed by tall yew and beech hedges. Mixed flower and shrub borders feature many roses and herbaceous plants around immaculately manicured lawns. A new garden incorporating several modern sculptures, planned around mature existing trees on a contoured and upward sloping site with open views, got off to a good start in 1991, with the lawns and shrubs enjoying the wet weather of early summer. The Lyde Garden (always open) is a water garden of great beauty and tranquillity supporting a variety of species plants.

THE MANOR HOUSE 13
Princes Risborough, Buckinghamshire.

The National Trust/Tenant Mr and Mrs R. Goode ＊ From High Wycombe take A4010 to Princes Risborough. Turn left down High Street, left at the Market Square and then towards the church. The Manor is next to the church on right ＊ Best season: mid-summer ＊ Public car park beside church ＊ Teas on charity open day ＊ Toilet facilities ＊ Suitable for wheelchairs ＊ Dogs by arrangement ＊ House open by written appointment only ＊ Garden open 28th June, 2 – 6pm and by appointment at weekends (08111) 3168 ＊ Entrance: £1, children 20p

A two-acre garden surrounds a seventeenth-century manor house restored by Lord Rothschild. Formal front garden with roses leads to walled garden with trees and mixed flower and shrub borders. The circular rose garden with box hedge surrounding the stone pool and fountain, planted in 1990, are well established. A special feature of the walled garden is the box balls and double herbaceous border. This theme is continued into the redesigned orchard where planting of a beech hedge is backed by a double blue and white border. Formal vegetable garden with mown paths leading from the walled garden to the old orchard, past a herbaceous border, via a small woodland area to a rose garden and gazebo with blue, white and pink flowering plants at the far end of the double border, returning towards the house past the new hedge-bordered vegetable garden.

MILTON'S COTTAGE 14
Deanway, Chalfont St Giles, Buckinghamshire. Tel: (02407) 2313

Milton Cottage Trust ＊ ¹/₂m W of A413, on road to Seer Green and Beaconsfield ＊ Best season: early summer ＊ Suitable for wheelchairs ＊ Shop ＊ Two museum rooms open ✳ *Garden open March to Oct, weekdays except Mon (but open Bank Holiday Mons), 10am – 1pm, 2 – 6pm, Sun, 2 – 6pm* ✳ *Entrance: £1.50, children under 15 60p, parties of 20 or more £1.20 per person*

An historic cottage where Milton completed *Paradise Lost*, it houses many of Milton's artefacts. The half an acre of attractive gardens contain a large mulberry tree which was a cutting from Milton's famous tree at Christ's College, Cambridge. Planting is informal cottage style with rose arches, vines and tapestry hedges.

NETHER WINCHENDON HOUSE 15
Nether Winchendon, Nr Aylesbury, Buckinghamshire. Tel: (0844) 290101

Mr and Mrs R. Spencer Bernard ✳ *7m SW of Aylesbury, 5m from Thame. Near the church in Nether Winchendon village* ✳ *Parking on road nearby* ✳ *Suitable for wheelchairs* ✳ *Open 26th April, 19th July, 2.30 – 6pm and at other times by appointment* ✳ *Entrance: £1, children 25p (1991 prices)*

These gardens surround a romantic brick and stone Tudor manor which is approached by an unusual avenue of dawn redwoods planted in 1973 continuing a centuries-old tree planting tradition by the Spencer Bernard family. Small orchards on either side of the house combine with fine specimen trees, including mature acers, catalpas, cedars, paulownias, liquidambars and, dominating the lawns at the back of the house, an eighteenth-century variegated sycamore and a late-1950s oriental plane of almost equal height. Well-kept lawns, shrub and flower borders, walled gardens including a productive kitchen garden.

SPINDRIFT 16
Jordans Village, Nr Beaconsfield, Buckinghamshire. Tel: (02407) 3172

Mr and Mrs E. Desmond ✳ *N of A40 in Jordans village, at far side of green turn right into cul de sac near school* ✳ *Best seasons: spring and summer* ✳ *Parking in school playground on open days* ✳ *Refreshments: coffee, lunches and tea* ✳ *Toilet facilities* ✳ *Partly suitable for wheelchairs* ✳ *Dogs* ✳ *Plants for sale* ✳ *Open 19th April, 28th June, 31st Aug, 11am – 5pm* ✳ *Entrance: £1, children under 12 30p*

The house, built in 1933, was surrounded with trees and hedges and the present owners have extended the mature gardens on a sloping site with particularly interesting well-kept fruit and vegetable area. Productive vines under glass. Unusual trees and shrubs positioned throughout the garden. Collections of hostas and hardy geraniums.

STOWE LANDSCAPE GARDEN ★★ 17
Buckingham, Buckinghamshire. Tel: (0280) 822850

The National Trust ✳ *3m NW of Buckingham via Stowe Avenue off A422*

Buckingham – Brackley road ✳ *Parking* ✳ *Light refreshments in temporary tearoom. Contact Administrator for party bookings. Picnic area in car park and Grecian Valley* ✳ *Toilet facilities inc. disabled* ✳ *Partly suitable for wheelchairs. Batricars available and may be pre-booked, free of charge* ✳ *Dogs on lead* ✳ *Shop* ✳ *House (Stowe School) may be open in holidays* ✳ *Garden open 28th March to 20th April, daily; 22nd April to 26th June, Mon, Wed, Fri; 28th June to 6th Sept, daily; 7th Sept to 23rd Oct, Mon, Wed, Fri; 24th Oct to 1st Nov, 19th Dec to 24th Dec, 27th Dec to 10 Jan 1993, daily, all 10am – 6pm or dusk if earlier (last admission 1 hour before closing)* ✳ *Entrance: parties £3 per person. All parties must book in advance*

The *Oxford Companion* says Stowe had an enormous influence on garden design especially after experiments there in 'natural' gardening in the 1730s. It continued to exhibit the changes of eighteenth-century taste and 'its final phase of idealized landscape still survives relatively intact'. It is a vast park with relatively few formal arrangements and the various changes made by the succession of distinguished designers who took a hand in it from the mid-seventeenth century is too long to describe here in detail. Viscount Cobham, Bridgeman, Vanbrugh (who decorated the area with temples and other features) were followed by Kent who certainly designed buildings and probably the garden. 'Capability' Brown was head gardener from 1741 and his plantings were thinned out when he left 10 years later by the new owner Lord Temple. The latter also built a triumphal arch on the horizon, a focus for the main vista. Inevitably, as the work continued into the nineteenth century, the family money ran out, and the estate was sold to become a school in 1923. The governors, supported by money from the parents and ex-pupils, did well in their attempt to restore the 32 surviving buildings and the grounds as far as possible to their 1800 condition. The money that its successive owners have poured into Stowe justifies its reputation as a classic English garden. Now that the grounds are in the hands of The National Trust, which has launched an appeal for £1 million for Stowe, we may expect even greater things. If possible, the visitor should approach the gardens via the south portico of the school. The view then before him has been described as 'sudden and breathtaking' with, beyond the lawn, the Octagon Lake, the Lake Pavilions and Corinthian Arch. He may advance to walk in, and examine in detail, the Elysian fields. The Trust warns that the complete route takes 2 hours to complete, and those who wish to stay even longer may do so by renting the Gothic temple owned by a private group.

THE THATCHED COTTAGE   18
Duck Lane, Ludgershall, Buckinghamshire. Tel: (0844) 237415

Mr and Mrs D. Tolman ✳ *6m from Bicester, 13m from Aylesbury, 2m S of A41* ✳ *Best season: early and mid-summer* ✳ *Parking on street* ✳ *Teas at owner's nursery nearby* ✳ *Toilet facilities* ✳ *Dogs on lead* ✳ *Plants for sale at nursery* ✳ *Open 17th, 24th May, 28th June, 5th July, 2 – 6pm. Parties by appointment on other days* ✳ *Entrance: £1, children free*

A picturesque cottage garden surrounding an equally picturesque and traditional thatched hovel, both restored by the owners over the last ten years, combine to provide the visitor with examples of interesting and rare herbaceous plants in an enchanting setting. Most of these plants, together with many other varieties, are produced at the Tolman's specialist plant nursery a mile away.

TURN END ★ 19
Townside, Haddenham, Buckinghamshire. Tel: (0844) 291383/291817

Mr and Mrs P. Aldington ＊ From A418 turn to Haddenham. From Thame Road turn at the Rising Sun into Townside. Turn End is 250 yards on left ＊ Best season: spring/early summer ＊ Parking on street ＊ Teas on charity open days ＊ Toilet facilities ＊ Plants for sale ＊ Open 19th, 20th April, 14th June, 27th Sept, 2 – 6pm. Also groups by appointment ＊ Entrance: £1.20, children 40p

Peter Aldington's RIBA award-winning development of three linked houses is surrounded by a series of garden rooms evolved over the last 25 years. A sequence of spaces, each of individual character, provides focal points at every turn. There is a fishpond courtyard, a shady court, a formal box court, an alpine garden, hot and dry raised beds and climbing roses. A wide range of plants is displayed to good effect against a framework of mature trees. This plantsman's garden is created within a one-acre village centre site.

WADDESDON MANOR ★★ 20
Waddesdon, Nr Aylesbury, Buckinghamshire. Tel: (0296) 651211/651282

The National Trust ＊ 6m NW of Aylesbury on A41, 11m SE of Bicester. Entrance in Waddesdon village ＊ Best season: spring – autumn ＊ Parking ＊ Refreshments: light lunches and teas. Picnics except on lawns at house ＊ Toilet facilities inc. disabled ＊ Suitable for wheelchairs ＊ Guide dogs only ＊ Plants for sale ＊ National Trust shop ＊ House closed until 1993 but free entry to stables for shop and tearoom open as grounds ＊ Grounds and aviary open 18th March to 23rd Dec, Wed – Fri, 12 noon – 5pm, weekends and Bank Holidays 12 noon – 6pm ＊ Entrance: £3, children 5 – 17 £1.50, under 5 free (grounds and aviary)

Baron Ferdinand de Rothschild's remarkable chateau (built 1874–1889), which houses a formidable art collection, is set in an appropriately grand park with fountains, vistas, terraces and walks. The gardens contain an extensive collection of Italian, French and Dutch statuary. An ornate, semi-circular aviary of sixteenth-century French style, built 1889, provides a distinguished home to many exotic birds. The park today benefits from its 100-year old plantings of native yews, limes and hornbeams with a liberal sprinkling of exotic pines, cedars, Wellingtonias and cypresses. The parterre has been replanted to restore it to its original style and appearance.

WEST WYCOMBE PARK ★ 21
West Wycombe, Buckinghamshire. Tel: (0494) 24411

The National Trust ＊ At W end of West Wycombe, S of A40 Oxford road ＊ Best season: spring – autumn ＊ Parking ＊ Suitable for wheelchairs ＊ Dogs in car park only ＊ House open June to Aug, Sun – Thurs, 2 – 6pm (last admission 5.15pm) ＊ Grounds open April to May, Sun and Wed, 2 – 6pm; June to Aug, Sun – Thurs, 2 – 6pm; Easter, May and Spring Bank Holiday Sun and Mon, 2 – 6pm (last admission 5.15pm). Closed Good Fri ＊ Entrance: £2.50 (grounds), £4 (house and grounds)

The park was largely created by the second Sir Francis Dashwood whose original designs, based on his experiences on the Grand Tour, were altered by Thomas Cook, a pupil of 'Capability' Brown, in 1779-80. Repton was called in by the next Dashwood but his plans never followed. The park survives as an important early example of the English Natural Landscape movement. Woodland and waterside walks lead to various classical temples. The music temple on an island in the lake is particularly fine. A small, pleasant park with views and vistas and a beautiful lake; this is not the place to visit if you seek flower gardens and rose beds.

THE WHITE COTTAGE   22
32 Nortoft Road, Chalfont Common, Chalfont St Peter, Buckinghamshire. Tel: (02407) 2520

Mr and Mrs A.W. Pardey ∗ Parking in road ∗ Teas ∗ Toilet facilities ∗ Suitable for wheelchairs ∗ Dogs on lead ∗ Plants for sale when available ∗ Open for charity 5th April, 25th May, 14th, 17th June, 2 – 6pm ∗ Entrance: 80p, children free

Beautifully maintained third-of-an-acre garden with shrubs, herbaceous plants, roses, climbers and traditional cottage garden plants. Small bog garden. Innovative design makes best of small site.

WINSLOW HALL   23
Winslow, Buckinghamshire. Tel: (029671) 2323

Sir Edward and Lady Tomkins ∗ 10m N of Aylesbury, 6m S of Buckingham on A413 ∗ Parking ∗ Teas served in village ∗ Partly suitable for wheelchairs ∗ Open June to Aug, Wed and Thurs, 2 – 6pm and by appointment ∗ Entrance: £1.50

The original gardens were created around the house completed in 1702 by Sir Christopher Wren. Apart from an English oak older than the house itself, the early London and Wise design has disappeared. Although set on a very busy main road the garden is exceptionally tranquil with a formal and high-walled terrace garden in front. Behind the house a sweep of lawn is bordered by shrubs and specimen trees mainly planted over the last 30 years by the owners and providing an unusual example of dedicated and consistent pruning to show the trees to their best advantage; among them American scarlet oak, *Prunus* 'Tai Haku' (single white cherry), willow oak, a fascinating weeping 'creeping' cedar resembling a prehistoric animal, and an 'immature' sequoia of only 100 years old. Where the 300-year old oaks and elms have died, low stumps remain and provide a base for honeysuckle, roses, clematis, berberis and other climbers which are regularly clipped to make unusual flowering domes. Planted chiefly for foliage effect and autumn colour, mixed shrub and flower borders and rose beds add summer interest.

CAMBRIDGESHIRE

LINCOLNSHIRE

⑭ Wisbech

NORFOLK

• Peterborough

⑯⑧

• March

NORTHANTS.

CAMBRIDGESHIRE

• Ely

⑩

• Huntingdon

⑪

• St. Neots

⑨⑮ ①

• Cambridge

④

⑰ ⑬

⑫

BEDFORDSHIRE

⑱

⑤⑥

③ ⑦

② SUFFOLK

*Two-starred gardens
are ringed in bold.*

ANGLESEY ABBEY ★   1
Lode, Cambridgeshire. Tel: (0223) 811200

*The National Trust * In village of Lode, 6m NE of Cambridge, on B1102 *
Parking * Refreshments: restaurant * Toilet facilities * Suitable for
wheelchairs * Plants for sale * National Trust shop * House open different
times * Garden open 28th March to 12th July, Wed – Sun and Bank Holiday
Mons; 13th July to 8th Sept, daily; 9th Sept to 18th Oct, Wed – Sun, 11am –*

5.30pm (last admission 5pm). Closed Good Fri ✳ *Entrance: Garden only Sun and Bank Holiday Mons £2.25 (house and garden: weekdays and Sat £4.60, Sun and Bank Holiday Mons £5.50. Parties £3.60 per person). Lode Mill free*

The grounds cover 100 acres and were created in the last 50 years in the park of an abbey which was later converted to an Elizabethan manor. A very visual garden with magnificent vistas down avenues of mature trees and statuary and hedges enclosing small intimate gardens. 4,500 hyacinths, spring bulbs and superb mature herbaceous borders. Silver pheasants.

BARTLOW PARK ★ 2
Nr Linton, Cambridgeshire. Tel: (0223) 891609

Brigadier and Mrs Alan Breitmeyer ✳ *6m NE of Saffron Walden, 1¹/₂m SE of Linton, off A604* ✳ *Parking* ✳ *Suitable for wheelchairs* ✳ *Open 12th April, 2 – 6pm* ✳ *Entrance: £1.50, children free*

This garden was started 25 years ago by the Breitmeyers, helped by the renowned designer John Codrington, the former neglected garden being incorporated into the scheme. From the terraces there are splendid views of the park, through which run the headwaters of the River Granta. Other features include a formal rose garden, a tapestry beech and holly hedge, an old yew hedge and an avenue of sorbus, combined with many interesting trees and shrubs such as kolkwitzias, Judas trees and viburnums. There are good colour contrasts with *Acer platanoides*, *A.p.* 'Drummondii' and 'Goldsworth Purple', *Pyrus salicifolia*, *Robinia pseudoacacia* and many more. Good colour contrasts again in the border below the terrace, with *Piptanthus laburnifolius*, *Cytisus battandieri*, *Clematis tangutica* and Michaelmas daisies for autumn interest.

BURY FARM ★ 3
Meldreth, Nr Royston, Cambridgeshire. Tel: (0763) 260475

Terry and Margaret Lynch ✳ *Just N of Royston on A10 to Cambridge, turn E signed to Meldreth. Opposite church* ✳ *Parking in back drive, or road* ✳ *Toilet facilities* ✳ *Suitable for wheelchairs* ✳ *Open April to July, 1st Sun in the month and by appointment* ✳ *Entrance: £1, children 20p*

A plantsman's garden full of interesting and architectural plants – acanthus, box, yew, euphorbias etc. A few ancient box trees remain from what was thought to be the parterre of the twelfth-century manor house. New yew avenue terminating in a box circle. Extensive shrub/herbaceous border in soft pinks and blues. Grey/white borders. Brick wall with appropriate planting. Good use of tender plants in garden and conservatory. Moat being developed recently. Collection of irises and campanulas. Monograph on campanulas published by the owner.

CAMBRIDGE COLLEGE GARDENS 4
Most colleges are helpful about free access to their gardens although the Masters' or Fellows' gardens are often strictly private or rarely open. Specific

viewing times are difficult to rely on because some colleges prefer not to have visitors in term time or on days when a function is taking place. The best course is to ask at the Porter's Lodge or to telephone ahead of visit. However, some college gardens will always be open to the visitor, by arrangement with porters, even if others are closed on that particular day.

It has been said that the Cambridge college gardens are superior to those of Oxford because at the former the Fellows spend money on their upkeep while at the latter it is the upkeep of the Fellows that has the priority. Be that as it may, Cambridge also has the advantage of the Backs. Although not a garden in the strictest sense of the word, this open stretch was, like many garden/parks, the subject of 'Capability' Brown's interest in the late eighteenth century. In 1779 he prepared a plan to develop this spendid stretch of land which contains the River Cam and the 'backs' of the line of colleges to the east, but the individual colleges were reluctant to collaborate. Nonetheless the Backs today are one of the country's finest pieces of green space and probably 'hardly less beautiful than even Brown could have made it' in the words of the *Oxford Companion*.

Amongst the College gardens of particular interest are the following: *Christ's*; note particularly Milton's mulberry; the cypress grown from seed from the tree on Shelley's grave in Rome; Charles Darwin's garden with canal and false perspective; roof garden on the new building [Open weekdays, 10.30am – 12.30pm and 2 – 4pm. Closed Bank Holidays, Easter Week and May to mid-June and 23rd Dec to 2nd Jan]. *Clare Fellows' Garden*; two-acre garden redesigned in 1946 [Open Mon – Fri, but not Bank Holidays, 2 – 4pm]. *Emmanuel Gardens*; large gardens with herb garden designed by John Codrington [Open daily, 9am – 5pm; College Gardens and Fellows' Garden open 11th July for charity]. *King's Gardens and Fellows' Garden*; one of the greatest British architectural experiences is set off by fine lawns and magnificent old specimen trees. Spring bulbs [Open daily until 6pm but access limited mid-April, mid-June and closed 10th, 11th Aug and 26th Dec to 2nd Jan. Fellows' Garden only 26th July]. *Leckhampton* (part of Corpus Christi) at 37 Grange Road. Laid out by William Robinson, originally seven acres with two acres added [Open only one day in the summer for charity]. *Magdalene Fellows' Garden* [Open daily 1 – 6pm. Closed May and June]. *Pembroke*; courtyard gardens with modern plantings [Daily during daylight hours]. *Peterhouse*; varied, smallish gardens and interesting octagonal court with hot and cool sides [Open Mon – Fri, 1 – 5pm. Limited access mid-April to mid-June]. *St John's*; huge park-like garden with eight acres of grass, fine trees and good display of bulbs in spring. Wilderness introduced by 'Capability' Brown. Rose garden [Open daily 10.30am to 5.30pm but College closed to visitors May and June]. *Trinity*; a garden and grounds of 45 acres with good trees. [Grounds open daily although restricted access April to Sept; opening times from Porter's Lodge. Fellows' Garden open 12th April, 2 – 6pm]

CROSSING HOUSE GARDEN ★   5
Meldreth Road, Shepreth, Cambridgeshire. Tel: (0763) 261071

Mr and Mrs Douglas Fuller ✳ *8m SW of Cambridge, ¹/₂m W of A10* ✳ *Some parking* ✳ *Suitable for wheelchairs* ✳ *Open daily* ✳ *Entrance by collecting box*

This is a tiny garden, started by the present owners 30 years ago. No matter what time of the year you visit it there is always something fascinating growing.

In all there are 5,000 species to see. It is also an eye-opener as to what can be achieved in such a small space – from the use of diminutive box edges, to the yew arches that are beginning to grow, to the three tiny greenhouses packed with unusual plants. Highly recommended – a delightful garden. Docwra's Manor (see below) is within easy walking distance.

DOCWRA'S MANOR 6
Shepreth, Royston, Hertfordshire. Tel: (0763) 261473, 261557, 260235

*Mrs John Raven * 8m SW of Cambridge, ¹/₂m W of A10. Opposite war memorial * Best season: May – July * Parking in street * Toilet facilities * Suitable for wheelchairs * Small nursery with hardy plants for sale * Open all year, Mon, Wed, Fri, 10am – 5pm and 5th April, 3rd May, 7th June, 5th July, 2nd Aug, 6th Sept, 2 – 6pm. Also by appointment. Parties welcome * Entrance: £1, accompanied children under 16 free*

This two and a half-acre garden round a Queen Anne house has been created by the owner since 1954. It is divided into different areas by using buildings, hedges and walls, thus enabling choice and tender plants to be protected from winds. Collections of euphorbias and clematis species. The garden has been encouraged to grow jungle-like and seedlings are left to grow where they will unless they are near something too small. Many bulbs and unusual plants. The Crossing House (see above) is within easy walking distance.

DUXFORD MILL 7
Mill Lane, Duxford, Cambridgeshire. Tel: (0223) 832325

*The Hon. Mrs S. Lea. Contact: Mr Terry Bailey * From M11 junction 10 take A505 towards Newmarket, taking the second turn to Duxford village * Best season: early July * Parking * Refreshments for parties by arrangement * Toilet facilities * Suitable for wheelchairs * Plants for sale occasionally * Open Bank Holiday weekends, 10am – 6pm * Entrance: £1, children 50p*

This nine-acre garden, started in 1948, took 20 years to complete and was planned to save upkeep with lawns which flow into each other for easy mowing and rose borders in long curves with access at front and back. Roses were bred at Duxford (there are over 2000) to give as constant a display as possible and to produce cut blooms. Vistas were planned to take advantage of the river and mill pools with statues and a Regency temple as focal points. Five hundred trees provide windbreaks, interest and winter colour, notably silver birch and other *Betula* species, such as *B. costata, B. jacquemontii* and *B. papyrifera*, the paper birch. Also a maple collection and specimens of the fossil tree, better known as dawn redwood (*Metasequoia glyptostroboides*), raised from cuttings from the first specimen sent to the UK in 1948. The gardens attract a variety of wildfowl.

ELTON HALL ★ 8
Peterborough, Cambridgeshire. Tel: (0832) 280454

*Mr and Mrs William Proby * 8m W of Peterborough in the village of Elton, just* *off the A605 ✳ Best season: July ✳ Parking ✳ Refreshments ✳ Toilet facilities ✳ Hall open ✳ Open Easter to August, Bank Holiday Suns and Mons; July, Wed and Sun; Aug, Wed, Thurs and Sun, 2 – 5pm ✳ Entrance: £1.40, children 70p (hall and garden £3, children £1.50)*

Elton Hall and gardens have many regular visitors enjoying the Proby family's progress in restoring the seventeenth-century hall which has been in their family ever since. The scent of more than 1000 roses in the Victorian rose garden is most memorable along with the sunken garden which is planted with an unusual selection of foliage and blue and white flowering plants, including *Crambe cordifolia* and *Romneya coulteri*. Restoration is advanced with feature areas, including the knot herb garden now well divided and set off by beech hedge, yew topiary and statuary. A 'must' for rose lovers. Arboretum and eight acres of grounds in total.

HARDWICKE HOUSE ★   9
High Ditch Road, Fen Ditton, Nr Cambridge, Cambridgeshire. Tel: (02205) 2246

Mr L. and Mr J. Drake ✳ 3¹/₂m NE of Cambridge. From A45 Newmarket Road turn N by the borough cemetery ✳ Best season: spring/summer ✳ Parking in road opposite ✳ Teas in Cambridge ✳ Partly suitable for wheelchairs ✳ Plants for sale ✳ Open by appointment and 24th May, 7th, 21st June, 2 – 6pm ✳ Entrance: £1.50, children 50p

This medium-sized garden can be visited at any season; the spring gives a stunning display of bulbs and the colchicums give September interest. Mr Drake holds the National collection of aquilegias – 120 different varieties. There are hedges everywhere to protect the garden from its very exposed position. These have been carefully planned to create varying environments. Within the hedged enclosures there are collections of plants available in this country prior to 1660, Turkish borders and tight plantings of ground cover interspersed with plants of great rarity.

THE HERB GARDEN   10
Nigel House, High Street, Wilburton, Ely, Cambridgeshire. Tel: (0353) 740824

Mrs Yate ✳ 5m SW of Ely on A1123 in the centre of Wilburton near the church ✳ Best season: May to July ✳ Parking in drive and by church ✳ Toilet facilities ✳ Suitable for wheelchairs ✳ Dogs on lead ✳ Plants for sale ✳ Open May to Sept, most days, 10am – 6pm. Telephone to check ✳ Entrance: free (collection box for charity)

For the enthusiast with a keen interest in herbs, Mrs Yate has created a small but very special garden. The narrow plot has been divided in such a way that surprise is just around each partition. The herbs are well displayed in named collections covering the aromatics, culinary, astrological, medicinal, biblical, dyers, Roman and Shakespearian herbs.

ISLAND HALL 11
Godmanchester, Nr Huntingdon, Cambridgeshire. Tel: (0480) 459676

Mr C. and the Hon. Mrs Vane Percy ∗ *On the main street in the centre of Godmanchester* ∗ *Parking in municipal car park* ∗ *Teas* ∗ *Toilet facilities* ∗ *House open* ∗ *Garden open 14th June to 6th Sept, Suns only, 2.30 – 5pm, and May to Sept for parties by appointment* ∗ *Entrance: £2, children £1.50 (house and garden). No children under 13 in house*

In a tranquil riverside setting with its own island, the garden has been reclaimed from neglect and from the Nissen huts put there when the house was requisitioned in World War II. The terrace has been removed and replaced at a lower level with gravel – to the benefit of the house. Formal shaped borders planted with different box are either side of the gravel terrace. Gaps have been left in the gravel for fastigiate yew. New shrubberies have been planted with a walk through to white and blue borders – urns, hedges and vistas are there. The island is being cleared and wild flowers encouraged. An exact replica of the original Chinese bridge over the millstream was completed in 1988. Visitors will especially enjoy the marvellous sense of history evoked by both house and garden, all of which is well documented in an excellent guide, with tales ranging from connections with William Tell and buried church plate to the restoration of the garden.

NORTH END HOUSE ★ 12
Grantchester, Nr Cambridge, Cambridgeshire. Tel: (0223) 840231

Sir Martin and Lady Nourse ∗ *2m SW of Cambridge. Approaching on the A10 from S, turn left at Trumpington (junction 11 on M11). If approaching from N on M11, take junction 12* ∗ *Parking* ∗ *Teas* ∗ *Suitable for wheelchairs* ∗ *Open 28th June, 2 – 6.30pm* ∗ *Entrance: £2*

A very well structured and maintained garden. It has the illusion of space, enhanced by a carefully placed mirror. Created almost solely by Sir Martin and Lady Nourse, the selection of shrubs and herbaceous plants is imaginative, illustrating what beauty can be created through a knowledgeable mixing of plants. The rockery is an excellent example of a feature which does not fall into the trap of domination but adds immensely to the charm of the garden. The use of plants to screen the tennis court shows what can be achieved in 10 years.

PADLOCK CROFT ★ 13
West Wratting, Cambridgeshire. Tel: (0223) 290383

Mr and Mrs P.E. Lewis ∗ *On the outskirts of the village by West Wratting Park. With the Chestnut Tree public house on your right take the first right and first right again. Signed on the left* ∗ *Best season: May to July* ∗ *Limited parking* ∗ *Toilet facilities* ∗ *Suitable for wheelchairs* ∗ *Plants for sale* ∗ *Open March to Oct, daily except Wed and Sun, 10am – 6pm. Wed and in winter by appointment* ∗ *Entrance: £1, children 50p on charity open days. Free at other times*

A two-thirds of an acre garden created during the last 12 years solely by the owners. Mrs Lewis holds the National collection of campanula and *Campanulaceae* and is a great plant enthusiast growing plants from all over the world including the St Helena ebony (once thought to be extinct). The garden offers a number of imaginative plantings for dry, damp and alpine collections. A new rockery and a *potager* are being created.

PECKOVER HOUSE★★   14
North Brink, Wisbech, Cambridgeshire. Tel: (0945) 583463

*The National Trust * In centre of Wisbech on N bank of the River Nene * House open (principal rooms only) as garden but Sun, Wed and Bank Holiday Mon, 2 – 5.30pm * Garden open 28th March to 1st Nov, Sat – Wed, 2 – 5.30pm * Entrance: £1 (garden only open days), £2.20 (house open days)*

For a hundred years or so this Victorian garden has been 'the product of prudent tidiness, a period piece'. Given in 1943 to The National Trust by Alexandrina Peckover, it had been in the same family since the second half of the eighteenth century. A town house, with two and a quarter acres of garden, it contains some very interesting trees. A maidenhair tree, one of the largest in England, was planted a century ago by the donor's Peckover grandfather. Hardy palms withstand the English winter, and in the Orange House is an orange tree bearing fruit which was bought at the Hagbeach Hall sale and is at least 200 years old. In the conservatory are billbergias, daturas and monsteras. Another small house contains tender ferns. Trees and plants are rather in the Victorian taste, such as fern-leaved beech, Wellingtonias and Lawson cypresses, yuccas and spotted-leaved aucubas. The garden is divided by walls; imaginative planting of bulbs, climbers and herbaceous plants make for continuous interest throughout the year. An elegant summer-house is joined to the conservatory by matching borders edged with pinks.

THE RECTORY   15
High Street, Fen Ditton, Nr Cambridge, Cambridgeshire. Tel: (02205) 3257

*The Revd. and Mrs L. Marsh * Off A45 Cambridge – Newmarket road. Turn N by cemetery into Ditton Lane * Best season: spring and early summer * Parking * Teas * Toilet facilities * Suitable for wheelchairs * Plants for sale when available * Open 21st June, 2 – 6pm and by appointment * Entrance: £1.50 (fee of £1.50 for June opening covers combined admission to Hardwicke House and Old Stables in the same village)*

The garden of this late seventeenth-century house is now reduced to one acre and is in the process of being restored. Some 70 varieties of old-fashioned roses and species roses have been planted with herbaceous plants to extend the flowering season. There are many rare plants including *Arisaema candidissimum*. Also good mature trees. Many fruit trees have been planted, mulberry, walnut, medlar and apricot among others. Vegetables are grown organically and in sufficient amounts to provide vegetables and fruit for the whole year. Masses of bulbs in the spring.

THORPE HALL   16
Longthorpe, Peterborough, Cambridgeshire. Tel: (0733) 330060

*The Sue Ryder Foundation * On W edge of Peterborough between A47 and A605*

Parking * *Refreshments* * *Toilet facilities* * *Suitable for wheelchairs* *
Shop * *Ground floor of house open as garden* * *Garden open daily except 25th,*
26th Dec and 1st Jan, 10am – 5pm * *Entrance: donations to home funds*

The Sue Ryder Foundation Home at Thorpe Hall opened in spring 1991 and
with it the Victorian gardens largely neglected since *c.* 1920 but now well into a
five-year restoration programme started in 1989. The garden's architecture,
proportions and vistas are elegant, and the restoration thus far promising,
although hampered by drought in 1990. Visits to see progress would be most
rewarding for Victorian garden enthusiasts. The adjacent garden centre is
separately managed with a good selection of well-labelled shrubs. One section
of the main garden is being restored to Cromwellian style.

UNIVERSITY BOTANIC GARDEN ★★   17
Cambridge. Tel: (0223) 336265

University of Cambridge * *In S Cambridge, on E side of A10 (Trumpington*
Road). There is also an entrance from Hills Road on the E * *Parking in road* *
Refreshments * *Toilet facilities* * *Suitable for wheelchairs* * *Open all year,*
Mon – Sat, 8am – 6pm in summer (dusk in winter) and Sun, from 10am *
Entrance: Mon – Sat, free, Sun, £1, children 50p

This garden covers a huge area (40 acres) and is so diverse that a brief
description will not do it justice. It admirably fulfils its three purposes –
research, education and amenity. A visit at any time is worthwhile – even in
winter when the stem garden, especially on a sunny day, is dramatic. The
various cornus with red, black, green and yellow-ochre stems contrast with
Rubus thibetanus, while the pale pink trunk of the birch *Betula albo-sinensis* var.
septentrionalis is stunning. There is a splendid collection of native trees as well
as exotic ones, including *Asimina triloba* and a good specimen of *Tetracentron*
sinense. Among the collections is a fine one of salix and poplars. *Populus nigra* is
now rare in England. A central area is reserved for research. There are also
rockeries (both sandstone and limestone), a collection of species tulips, a
scented garden, a fine range of glasshouses (hot and cool), a library and a
herbarium of cultivated plants. Every specimen is clearly labelled. The new
Gilmour building, named after a director who greatly expanded the garden in
the 1950s and 60s, was completed recently.

WIMPOLE HALL   18
Arrington, Royston, Cambridgeshire. Tel: (0223) 207257

The National Trust * *7m SW of Cambridge signposted off A603 at New*
Wimpole * *Best season: spring* * *Parking* * *Refreshments: teas and lunches* *
Toilet facilities * *Suitable for wheelchairs* * *Minimal number of plants for sale*
* *National Trust shop* * *House open* * *Garden open 28th March to 1st Nov,*
daily except Mon and Fri, 1 – 5pm but open Bank Holiday Sun and Mon, 11am –
5pm. Closed Good Fri. Pre-booked guided tours for parties with head gardener *
Entrance: £4.40, children £2.20 (hall and garden)

The gardens of this mid-seventeenth-century house followed almost every
fashion in landscaping from 1690 to 1810. Today it is much changed due to

Dutch elm disease. However, parterres, simplified by The National Trust, have been recently reinstated to the north of the house. Extensive and beautifully kept lawns but little else for the discerning plantsman, although the gardens are undergoing continuous restoration. The surrounding landscape is of great historic and aesthetic interest and includes a two and a quarter-mile avenue, originally planted in elm in 1792, recently replanted with limes by The National Trust. Grand folly and Chinese bridge. Today, the Hall is used as a farm centre with a children's corner and agricultural museum. Also adventure playground and film loft.

HOW TO FIND THE GARDENS
Directions to each garden are included in each entry. This information has been supplied by the garden inspectors and is aimed to be the best available to those travelling by car. However, it has been compiled to be used in conjunction with a road atlas. The unreliability of train and bus services makes it unrewarding to include details, particularly as many garden visits are made on Sundays. However, many properties can be reached by public transport and National Trust guides and the Yellow Book [NGS] give details. Future editions of the *Guide* may include a special list of gardens easily reached by public transport if readers indicate that this would be helpful. *The Maps*: The numbers on the maps correspond to the numbers of the gardens in each county. The maps show the proximity of one garden to another so that visits to several gardens can be planned for the same day. It is worthwhile referring to the maps of bordering counties to see if another garden visit can be included in the itinerary.

CHESHIRE

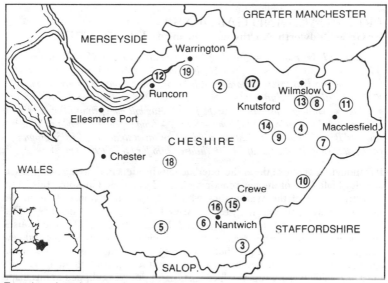

Two-starred gardens are ringed in bold.

ADLINGTON HALL   1
Macclesfield, Cheshire. Tel: (0625) 829206

Mr C.F. Legh ✳ 5m N of Macclesfield off the A523. Signposted in the village of Adlington ✳ Best season: May/early June ✳ Parking ✳ Refreshments in tea rooms ✳ Toilet facilities ✳ Partly suitable for wheelchairs ✳ Dogs on lead ✳ Small shop ✳ House open ✳ Garden open Good Fri to 4th Oct, Sun and Bank Holidays, 2 – 5.30pm ✳ Entrance: £2.50, children £1, parties of 25 or more £1.90 per person

To the front of the house (fifteenth and sixteenth-century with Georgian additions) a gravel drive encircles an oval of lawn with a sundial at its centre. Beyond there is more grass, then through a pair of iron gates is a short avenue of limes dating from 1688. After these a path leads eastwards to the Shell House, a small brick building dating from 1794, in which shells were stuck around its walls in the mid-nineteenth century. To the west is a wood through which there are walks open to the visitor. The walk along the small river bank is particularly pleasant. In the centre, close to a bridge is the Temple of Diana. East from the house across a cobbled area is a formal pool. A large statue of Neptune lies at the back with water pouring into the pool from a pitcher on which he leans. There are also bright beds of annuals and a small herb garden in this area. Not much interest, then, for the plantsperson but an attractive woodland park, mostly landscaped in the eighteenth century.

ARLEY HALL AND GARDENS★   2
Nr Great Budworth, Northwich, Cheshire. Tel: (0565) 777353

The Hon M.L.W. Flower ✻ *5m W of Knutsford off A50, 7m SE of Warrington off A49. Follow signs. Also signed from M6 junctions 19/20 and M56 junctions 9/10* ✻ *Parking* ✻ *Teas. More elaborate meals for pre-booked parties by arrangement* ✻ *Toilet facilities* ✻ *Suitable for wheelchairs* ✻ *Dogs on lead* ✻ *Plants for sale* ✻ *Shop* ✻ *Hall open as gardens except June to Aug but not open until 2pm* ✻ *Garden open Easter to early Oct, Tues – Sun, 2 – 6pm (open at 12 noon in June to Aug and Bank Holidays)* ✻ *Entrance: £2.10, children under 17, £1.05 (grounds, garden and chapel), additional £1.20, children 60p for Hall (1991 prices)*

It is thought that one of the earliest herbaceous borders in England was planted at Arley Hall. One of the few remaining landed estates in Cheshire, this is the ancestral house of the Warburtons who built their first house there in the fifteenth century, though the present Arley Hall dates only from 1840. The gardens cover 12 acres and were awarded the Christie's and Historic Houses Association Garden of the Year Award. Bounded by old brick walls and yew hedges, there is a special predilection for the tonsured, as evidenced in the splendid avenue of pleached limes which form the approach to the house and the remarkable ilex avenue which consists of 14 ilex trees clipped to the shape of giant cylinders. The walled garden, once a kitchen garden, now contains a variety of cordoned fruit trees, shrubs and herbaceous plants. There is also a collection of hybrid and species shrub roses, a rock garden planted with azaleas and rhododendrons, and a contemporary addition of a woodland garden which illustrates a continuous commitment to a family tradition.

BRIDGEMERE GARDEN WORLD   3
Bridgemere, Nr Nantwich, Cheshire. Tel: (09365) 239/381/382

Mr J. Ravenscroft ✻ *On A51 S of Nantwich. From M6 take junction 15 or 16 and follow signs* ✻ *Parking* ✻ *Refreshments: coffee shop* ✻ *Toilet facilities, inc. disabled* ✻ *Suitable for wheelchairs* ✻ *Plants for sale* ✻ *Shop* ✻ *Open daily except 25th, 26th Dec, summer 9am – 8pm, winter 9am – 5pm* ✻ *Entrance: £1 for Garden Kingdom*

Begun in 1961 with one field of roses, this 25-acre garden centre now claims to be Europe's largest. There are large areas with all types of plants for sale, garden ornaments, conservatories and greenhouses. Although some of these areas are attractively laid out, the main area of interest as a garden to view is the Garden Kingdom. This has been made mainly to show what the plants offered for sale will come to look like, and most plants are labelled. There is a rose garden, including modern and old-fashioned shrub roses, rhododendron garden, winter garden, large herbaceous border, white garden, rock and water garden, cottage garden and a vegetable and fruit garden demonstrating some unusual ways of growing your own food. Recently constructed is the 'Green and Pleasant Land', a garden that won the Chelsea gold medal in 1990, with a very notable folly built by John Bailey. Most of these areas are, as is to be expected, very well kept.

CAPESTHORNE HALL AND GARDENS ★ 4
Macclesfield, Cheshire. Tel: (0625) 861221/861779

*Mr W.A. Bromley Davenport * 7m S of Wilmslow, 1m from Monks Heath on A34 * Parking * Refreshments: lunch, afternoon teas, supper by arrangement * Toilet facilities * Suitable for wheelchairs * Dogs in park only * Shop * House open as gardens but 2 – 4pm only * Garden open April, Sun; May, Aug and Sept, Wed and Sun; June and July, Tues – Thurs and Sun, 12 noon – 6pm. Also open Good Friday and all Bank Holidays during the summer months * Entrance: £1.75, children 5 – 16, 50p (Hall extra £1.75, OAP £1.50, children 50p)*

Capesthorne is one of East Cheshire's fine historic parks showing the English style of eighteenth and nineteenth-century landscape design with belts of trees enclosing a broad sweep of park and with the house as the focal element. The gardens are best enjoyed by following the suggested woodland walks, because the outstanding features are the range of mature trees, and the views and plant-life associated with the series of man-made lakes. There is much, too, to interest those with a taste for the history of gardens – for example the site of a conservatory built by Sir Joseph Paxton. There is a pair of outstanding rococo Milanese gates, and more conventionally a formal lakeside garden planned in the 1960s by garden designer Vernon Russell-Smith.

CHOLMONDELEY CASTLE GARDENS ★ 5
Cholmondeley Castle, Malpas, Cheshire. Tel: (0829) 720 383/203

*The Marquess of Cholmondeley * On A49 between Tarporley and Whitchurch * Parking * Refreshments * Toilet facilities * Plants for sale * Shop * Open Easter Sun to Sept, Sun and Bank Holidays, 12 noon – 5.30pm * Entrance. £2, OAP £1, children 50p (1991 prices)*

In spite of the ancient family name (pronounced Chumley), the Castle and more particularly the gardens are of relatively recent development, and understandably therefore they lack the maturity of other Cheshire parklands. As a site, though, it is magnificent, with the castle straddling a hill-top and a view across parkland to a distant mere, and the classic cricket square in between. Much has been done by the present owners to develop the gardens which consisted in the 1960s of but a few (but splendid) cedars and oaks and the creation of the Temple Gardens in particular – bordered walkways around a water garden – is most satisfying with its rock garden with a fine view of the lake that leads into a stream garden planted with moisture-lovers. The grass round the tea room is filled with wild orchids and backing away from this is a good planting of rhododendrons. The rose garden contains an interesting mixture of old and new.

DORFOLD HALL 6
Nantwich, Cheshire. Tel: (0270) 625245

Mr R. Roundell ✻ *1m W of Nantwich, S of A534* ✻ *Best season: spring and early summer* ✻ *Parking* ✻ *Toilet facilities* ✻ *Partly suitable for wheelchairs (garden only)* ✻ *House open* ✻ *Garden open April to Oct, Tues and Bank Holiday Mons, 2 – 5pm* ✻ *Entrance: £2.50. children £1.50*

Dorfold Hall, impressive from the front, is approached through an avenue of limes with open parkland to each side and a large pool just to the west. The approach to the house is thought to have been laid out by William Nesfield who was chosen to design various parts of Kew. To the rear or south of the house is a large lawn at the east side of which is a statue of Shakespeare standing between two modern shrub borders. To the south is a low wall with a narrow border planted with shrub roses, beyond this is another large lawn from where there are views across a ha-ha to the flat countryside in the south. A broad grass walk leads eastwards to a dell. Here rhododendrons and other acid-loving shrubs have been planted amongst mature trees around a small stream, an area developed by the present owner. To the west is another grassed area with specimen trees and two fine gates lead to a disused walled garden.

GAWSWORTH HALL 7
Macclesfield, Cheshire. Tel: (0260) 223456

Mr and Mrs T. Richards ✻ *3m S of Macclesfield off A536. Signposted* ✻ *Best season: midsummer* ✻ *Parking* ✻ *Refreshments: tearooms at pavilion in car park* ✻ *Toilet facilities* ✻ *Suitable for wheelchairs* ✻ *Small shop* ✻ *House open* ✻ *Open Easter to 4th Oct, daily, 2 – 5.30pm* ✻ *Entrance: £1.50 (house and garden £3, children £1.50, parties of 20 or more £2.50)*

Gawsworth Hall is approached by a drive leading between two lakes which arrives at the north end of the hall where there is a large yew tree and lawns sloping down to one of the lakes. A formal garden on the west side of the house has beds of modern roses edged by bright annuals and many stone ornaments including a sundial and circular pool with a fountain. Stone steps lead to a sunken lawn area with borders of shrubs and perennials. To the south is another lawned garden surrounded by a high yew hedge and herbaceous borders. A grassed area containing mature trees lies to the west of these formal areas, from where there is a view of the medieval tilting ground and site of the Elizabethan pleasure gardens. A path back to the house passes a small conservatory containing classical statues.

HARE HILL GARDENS 8
Hare Hill, Over Alderley, Nr Macclesfield, Cheshire. Tel: (0625) 828981

The National Trust ✻ *N of B5087 between Alderly Edge and Prestbury at Greyhound Road* ✻ *Best season: spring/early June* ✻ *Parking* ✻ *Toilet facilities* ✻ *Partly suitable for wheelchairs* ✻ *Open April to 25th Oct, Wed, Thurs, Sat, Sun and Bank Holiday Mons, 10am – 5.30pm. Special for roses and* *azaleas, 18th May to 5th June, daily, 10am – 5.30pm. 31st Oct to March 1993, Sat, Sun, 10am – 5.30pm. Parties by appointment* * *Entrance: £1 per car*

This garden consists of two distinct areas, a walled garden, once used for growing vegetables, and surrounding it a large woodland garden. The walled garden is rather sparsely planted. Climbing plants around the walls include vines, roses, ceanothus and wisteria, and in the centre are a few small rosebeds. A seat set into the north wall is surrounded by a white trellis pergola and nearby are two wire statues. The woodland garden is perhaps of greater interest. It contains over 50 varieties of holly, many fine rhododendrons and magnolias and there are spring-flowering bulbs and some climbing roses growing high into their host trees. In the centre is a small pond spanned by two rustic wooden bridges. Much new planting carried out and the garden improves each year.

JODRELL BANK ARBORETUM 9
Jodrell Bank Science Centre and Arboretum, Macclesfield, Cheshire. Tel: (0477) 71339

Manchester University * *On the A535 between Holmes Chapel and Chelford, 5m from M6 junction 18. Signposted* * *Parking* * *Refreshments: self-service cafeteria* * *Toilet facilities* * *Partly suitable for wheelchairs* * *Shop* * *Open Easter to Oct, daily, 10.30am – 5.30pm. Otherwise Sat and Sun, 12 noon – 5pm* * *Entrance: £3, OAP £2.20, children £1.65 inc. science centre and planetarium. Family ticket £9*

The garden was begun in 1972 largely at the instigation of Professor Sir Bernard Lovell and with financial support from the Granada Foundation. It is set in a flat landscape with all views to the south dominated by the massive radio telescope. Large collections of trees, heathers and old-fashioned roses are its main attractions. There are broad grass walkways and many small natural ponds in this 40-acre garden. The National collections of malus and sorbus are here, together with the Heather Society calluna collection. A visit to Jodrell Bank represents good value when all its attractions are considered and is a day out for a family.

LITTLE MORETON HALL 10
Congleton, Cheshire. Tel: (0260) 272018

The National Trust * *4m SW of Congleton on the E side of the A34 between Congleton and Newcastle-under-Lyme* * *Parking* * *Refreshments: drinks and light meals* * *Toilet facilities* * *Suitable for wheelchairs. Wheelchair available on loan* * *Dogs in car park and areas outside moat only* * *Shop* * *Herbs usually for sale* * *Open April to Sept, Wed – Sun, 12 noon – 5.30pm. Bank Holiday Mons, 11am – 5.30pm. Oct, Wed, Sat and Sun, 12 noon – 5.30pm (last admission 5pm)* * *Entrance: £2.50, children £1.25 (weekends and Bank Holidays £3, children £1.50). Family £7.50*

Little Moreton Hall is one of the best-known timber-framed buildings in the country, and its gardens too are very pleasant in their own quiet way. They cover about an acre and are set within a moat. There is a cobbled courtyard in the centre of the hall and to the west a large lawn with fruit trees and an old grassed mound. To the north of the hall is a yew tunnel and the best feature of all, a knot garden, laid out under the guidance of Graham Stuart Thomas following a seventeenth-century model. It is a simple design of gravel and lawn separated by a low box hedge. Behind the knot garden, four new beds have been planted with medieval and culinary herbs and a selection of seventeenth-century vegetables. There are herbaceous borders around the hall and a gravel walk that follows the inside perimeter of the moat. The garden is largely the creation of the Trust and is a fitting complement to the house.

MELLORS GARDEN   11
Hough Hole House, Sugar Lane, Rainow, Nr Macclesfield, Cheshire. Tel: (0625) 572286

Mr and Mrs G. Humphreys ✳ *Ten minutes from the centre of Macclesfield. Take the Whaley Bridge road. In the village of Rainow turn off to the north, opposite the church into Round Meadow Lane. Then turn at the first left into Sugar Lane and follow this down to the garden* ✳ *Parking* ✳ *Refreshments* ✳ *Toilet facilities* ✳ *Partly suitable for wheelchairs* ✳ *Dogs on lead* ✳ *Open Spring and Aug Bank Holiday Sun and Mon, 2 – 5pm or by appointment for parties of more than 10* ✳ *Entrance: £1, children free*

Where can you pass through the valley of the shadow of death, climb Jacob's ladder, see the mouth of hell and visit the Celestial City all within 10 minutes of Macclesfield? Here in the second half of the nineteenth century, James Mellor, much influenced by Swedenborg, designed this allegorical garden which attempts to recreate the journey of Christian in Bunyan's *Pilgrim's Progress*. Most areas are grassed with stone paths running throughout. There are many small stone houses and other ornaments to represent features of the journey. At one end a large pond is overlooked by a small octagonal summerhouse. The garden stands in a small valley in a rugged but attractive part of the Peak District. Be sure to be shown round by the owner or buy one of the excellent guide books in order to get the best from this small garden.

NORTON PRIORY MUSEUM AND GARDENS   12
Tudor Road, Runcorn, Cheshire. Tel: (0928) 569895

Norton Priory Museum Trust ✳ *From M6 at junction 11 turn for Warrington and follow Norton Priory signs. From all other directions follow Runcorn then Norton Priory signs* ✳ *Parking* ✳ *Refreshments: teas and snacks in Museum* ✳ *Toilet facilities, inc. disabled* ✳ *Suitable for wheelchairs* ✳ *Dogs permitted but not in walled garden* ✳ *Plants for sale* ✳ *Shop* ✳ *Museum open* ✳ *Garden open April to Oct, weekdays, 12 noon – 5pm, Sat, Sun and Bank Holidays, 12 noon – 6pm, Nov to March, daily, 12 noon – 4pm. Walled garden closed Nov to Feb* ✳ *Entrance: £2.20, OAP and children £1.10. Museum and grounds £1.60, OAP, children and students 80p. Walled garden 90p, OAP, children and students 50p*

Norton Priory was built as an Augustan foundation in the twelfth century and transformed into a Tudor then Georgian mansion before being abandoned in 1921. The 16 acres of gardens contain the ruins of the Priory, and also an authentic eighteenth-century walled garden. Originally built by Sir Richard Brooke in 1757 it eventually fell into disrepair, but since 1980 the owners have restored it to reflect both the Georgian and modern designs and tastes. Its range of specialities include a culinary herb and medicinal herb garden, plants for household uses, a fruit arch and cordon fruit, a new orchard, and a number of herbaceous borders.

PENN 13
Macclesfield Road, Alderley Edge, Cheshire.

Mr R.W. Baldwin ✻ *³/₄m E of Alderley Edge village, N of B5087* ✻ *Parking on road* ✻ *Refreshments* ✻ *Partly suitable for wheelchairs* ✻ *Plants for sale* ✻ *Open 26th April, 24th, 25th May, 2 – 5.30pm* ✻ *Entrance: £1.50, OAP £1, children 50p*

This garden is most noted for its fine collection of rhododendrons and azaleas and there are over 500 varieties here. But the situation high on Alderley Edge and its layout contribute much to the garden's charm. An Edwardian house stands at the centre facing south and overlooks a large lawn, surrounded by banks of trees and shrubs including camellias and magnolias as well as rhododendrons. Behind the house is a steeply rising woodland garden with narrow paths running among the trees and shrubs, and it is here that the best views are obtained, both back across the Cheshire plain and over the Edge towards Manchester. A fruit and vegetable garden and some small herbaceous beds lie to the west of the house.

PEOVER HALL 14
Peover Hall, Over Peover, Nr Knutsford, Cheshire.

Mr R. Brooks ✻ *3m S of Knutsford on A50* ✻ *Teas on Mons* ✻ *Toilet facilities* ✻ *Partly suitable for wheelchairs (many grass paths)* ✻ *Dogs in park only* ✻ *Plants for sale on special occasions* ✻ *House open, Mon only, 2.30 – 4.30pm* ✻ *Gardens open May to Sept, Mon and Thurs, 2.30 – 4.30pm* ✻ *Entrance: £1 (hall and garden £2, children £1)*

Peover Hall and its gardens are surrounded by a large expanse of flat parkland laid out in the early eighteenth century, but the gardens are mainly Edwardian. On the northern side of the hall is a forecourt, from where a broad grass walk leads through an avenue of pleached limes to a summerhouse. This overlooks a small circular lawn and both are enclosed by a high yew hedge. On the west side of the gardens is a wooded area containing many rhododendrons and a grassed dell that is particularly attractive. Clustered around the south and west of the hall are several small formal gardens, separated by brick walls and yew hedges. Some contain yew topiary. There is a rose garden, a herb garden, a white garden and a pink garden. The lily pool garden has a summerhouse with a tiled roof supported by Doric columns. A church stands in the centre of the gardens and there are fine Georgian stables.

QUEEN'S PARK, CREWE ★ 15
Victoria Avenue, Wisterton Road, Crewe, Cheshire. Tel: (0270) 583191 ext 486

Crewe and Nantwich Borough Council ✻ *2m W of Crewe town centre, S of the*

A532 ✳ Parking off Queen's Park Drive ✳ Refreshments: cafeteria in park ✳ Toilet facilities, inc. disabled ✳ Partly suitable for wheelchairs ✳ Dogs on lead ✳ Open all year, 9am – sunset ✳ Entrance: free

Queen's Park is a very well landscaped Victorian park created in 1887-8 by the London & North Western Railway as a gift to the people of Crewe. It is oval in shape and covers 48 acres, with large grassed areas and a wide variety of mature trees. From an ornate entrance with two 'gothic' lodges and a clock tower, a drive leads through an avenue of birches to the centre of the park. Here a modern café with a terrace looks down upon the large boating lake that is surrounded by banks of trees and shrubs. From the west of the park a stream runs through a lightly wooded valley to join the lake. A path linking the entrance to this valley passes some raised beds of heathers and goes through a tunnel of laburnum. It merits a high grade for the quality of landscaping, the trees and the Victorian buildings, but in essence it is a large municipal park where a fight against vandalism and litter is fought hard.

REASE HEATH   16
Cheshire College of Agriculture, Nr Nantwich, Cheshire. Tel: (0270) 625131

Cheshire College of Agriculture ✳ 1¹/₂m N of Nantwich on A51 ✳ Parking ✳ Toilet facilities ✳ Partly suitable for wheelchairs ✳ Plants for sale ✳ Open for College Open Day 16th May, 1 – 5pm

Cheshire College of Agriculture is fortunate in being housed in the grounds of Rease Heath for its attractive gardens must constantly provide the students with inspiration. From the old brick hall a large lawn sweeps southwards to a lake, flanked on one side by a heather garden and by a rockery on the other. The lake is spanned by a wooden bridge and stocked with a good variety of water lilies and marginals. On the south side is a woodland garden, with many fine trees including a large cut-leaved beech. Underplanting is of primulas, hostas, azaleas and other shade loving plants. To the west of the lake is another lawned area; this has island beds with a variety of small trees, shrubs and perennials. There is also a formal rose garden enclosed by a berberis hedge. Other small gardens are scattered around the campus – altogether there is much here of interest and most plants are labelled.

TATTON PARK ★★   17
Knutsford, Cheshire. Tel: (0565) 654822

The National Trust ✳ Signposted from Knutsford and from A556 ✳ Parking £2 per car ✳ Refreshments: hot and cold lunches and snacks but from Oct to March, Suns only, 11.30am – 4.30pm ✳ Toilet facilities ✳ Partly suitable for wheelchairs ✳ Plants for sale ✳ Shop ✳ House open April to Sept open as gardens but 12 noon – 4pm. Oct to March 1993 open as gardens ✳ Gardens open April to Sept, daily except Mons (but open Bank Holiday Mons), 10.30am – 6pm. Oct to March 1993, daily except Mons and 24th, 25th Dec, 11am – 4pm. Open at other times by appointment ✳ Entrance: gardens £2.30, park £2 per car, Tatton Explorer (to house, park and gardens) £6

The gardens here cover 50 acres and warrant an extensive exploration. On passing through the entrance visitors see to their right the Orangery. Built in 1820 by Lewis Wyatt, it contains orange trees, lemon trees, a bougainvillaea and other exotics. Next door is Paxton's fernery of 1850. This has large New Zealand tree ferns in its distinctively Victorian interior. To the east passing a large L-shaped herbaceous and shrub border, the Edwardian rose garden is reached. This is formal in design with a pool at its centre and fine stone paths and ornaments around. To the south lie large informally planted areas, an arboretum contains many conifers and rhododendrons and a lake contains water lilies and has a good variety of marginal plants growing around its banks. On the west side of the lake is a unique Japanese garden built in 1910 by workers brought especially from Japan. To the south of the house is the Italian garden possibly designed by Paxton and best viewed from the top floor of the house. The garden also contains a maze and many other features of interest. It is surrounded by a great expanse of very attractive parkland.

TIRLEY GARTH ★ 18
Utkinton, Nr Tarporley, Cheshire. Tel: (0829) 732301

Tirley Garth Trust ＊ 2¹/₂m N of Tarporley, just N of village of Utkinton on the road to Kelsall. Signposted ＊ Parking ＊ Teas ＊ Toilet facilities ＊ Partly suitable for wheelchairs ＊ Dogs on lead ＊ Open 17th, 24th, 25th, 30th, 31st May, 2 – 6pm ＊ Entrance: £1.50, children 50p

Tirley Garth is a magnificent Edwardian house with gardens that complement it perfectly. They are still in much the same layout as originally designed by the architect T.H. Mawson and some of the stonework in the paths, ornaments and buildings is particularly notable. There is a circular courtyard at the western entrance and a small sunken garden to one side which leads to the large terrace on the south front which has lawns and rose beds. To the east is a lawned terrace with a view across the large semi-circular rose garden that spreads below it. In the centre of the house is a courtyard with a circular pool and fountain. Outside these formal gardens are areas of parkland and woodland; to the east is a stream running through a small valley planted with fine azaleas, rhododendrons and other acid-loving shrubs. There are good views of the surrounding countryside.

WALTON HALL GARDENS 19
Walton Lea Road, off Chester Road, Walton, Warrington, Cheshire. Tel: (0925) 601617

Warrington Borough Council ＊ 2m SW of Warrington on S side of A56 in the village of Walton ＊ Best season: spring and autumn ＊ Parking. A charge is made at weekends and Bank Holidays from Easter to Oct ＊ Refreshments ＊ Partly suitable for wheelchairs ＊ Toilet facilities ＊ Dogs on lead, some restricted areas ＊ Shop ＊ House open Easter to Sept, Thurs – Sun, 1 – 5pm (Easter, Bank Holidays) and Oct to Easter, Sun, 12.30 – 4.30pm. Extra charge ＊ Gardens open daily, 8am – dusk ＊ Entrance: free

Walton Hall, the former home of the Greenhall family, is a dark brick house with a distinctive clock tower. In front is a large lawn and to one side a modern pool and rockery, with a variety of shrubs, alpines and aquatic plants. Behind the Hall is a series of formal gardens separated by yew hedges and planted with bright annuals. Further south is a lawned area with herbaceous borders, with a path leading under some large beech trees to a rose garden. This has beds of modern roses set in an area of grass enclosed by a high conifer hedge. A walk back around the west side of the garden passes through an attractive area of shrubs and trees amongst which are many acers. Banks of mature woodland and large parkland surround the garden. The Council keeps the whole area in good condition.

OPENING DATES AND TIMES

Times of access given are the best available at the moment of going to press, but some may have been changed subsequently. In the entries, the times given are inclusive – that is, an entry such as May to Sept means that the garden is open from 1st May to 30th Sept inclusive and 2 – 5pm also means that entry will be effective during that period. Please note that many owners will open their gardens to visitors by appointment. They will often arrange to give a personally-conducted tour on these occasions.

CORNWALL

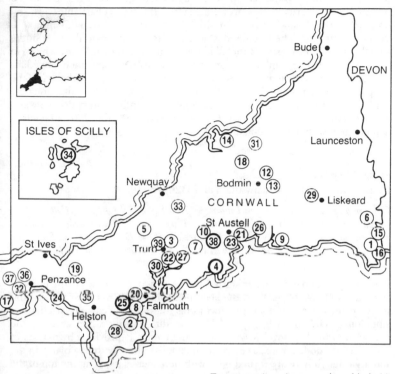

Two-starred gardens are ringed in bold.

ANTHONY HOUSE   1

Torpoint, Cornwall. Tel: NT office (0752) 812191; woodland garden office (0752) 812364

The National Trust and the Trustees of the Carew Pole Garden Trust ∗ From Plymouth use Torpoint car ferry. Anthony is 2m W of Torpoint on A374, 16m SE of Liskeard ∗ Best season: mid-March to mid-May ∗ Parking ∗ Toilet facilities ∗ Partly suitable for wheelchairs ∗ Shop ∗ House open as garden ∗ Garden open April to Oct, Tues, Wed, Thurs, and Bank Holiday Mons, 2 – 6pm. Also June to Aug, Suns 2 – 6pm ∗ Entrance: £3 (house and garden)

Anthony House is a little off the beaten track but it is well worth the effort to visit one of the country's finest eighteenth-century houses, in a truly magnificent natural setting. The great garden designer, Humphry Repton, was consulted by Reginald Carew Pole but they disagreed over the initial plans, and it has been successive generations of the Carew Pole family who have presided over the evolution of the formal garden, parkland and natural woodland. The house and formal garden with its terrace overlooking parkland which sweeps down to the River Lynher (glimpsed through a series of rides) are now owned by The National Trust. The Carew Pole family, through a charitable trust, still owns 100 acres of woodland garden, also open to the public in conjunction with the house gardens. The woodland is divided into two areas: to the west of the woodland garden car park is the Wilderness and Westdown Valley where, in late spring, one can ramble through a glorious array of specimen camellias, rhododendrons, azaleas and magnolias in a semi-wild setting. To the east of the car park are 50 acres of older natural woodland; here are lovely walks along the banks of the River Lynher, the Fishful Pond, a fifteenth-century dovecote and the Bath House – built by Thomas Parlby between 1788 and 1790 and open by appointment with The National Trust.

BOSAHAN ★ 2
Manaccan, Helston, Cornwall. Tel: (0326) 23330

Captain and Mrs H.R. Graham Vivian ✻ *10m SE of Helston, 1m NE of Manaccan village* ✻ *Parking in field if dry. If wet, firm area near farm* ✻ *Teas* ✻ *Toilet facilities* ✻ *Partly suitable for wheelchairs* ✻ *Dogs on lead* ✻ *Plants for sale* ✻ *Open 12th, 26th April, 17th May, 2 – 5.30pm* ✻ *Entrance: £1.50, children 50p*

This valley garden of five acres started 100 years ago leads down to the Helford river and will give pleasure to the keen plantsman as it has both mature and newer planted trees and shrubs, including some New Zealand varieties. Its situation is said to have inspired Daphne du Maurier when creating the background for her novel *Rebecca*. In spring colour is provided by masses of camellias, rhododendrons, azaleas and magnolias along with bog plants in the water garden. There are formal beds with herbaceous plants at the top of the garden and one walks down through the valley to find the more mature specimens including pittosporums and dicksonias. There is some additional colour from ornamental pheasants. Fine views from the top of the valley.

BOSVIGO HOUSE 3
Bosvigo Lane, Truro, Cornwall. Tel: (0872) 75774

Mr Michael and Mrs Wendy Perry ✻ *Approach from the outer road just before reaching the Higher Town, take turning into Dobbs Lane adjacent to Station Road. Entrance to Bosvigo House is clearly marked on the left* ✻ *Some parking in carriage drive, otherwise in lane* ✻ *Refreshments on charity Suns only* ✻ *Toilet facilities* ✻ *Partly suitable for wheelchairs* ✻ *Rare and unusual plants for sale at nursery, open every day* ✻ *Garden open June to Sept, 11am – 6pm* ✻ *Entrance: £1*

The three-acre garden surrounding a Georgian house consists of many delightful enclosed and walled areas. The 'hot garden' displays red, yellow and orange plants. The 'Vean Garden' has white and yellow flowers, and the walled garden many rare plants. Within this last section stands a Victorian conservatory where the owners have placed comfortable chairs for visitors. The woodland garden is resplendent with many plants, some rare. A garden with subtle mixtures of colour and foliage where the plantsman will find many unusual and rare specimens.

CAERHAYS CASTLE GARDEN★★   4
Caerhays, Gorran, St Austell, Cornwall. Tel: (0872) 501310

Mr F.J. Williams   ✳   10m S of St Austell. On the coast by Porthluney Cove between Dodman Point and Nare Head   ✳   Parking at beach car park   ✳ Refreshments at Beach Cafe   ✳   Toilet facilities   ✳   Partly suitable for wheelchairs ✳   Dogs on lead   ✳   Plants for sale   ✳   Open 29th March, 19th April, 4th May for charity, 2 – 5pm; also 30th March to 8th May, 11am – 4.30pm (last admission 4pm)   ✳   Entrance: £1.50 on charity days; £2.50, children under 16 £1.50 on other days

An internationally noted garden with unrivalled collections of magnolias and shrubs raised from seed and material brought back by such plant hunters as George Forrest and E.H. Wilson, who were assisted financially in their expeditions by the Williams. The house, a vast romantic castle in the 'Gothick' style, was built by John Nash between 1805 – 1807. The garden began to take on its present form from 1896. The woodland stretches down to the sea and there are many rare specimens to be seen including tree ferns, acers, oaks, azaleas and nothofagus. J.C. Williams originally specialized in the cultivation and hybridizing of daffodils, but turned his sheltered clearings over to a refuge for the nineteenth-century influx of new plants, and many in British gardens today originated at Caerhays. A place to be visited by the family as well as the plantsman.

CHYVERTON ★   5
Zelah, Truro, Cornwall. Tel: (0872) 54324

Mr and Mrs N. Holman   ✳   1m W of Zelah on A30. Turn off N at Marazanvose (end of new bypass), the entrance is ¹/₂m on right   ✳   Parking   ✳   Dogs on lead   ✳ Plants occasionally for sale   ✳   Open by appointment only March to June   ✳ Entrance: £2.50. For parties of 20 or more £2 per person. Bone fide horticultural students and children under 16 free. Visitors personally conducted around by owners

The outstanding feature of this garden originally landscaped in the eighteenth century is its collection of magnolias, including some bearing the name of the property and also the owner's father 'Treve' Holman. Superb trees of copper beech, cedars of Lebanon, eucryphia, and a collection of nothofagus make a beautiful backcloth to a vast collection of camellias and rhododendrons. The garden is planted to give vistas and is always being further developed. A collection of acers is being planted and there are good colour combinations with azaleas and photinias. There is an unusual hedge of *Myrtus luma* and by the stream are vast gunneras and lysichitums. Also of special interest is a Mexican *Magnolia dealbata* believed to be the best example outside Mexico. Trees and shrubs have room to develop freely here but it is hard to realise that this beautiful and vast garden is maintained solely by the owners.

COTEHELE ★ 6
St Dominick, Nr Saltash, Cornwall. Tel: (0579) 50434

The National Trust ✳ 1m W of Calstock, 8m SW of Tavistock, 4m from Gunnislake. Turn at St Anne's Chapel ✳ Best season: May/June ✳ Parking ✳ ☆Refreshments in the Barn Restaurant ✳ Toilet facilities (and mother and baby room) ✳ Partly suitable for wheelchairs ✳ Plants for sale ✳ Shop ✳ House open as garden ✳ Film Room: an eight-minute slide presentation of the history of the estate ✳ Garden open April to Oct, daily except Fri (but open Good Fri), 11am – 5.30pm ✳ Entrance: £2.20 (garden and mill), £4.40 (house, garden and mill) (1991 prices)

This ten-acre garden with terraces falling to a sheltered valley has developed gradually from Victorian times. It should give pleasure to most visitors with its combination of formal courtyards, fine terraces, walled garden, pools, herbaceous borders and valley garden. The grey granite walls of the house are a background to many climbers and from the rose terrace one walks down to the pool and dovecote. In the valley are giant conifers, hydrangeas, palms, acers and betula. There is a small acer plantation and yew hedges along with herbaceous borders.

COUNTY DEMONSTRATION GARDEN 7
Probus, Nr Truro, Cornwall. Tel: (0872) 74282

Cornwall County Council Education Committee ✳ Just E of Probus village on A390 ✳ Best season: summer ✳ Parking ✳ Refreshments: café ✳ Toilet facilities ✳ Suitable for wheelchairs ✳ Open May to Sept, daily, 10am – 5pm, Oct to April, Mon – Fri, 10am – 4.30pm ✳ Entrance: £2, children free

This seven and a half-acre demonstration garden was started from a field in the early 1970s to serve as an advisory and education centre. A unique and fascinating display garden covering methods of growing vegetables, pruning fruit, treating lawns, weed control, compost making, design of small gardens, layouts for many aspects and situations. Fencing and walls, artificial and natural windbreaks, heath and heather planting, hanging baskets, gardening for the disabled, tree planting and staking, cloches, mulches, shrubs for shade and pruning of shrubs, herbs, rock and scree garden – in fact all aspects of gardening including various plant collections and patio and container gardening. A place to visit to get ideas and advice on problems.

GLENDURGAN GARDEN 8
Helford River, Mawnan Smith, Nr Falmouth, Cornwall. Tel: (0208) 74281

The National Trust ✳ 4m SW of Falmouth, 1/2m SW of Mawnan Smith on the road to Helford Passage ✳ Best season: spring to Sept ✳ Parking ✳ Toilet facilities ✳ Open March to Oct, Tues – Sat, 10.30am – 5.30pm (last admission 4.30pm). Closed Good Friday but open Bank Holiday Mons ✳ Entrance: £2.50

This 40-acre valley garden was originally planted by Alfred Fox in the 1820s with the village of Durgan at its foot alongside the Helford river. The wooded valley contains many specimen trees including *Dicksonia antarctica*, drimys, embothrium, eucryphia, conifers and a *Davidia involucrata*. In spring there is colour from primroses, bluebells, Lenten lilies and small daffodils while in late summer there are masses of hydrangeas. An unusual feature is the laurel maze. Vast camellias and magnolias provide early colour in the garden.

HEADLAND 9
3 Battery Lane, Polruan-by-Fowey, Cornwall. Tel: (0726) 870243

Mr and Mrs J. Hill ✳ Use public car park. Turn left (on foot) down St Saviour's Hill, left again at intersection near Coastguard Office. Gate on right ✳ Best season: June/July ✳ Cream teas ✳ Beach for swimming ✳ Open June to Sept, Thurs 2 – 8pm ✳ Entrance: £1, children 50p

This cliff garden 100 feet above sea level, created from an old quarry on the headland, has been developed by the present owners since 1974. It is a great credit to the owners for the excellent range of plants they grow with sea on three sides of the garden where plants must withstand spray and gales. It is designed with narrow paths and archways leading round corners to discover secret areas with Australian and New Zealand plants – cordylines and olearias; sub-tropical succulents – agaves, echeverias, crassulas and lampranthus. There is a path with various eucalyptus trees. In crevices one sees sempervivum, sedum and erigeron. Monterey pines, tamarisk, Torquay palms, yuccas and a fatsia all thrive and there are good plant combinations. It is surprising to find vegetables and fruit trees and bushes doing well on such a windswept slope. With the vast range of plants and clever design it is hard to believe the garden is only one and a quarter acres.

THE HOLLIES 10
Grampound, Truro, Cornwall. Tel: (0726) 882474

Mrs N.B. and Mr J.R. Croggon ✳ 6m from St Austell on A390 Truro road in the village of Grampound next to post office ✳ Parking in side lanes – Creed Lane, Bosillian Lane, Pepo Lane ✳ Teas ✳ Toilet facilities ✳ Suitable for wheelchairs ✳ Plants for sale ✳ Open 24th May, 21st June, 12th July and by appointment, 2 – 5.30pm ✳ Entrance: £1, children free

This two-acre garden has a charming 'cottage' garden effect created by the unusual design. There are island beds containing a wide range of trees and shrubs with underplanting of bulbs to provide interest and beauty throughout the year, although spring is the peak time. There are many rare plants, including alpines, to be enjoyed here.

LAMORRAN HOUSE★ 11
Upper Castle Road, St Mawes, Cornwall. Tel: (0326) 270801

Mr and Mrs R. Dudley-Cooke ✳ At garage above village of St Mawes turn right – signposted at Castle. In about ¹/₂m Lamorran is on left of road set behind a line of pine trees ✳ Parking for cars in road. Coaches by prior appointment ✳ Toilet facilities ✳ *Partly suitable for wheelchairs* ✳ *Plants for sale* ✳ *Open for charity on 5th, 19th April, 19th, 24th May, 7th, 28th June, 10am – 5pm and coach parties at other times by arrangement* ✳ *Entrance: £2, children free*

This four-acre garden developed since 1980 contains a large and excellent collection of sub-tropical and warm temperate species which one would not expect to find on a hillside adjacent to the sea. In the main it has been designed in the Italian style with columns and other artefacts. There are 500 azaleas, many different palms and eucalyptus, yuccas, 250 rhododendrons, a wide range of conifers, a range of Australian and New Zealand plants and a fernery. There are little gardens and round every corner more unusual plants. A Japanese garden and water feature. The plantsman will enjoy this and so will other visitors as the owner has incorporated good design features and interesting colour and foliage combinations.

LANCARFFE ★   12
Nr Bodmin, Cornwall. Tel: (0208) 72756

Mr and Mrs R. Gilbert ✳ *2m NE of Bodmin. From W turn L off A30 signed Helland, then left at T-junction towards Bodmin. After 300 yards, turn right signposted Norton, Holton and Lancarffe* ✳ *Parking. No coaches* ✳ *Refreshments* ✳ *Toilet facilities* ✳ *Dogs on lead* ✳ *Open 17th May, 2 – 5pm* ✳ *Entrance: £1, children 50p*

Walking through this four and a half-acre garden one can enjoy its wide range of plants from *Davidia involucrata* (pocket-handkerchief tree) to beds of roses. Some beautiful trees form a backcloth to a fine collection of azaleas, camellias and rhododendrons. There is a delightful walled water garden with shrubs and climbers on the walls. Hydrangeas, eucryphias, acers, *Desfontainea spinosa*, *Campsis radicans*, a *Paulownia fargesii* (foxglove tree), various cornus and embothriums are some of the specimens to be enjoyed. The owners are continuing to develop this very pleasant garden.

LANHYDROCK ★   13
Bodmin, Cornwall. Tel: (0208) 73320

The National Trust ✳ *2¹/₂m SE of Bodmin off A38, or off B3268* ✳ *Best season: spring* ✳ *Parking 600 yards but inc. disabled adjacent to garden* ✳ *Refreshments* ✳ *Toilet facilities inc. disabled and mothers' and childrens' room* ✳ *Partly suitable for wheelchairs* ✳ *Dogs on lead in park* ✳ *Plants for sale* ✳ *Shop in house* ✳ *House open (closed Mon except Bank Holiday Mon and closed Nov to March 1993)* ✳ *Garden open April to Oct, daily, 11am – 5.30pm, Nov to March 1993, daily during daylight hours* ✳ *Entrance: £2.50 (garden and grounds), £4.30 (house and garden) (1991 prices)*

This superb 30-acre garden started in 1857 contains gardens within a garden and has some exceptional trees and shrubs both in the park, woodland and the more formal areas. The collection of trees started before 1634. Banks of colour are provided by magnolias, camellias and rhododendrons, and this is followed by roses which are in beds in the lawn adjacent to the house interspersed with cone-shaped Irish yews. In the terraces beds of annuals are edged with box. A circular yew hedge surrounds the herbaceous borders which contain a wide range of choice plants and provide summer colour. The woodland has walks amongst rare trees and hydrangeas and other flowering shrubs. There is a stream with moisture-loving plants.

LONG CROSS VICTORIAN GARDENS 14
Trelights, Nr Port Isaac, Cornwall. Tel: (0208) 880243

*Roger and Janet Warrillow * 7m N of Wadebridge on B3314 near St Endellion church and Trelights village. Well signposted * Parking * ☆Refreshments * Toilet facilities * Suitable for wheelchairs * Dogs on lead * Plants for sale * Open Easter to Nov, daily * Entrance: £1, OAP 75p for charity, accompanied children under 14 free*

In reconstructing this late-Victorian garden the owners discovered paths which were not known to exist, also rockeries, steps, shrubs and plants. Hedges act as effective windbreaks against the strong east winds in this salt-laden coastal region. The layout produces a maze-like effect. Among the many sections are a central area with an ornamental pond, a donkey paddock and a children's playground – in all, three acres. There is a good supply of attractive seats. Fine views of Port Quin to the west and Tintagel Head to the north. Long Cross is a hotel, open at all times.

MARY NEWMAN'S COTTAGE 15
Culver Road, Saltash, Cornwall.

*Caradon District Council for Tamar Protection Society * ¼m from Saltash town centre. Signposted from Fore Street * Parking on waterside nearby * Plants occasionally for sale * Open Easter and 2nd May to 26th Sept, Thurs, 12 noon – 4pm, Sats and Bank Holidays 11am – 4pm * Entrance: 50p, children 20p*

The cottage was built in the fifteenth century. Mary Newman, reputed to be Drake's first wife, lived here. The garden overlooks the River Tamar and Brunel's Royal Albert Bridge. Within a small area are herbaceous plants and such old-fashioned roses as 'Sir Walter Raleigh' and 'Fisherman's Friend', and a green santolina (cotton lavender). There is a well-stocked herb garden.

MOUNT EDGCUMBE HOUSE AND COUNTRY PARK ★ 16
Cremyll, Torpoint, Cornwall. Tel: (0752) 822236

*Plymouth City Council and Cornwall County Council * Access from Plymouth by Cremyll (pedestrian) Ferry to Park entrance. Access from Cornwall A38 to Trerulefoot roundabout then A374 and B3247 * Parking for cars and coaches, but advance booking for coaches helpful * Refreshments: lunches, teas and light refreshments April to Oct daily in Orangery (0752) 822586. Picnics * Toilet facilities * Suitable for wheelchairs * Dogs on lead in Country park and formal* *gardens only* ✳ *Shop* ✳ *House open as Earl's Garden* ✳ *Country park and formal gardens open daily, 8am – dusk. Earl's Garden open April to Oct, Wed – Sun and Bank Holidays, 11am – 5.30pm* ✳ *Entrance: Country park and formal gardens free. Earl's Garden and House £2.80, concessions £2.05, children (16 and under) £1.55*

The gardens and landscaped park were created by the Mount Edgcumbe family in the eighteenth century. They have been praised by Pepys, William Kent and Humphry Repton. The site covers 865 acres, and stretches from Plymouth Sound to Rame Head. The Earl's Garden contains a rare, recently restored, shell grotto. This garden which surrounds the house was re-established after having been terraced in 1941 and there are modern versions of late Victorian flower beds along the east front. The formal gardens at the lower end of the old tree-lined avenue encompass English, French and Italian Gardens (complete with ornamental orange trees) and two new gardens to commemorate the family's historical connection with America and New Zealand. Planted in the Amphitheatre is the National collection of camellias. There are fine sea views to Drake's Island from the Park, where fallow deer may sometimes be seen.

PENBERTH 17
St Buryan, Nr Penzance, Cornwall. Tel: (0736) 810208

Mrs J.M.M. Banham ✳ *Leave Penzance on A30 towards Lands End. After 2m turn left on B3283 to Porthcurno and St Buryan. Keep on B3315 through the village following signs to Porthcurno. Road descends into valley. Turn left at lane signed Penberth. Approach through gatehouse* ✳ *Best season: spring* ✳ *Parking in field* ✳ *Teas* ✳ *Toilet facilities* ✳ *Partly suitable for wheelchairs* ✳ *Plants for sale* ✳ *Open 5th, 19th April, 3rd May, 2 – 5pm and strictly by appointment* ✳ *Entrance: £1, children 30p*

A five-acre garden in a valley leading down to the sea, created by Dr Edward Vernon Favell 70 years ago. Water garden and rock garden. Camellias, azaleas and other shrubs. Bog plants. A rushing stream. Mass of daffodils in the spring. In the grounds stands an old mill dating from Doomsday.

PENCARROW ★ 18
Washaway, Bodmin, Cornwall. Tel: (020884) 369

The Molesworth-St Aubyn family ✳ *4m NW of Bodmin. Signposted from the A389 Bodmin – Wadebridge road and B3266 at Washaway* ✳ *Best season: spring* ✳ *Parking* ✳ *Refreshments in tearoom. Picnics* ✳ *Toilet facilities* ✳ *Partly suitable for wheelchairs* ✳ *Dogs on lead near house* ✳ *Plants for sale* ✳ *Shop* ✳ *House and Craft Centre open Easter to mid-Oct, daily except Fri and Sat, 1.30 – 5pm (June to 10th Sept and Bank Holiday Mons open 11am)* ✳ *Garden open daily dawn – dusk* ✳ *Entrance: £1, children 50p (1991 prices)*

The drive, one mile long, leads to the imposing Palladian mansion built in 1760. A formal garden with a circular lawn is laid out on two sides of the house. Nearby on a higher level, shrubs are placed in a rock garden made with boulders transported from Bodmin Moor when the gardens were designed by Sir William Molesworth from 1831 onwards. There are 50 acres of woodland and parkland where over 600 different species of rhododendrons and a large collection of camellias grow. Among the many trees stands a *Picea orientalis* (Caucasian spruce) the second earliest known to have been planted in Britain. There are a large number of Monkey Puzzle trees (*Araucaria araucana*). The English name is said to have originated at Pencarrow when, in 1834, the parliamentary barrister Charles Austin who was staying at Pencarrow rashly touched one of the prickly leaves and quickly withdrew his hand, saying: 'It would puzzle a monkey'.

PENPOL HOUSE 19
Penpol Avenue, Hayle, Cornwall. Tel: (0736) 753146

*Major and Mrs T.F. Ellis * 4m SE of St Ives. Turn left at White Hart, Penpol Road, then 2nd left into Penpol Avenue * Best season: May to July * Parking in adjacent field * Teas * Suitable for wheelchairs * Plants for sale * Open by appointment for parties mid-May to July and on 28th June for charity, 2 – 6pm * Entrance: £1, children 50p for charity*

This three-acre garden surrounding the sixteenth-century house has been developed over the past 100 years. It is made up of different small gardens and there are different design features including a white painted ship's figurehead, suspended on a small building, formerly the cider house. There is a grey garden, cottage garden, an old walled garden with fruit, vegetables and a pool, a rose garden and herbaceous borders with collections of iris, delphiniums, shrubs and perennials. The old greenhouses contain a 100-year-old vine and a geranium on the wall of the same age. This garden of unique charm has an alkaline soil, unusual for Cornwall.

PENWARNE 20
Mawnan Smith, Nr Falmouth, Cornwall. Tel: (0326) 250585/250325

*Mr and Mrs H. Beister * 3¹/₄m SW of Falmouth and 1¹/₂m N of Mawnan Smith off the Falmouth to Mawnan Smith road * Best season: spring * Parking. Coaches by prior arrangement * Toilet facilities * Partly suitable for wheelchairs * Dogs on lead * Open 14th May, 2 – 5pm * Entrance: £1, children 50p*

There are many large trees including *Cryptomeria japonica*, beeches and oaks which form a backcloth to this woodland garden planted about 1900 in which is set a fine Georgian house. The old walled garden has roses, clematis and lilies and there are banks of azaleas, rhododendrons, camellias and magnolias, together with shrubs from New Zealand. The pool with ornamental ducks and the stream running through the garden provide areas for primulas and tree ferns. There are fruit trees and bushes along with bamboos. Many new plantings.

PINE LODGE ★ 21
Cuddra, St Austell, Cornwall. Tel: (0726) 73500

*Mr and Mrs R. Clemo * Just E of St Austell off A390 between Holmbush and the* *turning to Tregrehan. Signs on open days* ✳ *Parking* ✳ *Teas* ✳ *Toilet facilities* ✳ *Suitable for wheelchairs* ✳ *Plants for sale* ✳ *Open 24th May, 12th July, 1 – 5pm or parties of 20 or more by appointment* ✳ *Entrance: £2, children free*

This four-acre garden, started 44 years ago but extended during the past 14 years, contains a wide range of plants and should be of interest to the keen gardener because there are good design features and original colour combinations. Plants labelled. Besides the usual rhododendrons and camellias so familiar in Cornish gardens there are herbaceous borders with rare and tender plants, a range of conifers, heathers, a pergola with clematis and ivies, and other climbers. A large wildlife pond, a bog garden, a vegetable garden and an arboretum with a large variety of trees are other features to enjoy.

POLGWYNNE 22
Feock, Nr Truro, Cornwall. Tel: (0872) 862612

Mr and Mrs P. Davey ✳ *5m S of Truro. Take A39, then B3289 to first crossroads. Carry straight on to ¹/₂m short of Feock* ✳ *Best seasons: spring and early summer* ✳ *Parking* ✳ *Refreshments on open days* ✳ *Toilet facilities* ✳ *Partly suitable for wheelchairs* ✳ *Plants for sale on open days only* ✳ *Open 26th April, 10th May, 7th June, 2 – 5.30pm and by appointment* ✳ *Entrance: £1.50 for charity, children free*

A three and a half-acre garden with woodlands extending to the shore of Carrick Roads. There is a *Gingko biloba* with a girth of 11ft 9ins, probably the largest specimen in Britain. Many fine trees and unusual shrubs. Beautiful setting with fine views.

PORTHPEAN 23
Porthpean House, St Austell, Cornwall. Tel: (0726) 72888

Mr and Mrs C. Petherick ✳ *Take A390 and then the road signposted Porthpean, past Mount Edgcumbe Hospice, turn left down Porthpean Beach Road. Porthpean House is the white building at the bottom of the hill just before the car park* ✳ *Best season: spring* ✳ *Parking in car park nearby* ✳ *Refreshments: teas for parties* ✳ *Toilet facilities* ✳ *Suitable for wheelchairs* ✳ *Dogs on lead* ✳ *Plants for sale* ✳ *Open 29th March and Sats and Suns in April and May, 2 – 5pm. Also by appointment* ✳ *Entrance: £1.50, children free*

This three-acre garden was first developed by Maurice Petherick some 40 years ago. It contains a special collection of camellias, also many azaleas and rhododendrons. The grounds have access to the beach and from the main lawn one has a magnificent view of St Austell Bay. On spring days cherry blossoms stand out sharply against the blue of the sea. There is also a nursery garden with Victorian greenhouses.

ST MICHAEL'S MOUNT 24
Marazion, Nr Penzance, Cornwall. Tel: (0736) 710507

The National Trust ✳ *¹/₂m from the shore at Marazion, ¹/₂m S of A394. Access by ferry or across causeway* ✳ *Best season: spring/early summer* ✳ *Parking in Marazion* ✳ *Refreshments: restaurant* ✳ *Toilet facilities* ✳ *Plants for sale* ✳ *Shop, March to Oct* ✳ *Castle and Abbey open but only to guided tours Nov to March when ferry may be difficult* ✳ *Open April to Oct, Mon – Fri, 10.30am – 5.45pm. Last admission 4.45pm. Open most weekends during April to Sept for charity when NT members expected to pay for admission. Nov to March guided tours can be arranged. Check by telephone* ✳ *Entrance: £2.90, children £1.45*

A unique and extraordinary 20-acre maritime garden which has been created in terraces just above the sea at the foot of a 300 ft perpendicular cliff. Here, in spite of apparent total exposure to gales and salt spray, sub-tropical species abound. The walled garden was planted in the eighteenth century by two young ladies, ancestors of the St Aubyn family who still live in the Castle. A remarkable example of micro-climate effect is in itself a fascinating study for the keen gardener. Planting has been done amongst granite boulders, some weighing hundreds of tons. There are yuccas, geraniums, euryops, hebes, phormium, fuchsias and in spring sheets of wild narcissus. Kniphofia grow wild in the bracken and provide great splashes of colour.

TREBAH ★★ 25
Mawnan Smith, Nr Falmouth, Cornwall. Tel: (0326) 250448

Major and Mrs J.A. Hibbert (The Trebah Garden Trust) ✳ *4m SW of Falmouth, 1m SW of Mawnun Smith and 500 yards W of Glendurgan Garden* ✳ *Best season: March to Oct* ✳ *Parking* ✳ *Refreshments* ✳ *Toilet facilities* ✳ *Partly suitable for wheelchairs* ✳ *Dogs on lead* ✳ *Plants for sale* ✳ *Open daily, 10.30am – 5pm* ✳ *Entrance: £2.50, disabled and children £1, children under 5 free (Nov to Feb, £1, disabled and children 50p)*

A 25-acre ravine garden started by Charles Fox in the 1840s which contains many beautiful and mature trees and shrubs that provide an undulating carpet of colour. The deep ravine leads to a private beach on the Helford River. A stream runs through a water garden and a series of ponds with mature Koi carp. Extensive plantings of sub-tropical Mediterranean plants at the top of the garden blend into the rain forest of the lower reaches with glades of giant tree ferns, bananas and bamboos. Three acres of blue and white hydrangeas carry the colour through to Christmas. A paradise for the artist, the plantsman and the family.

TREGREHAN 26
Par, Cornwall. Tel: (072681) 2438 or 4389

The Carlyon Estate. Mr T. Hudson ✳ *On A390 Lostwithiel to St Austell road. The entrance is opposite the Britannia Inn* ✳ *Best season: spring* ✳ *Parking* ✳ *Toilet facilities* ✳ *Partly suitable for wheelchairs* ✳ *Plants for sale, esp. camellias* *Open mid-March to June and Sept, Wed – Sun, 10.30am – 5pm* ✳ *Entrance: £2, children 75p. Guided tours by prior arrangement*

The 20-acre garden contains many large and interesting trees and rhodo-dendrons in addition to the large collection of camellias raised by the late owner. There are woodland walks carpeted with bluebells in spring and a walled garden. Other plants include clivias and nerines, but the camellias, rare trees and vast rhododendrons are of particular interest to the keen plantsman. Magnificent Victorian greenhouses.

TREHANE 27
Nr Probus, Cornwall. Tel: (087252) 270

*David and Simon Trehane * Turn N off A39 between the Wheel Inn and Tresillian Bridge. Signposted * Best season: spring/summer * Parking in field. Coaches by special arrangement for a different route * Teas * Toilet facilities * Partly suitable for wheelchairs * Dogs on lead * Plants for sale * Open by appointment and 29th March, 12th, 26th April, 10th, 24th May, 7th, 22nd June, 5th, 19th July, 16th Aug, 2 – 5pm * Entrance: £1, children 50p*

This is a plantsman's garden containing a wonderful variety and many good collections – geraniums, hemerocallis, romneyas and trilliums. There are lovely camellias, many actually raised here. Interesting climbers cover the old walls and in spring the woodland area is carpeted with bluebells, claytonias and campions. A very old *Pieris japonica* and a davidia and vast rhododendrons, azaleas and magnolias provide a background to a large collection of herbaceous plants. This garden will also be enjoyed by the general visitor as it has a great sense of peace and half of its 10 acres is woodland.

TRELEAN 28
St Martin-in-Meneage, Nr Helston, Cornwall. Tel: (032623) 255

*Squadron Leader and Mrs G.T. Witherwick * 7m SE of Helston on B3293. After 4m turn left for Mawgan. 1m from the village of St Martin-in-Meneage * Parking in field * Teas * Toilet facilities * Dogs on lead * Plants for sale * Open 23rd May, 24th Oct, 12 noon – 5pm or garden tours with the owner by appointment * Entrance: £1, children free*

This three-acre garden set in a wooded estate with superb views of the River Helford is for the keen plantsman as it contains a superb collection of beautiful and rare trees and shrubs including 14 different nothofagus, 50 different acers, various eucalyptus, cistus, enkianthus, olearias and robinias. The winding steep paths are bordered on either side by ilex, hazels, Scots pine and many varieties of rhododendrons and 70 different conifers. The owner, who started this garden from an area of woodland and bracken in 1980, is certainly creating a paradise for the botanist.

TRELIDDEN 29
Trelidden Coombe, Liskeard, Cornwall. Tel: (0579) 42251

*Mr and Mrs P. Blamey * Turn off the western end of the Liskeard bypass into Moorswater Industrial Estate. Aim for the right-hand arch of the viaduct. The garden is 200 yards on the right * Parking 200 yards by arrangement * Original paintings and books illustrated by Marjorie Blamey for sale * Open last Sun in June and by appointment * Entrance: £1, children 50p for charity*

A stream at the bottom of this one and a half-acre garden supplies a constant flow of water to a well-stocked fish pond. The garden has been constructed on a sloping site and this affords the visitor a great variety of bright vistas. Scent is considered as important as colour by the owners, and they have achieved much in the development of a garden from what was a simple meadow 20 years ago.

TRELISSICK ★   30
Feock, Nr Truro, Cornwall. Tel: (0872) 862090

The National Trust ✳ 4m S of Truro on B3289 above King Harry Ferry ✳ Best season: April/May ✳ Parking £1 (refundable) ✳ Refreshments: restaurant open 10.30am – 5.30pm, Sun, 12 noon – 5.30pm. Limited opening Nov and Dec, phone (0872) 863486 ✳ Toilet facilities ✳ Partly suitable for wheelchairs ✳ Dogs on lead on woodland walk and park only ✳ Plants for sale ✳ Art and Craft Gallery in grounds open ✳ Garden open March to Oct, Mon – Sat, 10.30am – 5.30pm, Sun, 1 – 5.30pm ✳ Entrance: £2.80

This 25-acre garden with woodland was originally planted with exotic things and became known as the fruit garden of Cornwall. Now it contains a wide variety of interest with its collection of hydrangeas, a dell, aromatic, fern and fig gardens along with some very large trees including *Quercus ilex*, *Fagus sylvatica* and a beautiful Japanese cedar *Cryptomeria japonica* in a lawn backed by herbaceous borders containing a range of perennials. Near the entrance is a lovely border of heliotrope – a tradition of Trelissick. The dell has tree ferns, hostas and hellebores and there are many beautiful shrubs. Small walled garden with aromatic plants.

TREMEER   31
St Tudy, Nr Bodmin, Cornwall. Tel: (0208) 850313

The Haslam-Hopwood family ✳ NW of St Tudy between A39 and B3266. Take Wadebridge road from the centre of St Tudy ✳ Best season: April to June ✳ Parking in garden. Coaches at village hall by arrangement ✳ Toilet facilities ✳ Dogs on lead ✳ Open April to Sept, daily, 9 – 6pm ✳ Entrance: free. Donations to charity at the entrance

By Cornish standards this seven-acre garden is exposed and cold and has a high rainfall, but manages to produce vivid colour and pervading scent. A large bank of heathers is backed by dwarf rhododendrons and camellias. The terrace beneath the house looks out to a backcloth of fine mature trees. After crossing the lawn, walks meander through beautiful shrubs – rhododendrons, azaleas, camellias – and at the bottom of the garden is a small lake with ducks. Primulas, hostas and other water plants. Herbaceous borders provide summer colour and the walls have good climbers and perennials beneath.

TRENGWAINTON GARDEN ★   32
Nr Penzance, Cornwall. Tel: (0736) 63021

The National Trust ✳ 2m NW of Penzance on B3312, or ¹/₂m off A3071 ✳ Best season: spring ✳ *Parking* ✳ *Teas usually at Trengwainton Farm* ✳ *Toilet facilities* ✳ *Suitable for wheelchairs* ✳ *Dogs on lead* ✳ *Open March to Oct, Wed – Sat, Bank Holiday Mon and Good Fri, 10.30am – 5.30pm (closes 4.30pm in March and Oct)* ✳ *Entrance: £2.20*

Trengwainton means 'House of the Spring' and was acquired by the Bolitho family in 1867. It will appeal to both the plantsman and the ordinary gardener because it contains a magnificent collection of magnolias, rhododendrons and camellias and a series of walled gardens with many tender and exotic shrubs and plants that would not survive in less mild areas of England. The stream garden alongside the drive backed by a beech wood provides masses of colour from candelabra primulas, lilies, lysichitum and other bog plants. Many of the rhododendrons were raised from seed collected by Kingdon Ward's expedition to NE Assam and the Mishmi Hills of Burma. New Zealand tree ferns, pittosporums from China, Japanese maples, embothriums, olearia, acacia, eucryphia, and Chatham Island forget-me-not are just a few of the beautiful plants to be seen during the spring and summer. There are magnificent views of the hills leading down to the sea and a space has been cut in the woodland to reveal St Michael's Mount.

TRERICE   33
Nr Newquay, Cornwall. Tel: (0637) 875404

The National Trust ✳ *3m SE of Newquay via A392 and A3058. Turn right at Kestle Mill* ✳ *Best season: summer* ✳ *Parking* ✳ *Refreshments* ✳ *Toilet facilities* ✳ *Partly suitable for wheelchairs* ✳ *Plants for sale* ✳ *Shop in house* ✳ *House open* ✳ *Garden open April to Oct, daily except Tues, 11am – 5.30pm (5pm in Oct) (last admission ¹/₂ hour before closing)* ✳ *Entrance: £3.40*

A small garden by Cornish standards developed around an Elizabethan manor house where one can enjoy many unusual and lovely rare plants. It has been planted with shrubs, climbers and perennials to provide very good foliage and colour combinations. In the front walled courtyard are herbaceous borders. The back court has a range of cottage garden plants – fuchsia, lonicera, roses and climbers on the house. An orchard has been planted with apples, pears, quince, plums in the quincunx pattern used in the seventeenth century, and there are figs elsewhere in the garden. The design features of the garden are of particular interest. Lawn mowers of different sizes and from different periods are displayed in the former stable hay loft.

TRESCO ABBEY ★★   34
Tresco, Isles of Scilly. Tel: (0720) 22849 Mike Nelhams (Head Gardener)

Mr R.A. Dorrien-Smith ✳ *On the Island of Tresco. Travel: by helicopter from Penzance Heliport to Tresco Heliport – 12 months (reservations (0736) 63871 and (0720) 22646) or from St Mary's by launch* ✳ *Refreshments* ✳ *Toilet facilities* ✳ *Suitable for wheelchairs (available at garden gate)* ✳ *Dogs on lead* ✳ *Plants for sale* ✳ *Shop* ✳ *Open daily, 10am – 4pm* ✳ *Entrance: £3, children £1.50*

One of the most spectacular of all Britain's 'sub-tropical' gardens on an island which lies in the warming Gulf Stream. Protected from the Atlantic gales by windbreaks, the garden is arranged on several terraces mounting a hillside which are linked by flights of steps. They serve as a home for myriad exotic plants like proteus from South Africa, the tender geranium *G. maderense* from Madeira and trees and shrubs from the North Island of New Zealand and Australia which could not thrive out-of-doors in many places on the British mainland. This 17-acre garden is both formal and informal. Many of the plants are self-seeded. The grounds also house the Valhalla collection of ship figureheads from the National Maritime Museum.

ISLES OF SCILLY

There are over one hundred islands in addition to Tresco. Only five are inhabited. Spring comes very early, bringing abundant flowering of daffodils and narcissi. In 1868 William Trevellick of St Mary's sent some flowers to Covent Garden in a hat box and since then the industry has grown steadily and now between December and April some 800 tons of flowers are transported, many in bud so as to reach market in peak condition. February is perhaps the best month for the visitor. Then there is a wide variety of wild flowers in the fields and hedgerows. The *soleil d'or* grows in the bulb fields and the pink sea thrift is everywhere on the cliffs. One mile from Hugh Town, St Mary's, a two-acre garden is being created in a quarry by volunteer gardeners. Entrance is free. Contact Mr R Letherbridge (0270) 22404.

TREVARNO   35
Helston, Cornwall. Tel: (0326) 572022

Mr and Mrs P. Bickford-Smith ∗ 3m N of Helston on B3303 and E of Crowntown ∗ Best season: spring ∗ Parking. Coaches by arrangement ∗ Refreshments ∗ Toilet facilities ∗ Open 19th April, 10th May for charity, 1.30 – 5pm. Parties by arrangement ∗ Entrance: £1.50, children 50p

This fine woodland garden of 15 acres includes a large ornamental lake at the foot of the garden and alongside is the bog garden. It contains a vast range of rare trees and shrubs along with a collection of oaks, species rhododendrons and *Acer palmatum* 'Dissectum Nigrum'. There is a collection of ilex, a shady garden and a grotto, and a collection of geraniums. Beside the waterfall are primulas, rheums, astilbes and aruncus. A plantsman's garden.

TREVEGEAN   36
9 Manor Way, Heamoor, Penzance, Cornwall. Tel: (0736) 67407

Mr and Mrs P.G. Cousins ∗ Take Penzance bypass, turn left at first roundabout towards Treneere, turn sharp right, straight up hill to Manor Way. Concealed entrance to garden marked 7 and 9 ∗ Parking on road ∗ Cream teas ∗ Toilet facilities ∗ Plants for sale ∗ Open 7th June, 19th July, 2 – 5 pm ∗ Entrance: £1, children free

This third-of-an-acre garden is a delight for the plantsman as well as being of great interest to the general gardener. The different concealed sections are edged with box hedging and they intercommunicate by brick paths. This remarkable garden, placed at the rear of a housing estate, is completely concealed from the outside by trees and hedges. There are many interesting shrubs: *Viburnum odoratissimum*, *Muehlenbeckia*, and among the flowers you find *Rosa chinensis* 'Mutabilis', *Geranium paramatum* and *Lobelia tupa*.

TREWIDDEN 37
Penzance, Cornwall. Tel: (0736) 62087 (Head Gardener)

Captain A.R. Bolitho * *Follow the Penzance distributor road as for Land's End. Entrance is on the right beyond crossroad to Newlyn. Signed 'Trewidden Nursery'* * *Best season: spring* * *Parking. Coaches by appointment* * *Toilet facilities* * *Dogs on leads* * *Woodland garden open Mon – Sat, 8am – 1pm, 2 – 5pm* * *Entrance: £1, children 50p*

This woodland garden contains a large number of fine specimens of the best kinds of flowering shrubs. A *Magnolia* x *veitchii*, possibly the largest in Britain, overshadows a large pond. In this section, too, one finds other fine magnolias. In the Fern Pit, once an open tin mine, stands a magnificent group of *Dicksonia antarctica* (tree ferns) which are 100 years old. The nurseries, originally a kitchen garden, are now used to produce a wide range of trees and shrubs for sale. The private garden of the house is also open for three afternoons during the year.

TREWITHEN ★★ 38
Grampound Road, Nr Truro, Cornwall. Tel: (0726) 882418/882763/ 882764

Mr A.M.J. Galsworthy * *On A390 between Truro and St Austell, adjacent to the County Demonstration Garden* * *Parking* * *Toilet facilities* * *Suitable for wheelchairs* * *Dogs on lead* * *Plants for sale* * *Garden shop (0726) 883794* * *House open April to July, Mon, Tues, 2 – 4.30pm. £2.75* * *Gardens open March to Sept, Mon – Sat, 10am – 4.30pm* * *Entrance: £2 (£1.75 in Sept), children £1*

This is an internationally famous garden, known for its great collection of magnolias, rhododendrons and camellias along with many other beautiful and rare trees and shrubs. It is fitting that its founder George Johnstone named a camellia after his daughter 'Elizabeth Johnstone', and there are rhododendrons 'Alison Johnstone' after his wife, 'Trewithen Orange' and 'Jack Skelton' after his head gardener. The lawn in front of the house is edged with banks of a wide range of shrubs including viburnums, azaleas, potentillas, euonymus, berberis. There is a sunken garden with tree ferns, azaleas and acers. There are many nothofagus, embothriums, pieris, enkianthus, eucryphias, griselinias. The walled garden has a pool and some choice climbers including *Clianthus puniceus*, and *Mutisia decurrens*, and there is a pergola with wisteria. Newly planted beds of young trees of sorbus and birch, mahonia, cornus, phygelius and roses and island beds with heathers and dwarf conifers. The beech trees that provide shelter for the garden are magnificent. A half hour video describes the creation of the garden over the years.

VICTORIA GARDENS 39
Truro, Cornwall. Tel: (02807) 72049

Carrick District Council leased to Truro City Council * *In Truro city centre, next*

*to Crown Court ✳ Car park next to Crown Court ✳ Toilet facilities ✳ Partly
suitable for wheelchairs, but a few steps. Enter by SW or N gate ✳ Dogs on lead ✳
Open daily, weekdays, 8am – dusk, Sun, 8am – 5pm or dusk if earlier ✳
Entrance: free*

A delightful Victorian public park of seven acres complete with a contemporary fountain in a circular pond adjacent to a fine bandstand still very much in use during summer. The park rises steeply from a brook at the bottom to a large fishpond at the top. At the lower level beneath the brook there is a small additional section of grass and flower beds. Apart from the numerous flower beds throughout the park there are some fine mature trees including copper beeches and a weeping beech.

TELEPHONE NUMBERS
Except where owners have specifically requested that they be excluded, telephone numbers to which enquiries may be directed are given for each property. To maintain the support and cooperation of private owners it is suggested that the telephone be used with discretion. Where visits are by appointment, the telephone can of course be used except where written application, particularly for parties, is specifically requested. Code numbers are given in brackets. For the Republic of Ireland phone 010353 followed by the code (Dublin is 1) followed by the subscriber's number. In all cases where visits by parties are proposed, owners should be advised in advance and arrangements preferably confirmed in writing.

CUMBRIA
& THE ISLE OF MAN

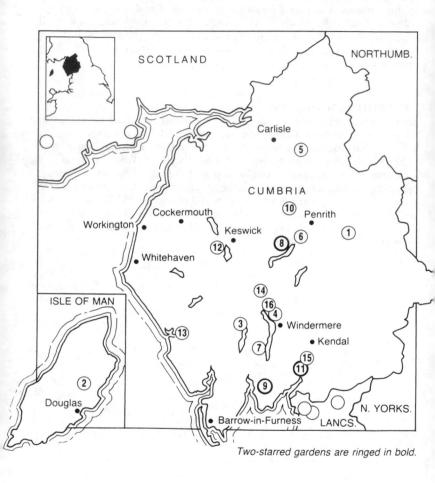

Two-starred gardens are ringed in bold.

ACORN BANK GARDEN
Temple Sowerby, Penrith, Cumbria. Tel: (07683) 61893

The National Trust ✳ *6m E of Penrith off A66 N of Temple Sowerby* ✳ *Best season: spring and early summer* ✳ *Parking* ✳ *Picnic area only* ✳ *Toilet*

1

facilities inc. disabled ✳ *Mostly suitable for wheelchairs* ✳ *Guide dogs only in gardens, on lead in picnic area* ✳ *Plants for sale* ✳ *Shop* ✳ *Admission to house by prior written permission Sue Ryder Society* ✳ *Garden open 17th April to Oct, 10am – 5.30pm* ✳ *Entrance: £1.30, children 60p (1991 prices)*

The 'acorn bank' is the ancient oakwood sloping down to the Crowdundle Beck behind the house. In spring it is a mass of daffodils and narcissi in many varieties planted profusely in the 1930s (e.g. some 60,000 Lenten lilies). The walled gardens are then also a mass of blossom from the old varieties of apple, medlar, pear and quince in the sheltered orchards, with their carpet of wild tulips, anemones and narcissi. The orchard's trees include apple varieties which blossom late and are therefore suitable for cooler northern areas. Along the three sheltering walls are carefully modulated herbaceous and shrub borders, with good clematis and climbers. A bed of species roses (*rugosa* and others) flanks the steps to a picturesque sunken garden (a pond and alpine terraces). Through a gateway lies a splendid herb garden – a well tended collection of some 250 medicinal and culinary herbs, all comprehensively labelled and documented.

BALLALHEANNAGH ★ 2
Glen Roy, Lonan, Isle of Man. Tel: (0624) 861875

Clif and Maureen Dadd ✳ *In Glen Roy on E side of island, 2m inland from Laxey* ✳ *Best season: spring* ✳ *Parking* ✳ *Plants for sale at nursery* ✳ *Open daily, 10am – 1pm and 2 – 5pm, but closed weekends from Nov to Feb* ✳ *Entrance: £1*

Take a steep-sided valley, a ladder, some seedlings of exotic rhododendrons and forget all about digging pits to accomodate the roots. Just stick them into crevices among the mosses and ferns. Wait a few years, never giving up. Outcome – paradise for plant-lovers. You expect to find a garden like Ballalheannagh in Cornwall or Kerry but this is in the middle of the Isle of Man. Every visitor with an interest in gardening, who is marooned on that island, need not fear boredom. This is a botanical garden, not in name, but surely in content. Steep winding paths cling to the valley sides. Crystal water cascades below carry the bells of pieris to the Irish Sea. The lower portion is well stocked with lofty rhododendrons while the upper parts of the valley contain newer plantings that will certainly delight in years to come. Here are pieris, eucalyptus, drimys, epacris, epigaea, megacarpea and betula (species with wonderful names like *Betula tatewakiana*), and a host of others. It's not all shrubs and trees, there are choice bulbs too, and the native mosses and ferns are a wonderful sight.

BRANTWOOD 3
Coniston, Cumbria. Tel: (05394) 41396

Brantwood Trust ✳ *E side of Coniston Water off B5285, signposted. Steam yacht 'Gondola' sails regularly from Coniston Pier* ✳ *Best season: spring, autumn* ✳ *Parking* ✳ *Tea room and restaurant* ✳ *Toilet facilities inc. disabled* ✳ *Dogs* ✳ *Plants for sale planned* ✳ *Shop* ✳ *House open, £2.50, children £1.25, family*

£6.50 (2 plus 5 maximum) ✳ Garden open mid-March to mid-Nov, daily, 11am – 5.30pm, winter, Wed – Sun, 11am – 4pm ✳ Entrance: 50p, children 25p (nature trail)

This is a superb site with wonderful views, atmosphere and potential. The rocky hillside behind the house is threaded with a wandering network of paths created by Ruskin (who lived here 1872 – 1900) to delight the eye and please the mind. Rhododendrons and azaleas flourish in the acid soil to make a lovely woodland garden. Now in the capable hands of Sally Beamish, it is being restored to its former glory after long neglect and enhanced by imaginative planting. The water features will also be revived. Given time and hard work it should become a classic.

BROCKHOLE ★ 4
Lake District National Park Centre, Windermere, Cumbria. Tel: (09662) 6601

Lake District National Park Authority ✳ 1 1/2m N of Windermere on A591 ✳ Parking ✳ Refreshments: restaurant and cafeteria ✳ Toilet facilities inc. disabled ✳ Partly suitable for wheelchairs ✳ Dogs on lead ✳ Shop ✳ Exhibition and slide theatres ✳ Open Easter to early Nov, daily, 10am – 5pm (evening opening in July and Aug) ✳ Entrance: £2, children £1, family and group rates available

A garden blessed with the Lakeland combination of western aspect and water to the hills beyond, in this case notably the Langdale Pikes. To frame this view Mawson worked closely (c.1900) with his architect colleague, Gibson. The ornamental terraces drop through rose beds, herbaceous borders and shrubbery to a wild flower meadow flanked by mature woodland. The original kitchen and herb garden has been restored by Sue Tasker. Special features are rock plants, Chilean and other half-hardy shrubs and rarities and the constantly changing colour from spring rhododendrons and azaleas through to the late Chilean hollies.

CORBY CASTLE 5
Great Corby, Cumbria. Tel: (0228) 560246

Sir John Howard-Lawson, Bart, and Lady Howard-Lawson ✳ 6m E of Carlisle, turn off A69 at Warwick Bridge to Great Corby village ✳ Best season: spring, early summer ✳ Parking ✳ Dogs on lead ✳ Open April to Sept, daily, 12 noon – 5pm ✳ Entrance: 50p (honesty box)

Created by Thomas Howard in the early eighteenth century the grounds run along the River Eden for about one mile, with fine trees and architectural features. The cascade was restored in 1957 and takes the water from the park down a series of steps to the river.

DALEMAIN ★ 6
Dalemain Estate, Dacre, Penrith, Cumbria. Tel: (07684) 86450

Mr and Mrs Bryce McCosh ✳ On A592 2m N of Pooley Bridge on Penrith road

* *Best season: early summer* * *Parking* * *Licensed restaurant and tea room* *
Toilet facilities * *Suitable for wheelchairs* * *Plants for sale* * *Shop* * *House open* * *Garden open Easter Sun to 4th Oct, Sun – Thurs, 11.15am – 5pm* *
Entrance: £2.50, children free (house and garden £3.50, children £2.50, family £9.50 (2 plus own children)). Special prices for pre-booked parties. Guided tours of gardens £3 per person

Dalemain has evolved in the most natural way from a twelfth-century pele tower with its kitchen garden and herbs. The Tudor-walled knot garden is there, as is the Stuart terrace (1680s) and the walled orchard where apple trees like 'Nonsuch' and 'Keswick Codling', planted in 1728, still bear fruit. The gardens have been finely re-established by Mrs McCosh with shrubs, species roses and other rarities, together with herbaceous replanting along the terraces and around the orchard. There is a wild garden on the lower ground featuring the Himalayan blue poppy in early summer and a walk past the Tudor gazebo into woods overlooking the Dacre Beck.

GRAYTHWAITE HALL ★   7
Ulverston, Hawkshead, Cumbria. Tel: (05395) 31248

Esthwaite Estate Company * *4m up W side of Windermere from Newby Bridge, A590* * *Best season: spring* * *Parking* * *Toilet facilities* * *Dogs on lead* *
Open April to mid- or late-July, daily, 10am – 6pm * *Entrance: £2, children free*

Essentially a spring garden landscaped by the late Victorian Thomas Mawson in partnership with Dan Gibson in a beautiful parkland and woodland setting. Azaleas and rhododendrons lead to late cultivars of spring-flowering shrubs. Formal terraced rose garden. The finely wrought sundials and gate by Gibson, the Dutch garden and the stream and pond all add charm to this serene garden. For topiary admirers, Mawson employed interesting effects to contrast with his more billowy plantings. Notable are the battlemented yew hedge and some globe yews with golden yews in the top half and green in the bottom.

HOLEHIRD ★★   8
Troutbeck, Windermere, Cumbria. Tel: (05395) 46238

Lakeland Horticultural Society * *2m N of Windermere on A592 Troutbeck road* * *Parking* * *Toilet facilities* * *Partly suitable for wheelchairs* * *Dogs on lead* *
* *Annual plant sale 1st Sat in May in local school* * *Open all year, daily, sunrise – sunset. Garden guides available April to Oct, 11am – 5pm* * *Entrance: free*

This is a garden run by members of a Society dedicated to promoting 'knowledge on the cultivation of plants, shrubs and trees especially those suited to Lakeland conditions'. It lies on a splendid site with a natural water course and rock banks looking over Windermere to Scafell Pike. The Society has part of the former orchard, the rock garden and now the walled kitchen garden. Much earlier planting has been preserved, including survivors from plant-hunting expeditions to China and many fine specimen trees (e.g. 60ft handkerchief tree). Highlights are the summer-autumn heathers, winter-flowering shrubs, alpines and the national astilbe and hydrangea collections.

The walled garden now has herbaceous specimens, herbs and climbers. Good ferns.

HOLKER HALL ★★   9
Cark-in-Cartmel, Grange-over-Sands, Cumbria. Tel: (05395) 58328

Lord and Lady Cavendish ✻ 4¹/₂m W of Grange-over-Sands on B5278 between Haverthwaite (A590) and Grange-over-Sands ✻ Best season: spring, summer ✻ Parking ✻ Refreshments: cafeteria lunches, snacks and teas ✻ Toilet facilities inc. disabled ✻ Mostly suitable for wheelchairs ✻ Dogs ✻ Plants for sale ✻ Shop ✻ Hall and Motor Museum open. Extra charge ✻ Open April to Oct, Sun – Fri, 10.30am – 4.30pm ✻ Entrance: £2.55, children over 6 £1.45. Group rates £2, OAP £1.65, children over 6 £1.50 (gardens, grounds and exhibitions) (1991 prices)

Set in acres of parkland, the woodland walks and formal gardens have been constantly developed by the family ever since Lord George Cavendish established his 'contrived natural landscape' some 200 years ago. The woods now contain many rare and beautiful specimens, all tagged and chronicled in the excellent guide to the walks. Other features are the recent cascade, evocative of the Villa d'Este, and a beautifully contrived transformation of the croquet lawn into summer gardens. This combination of formal beds and inventive planting (e.g. spire lilies rising out of massed rue) makes a wonderful Italianate-cum-English garden that typifies the spirit of Holker. There is also Mawson's rose garden, now being sensitively renewed (his pergola and balustrade still survive). The early blaze of rare rhododendrons and azaleas, carpets of spring bulbs and the colour and scent of summer and autumn displays provide year-round interest and pleasure. A Great Garden and Countryside Festival will be held for the first time 5th to 7th June 1992.

HUTTON-IN-THE-FOREST ★   10
Skelton, Penrith, Cumbria. Tel: (08534) 449

Lord and Lady Inglewood ✻ 3m from M6 junction 41, along B5305 to Wigton ✻ Best season: early summer ✻ Parking ✻ Teas when house open. Other meals on request ✻ Toilet facilities ✻ Possible for wheelchairs – gravel paths ✻ Dogs on lead ✻ House open: 28th May to 27th Sept, Thurs, Fri and Sun, 1 – 4pm and Bank Holiday Suns and Mons. Private parties by arrangement from April ✻ Garden and grounds open daily, except Sat and 25th Dec, 11am – 5pm ✻ Entrance: £1, children free (house and grounds £2.80, children 7-16 £1) (1991 prices)

This garden was inspired by William Gilpin, eighteenth-century pioneer of the picturesque, who was brought up in the Border Country. It has great visual appeal, with a magnificent view from the Victorian topiary terraces. There are good herbs and fruit trees and excellent beds and borders in the walled garden. Some of the mature woodland trees were imported from the Indies by Henry Fletcher, an ancestor of the owners, in the early eighteenth century. Recent planting includes rhododendrons and other spring displays in the woodland low garden and there is an extensive park with forest walks, where conducted tours take place by arrangement. Other features include a seventeenth-century dovecote and pools.

LEVENS HALL ★★ 11
Levens Hall, Kendal, Cumbria. Tel: (05395) 60321

Mr C.H. Bagot ✻ *5m S of Kendal on A6 (M6 junction 36)* ✻ *Best season:
summer* ✻ *Parking* ✻ *Teas* ✻ *Toilet facilities inc. disabled* ✻ *Suitable for
wheelchairs* ✻ *Plants for sale* ✻ *Shop* ✻ *House open. Combined ticket £3.25,
children and students £1.65, groups of 20 or more and others £2.65 per person* ✻
Garden open Easter Sun to Sept, Sun – Thurs, 11am – 5pm ✻ *Entrance: £1.90,
children 95p, groups of 20 or more and others £1.70 per person (1991 prices)*

James II's gardener, Guillaume Beaumont, designed this famous topiary
garden in 1692. It is one of very few to retain its original trees and design. The
impeccably clipped yews and box hedges are set off by colourful spring and
summer bedding and borders. Massive walls of beech hedge open to vistas over
parkland. One avenue leads to the earliest designed ha-ha. There is a
picturesque herb garden behind the house, and another now planted up to
match the recently discovered seventeenth-century plan. The record of only 10
gardeners in 300 years, and the affectionate care by the Bagot family, account
for the rare harmony of this exceptional garden.

LINGHOLM GARDENS ★ 12
Lingholm, Keswick, Cumbria. Tel: (07687) 72003

The Viscount Rochdale ✻ *W side of Derwentwater, 3m from Keswick off A66* ✻
Best season: spring, early summer and autumn ✻ *Parking* ✻ *Teas* ✻ *Toilet
facilities* ✻ *Suitable for wheelchairs* ✻ *Plants for sale* ✻ *Open April to Oct,
daily, 10am – 5pm* ✻ *Entrance: £2.20, accompanied children free, groups £1.80
per person*

A most pleasing lakeland garden with view south to Borrowdale. Colour from
early spring with bulbs and long-lasting display of azaleas and rhododendrons
(note *Rhododendron auriculatum* and *Rhododendron* 'Shilsonii') right through to
August. Much other blossom and a particularly good mix of trees (e.g. silver
firs, cedars and maples) keep up the interest throughout the season. Careful
labelling in the formal gardens and along the delightful woodland walk
enhances the pleasure. Beatrix Potter stayed and wrote 'Squirrel Nutkin' here.

MUNCASTER CASTLE ★ 13
Ravenglass, Cumbria. Tel: (0229) 717/614/203

Mr and Mrs Gordon-Duff-Pennington ✻ *15m S of Whitehaven on A595* ✻ *Best
season: May and June* ✻ *Parking* ✻ *Teas* ✻ *Toilet facilities* ✻ *Suitable for
wheelchairs* ✻ *Dogs on lead* ✻ *Garden centre plants for sale* ✻ *Shop* ✻ *Castle
open: Tues – Sun, 1 – 4pm. Combined ticket £3, children £1.50* ✻ *Garden open
April to Oct, daily, 11am – 5pm* ✻ *Entrance: £1.50, children £1 (1991 prices)*

The splendid backdrop of Scafell and the hills, the acid soil and the Gulf
Stream warmth provide ideal conditions. One of the finest collections of
species rhododendron in Europe has been built up, many from plant-hunting
expeditions to Nepal in the 1920s (Kingdon-Ward, Ludlow and Sheriff).

There are excellent azaleas, camellias, magnolias, hydrangeas and maples, plus many unusual trees (e.g. *Nothofagus* species). The garden is at its best in May and June but intensive new planting is ensuring constant pleasure for visitors in all seasons. Tony Warburton of TV fame also runs an Owl Centre here – a national centre for breeding and conservation of endangered owls, including many worldwide species.

RYDAL MOUNT 14
Ambleside, Cumbria. Tel: (05394) 33002

*Mrs Henderson * 1m N of Ambleside on A591 * Best season: spring * Parking * Toilet facilities * Dogs on lead * Shop * House open * Gardens open Mar to Oct, daily, 9.30am – 5pm, Nov to Feb, daily except Tues, 10am – 4pm * Entrance: £2, children 80p, groups £1.70 per person*

The carefully maintained grounds of Wordsworth's house still follow the lines of his own plan and it is easy to imagine the poet wandering along the upper terrace walk (Isabella's) and down through winding, shaded paths to the lawns, or across a terrace to the ancient mound with its distant glimpse of Windermere. Apart from its poetic association the garden is also a visual delight with good herbaceous borders, shrubs and unusual trees (e.g. the fern-leaved beech). An addition to the spring display is the bank of dancing daffodils in nearby Dora's field. A word of praise for some good labelling.

SIZERGH CASTLE ★ 15
Kendal, Cumbria. Tel: (05395) 60070

*The National Trust * 1m S of Kendal on A591 (M6 junction 36) * Best season: spring to autumn * Parking * Teas: 1.30 – 5pm * Toilet facilities * Partly suitable for wheelchairs * Shop * Castle open same days, 1.30 – 5.30pm * Open April to 29th Oct, Sun to Thurs, 12.30 – 5.30pm (last admission 5pm) * Entrance: £1.60 (castle and garden £3.10). Parties of 15 or more reduced rate by arrangement*

An exceptionally varied garden with colour from early spring daffodils to summer borders and climbers culminating in glorious autumn tints (the vine-clad tower all fiery red is a memorable spectacle). Other features encountered along shady paths are the Hayes' rock garden (Japanese maples, dwarf conifers, primulas, gentians, etc.) the long wall (*Clematis flammula*, *Hydrangea petiolaris*, brooms and much else) and the rose garden (specimen roses and clematis). The pond and rockery are now being refurbished.

STAGSHAW 16
Ambleside, Cumbria. Tel: (05394) 35599

*The National Trust * ¹/₂m S of Ambleside on A591 * Best season: spring, early summer * Limited parking, access dangerous * Open April to June, daily, 10am – 6.30pm, July to Oct, by appointment (please send SAE to The National Trust North West Regional Office, The Hollens, Grasmere, Cumbria) * Entrance: £1*

Created by C.H.D. Acland, this is a carefully blended area of azaleas and rhododendrons among camellias, magnolias and other fine shrubs on a west-facing hillside of oaks looking over the head of Lake Windermere. Rather difficult of access but worth the effort.

HOW TO FIND THE GARDENS

Directions to each garden are included in each entry. This information has been supplied by the garden inspectors and is aimed to be the best available to those travelling by car. However, it has been compiled to be used in conjunction with a road atlas. The unreliability of train and bus services makes it unrewarding to include details, particularly as many garden visits are made on Sundays. However, many properties can be reached by public transport and National Trust guides and the Yellow Book [NGS] give details. Future editions of the *Guide* may include a special list of gardens easily reached by public transport if readers indicate that this would be helpful. *The Maps*: The numbers on the maps correspond to the numbers of the gardens in each county. The maps show the proximity of one garden to another so that visits to several gardens can be planned for the same day. It is worthwhile referring to the maps of bordering counties to see if another garden visit can be included in the itinerary.

DERBYSHIRE

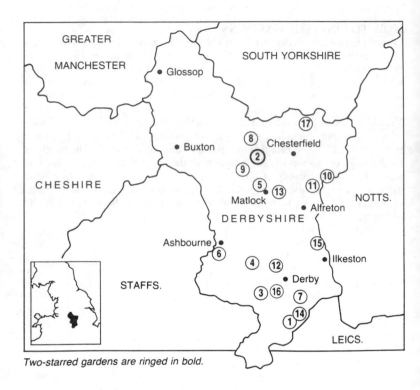

Two-starred gardens are ringed in bold.

CALKE ABBEY 1

Ticknall, Derbyshire. Tel: (0332) 864444 (24hr recorded information or (0332) 863822 (office)

The National Trust ✳ 9m S of Derby, off A514 at Ticknall ✳ Parking ✳ Refreshments: restaurant ✳ Toilet facilities ✳ Partly suitable for wheelchairs ✳ National Trust shop ✳ House open as garden but 1 – 5pm (tickets are timed and there may be some waiting) ✳ Garden open 30th March to Oct, Sat – Wed and Bank Holiday Mons, 11am – 5pm. Closed Good Friday ✳ Entrance: £1.70, children 80p (house and garden £4, children £2). £1.50 vehicle charge entry to park, which is open during daylight hours all year, refundable on entry to house.

Previously owned by an eccentric family and recently taken on by the Trust, Calke House and park overshadow the gardens at present. These latter have a long history and with a sympathetic approach could be another Trust jewel. There are frames, pits, an orangery and grotto, and an auricula stand all waiting to be restored. Only two gardeners are on the staff at present but the work done in recent years is magnificent. The flower garden is delightful with a pattern of beds and basket-weave ironwork round a little fountain pond. The Trust hopes to restore the gardens to their former glory given enough funds, and for locals it will be worth making periodic visits to see its resurrection to eighteenth and nineteenth-century status.

CHATSWORTH ★★ 2
Bakewell, Derbyshire. Tel: (0246) 582204

The Duke and Duchess of Devonshire ✳ *4m E of Bakewell, 10m W of Chesterfield on B6012, off A619 and A6* ✳ *Parking: cars £1, coaches free* ✳ *Refreshments: hot meals and salads in the Carriage House restaurant, snacks near Orangery Shop* ✳ *Toilet facilities* ✳ *Suitable for wheelchairs (but not house)* ✳ *Dogs on lead* ✳ *Plants for sale* ✳ *Shop* ✳ *House open* ✳ *Open 29th March to 1st Nov, daily, 11am – 5pm* ✳ *Entrance: £2.75, OAP and students £2.25, children £1.25, family £7 (house and garden £4.75, OAP and students £4, children £2.25, family £12)*

The 100 acres of garden at Chatsworth have developed over 300 years and many areas still reflect the garden fashions of each century. The seventeenth-century gardens of London and Wise remain only as the cascade and canal pond to the south. During the eighteenth century 'Capability' Brown destroyed much of the formal gardens to create a landscaped woodland park. Notable is the vista created by Brown from the Salisbury Lawn to the horizon, which remains unchanged as does the lawn itself since no liming or fertilizer has been used, allowing many varieties of wild flowers, grasses, moss and sedges to thrive. The orange borders and blue and white borders are twentieth-century additions as is the terrace, display greenhouse, rose garden and old conservatory garden which has lupin, dahlia and Michaelmas daisy beds. The Duke and Duchess continue to work on the garden improving the arboretum and pinetum by removing the suffocating rhododendron, laurels and sycamores and planting many new trees – labelling of these different trees is excellent. The serpentine hedge of beech was planted in 1953 and the double rows of pleached red-twigged limes were planted in 1952, both now rewarding features. Paxton's work still gives pleasure: there is the large rockery, some rare conifers, the magnificent 276 ft water jet from the Emperor fountain. Alas, the Great Conservatory was a casualty of the 1914-18 war and three and a half foot stone walls in the old conservatory garden are all that remain to give an idea of its size. The epitome of a cottage garden has been created near the 'Plant Sales' area. A useful booklet 'The Garden at Chatsworth' can be bought in the shop before entering the garden.

CHERRY TREE COTTAGE 3
18 Sutton Lane, Hilton, Derbyshire. Tel: (0283) 733778

Mr and Mrs R. Hamblin ✳ *8m SW of Derby. Take A516 from Derby. Sutton*

Lane is on the right in Hilton opposite The Old Talbot pub. Cherry Tree Cottage is a few yards down on the right ✳ *Parking in Hilton car park* ✳ *Toilet facilities* ✳ *Plants for sale* ✳ *Open 3rd May, 7th June, 5th July, 2 – 6pm and by appointment. Groups welcome* ✳ *Entrance: 50p, children free*

Despite being a small area, there are large collections of many plants, especially snowdrops, hellebores, aquilegias, dianthus and variegated plants, as well as room for a scree garden, pool and large herb garden. The garden achieves so much yet remains neat and charming and was deservedly featured in *Small Gardens* in Summer 1990 and on *Gardener's World* in 1991.

DAM FARM HOUSE   4
Yeldersley Lane, Brailsford, Derbyshire. Tel: (0335) 60291

Mrs S.D. Player ✳ *5m SE of Ashbourne on A52. Opposite the Ednaston village turn, the gate is 500 yards on right* ✳ *Parking in field next to garden* ✳ *Teas on Sun* ✳ *Suitable for wheelchairs* ✳ *Plants for sale* ✳ *Open by appointment and 26th April, 31st May, 28th June, 12th July, 2 – 5pm* ✳ *Entrance: £1, children 25p*

The scree garden has a large number of choice alpines. Climbers are used abundantly for clothing walls, trees, pergolas – even spilling down over high retaining walls and all achieved in 10 years. Collections of plants, shrubs and roses. Plenty of informative labelling. This garden promises to be a most important one as it continues to develop under the expertise of Mrs Player.

DARLEY HOUSE ★   5
Darley Dale, Matlock, Derbyshire. Tel: (0629) 733341

Mr and Mrs G.H. Briscoe ✳ *2m N of Matlock on A6 to Bakewell, on right just past Whitworth Hospital* ✳ *Best season: spring/summer* ✳ *Limited parking beside entrance* ✳ *Refreshments: tea and biscuits* ✳ *Partly suitable for wheelchairs* ✳ *Plants for sale. Extensive seed list* ✳ *Open 25th April to Oct by appointment* ✳ *Entrance: 60p, children 20p. Special arrangements for private parties*

This serene garden was originally set out by Paxton in 1845. Plantsman's gardens can be bogged down by the sheer number of different plants but here, although there is a wealth of beautiful and unusual plants, all harmonise. There are a number of mature tender shrubs and plants which surprisingly survive the Derbyshire weather – thoughtful planting obviously paying dividends. Extensive seed list.

DOVE COTTAGE GARDENS   6
Clifton, Ashbourne, Derbyshire. Tel: (0335) 43545

Mr and Mrs S.G. Liverman ✳ *1¹/₂m SW of Ashbourne off A515. In Clifton turn right at crossroads then first left (signposted Mayfield Yarns). The house is 200 yards down lane on the left by the River Dove* ✳ *Parking* ✳ *Teas* ✳ *Toilet facilities* ✳ *Plants for sale* ✳ *Open by appointment for party bookings of 10 or more and for*

charity 17th May, 21st June, 26th July, 16th Aug, 1.30 – 5pm ✳ Entrance:
Parties £1.50 per person for guided tour and for charity £1, children free

It is only to be expected that this richly-stocked cottage garden is above average
for it has had the benefit of being developed and nurtured by an owner who is a
qualified horticulturalist. He began replanting in 1979. There are several hardy
plant collections including alliums, euphorbias and variegated plants.

ELVASTON CASTLE COUNTRY PARK ★   7
Nr Derby, Derbyshire. Tel: (0332) 571342

Derbyshire County Council ✳ 6m SE of Derby on B5010 between Borrowash
A6005 and Thulston A6. Signposted from A6 and A52 ✳ Parking: mid-week
60p, weekends and Bank Holidays £1.20 (1991 prices) ✳ Refreshments: Parlour
tearoom, Easter to Oct ✳ Toilet facilities ✳ Suitable for wheelchairs ✳ Dogs on
lead in Old English Garden ✳ Shop ✳ Estate Museum open Easter to Oct, daily
except Mon and Tues (but open Bank Holiday Mons) ✳ Open all year, daily, 9am
– dusk ✳ Entrance: free

A fine garden to visit at any time of the year. Within the 200 acres there is a large
variety of mature trees with many recent trees planted from donations as a
memorial to a loved one – an excellent idea. A tree trail is planned. The Italian
garden with its clipped yews has limited appeal visually. The original walled
kitchen garden is now the Old English Garden containing herbaceous borders,
rose garden and herb garden. The history of the garden is diplayed in the
Information Centre; of particular interest is that in 1851 there were 90
gardening staff. William Barron, the professional gardener who developed the
garden at that time, was an expert on transplanting mature trees – the cedars
here were moved by the Barron method – Kew has a 'Barron transplanter'. He
had erected 11 miles of yew hedge by 1850 and in 1880, when he had left his
employment here, he caused a controversy by transplanting a 1000-year-old
yew tree in Buckland churchyard to save the church

FIR CROFT   8
Froggatt Road, Calver, Derbyshire.

Dr and Mrs S.B. Furness ✳ 4m N of Bakewell. Between the Q8 filling station and
the junction of B6001 and B6054 ✳ Best season: spring/early summer ✳ Limited
parking ✳ Partly suitable for wheelchairs ✳ Plants for sale at adjoining nursery
✳ Open 26th April, 17th May, 21st June, 12th July, 2– 6pm ✳ Entrance: by
collection box for charity

The owner is a botanist and botanical photographer who has put his expertise
into an extensive alpine garden – a 'must' to visit if interested in alpine and scree
gardens, particularly as the garden was started from scratch in 1985.

HADDON HALL   9
Bakewell, Derbyshire. Tel: (0629) 812855

The Duke of Rutland ✳ 2m SE of Bakewell, 6¹/₂m N of Matlock on A6 ✳

Parking: cars 50p, coaches free ✳ *Refreshments: lunches and teas in Stables tearoom* ✳ *Toilet facilities* ✳ *House open* ✳ *Garden open Easter to Sept, daily except Mon in April to June, and except Sun and Mon in July and Aug, but open Bank Holiday Sun and Mon, 11am – 6pm* ✳ *Entrance: £3.20, OAP £2.60, children £1.90 (house and garden – inclusive ticket only)*

The castle and gardens of seventeenth-century origin – reconstructed this century – stand on a limestone bluff. The gardens are mainly on the south side and are laid out in a series of stone-walled terraces with the River Wye at their feet. The thick stone walls of the castle and terrace walls face south and west and look well as a background for the extensive collection of climbing and rambling roses. The plants, shrubs and roses all have legible labels. The upper terrace with balustraded parapet and fine stairway is particularly memorable.

HARDWICK HALL ★   10
Doe Lea, Chesterfield, Derbyshire. Tel: (0246) 850430

The National Trust ✳ *6¹/₂m NW of Mansfield, 9¹/₂m SE of Chesterfield. Approach from M1 junction 29 then A617* ✳ *Best season: summer* ✳ *Parking. Gates close at 6.30pm* ✳ *Refreshments in Great Kitchen of Hall on days Hall is open 12 noon – 4.45pm* ✳ *Toilet facilities* ✳ *Suitable for wheelchairs* ✳ *Dogs in park only, on lead* ✳ *National Trust shop* ✳ *House open April to Oct on Wed, Thurs, Sat, Sun and Bank Holiday Mon, 12.30 – 5pm or sunset if earlier (last admission 4.30pm)* ✳ *Garden open April to Oct, daily, 12 noon – 5.30pm. Country park open, daily, dawn – dusk* ✳ *Entrance: £2 (house and garden £5, children £2.50). No reduction for parties*

This famous Elizabethan mansion house was built for Bess of Hardwick by Robert Smythson in the late sixteenth century. Mature yew hedges and brick walls provide necessary shelter to an otherwise exposed hilltop site. The borders of the Great Court have spring-flowering shrubs to give colour for a longer period than herbaceous plants can provide. Some herbaceous borders have strong, hot colours as an overall grouping, others have soft hues. In order to rest the soil to rid it of a build-up of pests and diseases the borders were replanted in October 1989. The herb garden is outstanding in variety of plants and display. There is some 300 acres of country park. One of the two magnificent cedars has been badly wind-damaged.

THE HERB GARDEN   11
Hall View Cottage, Hardstoft, Pilsley, Nr Chesterfield, Derbyshire. Tel: (0246) 854268

Mrs Raynor ✳ *5m SE of Chesterfield on B6039 Holmewood – Tibshelf road. 3m from M1 junction 29* ✳ *Parking* ✳ *Suitable for wheelchairs* ✳ *Plants for sale* ✳ *Shop* ✳ *Garden open March to Sept, daily, 10am – 6pm; Oct to Christmas, weekdays. Closed Jan and Feb* ✳ *Entrance: free*

A rich herb garden in a rural setting with a now established parterre. Three new speciality gardens have been added: a physic garden, a scented pot pourri garden and a lavender garden. A very large range of herbs for sale including rare and unusual species. This garden is only a short distance from the other excellent herb garden in Hardwick Hall (see above).

KEDLESTON HALL ★   12
Kedleston, Derbyshire. Tel: (0332) 842191

The National Trust ∗ 4¹/₂m NW of Derby on the Derby – Hulland road between A6 and A52. Well signposted ∗ Best season : summer/autumn ∗ Parking ∗ Refreshments: tearoom, 12 noon – 5pm ∗ Toilet facilities ∗ Not suitable for wheelchairs unless by prior written arrangement ∗ Shop ∗ Hall open, April to Oct, Sat – Wed, 1 – 5.30pm, contains Curzon's Indian Museum ∗ Park open April to Oct, daily, 11am – 6pm and Nov to 23rd Dec, Sat and Sun only, 12 noon – 4pm. Garden open April to Oct, Sat – Wed, inc Bank Holidays, 11am – 6pm ∗ Entrance: park: £1 vehicle entry charge on Thurs and Fri. Hall and garden: £3.75, children £1.80. Coach parties must pre-book by writing to the Administrator

The ancient home of the Curzon family, their most famous member being George Nathaniel, one time Viceroy of India. The extensive gardens do not compete with this classical Robert Adam palace, but are of mature parkland where the eye is always drawn to the house. The rhododendrons when in flower are worth visiting in their own right, otherwise use the gardens as a pleasurable way not only to view Adam's magnificent south front but his octagonal-domed summerhouse, his orangery, a Venetian-windowed waterside house, the bridge across the lake, the aviary – now a loggia – and the main gateway. The formal gardens have a heart-shaped sunken rose garden and beds by Lutyens (1925). The Hackforth Fountain is another attraction.

LEA GARDENS   13
Lea, Nr Matlock, Derbyshire. Tel: (0629) 534380/534260

Mr and Mrs Tye ∗ 5m SE of Matlock E off A6 ∗ Parking. Coaches by appointment ∗ Refreshments: light lunches, teas ∗ Suitable for wheelchairs ∗ Plants for sale ∗ Open 20th March to July, daily, 10am – 7pm, Oct and Nov, Wed, Thurs and Sun, 2 – 5pm ∗ Entrance: season ticket £1.50, children 50p

This garden, featured in a 1990 *Gardener's World* programme, has a comprehensive collection of rhododendrons, azaleas, alpines and conifers all brought together here in a beautiful woodland setting. The excellent booklet describes the contents of the garden with a suggested route. John Marsden Smedley started his rhododendron garden in 1935, inspired by his visits to Bodnant and Exbury. Under the Tye family the collection now comprises some 550 varieties of rhododendrons and azaleas.

MELBOURNE HALL ★   14
Melbourne, Derbyshire. Tel: (0332) 862502

Lord Ralph Kerr ∗ 8m S of Derby off B587 in village of Melbourne (between A514 and A453) ∗ Best season: spring/summer ∗ Limited parking ∗

Refreshments: hot and cold meals in tea room ✳ *Toilet facilities* ✳ *Suitable for wheelchairs* ✳ *Shop* ✳ *House open, Aug, most days, 2 – 5pm, £2, OAP £1.50, children 75p* ✳ *Garden open April to Sept, Wed, Sat, Sun and Bank Holiday Mon, 2 – 6pm* ✳ *Entrance: £2, OAP £1*

There has been very little alteration to Sir Thomas Coke's formal garden so this is a visual record of a complete late seventeenth-century/early eighteenth-century garden in the style of Le Nôtre laid out by London and Wise. It is in immaculate condition with avenues culminating in exquisite statuary and fountains, including the lead urn The Four Seasons by van Nost, whose other lead statuary stands in niches of yew. A series of terraces run down to a lake, the Great Basin. A grotto has an inscription thought to be that of Byron's troublesome mistress Caroline Lamb. Unique in English gardens is the Birdcage iron arbour of 1706 which can be seen from the house along a long walk hedged with yews. It is well worth buying the booklet 'Melbourne Hall Gardens' at the entrance, giving the history and a suggested guided tour.

210 NOTTINGHAM ROAD 15
Woodlinkin, Langley Mill, Derbyshire. Tel: (0773) 714903

Mr and Mrs R. Brown ✳ *12m NW of Nottingham on A610 near Codnor. It is the first house past a garage on the left* ✳ *Best season: late spring/early summer* ✳ *Limited parking* ✳ *Suitable for wheelchairs* ✳ *Dogs on lead* ✳ *Open 24th May, 28th June, 2 – 5pm* ✳ *Entrance: £1*

A plantsman's garden of half an acre with an emphasis on shrub roses – the garden is packed with many good examples. There are also some rarer shrubs and trees. Geraniums, hellebores, symphytums and similar plants provide all-year interest in the herbaceous section. The brick base of a disused greenhouse is used for a display of alpines.

57 PORTLAND CLOSE 16
Mickleover, Derbyshire. Tel: (0332) 515450

Mr and Mrs A.L. Ritchie ✳ *From A111 (Derby ring road) take A516. At first roundabout take B5020 (signposted Mickleover). In Mickleover take right turn into Cavendish Way, then second left into Portland Close* ✳ *Best season: spring/summer* ✳ *Limited parking* ✳ *Plants for sale* ✳ *Open by appointment and 26th April, 31st May, 2 – 5pm* ✳ *Entrance: 50p, children free*

A plantsman's small garden with something unusual planted in almost every inch of it. The knowledgeable owner propagates most of the huge variety of hostas, primulas, auriculas, violas and cyclamen, with many of the plants for sale. Alpines, sink gardens.

RENISHAW HALL 17
Eckington, Derbyshire.

Sir Reresby and Lady Sitwell ✳ *6m from Sheffield and Chesterfield on A616.*

From M1 at junction 30, take A616 towards Sheffield for 3m, over the railway bridge S-bend, and immediately turn left. From the traffic lights in Eckington take the third turning right – up a slight rise and the entrance is ahead ✱ Best season: summer ✱ Parking ✱ Teas ✱ Toilet facilities ✱ Partly suitable for wheelchairs ✱ Dogs on lead ✱ Plants for sale ✱ Open 26th April, 31st May, 7th, 14th, 21st, 28th June, 26th July, 30th Aug, 2 – 5pm ✱ Entrance: £1.50, OAP £1, children 50p

An entry in *The Guinness Book of Records* states that Renishaw has 'the most northerly vineyard in western Europe'. Also astonishing to see at this northerly latitude and on top of a hill (albeit on a south-facing wall) are enormous specimens of *Acacia dealbata*, *Cytisus battendieri* and *Fremontodendron californicum*. There are other rare, slightly tender specimen shrubs within the garden. Presumably the fact that the soil is light, the aspect southerly and shelter provided by yew hedges and parkland trees overcome the disadvantages of latitude and height. Sir George Sitwell spent much of his life in Italy and hence this is the style he recreated at Renishaw. The sound of splashing water, always in the background, adds to the Italianate atmosphere. Osbert Sitwell's memoirs give amusing anecdotes about his father's plans for the gardens which could certainly have included, had he been alive today, the attainment of ★★ in the *Guide*.

CUTTINGS

Readers may wish to be reminded that the taking of cuttings without the owner's permission can lead to embarrassment and, if it continues on a large scale, may cause the owners to close their gardens to the public. This has to be seen in the context of an increasing number of thefts from gardens. At Nymans, the famous Sussex garden, thefts have reached such a level that the gardener will not now plant out any shrub until it is semi-mature and of such a size that its theft would be very difficult. Other owners have reported the theft of artifacts as well as plants.

DEVON

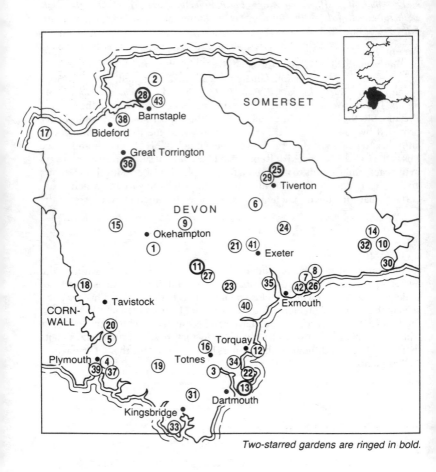

SOMERSET

DEVON

CORN-WALL

Two-starred gardens are ringed in bold.

ANDREW'S CORNER

Belstone, Nr Okehampton, Devon. Tel: (0837) 840332

H.J. and Mr and Mrs R.J. Hill ✳ 3m E of Okehampton, signposted to Belstone
✳ Parking ✳ Teas on open days ✳ Suitable for wheelchairs ✳ Plants for sale
✳ Open by appointment and 26th April, 3rd, 24th, 25th May, 7th, 21st June,
19th July, 2.30 – 6pm ✳ Entrance: 50p, children 25p

Nine hundred feet above sea level, on north Dartmoor, facing to the Taw valley and across to the high moor. In only a little over an acre (amazing that it is not larger) grow a wide variety of plants of all sorts not normally seen at such an altitude. The sense of space is achieved by the division of the garden into different levels by rhododendrons and trees, each area being a small region with its own micro-climate, and all with glimpses through to other areas and to the wide landscape. There are herbaceous plants and lilies, conifers and heathers in island beds; in spring flowering bulbs and meconopsis; in autumn colour from maples (many grown from seed) and gentians. There are dry stone walls (a speciality of the area), a paved area and a pond with water plants; among the stone and paving are lewisias and other alpines. The owner does not like the description 'plantsman'; he says it is a hobby he loves – it is certainly an inspiration.

ARLINGTON COURT 2
Arlington, Nr Barnstaple, Devon. Tel: (0271) 850296

*The National Trust * 7m N of Barnstaple on A39, turn E * Parking 300 yards away * Refreshments: in tearoom when house open * Toilet facilities near house * Dogs in grounds only on leads * Shop open during open hours, and weekends before Christmas * House open * Garden open April to 1st Nov, daily except Sat (but open Sat of Bank Holiday weekends), 11am – 5.30pm (last admission ¹/₂ hour before closing). Park open all year, daily during daylight hours * Entrance: Garden and Carriage Museum £2.20, children £1.10 (house, museum and garden £4.10, children £2.20, parties £3.30 per person)*

The Georgian house is set in a magnificent park where Shetland ponies and Jacob sheep graze. There are a number of woodland walks with many remains of the old stone-built water courses or leats that were used to irrigate the park in times of drought two centuries ago. The planned 'wilderness' was a popular eighteenth-century feature, a semi-wild area between the garden and the parkland. The woodland is managed to protect wildlife including red deer. The lake is approached by an avenue of monkey puzzle (araucaria) trees.

AVENUE COTTAGE GARDENS 3
Ashprington, Totnes, Devon. Tel: (0803) 732769

*Mr R.C.H. Soans and Mr R.J. Pitts * Take the A381 from Totnes towards Kingsbridge. Turn left to Ashprington. Facing the Durant Arms in Ashprington turn left uphill past the Church (No through road). The gardens are 300 yards on the right * No coaches * Plants for sale * Open April to Sept, Tues – Sat, 11am – 5pm. Also by appointment * Entrance: by donation*

These gardens were originally part of the eighteenth-century landscape gardens of Sharpham House, separated 50 years ago. They are approached along a splendid avenue of Turkey oaks planted in 1844. Many of the rhododendrons and azaleas planted in the last century are enormous and magnificent. Over the years the garden had become overgrown in some places and it is now undergoing a major transformation with overcrowded areas being cleared to give more space and light to new plantings and to open up new vistas.

There are new plantings of many unusual herbaceous plants including species asters, hydrangeas and several giant grasses including pampas and miscanthus. It is probably best in spring and early summer but there is late summer colour, too, particularly in the large acers.

41 BEAUMONT ROAD 4
St Judes, Plymouth, Devon. Tel: (0752) 668640

Mr and Mrs A.J. Parsons ✳ *¹/₂m from Plymouth city centre, 100 yards from Beaumont Park. Take Ebrington Street exit from Charles Cross roundabout in city centre* ✳ *Parking in nearby street* ✳ *Teas* ✳ *Open 7th June, 2 – 6pm* ✳ *Entrance: 50p*

A prize-winning garden in a north-facing, narrow Victorian backyard, 60 feet long. Plants intensively grown in pots and containers include clematis, ceanothus, parthenocissus. Variagated ivies grow out of tubs over arches; there is a rockery and even a pool and waterfall. Pieris, viburnums, camellias, many clematis, and scented plants, such as philadelphus, *Viburnum farreri* and Regal lilies, make this matchbox garden an inspiration for small town garden owners. Mr and Mrs Parsons aptly quote Horace: 'This is one of my prayers: for a parcel of land, not so very large'.

BICKHAM HOUSE 5
Bickham, Roborough, Plymouth, Devon.

Lord and Lady Roborough ✳ *8m N of Plymouth on A386. Take Maristow turn left on Roborough Down and follow poster directions* ✳ *Parking* ✳ *Teas* ✳ *Toilet facilities* ✳ *Plants for sale* ✳ *Open Sun only 29th March to 7th June, and 20th April, 4th, 25th May, 21st June, 2 – 5.30pm* ✳ *Entrance: £1*

This is a spring garden in a valley with magnificent views. There is a mass of bulbs and many camellias as well as magnolias and rhododendrons. There are two ponds with aquatic plants and a walled garden with old roses.

BICKLEIGH CASTLE 6
Nr Tiverton, Devon. Tel: (0884) 855363

Mr O.N. Boxall ✳ *4m S of Tiverton off A396. At Bickleigh Bridge take A3072 and follow signs* ✳ *Best season: spring/early summer* ✳ *Parking* ✳ *Teas* ✳ *Suitable for wheelchairs (ground floor of house only)* ✳ *House open. Private tours for groups by appointment* ✳ *Garden open Easter week (Good Friday – Fri), then Suns, Weds and Bank Holiday Mons, 2 – 5pm until late May Bank Holiday and then daily except Sat until early Oct, 2 – 5pm* ✳ *Entrance: £2.80, children 5 – 15 £1.40 (house, garden and exhibitions). Family tickets available*

These gardens are situated in the valley of the Exe around the ancient buildings which are historically fascinating with much to see. The gatehouse is fourteenth-century, the thatched chapel eleventh and twelfth-century, and the Castle became the home of the Carew family, Sir George Carew being the Vice Admiral of the Mary Rose. Beyond the eighteenth-century Italian wrought iron courtyard gates is a large mound planted in the 1930s with every known variety of rhododendron. There is a 300-year-old wisteria and many more mature trees including *Gingko biloba*, magnolias, a Judas tree and a tulip tree. The Castle moat is planted with iris and water lilies.

BICTON COLLEGE OF AGRICULTURE　　　7
East Budleigh, Devon. Tel: (0395) 68353

By Sidmouth Lodge, halfway between Budleigh Salterton and Newton Poppleford on A376　✷　Parking main college car park, short walk to gardens　✷　Toilet facilities　✷　Suitable for wheelchairs　✷　Wide range of plants for sale　✷　Opening times are under review but will include all year Wed and Fri only, 2 – 5pm. Closed Christmas　✷　Entrance: £1, children free (1991 prices). Membership of Friends of the College gives unlimited access and free gardening advice on Fri afternoons

The gardens of this Georgian house form the horticultural department of Bicton Agricultural College, and as such contain a large number of plants laid out for both study and general interest. As well as the fascinating herbaceous beds there is an arboretum with spring-flowering trees and an old walled garden with glasshouses, all approached by an avenue of araucarias (monkey puzzle trees). Amongst the plants which provide both information and effect are the NCCPG collections of agapanthus and pittosporums. Garden and arboretum guides are available.

BICTON PARK ★　　　8
East Budleigh, Budleigh Salterton, Devon. Tel: (0395) 68465

Bicton Park Trust Company　✷　2m N of Budleigh Salterton on A376　✷　Parking　✷　Refreshments: self-service restaurant and licensed bar, picnic areas　✷　Toilet facilities　✷　Suitable for wheelchairs (wheelchair loan available)　✷　Dogs on lead　✷　Shop　✷　Museum open, extra charge　✷　Open March to Oct, daily, 10am – 6pm　✷　Entrance: £3.75, OAP £3.50 (OAP 'Golden Days' (Wed and Thurs) £2.50), children 3 – 15 £2.75. Family ticket £2.75 per person. Special rates for parties of 20 or more (1991 prices)

There is much to see here in the 50 acres – don't be put off by the 'fun and family entertainment'. The formal and informal gardens date from 1734 and the Italian garden is attributed to Le Nôtre; there is an Oriental garden with a 150 year old mulberry, azaleas, camellias, flowering cherries and a paeony border (bush and tree); an American Garden established in the 1830s with a snowdrop tree (*Halesia carolina*), calico bushes and a handkerchief tree (*Davidia involucrata*); a Hermitage Garden with lake and water garden and a pinetum with some rare conifers including a Mexican juniper, yuccas, Korean thuya and Tasmanian cedar. The pinetum was established in 1838 and extended in 1910 to take the collection of the famous botanist and explorer 'Chinese' Wilson. Perhaps Bicton's greatest glory is the Palm House built between 1815 and 1820, one of the oldest in the country and recently refurbished; in it, Kentia palms up to 20 feet, tree ferns and bromeliads, and outside an Assam tea plant. There are also geranium and fuchsia houses and a tropical and a temperate house for bananas, coffee trees and bougainvilleas. Bicton College of Agriculture is also open (see above).

THE BUNGALOW 9
9 Bouchers Hill, North Tawton, Nr Okehampton, Devon. Tel: (0837) 82701

Dr and Mrs M.C. Corfield ✳ *6m NE of Okehampton on A3072, 3m W of Bow. In the square past the clock tower turn into North Street (Nat West Bank on right). ¹/₄m up hill, sharp left, 100 yards to the bungalow* ✳ *Parking* ✳ *Teas* ✳ *Toilet facilities* ✳ *Plants for sale* ✳ *Open 21st June, 12 July, 2 – 6pm* ✳ *Entrance: 50p, children 25p*

There is a wealth of interest for the dedicated plantsman in this acre of red earth garden with lovely views across Dartmoor. Created by the owners over a six-year period, it is still developing. It supports a wide range of herbaceous perennials and shrubs, a fine collection of hardy geraniums and ornamental grasses. The 100-foot long herbaceous border has been featured on local television. Given the difficult soil conditions (very dry, and hardpan at 18 inches) and the cold winds which blow in from the moor, the Corfields have succeeded where many less dedicated gardeners would have failed.

BURROW FARM GARDENS ★ 10
Dalwood, Axminster, Devon. Tel: (040483) 285

Mr and Mrs John Benger ✳ *4m W of Axminster. Take A35 Honiton road from Axminster. After 3¹/₂m turn north near Shute garage on to the Stockland road. Garden is ¹/₂m on right* ✳ *Parking* ✳ *Cream teas on Weds and Suns* ✳ *Toilet facilities* ✳ *Suitable for wheelchairs (not woodland garden)* ✳ *Dogs on leads* ✳ *Plants for sale in nursery* ✳ *Open April to Sept, daily, 2 – 7pm and mornings by appointment* ✳ *Entrance: £1.50, children 50p, parties (discount rate) by appointment*

These lovely gardens, created from pasture land, are the inspiration of Mary Benger and her family, who have all contributed to this incredible feat of imagination and hard work. The five-acre site is still being developed and from all angles affords magnificent views of the surrounding countryside. Foliage effect was the prime consideration during the planning stages and this has been admirably achieved with a lovely array of azaleas and rhododendrons. A former Roman clay pit is graded from top to bottom through mature trees and shrubs to an extensive bog garden which boasts a marvellous show of candelabra primulas and native wild flowers during the early part of the season. In summer the pergola walk, with its old-fashioned roses and herbaceous borders, is a picture. Burrow Farm Gardens are home to a huge range and variety of shrubs and the setting and sense of grandeur are more typical of gardens of greater repute.

CASTLE DROGO ★★ 11
Drewsteignton, Devon. Tel: (0647) 433306

The National Trust ✳ *4m S of A30 or 4m N of Moretonhamstead on A382, follow signs from Sandy Park* ✳ *Parking. Coaches by appointment only* ✳ *Refreshments: coffee and light lunches (licensed) and teas, 10.30am – 5pm* ✳ *Toilet facilities inc.*

disabled ✳ *Suitable for wheelchairs. Special parking and access by arrangement at reception. Scented plants for visually handicapped* ✳ *Shop* ✳ *House open at extra charge (but closed Fri). Croquet can be played with hired equipment* ✳ *Garden open April to 1st Nov, daily, 10.30am – 5.30pm (last admission ¹/₂ hour before closing)* ✳ *Entrance: £1.80 (garden and grounds only). Reduced rates for parties by appointment*

The last castle to be built in England (begun 1910) was designed by Sir Edwin Lutyens. Gertrude Jekyll had some involvement with the planting of trees around the drive, but the plans for the planting of the garden were by George Dillistone of Tunbridge Wells. Apart from the evergreen oaks above the magnificent views over the Teign Gorge, and a valley planted with rhodo-dendrons, magnolias, camellias, cherries and maples, there is a series of formal terraces and borders with walls of granite and sharp-edged yew hedges. One terrace has rose beds, with white flowers and arbours of yew and *Parrotia persica*, 'the iron tree'. In the main formal gardens, with galleries round a sunken centre, paths are serpentine (an Indian touch typical of Lutyens who built New Delhi in the 1920s when he was supervising here), and herbaceous borders are full of old varieties of lupins, lychnis, campanula, hollyhocks and red hot pokers. Under the granite walls are perennials like euphorbias, hellebores, alchemilla and veronica, with spring bulbs. Steps lead to a second terrace with yucca and wisterias and herb borders; more steps to shrub borders of lilac, azaleas, magnolias and lilies, and finally a splendid circular lawn surrounded by a tall yew hedge at the top, a huge green circle and a perfect stage set for croquet.

CASTLE TOR 12
Wellswood, Torquay, Devon. Tel: (0803) 214858

Mr L. Stocks ✳ *In Torquay. From Higher Lincombe Road, turn E into Oxlea Road. Entrance is 200 yards on right with eagle-topped pillars* ✳ *Parking* ✳ *Open by appointment* ✳ *Entrance: 50p, children 25p*

Half a century ago the then owner of Castle Tor approached Sir Edwin Lutyens and asked him to design a smaller version of Castle Drogo; being too busy Sir Edwin nominated a pupil of his, Frederick Harrild, and the result is this fascinating architectural garden with magnificent views over Lyme Bay and Tor Bay. Gertrude Jekyll's ideas about garden colour – no violent juxtapositions or circular beds full of salvias – were incorporated, and the whole is framed in terraces of Somerset limestone (a pleasant change from granite) and cubic green walls of yew hedges; there is topiary in both green and golden (Irish) yew. There are architectural type follies like a pillared orangery with a domed roof and a tower with portcullis and gatehouse; best of all a long ornamental water course or small canal. Over the years the owner has collected suitable statuary and bright annual flowers are seen as accents in urns and tubs against the stone background.

COLETON FISHACRE GARDEN ✳✳ 13
Coleton, Kingswear, Dartmouth, Devon. Tel: (080425) 466

The National Trust ✳ *2m from Kingswear, take Lower Ferry Road and turn off at toll house* ✳ *Parking* ✳ *Very limited for wheelchairs* ✳ *Open 1st, 8th, 15th, 22nd, 29th March, 2 – 5pm, and April to Oct, Wed – Fri and Sun, 11am – 6pm* ✳ *Entrance: £2.40, children £1.20, pre-arranged coach parties of 15 or more £1.80 per person*

Oswald Milne who was a pupil of Edwin Lutyens designed the house and the architectural features of this garden for Sir Rupert and Lady D'Oyly Carte; the house was completed and the garden begun in 1926. Exceptionally mild and sheltered, it is in a Devon combe, sloping steeply to the cliff tops and the sea, and sheltered by belts of Monterey pine and holm oaks planted in 1925. There are many streams making a humid atmosphere for the moisture-loving plants like the magnificent bamboos (inch thick canes) and mimosas, and many other sub-tropical plants, rarely growing outside in this country. There is a collection of unusual trees like dawn redwood and swamp cypress and Chilean myrtle, and dominating all a tall tulip tree the same age as the house. Formal walls and terraces make a framework round the house for a large number of sun-loving tender plants; there are various water features, notably stone-edged channels and a circular pool in the lawn in the herbaceous-bordered walled garden. Scented herbs and plants.

CROFTDENE 14
Ham, Nr Dalwood, Axminster, Devon. Tel: (040483) 271

Mr and Mrs P. Knox ✳ *3¹/₂m W of Axminster turn N from A35 near Shute garage and immediately turn right, signposted Dalwood. After ³/₄m mile turn left at T-junction and proceed across Dalwood crossroads, signposted Ham. Garden just before phone box on left* ✳ *Parking on road* ✳ *Cream teas at Burrow Farm Gardens (see entry)* ✳ *Toilet facilities* ✳ *Open 31st May, 5th July, 2 – 6pm and by appointment* ✳ *Entrance: 60p, children 20p*

It is hard to believe that this garden is less than five years down the road to maturity. Near fanatical devotion on the part of the owners has resulted in the creation of a plantsman's paradise. The one and a half-acre garden supports a huge range of shrubs, herbaceous and ericaceous plants, a marvellous rock garden (still in the making) with a fine collection of alpines; island beds and pond and waterside plants. A delightful acre of natural woodland provides the perfect contrast to the more formal setting.

CROSSPARK 15
Northlew, Nr Okehampton, Devon. Tel: (0409221) 518

Mrs G. West ✳ *8m NW of Okehampton. From Okehampton take old A30 Launceston road for 1m, turn right onto Holsworthy road for 6m and right to Northlew by telephone mast, go over bridge and left to Kimber, then follow road for 2 ¹/₂m* ✳ *Parking* ✳ *Toilet facilities* ✳ *Only a small area suitable for wheelchairs* ✳ *Plants for sale* ✳ *Open end March to Sept, Fri and Sun and Bank Holiday Mons, 2 – 6pm, and Easter to mid-Sept by appointment* ✳ *Entrance: 50p*

This plantswoman's garden, created from a field by the owner, would provide interest for a visit at most times of the year. A heather bed and pleasant separate colour beds and also an attractive white garden. The pool and waterfall are surrounded by a range of bog plants and there is a good selection of climbers on the house. Also dwarf conifers and a rockery.

DARTINGTON HALL ★   16
Dartington, Nr Totnes, Devon. Tel: (0803) 862271

Dartington Hall Trust ✳ 2m NW of Totnes, E of A384 ✳ Parking. Coaches by appointment (0803) 863614 ✳ Refreshments by appointment ✳ Toilet facilities ✳ Plants for sale ✳ Open daily, dawn – dusk ✳ Entrance: by donation

The gardens were begun by Dorothy and Leonard Elmhirst in 1925 when the Hall was derelict and the estate and parkland overgrown. Several garden designers have been advisers – Beatrix Farrand designed the courtyard and cobbled drive round the central lawn and opened up the woodland walkways. There are three woodland walks using bay, yew, and hollies as a background for a collection of camellias, magnolias and rhododendrons. Landscape designer Percy Cane made the glade and the azalea dell. The overall design is strongly architectural with sunken lawns and terraces and formal clipped yews contrasting with the mature woodland. Fine sculpture by Henry Moore and others.

DOCTON MILL ★   17
Spekes Valley, Nr Hartland, Devon. Tel: (0237) 441369

Mr N.S. and Mrs I.D. Pugh ✳ Off A39 from north Devon via Hartland to Stoke or from north Cornwall to West Country Inn, turn left and follow Elmscott signs towards Lymebridge in Spekes Valley ✳ Parking ✳ Open March to Sept, daily, 10am – 5pm ✳ Entrance: £1.50, children free

Mr and Mrs Pugh took over this then derelict water mill nine years ago and embarked upon a large scale clearance of the waterways; there are ponds, leats, footbridges over the river and many smaller streams as it is only 1500 yards from Speke's Mill Mouth coastal waterfall and the beach. A boggy area was drained to make a stream and a bog garden with ligularias and primulus and ferns; the whole purpose has been to make everything as natural as possible, integrating the garden into the wild with indigenous plants such as brooms, cytisus and many grasses. Near the house the garden abounds in roses, mostly old shrub roses, there is a hedge of 'Felicia' and 'Pax' hybrid musk roses and a climbing 'Felicia' – a rarity. Roses are underplanted with many varieties of perennial geraniums, another favourite plant, and these are also used on the rockery which is wet clay and north facing and not suitable for alpines, together with hebes and small conifers.

ENDSLEIGH HOUSE AND GARDENS   18
Milton Abbot, Nr Tavistock, Devon. Tel: (082287) 248

Endsleigh Charitable Trust ✳ 4m W of Tavistock on the A384 ✳ Parking ✳ Refreshments: hotel open by appointment for lunch and tea ✳ Garden open April to

Sept, Sat, Sun and Bank Holidays, 12 noon – 4pm, and by appointment, Tues and Fri, 12 noon – 4pm ∗ *Entrance: by donation (suggested minimum £1)*

Endsleigh was built, starting in 1811, for the 6th Duke of Bedford from designs by architect Jeffry Wyatville and landscape designer Humphry Repton. The house is a good example of the 'Cottage Orné' and was used as a fishing and hunting lodge by the Duke. It is now a Country House Hotel popular with salmon fishermen. The park and garden have magnificent views over the Tamar Valley. There is a shell house with a terrace, an arboretum mainly planted in the first years of the last century, a rock pool with alpines and newly-planted ferns, an ornamental pool with carp, a waterfall and a yew walk. These gardens will also be of great interest to birdwatchers.

FARDEL MANOR   19
Ivybridge, Devon.

Dr A.G. Stevens ∗ *1¹/₄m NW of Ivybridge, 2m SE of Cornwood, 200 yards off railway bridge* ∗ *Parking* ∗ *Teas* ∗ *Plants for sale* ∗ *Open 27th July, 11am – 4.30pm* ∗ *Entrance: £1, children 50p*

A five-acre garden, half of it recently planted, with secluded areas or 'rooms', including a herb garden, a formal pond garden, herbaceous borders and shrubberies surrounding the fourteenth-century manor house. Climbing roses cover the garden walls together with Canary creeper and clematis. There is an orangery with pond and fountain and many established tender plants. Vegetable and fruit gardens and an orchard, a bog area with parsley, thistles, day lilies and wild iris and the giant *Gunnera manicata*. A stream leads to a lake with iris and native plantings – a habitat for waterfowl of all kinds. The cultivation is totally organic.

THE GARDEN HOUSE ★★   20
Buckland Monachorum, Yelverton, Devon. Tel: (0822) 854769

The Fortescue Garden Trust ∗ *10m N of Plymouth, W of Yelverton off A386* ∗ *Parking* ∗ *Refreshments: coffee, light lunches and cream teas* ∗ *Plants for sale* ∗ *Open March to Oct, daily, 10.30am – 5pm* ∗ *Entrance: £2.50, children 50p*

An eight-acre garden created after 1945 by Lionel Fortescue, a great plant collector and perfectionist. The walls, thatched barn and tower date from the sixteenth century, and the tower was once part of a vicarage. The delightful two-acre walled garden has been described as one of the most beautiful in the country. It contains a fine collection of herbaceous plants, and hedges planted for shelter on different levels have enhanced the 'secret' ambience of this very special garden. There are some lovely old specimen trees and shrubs, herbaceous plants and alpines. This gem of a garden should not be missed.

THE GLEBE HOUSE   21
Whitestone, Nr Exeter, Devon. Tel: (039281) 200

Mr and Mrs S.J. West ∗ *4m W of Exeter, adjoining Whitestone church* ∗

Parking but narrow lanes unsuitable for coaches ✻ *Open 31st May to 26th July, Suns only and by appointment, 2 – 5pm* ✻ *Entrance: £1, children free*

A two-acre garden round a former rectory, fifteenth-century with a Georgian facade, and a fourteenth-century tithe barn (Ancient Monument), with magnificent views to the south over the estuary of the Exe, and towards Dartmoor. On the lower level are lawns, trees and a heather garden; above, divided by coniferous hedges and windbreaks, are walks among clematis, vitis and a collection of over 200 varieties of shrub roses – old-fashioned, species and modern hybrid. The middle level of the garden, with the house and tithe barn, features many varieties of climbing roses, clematis, jasmine and honeysuckle. The most impressive and memorable plant is an enormously vigorous *Rosa filipes* 'Kiftsgate' which is trained along the tithe barn, and extends over 120 feet. Flooding the courtyard with scent when in flower in early July this must be one of the largest climbing roses in the South West.

GREENWAY HOUSE 22
Nr Greenway Ferry, Churston Ferrers, Brixham, Devon. Tel: (0803) 842382 (Greenway Gardens)

Mr and Mrs A.A. Hicks ✻ *4m W of Brixham. From B3203 Paignton – Brixham road, take road to Galmpton, then towards Greenway Ferry* ✻ *Parking* ✻ *Tea and biscuits* ✻ *Suitable for wheelchairs* ✻ *Plants for sale in nursery open Tues, Wed, Fri pm, Sat am and by appointment* ✻ *Open 30th April, 7th May, 2 – 6pm* ✻ *Entrance: £1, children 50p*

Another large (30-acre) and ancient Devon garden on a steep slope, on the bank of the tree-lined Dart river which has woodland walks. There are a large number of indigenous trees over 150 years old and a giant tulip tree. In the walled garden are many camellias, 30 varieties of early magnolias, ceanothus, wisterias and abutilons, and a cork oak. The banks of primroses and bluebells make it magical in spring. On the Georgian facade are *Magnolia grandiflora*, *Akebia quinata* and *Mutisia oligodon*; in the natural glades are foxgloves, white iris, herb Robert, pennywort, ivy and hart's tongue and male ferns.

HIGHER KNOWLE 23
Lustleigh, Devon. Tel: (06477) 275

Mr and Mrs D.R.A. Quicke ✻ *8m NW of Newton Abbot, 3m NW of Bovey Tracey on A382 towards Moretonhamstead. In 2¹/₂m, turn left at Kelly Cross for Lustleigh; after ¹/₄m straight on at Brookfield for Manaton; after ¹/₂m steep drive on left* ✻ *Teas in village* ✻ *Open 19th April to May, Sun and Bank Holiday Mons, 2 – 6pm* ✻ *Entrance: £1, children 50p*

A woodland garden only 30 years old situated on a steep hillside with Dartmoor views. The old beech wood is carpeted with bluebells in spring, and magnolias and rhododendrons, ornamental cherries and heather banks; there is also a tall *Embothrium coccineum* flowering in early summer. A beech hedge encloses a lawn, with the main display of deciduous and evergreen azaleas. Giant Dartmoor granite boulders add much natural sculpture to the woodland walks.

KILLERTON ★ 24
Broadclyst, Nr Exeter, Devon. Tel: (0392) 881345

*The National Trust * 7m NE of Exeter, on W side of B3181 * Parking *
Licensed refreshments same time as house. Tearoom limited opening in winter *
Toilet facilities * Partly suitable for wheelchairs but motorised buggy with driver
available for higher levels * Shop * House and costume museum open April to
1st Nov, daily except Tues, 11am – 5.30pm (last admission ¹/₂ hour before closing)
* Park and garden open all year during daylight hours * Entrance: £3.20 (winter
rate £1) (house, park and garden £4.20)*

This large garden was made on a hill with woods extending in all to 4000 acres,
first by John Veitch in the 1770s and then by the famous Victorian William
Robinson. The actual garden area of 15 acres will provide interest and pleasure
to all, but to the tree and shrub enthusiast it is a haven of delight. Beside the
avenues of beeches there are Wellingtonias and Lawson cypresses which
provide colour and form and many fine broad-leaved trees including oaks and
maples, as well as the usual conifers. Terraced beds provide summer colour
and there are dwarf shrubs and herbaceous specimens to follow the fine display
of rhododendrons. There is a bear house. A garden to give pleasure at most
times of the year.

KNIGHTSHAYES ★★ 25
Bolham, Tiverton, Devon. Tel: (0884) 254665

*The National Trust * 2m N of Tiverton, turn right off A396 at Bolham *
Parking inc. disabled * Refreshments: restaurant for coffee, lunches and teas.
Licensed * Toilet facilities * Suitable for wheelchairs * Dogs on lead in park
only * Plants for sale * Shop * House open, daily except Fri but open Good
Friday, 1.30 – 5.30pm (last admission 5pm) * Garden open April to 1st Nov,
daily, 10.30am – 5.30pm * Entrance: £2.60 (garden and grounds only)*

This 50-acre garden is the setting for a most extraordinary late-Victorian
gothic-style house in warm red Devon stone. On the terrace nearest to the
house subtly-coloured borders reflect the sensitivity and skill of Lady
Heathcoat Amory's original planting. In bold contrast, the famous pool garden
is enclosed by tall, dark battlemented hedges while on a lower terrace hedge,
topiary hounds in full cry chase a fox they will never catch. Extensive woodland
gardens shelter magnolias and rhododendrons; acers and tree peonies flourish,
together with many tender and rare plants, some in raised peat block beds, and
in parkland magnificent trees, including Douglas firs and nothofagus, abound.
The only disappointment is the neglected and overgrown state of the Willow
Garden, which it is hoped will soon be restored by the enthusiastic team of
gardeners.

LEE FORD 26
Budleigh Salterton, Devon. Tel: (03954) 5894

*Mr and Mrs N. Lindsay-Fynn * 3¹/₂m from Exmouth * Parking * Teas on
open days, 3 – 5.30pm * Suitable for wheelchairs * Plants for sale * Open by*

prior appointment for parties only and 24th May, 1.30 – 5.30pm ✳ Entrance:
£1.20, OAP £1, children 60p. Parties of 20 or more £1 per person

Inspired by the Savill Gardens at Windsor, the present owner's father developed this wild woodland garden in the 1950s and 60s and it is one of the longest established open-to-the-public gardens in Devon, best seen perhaps in early summer when the magnolias are in flower. The mown glades are surrounded with masses of species and ponticum rhododendrons, and there is a large collection of camellias, many from the Channel Islands, including white camellias which are often in flower on Christmas Day. There is also a treat of an old-fashioned walled vegetable garden with an Adam pavilion.

MARDON   27
Moretonhampstead, Devon. Tel: (0647) 40239

His Honour and Mrs A.C. Goodall ✳ At Moretonhamstead, coming from Bovey Tracey on A382, turn first right 30 yards after crossroads then immediately left, down hill, over a stream and enter over cattle grid on right before hill ✳ Best season: May and June ✳ Parking ✳ Teas at Moretonhamstead ✳ Toilet facilities ✳ Open 24th, 31st May, 7th June, 2 – 5.30pm ✳ Entrance: £1, children free

The house was built in 1902 by Lord Hambledon as a rectory. Mrs Goodall's godmother was largely responsible for creating the garden, and the present owners have continued her work. The house and its two-acre garden are beautifully situated just outside the charming moorland village of Moretonhamstead. From the terrace an imposing lawn sweeps down to a stream which has given rise to a wild marshy area planted with astilbes, candelabra primulas and many native species. The trout pond is home to visiting Canada geese who enjoy fine views of Moretonhampstead church from their tranquil temporary residence. There is a pleasantly rampant herbaceous border running the length of the lawn and a fine collection of old-fashioned shrub roses along the entrance drive. But in this essentially low-maintenance garden pride of place goes to the rhododendrons which are a picture during the late spring just after the mass of bulbs have lost their bloom.

MARWOOD HILL ★★   28
Marwood, Nr Barnstaple, Devon. Tel: (0271) 42528

Dr J.A. Smart ✳ 4m NW of Barnstaple. Turn off B3230 to Marwood ✳ Best season: April to Aug ✳ Parking in roadway ✳ Teas on Sun and Bank Holidays or for parties by prior arrangement ✳ Partly suitable for wheelchairs ✳ Dogs on lead ✳ Plants for sale ✳ Open daily except 25th Dec, dawn to dusk ✳ Entrance: £1, children 10p

With the wonderful collection of plants this 20-acre garden is of special interest to the connoisseur but could not fail to give pleasure to any visitor. Over 3000 different varieties of plants covering collections of willows, ferns, magnolias, embothriums, rhododendrons and hebes, and fine collection of camellias in a glasshouse. Large planting of eucalyptus and betulas. Recently-built pergola with 12 varieties of wisteria. Raised alpine scree beds. Three small lakes with extensive bog garden and National collections of astilbe and *Iris ensata*.

MIDDLE HILL 29
Washfield, Nr Tiverton, Devon. Tel: (03985) 380

Mr and Mrs E. Boundy ✳ *4¹/₂m NW of Tiverton, via B3221. Through the village of Washfield and the garden is 1¹/₂m on left* ✳ *Best season: May* ✳ *Parking* ✳ *Partly suitable for wheelchairs* ✳ *Plants for sale* ✳ *Open 26th April to 30th Aug, most Suns, 2 – 5pm and by appointment* ✳ *Entrance: 50p, children 25p*

This small garden has been created over 20 odd years to include some specialist plants. There are raised beds, a rockery, island beds growing gentians, ferns, hostas, clematis, crocosmias, penstemons, pittosporums and, being so exposed, shelter has been provided. Interesting colour and foliage combinations offer some good tips.

THE MOORINGS 30
Rocombe, Uplyme, Lyme Regis, Dorset. Tel: (0297) 443295

Mr and Mrs A. Marriage ✳ *2m NW of Lyme Regis. Take A3070 out of Lyme Regis, turn right 150 yards beyond Black Dog pub, over crossroads, fork right into Springhead Road. Top gate to garden is 500 yards on left* ✳ *Parking* ✳ *Open 19th, 20th April, 3rd, 4th, 24th, 25th May, 1st Nov, 11am – 5pm and by appointment* ✳ *Entrance: 75p, accompanied children free*

Especially rewarding to visit in spring and autumn, this garden has been made by Mr Marriage since 1965 out of three fields on a sheltered, steep, west-facing slope. Impressively, most of the newly-planted arboretum trees have been grown from seed; there is a collection of eucalyptus, many unusual pines including umbrella and maritime pines (grown from seed gathered in the south of France) and nothofagus, including *N. obliqua* and *N. procera*, and the woodland is underplanted with snowdrops. *Hibiscus paramutabilis*, a hardy shrub with very large flowers in August, is very rare in this country; there are camellias and a 35 foot high magnolia, and a buddleia flowering rose-red in June. A great point of interest is the collection of over 50 different species of fern, all grown from spores.

THE OLD RECTORY 31
Woodleigh, Nr Loddiswell, Devon. Tel: (0548) 550387

Mr and Mrs H.E. Morton ✳ *3¹/₂m N of Kingsbridge, E off Kingsbridge – Wrangaton road at Rake Cross (1m S of Loddiswell), 1¹/₂m to Woodleigh itself* ✳ *Parking* ✳ *Suitable for wheelchairs* ✳ *Open by appointment only* ✳ *Entrance: 50p, children 10p*

A three-acre woodland garden, and walled garden, rescued from neglect 27 years ago. In the woodland are several individual glades of mature trees, underplanted with magnolias, azaleas, camellias and rhododendrons. There is great attention to form in the planting; evergreens and shrubs are planted for scent and winter effect, and the wild garden is most colourful in spring with crocus and daffodils, while the walled garden is designed with summer in mind. The garden is a haven for wildlife, and chemicals have never been used.

THE OLD VICARAGE   32
Shute, Nr Axminster, Devon.

Mr and Mrs R. Ingram ＊ 3m W of Axminster on A35, 6m E of Honiton, turn S on to B3161 at Shute Garage, signposted Shute and Colyton. House on right 1/4m past tall gate pillars ＊ Parking in adjacent field ＊ Cream teas ＊ Toilet facilities ＊ Suitable for wheelchairs but sloping site ＊ Plants for sale ＊ Open 14th, 21st June, 2 – 5pm, 17th June, 10am – 5pm ＊ Entrance: 75p, children 30p

Since the autumn of 1989 the owners of this lovely stone-built Victorian rectory, with superb views down the Umbourne valley to the sea, have been extending the existing one-acre formal Victorian garden to include an adjoining two-acre field. Formal features in the early stages of development include an ambitious parterre, a delightful rose garden, with mainly old garden varieties, an Elizabethan-style bowling alley, a maze and a new avenue of limes. Given the extent of recent tree-planting – both woodland and foliage shrubs – this is a garden in its infancy. But it is no less interesting for that.

OVERBECKS MUSEUM AND GARDEN ★   33
Sharpitor, Salcombe, Devon. Tel: (054884) 2893

The National Trust ＊ 1 1/2m S of Salcombe, SW to South Sands ＊ Best season: spring – early summer ＊ Parking. Coaches by appointment ＊ Picnic area ＊ Toilet facilities ＊ Shop ＊ Museum open, April to 1st Nov, 11am – 5pm. £3 ＊ Garden open daily 10am – 8pm or sunset if earlier ＊ Entrance: £2, children £1 (garden only). Parking charge refundable

Palms stand among the bluebells in this exotic garden high above the Salcombe estuary, giving a strongly Mediterranean atmosphere. The mild, maritime climate enables it to be filled with exotics such as myrtles, daturas, agaves and an example of the large camphor tree, *Cinnamomum camphora*, a great rarity. The Himalayan *Magnolia campbellii* is nearly 90 years old and 40 feet high and wide and a sight to see in March. The steep terraces were built in 1901 and lead down through fuchsia trees, fruiting banana palms and myrtle trees to a wonderful *Cornus kousa*. In formal beds near the house is the Chatham Island forget-me-not – *Myosotidium hortensia* (hydrangea-like) with flowers as clear as blue china, phormiums, and tender roses among the rocks.

PAIGNTON ZOO AND BOTANICAL GARDEN   34
Totnes Road, Paignton, Devon. Tel: (0803) 527936

Parking ＊ Refreshments: restaurants ＊ Toilet facilities ＊ Suitable for wheelchairs ＊ Shops ＊ Open daily except 25th Dec from 10am (closing times vary according to season) ＊ Entrance: £4.90, OAP £4.20, children £3 (1991 prices). Group rates available

Those not keen on zoos may be won over by Paignton; it is in the forefront of animal and plant conservation and one of the zoos worldwide involved in the breeding of endangered species. As well as the very healthy and happy animals there are some interesting trees and shrubs. Paignton (over 100 acres in size) was the first zoo in the country to combine animals and a botanic garden, laid out 60 years ago and added to over the years. Choice of plants has been dictated by their harmlessness to teeth and beaks and their ability to provide shade, perches and swinging and basking places; there are geographical collections of plants in the paddocks, and plants also make the fences safer. Hardy Chinese plants surround the baboon rocks. Paignton has the R.H.S. National Collection of sorbaria and buddleia. There are two large plant houses, one sub-tropical with tender plants and trees and magical birds flying, and a tropical house with a jungle pool and areas of tropical plants. At Paignton Zoo the fauna and flora enjoy a complementary relationship – resist the temptation to judge the garden in isolation.

POWDERHAM CASTLE 35
Kenton, Exeter, Devon. Tel: (0626) 890243

Lord and Lady Courtenay * *From Exeter take the A379. Signposted* * *Parking* * *Teas, ices and soft drinks* * *Toilet facilities* * *Shop* * *House open* * *Garden open late-May to mid-Sept, daily except Fri and Sat, 2 – 5.30pm* * *Entrance: £3.20 (house and garden), children £1 (1991 prices)*

The house is believed to date back in parts to 1390, with major additions and a terraced garden in 1840. Broad steps lead down from the terrace to a formal rose garden (formerly another terrace) with gravelled paths and rose beds in a raised lawn; the roses include modern (flowering in September) and a good selection of old-fashioned shrub roses. The garden has urns, a sundial and topiary and one wing of the house is covered in a giant wisteria where lives a grand tortoise aged over 150. More climbing roses and honeysuckles grow from the gravel along the castellated wall which gives a magnificent view over the park with its splendid trees and large herd of fallow deer to the sailing boats on the Exe estuary.

ROSEMOOR GARDEN ★★ 36
Great Torrington, Devon. Tel: (0805) 24067

The Royal Horticultural Society * *1m SE of Great Torrington on B3220* * *Best season: May to Sept* * *Parking* * *Refreshments: in restaurant (licensed)* * *Toilet facilities* * *Suitable for wheelchairs* * *Plants for sale in plant centre* * *Shop in Visitors' Centre open March to Oct, 10am – 6pm (summer)* * *Garden open all year* * *Entrance: £2.25, children 50p*

First opened to the public 35 years ago, the original eight-acre garden was made by Lady Anne Palmer; it contains a collection of 3500 plants from all over Europe, North and South America, New Zealand and Japan. There is a large collection of rhododendrons, heathers, waterside plants and old roses; it is also the home of specialist collections of ilex (hollies) and cornus (dogwoods) – over 100 varieties. There arc scree gardens, an arboretum, alpines and bulbs.

Recently Rosemoor was given to the Royal Horticultural Society as its first regional centre, second only to Wisley. An extra 32 acres have been given, and after much moving and drainage work the extensions have begun, including a new rose garden and a visitors' centre, and there is a developing plan to include cottage and herb gardens, a *jardin potager*, alpine lawns, fruit and vegetables and a trial garden to illustrate how specific groups of plants will perform in different conditions. This is truly a great National Garden in the making.

SALTRAM HOUSE ★   37
Plympton, Plymouth, Devon. Tel: (0752) 336546

The National Trust ✳ 3m E of Plymouth. On A379 turn N to Billacombe. After 1m turn left to Saltram ✳ Best season: April to June ✳ Parking ✳ Licensed refreshments ✳ Toilet facilities ✳ Suitable for wheelchairs ✳ Shop ✳ House open April to 1st Nov, 12.30 – 5.30pm. £4.40 ✳ Garden open April to 1st Nov, daily except Fri and Sat, 10.30am – 5.30pm (last admission 5pm) ✳ Entrance: £1.60 garden only (1991 prices)

The original garden dates from 1770, slightly altered in the last century; there are three eighteenth-century buildings – a castle or belvedere, an orangery (due to the mild climate the orange and lemon trees are moved outside in the summer) and a classical garden house named Fanny's Bower after Fanny Burney who came here in 1789 in the entourage of George III. There is a long lime avenue underplanted with narcissi in spring, *Cyclamen linearifolium* in autumn and a central glade with specimen trees like the stone pine and Himalayan spruce. There is a beech grove, a Melancholy Walk, and walks with magnolias, camellias, rhododendrons and Japanese maples which, with other trees, make for dramatic autumn colour.

TAPELEY PARK ★   38
Instow, Devon. Tel: (0271) 860528

Mr H.T.C. Christie ✳ 2m N of Bideford S off A39 Barnstaple – Bideford road ✳ Parking ✳ Teas in Queen Anne dairy. Picnic places ✳ Toilet facilities ✳ Suitable for wheelchairs ✳ Dogs ✳ Plants for sale ✳ House open. £1.50, children £1. Tours for parties of 6 or more ✳ Medieval jousting displays ✳ Open Easter to Oct, daily except Sat, 10am – 6pm ✳ Entrance: £1.90 (non-jousting days) to £4.50 (Bank Holiday Sun and Mon competitive jousting days), OAP £1.50 to £3.50, children £1 to £2

The house is basically William and Mary, set on a splendid site above the River Torridge and Bideford, with much to see and a family with a fascinating history – the Christies of Glynbourne. There are three formal terraces, an Italian garden with ornamental water, yew hedges, an ilex tunnel, a shell house, ice house, and a variety of roses, fuchsias. lavender, dahlias as well as more exotic plants like *Abelia floribunda*, sophora and feijoa from Brazil. On the south of the house are yuccas, *Magnolia grandiflora*, agapanthus and mimosas; on the east, wisteria and *Drimys winteri*, a rare honeysuckle. A woodland walk is lined with camellias, hydrangeas and rhododendrons with primroses and primulas in spring under the giant beeches and oaks; this leads to a water-lily-covered pond in late summer, in the background tall firs and *Thuya plicata*. Walled kitchen garden.

TUDOR ROSE TEA ROOMS AND GARDEN 39
36 New Street, The Barbican, Plymouth, Devon.

*Plymouth Corporation * In the centre of the old town * Parking difficult * Dogs * Open daily, 10am – 6pm * Entrance: free*

An integral part of an area of Plymouth that is being refurbished, this is an interesting reconstruction of the type of Tudor garden that would have existed behind the house in this ancient street. As far as possible only plants which grew in Elizabethan England have been established. Elsewhere in Plymouth the Corporation commemorates great Victorian seaside gardening with colourful carpet bedding by traditional methods.

UGBROOKE PARK 40
Chudleigh, Devon. Tel: (0626) 852179

*The Lady Clifford * Follow signs on A380 Exeter – Torbay road, and on A38 Exeter – Plymouth road * Parking * Refreshments 1.30 – 5pm * Toilet facilities * Suitable for wheelchairs * Dogs * House open. Private tours for groups by appointment * Garden open Sat, Sun and Bank Holiday Monday from late May Bank Holiday to Aug Bank Holiday * Entrance: £2, children 75p*

The magnificent park around this house (originally twelfth-century and redesigned by Robert Adam) was laid out by 'Capability' Brown. There are extensive lakeside walks. Much new planting is going on, including an interesting Japanese water garden at the entrance gates. There is an eighteenth-century orangery and the conservatory houses tropical plants. Much of the outside planting is semi-tropical.

UNIVERSITY OF EXETER ★ 41
Northcote House, The Queen's Drive, Exeter, Devon. Tel: (0392) 263263

*University of Exeter * On N outskirts of Exeter on A396, turn E on to B3183 * Best season: April to June * Parking * Dogs on lead * Shop open weekdays sells guide book * Open daily * Entrance: free. Coaches by appointment only*

There is much to see on a one mile tour of these extensive gardens based on those made in the 1860s by an East India Merchant millionaire who inherited a fortune made by blockade-running in the Napoleonic wars. The landscaping and tree planting was carried out by Veitch whose plant collectors went all over the world (among them E.H. 'Chinese' Wilson) and at that time many of the trees were unique in Europe. There is a series of lakes with wildfowl, dogwoods, birches, hazel and alder, callistemon shrubs (bottle brushes) wingnut trees (*Pterocarya stenoptera*) brought from China in 1860 and a maidenhair tree (*Gingko*) sacred in Buddhist China. Rockeries have collections of alpines; there is a banana tree (*Musa basjoo*), a large *Gunnera chilensis* and palm trees introduced by Robert Fortune in 1849. Formal gardens and bedding plants lead to a sunken, scented garden. Exeter will house the National collection of Azara, evergreens from Chile, with scented yellow flowers. There are, of course, rhododendrons, magnolias, camellias in a woodland walk; roses, eucalyptus and *Opuntia humifusa*, the prickly pear cactus flowering in summer.

VICAR'S MEAD   42
Hayes Lane, East Budleigh, Devon. Tel: (03954) 2641

*Mr and Mrs H.F.J. Read * From A376 Newton Poppleford – Budleigh Salterton road, turn off left for East Budleigh * Car park 50 yards from entrance * Teas in village * Toilet facilities * Partly suitable for wheelchairs * Plants for sale * Open 19th, 20th April, 3rd, 4th, 24th, 25th May, 14th, 21st, 28th June, 5th, 12th July, 2nd, 30th, 31st Aug, 6th, 13th Sept, 2 – 6pm * Entrance: £1, children free*

On and around a red sandstone escarpment this three and a half-acre garden has been created since 1977. It is most interesting to keen plantsmen in that it contains many rare and unusual shrubs and houses four National collections – dianellas, libertias, liriopes and ophiopogons.

WOODSIDE   43
Higher Raleigh Road, Barnstaple, Devon. Tel: (0271) 43095

*Mr and Mrs M. Feesey * Off A39 Barnstaple to Lynton road, turn right 300 yards above fire station * Parking in road outside * Open 10th May, 21st June, 19th July, 2 – 5.30pm * Entrance: 60p, children 20p*

A sloping two-acre garden in a suburban area with an unusual collection of plants including ornamental grasses, bamboos and sedges. Many parts of the garden are shaded but rare dwarf shrubs, trees and conifers survive. There are raised beds and troughs with alpines and peat-loving opoulmum. A collection of New Zealand plants along with peat-loving shrubs make this a garden with a difference.

DOGS, TOILETS & OTHER FACILITIES
If these are *not* mentioned in the text, then facilities are not available. For example, if dogs are not mentioned, owners will probably not permit entry, even on a lead.

DORSET

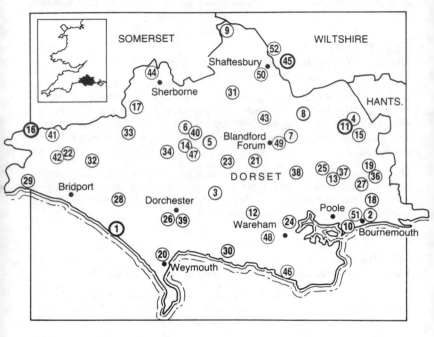

Two-starred gardens are ringed in bold.

ABBOTSBURY GARDENS ★★   1
Abbotsbury, Dorset. Tel: (0305) 871387

*Ilchester Estates   ✳   9m NW of Weymouth, 9m SW of Dorchester off B3157   ✳
Parking   ✳   Refreshments   ✳   Toilet facilities   ✳   Partly suitable for wheelchairs   ✳
Dogs on lead   ✳   Plants for sale   ✳   Shop   ✳   Open March to Oct, daily, 10am –
5pm, Nov to Feb, daily except Mon, and 25th, 26th Dec, 10am – 4pm   ✳
Entrance: £2.50, OAP £2, children 60p. Joint tickets with Swannery and group
booking discounts available*

Proximity to the sea helps to provide the 'micro-climate' which makes
Abbotsbury so special. Within its 20 acres there is much of great interest to the
plantsperson in the many rare species on display, while amateur gardeners can
get pleasure from the banks of colour and the shaded walks – particularly in the
spring, but also at other seasons. People travel a long way to visit these gardens –

often called 'sub-tropical', but probably technically better described as 'wet Mediterranean'. The new visitor centre, shop and refreshment area are an excellent additional bonus for the many coach parties who come for both gardens and nearby Swannery (not to be missed when open!). Pure garden enthusiasts will be more interested in the redesigned plant sales area which, while not extensive, has a good range of healthy stock on tempting display. It is good to see that the recent severe damage from wind and flood has not diminshed the tranquillity of this fascinating garden.

ARNMORE HOUSE   2
57 Landsdowne Road, Bournemouth, Dorset. Tel: (0202) 551440

Mr and Mrs David Hellewell ✳ *On B3064 just S of the hospital* ✳ *Parking in road* ✳ *Toilet facilities* ✳ *Suitable for wheelchairs* ✳ *Open all year by appointment only* ✳ *Entrance: £1, children free*

The special features of this garden have developed through a mixture of the owner's interest in Chinese gardening and a pragmatic approach to ease of management. Trees and shrubs have been chosen for their shape and foliage, and, where desired, have been trained or pruned to fit the over-all picture. Flower borders are eschewed in favour of grey slab paths alongside raised beds containing rows of shaped yew and privet, box and bay. Wherever possible these small to medium-sized trees are grown in pots so that trimming can take place over a suitable receptacle for the clippings. The formal parterre consists of neat diagonals of *Buxus* 'Aureovariegata' and again features grey concrete slabs to minimise maintenance. A yew hedge at the end of the level lawn screens a grove of beech trees rising from a 'moss garden' (little else will grow here in the limited light, so mosses are encouraged). All this may sound rather austere, but it nevertheless suits the composer/owner who has created it and published a book about its development. It is worth a visit for its originality.

ATHELHAMPTON ★   3
Puddletown, Dorchester, Dorset Tel: (0305) 848363

Lady Du Cann ✳ *On A35 1m E of Puddletown, near Dorchester* ✳ *Best season: May/June* ✳ *Parking* ✳ *Refreshments* ✳ *Toilet facilities* ✳ *Partly suitable for wheelchairs* ✳ *Shop* ✳ *House open* ✳ *Garden open Easter to Oct, Wed, Thurs, Sun and Bank Holidays (also Mons in Aug and Tues May to Sept), 2 – 6pm* ✳ *Entrance: £1.60, children free (£3.20 house and gardens)*

Athelhampton garden was rescued and re-designed by Alfred La Fontaine in 1891, a process continued by subsequent owners, latterly the late Robert Cooke. Courts and walls follow the original plan with beautiful stonework in walls and arches. Apart from some of the most impressive topiary in England there are pools, fountains, a rectangular canal with water lilies and a pleached lime walk. It is not a great flower garden but rambling roses, clematis and jasmine (in their seasons) make it memorable. With one and a half gardeners instead of the original 12 you can't have everything!

BOVERIDGE FARM   4
Cranborne, Dorset. Tel: (07254) 241

Mr D.J. Dampney ✳ *Nr Cranborne on Martin Road (unclassified). Take 2nd turn on right* ✳ *Parking* ✳ *Teas at Ashley Park in next village of Damerham* ✳ *Toilet facilities* ✳ *Plants for sale at Ashley Park* ✳ *Open 19th April, 17th May, 14th June, 2 – 5.30pm* ✳ *Entrance: 75p, children free*

The house lies on a steep north-facing slope, and the garden has been laid out below it, to the west of it and above. The plants and shrubs on the lower side are on chalk, whilst the fern bank and shrubbery above is on neutral clay. There is a fine view across the rooftops and along the valley, which is largely arable with wooded hilltops. As a busy farmer, Mr Dampney has had to fit his enthusiasm for uncommon plants around his working life. It has taken over 35 years to create the garden as it is today, a colourful and interesting collection much of which he has himself grown from seed or cuttings. He has recently developed a farm and woodland walk at Damerham (3 miles away). The walk leads through ancient woods which now include 40 different varieties of oak tree, with underplanting of spring shrubs.

BROADLANDS ★   5
Hazelbury Bryan, Nr Sturminster Newton, Dorset. Tel: (0258) 817374

Mr and Mrs M.J. Smith ✳ *4m S of Sturminster Newton off A357 Blandford – Sherborne road at signpost. ¹/₂m beyond Antelope pub* ✳ *Parking* ✳ *Toilet facilities* ✳ *Suitable for wheelchairs* ✳ *Plants for sale* ✳ *Open by appointment and 5th, 26th April, 17th May, and every Wed in June, July and Aug, 2 – 5.30pm* ✳ *Entrance: £1.20, accompanied children free*

This is a two-acre garden in which the design and planting have the intriguing effect of obscuring the full size of the area while at the same time extending the apparent distance the visitor covers in walking round it. This is achieved by the clever siting of island beds, with grass walkways leading to features such as ponds, rockeries and paved seating areas. There are screening hedges to enhance the surprise of discovering the greenhouse, the vegetables, the ornamental woodland. Round every corner the visitor comes upon some new feature of interest and delight, and everywhere there are uncommon plants to give pleasure in all seasons. Begun in 1975, this is a most successful layout, excellently labelled and refreshingly imaginative, which should inspire gardeners of all levels of competence. New features include an area devoted to shrub and climbing roses with an attractive but simply-constructed pergola, and further development and underplanting in the woodland area. There are plans for a scree garden, which would extend still further the range of interesting plants on view.

CANNINGS COURT   6
Pulham, Nr Sherborne, Dorset. Tel: (0258) 817210

Mr and Mrs J.D. Dennison ✳ *13m N of Dorchester, 8m SE of Sherborne. Turn E at crossroads in Pulham* ✳ *Parking* ✳ *Refreshments* ✳ *Toilet facilities* ✳ *Suitable for wheelchairs* ✳ *Plants for sale* ✳ *Open 17th May, 28th June, 19th July, 2 – 6pm and 20th May, 1st, 22nd July, 11am – 6pm* ✳ *Entrance: £1*

Over twenty years of loving labour have gone into this farmhouse garden, developed virtually from scratch at the same time as the owners were busy with the rescue of the farm itself. The bare walls of the Georgian facade have been clothed with thriving creepers, the open land behind is sheltered by tree screens and contains colourful borders and shrubberies, a pond and an arboretum. The *potager* has now been developed into a thriving plot of unusual and colourful vegetables. Based on those at Villandry, it is being edged with box and cotton lavender. Not content, they have plans for a woodland walk, more tree screens and arbours – probably enough to occupy the next 20 years. Do not leave without looking in the tool store-cum-workshop which is entered through a huge Elizabethan fireplace rising 20 feet up a blackened chimney. The farm name is a corruption of 'Canon's Court' and it has probably been in continuous occupation for over 1000 years, as the surrounding buildings could testify.

CHARLTON COTTAGE 7

Tarrant Rushton, Blandford Forum, Dorset. Tel: (0258) 452072.

The Hon. Penelope Piercy ✻ *3m SE of Blandford on B3082. Fork left at top of hill, right at T-junction, first left to village* ✻ *Parking in adjacent field* ✻ *Suitable for wheelchairs* ✻ *Open 14th, 28th June, 2 – 6pm* ✻ *Entrance: £1, children 25p*

Charlton Cottage lies at the end of the village where the garden surrounds what used to be two terraced cottages, now all one property. In place of the long narrow cottage strips, the back garden has two lawn areas separated by colourful borders and leading up a gentle slope among shrubs and trees to a vegetable area. In front of the house the road from the village peters out into a narrow track, so the owner has acquired land on the other side where there are further borders through which the visitor descends to a shady water garden and wild area.

CHETTLE HOUSE 8

Blandford Forum, Dorset. Tel: (0258) 89209

Mr and Mrs P. Bourke ✻ *6m NE of Blandford on A354, turn left to Chettle* ✻ *Parking* ✻ *Refreshments at weekend* ✻ *Toilet facilities* ✻ *Suitable for wheelchairs* ✻ *Plants for sale* ✻ *Art gallery* ✻ *House open* ✻ *Garden open Easter to mid-Oct, daily except Tues, 11am – 5pm* ✻ *Entrance: £1.50, children free*

The wide lawns frame the attractive Queen Anne house with many chalk-loving varieties of shrubs and herbaceous plants (some quite rare) in the borders. Visitors can experience a very peaceful and relaxing atmosphere in this garden, and if interested can purchase plants raised from garden stock in the good small nursery not far from the house.

CHIFFCHAFFS 9

Chaffeymoor, Bourton, Gillingham, Dorset. Tel: (0747) 840841

Mr and Mrs K.R. Potts ✻ *3m E of Wincanton off A303 at W end of Bourton village* ✻ *Best season: spring* ✻ *Parking in road* ✻ *Teas on last Sun in month and Bank Holiday weekends ＊ Toilet facilities ＊ Plants for sale ＊ Open 22nd Mar to 27th Sept, Sun, Wed and Thurs (except first Sun, Wed and Thurs in each month),2 – 5.30pm ＊ Entrance: £1, children 25p*

An impressive avenue of flowering cherries leads to the house and garden, the nursery and the woodland walk through the surrounding fields, which extend to a total of 12 acres. The terraces and viewpoints afford fascinating glimpses of open country around and the varied and colourful beds and borders are delightful. Special interest is provided by the new underplanting in the woodland area and by the collection of dwarf rhododendrons and old-fashioned roses. The nursery is well-stocked with a wide variety of healthy-looking plants.

WHEELCHAIR USERS
Please note that entries which describe a garden as 'suitable for wheelchairs' refer to the garden only. If there is a house open, it may or may not be suitable.

COMPTON ACRES ★   10
Canford Cliffs, Poole, Dorset. Tel: (0202) 700778

Mr and Mrs L. Green ＊ From Poole/Bournemouth road onto Canford Cliffs road (near Sandbanks) ＊ Parking ＊ Refreshments ＊ Toilet facilities ＊ Suitable for wheelchairs (can be supplied) ＊ Guide dogs only ＊ Plants for sale ＊ Shop ＊ Open March to Oct, daily, 10.30am – 6.30pm ＊ Entrance: £3, OAP £2.20, children £1 (1991 prices)

Keen gardeners might be put off by the huge coach park, the frankly commercial and rather down-market approach. They should persevere, because the gardens themselves are well-designed, immaculately kept and stocked with many interesting and well-labelled plants, trees and shrubs. Water abounds in streams, waterfalls, ponds and formal lakes, the home of fat, multi-coloured carp. An enterprise aimed obviously (and very accurately) at the tourist, Compton Acres has the feel of a very opulent public park, a sort of pop-concert of the gardening world – but none the worse for that.

CRANBORNE MANOR GARDENS ★★   11
Cranborne, Dorset. Tel: (07254) 248

The Viscount and Viscountess Cranborne ＊ 10m N of Wimborne on B3078 ＊

Parking ✳ *Toilet facilities* ✳ *Partly suitable for wheelchairs* ✳ *Garden centre open all year* ✳ *Shop* ✳ *Gardens open 13th June for charity and March to Sept, Weds, 9am – 5pm* ✳ *Entrance: £2.50, OAP £2*

Tradescant established the basic framework in the early seventeenth century, but little is left of the original plan. Neglected for a long period, the garden has been revived in the last three generations and now includes several smaller areas surrounded by tall clipped yew hedges, a walled white garden at its best in midsummer, wide lawns (again yew-lined) and extensive woodland and wild areas. Best of all is the high-walled entrance courtyard to the south which is approached through an arch between the two Jacobean gate houses. Here the plant selection along the lengthy borders is delightfully imaginative, providing the perfect introduction to what has been called 'the most magical house in Dorset' (not least for the garden which surrounds it). The excellent nursery garden specializes in traditional rose varieties, but also carries a wide selection of other plants. Italian statuary and stone ornaments are also featured, together with very high quality garden furniture.

CULEAZE   12
Bere Regis, Dorset. Tel: (0929) 471209

Col. and Mrs A.M. Barne ✳ *1¹/₂ S of Bere Regis on the road to Wool. Take 2nd left (signposted) then right* ✳ *Parking* ✳ *Refreshments in Bere Regis* ✳ *Toilet facilities* ✳ *Suitable for wheelchairs* ✳ *Dogs on lead* ✳ *Plants for sale* ✳ *Farm shop* ✳ *Open 2nd, 3rd May, 2 – 6pm* ✳ *Entrance: £1*

Most of the trees and plants in this well-established garden have been grown from seeds or cuttings raised by the owners. They include some rare and unusual specimens successfully reared despite the warning advice of experts – always ready to say it couldn't be done. There is a large lawn bordered by interesting trees, and a good-sized walled area with many more special and often sought-after plants, not to mention an extensive cut flower and Christmas tree plantation. This is a very large enterprise to be attempted with part-time staff, and the visitor will readily appreciate the effort required to maintain it.

DEAN'S COURT   13
Wimborne Minster, Dorset.

Sir Michael and Lady Hanham ✳ *In the centre of Wimborne off B3073* ✳ *Parking nearby* ✳ *Wholefood teas* ✳ *Toilet facilities* ✳ *Suitable for wheelchairs* ✳ *Organically-grown herb plants for sale* ✳ *Open Easter to Sept, Bank Holidays and certain Thurs and Suns. Contact Wimborne Tourist Information Office for details. Tel: (0202) 886116* ✳ *Entrance: £1, children 50p*

A mellow brick house set in 13 acres of parkland containing a number of interesting and very large trees. A swamp cypress towers near the house, and a 92 foot tulip tree covers one wall. The many fine specimens include Lucombe oak, Wellingtonias, Caucasian wing nut, Chilean fire bush, Japanese pagoda tree, blue cedars and horse chestnuts. There are few formal beds, but a courtyard contains an unusually comprehensive herb garden with almost 100 different plants. The walled kitchen garden, in which many of the old varieties of vegetable are grown by organic production methods, is extensive and obviously successful. A peaceful haven from the busy town just a few yards away, and well worth a visit.

DOMINEY'S YARD   14
Buckland Newton, Dorset. Tel: (03005) 295

Captain and Mrs W. Gueterbock ✳ 11m from both Dorchester and Sherborne, 2m E of A352 or take B3143 from Sturminster Newton. Take 'no through road' between church and pub next to phone box. Opposite new houses ✳ Parking in lane ✳ Teas ✳ Toilet facilities ✳ Partly suitable for wheelchairs ✳ Open 28th June, 16th Aug, 2 – 6pm ✳ Entrance: £1.30, children 30p

An inviting swimming pool and an immaculate lawn tennis court are features of this attractive family garden; they are so placed that they neither dominate nor detract from the borders and shrubberies which will interest and delight amateurs and plantsmen alike. Blessed with three different soil types within two acres, the owners have been able to grow a wide variety of unusual plants during the 30 years they have lived here. Camellias and magnolias grow on greensand here. Shrubs and trees provide year round colour to enhance the lovely seventeenth-century cottage. Decorative kitchen garden.

EDMONDSHAM HOUSE   15
Edmondsham, Nr Cranborne, Dorset. Tel: (07254) 207

Mrs J. Smith ✳ 2m S of Cranborne. From the A354 turn at Sixpenny Handley crossroads to Ringwood and Cranborne ✳ Best season: spring ✳ Parking ✳ Refreshments on open days ✳ Toilet facilities ✳ Suitable for wheelchairs ✳ Plants and vegetables for sale ✳ House open 15th April, all Bank Holiday Mons, Weds in April and Oct, 2 – 5pm ✳ Garden open April to June and Oct, Wed – Sat, 10am – 12 noon. Also by appointment ✳ Entrance: £1, children 50p (£2, children £1 house and garden)

A vast, walled kitchen garden in which only organic methods are used provides the major interest here. This is very much a Victorian kitchen garden in origin, having been intensively cultivated since the mid-nineteenth century, but several modern and interesting vegetable variants are grown for sale. Herbaceous borders line the walls. Wide lawns surround the house, bordered by many fine and rare trees growing to a good height. An unusual circular grass hollow is said to be a cockpit, one of only a very few 'naturalised' areas of the sort in the country. The massed spring bulbs together with the many spring-flowering shrubs make this the best season to visit, but the peaceful, mellow atmosphere pervades the garden at all seasons. The house is of Tudor origin and the church nearby is also of historic interest.

FORDE ABBEY ★★   16
Chard, Somerset. Tel: (0460) 21366

Mr M. Roper ✳ 7m W of Crewkerne, 4m SE of Chard off A30 ✳ Parking ✳

*Refreshments * Toilet facilities * Suitable for wheelchairs * Dogs * Plants for sale * House open * Open all year, daily, 10am – 4.30pm * Entrance: £2.80, OAP £2.20, children free (1991 prices)*

This unique and fascinating former Cistercian abbey, inhabited as a private house since 1649, is set in a varied and pleasing garden. Old walls and colourful borders, wide sloping lawns, lush ponds and cascades, graceful statuary and huge mature trees combine to create an atmosphere of timeless elegance. There is something here for every gardener to appreciate; the bog garden displays a large collection of primulas and other Asiatic plants; the shrubbery contains a variety of magnolias, rhododendrons and other delightful specimens. The rock garden has been revolutionised by Mr Jack Drake now retired from Aviemore and a very fine arboretum has been built up since 1947; at the back of the abbey is an extensive kitchen garden and a nursery selling rare and unusual plants which look in fine health.

FRANKHAM FARM 17
Ryme Intrinseca, Nr Sherborne, Dorset. Tel: (0935) 872304

*Mr and Mrs R.G. Earle * 3m S of Yeovil, turning off A37 at crossroads with garage. Drive ¹/₄m on left * Best season: spring/summer * Parking * Suitable for wheelchairs * Open 5th April, 10th May, 21st June, 2 – 5.30pm * Entrance: £1, children free*

Approached by an impressive tree-lined drive the entrance yard has colourful climbing plants clinging to its grey walls. There is more colour and greenery in the beds and screening hedges that help to distance the farm house itself from the working buildings behind. To the south of the house, a lawn has curving borders on each side framing a low wall and leading the eye on to the fields beyond. The variety and success of the planting in the borders is evidence of the owners' flair for colour and form as well as their knowledge of unusual and interesting plants. From the end wall the visitor can begin to see the extent of the tree-screening which protects the garden on either side. This is a very exposed site around which shelter belts of quick-growing species have gradually been extended to allow replacement by a variety of plantings that should interest keen tree-lovers. On the west side, beyond the drive, a small orchard has been enlarged by the same means into a delightful arboretum, underplanted with spring bulbs, camellias and other shrubs. There is much to learn and admire for gardeners facing the problems of an exposed position.

37 THE GLADE 18
Ashley Heath, Ringwood, Nr Bournemouth, Dorset. Tel: (0425) 475803

*Mrs Sally Tidd * Take A31 Wimborne – Ringwood road, turn left at roundabout 3m W of Ringwood into Woolsbridge Road, then left after ¹/₂m into The Glade * Parking in road * Toilet facilities * Partly suitable for wheelchairs * Dogs on lead * Open 21st June, 19th July, 2 – 6pm * Entrance: 50p*

It is always a special delight when a modern bungalow, from the front much the same as all the others in the row, opens at the rear on to a treasure trove of colourful plants of every shape, size and decorative quality. Within only one third of an acre Mrs Tidd has plants to give interest in all seasons, and this on poor heath soil which has demanded endless attention to keep it in good heart. Despite all the differences of colour and shape, each plant seems to grow to full effect within its own allotted space as if following firm and detailed instructions; this is a credit to the owner's care and hard work, though the result is to lose that apparently natural disorder which can sometimes help to bring tranquillity to eye and mind.

HIGHBURY 19
West Moors, Dorset. Tel: (0202) 874372

Mr and Mrs S. Cherry ✳ 8m N of Bournemouth off B3072. In Woodside Road, the last road at the N end of West Moors village ✳ Parking in road ✳ Refreshments ✳ Toilet facilities ✳ Suitable for wheelchairs ✳ Plants for sale ✳ Open by appointment for parties and on Suns and Bank Holidays, from 5th April to 6th Sept, 2 – 6pm ✳ Entrance: 65p, OAP and parties 45p, children 25p

Mr and Mrs Cherry have amassed in their small botanical garden a fascinating collection of unusual specimens which will interest plantsmen and botanists rather than amateurs. With excellent labelling and much other general information available, this is a garden which delivers more to the enthusiast than is conveyed by the initial impression. It must be admitted that the average gardener might find the closely surrounding trees and the emphasis on rarity as against form and colour rather less than exciting.

HIGHER MANOR FARM 20
Littlemead, Broadwey, Weymouth, Dorset. Tel: (0305) 812408

Mrs Sarah Studley ✳ Take A354 Dorchester – Weymouth road, turn W by Swan Inn in Broadwey into Littlemead (end of lane) ✳ Parking ✳ Teas ✳ Plants for sale ✳ Open 7th June, 12th July, 2nd Aug, 2 – 5.30pm ✳ Entrance: 75p, children 10p

This tiny garden (probably less than a quarter of an acre of planted ground) is a notable example of quarts into pint pots. Features within such a limited space include a pond, rockeries, a pergola and an alpine scree garden, together with lawn areas and borders stocked to bursting point with unusual and rare plants mixed with thriving old favourites. Being part of a busy farm, the contrast with the workaday yards and buildings around provides a lush oasis of gardening skill and enthusiasm.

HILTON HOUSE 21
Hilton, Milton Abbas, Dorset. Tel: (0258) 880229

Mr and Mrs S.N. Young ✳ 10m SW of Blandford. Take A354 to Winterborne Whitechurch through Milton Abbas past Milton Abbey. Hilton House is next to the church in Hilton ✳ Parking ✳ Teas ✳ Suitable for wheelchairs ✳ Plants for sale ✳ Open 24th May, 14th June, 5th July ✳ Entrance: £1, children free

Surrounded by wooded hills, the house stands before a wide lawn bordered on the right by a sheltering wall. Beneath this runs a paved walk between beds filled with scented roses and other shrubs, intermingled with colourful border plants. From this vantage point visitors can view fields and wooded hills along the valley, or turn to look across the lawn to a truly magnificent, spreading oak tree which might be considered justification in itself for a visit to this lovely, mature garden. Walled vegetable garden and shrub-lined path to the nearby church. Teas on open days in a recently-added low-walled paved area surrounding a pond and fountain.

HORN PARK 22
Beaminster, Dorset. Tel: (0308) 862212

*Mr and Mrs John Kirkpatrick * On A3066 1¹/₂m N of Beaminster on left before tunnel * Best season: spring * Parking * Teas in Beaminster and in Craft Centre, Broadwindsor * Toilet facilities * Open April to Oct, Tues and Thurs and first and third Suns in month, also Bank Holidays 2 – 5.30pm * Entrance: £2*

Although the impressive house by a pupil of Lutyens dates from 1910, the garden is a developing re-creation based partly on features discovered as the work progresses. A drive through parkland leads to the wide gravel sweep before the entrance porch, with terraced lawns to the front of the house and a panoramic view east and south towards Beaminster and the distant coast. Other features, many of recent construction, include rock areas, herbaceous and rose borders, a small water garden beneath a steep azalea bank, ponds and an organic orchard. This garden is open regularly and has the potential to become a magnet for visitors, as Mrs Kirkpatrick is a member of the Loder family, so well-known in Somerset and Sussex for their great gardens developed over several generations.

IVY COTTAGE ★ 23
Aller Lane, Ansty, Dorset. Tel: (0258) 880053

*Mr and Mrs A. Stevens * 8m W of Blandford, 12m N of Dorchester. Take A354 Puddletown/Blandford road, turn first left after Blue Vinney, through Cheselbourne * Parking in road * Teas on Suns only * Partly suitable for wheelchairs * Plants for sale * Open April to Oct, Thurs, 10am – 5pm and on 12th April, 24th May, 30th Aug, 27th Sept, 2 – 5.30pm. Parties by appointment only * Entrance on Thurs, April to Oct, £1.25, on Sun, £2 (combined with Aller Green)*

Mrs Stevens trained and worked as a professional gardener before coming to her cottage 27 years ago. Although chalk underlies the surrounding land, this garden is actually on greensand; it has springs and a stream that keep it well watered and is therefore an ideal home for plants such as primulas, irises, gunneras, and in particular trollius and moisture-loving lobelias, for both of which this is the NCCPG National collection. A thriving and ordered vegetable garden (which never needs a hose), large herbaceous borders giving colour all year round, drifts of bulbs and other spring plants surrounding specimen trees and shrubs and two most interesting raised beds for alpines. This garden has been justifiably featured in print and on television, and merits a wide detour. Just up the road is Aller Green, a typical peaceful Dorset cottage garden of approximately one acre in an old orchard setting. The two share some charity opening days with a combined admission charge.

KESWORTH 24
Kesworth Farm House, Sandford, Wareham, Dorset. Tel: (0929) 551577

Mr H.J.S. Clark ✳ *1¹/₂m N of Wareham off A351 opposite Sandford School (Keysworth Drive)* ✳ *Parking* ✳ *Toilet facilities* ✳ *Dogs* ✳ *Open 10th, 17th May, 12.30 – 7pm (last admission 5.30pm)* ✳ *Entrance: £1, children free*

Kesworth is a twentieth-century park and garden scheme conceived on the scale of 'Capability' Brown, but carried out under unfavourable conditions. Bordered on the south side by the marshy edge of Poole Harbour, to the north by a busy road and railway line, and with industrial estates, both active and derelict formerly in full view, it is hardly surprising that Mr Clark's friends feared for his sanity when he acquired Kesworth. His intention of revitalising the farmland and building his own residence there was to prove even more difficult than he imagined. Poor soil, voracious wildlife, wind and fire took constant toll of his plantings. Twenty-five years of effort and 40,000 trees have gone into the project, with the result that Kesworth farmhouse (a modern evocation of the mid-eighteenth century) now stands fronted by a wide yew-lined lawn, with flagged courts and borders to the rear linking it with the original farm outbuildings. On all sides are graduated screens of trees set in broad grassland. The eyesores have been successfully obliterated, the land revived. Kesworth may not stand among the foremost as a gardener's treasure trove, but with its avenue, groves and marshland scenery and wildlife it provides a wonderful example of conservation started 20 years before the concept became generally fashionable.

KINGSTON LACY ★ 25
Wimborne, Dorset. Tel: (0202) 883402

The National Trust ✳ *1¹/₂m W of Wimborne on B3082* ✳ *Best season: spring* ✳ *Parking 100 yards* ✳ *Licensed refreshments and teas, 11.30am – 5.30pm. Picnics in north park only* ✳ *Toilet facilities* ✳ *Suitable for wheelchairs* ✳ *Dogs on lead and in car park and north park only* ✳ *Shop* ✳ *House open as garden (£4.80)* ✳ *Garden open April to 1st Nov, daily except Thurs and Fri, 12 noon – 5.30pm (last admission 4.30pm). Park 11.30am – 6pm* ✳ *Entrance: £1.60 (park and garden)*

The terrace, modelled by Barry on the Queen's House at Greenwich, displays urns, vases and lions in bronze and marble. There are six interesting marble wellheads or tubs for bay trees, also an Egyptian obelisk and a sarcophagus. The small informal 'Dutch Garden' was laid out in 1899 for Mrs Bankes in memory of her husband and is still planted in the seasonal schemes designed for her. The restored Victorian fernery leads to the once fine Cedar Walk where one of the trees was planted by the Duke of Wellington in 1827, others by visiting royalty and family members. Sadly many of these trees were among the

1000 or so lost in the storms of January 1990. However, there is still the laurel walk, the ancient lime avenue, and many areas of spring bulbs in the 400-acre park to enjoy.

KINGSTON MAURWARD ★   26
Dorset College of Agriculture, Dorchester, Dorset. Tel: (0305) 264738

Dorset County Council ∗ E of Dorchester off A35. Turn off at roundabout at end of bypass ∗ Best season: spring/summer ∗ Parking ∗ Toilet facilities ∗ Partly suitable for wheelchairs ∗ Open Easter to Sept, 11am – 5pm. Guided tours by appointment ∗ Entrance: £2, children £1 (inc. Farm Animal Park)

As might be expected, the requirements of a busy agricultural and horticultural teaching centre have inevitably altered the character of what was for many generations an impressive private mansion. The garden, with its splendid stone terraces, balustrades and steps, was laid out to the west of the house during and soon after World War I and the hedges and topiary of box and yew which form such a feature also date from this period. From 1939 to 1947 the property suffered misuse and total neglect, and it has taken many years of dedicated work by staff and students to restore it to something of its former glory. Sadly, features such as statuary and a Grecian temple have gone for good, with the result that recesses in the hedges stand empty, carefully planned vistas lead to nothing. Nevertheless, the planting is colourful and interesting (the National Collection of penstemons and salvias is held here); drifts of bulbs in spring, mainly crocus and anemone species and later cyclamen and autumn crocus surround some fine specimen trees. The large lake below the wide, sloping lawn dates back to the late eighteenth century. The nature trail provides shady walks around its margin, is full of wildlife and gives superb views over the lake and water meadows. Also surviving are the remains of what was once a Japanese garden, and a graceful folly and pond. The former walled kitchen garden provides a demonstration and practical working area for students. Much good restoration work is still being done, but to return it to its former status this garden needs the sort of lavish resources which are not available to a local authority in these times. Linked to the garden is the Farm Animal Park which contains unusual breeds.

KNOLL GARDENS ★   27
Stapehill Road, Wimborne, Dorset. Tel: (0202) 873931

Mr K. Martin ∗ Between Wimborne and Ferndown, near village of Hampreston ∗ Parking ∗ Refreshments ∗ Toilet facilities ∗ Suitable for wheelchairs ∗ Plants for sale ∗ Shop ∗ Gardens open March to Oct, 10am – 6pm ∗ Entrance: £2.95, OAP £2.40, children £1.45

Alterations and new developments continue to provide added interest to what has already become a magnet for garden-loving tourists. The waterfall and ponds have been re-designed to feature a striking dragon sculpture, beneath whose arched body thin streams of water form the strings of a harp. A brick 'ruin' provides a backcloth to yet another pond below, and all around are borders and shrubberies, island beds and rockeries, interesting trees (particularly in the Australian section) and pleasant lawns. Everywhere the condition is immaculate, the labelling informative – a thoroughly professional production backed by a well-stocked nursery, restaurant and shop. As this garden is now a tourist attraction, to rival any similar establishment, plant- and garden-lovers who can choose the time of their visit should avoid holiday weekends and the busy summer season if they wish to study it at best advantage.

LANGEBRIDE HOUSE 28
Long Bredy, Nr Bridport, Dorset. Tel: (0308) 482257

Major and Mrs John Greener ✳ *Off A35 Dorchester – Bridport road, turn S to Long Bredy* ✳ *Best season: early spring* ✳ *Parking* ✳ *Toilet facilities* ✳ *Partly suitable for wheelchairs* ✳ *Open 22nd March, 5th April, 2 – 5pm, 19th April, 3rd, 24th May, 9th Aug, 2 – 6pm and by appointment March to July* ✳ *Entrance: £1*

This garden has so many desirable features it is difficult to avoid making a list: 200 year-old copper beeches rising from wide, lush lawns, underplanted with carpets of spring bulbs; a thriving enclosed vegetable garden of manageable size, backing onto a sloping grass area with colourful mixed borders along the old tile-topped walls; a rising slope to the mixed wild woodland behind, where favourite trees have been planted in groups to allow for culling as they enlarge; a formal yew-lined lawn with pond, fountain and old stone features, from which steps descend through sloping shrubberies towards the front of the house; a miniature area of greensand allows a patch of acid-loving plants to provide contrast; a long line of pleached limes runs parallel with the bi-colour beech hedge along the road; there is a sloping orchard, a tennis court with a tall rockery behind as a viewing point and sun-trap, there are beds and borders, trellises for climbing plants and low stone walls for those that prefer to hang; and all around thousands of bulbs hide in waiting for the spring explosion which, in the owners' opinion, is the best season to visit.

LANGMOOR MANOR 29
Charmouth Manor, Charmouth, Dorset. Tel: (0297) 60229

Simon and Victoria Connell ✳ *Take A35 W from Bridport, second exit off the Charmouth bypass, signposted to Lyme Regis; entrance is 200 yards on the left* ✳ *Best season: spring* ✳ *Parking off road* ✳ *Refreshments* ✳ *Toilet facilities* ✳ *Dogs on lead* ✳ *Plants for sale* ✳ *Shop* ✳ *Open end March to Sept, most Suns and Tues to Thurs, 11am – 5.30pm and by appointment* ✳ *Entrance: £2, children £1*

The recently-completed Charmouth bypass running nearby caused this property to lie blighted over a long period. Four years ago the present owners began a mammoth task of restoring the house and garden towards their former Georgian glory, and have made great strides in so short a time. Uncovering the area near the house they have found many unexpected plants, particularly species of fern which may date back to a former owner, James Moly, 'the handsomest man in Dorset'. Moly, an ardent pteridologist, is reputed to have introduced the agapanthus into England in the late-nineteenth century. Much of this garden is inevitably immature or under development, but the home garden and fruit/vegetable areas are thriving and colourful; the long pond and the bog garden attract wildlife below the wooded hills, and the friendly livestock, Vietnamese black pigs among them, are an amusing bonus.

THE MANOR HOUSE 30
East Chaldon, Dorchester, Dorset.

Dale and Alice Fishburn ✳ *Take A352 Dorchester – Wareham road. After dual carriageway take second turn right to East Chaldon. House is next to church* ✳ *Best season: summer* ✳ *Parking in road* ✳ *Teas* ✳ *Toilet facilities* ✳ *Open 4th July, 4 – 8pm, 25th July 2 – 6pm* ✳ *Entrance: £1.50, children free*

The walk up to the house is a long curving drive overhung by mature trees, with shrubs and grassland to the right. A stone terrace in front of the house gives views northwards to the heathland, while to the west lies the fine vegetable garden running down to the churchyard wall with lovely flower borders, full of colour. Behind and between outhouses and the house are small areas and courtyards brimming with shrubs and climbers – roses, honeysuckles, clematis and vines. A magnificent deep border, backed by a screening hedge, runs eastward beside the lawn to a wall and arch surmounting an ornamental trough, a focal point through which can be viewed fields and rolling hills. Yews line another lawn leading back to the house and a pergola massed with climbers. Although rarely open to visitors, this is a garden enthusiasts should make special efforts to see.

THE MANOR HOUSE 31
Hinton St Mary, Sturminster Newton, Dorset. Tel: (0258) 72519

Mr and Mrs A. Pitt-Rivers ✳ *1m NW of Sturminster Newton on B3092* ✳ *Parking* ✳ *Toilet facilities* ✳ *Suitable for wheelchairs* ✳ *The garden may be undergoing reconstruction in 1992 but check local press for possible weekend opening. Also open by appointment.*

The Manor House lies in the Blackmore Vale and has splendid views. There is a pleasant sunken pond with fountains, an interesting arboretum to the side of the house, a further sunken rose garden, again with statuary and fountains screened by yew trees, a lime tree walk and an unusual stone gazebo as part of a walled garden by the barn. Individually each part of this garden has interest and attraction for the visitor, but taken together the result is somehow rather disappointing. Perhaps the loss of some fine elm trees which used to surround the garden has something to do with it; perhaps it may need the application of an overall design to link the various sections. Plans are in hand to replant in some areas, and hopefully the opportunity can be taken to provide the coherence and 'heart' which currently this garden seems to lack. Events are held from time to time in the large restored barn.

MAPPERTON ★ 32
Beaminster, Dorset. Tel: (0308) 862645

The Montagu family ✳ *5m NE of Bridport, 2m SE of Beaminster* ✳ *Parking* ✳

Toilet facilities ∗ *House open to parties of 15 or more by appointment* ∗ *Garden open March to Oct, daily, 2 – 6pm* ∗ *Entrance: £2.50, children under 18 £1.50, children under 5 free*

A garden with a difference, Mapperton runs down a gradually steepening valley dominated by the delightful sixteenth/seventeenth-century manor house. Terraces in brick and concrete descend through formal Italian-style borders towards the summer house, which itself stands high above two huge fish tanks (how have they resisted turning them into an Olympic-length swimming pool?) On all sides there is topiary in yew and box. Beyond the tanks, the valley becomes a shrubbery and arboretum, much of it recently planted by the present owners. Many of the concrete features depicting animals and birds, both natural and stylistic, are in need of attention, but in general the numerous ornaments provide interest and surprise.

MELBURY HOUSE 33
Evershot, Dorset. Tel: (0935) 83222 (Estate Office)

The Hon. Mrs Morrison ∗ *13m N of Dorchester on A37 Yeovil – Dorchester road. Signposted* ∗ *Best season: spring/summer* ∗ *Parking* ∗ *Toilet facilities* ∗ *Suitable for wheelchairs* ∗ *Plants for sale* ∗ *Open 5th May to 27th Aug, Tues and Thurs, 2 – 5pm* ∗ *Entrance: £2, OAP and children £1*

This historic house (not open to the public) is approached from the north by a long drive through open parkland. Visitors are directed round the east side, passing the ancient family church (open) set above a wooded valley. Lawns sweep down to a small lake beyond which rise more wooded hills. A shrub-enclosed lawn leads to a flower garden on the west side, with colourful herbaceous borders beneath mellow brick walls. Beyond this are two other vast walled areas largely used as paddock or open lawn, but with a small part still maintained as a productive kitchen garden. To the south-west of the house lies an interesting arboretum with shrubs and massed spring bulbs. Plans are now afoot for extensive renovation, alteration and replanting throughout the garden. It will take many years before the full effect is achieved, but it will be a source of continuous interest to watch the garden become once more a worthy foil to the fascinating and historic building it enfolds.

MINTERNE 34
Minterne Magna, Dorchester, Dorset. Tel: (0300) 341370

Lord and Lady Digby ∗ *9m N of Dorchester on A352* ∗ *Parking* ∗ *Toilet facilities* ∗ *Dogs on lead* ∗ *Open April to Oct, daily, 10am – 7pm* ∗ *Entrance: £2, children (accompanied only) free*

An interesting collection of Himalayan rhododendrons and azaleas, spring bulbs, cherries and maples. Many rare trees. One and a half miles of walks with palm trees, cedar, beech, etc. Alas no labelling to help the amateur. The first half of the walk is disappointing in midsummer although evidence remains of some spectacular spring colour. At the lower end of the valley the stream with its lakes and waterfalls is surrounded by splendid tall trees among which the paths wind back towards the house. A very restful and attractive atmosphere, but both lakes and undergrowth could do with attention. Tree colour in autumn should be special.

THE MOORINGS
(see Devon)

MOULIN HUET 36
15 Heatherdown Road, West Moors, Dorset. Tel: (0202) 875760

*Mr H. Judd * 8m N of Bournemouth. Look for cul-de-sac off the road *
Parking in road * Open by appointment for parties and on Sun 10th, 17th, 24th
May, 2 – 5pm * Entrance: 50p, children free*

Mr Judd (more than 85 years old) and his late wife built their garden from open heath over 20 years. Although only a third of an acre and triangular in shape, it seems to stretch and enlarge as the visitor is conducted from area to area through archways and along winding paths. All the plants, some of them quite rare, have been grown from seed or cuttings. There is also a fine collection of bonsai, grown by Mr Judd's own unique method which apparently defies all the rules.

NORTH LEIGH HOUSE 37
Colchill, Wimborne, Dorset. Tel: (0202) 882592

*Mr and Mrs S. Walker * 1m NE of Wimborne. Turn off B3073 by Sir Winston
Churchill pub into North Leigh Lane (³/₄m) * Parking * Refreshments *
Toilet facilities * Partly suitable for wheelchairs * Dogs on lead * House open
by appointment * Open 5th April, 3rd May, 2nd Aug, 2 – 6pm * Entrance:
75p, children 20p*

The restoration of this delightful house and its once impenetrable grounds has taken over 22 years to achieve, and the work continues. There are five acres of informal parkland, with mature trees, a small lake and grassy banks covered in drifts of wild orchids and naturalised spring bulbs. The Victorian features include a balustraded terrace, a fountain, a small walled garden and a magnificent conservatory in which a heavy-fruiting vine flourishes alongside other interesting specimens. There is a strong sense of the past being recaptured here; it is not difficult to imagine in such surroundings the tennis or croquet parties of 100 years ago, and the urbane butler bringing forth cooling drinks on a long-distant summer afternoon. Today, figs from the tree may be taken with afternoon tea.

THE OLD MILL 38
Spetisbury, Blandford, Dorset. Tel: (0258) 453939

*The Rev and Mrs J. Hamilton-Brown * Take A350 Blandford – Poole road.*

Opposite school at entrance to the village, sign marked Footpath ✳ *Best season: summer* ✳ *Parking* ✳ *Toilet facilities* ✳ *Partly suitable for wheelchairs* ✳ *Dogs on leads* ✳ *Plants for sale* ✳ *Open June to Sept, Weds, 2 – 5pm and for charity 19th July, 2 – 5pm. Other days by appointment* ✳ *Entrance: £1, children free*

For best effect approach along the public footpath, a narrow concrete bridge four feet above the undulating grass. From this vantage point the visitor can immediately appreciate the quiet mill stream glowing with well-chosen, water-loving plants along its banks, the ponds and dips sheltering lushly-planted boggy areas, the graceful willows rising and weeping above banks of balsam, rushes and tall grasses, the river Stour flowing clear and full inches below the mown lawns. Water naturally predominates (and sometimes overwhelms!) in this fascinating garden, developed over 17 years by the owners who have recently retired from their busy parish of Dorchester. To see the results of their labours on a late afternoon of golden sunshine must encourage the hope that they may long derive as much pleasure from the garden as it affords their privileged visitors.

THE OLD RECTORY   39
Litton Cheney, Nr Dorchester, Dorset. Tel: (0308482) 383

Mr and Mrs H. Lindsay ✳ *1m S of A35, beside the village church* ✳ *Best season: spring* ✳ *Limited parking in centre of village* ✳ *Teas* ✳ *Plants for sale* ✳ *Open 19th April, 17th May, 2.30 – 5.30pm* ✳ *Entrance: £1, children 20p*

The Rectory rests comfortably below the church and is approached by a gravel drive which circles a small lawn. A thatched summer house stands to one side, like a massive beehive. A small walled garden has outhouses on two sides and borders around three, prolifically stocked with well-chosen and favourite plants in specific colour bands. A steep path leads in to the four acres of natural woodland, a surprisingly extensive area of mature trees with many springs, streams and ponds – never a water shortage here, even in the driest of summers. This area was 'rescued' by the current owners, who are adding new young trees and shrubs as well as successfully encouraging many spring-flowering plant colonies. Climbing back up to the house, the visitor arrives at the terrace – a belvedere giving views over the trees to open farmland on the other side of the valley. Spring and autumn are the best times to see this garden, from which Reynolds Stone, the engraver, drew the inspiration for much of his best work.

THE OLD RECTORY   40
Pulham, Dorchester, Dorset. Tel: (0258) 817595

Sir John and Lady Garnier ✳ *13m N of Dorchester, 8m SE of Sherborne on B3143. Turn E at crossroads in Pulham* ✳ *Parking* ✳ *Refreshments* ✳ *Toilet facilities* ✳ *Suitable for wheelchairs* ✳ *Dogs on lead* ✳ *Plants for sale* ✳ *Open 17th, 20th, 27th May, 21st, 24th June, 2 – 6pm* ✳ *Entrance: £1, children free*

A wide lawn runs away southward from this delightful Georgian building, leading to a ha-ha and a really spectacular view over open countryside to distant hills. The main part of the three-acre garden is set to the west and includes some fine mature trees as well as interesting younger ones, a fenced pond, a rose arbour containing many varieties of bush, shrub and climbing plants, and a pleasant vista down a yew-lined lawn, back towards the west front. This is a lovely, peaceful, mature garden which fully compensates for the somewhat startling impression some visitors may experience when greeted by the castellated Gothic facade of the north front.

THE OLD RECTORY   41
Seaborough, Nr Beaminster, Somerset. Tel: (0308) 68426

Mr and Mrs C.W. Wright ✳ 3m S of Crewkerne. Take B3165, turn second left after derestriction sign, first right after ¹/₂m, second left in Seaborough village (house on corner). Signposted on open days ✳ Best season: April to July ✳ Parking but no coaches ✳ Teas on open day ✳ Toilet facilities ✳ Dogs on lead ✳ Open once a year in spring or early summer and by appointment all year ✳ Entrance: £1, children 20p

Pleasant views from the terraces, with stone steps down to the lower garden. Magnolias, rhododendrons and camellias give colour in their season, and the Himalayan plants and over 1000 species of ferns provide a wealth of interest later in the year. The Seaborough yellow violet is found here together with the more usual hues. This garden specialises in providing suitable conditions for interesting plants rather than their arrangement in colour schemes.

PARNHAM HOUSE ★   42
Beaminster, Dorset. Tel: (0308) 862204

Mr and Mrs J. Makepeace ✳ ¹/₂m S of Beaminster on A3066 ✳ Parking ✳ Refreshments: licensed buttery ✳ Toilet facilities ✳ Partly suitable for wheelchairs ✳ Dogs on lead ✳ Shop ✳ House and workshop open ✳ Open April to Oct, Wed, Sun and Bank Holidays, 10am – 5pm ✳ Entrance: £3, children 10 – 15 £1.50, under 10 free (house, workshop and garden)

The imposing stone terracing to the west of the house frames the many large clipped yews through which descend spring-fed water channels. A wide lawn leads to a balustrade and a small lake. There are large woodland and wild areas to the north and east, and sheltered borders along the brick wall of the old kitchen garden – the earliest part. Here Mrs Makepeace has used her gift for colour and form to create some splendid displays, notable as much for their shape and texture as for the well-chosen colour schemes. There are also delightful small and large courtyards to the south of the house with interesting plantings. Because the house is regularly open to the public in connection with John Makepeace's furniture design and workshops, there are asphalted drives and parking areas near the house, as well as a large grassed car park. This together with the proximity of the southern fencing to the house itself creates a somewhat disturbed and truncated effect which tends to take away from the overall excellence. Mr Makepeace, as well as being a designer with an international reputation, has recently taken an interest in the use of woodland thinnings for structural and manufacturing uses, and has founded the Parnham Trust to establish nearby Hooke Park College where students are trained in forestry, building and furniture design using radically new techniques.

RUSSETS 43
Rectory Lane, Child Okeford, Nr Blandford, Dorset. Tel: (0258) 860703

Mr and Mrs G.D. Harthan ✳ 6m NW of Blandford off A357. Turn N after Shillingstone ✳ Best season: June/July ✳ Parking in Rectory Lane ✳ Teas ✳ Suitable for wheelchairs ✳ Dogs on lead ✳ Plants for sale ✳ Open by appointment and 20th April, 26th July, 31st Aug, 2.30 – 5.30pm ✳ Entrance: £1, children free

This property, which used to be part of an old orchard, was acquired as a building plot in the early seventies. The garden has been more than 16 years in the making, and under the care of compulsive plant lovers now surrounds the house in a delightful variety of colour and shape. Although described as a 'plantsman's garden' this is much more than just a collector's display, and should give pleasure to any gardener who, like the owners, cannot resist acquiring plants simply for the love of their infinite variety.

SANDFORD ORCAS MANOR 44
Nr Sherborne, Dorset. Tel: (096322) 206

Sir Mervyn Medlycott, Bart. ✳ 2¹/₂m N of Sherborne, turning off B3148, next to village church ✳ Parking ✳ Toilet facilities ✳ Dogs on lead ✳ House open ✳ Garden open Easter Mon, 10am – 6pm, then May to Sept, Sun, 2 – 6pm and Mon, 10am – 6pm ✳ Entrance: £1.60, children 80p (house and garden). Pre-booked parties of 10 or more at reduced rates on other days if preferred

Looked at purely as a garden, Sandford Orcas is not exceptional. An old, flagged path slopes up between bordered lawns towards an open field. The stone walls at either side are attractive enough, but they stop suddenly at the wire fence and the view lacks a frame and a focal point. There is a herb garden with small box-bordered beds and a pleasant view across a lower lawn along the south side of the house. At the end of this lawn another viewpoint back towards the south front allows the attractive planting below the herb garden to show at its best. Roses and other climbing plants clinging to the honey-grey walls harmonize well with this gracious setting. It is the house, ancient and redolent of its long history, which permeates the scene and transforms the garden. On its own the visitor might enjoy but remain unmoved by the garden; but to see house and garden in perfect harmony on a warm summer's day is a pleasure not to be lightly forgone.

SHUTE HOUSE ★★ 45
Donhead St Mary, Shaftesbury, Dorset.

Lady Anne Tree ✳ 4m E of Shaftesbury, N off A30 on far side of village ✳ Parking on road ✳ Partly suitable for wheelchairs ✳ Open 25th May, 2.30 – 5pm ✳ Entrance: £2, OAP £1, children 50p (1991 prices)

Designed by Sir Geoffrey Jellicoe in the 1960's the beauty of Shute House garden depends entirely upon the water supplied by a bountiful spring. It is used throughout, in streams, in formal and informal pools, and above all in the 'Kashmiri' garden – the centrepiece of the design – where it falls from level to level over cascades arranged to vary the sound it makes; it runs through channels between octagonal pools, each with its own source so that the surface is never still; framed by grass and trees, reflecting and refracting the sunlight and culminating in a statue, beyond which are the fields and hills of open countryside. Vistas abound in this garden. There are statues to draw and satisfy the eye, varied and interesting trees to frame the view. Although there is colour particularly in spring, form is the key, in timberwork, in stone, in plant-entwined arches, in box-bordered flower beds, shaped pools and twisting paths. This theme is still being developed in a new area, where tall metal frames are to support ivy and other climbing plants in geometrical patterns. Even in the bog garden, perhaps the least ordered area, a primitive African figure enigmatically presides, and near to the house is an amusing 'bedroom' of clipped box, furnished with a dressing table and a four poster bed framed with climbing vines. Conceived with skill and wit, this is a garden not to be missed.

SMEDMORE HOUSE 46
Kimmeridge, Nr Wareham, Dorset.

Dr Philip Mansel ✳ *7m S of Wareham. Right off A351 at sign to Kimmeridge* ✳ *Best season: June to July* ✳ *Parking* ✳ *Refreshments at post office in Kimmeridge* ✳ *Toilet facilities* ✳ *Suitable for wheelchairs* ✳ *Organised parties in summer by appointment with the Administrator Tel: (0929) 480719* ✳ *Entrance: by arrangement*

The gardens at Smedmore are of necessity either surrounded by walls or protected by screens of trees in order to mitigate the damage from sea winds. The mellow walls are admirably used to display many attractive and interesting climbing plants, including fine double mauve and white wisterias and the tender *Clianthus puniceus*, while among the trees are some splendid mature and unusual specimens. The large kitchen garden is now being prepared for use as a nursery. There are three very pretty small walled gardens as well, but the main pleasure at Smedmore is derived from the colourful principal garden with its air of age and tranquillity.

STICKY WICKET 47
Buckland Newton, Dorset. Tel: (03005) 476

Peter and Pam Lewis ✳ *11m from Dorchester and Sherborne, 2m E of A352 or take B3143 from Sturminster Newton. At T-junction midway between church and school* ✳ *Parking in road* ✳ *Refreshments* ✳ *Toilet facilities* ✳ *Partly suitable for wheelchairs* ✳ *Plants for sale* ✳ *Open June to Sept, Thurs, and some Suns for charity, 10.30am – 6pm* ✳ *Entrance: £1, children 50p*

A design of concentric circles and radiating paths has enabled the creation of many separate beds showing different planting styles. A very fragrant and colourful display is enhanced by many unusual and/or variegated plants and bordered by species roses. The garden is designed to attract birds, butterflies and bees and to provide spectacular flowerheads for drying. There is a small pond and a wet area which is also attractive to wildlife. This is very much the garden of conservationist-minded plantlovers; plans are afoot to develop a white woodland area to carry the idea further. If the progress of recent years is maintained this garden is destined to become outstanding.

STOCKFORD 48
East Stoke, Wareham, Dorset. Tel: (0929) 462230

Mrs A.M. Radclyffe ✳ *3¹/₂m W of Wareham on A352 opposite Stokeford Inn* ✳ *Parking* ✳ *Toilet facilities* ✳ *Partly suitable for wheelchairs* ✳ *Dogs on lead* ✳ *Open 19th April, 3rd, 24th May, 2 – 6pm* ✳ *Entrance: 50p, children 25p*

A longish drive through woodland leads to this large, quaint, thatched house closely surrounded by mature trees. Underplanting of camellias, rhododendrons and azaleas among the lush grass gives evidence of attractive spring colour, while in the part-walled garden well-established shrubs and border plants nestle in the dappled shade. The woodland, three acres in extent, is obviously proving difficult to manage following the disastrous storms of recent years, but the immediate surroundings of this unusual house make an attractive picture in summer sunshine.

STOUR HOUSE 49
East Street, Blandford, Dorset. Tel: (0258) 452914

Mr T.S.B. Card ✳ *In Blandford, 100 yards from Market Place on the one-way system* ✳ *Parking in town* ✳ *Toilet facilities* ✳ *Suitable for wheelchairs* ✳ *Open 5th April, 12th July, 16th Aug, 2 – 6pm* ✳ *Entrance: 60p, children 20p*

A wooden bridge of unusual design leads onto a long island set in the River Stour at the end of this garden. Mature trees and shrubs flourish on a lush green sward underplanted with massed spring bulbs. Walk westwards to the end of the island to enjoy a perfect view of the weir below a distant, graceful bridge. It is easy to imagine the romantic picnic parties that must have been held here in the past. The main garden has wide-bordered lawns with some interesting plants and shrubs, and an orchard and vegetable area. It might perhaps benefit by offering more interesting focal points, and needs some further screening from the presence of a supermarket and car park alongside, but the surprise and pleasure afforded by discovering such a pleasing, tranquil area in the heart of a busy market town makes this hidden garden well worth a visit.

14 UMBERS HILL 50
Shaftesbury, Dorset. Tel: (0747) 53312

Mrs K. Bellars ✳ *From Shaftesbury take B3091. Turn right into Breach Lane at small crossroads, then right into Umbers Hill* ✳ *Best season: April to Sept* ✳ *Parking* ✳ *Toilet facilities* ✳ *Open by appointment only* ✳ *Entrance: 75p inc. tea and coffee*

Mrs Bellars and her husband have created a garden worthy of the splendid position in which their bungalow was built more than 20 years ago. Although only a small plot it has shrubberies, beds and borders filled with thriving and well-chosen plants. There are over 50 varieties of clematis and also numerous stone sinks containing alpines and rock plants. A new Japanese corner has aroused much interest among visitors. (Mrs Bellars lectures frequently on alpines and other plants about which she is a recognised authority.) From the sunny terrace visitors can view 25 miles down the lovely Blackmore Vale.

WATERFALLS 51
59 Branksome Wood Road, Bournemouth, Dorset. Tel: (0202) 762667

*Mr and Mrs Roger Butler * From the centre of Bournemouth take the road leading NW called Bourne Avenue. This becomes Branksome Wood Road. Continue 1m to No 59 * Parking in road * Dogs on lead * Open 2nd Aug, 2 – 6pm * Entrance: 60p, children 30p*

Here is a new angle on gardening – 60 degrees at a rough guess! In order to make use of what they euphemistically refer to as a 'steeply-inclined' site, the owners have created a waterfall tumbling through stepped greenery to a small pond. Around this they have built flights of stone steps to two small terraces from which visitors can look over the house roof (sadly, nothing special in view). A lopped pine above the water source is covered with a mass of clematis seedheads giving evidence of what must be a spectacular early summer show, but at the August opening day the hydrangeas have pride of place with an outstanding display of brilliant and subtle hues. Tall, older trees along each side emphasise the narrowness of the plot, but do not seem to inhibit the arching fronds of new growth which the owners obviously find special delight in encouraging. The high trees and lush planting all around have not, unfortunately, deterred marauding herons from attempting daylight robbery in the fishpond; this is now surrounded by trellis and chain which in no way detracts from the unique interest of this unusual garden.

WINCOMBE PARK 52
Shaftesbury, Dorset. Tel: (0747) 52161

*The Hon Martin and Mrs Fortescue * 2m from Shaftesbury signed to Wincombe off A350 to Warminster * Best season: summer * Parking * Teas * Toilet facilities * Dogs on lead * Unusual plants occasionally for sale * Open 7th June, 2 – 6pm and to groups by appointment * Entrance: £1, children 25p*

This is essentially a beautifully landscaped park. The house is set upon the side of a valley, screened behind tall trees and approached by a winding drive. There is a high bank beside the drive containing an interesting and well-judged selection of shrubs and small trees. Below and to the side of the house are small lawns and a walled kitchen-garden, itself worth a look. The borders are full of specimens to interest the plantsperson. But the real pleasure for the visitor lies in the wide, sloping lawn below the lake, and then up the steep wooded valley side beyond. In addition to the newly planted walled garden, the owners are heavily involved in removing and replacing the 1500 trees destroyed in winter storms around the valley. The garden alone would not justify a long detour but the ensemble is memorable.

DURHAM

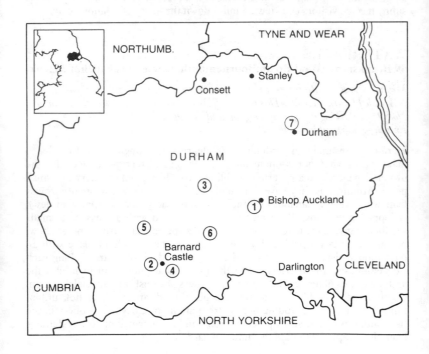

AUCKLAND PARK 1
Auckland Castle, Bishop Auckland, Co. Durham.

Bishop of Durham; Managed by Wear Valley District Council ✳ Leave A1/M at Bishop Auckland sign and follow A689 west, through Rushyford, past Windlestone Hall and Coundon into Bishop Auckland ✳ Best season: early summer ✳ Parking in Market Square, W of Castle ✳ Refreshments: cafés in Market Square ✳ Toilet facilities in bus station ✳ Partly suitable for wheelchairs ✳ Dogs on lead ✳ Auckland Castle State Rooms and Chapel open during summer, Suns and Weds, pm and Tues, am ✳ Gardens open daily throughout year: summer, 7.30am – 9pm; winter, 7.30am – dusk ✳ Entrance: free (castle £1.50)

A remarkable survival, poorly maintained, of an eighteenth-century and earlier deer park in the well-wooded valleys of the Coundon Burn and Gaunless River, tributary to the River Wear. Enter the park via a gatehouse designed by Sir

Thomas Robinson with touches of Thomas Wright, and walk past Auckland Castle, glimpsed through a *clairvoyée*. Suddenly, through the gateway in James Wyatt's screen of 1796 for Bishop Barrington there is a glimpse of the twelfth century chapel of Bishop Pudsey enriched by Bishop Cosin in the late seventeenth century. There is an inner and an outer park covering 70 acres, all that remains of a deer park that once extended to 500 acres. Within them the River Gaunless traces a meandering course with precipitate bluffs such as Kitty Heugh and craggy outcrops. The river has been canalised in places with a weir, dating from the eighteenth century. There are avenues of Austrian pine and sweet chestnut and circular platoons of trees. There are groves of ancient alders and clumps of holly trees among which dog roses climb. The gnarled and ancient clumps of hawthorns are also a feature. Ornamental, but functional, buildings in the park are the deer shelter (now in the care of English Heritage), designed by Thomas Wright (the Wizard of Durham) of 1757, and a stone pyramid built as a deer hide.

BARNINGHAM PARK 2
Barningham, Barnard Castle, Co. Durham. Tel: (0833) 21202

*Sir Anthony Milbank * 5m SE of Barnard Castle, 10m NW of Scotch Corner off A66 at A66 Motel crossroads * Parking * Teas * Partly suitable for wheelchairs * Plants for sale * Open 31st May, 7th June, 20th, 27th Sept, 2 – 6pm * Entrance: £1, children 50p*

The house is set down in an early eighteenth-century landscape on a north-facing, steep slope of the River Tees Valley, with remarkable views north and east to the North Sea. There are grass terraces to the south east of the house, reminiscent of Claremont, and a grass terrace walk to a mount, on the top of which was a bowling green, similar to the ascent to Wray Wood, Castle Howard. Extensive woodland to the south is a deer park with circumuallating wall. Paths and mounts. Rock garden and stream with waterfalls was laid out by Sir Frederick and Lady Milbank in the late 1920s and 1930s: did Col. Charles Hervey Grey of Hocker Edge and Harlow Carr advise and supply plants? A very interesting garden and landscape.

BEDBURN HALL GARDENS 3
Hamsterley, Bishop Auckland, Co. Durham. Tel: (038888) 231

*Mr I. Bonas * 9m NW of Bishop Auckland. W off A68 at Witton-le-Wear. 3m SE of Wolsingham off B6293 * Parking * Teas * Partly suitable for wheelchairs * Open by appointment and as advertised on certain days in summer, 2 – 6pm * Entrance: £1, children 25p*

A medium-sized terraced garden, largely developed by the present owner, it is beautifully situated by Hamsterley Forest. The garden is dominated by a lake with associated rhododendrons and bamboos. A new conservatory contains figs, bougainvilleas, passion flowers and other exotics. Woodland.

BOWES MUSEUM GARDENS ★ 4
Barnard Castle, Co. Durham. Tel: (0833) 690606

*Durham County Council * From Barnard Castle E on the road towards*

Westwick ✳ *Best season: spring/summer* ✳ *Parking* ✳ *Refreshments: coffee, lunch, teas in museum restaurant and picnic areas all during summer* ✳ *Toilet facilities* ✳ *Suitable for wheelchairs* ✳ *Shop in museum* ✳ *Open daily, dawn – dusk* ✳ *Entrance: free*

The formal gardens reflect the grandeur of the museum buildings (built in the 1870s) which are like a large French chateau. The parterre has been recut in the style of the seventeenth century using elaborate shapes formed by box hedges and coloured gravels. The nineteenth-century tradition is continued by planting a succession of flowers during the spring and summer months and the whole impression is of a period-piece. Bowls and tennis facilities available.

EGGLESTON HALL GARDENS 5
Eggleston, Barnard Castle, Co. Durham. Tel: (0833) 50378

Mrs W.T. Gray ✳ *5m NW of Barnard Castle on B6278* ✳ *Parking* ✳ *Catering for parties can be arranged* ✳ *Partly suitable for wheelchairs* ✳ *Plants for sale at Eggleston Hall* ✳ *Shop in Barnard Castle: 'Partners', 26 Horsefair, open 9.30am – 5pm* ✳ *Gardens open daily, 10am – 5pm* ✳ *Entrance: £1, children 50p*

The current garden was developed by the present owner within the framework of an older garden that, apart from mature trees and an original walled garden, retains little of its early identity. It is largely informal with an excellent collection of unusual plants and flowers suitable for floral art. Extensive lawns and a kitchen garden run on organic lines to produce ingredients for the cookery courses run at the Hall. Interesting cool greenhouse. In the walled garden both the plantings and the nursery area have been extended.

RABY CASTLE GARDENS 6
Staindrop, Co. Durham. Tel: (0833) 60202

The Rt Hon. The Lord Barnard ✳ *1m N of Staindrop on A688 Barnard Castle – Bishop Auckland road* ✳ *Parking* ✳ *Teas* ✳ *Toilet facilities* ✳ *Partly suitable for wheelchairs* ✳ *House open (extra charge)* ✳ *Garden open 18th to 22nd April (closed rest of April), May and June, Weds and Suns only, July to Sept, daily except Sat, 11am – 5.30pm* ✳ *Entrance: £1, OAP and children 75p*

This formal garden dating from the mid-eighteenth century was designed by Thomas White for the 2nd Earl of Darlington, and has a wide array of trees, shrubs and herbaceous plants. White (the Wizard of Durham) also advised on the landscaping, along with Joseph Spence. The garden walls from locally hand-made bricks have flues which used to enable sub-tropical fruits to be grown on the south terrace. The famous white Ischia fig tree brought to Raby in 1768 still survives. Rose garden, shrub borders, original yew hedges and ornamental pond, though the best bits (*ferme ornée*) lakes, gothic cottage and Roman baths) are alas not open to the public.

UNIVERSITY OF DURHAM BOTANIC GARDEN ★ 7
Hollingside Lane, Durham, Co. Durham. Tel: (091) 3742670

Durham University ✳ *1m from centre of Durham City. Turn off A167 at Cock O'*

The North roundabout towards the city for 1m, garden off Hollingside Lane ✳
Parking ✳ *Toilet facilities* ✳ *Partly suitable for wheelchairs* ✳ *Open all year.*
Glasshouses open daily, 9am – 4pm. Visitor Centre open May to Oct, daily,
10.30am – 5.15pm, Nov to April, Mon – Fri, 10am – 12 noon, Sat and Sun,
except Christmas week and bad weather, 2 – 4pm ✳ *Entrance: suggested 50p*
donation

Established in 1970 as a centre for botanical study, this is now one of the few
botanical gardens in the north of England. It contains fine labelled collections,
especially of trees and shrubs, and conducts basic research into many aspects of
the plant kingdom. There are demonstrations of major forest systems and
cactus and tropical greenhouses. A garden for the keen plant lover rather than
the landscape designer. On economic grounds, some of its previous collections
and features have been rationalized. Within walking distance from the Botanic
Gardens, through an area of fine views, is the Durham College of Agriculture
and Horticulture (Open Weds, Sats and Suns throughout the year, 1.30 –
4.30pm) where a parkland has been laid out between the A177 main road and
the College. To the west, there are formal rose gardens, an island bed of
fuchsias and some malus trees. To the south and south west of the Conference
Hall an area of Ericales has been laid out, over which St Columba presides
rather incongruously. To the south are trial grounds and specimen trees are
dotted around. An area enclosed by beech and hawthorn has many island beds
with a tufa rock garden, a sandstone rock garden, dahlias, conifers, a small pond
and shrub beds. Here is the National collection of meconopsis. To the south
again are greenhouses and plants for sale. West of an access track is a pine
plantation, now with a rich ground flora and bark paths. The plants are
generally well-labelled but the garden lacks structure and form, there are no
plans or guides and the route for visitors is not marked. However, there is an
excellent collection of plants, well-displayed, in the Houghall frost hollow.

ESSEX

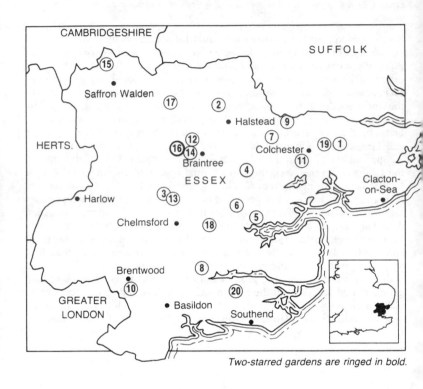

CAMBRIDGESHIRE

SUFFOLK

⑮

Saffron Walden

⑰ ②

HERTS.

● Halstead ⑨

⑦

⑯⑭ ⑫ Colchester ● ⑲①
Braintree

④ ⑪

ESSEX

Clacton-
on-Sea

● Harlow

③⑬

Chelmsford ● ⑱ ⑥

⑤

Brentwood ⑧

⑩

GREATER
LONDON

● Basildon

⑳

Southend

Two-starred gardens are ringed in bold.

THE BETH CHATTO GARDENS ★ 1
Elmstead Market, Colchester, Essex. Tel: (0206) 822007

Mrs Beth Chatto ✳ *¹/₄m E of Elmstead Market on A133* ✳ *Parking* ✳ *Toilet facilities* ✳ *Plants for sale in nursery adjoining gardens* ✳ *Open March to Oct, Mon – Sat, 9am – 5pm, Nov to Feb, Mon – Fri, 9am – 4pm. Closed Bank Holidays. Groups by arrangement* ✳ *Entrance: £1, children free*

Beth Chatto, the Gertrude Jekyll of today, designed this garden in the 1960s from a neglected hollow which was either boggy and soggy or exceedingly dry. She, more than anyone else, has influenced gardeners by her choice of plants for any situation – dry, wet or shady – and her ability to show them off to perfection. The planting of her garden is a lesson to every gardener on how to use both leaf and flower to best advantage.

142

CRACKNELLS ★   2
Great Yeldham, Essex. Tel: (0787) 237370

Mr and Mrs T. Chamberlain ✳ *Off A604 between Halstead and Haverhill* ✳ *Parking* ✳ *Suitable for wheelchairs* ✳ *Open by appointment* ✳ *Entrance: by charity box donation*

Mr Chamberlain started contouring this large garden even before he started building his house. The garden rolls away from the house down to the lake, also excavated at the start. This is not a garden in the accepted sense but 'a garden picture painted with trees', to use Mr Chamberlain's own words. He has collected trees from all over the country and has an impressive collection. Here is the rare cut-leaved beech, *Fagus sylvatica* var. *heterophylla* and its purple and pink-leaved forms, 'Rohanii' and 'Roseomarginata' as well as the variegated tulip tree *Liriodendron tulipifera* 'Aureomarginatum'. There are also collections of birches, acers, sorbus and oaks. If you are a lover of trees, make your pilgrimage.

FANNERS GREEN   3
Great Waltham, Nr Chelmsford, Essex. Tel: (0245) 360035

Dr and Mrs T.M. Pickard ✳ *4m N of Chelmsford. Take the old A130 from Chelmsford to Great Waltham, turn left into South Street, opposite Six Bells pub. Drive 1¼m* ✳ *Limited parking* ✳ *Plants for sale* ✳ *Open 17th, 18th May, 14th, 15th June, 12th, 13th July (Suns and Mons), 2 – 6pm* ✳ *Entrance: 60p, children 30p*

Mrs Pickard is a garden designer and it certainly shows in this small country garden. Here are compartments in miniature with hedges of thuya and beech, each compartment having a different theme. The vegetable garden is divided by paths into tiny squares with vegetables grown for their decorative qualities as well as their culinary uses. There is a large range of plants and shrubs, including a half-standard purple-leaved sambucus, a herb garden and a well-kept conservatory.

FEERINGBURY MANOR ▲   4
Coggeshall Road, Feering, Essex. Tel: (0376) 561946

Mr and Mrs Giles Coode-Adams ✳ *On B1024 between Coggeshall and Feering* ✳ *Parking* ✳ *Toilet facilities* ✳ *Suitable for wheelchairs* ✳ *Open May to July, weekdays, 9am – 1pm and by appointment. Closed Bank Holidays* ✳ *Entrance: £1.50*

For all its size (seven acres) and variety this is a peaceful garden. The large natural ponds are well planted with rare and unusual bog plants – gunneras and primulas, blue and yellow meconopsis, and kirengeshomas. There are fine trees, shrub borders and a long 'old rose' border backed up by a trellis with clematis growing up it. Clematis are Mr Coode-Adams' speciality. Here are many exciting plants tucked into corners, by walls or on the terrace.

FOLLY FAUNTS HOUSE   5
Goldhanger, Maldon, Essex. Tel: (0621) 88213

Mr and Mrs J.C. Jenkinson ✳ *On B1026 between Maldon and Colchester* ✳

ESSEX

Parking ✻ *Teas* ✻ *Toilet facilities* ✻ *Suitable for wheelchairs* ✻ *Dogs on lead*
✻ *Plants for sale* ✻ *Open 24th May, 7th, 28th June, 5th July, 2 – 5pm and by*
appointment for small or large parties ✻ *Entrance: £1.50, children 50p*

A large five-acre garden around an eighteenth-century manor house has been
created by the owners since 1963. The garden is divided into 'compartments'
each with a different theme and has a wide variety of unusual trees and shrubs.
The plantings around the informal and formal ponds are a special feature. In
recent years a further 20 acres of park and woodland divided by five double
avenues has been planted to make attractive walks.

GLEN CHANTRY 6
Wickham Bishops, Nr Witham, Essex. Tel: (0621) 891342

Mr and Mrs W.G. Staines ✻ *SE of Witham. Turn left off B1018 towards*
Wickham Bishops. Cross River Blackwater bridge and turn left up track by Blue
Mills ✻ *Parking* ✻ *Teas* ✻ *Toilet facilities* ✻ *Suitable for wheelchairs* ✻
Large range of unusual plants for sale ✻ *Open 19th April, 3rd, 17th, 31st May,*
14th, 28th June, 12th, 26th July, 23rd Aug, 6th, 20th Sept, 2 – 5pm ✻
Entrance: £1, children 50p

This large undulating garden has been created by the owners since 1977. The
huge informally-shaped borders are filled with a variety of plants and colours.
Kniphofia 'Little Maid' was looking pretty, mixed with monardas, eryngiums,
roses and hemerocallis. The unusual *Stokesia laevis* 'Blue Star' was particularly
noticeable. Large rock gardens and a stream with waterfalls running through
them to a pond make a dominant feature amongst the very wide selection of
herbaceous plants and heather and conifer beds.

HILL HOUSE 7
Chappel, Nr Colchester, Essex. Tel: (0787) 222428

Mr and Mrs R. Mason ✻ *On A604 between Colchester and Earl's Colne* ✻
Limited parking ✻ *Plants for sale* ✻ *Open by appointment* ✻ *Entrance:*
donation to charity

This is a large garden at the beginning of its life. It has been designed by the
owners on formal lines using yew hedging and walls to create vistas. A mixed
planting of tough native trees, sorbus and hawthorn, etc. has been established
as a windbreak. A new lime avenue is the latest addition – sited to lead the eye
out into the country. The pond area will be planted next. The bones of the
garden are now in place including urns, statues and seats. All the colour and
secondary planting will come next. In a small courtyard, reminiscent of a
London garden, is a raised pool planted only with green-leaved plants and
white flowers.

HYDE HALL GARDEN ★ 8
Rettendon, Nr Chelmsford, Essex. Tel: (0245) 400256

Hyde Hall Garden Trust ✻ *7m SE of Chelmsford, signposted from A130 and*

A132 ✱ *Parking* ✱ *Light refreshments* ✱ *Toilet facilities* ✱ *Suitable for wheelchairs* ✱ *Dogs on lead* ✱ *Plants for sale* ✱ *Open April to Oct, Wed, Sat, Sun and Bank Holidays, 11am – 6pm. Open at other times by appointment* ✱ *Entrance: £1.50, OAP £1, children free*

An attractively landscaped, all-year-round garden of eight acres set on a hill top with very fine views across the surrounding countryside. Large plantings of roses including modern HTs and floribundas, old-fashioned and modern shrub roses, climbers and patio roses; fine herbaceous collections including irises and peonies; wide ranging plantings of trees and shrubs including the National collections of malus and viburnum and many less frequently seen willows and dwarf conifers. All-year garden with rhododendrons, camellias, magnolias, hellebores and trilliums; interesting and attractive tender and half-hardy wall plants; underplantings of bulbs in many areas including magnificent stands of the pink-flowered *Eremurus robustus* and the large purple *Allium christophii*; collections of many half-hardy summer and autumn-flowering perennials, including cultivars of osteospermums, argyranthemums and gazanias both in containers and planted out. Glasshouses with a range of attractive tender winter and summer-flowering pot plants, shrubs and climbers; small alpine house.

LOWER DAIRY HOUSE 9
Little Horkesley, Colchester, Essex. Tel: (0206262) 220

Mr and Mrs D.J. Burnett ✱ *7m N of Colchester off A134. Left at bottom of hill before Nayland Village, into Water Lane. Garden ¹/2m on left after farm buildings* ✱ *Parking* ✱ *Teas* ✱ *Toilet facilities* ✱ *Plants for sale* ✱ *Open by appointment and 4th, 5th, 18th to 20th April, 2nd to 4th, 16th, 17th, 23rd to 25th, 30th, 31st May, 13th, 14th, 20th, 21st June, 4th, 5th, 11th, 12th July , 2 – 6pm* ✱ *Entrance: £1, children 50p*

This immaculately-kept garden of one and a half acres is a riot of colour. Mrs Burnett fills any spaces in between the perennials with annuals – marigolds and larkspur and geraniums all old fashioned plants. Many unusual plants intermix with cottage garden varieties, including a good selection of cistus, diascias and other sun lovers. There is a newly-created pond where the thick planting consists of primulas, hostas and mimulus. A bridge crosses a natural stream to a path which runs along the bank, much loved by the children who visit the garden.

THE MAGNOLIAS 10
18 St Johns Avenue, Brentwood, Essex. Tel: (0277) 220019

Mr and Mrs R.A. Hammond ✱ *From A1023 turn S to A128. After 300 yards turn right at traffic lights, over railway bridge. St Johns Avenue is third on right* ✱ *Restricted parking* ✱ *Teas* ✱ *Plants for sale* ✱ *Open 5th, 19th April, 3rd, 17th, 24th May, 7th, 21st June, 19th July, 9th, 30th Aug, 20th Sept, 18th Oct, 10am – 5pm. Parties by appointment* ✱ *Entrance: 70p, children 30p*

This fascinating half-acre plantsman's garden illustrates what can be achieved in a small space. Lawns are minimal. Paths wind through jungle-like borders filled with acers, camellias and magnolias underplanted with smaller shrubs and ground-cover plants. There is a large collection of hostas and unusual and rare bamboos. Mr Hammond also keeps the National collection of Arisaemas. Some huge koi live in raised pools and turtles swim happily in their greenhouse. Something of interest here at any time of the year.

OLIVERS ★   11
Olivers Lane, Colchester, Essex. Tel: (0206) 330575

*Mr and Mrs David Edwards * 3m SW of Colchester between B1022 and B1026 (signposted). From Colchester via B1022 Maldon Road turn left at Leather Bottle pub miniroundabout into Gosbeck's Road, right into Olivers Lane * Parking * Teas at weekends * Toilet facilities * Suitable for wheelchairs * Plants for sale * Open May to July, Wed, 10am – 5pm, also 9th, 10th May and 21st June, 2 – 6pm. Other times and parties by appointment * Entrance: £1, children free*

The moment you drive down to the attractive Georgian-fronted house and step on to the large York paved terrace, beautifully planted in soft sympathetic colours, you are entranced. Around you are 20 acres of garden and woodland in fine condition. From the terrace you look down over lawn, pools and woods to a natural meadow (cut only to encourage wild flowers and grasses) and to trees bordering the river. A 'willow pattern' bridge crosses the first of a succession of pools which drop down to an ancient fish pond. *Taxodium distichum*, metasequoia and gingko flourish by the pools. There are yew hedges and the delightful woodland walk. Here mature native trees shelter rhododendrons, azaleas and shrub roses in the rides.

PANFIELD HALL   12
Nr Braintree, Essex. Tel: (0376) 24512

*Mr and Mrs R. Newman * 2m from Braintree. N off A120 through Great Saling, right to Panfield, through village and right into Hall Road * Parking * Cream teas * Toilet facilities * Suitable for wheelchairs * Dogs on lead * Plants for sale * Open 11th July, 2 – 6pm * Entrance: £1, OAP and children 50p*

This four-acre garden surrounding an old house (1520) has been restored in the last few years. There are plans for further development. The rose garden is completed. Leading from there is a pergola with laburnum, wisterias and clematis already looking established. Crossing the bridge over the ponds is a sunken garden near the house, box-edged, with rose 'Little White Pet' and soft-coloured ground-cover. There is a box and topiary maze here too. The long formal canal-like pool and statue are in memory of Mr Newman's parents. The clipped box crowns add to the formality.

PARK FARM   13
Chatham Hall Lane, Great Waltham, Chelmsford, Essex.
Tel: (0245) 360871

*Mr D. Bracey and Mrs J.E.M. Cowley * 5m N of Chelmsford. Leaving*

Chelmsford take road to Braintree via Broomfield (B1008). On Little Waltham bypass turn left into Chatham Hall Lane ✳ *Parking* ✳ *Teas* ✳ *Toilet facilities* ✳ *Plants for sale* ✳ *Open 19th, 20th April, 3rd, 4th, 17th, 18th, 31st May, 1st, 14th, 15th, 28th, 29th June, 13th, 14th, 27th, 28th July, 2 – 6pm* ✳ *Entrance: 75p, children 30p*

Mrs Cowley immediately infects the visitor with her enthusiasm and energy. She is still creating her two-acre garden on the site of an old farmyard. Each part of her garden is different. A small copse by the drive leads to raised borders for plants that like hot dry conditions, which in turn lead back to the house. The garden surrounds the house and is divided up by hedges. Climbing roses cover the trees. The difficult *Romneya coulteri* mingles happily with other herbaceous plants. Shrub roses abound as they are special favourites. There are vistas and cross vistas all cleverly combined to lead you on. After visiting China and getting some cuttings (legally) Mrs Cowley has made her own Chinese garden. Giant hogweed and *Crambe cordifolia* fight over the pool.

POUND FARM HOUSE   14
Rayne, Nr Braintree, Essex. Tel: (0376) 26738

Mrs J.F. Swetenham ✳ *Off A120, 2m W of Braintree* ✳ *Parking* ✳ *Suitable for wheelchairs* ✳ *Open by appointment* ✳ *Entrance: donation to charity*

Mrs Swetenham has created an interesting medium-sized garden. It is imaginatively planted and beautifully kept. Her purple and orange border works well, using purple-leaved cotinus and purple berberis with orange and yellow herbaceous plants including African marigolds. She also plants vegetables in her borders in unexpected places. She is developing a large natural pond at the far end of the garden and is making a stem and willow garden.

REED HOUSE   15
Manor Lane, Great Chesterford, Saffron Walden, Essex. Tel: (0799) 30312

Mrs Felicity Mason ✳ *11m S of Cambridge, 4m N of Saffron Walden, 1m S of Stump Cross M11 junction. On B184 turn into Chesterford High Street. Turn left at Crown and Thistle public house into Manor Lane* ✳ *Open by appointment and combined opening with Manor Farm nearby 5th July, 2 – 6pm. The owners of Manor Farm are Mr and Mrs W. Hamilton. Tel: (0799) 30279* ✳ *Entrance (to both) £1.75, children 50p*

Mrs Mason moved to her present house a few years ago, leaving a large garden (crammed with treasures) that used to be open to the public four times a year. Her new garden is a revelation as to what can be achieved in a short time. She designed the garden and planted everything herself. Features include sink gardens, koi carp in the pool, bulbs everywhere, clematis, a greenhouse bursting at its panes, and a new conservatory rapidly filling up with rare plants.

SALING HALL ★★   16
Great Saling, Nr Braintree, Essex.

Mr and Mrs Hugh Johnson ✳ *6m NW of Braintree, halfway between Braintree* *and Dumnow on A120 turn N at the Saling Oak * Parking * Suitable for wheelchairs * Open for charity May to July, Wed, 2 – 5pm and 5th July, 2 – 6pm. Parties by appointment * Entrance: £1, children free*

Hugh Johnson's wonderful garden is essentially for tree lovers. The huge elms died, and he turned the 12 acres of chalky boulder clay into an arboretum of genera that thrive on alkaline clay or gravel. A marvellous collection of pines, quercus, sorbus, aesculus, robinias, prunus, salix and betula. Many rarities like *Cercis canadensis* 'Forest Pansy', *Eriobotrya japonica*, *Staphylea pinnata*, an unknown weeping juniper, incense cedars from Oregon seed and unusual pines on the east slope. The walled garden faces south west. Fruit trees are trimmed into mushroom shapes to contrast with a file of clipped cypress and a matching file of Irish junipers and pyramid box bushes. The borders are informal with grey and blue plants of rather typical Mediterranean associations – agapanthus, euphorbias, etc. The disciplined planting in the various sections creates a distinct atmosphere in each. There is a vegetable garden, a Japanese garden, a water garden (recently planted with gunnera, primulas, irises, etc.), a valley garden and a rose glade. This last is mainly dedicated to pink shrub roses, including *Rosa* 'Complicata', *R.* 'Constance Spry' and *R. glauca* (*rubrifolia*) and tree-climbing varieties of *R. moschata*. The old moat with its cascade boasts some substantial carp.

SPAINS HALL 17
Finchingfield, Essex. Tel: (0371) 810266

*Colonel Sir John Ruggles-Brise, Bart * 1m NW of Finchingfield. Signposted * Parking * Toilet facilities * Suitable for wheelchairs * Dogs on leads * Open May to July, Sun, 2 – 5pm * Entrance: 50p, children 25p*

The flower garden by the charming Elizabethan house includes a large cedar of Lebanon, planted in 1670, with a spread of 186 feet. At each side of the sundial (made in 1799 by Adams, who also made those in the gardens of Buckingham Palace) are perpetually-flowering pink China roses 'Hermosa' from Sir Walter Gilbey's vineyard in France. The park (private) and kitchen garden were landscaped by Humphry Repton in 1807, and walled in 1828. The greenhouse contains bougainvillaeas brought from Sir John's sister's previous home in Kenya. The Chinese *Paulownia* occasionally produces its blue foxglove-shaped flowers.

STONE PINE ★ 18
Hyde Lane, Danbury, Chelmsford, Essex. Tel: (024541) 3232

*Mr and Mrs David Barker * E of Chelmsford 1m off A414 * Limited parking * Plants for sale occasionally * Open by appointment * Entrance: by charity box*

This small plantsman's garden is owned by the Chairman of the Hardy Plant Society. Mr Barker has filled it with choice and unusual plants. The area of grass is minimal and paths wind around borders crammed with trees, acers being particularly popular, and shrubs. Surprising plants appear around each corner like the rarely-seen *Paris quadrifolia*. Mr Barker is also knowledgeable on lilies, hemerocallis, hostas and grasses of all kinds. National reference collections of epimedium and Japanese anemones.

TYE FARM 19
Elmstead Market, Colchester, Essex. Tel: (0206) 222400

*Mr and Mrs C. Gooch * 2m from Colchester on A133, ¹/2m before Elmstead Market * Parking * Teas * Suitable for wheelchairs * Open 27th, 28th June, 2 – 6pm * Entrance: £1, children 50p*

This one-acre garden is cleverly planted with hedges to make compartments to break the prevailing wind. There is a neat vegetable garden with espaliered peach trees, a white garden and over 60 varieties of old roses planted with spring-flowering or autumn-flowering shrubs. Outside the conservatory is a formally-planted area for herbs, box-edged. The conservatory has many unusual plants in it, including a lemon tree, a mature *Rhododendron fragrantissima*, a frangipani and a *Grevillea banksii*.

VOLPAIA ★ 20
54 Woodlands Road, Hockley, Essex. Tel: (0702) 203761

*Mr and Mrs D. Fox * 2³/4m NE of Rayleigh. On B1013 Rayleigh – Rochford road, turn S from Spa Hotel into Woodlands Road * Limited parking * Teas * Open 16th April to 5th July, Thurs and Sun, 2.30 – 5.30pm and by appointment * Entrance: 70p, children 30p*

Here is a garden for plant lovers – not a garden for lovers of massed colour. From the lawn at the rear of the house, paths lead into natural woodland of mature oak, hornbeam and birch where all kinds of rhododendron, camellia and magnolia have been planted and now flourish. *Davidia involucrata*, cornus and eucryphia flower in turn. Woodland plants seldom seen elsewhere are at home here: trilliums, uvularias, disporums, erythroniums and Solomon's seal. Corners have been cut back to allow lilies to flower in summer and the willow gentian in autumn. There is a bog garden where primulas, gunnera, ferns, and hostas and the skunk cabbage find the moisture they love. Reports say it has become rather overgrown.

GLOUCESTERSHIRE

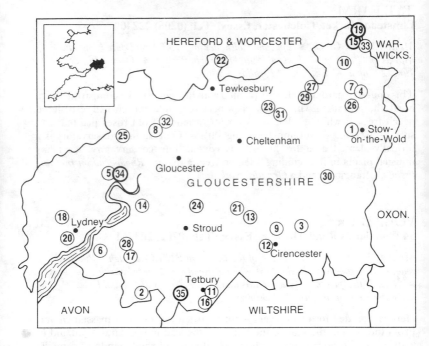

Two-starred gardens are ringed in bold.

ABBOTSWOOD ★   1
Stow-on-the-Wold, Gloucestershire. Tel: (0451) 30366

Dikler Farming Co ✳ *1m W of Stow-on-the-Wold on B4077* ✳ *Best season: spring* ✳ *Parking free in grounds but no coaches. Coaches can drop passengers at the top gate and park in Stow* ✳ *Teas* ✳ *Toilet facilities* ✳ *Partly suitable for wheelchairs* ✳ *Open 19th April, 3rd, 17th, 31st May, 1.30 – 6pm* ✳ *Entrance: £1.50, children free*

The house is in one of the most beautiful of Cotswold settings. From the car park it is approached up a descending stream and pools towards the woodland carpeted with spring flowers and bulbs, including one of the world's largest displays of fritillaries. The woods continue above and beyond the house and have been planted with rhododendrons, flowering shrubs and specimen trees. Near the house are formal gardens and terraces including a box-edged rose garden and a water garden. Extensive heather plantings. The house (not open) was formerly owned by Harry Ferguson, inventor of the modern tractor, who spent part of his considerable fortune developing the estate which has a somewhat park-like character. Nearby are the Swells, Cotswold villages renowned for their floral decoration.

ALDERLEY GRANGE ★   2
Alderley, Gloucestershire. Tel: (0453) 842161

Mr Guy and the Hon. Mrs Acloque ✳ *2m S of Wotton-under-Edge. Turn NW off A46 Bath – Stroud road at Dunkirk* ✳ *Best season: April to July* ✳ *Parking* ✳ *Suitable for wheelchairs* ✳ *Open by appointment during June* ✳ *Entrance: £1, children free (1991 price)*

Garden of exceptional beauty and character in tranquil walled setting, renowned for its collection of aromatic plants and scented flowers. Designed by Alvilde Lees-Milne and believed to be the last garden in which Vita Sackville-West had a hand, Alderley Grange was acquired by the present owners in 1974 and has been immaculately maintained and developed with discretion and style. The fine house and a mulberry tree date from the seventeenth century; a pleached and arched lime walk leads to a series of enclosed gardens. There is a notable hexagonal herb garden with many delightful perspectives of clipped, trained or potted shrubs and trees. There are abundant plantings of old roses. Many tender and unusual subjects flourish in this cherished and exquisite space, which has been much photographed and drawn.

BARNSLEY HOUSE ★★   3
Barnsley, Gloucestershire. Tel: (0285) 740281

Mrs Rosemary Verey ✳ *4m NE of Cirencester on B4425 in village of Barnsley* ✳ *Parking, inc. coaches* ✳ *Toilet facilities* ✳ *Partly suitable for wheelchairs* ✳ *Plants for sale* ✳ *Open Mon, Wed, Thurs and Sat, 10am – 6pm* ✳ *Entrance: £2, OAP £1, children free. Season ticket £4. Dec to Feb no charge. Parties by appointment*

A splendid small garden under three acres, but comprising many garden styles from the past, carefully blended by the Verey's since they acquired the house and garden in the early 1960s. The Queen Anne stone house is set in an array of small gardens and vistas that blend perfectly to give a harmonious overall effect. The standard of horticulture and maintenance is very high. Great attention has been given to colour and texture. The kitchen garden is a particular delight with numerous small beds, ornate paths, box hedges, trained fruit trees etc. This garden was the recipient of the Christie's Award for the Best Garden in 1988.

BATSFORD ARBORETUM ★   4
Moreton-in-Marsh, Gloucestershire. Tel: (0386) 700409/(0608) 50722

The Batsford Foundation ✳ *1½m NW of Moreton-in-Marsh on A44 to Evesham. Opposite the entrance to Sezincote (see entry)* ✳ *Best season: spring and autumn* ✳ *Parking* ✳ *☆Refreshments: coffees, light lunches and teas except Mons. Picnic area* *garden centre* ✳ *Toilet facilities* ✳ *Dogs on lead in arboretum* ✳ *Plants for sale at garden centre open all year 10am – 5pm* ✳ *Open March to Oct, daily, 10am – 5pm* ✳ *Entrance: £2, OAP and children £1 (1991 prices)*

Over 1000 species of different trees in 50 acres of typical Cotswold countryside plus an unusual collection of exotic shrubs and bronze statues from the Far East, originally collected for the garden by Lord Redesdale. It was expanded into an arboretum by Lord Dulverton in the 1960s. For students, a guidebook gives the details, but everyone will enjoy the effects, particularly the autumn colours. Fine views of the house (not open). There is also a water garden and, nearby, a falconry centre.

BELL HOUSE 5
Westbury-on-Severn, Gloucestershire. Tel: (0452) 760388

Mr and Mrs G.J. Linklater ✳ *9m S of Gloucester off A48, beside church close to Westbury Court Gardens* ✳ *Refreshments* ✳ *Toilet facilities* ✳ *Suitable for wheelchairs* ✳ *Plants for sale* ✳ *Open 22nd March, 19th, 20th April, 3rd, 4th, 24th, 25th May, 21st June, 12th July, 2nd, 30th, 31st Aug, 20th Sept, 11am – 5pm and parties by appointment* ✳ *Entrance: £1, children 50p*

Attractively laid-out two-acre mature garden in process of restoration and extension by present owners with help from their young family. The Bell House is near the village church and the garden contains mature trees, a stream, an interesting water garden and ponds. Established colonies of cyclamen, daffodils and fritillaries flourish among specimen shrubs and trees whose strong outlines and contrasting textures are now fulfilling the promise of a design laid out 50 years ago. The relaxed and welcoming atmosphere here is a pleasant complement to the prevailing sense of formality at nearby Westbury Court (see entry).

BERKELEY CASTLE 6
Berkeley, Gloucestershire. Tel: (0453) 810332

Mr R.J.G. Berkeley ✳ *W of M5 between junctions 13 and 14 just off A38* ✳ *Parking* ✳ *Tea rooms and picnic area* ✳ *Toilet facilities* ✳ *Shop* ✳ *House open* ✳ *Butterfly house* ✳ *Garden open April, daily except Mon, 2 – 5pm, May to Sept, Tues – Sat, 11am – 5pm, Sun, 2 – 5pm, Oct, Sun, 2 – 4.30pm, Bank Holiday Mon, 11am – 5pm* ✳ *Entrance: £1, children 50p (castle and gardens £2.90, OAP £2.60, children £1.45) (1991 prices). Special prices for parties*

Apart from Windsor, Berkeley is the oldest inhabited castle in Britain. Its history, full of incident, includes the brutal murder of Edward II after his failure to succumb to the stench of putrefying carcasses in the dungeon below his prison room. The castle grounds remain the home of the Berkeley Hunt, distinguished by their yellow jackets since the eighteenth century when Berkeleys hunted their hounds to Charing Cross and back on their own land. An entertaining guided tour of the immaculately-maintained castle may be followed by a walk in the extensive parkland, with lovely views over gentle, unspoilt Gloucestershire landscape. There is an Elizabethan bowling lawn, a lily pond and terraced beds simply planted with many unusual shrubs and ramblers which tumble and climb against the imposing castle walls, their colours in the sun reminiscent of rose and lavender pot pourri.

BOURTON HOUSE   7
Bourton-on-the-Hill, Nr Moreton-in-Marsh, Gloucestershire.

*Mr and Mrs R. Paice * 2m W of Moreton-in-Marsh on A44 * Parking across road * Refreshments: DIY tea and coffee in historic barn * Toilet facilities * Suitable for wheelchairs * Open 28th May to 24th Sept, Thurs, 12 noon – 5pm * Entrance: £1.50, children free*

This exceptionally handsome eighteenth-century Cotswold village house with fine views is enhanced by a medium-sized garden largely created under the present ownership. The diminutive geometrical *potager* is a particular delight. Well-kept lawns, quiet fountains, a knot garden in the making and Cotswold stone walls set off a number of herbaceous borders in which the choice and arrangement of plants and shrubs skilfully use current fashions in garden design. Nearby Sezincote and Batsford, and Hidcote as well as Kiftsgate less than half an hour away, make Bourton House a sensible location to include in garden touring in this part of Gloucestershire.

CAMP COTTAGE   8
Highleadon, Gloucestershire. Tel: (0452) 79352

*Mr L.R. Holmes and Mr S. O'Neill * 6m W of Gloucester. From Gloucester take A40 Ross road, turn right onto B4215 Newent road. 2¹/₂m along, turn right at sign for Upleadon (Highleadon garage on left side at turn). Cottage is 100 yards up lane on left hand side * Best season: May to July * Parking on main road outside * Refreshments: tea and soft drinks * Suitable for wheelchairs * Plants for sale * Open all year, Sun, and 31st March to 29th Oct, Tues, Thurs and Bank Holidays, 2 – 6pm or dusk * Entrance: 75p, children 25p*

Picturesque seventeenth-century timbered cottage in a sheltered setting surrounded by richly-planted cottage garden. An extensive network of pergolas and arches bears a splendid collection of old roses, honeysuckles, unusual climbers and ramblers. Old-fashioned herbaceous plants and self-sown annuals pack every niche in the garden, whose rich river silt base supports prodigious colonies of opium and Welsh poppies. It is hard to believe that the present owners have built up this lavish, multi-tiered display only since 1988.

CERNEY HOUSE   9
North Cerney, Nr Cirencester, Gloucestershire. Tel: (0285) 831300

*Sir Michael and Lady Angus * 4m N of Cirencester on A435 Cheltenham road, behind famous thirteenth-century church * Best season: Feb * Parking * ☆Teas * Toilet facilities * Suitable for wheelchairs * Plants for sale * Shop * Open Wed, 2 – 6pm and one Sun in May for charity (when adjacent Scrubditch Farm is also open) and by appointment * Entrance: £1, children free*

The house, instead of being the expected traditional Cotswold stone, was remodelled in 1791 by Decimus Burton, who designed the Palm House at Kew. Goats (from whose milk Lady Angus makes delicious cheese) graze on one side of the drive, and there is a wild flower meadow on the other. The pleasantly unmanicured three and a half-acre garden is not for those who like everything tickety-boo – the plants are happy and unrestrained. There are lawns, shrubs and trees around the house, and behind it a large walled garden started only three years ago with riotous herbaceous borders, vegetables, many old roses, clematis and a delightful children's story-book pig (a Gloucester Old Spot, of course) beneath the apple trees nearby. A woodland walk leads to the adjacent Scrubditch Farm (also open one day for charity) carpeted with snowdrops in February and bluebells in May. There is a somewhat overgrown rockery behind the house, with a waterfall. A herb garden is planned for next year, and a new pink border beside the swimming pool. The area is rich in Roman history, with Chedworth Roman Villa a few miles away.

CHIPPING CAMPDEN GARDENS 10
Chipping Campden, Gloucestershire.

N of A44 between Evesham and Stow-on-the-Wold and S of Stratford-upon-Avon off A46 E of Broadway ＊ *Parking* ＊ *Refreshments: ample facilities in town for all needs* ＊ *Public toilets in town*

Because of its position near Hidcote, Kiftsgate and Stratford the town is a popular holiday stopping-off point for garden visitors, so it is fortuitous that it has two small gardens frequently open. Mr and Mrs Lusty's is entered through their house The Martins in the main street which is itself next door to Mrs Lusty's interior decorating shop The Green Dragon and behind the butter market. It is a long, narrow town garden, with houses and a drive on one side, which has triumphed over its location by being cleverly designed to give surprises, informality, shelter and a wide variety of plants. Two levels are used, forming divisions with grass paths around small borders and beds. There is a spendid mulberry tree. Visitors are invited to contribute to charity, and the garden is open in the summer 'when it looks good' and is closed when it rains so check with the shop (0386) 840379.

Another town garden normally open during the year is the Ernest Wilson Memorial Garden, also in the High Street. It was opened in 1984 in memory of 'Chinese' Wilson, who was born in Chipping Campden in 1876. The famous collector is estimated to have introduced 1200 species of trees and shrubs during his career and the garden includes several of his finds including *Acer griseum*, the paperbark maple, *Davidia involucrata*, the handkerchief tree, and the plant for which he wished to be remembered, the *Lilium regale*. It is a peaceful oasis, with seats and shade, backed by the beautiful church tower. Admission is free with a box for contributions to its upkeep set in the stone wall beside the entrance arch.

Other gardens in Campden and neighbouring Broad Campden are open for charity and for the past three years a charity has arranged for 30 gardens to open over a June weekend. This will probably become an annual event. The choice of gardens appears to have been dictated by a desire for quantity rather than quality, and in general their appeal will be to those who like what is now called the traditional Cotswold style.

THE CHIPPING CROFT   11
The Chipping, Tetbury, Gloucestershire. Tel: (0666) 503570

*Dr and Mrs P. Taylor ✳ In the centre of town proceed between The Snooty Fox and
Barclays – past parking in Chipping Square – garden is on left at bottom behind
stone wall with tall trees, entrance in driveway to courtyard ✳ Teas on 26th April
and 7th June ✳ Dogs ✳ Open 26th April, 7th, 14th June, 2 – 6pm. Other dates
by appointment ✳ Entrance: £1*

This is a most unusual town garden because of its size and character. Entering
through a courtyard leading to a large and immaculately-maintained lawn
bordered by mature trees and a wooded walk, it extends to about two acres and
is on three levels. At one time, the eighteenth-century house was used as a
school, and since 1984 Dr Taylor has transformed a hard-surfaced playground
area into a courtyard with a small rectangular raised pool, and where there was a
giant old fruit cage and a sea of thistles are now three formal terrace-gardens
containing a variety of cottage garden flowers as well as unusual plants,
vegetables and herbs with the kitchen garden proper on a higher level. Beneath
the terraces is a wide walk with borders either side and arches covered with
roses, honeysuckle and clematis leading back to the house. A peaceful oasis
hidden among the streets of Tetbury, neither a conventional town garden nor a
country garden transported to urban surroundings.

CIRENCESTER GARDENS   12
Cecily Hill, Cirencester, Gloucestershire. Tel: see below

*On W side of Cirencester, leading up to entrance to Cirencester Park ✳ Parking ✳
Teas only on 19th July ✳ Toilet facilities ✳ Plants for sale ✳ Open:
Little Tulsa, 38 Cecily Hill: 7th, 14th, 21st, 28th June, 5th, 12th, 19th, 26th
July, 2nd, 9th, 16th, 23rd Aug, 2 – 5.30pm (except 19th July when 2 – 6pm). Also
by appointment May to Sept. Cecily Hill House: 19th July only, 2 – 6pm*

The grandest garden in the town, Cirencester Park, is usually only open once a
year in aid of charity but the park is open all the year round, courtesy of Lord
Apsley. Note the perimeter hedge, claimed to be the largest in the world,
planted in 1720 by the first Earl Bathurst. It is 40ft high. Three gardens in
Cecily Hill are open occasionally for charity and one of them, the most
publicised in the media, is at No 38 (Little Tulsa). For those who like to see a
garden full of flowers and colour this could be their Mecca, although another
name would be more appropriate as it is owned by the Rev. and Mrs John Beck.
Entered through the house is a small walled garden of great interest, but
beyond this and concealed from view is a long low flower garden with some 500
perennials including many varieties of geranium. Mrs Beck is pleased to open
the garden by appointment, (0285) 653778. One of the other gardens open,
Cecily Hill House owned by Mr and Mrs Rupert de Zoete, has a small
ornamental kitchen garden of original design and unusual vegetables. Five to
ten minutes walk from Cecily Hill at 20 St Peter's Road is a tiny 70 foot garden
entirely without grass, with a small rockery, cascade and pond and 18 varieties
of clematis which would be of considerable interest to anyone having to design
for such a small space. Meg and Jeff Blumson open by appointment as well as
their charity Sunday openings twice in the summer. Telephone (0285) 657696.

CONDERTON MANOR
(See Hereford and Worcester)

COTSWOLD FARM   13
Duntisbourne Abbots, Gloucestershire. Tel: (0285) 653856

Major and Mrs P.D. Birchall ✱ *5m N of Cirencester on A417; signed immediately W of Five Mile House Inn* ✱ *Best season: May to July* ✱ *Parking at house* ✱ *Toilet facility* ✱ *Open by appointment* ✱ *Entrance: £1.50*

Mature garden planted in grand style and sustained with sensitive artistry surrounding fine old house in superb Cotswold setting. Formal walled gardens with pools and planted with shrub roses, lavender and a collection of scented flowers. Established plantings of shrubs, herbaceous plants and many small treasures overlooking an unspoilt wooded valley. A charmed garden redolent of another age in a remote and lovely situation.

FRAMPTON COURT   14
Frampton-on-Severn, Gloucestershire. Tel: (0452) 740267

Mrs Peter Clifford ✱ *SW of Gloucester near Stonehouse, 2m from M5 junction 13. Signposted. Left hand side of village green, entrance through imposing gates in long wall between two large chestnut trees* ✱ *Best season: May to Sept* ✱ *Parking* ✱ *Refreshments in village hall on selected days* ✱ *Suitable for wheelchairs* ✱ *House open by appointment. £3* ✱ *Garden open all year by appointment* ✱ *Entrance: £1*

Home of the lady artists who painted *The Frampton Flora*, Frampton Court remains an elegant family establishment on land owned by the Clifford family since the twelfth century. The house, dating from the 1730s, is of the Vanbrugh school, with exquisite interior woodwork and furnishings which may be shown by appointment to visitors, preferably in parties, by the present owner Mrs Peter Clifford. The five-acre grounds are maintained with a minimum of labour and contain a lake, fine trees and a formal water garden of Dutch design, believed to have been built by the architects of the larger Westbury Court Garden on the other side of the Severn. A Strawberry Hill Gothic Orangery (not open but available for letting) where the ladies are believed to have executed their work, stands reflected in the still water, planted with lilies and flanked by a mixed border. This garden is open in association with that of Frampton Manor, also occupied by Cliffords, where a strongly-planted walled garden with many old roses is splendidly set off by a fine fifteenth-century timbered house.

HIDCOTE MANOR GARDEN ★★   15
Hidcote Bartrim, Chipping Campden, Gloucestershire. Tel: (0386) 438333

The National Trust ✱ *Follow signposts from Chipping Campden or Mickleton near Stratford-on-Avon* ✱ *Parking but coaches by prior arrangement* ✱ *Refreshments: café for morning coffee, licensed light lunches, teas 11am – 5pm Party bookings. No picnics* ✱ *Toilet facilities* ✱ *Partly suitable for wheelchairs* ✱ *Plants for sale* ✱

Shop ∗ *Open April to Oct, daily except Tues and Fri, 11am – 7pm (last admission 6pm or 1 hour before sunset if earlier)* ∗ *Entrance: £4.20, children £2.10, family (2 adults and up to 4 children) £11.60*

It is unnecessary to describe this garden in detail, one of the most famous in Britain and an essential visit for garden lovers of every persuasion. Created by Lawrence Johnston in the early years of the twentieth century, the original condition of the site may be judged from the early photographs in the entrance area. Johnston had a strong sense of design and great skill in planting, using mainly nineteenth-century specimens. Many varieties now bear the name Hidcote. Given to the National Trust in 1948, its splendid architectural effects and bold plantings have been retained, although these days some visitors are offended by the use of annuals. Johnston's achievement is all the more remarkable because of the isolation of the hill-top site whose scale can be appreciated by the view from the entrance to Kiftsgate garden which is within walking distance (see entry). See also Vale House.

HODGES BARN 16
Shipton Moyne, Tetbury, Gloucestershire. Tel. (066688) 202

Mr and Mrs Charles Hornby ∗ *3m S of Tetbury on the Malmesbury side of Shipton Moyne. From the A133 Tetbury – Bath road, Shipton Moyne is signposted. Drive through the village, past the Cat & Custard Pot pub, bear left and a few hundred yards after leaving the village, the towers of Hodges Barn will be visible on the left* ∗ *Parking* ∗ *Suitable for wheelchairs* ∗ *Open 19th, 20th April, 3rd, 4th, 24th, 25th May, 28th June, 2 – 6pm and by appointment* ∗ *Entrance: £1.50 for charity, children free*

In 1499 this was built as a dovecote or columbarium to a large house nearby, the latter burnt down in 1556. It was converted to a home in 1938 and bought by the Hon Mrs Arthur Strutt, the present owner's grandmother, in 1946, and she set about creating the basic structure of the garden with good stone walls and topiary. She also planted most of the trees before her death in 1973. Another influence on the present garden was the once-famous Pusey House, near Faringdon, owned by Mr Hornby's parents, who supplied some of the fine plants at Hodges Barn. It is an extensive six-acre garden, with plenty of interest for everyone – above all those who like roses. The spring garden, water garden, little wild woodland, the large cleared wood, the topiary and the splendid lawns are all enjoyable. The plantings reflect the owners' interest in colour, scent and variety, and they have not been inhibited by a desire to prevent one flower or shrub from growing into another. Note the planting in gravel along some of the many beds, and the tapestry hedges. This is a garden which reeks of enthusiasm and long may it continue.

HUNTS COURT 17
North Nibley, Dursley, Gloucestershire. Tel: (0453) 547440

Mr and Mrs T.K. Marshall ∗ *2m NW of Wotton-under-Edge nr North Nibley. Turn E off B4060 in Nibley at the Black Horse Inn and fork left after ¼m* ∗ *Best season: June* ∗ *Parking* ∗ *☆Teas on Suns only* ∗ *Toilet facilities* ∗ *Suitable*

GLOUCESTERSHIRE

for wheelchairs ✱ *Plants for sale* ✱ *Open all year except Aug, Tues – Sat, 2 – 6pm. Also for charities on last three Suns in June and first two in July and by appointment* ✱ *Entrance: £1*

An informal garden next to a nursery and working farm, designed to show off a fine collection of more than 400 varieties of old roses, climbers, species and shrubs. In June, there is a stunning display of fully grown climbers cascading from old apple trees.

JASMINE HOUSE 18
Bream, Nr Lydney, Gloucestershire. Tel: (0594) 563688

Mr V.M. Bond ✱ *W of the Severn estuary, 3m N of Lydney. At Bream Maypole Garage turn right to Park End. Immediately after crossroads, turn right by insurance office. House is 200 yards on left* ✱ *Best season: summer* ✱ *Parking in village only* ✱ *Plants for sale* ✱ *Open 19th, 20th, 30th April, 3rd, 4th, 21st, 24th, 25th May, 11th, 14th, 25th, 28th June, 9th, 12th, 23rd, 26th July, 6th, 9th, 27th, 30th, 31st Aug, 19th, 10th, 13th Sept, 2 – 6pm* ✱ *Entrance: 75p*

A plantsman's garden developed over the last few years, virtually from scratch, on a three-quarters of an acre cottage garden. Naturally there are cottage plants but the main interest is the alpines, heathers and fuchsias. There are many species of herbaceous plants. Among the fruit trees in the orchard are 'beds' – small wild gardens of differing types. Not far away is Lydney Park, a rather grand garden at its most spectacular in spring (see entry).

KIFTSGATE COURT ★★ 19
Chipping Campden, Gloucestershire. Tel: (0386) 438777

Mr and Mrs A.H. Chambers ✱ *3m NE of Chipping Campden and near Mickleton. Kiftsgate is next to Hidcote Manor which is signposted* ✱ *Parking* ✱ *Plants for sale* ✱ *Open April to Sept, Wed, Thurs, Sun, 2 – 6pm. Also Sat in June and July, and Bank Holiday Mons (NB not identical opening times with Hidcote)* ✱ *Entrance: £2.20, children 80p*

The house was built mid-nineteenth century on this magnificent site surrounded by three steep banks. The garden was largely created by the present owner's grandmother who with her husband moved there after World War I. Her work was continued by her daughter, Diana Binny, who made a few alterations but continued the colour schemes of the borders. In spring, the white sunken garden is covered with bulbs and there is a fine show of daffodils along the drive. June and July are the peak months for colour and scent but the magnificent old and species roses are the glory of this garden, home of *Rosa* 'Kiftsgate'. Other features are perennial geraniums, a large wisteria and many species of hydrangea, some very large. In autumn, Japanese maples glow in the bluebell wood. This garden should not be missed, not only because of its proximity to Hidcote, but because of its profusion of colour and apparent informality. Unusual plants are sometimes amongst those available for sale. Vale House (see entry) is nearby.

LYDNEY PARK GARDENS 20
Lydney, Gloucestershire. Tel: (0594) 842844

Lord Bledisloe ✱ *20m SW of Gloucester. N of A48 between Lydney and*

Aylburton ✳ *Parking* ✳ *Refreshments: teas. Picnics in deer park* ✳ *Toilet facilities* ✳ *Dogs on lead* ✳ *Shrubs for sale* ✳ *Shop* ✳ *Roman site and museum open* ✳ *Open 5th April to 7th June, Suns and 24th to 31st May, daily, 11am – 6pm. Parties by appointment in season* ✳ *Entrance: £1.50 except Wed when £1. Car and accompanied children free*

The park dates back to the seventeenth century and although it has been in the hands of one family since 1723, a new house was built in 1875 and the old one demolished. A new start was made on the garden in 1950 when the terrace was paved and a line of cypresses 'Kilmacurragh' planted to frame the view. An area near the house has an interesting collection of magnolias but the most picturesque sight is the bank of daffodils and cherries, splendid in season. From 1957, a determined attempt has been made to plant rhododendrons and azaleas in the wooded valley, behind and below the house, with the aim of achieving bold colour at different times between March and June. Near the entrance to the main part of the gardens there is a small pool surrounded by azaleas and a collection of acers. From here the route passes through carefully-planted groups of rhododendron and by a folly, brought from Venice as recently as 1961. This overlooks a valley and bog garden. Criss-crossing the hillside, there are rare and fine rhododendrons and azaleas, including an area planted with un-named seedlings. Enormous effort has gone into the plant design, colour combination and general landscaping, and those who are enthusiastic about rhododendrons, azaleas and camellias will find enough to enjoy for a whole day. Another interest for visitors is the Roman camp, excavated by Sir Mortimer Wheeler, and the museum which contains the famous bronze Lydney Dog, one of the finest pieces of Romano-British sculpture. Guide book with map available.

MISARDEN PARK GARDENS ★   21
Miserden, Stroud, Gloucestershire. Tel: (0285) 821309

Major M.T.N.H. Wills ✳ *7m SW from Gloucester, 3m from A417. Signposted* ✳ *Parking* ✳ *Toilet facilities* ✳ *Suitable for wheelchairs* ✳ *Nursery adjacent to garden* ✳ *Open April to Sept, Wed and Thurs, 9.30am – 4.30pm and 5th April, 5th July, 2 – 6pm* ✳ *Entrance: £1.50 (inc. printed guide), children free. Reduction for booked parties of 10 or more*

This lovely, timeless English garden has most of the features that one expects from a garden of the early twentieth century. There are extensive yew hedges, a York stone terrace, a loggia overhung with wisteria, a fine specimen of *Magnolia* x *soulangiana*. The south lawn sports very fine grass stairs. The west of the house descends to the nursery in a series of fine grassed terraces. There are two very good herbaceous borders leading to a traditional rose garden beyond. The grounds are planted with many fine specimen trees. The spring show of blossom and bulbs is particularly good. The gardens command excellent views over the famous Golden Valley.

THE OLD MANOR   22
Twyning, Nr Tewkesbury, Gloucestershire. Tel: (0684) 293516 or (0684) 299878

Mrs Joan Wilder ✳ *3m N of Tewkesbury via A38; follow signs to Twyning. The garden is at the T-junction at west end of the village* ✳ *Best season: April to June* ✳ *Parking* ✳ *Tea and biscuits on Bank Holiday Mons only* ✳ *Toilet facilities* ✳ *Suitable for wheelchairs* ✳ *Small specialist nursery* ✳ *Open all year, Mon, 2 – 6pm (or dusk if earlier)* ✳ *Entrance: £1.20, children free*

Plantswoman's garden packed with treasures developed over 35 years partly on the site of a Queen Anne Manor. Ancient abbey masonry, churchyard headstones and old brick walls with pineapples give atmosphere to a series of separated contained spaces featuring a pool garden, fern, peat and scree beds, troughs and a renowned 'snake bed'. A connoisseur's collection of plants including many species; unusual plants are available from the small nursery.

ORCHARD COTTAGE 23
Duglinch Lane, Gretton, Nr Winchcombe, Gloucestershire. Tel: (0242) 602491

Mr Rory Stuart ✳ *In Gretton (off B4078) up Duglinch Lane to the left of the Bugatti Inn. Approximately 300 yards up lane on right opposite black railings* ✳ *Limited parking in driveway* ✳ *Plants for sale* ✳ *Open all year by appointment only* ✳ *Entrance: £1 for charity*

Well past the somewhat unpromising suburban beginnings of Duglinch Lane and tucked into the hillside near the famous Bugatti Club's Prescott Hill Climb is this cottage garden created largely by the present owner's aunt, the late Mrs Nancy Saunders, in the 1950's, and featured in *The Englishwoman's Garden*. She was helped by the late John Codrington, whom she met on a botanical expedition. Its approximately one and a half acres consist of an old orchard with a variety of unusual shrubs and trees, from which there is a splendid view towards Bredon Hill, and the garden around the cottage. Mrs Saunders derived great pleasure from collecting plants during her travels abroad, bringing them home in her sponge-bag. The wide range of planting is for all-year interest (35 plants in bloom last 1st January), but if hellebores are your particular passion February to March would be the best time to see the extensive collection. Sudeley Castle (see entry) is nearby.

PAINSWICK ROCOCO GARDEN 24
The Stables, Painswick House, Painswick, Gloucestershire.

Lord and Lady Dickinson ✳ *¹/₂m from Painswick on B4073. Signposted* ✳ *Best season: spring* ✳ *Parking* ✳ *Refreshments: teas and lunches* ✳ *Toilet facilities* ✳ *Plants for sale* ✳ *Shop* ✳ *Open Feb to mid-Dec, Wed – Sun and on Bank Holiday Mons, 11am – 5pm* ✳ *Entrance: £2.40, OAP £2, children £1.20. Coaches by appointment*

A great deal of time, money and effort is going into the restoration (almost complete redevelopment) of this rare rococo survival. Most of the work is new, plantings are incomplete and very young. Whole sections are yet to be restored. But, given time, it will be splendid. At present, the best features are the eighteenth-century garden buildings, the views into especially beautiful surrounding countryside, and the marvellous snowdrop wood spanning a stream that flows from a pond at the lower end. This must be one of the best displays of naturalized snowdrops in England. There are some splendid beech woods and older specimen trees. Wildflowers are allowed complete freedom. Rococo gardening was an eighteenth-century combination of formal geometric features with winding woodland paths, revealing sudden incidents and vistas – in essence, a softening of the formal French style, apparent from about 1715 onwards in all forms of art. A painting by Thomas Robins (1716-1778) is the basis for Painswick's restoration.

THE PRIORY, Kemerton
(see Hereford and Worcester)

RYELANDS HOUSE   25
Taynton, Gloucestershire. Tel: (045279) 251

Captain and Mrs E. Wilson ✳ 8m W of Gloucester, midway betwen Huntley (A40) and Newent (B4215) ✳ Best season: spring ✳ Parking ✳ Refreshments ✳ Toilet facilities ✳ Suitable for wheelchairs in dry weather ✳ Dogs welcome on country and woodland walk ✳ Plants for sale ✳ Open by appointment for parties and on 5th, 12th, 19th, 20th, 26th April, 3rd, 4th May, 28th June, 5th, 12th July, 2 – 6pm ✳ Entrance: £1.50, children free

Carefully cultivated garden designed, developed and maintained by owners since 1964 surrounding a fine creeper-clad early-nineteenth-century house in a peaceful country setting. Yew and box hedges subdivide a sunken garden, pergolas and arches frame well-placed statuary and lead the eye to inviting seats, a water garden and specimen shrubs. Mature trees shade immaculately-maintained beds planted with an experienced eye, in sophisticated tonal harmonies. A mile walk across the owners' land to a tranquil two-acre secluded lake, rich with wildlife, should not be missed especially in spring when the wild daffodils carpet the surrounding woodland. A garden of character with a warm welcome from the owners.

SEZINCOTE ★   26
Bourton-on-the-Hill, Nr Moreton-in-Marsh, Gloucestershire.

Mr and Mrs D. Peake ✳ 1¹/₂m from Moreton-in-Marsh on A44 just before reaching Bourton-on-the-Hill ✳ Parking ✳ Teas on charity open day ✳ Toilet facilities ✳ House open May to July and Sept, Thurs, Fri, 2.30 – 6pm (no children in house) ✳ Garden open Jan to Nov, Thurs, Fri and Bank Holiday Mons, 2 – 6pm (or dusk if earlier). Also 12th, 25th July for charity. Closed Dec ✳ Entrance: £2.50, children £1, children under 5 free (house and garden £3.50)

The estate, acquired in the early nineteenth century, was developed in the Indian style by the architect, Thomas Daniell, who combined this with Palladian motifs. In the twentieth century a canal pool, a curving conservatory and a little pavilion also in Indian style have been added. The garden reflects what the *Oxford Companion* calls its architectural dichotomy, and, despite some

GLOUCESTERSHIRE

work by Repton, the mixture of traditional landscape with eastern ornamentation, such as the Indian bridge, is not one which every visitor finds satisfactory. However it is certainly unique, although there are echoes of Brighton Pavilion, for which Repton drew designs of an oriental nature.

SNOWSHILL MANOR ★ 27
Nr Broadway, Gloucestershire. Tel: (038685) 2410

The National Trust ✳ 3m S of Broadway off A44 ✳ Parking. No coaches ✳ No refreshments but nearby pub serves morning coffee and lunches ✳ Liable to overcrowding on Suns and Bank Holiday Mons ✳ Open Easter Sat, Sun and Mon, 11am – 1pm and 2 – 6pm, April and Oct, Sat, Sun, 11am – 1pm and 2 – 5pm. May to Sept, Wed – Sun and Bank Holiday Mon, 11am – 1pm and 2 – 6pm. Last admission ½ hour before closing ✳ Entrance: £3.80. Parties by written appointment only and no concessions

From a design by MH Baillie-Scott, the owner Charles Wade transformed a 'wilderness of chaos' on a Cotswold hillside into an interconnecting series of outdoor 'rooms' in Hidcote style from the 1920s onwards. Wade was, according to the *Oxford Companion*, a believer in the arts and crafts rustic ideal and the garden, like the house, expresses his eccentricities. Seats and woodwork are painted 'Wade' blue, a powdery dark blue with touches of turquoise which goes well with the Cotswold stone walls. The simple cottage style conceals careful planting with blue, mauve and purple as the motif. Organic gardening is employed here. The visitor may care to contrast Wade's success with some of the less happy attempts at the Cotswold garden style by others in this picture-postcard village no longer inhabited by traditional villagers.

STANCOMBE PARK 28
Stinchcombe, Gloucestershire. Tel: (0453) 542815

Mr and Mrs Barlow ✳ Between Wotton-under-Edge and Dursley on B4060 ✳ Best season: June ✳ Parking in field by park ✳ Teas and home-made cakes ✳ Toilet facilities ✳ Partly suitable for wheelchairs ✳ Plants for sale ✳ Open 14th June, 2 – 6pm and by appointment for parties ✳ Entrance: £1.50 for both gardens

When Stancombe Park – built in the 1840s – was open for charity last June, 1400 people rushed to view the most curious park and garden south of Biddulph Grange. Set on the Cotswold escarpment, Stancombe Park boasts the ingredients of a Gothic best-seller. A narrow path drops into a dark glen, roots from enormous oaks, copper beeches and chestnuts trip your feet, ferns brush your face, walls drip water, and amonites and fossils loom in the gloom. A dark lake reflects an eerie Doric temple. Rocks erupt with moss. Egyptian tombs trap the unwary. Tunnels turn into gloomy grottos. Even plants live in wire cages. Metal arches flake with rust. Family parties become confused, divided and lost. Folly freaks are in their element. Everyone has a good time in this Victorian theme park turned horror movie. Escape can be found in the pretty rose garden, tea and further twentieth-century follies around the charming house.

STANWAY HOUSE 29
Cheltenham, Gloucestershire. Tel: (038673) 469

Lord Neidpath ✳ *1m E of B4632 Cheltenham – Broadway road, 4m from Winchcombe* ✳ *Parking* ✳ *Refreshments: coffee and tea, Bakehouse tea rooms in village. Picnics permitted in park* ✳ *Toilet facilities* ✳ *Partly suitable for wheelchairs* ✳ *Dogs* ✳ *House open* ✳ *Garden open June to Aug, Tues and Thurs, 2 – 5pm. Other times by appointment* ✳ *Entrance: £2, OAP £1.75, children £1 (house and garden)*

Stanway is a honey-coloured Cotswold village with its Jacobean 'great house' which has been in the hands of only two families since. It was much frequented by Arthur Balfour and 'The Souls' in the latter years of the last century. More recently, the garden was used to film part of *The Draughtsman's Contract* so one need to say no more to those who favour grand design and effects. Contrariwise it offers nothing to the plantsperson as there is hardly a flower in sight. Behind the house, the garden rises in a series of dramatic lawns and a (rare) formal terraced mound to the pyramid folly which, in the eighteenth century was the pivot of the vast cascade descending to a lake by the house. The present owner plans to restore this with its 170m-long waterfall, its canal 35m wide, and to extend the lime avenue and vista. Alas the estimated cost is £¹/₄ million. Other features include the fourteenth-century tithe barn, church and a dog cemetery whose inmates go back to 1700.

STOWELL PARK 30
Northleach, Gloucestershire. Tel: (0285) 720360

The Lord and Lady Vestey ✳ *2m SW of Northleach on A429. The drive entrance is on right after a long stone wall* ✳ *Parking to the right of drive* ✳ *Teas* ✳ *Toilet facilities* ✳ *Open 28th June, 9th Aug, 2 – 6pm* ✳ *Entrance: £1.50, children free*

The original house dates from around 1600 but it was enlarged for the Earl of Eldon in the 1880s and 90s by Sir John Belcher, the architect of the Mappin & Webb building in the City of London. Stowell Park was used as a shooting lodge. This is a large garden in a magnificent setting: the terrace on the south side of the house overlooks the River Coln, with Chedworth Woods across the valley. The original garden is thought to have been laid out in the 1870s, but since 1981 Lady Vestey has introduced new ideas and new plantings. Rosemary Verey helped with the planting on the broad terrace which has a herbaceous border running the length of the balustrading. The approach to the house is along an avenue of pleached limes planted in 1983, and there are fine walled kitchen gardens containing vegetables, fruit, flowers for cutting and a range of glasshouses. A good collection of old-fashioned and climbing roses. The twelfth-century church nearby has original wall paintings of the same date.

SUDELEY CASTLE ★ 31
Winchcombe, Gloucestershire. Tel: (0242) 604357/8

Lord and Lady Ashcombe ✳ *8m N of Cheltenham Spa on B4632. Entry through the town of Winchcombe* ✳ *Parking* ✳ *Meals and refreshments. Picnic facilities in play area only* ✳ *Toilet facilities* ✳ *Suitable for wheelchairs* ✳ *A good selection of plants for sale. Plant centre open mid-Feb to Nov, 10am – 5.30pm. Information (0242) 602308* ✳ *Shop* ✳ *Castle open 12 noon – 5pm* ✳ *Open April to Oct, 11am – 5.30pm* ✳ *Entrance: £2.80, children £1.25 (castle and grounds £4.30, children £2.25) (1991 prices)*

There has been a house on this magnificent site for over 1000 years and today the emphasis is on tourism with pleasant facilities, craft and other exhibitions such as falconry. The main attraction of the extensive grounds are the clipped yews by the park balustrade and the sculptural yew hedges with openings and tunnel walks round the so-called Queen's garden. This imitation of a medieval knot garden, made in the nineteenth century by an ancestor of the owners, has well-clipped rosemary, lavender and other herbs. Otherwise, the planting is rather patchy. The owners have renovated the Queen's garden under the guidance of Jane Fearnley-Whittingstall to 'become one of the major rose gardens of England'.

TREVI GARDEN 32
Hartpury, Gloucestershire. Tel: (0452) 700370

Mr and Mrs G.D. Gough ✳ *5m NW of Gloucester via A417. In village turn sharp back right over Old Road before war memorial* ✳ *Parking in road outside* ✳ *☆Teas* ✳ *Toilet facilities* ✳ *Suitable for wheelchairs* ✳ *Plants for sale* ✳ *Open 19th March to 24th Sept, Thurs, 2 – 6pm. Also 3rd May to 2nd Aug, Suns, 2 – 6pm. Coaches and groups at other times by appointment* ✳ *Entrance: £1, accompanied children free*

This carefully-planned and maintained garden gives the impression of more space than its one acre and aims to be full of interest and variety at all times of the year. Meandering paths lead through arches, around well-planted beds, under a laburnum and clematis walk, through a stream garden and alongside a decorative vegetable garden flanked with espaliered fruit trees. The owners have invested much hard work in achieving a garden displaying colour and good-looking plants at every season and have created a sense of enclosed and charmed oasis within an area of recently-built housing. There are unusual species and cultivars to catch the plantsman's eye as well as colourful annuals and old favourites, and there is a welcoming informality here to make any visitor feel at home.

VALE HOUSE 33
Hidcote Boyce, Chipping Campden, Gloucestershire. Tel: (0386) 438 228

Miss Bettine Muir ✳ *On the road from Chipping Campden to Hidcote Manor and Kiftsgate Gardens (see entries). On the edge of Hidcote Boyce* ✳ *Parking in mown paddock* ✳ *Partly suitable for wheelchairs* ✳ *Open May to July, Wed, 2 – 5pm* ✳ *Entrance: £1, children 50p*

Miss Bettine Muir is the second daughter of Heather Muir, the creator of Kiftsgate and remembers the planting of the famous rose. She is a born gardener and her skill is reflected in the most unusual and exciting planting in her own garden. She moved to Vale House in the early 1970s, beginning work on the 'flat field' which surrounded it in 1972. Within dense windbreaks which do not impede the lovely view west across the Cotswolds to Bredon are a series of small gardens linked by grass paths. Around the house are climbers and borders of unusual plants, to the east more hedges and new shrub plantings.

WESTBURY COURT GARDEN ★★   34
Westbury-on-Severn, Gloucestershire. Tel: (045276) 461

The National Trust ✳ 9m SW of Gloucester on A48, close to the church ✳ Parking ✳ Picnic area ✳ Toilet facilities ✳ Suitable for wheelchairs ✳ Open April to Oct, Wed – Sun and Bank Holiday Mon, 11am – 6pm ✳ Entrance: £1.80, children 90p. Groups of 15 or more by prior arrangement

Seventeenth-century Dutch water garden restored and maintained in pristine condition by The National Trust. Formally-clipped yew hedges sporting stalked pyramids and globes flank rectangular canals planted with water lilies and containing huge carp. A contemporary tall pavilion gives an overview of the parallel canals, one widening to a T-shaped lake with Neptune rising from the deep. The Forest of Dean makes a spectacular backdrop but the great house has gone, alas, and has been replaced by a purpose-built residential home for elderly people. Carefully selected contemporary plants and fan-trained fruit trees flourish against the old walls, and a collection of herbs and medicinal plants, old tulips, dianthus and roses has been assembled and planted in a parterre in an enclosed garden which gives the feel of an outdoor room.

WESTONBIRT ARBORETUM ★★   35
Westonbirt, Gloucestershire. Tel: (066688) 220

The Forestry Commission ✳ 3m SW of Tetbury on A433, 5m NE of junction with A46 ✳ Best seasons: spring and autumn ✳ Parking ✳ Light refreshments at cafe (closed late Nov to Easter). Picnic area ✳ Toilet facilities ✳ Suitable for wheelchairs ✳ Dogs allowed in most areas ✳ Visitor Centre with exhibition and shop (closed late Nov to Easter) ✳ Open all year, 10am – 8pm or dusk ✳ Entrance: £2, OAP and children 5 – 16, £1 (1991 prices)

This is perhaps the finest arboretum in Britain. Started in 1829 by R. Staynor-Holford, Westonbirt was expanded and improved by successive generations of the same family until it was taken over by the Forestry Commission in 1956. Numerous grass rides divide the trees into roughly rectangular blocks, within which are various open spaces and glades used for special plantings such as the famous Japanese maple collection. Westonbirt is noted for its vast range of notable mature specimen trees. Colour is best in spring (rhododendron, magnolias etc) and autumn (Japanese maples, fothergilla) The Forestry Commission is continuing with new planting, for example the Hillier Glade with ornamental cherries. Across the valley from the original arboretum is Silk Valley with collections of native and American species that in spring are carpeted with primroses, wood anemones and bluebells. 17,000 numbered trees and 17 miles of paths.

HAMPSHIRE
& ISLE OF WIGHT

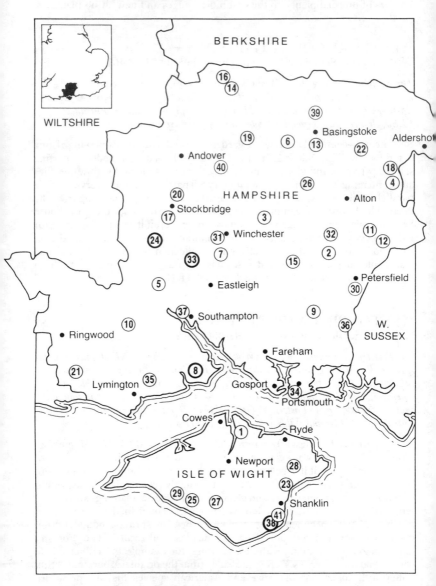

Two-starred gardens are ringed in bold.

BARTON MANOR ★ 1
Whippingham, East Cowes, Isle of Wight. Tel: (0983) 292835

*Robert Stigwood * From E. Cowes A3021, 500 yards beyond Osborne House on left * Best season: mid-May/Aug * Parking * Refreshments: cafeteria and wine bar – all day licence * Toilet facilities * Suitable for wheelchairs * Plants for sale * Shop * Open Easter; 6th to 30th April, Sat and Sun; May to 11th Oct, daily, 10.30am – 5.30pm * Entrance: £3.50 (inc. souvenir tasting glass, wine tasting and guide leaflet), children (one per adult) free (1991 prices)*

Prince Albert's original design included fine trees and the cork grove. The grand terraces were added by Edward VII, and slope down towards Osborne Bay. In 1924 no less than 225,000 daffodils were planted around the lake, which give a fine display in spring. There is also a secret garden planted with azaleas and roses, impressive herbaceous borders and a productive vineyard, wine from which is on sale. In 1968 Hilliers laid out an intriguing water garden on the far side of the lake, on what was originally Queen Victoria's skating rink. The present owners, running the garden and vineyard as a commercial operation, have spared no effort in restoring and maintaining the estate to an immaculate standard. The NCCPG's National collection of red hot pokers (kniphofia) is here.

BRAMDEAN HOUSE ★ 2
Bramdean, Nr Alresford, Hampshire. Tel: (0962 771) 214

*Mr and Mrs H. Wakefield * 10m E of Winchester on A272 at W end of Bramdean * Best season: summer * Parking * Refreshments * Toilet facilities * Plants for sale * Open 15th March, 19th, 20th April, 17th May, 21st June, 19th July, 16th Aug, 2 – 5pm * Entrance: £1, children free*

A bumbling hedge of yew and box swelling out between a pair of armorial gates lends a slightly eccentric air to the south front of the eighteenth-century house and effectively conceals the fine country house garden to the north. A grass path rises steadily from the centre of the garden front forming a vista through the three main sections. The first is dominated by the famous double herbaceous border, lawns and mature trees; a walled kitchen garden defines the second and an orchard watched over by a cupola'ed gazebo the last. The careful composition of colours, foliage and views is a continuous and successful feature of these 'gardens', from *Crambe cordifolia* and onopordums, the spreading *Prunus subhirtella*, yew topiary and huge beeches to the classical and meticulously maintained kitchen garden. The view from the orchard through the wrought iron gates of the walled garden with sundial to the herbaceous borders and lily pond in midsummer is much admired.

BRANDY MOUNT HOUSE 3
Brandy Mount, Alresford, Hampshire. Tel: (0962) 732189

*Mr and Mrs M. Baron * In Alresford town centre. First right in East Street before Sun Lane. No vehicular access * Best season: spring * Parking in Broad Street * Suitable for wheelchairs * Plants for sale * Open 16th Feb, 22nd March,*

12th April, 26th April, 14th June, 2 – 5pm and by appointment on Sats ✳
Entrance: £1, children free

At the end of a small lane is the glade-like garden of Brandy Mount House, with mature trees and shrubs gathered about a well-tended lawn. Daffodils, tulips, snowdrops and hellebores amongst much else bridge the early months as the many and varied herbaceous borders first swell then burst with a true plantsman's collection. At Northington, north of old Alresford, can be found a seminal work in Architectural and Landscape History. Built in 1804 to 1809 to the design of William Wilkins, The Grange was the first country house in Europe designed in the Greek Revival style. Though neglected for many years before restoration the combination of pastoral park and Greek temple is irresistible. Details of Northington Grange available from English Heritage (0962) 734720.

BROADHATCH HOUSE 4
Bentley, Nr Alton, Hampshire. Tel: (0420) 23185

Bruce and Elizabeth Powell ✳ *4m NE of Alton on A31. Turn right at pond ¹/₂m up School Lane, bear right at fork* ✳ *Parking* ✳ *Suitable for wheelchairs* ✳ *Dogs on lead* ✳ *Plants for sale* ✳ *Open 21st June, 2 – 6pm, 22nd June, 11am – 6pm, 11th July, 2 – 6pm, 12th July, 11am – 6pm and by appointment* ✳ *Entrance: £1, children free*

Spreading from the east, south and west of the house the three and a half acres are divided into a series of garden rooms which, although extremely well laid out, are sometimes let down by the absence of a strong feature. However the view through the sunken rose garden with its 'Peace' and hybrid musks to the double herbaceous borders will be sufficient reward for any visitor. The kitchen garden is well-maintained.

BROADLANDS ★ 5
Romsey, Hampshire. Tel: (0794) 516878

Lord Romsey ✳ *S of Romsey on A31. Signposted* ✳ *Parking* ✳ *Refreshments and picnic site* ✳ *Toilet facilities* ✳ *Suitable for wheelchairs* ✳ *Shop* ✳ *Open 16th April to 27th Sept, daily except Fri (but open Good Fri and Fri in Aug), 10am – 4pm* ✳ *Entrance: £4.75, OAP £3.80, children (12 – 16) £3.15*

This former home of Lord Louis Mountbatten has a smooth lawn running from the steps of the porticoed west front to the River Test and spreading parkland trees of beech and cedar come together in a composition that epitomises the eighteenth-century English Landscape School. The elegant Palladianism of Broadlands could only be the work of 'Capability' Brown. To the south of the house a large circular pool and fountain hold centre stage within an enclosure of topiary yew hedges and, to the north and east a series of disappointing walled gardens. In addition to the house, arguably the finest in Hampshire, a classical orangery, ice house and a small garden are perfectly sited in the immaculate lawns amongst noteworthy specimens of magnolias, taxodiums, limes and huge plane trees. It is for these overall impressions rather than details that Broadlands has gained its popularity.

CHURCH OAKLEY GARDENS 6
The Barn House and Oakley Manor, Church Oakley, Nr Basingstoke, Hampshire.

Brigadier and Mrs H.R.W. Vernon and Mr and Mrs R.H. Priestley ✳ *5m W of Basingstoke on B3400. Turn left at Station Road $^{1}/_{2}m$ W of Newfound* ✳ *Parking at Oakley Manor* ✳ *Refreshments* ✳ *Oakley Manor suitable for wheelchairs* ✳ *Plants for sale* ✳ *Open: The Barn House – 2nd Aug; Oakley Manor – 26th April, 2nd Aug, 2 – 6pm* ✳ *Entrance: £1, children 50p (combined admission)*

Lying in the shadow of St Leonards church tower, Oakley Manor and The Barn House are perfectly paired. The Manor, sophisticated and seductive, has sentinel yews, topiary and walled gardens, lavender and limes, and striped lawns and lichen-splashed steps. A short walk away, The Barn House awaits, eager to please with herbaceous borders crammed with clematis, crocosmias, astrantias, alchemillas and lavateras jostling in colour schemes of blue, yellow and red.

HOW TO FIND THE GARDENS
Directions to each garden are included in the entry. This information has been supplied by the garden inspectors and is aimed to be the best available to those travelling by car. However, it has been compiled to be used in conjunction with a road atlas. The unreliability of train and bus services makes it unrewarding to include details, particularly as many garden visits are made on Sundays. However, many properties can be reached by public transport, and National Trust guides and the Yellow Book [NGS] sometimes give details. Future editions of the *Guide* may include a special list of gardens easily reached by public transport if readers indicate that this would be helpful. *The Maps*: The numbers on the maps correspond to the numbers of the gardens in each county. The maps show the proximity of one garden to another so that visits to several gardens can be planned for the same day. It is worthwhile referring to the maps of bordering counties to see if another garden visit can be included in the itinerary.

COMPTON END 7
Compton Street, Compton, Nr Winchester, Hampshire. Tel: (0962) 713342

Captain and Mrs G.A. Kitchin ✳ *3m S of Winchester at end of Compton village* ✳ *Parking, unofficial, along road* ✳ *Partly suitable for wheelchairs* ✳ *Dogs on lead* ✳ *Open 3rd, 4th May, 5th, 6th July, 30th, 31st Aug, 12 noon – 6pm* ✳ *Entrance: £1, children 25p*

Designed and laid out by George Herbert Kitchin from 1895 onwards. That he was a successful architect practised in the Arts and Crafts tradition is obvious in the confident manner of the layout and the assuredness behind the unity of the formal garden with the cottage garden. The garden can be divided into principally three levels, a series of 'rooms' on the upper, croquet/tennis lawn at the mid-point and vegetable/orchard to the south west. The garden is in the style of Hidcote with yew, box hedges, topiary and herbaceous borders, and will not fail to delight every garden lover as well as history enthusiasts.

EXBURY GARDENS ★★ 8
Exbury, Nr Southampton, Hampshire. Tel: (0703) 891203

Mr E.L. de Rothschild ✳ 2¹/₂m SE of Beaulieu, 15m SW of Southampton, via B3054 SE of Beaulieu after 1m turn right for Exbury ✳ Best season: spring/ autumn ✳ Parking ✳ Refreshments ✳ Toilet facilities ✳ Suitable for wheelchairs ✳ Dogs on lead ✳ Plants for sale ✳ Shop ✳ Open early March to late Oct, but part of garden closed early July to early Sept, 10am – 5.30pm ✳ Entrance: £3.50, OAP and children (10 – 16) and parties £2.50 per person (seasonal discounts)

Established in the 1920s and 1930s these outstanding gardens are synonymous with the name of Rothschild and with the development of new hybrid rhododendrons and azaleas over the last 70 years or so. Work on this most beautifully tended woodland garden is continuing and the 200 acres provide aspects of planting from early nineteenth-century cedars and *Sequoiadendron gigantium* (Wellingtonias) to huge swathes of colour such as the apricot or the spectacular 'Lady Chamberlain's Walk' beneath the high canopy of oak and pine. In compositional terms it would be hard to better the layout of the area around the high and low ponds where Japanese maples, cercidiphyllum, *Salix fargesii* and primulas are the pick of the plants and the glimpsed views across the Beaulieu river refreshing. Three separate walks amongst conifers, camellias, wisteria, rock gardens, winter gardens and pools demand that nothing less than a day is spent here.

FAIRFIELD HOUSE ★ 9
Hambledon, Portsmouth, Hampshire. Tel: (0705) 632431

Mr and Mrs P. Wake ✳ 10m SW of Petersfield on B2150 ✳ Best season: June to July ✳ Parking ✳ Refreshments ✳ Toilet facilities ✳ Suitable for wheelchairs ✳ Dogs on lead ✳ Plants for sale ✳ Open by appointment, 2 – 6pm ✳ Entrance: £1, children 50p (suitable for groups)

There can be little doubt that Lanning Roper, who assisted in the establishment of this excellent garden, would approve of the continuing development of the planting at Fairfield, particularly the climbing, shrub and bush roses around and on the elegant white Regency 'colonial' house. Set on a south-facing slope beneath chalk down and sheltered by hedges, walls and a legacy of fine trees, cedars of Lebanon and a stooled lime tree worthy of note, this largely informal garden has been skilfully shaped by the Wakes. The four acres not only host an impressive range of shrub roses, of which there are over 160 in number, but mixed borders of choice specimens, clematis and solanum are very successful, and in spring drifts of bulbs.

FURZEY GARDENS ★ 10
Minstead, Nr Lyndhurst, Hampshire. Tel: (0703) 812464

Mrs M.A. Selwood (Manager) ✳ 8m SW of Southampton, 1m S of A31, 2m W of Cadnam and the end of M27, 3¹/₂m NW of Lyndhurst ✳ Best season: spring ✳ Parking ✳ Refreshments at Honey Pot café ¹/₂m away ✳ Toilet facilities ✳ Plants for sale ✳ Gallery of crafts ✳ Sixteenth-century cottage open daily in summer, weekends in winter ✳ Open daily except 25th and 26th Dec, 10am – 5pm. Dusk in winter ✳ Entrance: £1.95, children 95p, winter £1, children 50p. Reductions for parties by arrangement

This eight-acre garden was laid out by Hew Dalrymple in the early 1920s using plants from the nursery at nearby Bartley. The range of plants, particularly those of Australasian descent, make this garden a must for horticulturalists and plant historians. Situated on a south-facing slope, winding paths lead to many noteworthy and surprisingly large specimens. There is relatively little herbaceous planting but this is more than compensated for by the boldness and density of some of the most colourful planting schemes with the vermilion of Chilean Fire trees in May/June outstanding. Recent replanting has left some gaps in the borders but there does not seem to be anything from lawns to the shaded plants of the water garden that will not flourish here.

THE GILBERT WHITE MUSEUM 11
'The Wakes', Selborne, Alton, Hampshire. Tel: (042050) 275

Oates Memorial Trust ✳ 4¹/₂m S of Alton, 8m N of Petersfield on B3006 ✳ Best season: spring ✳ Parking: public car park behind Selborne Arms ✳ Toilet facilities ✳ Suitable for wheelchairs ✳ Shop ✳ House open ✳ Open Easter to Oct, Wed – Sun and Bank Holidays, 11am – 5.30pm (last admission 5pm). Also open Tues in July and Aug ✳ Entrance: £1.60, OAP/student £1, children 80p

'The Wakes' through the great naturalist Gilbert White's 'Garden Kalender' is probably one of the best documented gardens of the eighteenth century. Since their purchase in 1954 the gardens have been steadily restored to period form and now show many of the flowers described in White's journals. Of the many interesting and period features, the yew topiary, laburnum arbour, herb garden and rose garden should be noted. An original brick path may be followed past an ancient yew and out into the 'Great Mead' where from the shelter of an arbour Selborne Hanger, the parkland trees and the early ha-ha can be enjoyed. Visitors may ponder on the fact that it was at 'The Wakes' that White made the first observations of the value of the earthworm to gardens and farms.

GREATHAM MILL ★ 12
Greatham, Nr Liss, Hampshire. Tel: (04207) 219

Mrs E.N. Pumphrey ✳ 7m SE of Alton. From Alton take B3006 signposted Liss. Through Empshot to bottom of hill. Then ¹/₂m to conspicuous poplar tree where two lanes join road from right. Take first lane (No Through Road) to garden. Or 5m N of Petersfield. At Greatham turn off A325 Petersfield – Farnham road to B3006 signposted Alton and Selbourne. After ¹/₄m turn left into lane marked No Through

Road to garden ✳ *Parking* ✳ *Refreshments: picnic area* ✳ *Toilet facilities* ✳
Plants for sale ✳ *Open mid-April to Sept, Sun and Bank Holiday, 2 – 6pm. Also
by appointment* ✳ *Entrance: £1, children free*

Seemingly protected by the moat-like River Rother and a mill race the 'cottage-
style' garden of Greatham Mill harbours a wide-ranging collection of many
unusual varieties as well as attractive planting associations of the more usual
kind. The seventeenth-century mill half hidden by wisteria provides a romantic
backdrop to a water garden at the front where large leaves and luxuriance of
hostas, royal ferns, rodgersias and gunnera dominate more sensitive planting.
Passing beside and behind the house the full extent of the Pumphrey's
achievements since their arrival here in 1949 can be appreciated. Alpines, in
spreading middle age, grasses and herbaceous plants provide constant ground
cover interest amongst carefully laid out grass paths, enticed by groupings of
choice foliage shrubs, including a curious pencil-thin hedge, and trees.

HACKWOOD PARK (The 'Spring Wood')   13
Basingstoke, Hampshire. Tel: (0256) 23107

The Viscount and Viscoutess Camrose ✳ *1m S of Basingstoke. Entrance is off
Tunworth Road. Signposted* ✳ *Best seasons: spring/autumn* ✳ *Parking* ✳
Refreshments ✳ *Toilet facilities* ✳ *Suitable for wheelchairs* ✳ *Open 12th April
and one day in May, 2 – 6pm and one day in Oct, 1.30 – 5.30pm* ✳ *Entrance:
£1.50, children free*

Furnished with follies to the design of James Gibbs, architect of St Martin-in-
the Fields, and almost certainly laid out under his direction, 'Spring Wood' is
the only complete example in England of a garden wood in the French manner.
Eight Le Nôtre-styled avenues radiate from a central round point leading the
visitor beneath an impressive canopy of specimen and forest trees and revealing
in turn the surprisingly subdued follies by Gibbs and others, the impressive
earthworks of the woodland boundary and of Hackwood House. The nation
probably has Lord Curzon to thank for the preservation of the house, which he
leased after his return from India, much depressed by his treatment by the
wretched Kitchener and by the death of his wife.

HIGHCLERE CASTLE   14
Highclere, Nr Newbury, Hampshire. Tel: (0635) 253210

Lord and Lady Carnarvon ✳ *4¹/₂m S of Newbury on W side of A34* ✳ *Parking*
✳ *Refreshments and picnic area* ✳ *Toilet facilities* ✳ *Suitable for wheelchairs* ✳
Plants for sale at plant centre ✳ *Shop* ✳ *House open* ✳ *Garden open July to
Sept, Wed – Sun and Bank Holidays (Easter and May: Sun and Mon; Whitsun:
Sat – Mon; August: Mon), 2 – 6pm. Last admission 5pm* ✳ *Entrance: £3.50,
OAP £3, disabled and children under 16, £2 (1991 prices). Garden only tickets
available and special group rates*

Though much altered by 'Capability' Brown in the 1770s, Highclere Park will
still reward students of the earlier rococo style with a rare and fine collection of
early eighteenth-century follies. Around Charles Barry's huge battlemented

house an equally fine collection of cedars – North Indian Deodar, Mount Atlas and Lebanon – may be identified, the near horizontal branches of the latter framing views to first of the house and then seemingly of all the district. Relegated to the slopes away from the house, the walled and secret garden is planted in an uncharacteristically cautious manner for Highclere and saved only by James Russell's eye for good spring and summer colour. It was on Lord Carnarvon's estate here that in 1909 the young Geoffrey de Havilland made some of the early powered tests in his wood and fabric flying machine. The savage winter storm of 1990 damaged many lime and beech avenues and tragically destroyed more than 50 cedars of Lebanon depriving the house and estate of many of its memorable and stately vistas. See also entry for Hollington Herb Garden.

THE HILLIER GARDENS AND ARBORETUM
(see The Sir Harold Hillier Gardens and Arboretum)

HINTON AMPNER ★   15
Hinton Ampner, Bramdean, Nr Winchester, Hampshire. Tel: (0962) 771305

The National Trust ✻ *1m W of Bramdean village, 8m E of Winchester on A272* ✻ *Parking. Special entrance for coaches through village* ✻ *Homemade teas in tearoom 2 – 5pm* ✻ *Toilet facilities* ✻ *Suitable for wheelchairs* ✻ *House open Tues and Wed only and Sat and Sun in Aug, 1.30 – 5.30pm (last admission 5pm) £1.30 extra* ✻ *Garden open April to Sept, Sat, Sun, Tues, Wed and Bank Holiday Mons, 1.30 – 5.30pm (last admission 5pm)* ✻ *Entrance: £2. Pre-booked parties to house and garden £2.80 per person. Bookings and enquiries to: The Administrator, Hinton Ampner House, Alresford, Hampshire SO24 0LA*

Located on the shoulder of a ridge, the ascent to the house through almost routine parkland in no way prepares the visitor for the view to the south of classic English downland scenery over a series of descending terraces laid out in the Hidcote style. From his inheritance of the estate in 1935 onwards Ralph Dutton, later Lord Sherborne, set about transforming the remnants of a Victorian/Edwardian park into a series of gardens on different levels linked by the 'Long Walk' and the 'main terrace'. The skill with which features such as the temple, obelisk and statue of Diana are sited and with which many surprise vistas were created is testimony to Lord Sherborne's knowledge of garden history. Although areas of the garden are in the process of restoration and some large shrubs need to be rescued, both from rampant climbers, Russian vine and Kiftsgate roses and undisciplined pruning, the masterly design of this garden and the elegance of its topiary, yew and box hedges deserve wide recognition.

HOLLINGTON HERB GARDEN   16
Woolton Hill, Nr Newbury, Berkshire. Tel: (0635) 263908

Mr and Mrs S.G. Hopkinson ✻ *4m S of Newbury off A343. Follow signs to Herb*

Garden ✳ *Best season: summer* ✳ *Parking* ✳ *Refreshments* ✳ *Toilet facilities* ✳ *Suitable for wheelchairs* ✳ *Plants for sale* ✳ *Shop* ✳ *Open March to Sept, daily, 10am – 5.30pm, Sun and Bank Holidays, 11am – 5pm, Oct to Mar, Mon – Fri, 10am – 5pm* ✳ *Entrance: free. Collecting box for charity*

Interestingly laid out, this small garden modestly but successfully combines the function of a sales pitch for its specimen plants with the art of garden design. Set within an old walled garden, a small fountain, knot garden and rampant hop climbing over gnarled espalier provide the visual treats, but it is the pot-pourri of aromas that distinguishes this garden and nursery. It could be combined with a visit to Highclere Castle nearby (see entry).

HOUGHTON LODGE ★ 17
Stockbridge, Hampshire. Tel: (0264) 810177/(0264) 810502

Captain and Mrs M. Busk ✳ *6m S of Andover, 1¹/₂m S of Stockbridge on minor road signposted Houghton* ✳ *Best season: spring* ✳ *Parking* ✳ *Refreshments on Easter Sun, Bank Holidays and charity days. Picnic area* ✳ *Suitable for wheelchairs* ✳ *Plants for sale* ✳ *House open by appointment only* ✳ *Gardens, greenhouse and hydroponicum open March to Sept, Sats and Suns, 10am – 5pm, Mon, Tues and Fri, 2 – 5pm. Other times by appointment. Coach parties welcome by prior appointment* ✳ *Entrance: £2.50*

Built shortly before 1801 Houghton Lodge is probably among the most 'picturesque' of Gothic cottage ornés both in its architectural fantasy and its perfect garden setting alongside the River Test. Marie Antoinette would certainly have approved of this idyll. A succession of snowdrops and massed daffodils beneath fine parkland specimens of plane, oaks and horse chestnuts clothe the ridge beyond the lawns from where a unique rustic flint grotto can be reached; in autumn the colours of Indian gums and maples can be observed reflected in the river. The Hampshire Hydroponicum, believed to be the first set up for public display of plant culture without soil in England, was opened in early 1990 within the chalk cob walls of the kitchen garden. Replanting of the gardens is being undertaken with the advice of the landscape historian David Jacques.

JENKYN PLACE ★ 18
Bentley, Nr Alton, Hampshire. Tel: (0420) 23118

Mrs Patricia Coke ✳ *4m SW of Farnham on A31, signposted 400 yards N of Bentley crossroads* ✳ *Parking* ✳ *Toilet facilities* ✳ *Suitable for wheelchairs* ✳ *Plants usually for sale* ✳ *Open 9th April to 6th Sept, Thurs – Sun and Bank Holiday Mons, 2 – 6pm* ✳ *Entrance: £2, children 75p*

Since their arrival just after World War II Mr and Mrs Coke have created a remarkable garden that is somewhat reminiscent of Hidcote, both in spirit and structure. Falling steadily to the south-east the high ground of this garden is dominated by a series of formal rooms arranged on terraces of which the sundial garden, an elegant rose garden (note the *Caesalpinia japonica* and loquat shrub), and a scented Dutch garden are the pick. A classically-perfect double herbaceous border backed by high hedges ends the sequence of walled and hedged enclosures and leads by way of cross axis to a succession of less intensively and informally planted areas which do tend to be less successful in design. A long sloping lawn returns to the house revealing the handsome seventeenth-century facade and a superb Cedar of Lebanon planted in 1828. This is a garden to be visited more than once.

LAVERSTOKE HOUSE 19
Laverstoke, Nr Whitchurch, Hampshire. Tel: (0256) 770245

Mr and Mrs Julian Sheffield ✳ 2m E of Whitchurch, 10m W of Basingstoke on B3400 ✳ Parking ✳ Suitable for wheelchairs ✳ Dogs on lead ✳ Open by appointment, 2 – 5.30pm ✳ Entrance: 80p, children 20p

Rebuilt by Joseph Bonomi in 1796-98, Laverstoke was home to the Portal family, founders of the nearby paper mills where Bank of England notes were made for over 200 years. Beneath the imposing yellow brick facades and giant portico, the owners have laid out a terrace and garden of great style and poise; a collection of old-fashioned shrub roses underplanted with *Alchemilla mollis* is particularly effective. If it is the great imagination of the Sheffields that is shaping the gardens immediately around the house, it is their good fortune that many good hands planted the impressive parkland trees that accompany the descent from Laverstoke to the River Test.

LONGSTOCK PARK GARDENS ★ 20
Longstock, Nr Stockbridge, Hampshire. Tel: (0264) 810894

John Lewis Partnership (Leckford Estates Ltd) ✳ 2m N of Stockbridge. From A30 turn N on A3057. Signposted ✳ Parking ✳ Refreshments at Leckford ✳ Toilet facilities ✳ Suitable for wheelchairs ✳ Plants for sale ✳ Open April to Sept, 3rd Sun of each month, 2 – 5pm ✳ Entrance: £1.50, children 50p (1991 prices)

The huge leaves of gunnera, the stilts (pneumatophores) of *Taxodium distichum*, varied nymphaeas and a giant white lily, *Cardiocrinum giganteum*, are just a few of the many interesting features and unusual plants to be found in this most immaculate and loveliest of water gardens. Developed between 1946 and 1953 the garden is fed by the River Test and is located some way from the house. Approached with an air of increasing expectation between a high hedge and old oak trees the garden reveals itself all at once as a veritable archipelago connected by narrow bridges and causeways beneath which clear waters and golden carp slowly move. The background is formed by woodland trees into which a variety of acid-loving trees and shrubs and wild flowers have been introduced as a contrast to the sometimes over-disciplined planting of this successful garden.

WHEELCHAIR USERS
Please note that entries which describe a garden as 'suitable for wheelchairs' refer to the garden only. If there is a house open, it may or may not be suitable for wheelchairs.

MACPENNYS NURSERIES AND WOODLAND GARDENS 21
Burley Road, Bransgore, Nr Christchurch, Hampshire.

Mr and Mrs T.M. Lowndes ✳ *Midway between Christchurch and Burley. Turn N off A35 Lyndhurst – Bournemouth road at Hinton Admiral (Cat and Fiddle), right at Bransgore crossroads (Crown) on ¹/₄m on right* ✳ *Best season: spring* ✳ *Parking* ✳ *Teas at Holmsley Old Station Tearooms or Burley Forest Tearooms* ✳ *Suitable for wheelchairs* ✳ *Dogs on lead* ✳ *Plants for sale* ✳ *Open daily except 25th, 26th Dec and 1st Jan, Mon – Sat, 9am – 5pm, Sun, 2 – 5pm* ✳ *Entrance: collecting box for donations to charity which are not required for customers visiting nursery*

There is something about the very name Macpennys that promises the well-stocked nursery that one finds at Bransgore. The gravel pit alongside provides a highly successful way of extending the plant collection into a most unusual woodland garden. Magnolias, camellias, pieris and rhododendrons all flourish beneath a canopy of pine somewhat savaged by the recent severe winter storms. A labyrinthine series of paths (from which one is invited to scramble to reach labels) eventually return to the nursery where many of the plants seen can be purchased.

THE MANOR HOUSE 22
Upton Grey, Nr Basingstoke, Hampshire. Tel: (0256) 862827

Mr and Mrs J. Wallinger ✳ *6m SE of Basingstoke in Upton Grey village on hill immediately above church* ✳ *Best season: May to July* ✳ *Parking. Coaches by appointment only* ✳ *Teas available if notice given* ✳ *A few plants for sale* ✳ *Open by appointment and 20th, 27th May, 3rd, 10th, 24th June, 29th July, 23rd September, 2 – 5pm* ✳ *Entrance: £1.50*

Here are formal gardens and terraces with excellent herbaceous borders and dry-stone walling. They have been meticulously restored by the present owners over the past five years to the original plans prepared by Gertrude Jekyll in 1908 – 1910 and this garden illustrates many of the designer's favourite herbaceous planting combinations. The yew hedging in the formal garden is far from maturity and consequently deprives the scene of much needed structure but the colour and shape are clearly evident. To the south-west is an informal wild garden and pool. The house was designed by Ernest Newton for Charles Holmes, editor of *The Studio* magazine.

MORTON MANOR 23
Brading, Sandown, Isle of Wight. Tel: (0983) 406168

J.B., J. and J.A. Trzebski ✳ *3m from Ryde on A3055, turn right at Brading traffic lights, signposted 100 yards up hill* ✳ *Best season: April to June* ✳ *Parking* ✳ *Refreshments: morning coffee, lunch, cream teas. Fully licensed* ✳ *Toilet facilities* ✳ *Suitable for wheelchairs* ✳ *Dogs on lead* ✳ *Home-grown plants and vines for sale* ✳ *Shop* ✳ *House open* ✳ *Vineyard and winery* ✳ *Garden open 5th April – Oct, daily except Sat, 10am – 5.30pm* ✳ *Entrance: £2.20, OAP £1.75, children £1 (1991 prices)*

The history of Morton dates back to the thirteenth century. The Elizabethan sunken garden is surrounded by a 400 year old box hedge and old-fashioned roses and shaded by a magnificent *Magnolia grandiflora*. The terraces are nineteenth-century with extensive herbaceous borders and a huge London plane. Masses of spring bulbs are followed by rhododendrons and traditional herbaceous displays. Among the wide range of fine trees is an Indian Bean (*Catalpa bignonioides*). Little remains of the old walled garden but in the corner behind the herbs are the restored bee boles; also a turf maze has been made for children, and there is a vineyard. A recent addition is a range of Japanese maples.

MOTTISFONT ABBEY GARDEN ★★   24
Mottisfont, Nr Romsey, Hampshire. Tel: (0794) 40757

The National Trust ✳ *4¹/₂m NW of Romsey, ¹/₂m W of A3057* ✳ *Best season: midsummer* ✳ *Parking* ✳ *Refreshments at local post office* ✳ *Toilet facilities* ✳ *Suitable for wheelchairs* ✳ *Dogs in car park only* ✳ *Shop* ✳ *Open April to Sept, daily except Fri and Sat, 2 – 6pm (last admission 5pm). Evening opening of rose garden Tues, Wed, Thurs and Sun, 7 – 9pm during rose season only (check first) (last admission 8.30pm)* ✳ *Entrance: £2.30. Bookings and enquiries to The Head Gardener, The White House, Hart Lane, Mottisfont, Nr Romsey S051 OLJ. Tel: (0794) 41220 during opening hours, other times (0794) 40757*

Established in only 1972, the walled rose garden designed by Graham Stuart Thomas is already famous and deservedly so. Between the gravel paths, meeting at a small pool and fountain, are assembled one of the most comprehensive collections of old French roses of the nineteenth century, seen and smelt at its best in midsummer when the scent is trapped within its walls. Broad herbaceous borders containing pinks, aubretias, saponarias and much else ensure that from very early in the season there is always something to enjoy. It is to be hoped that the visitor will not miss, if it is possible to miss, the enormous London plane trees, *Platanus x hybrida (acerfolia)* (the largest in the country) that occupy parkland sweeping down to the River Test. Pockets of formal gardens can be found around the house created by such accomplished designers as Geoffrey Jellicoe (the pleached lime walk underplanted with *Chionodoxa luciliae*) and Norah Lindsay. The Abbey (tenanted) contains a drawing room decorated by muralist Rex Whistler but access is limited.

MOTTISTONE MANOR   25
Mottistone, Newport, Isle of Wight. Tel: (0983) 740946

The National Trust ✳ *SW of Newport on B3399 between Brighstone and Brook* ✳ *Best season: May/June* ✳ *Parking* ✳ *House open Aug Bank Holiday only. £1.50 extra* ✳ *Garden open April to Sept, Wed only and Bank Holiday Mon, 2 – 5.30pm (last admission 5pm)* ✳ *Entrance: £1.70, children 85p*

A terraced garden, best seen in late spring for a glorious display of irises, laid out to gain maximum effect from the views over the Needles, Channel and south-west coast of the island. Not so much a plantsman's garden as an impressive frame for the Manor.

MOUNDSMERE MANOR   26
Preston Candover, Nr Basingstoke, Hampshire. Tel: (025687) 207

Mr and Mrs Andreae ✳ *6m S of Basingstoke on B3046. Drive gates on left just after Preston Candover sign* ✳ *Parking. Coaches by appointment* ✳ *Suitable for wheelchairs* ✳ *Dogs on lead* ✳ *Open 5th July, 2 – 6pm* ✳ *Entrance: £1, children 50p*

Inspired by Hampton Court and designed in 1908, the pleasing relationship of house to garden to landscape marks Moundsmere Manor as one of Sir Reginald Blomfield's (1856-1942) best surviving gardens. To the south of the 'Wrenaissance' house the principal formal garden descends in terraces framed by clipped yews with deep herbaceous borders. This is Edwardian gardening on a grand scale, characteristically architectural, and will not disappoint students of Blomfield's *The Formal Garden in England* in which he attacked the informal style of gardening supported by William Robinson. For Blomfield, gardens were primarily works of art. Other examples of his work are found at Godington Park (Kent) and Athelhampton (Dorset) (see entries). There is a pinetum to the north.

WHEELCHAIR USERS
Please note that entries which describe a garden as 'suitable for wheelchairs' refer to the garden only. If there is a house open, it may or may not be suitable.

DOGS, TOILETS & OTHER FACILITIES
If these are *not* mentioned in the text, then facilities are not available. For example, if dogs are not mentioned, owners will probably not permit entry, even on a lead.

NORTHCOURT ★   27
Shorwell, Newport, Isle of Wight. Tel: (0983) 740415

Mr and Mrs J. Harrison ✳ *4m S of Newport on B3323. Entrance on right after rustic bridge, opposite thatched cottage* ✳ *Best season: May/June* ✳ *Parking* ✳ *Refreshments* ✳ *Partly suitable for wheelchairs* ✳ *Dogs on lead (under sufferance)* ✳ *Plants sometimes for sale* ✳ *Open 24th May, 20th June, 2 – 5pm. (The period 15th to 21st June is Heritage Week for the Isle of Wight Gardens Trust and John Harrison has arranged for several beautiful Isle of Wight gardens to be open at that time which are not normally open to the public). Groups of 10 or more can book for special opening May and June only* ✳ *Entrance: approx. £1.20 (varies according to charity)*

Twelve acres of wooded grounds surround a Jacobean manor house. There are three varied gardens (divided between members of the Harrison family) consisting of landscaped terraces leading down to the stream and water gardens; herbaceous borders, woodland walks, walled rose garden and walled kitchen garden containing over 50 varieties of apples. The more interesting plants include *Echium pininana* (biennial from the Canaries) on the top terrace by the pond; eucryphias; and the dainty little daisy *Erigeron mucronatus* in the rose garden that may have been inspired by Gertrude Jekyll. Northcourt offers bed and breakfast accomodation and could be the ideal spot for a gardener's tour of the Isle of Wight.

NUNWELL HOUSE 28
Coach Lane, Brading, Ryde, Isle of Wight. Tel: (0983) 407240

Col. and Mrs J.A. Aylmer ✻ *3m S of Ryde, signed off the A3055 in Brading into Coach Lane* ✻ *Best season: July and September* ✻ *Parking* ✻ *Toilet facilities* ✻ *Shop* ✻ *House open* ✻ *Garden open 5th July to 24th Sept, daily except Fri and Sat, 10am – 5pm* ✻ *Entrance: £2.30, OAP £1.80, children 60p (house and garden)*

Nunwell House stands in six acres of gardens with wonderful views across the park to Spithead. The rose garden (originally a bowling green in the seventeenth century) is set at the top of a slope, in front of the walled garden (not open), which leads down the Long Walk past the side of the house, where stand two very handsome paulownias, to the front. The fountain came from the Crystal Palace and below the balustrade is a lily pond, formerly a swimming pool. Among the varied plants in the borders there is the pretty mallow 'Barnsley' and on the front of the house are two large myrtles. A steep flight of steps bordered by lavender leads up to the woods. To the rear of the house is an arboretum laid out by Russel Vernon Smith in 1963. The Aylmers are gradually restoring the gardens to their former glory.

OWL COTTAGE ★ 29
Hoxall Lane, Mottistone, Newport, Isle of Wight. Tel: (0983) 740433

Mrs A.I. Hutchinson, Miss S.L. Leaning ✻ *From B3399 turn down Hoxall Lane by Mottistone green. Owl Cottage is 200 yards on right* ✻ *Best season: late June/ early July* ✻ *Refreshments: homemade teas by appointment* ✻ *Toilet facilities* ✻ *Suitable for wheelchairs* ✻ *Dogs* ✻ *Open May to Aug, 2 – 6pm, by appointment for parties of 10 or more (max. 24)* ✻ *Entrance: £1*

A brilliant cottage garden with sea views (the thatched cottage is sixteenth-century), planted to give year round colour. There are 23 flowering cherries and over 50 varieties of clematis, including the *balearica* flowering in sequence from January to October and the *armandii*. In addition to a large herbaceous section there are colourful bulbs and flowering shrubs, euphorbias, amaryllis lilies, agapanthus and delphiniums. The garden is the creation of the present owners.

PETERSFIELD PHYSIC GARDEN 30
16 High Street, Petersfield, Hampshire. Tel: (0730) 64709

Hampshire Gardens Trust ✻ *Located to the rear of No 16 High Street with access*

from High Street ✳ *Best season: spring and summer* ✳ *Suitable for wheelchairs*
✳ *Plants for sale* ✳ *Open all year except 25th Dec, 9am – 5pm* ✳ *Entrance: free,*
donations welcome

Held within the arms of a walled garden that reach out to the rear of Petersfield High Street is the latest of a series of remarkable historic garden recreations undertaken by the Hampshire Gardens Trust. A small physic garden attended by beds holding the John Goodyer collection, named after the seventeenth-century Petersfield botanist, is rapidly establishing itself as a retreat for research or pleasure, for local residents, horticulturalists and latterday students of medicine and botany. The care and attention to detail is worthy of note and promises much for the knot garden and topiary walk to follow. Such ambition should be encouraged by contributing to the collection box and returning often.

QUEEN ELEANOR'S GARDEN   31
Great Hall, Castle Avenue, High Street, Winchester, Hampshire. Tel: (0962) 846476

Hampshire County Council (sponsored by Hampshire Gardens Trust) ✳ *Through the Great Hall, central Winchester* ✳ *Public car park nearby in Sussex Street* ✳ *Suitable for wheelchairs* ✳ *Shop* ✳ *Open daily except Good Fri and 25th, 26th Dec, 10am – 5pm, (4pm on winter weekends)* ✳ *Entrance: free*

Faced with a wedge of land 90 x 30 feet and bounded by buildings, the designer, Dr Sylvia Landsberg, has achieved the only authentic recreation of its type in Britain of a thirteenth-century medieval pleasure garden. When viewed against the neighbouring wall of the Great Hall the maturing Queen's herber, tunnel arbour and the detailed research behind the rill and fountain make it possible to forget that this is a garden of recent creation.

ROTHERFIELD PARK   32
East Tisted, Alton, Hampshire. Tel: (042058) 204

Sir James and Lady Scott ✳ *4m S of Alton on A32* ✳ *Parking* ✳ *☆Teas when house open. Picnickers welcome* ✳ *Dogs on lead* ✳ *Plants for sale* ✳ *House open Bank Holiday Suns and Mons and 1st to 7th June, 1st to 7th July, 1st to 7th Aug, 2 – 5pm* ✳ *Gardens open as house but also April to Sept, Sun and Thurs, 2 – 5pm* ✳ *Entrance: £1, children free (house and gardens £2.50)*

Living at Chawton, less than 10m north, Jane Austen would have counted herself a neighbour, and an approving one, to Rotherfield estate which underwent picturesque improvement at the hands of J.T. Parkinson from 1815-1821. The elevated and exposed position of the house is superb and ideally suited to the lofty gothic architecture if not the sweet chestnuts and oaks which just survived the hurricanes of 1987 and 1990. The garden sensibly leaves the slopes to parkland and finds shelter in the walled area away from the watchful castellations, colonnades and turrets of the house. Approached between yew hedges, buttressed with the golden variety, wrought-iron gates open to herbaceous borders, fan-trained apricots and apples and espalier fruit trees. Mindful of the disapproval of Miss Austen, remnants of the earlier eighteenth-century gardens are hidden in the park's woodlands.

THE SIR HAROLD HILLIER GARDENS AND ARBORETUM ★★ 33
Jermyns Lane, Ampfield, Nr Romsey, Hampshire. Tel: (0794) 68787

*Hampshire County Council * 3m NE of Romsey, 9m SW of Winchester, ³/₄m W of A31 along Jermyns Lane. Signposted from A31 and A3057 * Parking * Light refreshments at weekends and Bank Holidays April to Oct, 12 noon – 5pm * Toilet facilities * Suitable for wheelchairs * Plants for sale at Hilliers Nursery/ Garden Centre * Open all year Mon – Fri, 10.30am – 5pm. Weekends and Bank Holidays, March to Nov, 10.30am – 6pm. For summer evening and winter weekend opening telephone for further details. Brentry Woodland open late spring only * Entrance: £2, OAP £1.50, children under 15, 75p at weekends and Bank Holidays, free on weekdays. Season tickets £7.50. For parties exceeding 30 adults, £1.50 per head*

Administered by Hampshire County Council since 1977 this enormous collection of trees and shrubs was begun in 1953 by the late Sir Harold Hillier using his house and garden as a starting point. Extends to 160 acres and includes approximately 14,000 different species and cultivars, with many rarities. With a total of 36,000 plants it is impossible not to be impressed or to learn something about how, what and where to plant. Seasonal interest maps and labelling will lead the visitor to herbaceous, scree, heather and bog gardens. Amongst the trees and shrubs *Eucalyptus nitens* and *niphophila*, *Magnolia cylindrica* and the acers are worthy of note. Much more than an arboretum this attractively laid-out garden can be enjoyed at many levels and can only increase in interest as the immense collection of young trees gains in maturity. Keen gardeners should partake little and often and always be armed with a notebook.

SOUTHSEA COMMON AND ESPLANADE SEAFRONT GARDENS 34
Clarence and Southsea Esplanade, Portsmouth, Hampshire. Inquiries to Tourist Information Centre. Tel: (0705) 826722/832464/838382

*Follow directions for Old Portsmouth but from Anglesey Road one way system turn left into Hampshire Terrace, continue to Pier Road and turn left down Clarence Esplanade * Best season: June to Sept * Southsea Castle car park and public parking nearby * Toilet facilities * Suitable for wheelchairs * Dogs * Open all year * Entrance: free*

The heathland origins of Southsea Common and Esplanade could not be further from the minds of the many thousands of tourists as they admire year after year the extensive bedding out and manicured gardens. Quintessentially English, a tour of approximately four and a half miles will brazenly confirm the highest, or worst, expectations of what the pleasure grounds of a seaside resort should be.

SPINNERS ★ 35
School Lane, Boldre, Nr Lymington, Hampshire. Tel: (0590) 673347

*Mr and Mrs P.G.G. Chappell * 1¹/₂m N of Lymington. From A337 Brockenhurst*

*– Lymington road, turn E for Boldre. Signposted * Parking * Wide selection of plants for sale in nursery * Open mid-April to Aug, daily, 9am – 6pm. Other times by appointment. Nursery open all year * Entrance: £1*

Created and developed by the Chappells on a wooded slope falling westwards towards the Lymington river it is not difficult to understand why Roy Lancaster and many other plantsmen have so highly praised this garden. The spirit of the nearby New Forest has been carefully maintained and shade and acid-loving plants flourish beneath a canopy of indigenous and specimen shrubs and trees. *Cornus kousa chinensis*, a grove of eucalyptus and unusual magnolias catch the eye amongst many other specimens that are improved by good plant associations. Cyclamen, erythroniums, trillium and hellebores in spring; lush hostas, primulas, ferns and rodgersias in the bog garden; magnolias in summer and the autumn colours of *Nyssa sinensis* and many maples ensure that wherever the meandering paths lead in this excellent informal garden there is always something of interest and apparently something of everything.

STANSTED PARK   36
Rowlands Castle, Hampshire. Tel: (0705) 412265

*The Earl and Countess of Bessborough * 1m N of Emsworth, just off the B2149 * Best season: early summer * Parking * Refreshments * Toilet facilities * Plants for sale * Shop * House open * Garden open Easter Sun and Mon, May to Sept, Sun – Tues inc. Bank Holidays, 2 – 5.30pm (last admission 5pm) * Entrance: £2, children under 12 £1 (house and gardens £3.50, OAP £3, children under 12 £1.50. Parties of 20 or more £3, children £1 per person)*

A woodland walk with fine spring bulbs encloses walled gardens with good greenhouses with muscat vines and other organically-grown produce. There is an elegant Dutch-style rose garden, which is set off beautifully by the mellow red brick eighteenth-century house, and a fine arboretum which is quickly recovering from the gale damage of 1987. There is also a prettily set cricket ground with cricket every Sunday, taking place in view of the tea room.

THE TUDOR HOUSE MUSEUM   37
Tudor House, Bugle Street, Southampton, Hampshire. Tel: (0703) 332513

*Southampton City Council * A36 to West Quay Road or Western Esplanade or A33, follow signs to Docks and Town Quay * Public car park on Western Esplanade * Toilet facilities * Suitable for wheelchairs * Shop * Museum open * Open Tues – Fri, 10am – 12 noon, 1 – 5pm, Sat, 10am – 12 noon, 1 – 4pm, Sun, 2 – 5pm * Entrance: free*

This must be many people's favourite museum, not particularly for its collection although it is good, but for its timber-framed building and garden setting. Designed by Dr Sylvia Landsberg and completed in 1982, the garden is a convincing distillation of ornamental gardens of the Tudor period. Packed with authentic details, heraldic beasts, camomile lawn, knot garden and many old English flowers and sixteenth-century roses this is a surprisingly peaceful place.

VENTNOR BOTANIC GARDEN ★★ 38
The Undercliffe Drive, Ventnor, Isle of Wight. Tel: (0983) 855397

South Wight Borough Council ✻ Follow signs from A3055 ✻ Paying car park ✻ Refreshments: restaurant/café, licensed bar ✻ Toilet facilities ✻ Suitable for wheelchairs ✻ Dogs on lead ✻ Limited plants for sale ✻ Shop ✻ Open all year. Temperate House, Easter to Oct, daily, 10am – 5pm, Nov to Easter, Tues – Thurs, 11am – 3pm and Sun 1 – 4pm ✻ Entrance: free (Temperate House 50p, children 20p subject to variation)

Twenty-two acres, sheltered from north and east and planted with *Quercus ilex*, *Pinus nigra* and cypresses interspersed with escallonia, griselinia and viburnums to give shelter from sea winds to the south. Many tender plants (including olives; *Berberis asiatica* and *Acer sikkimensis* from the Himalayas; *Cestrum elegans* from Mexico; *Pittosporum daphniphylloides* from China all of which flourish in the mild climate). The rose garden has over 700 hybrid teas and floribundas also modern shrub, Banksian, climbing, rambler, rugosa, etc. The pinetum has many exotic species from the Canary Islands, New Zealand and China and in the palm garden banana plants from Japan and *Citrus ichangensis* are but a few of the rare plants displayed to maximum effect in surroundings designed by Geoffrey Hillier. There is also a magnificent temperate house with a worldwide collection of plants from the warmest zones of the world, together with impressive written and pictorial displays. There is an Australian section, a central bed of flowers from southern Africa, an island section with palms from Crete and a unique collection from St Helena. Damage by gales in 1987 and 1990 has caused the management to begin replanting with windproof varieties.

THE VYNE 39
Sherborne St John, Nr Basingstoke, Hampshire. Tel: (0256) 881337

The National Trust ✻ 4m N of Basingstoke between Sherborne St John and Bramley on A340, turn E at NT signs ✻ Parking ✻ Refreshments: light lunches, homemade teas, 12.30 – 2pm, 2.30 – 5.30pm ✻ Toilet facilities ✻ Suitable for wheelchairs ✻ Dogs in car park only ✻ Shop ✻ House open 1.30 – 5.30pm (last admission 5pm) ✻ Garden open April to 24th Oct, daily except Mon and Fri (but open Good Fri), 12.30 – 5.30pm. Open Bank Holiday Mon (but closed Tues following), 11am – 5.30pm ✻ Entrance: £1.90 (house £3.80). Parties £2.50 per person Tues – Thurs only

This example of the English School was landscaped by John Chute between 1755 and 1776 to complement the early classical portico and garden houses designed by John Webb, disciple of Inigo Jones. Though not as grand or extensive as many country houses in the ownership of The National Trust this early sixteenth-century house provides to the west of its modest entrance one of the best though small, herbaceous borders of such properties and to the north broad lawns and fine trees that perfectly match the famous Corinthian portico. The framed views to the house from across the lake will amply reward those who venture on the woodland walk. Other features include stone seats in architectural yews, great oaks, the Garden House lake and *Phillyrea latifolia* specimens.

WHITE WINDOWS 40
Longparish, Nr Andover, Hampshire. Tel: (026472) 222

Mrs J. Sterndale-Bennett ✳ 5m E of Andover. Off A303 to Longparish village on B3048 ✳ Parking ✳ Refreshments on Suns ✳ Suitable for wheelchairs ✳ Plants for sale ✳ Open 6th, 7th Sept, 2 – 6pm and by appointment April to Sept, Weds, 11am – 5pm ✳ Entrance: £1, children 10p

There is a curiously theatrical air to the garden at White Windows. So carefully staged is the layout and the planting combinations that the whole display is like a series of windows swung open to public view. Begun in 1980, the Sterndale-Bennetts have already assembled an impressive collection of plants. The best has still to be seen of the many specimen plants which, young in years, mingle with the herbaceous 'chorus line'. However, the scene has been busily and cleverly set for their ascendency.

YAFFLES 41
Bonchurch, Ventnor, Isle of Wight. Tel: (0983) 852193

Mrs Wolfenden ✳ Immediately above St Boniface Church in Bonchurch ✳ Best season: April/May ✳ Parking in road ✳ Refreshments: home-made teas ✳ Dogs on lead ✳ Plants for sale ✳ Shop ✳ Open 3rd May, 14th June, 2.30 – 5pm ✳ Entrance: £1, children free

A quarter of an acre of sheltered cliff garden with spectacular sea views, sculpted by Mrs Wolfenden from a precipice overgrown with weeds and scrub. Years of very hard work have made this garden of ledges and glades, with a variety of flowering shrubs, spring bulbs and plants of botanical interest. Taking advantage of the mild climate of the island's undercliff the owner has succeeded in creating a sheet of colour all the year round.

HEREFORD
AND WORCESTER

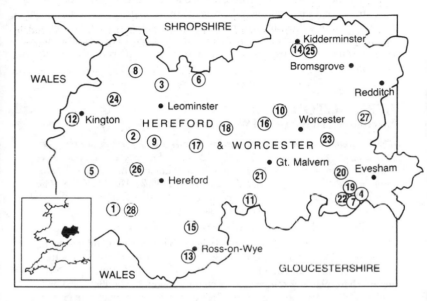

Two-starred gardens are ringed in bold.

ABBEY DORE COURT 1
Abbey Dore, Hereford, Hereford and Worcester. Tel: (0981) 240419

Mrs C.L. Ward ✳ 11m SW of Hereford ✳ Parking ✳ Refreshments: from 11.30am ✳ Toilet facilities ✳ Partly suitable for wheelchairs ✳ Plants for sale ✳ Gift gallery ✳ Garden open 21st March to 18th Oct, daily except Wed, 11am – 6pm ✳ Entrance: £1.50, children 50p

Mrs Ward is a noted plantswoman and the large garden has much of interest. Two old sequoias dominate the garden once edged by the river but now extended into a meadow with a pool and well-planted rockery. Another recent area of expansion contains a more formal arrangement in which greys and whites are much in evidence and in large beds near the walled fruit garden there is the NCCPG collection of sedums.

ARROW COTTAGE GARDEN 2
Ledgemoor, Weobley, Hereford and Worcester. Tel: (0544) 318468

*Mr and Mrs L. Hattatt * 10m NW of Hereford * Best season: May/June *
Parking on roadside * Open March to July, Sept, Wed – Fri and Sun, 2 – 5pm.
Closed Aug. At other times by appointment * Entrance: £1, children free*

Designed as a series of small gardens by the present owner and his family since
1972. The older part of the garden, planted long before the expansion over the
little stream that winds through the property is, perhaps, rather reminiscent of
the surroundings of an ideal Wendy House and there is a marked contrast on
crossing the tiny bridge to later and more formal areas. The one and a half acres
contain some interesting flowers, trees and shrubs and everything is very well
maintained.

BERRINGTON HALL 3
Leominster, Hereford and Worcester. Tel: (0568) 5721

*The National Trust * 3m S of Leominster on W side of A49 * Parking *
Refreshments: lunches and teas (opening 12.30pm) Picnic tables in car park *
Toilet facilities * Suitable for wheelchairs * National Trust shop * House
open * Garden open April, Sat, Sun and Bank Holiday Mon, 1.30 – 5.30pm.
May to Sept, Wed – Sun and Bank Holiday Mon, 1.30 – 5.30pm. Oct, Sat and
Sun, 1.30 – 4.30pm (last admission $^1/_2$ hour before closing). Grounds open from
12.30pm * Entrance: £1.20 (house and grounds £3.10)*

This late eighteenth-century house designed by Henry Holland is set in mature
grounds landscaped by 'Capability' Brown. The gardens have seen better times
but are well-maintained. The new woodland area needs time to mature and a
new orchard planting scheme has been undertaken by the Hereford branch of
the NCCPG in the walled garden. There is a joint entry ticket with Croft Castle
nearby (see entry) and the best value for intending visitors is the joint ticket
giving entry to both houses and gardens, although those not interested in the
houses may feel that the afternoon becomes a little expensive.

BREDON SPRINGS 4
**Ashton-under-Hill, Evesham, Hereford and Worcester. Tel: (0386)
881328**

*Mr R. Sidwell * 6m SW of Evesham * Best season: early summer * Small
free car park 300 yards from garden * Dogs * Open April to Oct, Sat, Sun,
Wed, Thurs, also Bank Holiday Mons and following Tues, 10am – dusk *
Entrance: 75p, children free*

A plantsman's garden created by the owner over the last 40 years with a diverse
collection of material, carefully arranged and planted in an old cottage garden.
Areas of woodland have been added to increase the range of growing
conditions. There are signs of a decline and some of the plantings are becoming
overgrown. In several parts of the garden the aggressive weed *Hippuris vulgaris*,
marestail or horsetail, is becoming well established. Nevertheless, a garden
which still retains some unusual and interesting plants.

BROBURY GARDENS AND GALLERY   5
Brobury, Hereford and Worcester. Tel: (09817) 229

Mr E. Okarma ＊ 11m W of Hereford ＊ Parking ＊ Toilet facilities ＊ Art Gallery open ＊ Open May to Sept, Mon – Sat, 9am – 4.30pm ＊ Entrance: £1.50, OAP £1, children 50p

The garden is what might be expected to be enjoyed by a well-to-do Victorian gentleman. Conifers, some formal terracing, good trees, herbaceous borders as well as modern planting including a nice young stand of *Betula jacquemontii* and clever use of conifers to conceal electricity poles. More interesting plants can be found in antique prints in the Gallery which has a very wide selection, both horticultural and general. Brobury, facing, as it does, both Moccas and Bredwardine where the diarist Kilvert was vicar for the last few months of his life and where he is buried, is a convenient stop on the Kilvert Trail. A walk through the famous avenue of Scots Firs to Monnington will take the literary pilgrim to where he baptised, in 1879, Frances Theodora, the daughter of his brother-in-law, the Rector. More than half-a-century later she destroyed the major part of his voluminous diary before publication.

BURFORD HOUSE GARDENS ★   6
Tenbury Wells, Hereford and Worcester. Tel: (0584) 810777

Mr J. Treasure ＊ 1m W of Tenbury Wells on A456 ＊ Best season: summer ＊ Parking close to garden ＊ Refreshments: tea room ＊ Toilet facilities ＊ Suitable for wheelchairs ＊ Plants for sale in nursery open Mon – Sat, 9am – 5pm, Sun, 2 – 5pm ＊ Garden open April to Sept, 10am – 5pm, Sun, 1 – 5pm ＊ Entrance: £1.95, children 80p. Parties of 25 or more £1.60 per person (1991 prices)

The Georgian house dates from 1728 but the present gardens from only 1954 when the current owners took over. The garden and adjoining nursery is best known for its collection of clematis. However, it is very diverse in its plants and plantings. Formal water gardens at the rear of the house give way to a variety of informal shrub and herbaceous borders. Good autumn colour is provided by the woodland planting. A garden that cannot fail to please throughout the growing season.

CONDERTON MANOR   7
Conderton, Tewkesbury, Gloucestershire. Tel: (0386 89) 389

Mr and Mrs William Carr ＊ 5¹/₂m NE of Tewkesbury between the A435 and the B4079 ＊ Best season: spring and summer ＊ Parking ＊ Toilet facilities ＊ Suitable for wheelchairs ＊ Open 16th April, 14th May, 11th June, 9th July, 6th Aug, 2 – 6pm and by appointment for groups ＊ Entrance: £1, children 25p

A very fine example of what most people think of as *the* traditional Cotswold Manor House. The seven-acre garden has interesting plantings of trees, mixed beds and a long border with some unusual plants. There is a newly-built formal terrace, a stream garden, and, above all a position commanding a panorama of the countryside. A public house is situated conveniently close to the entrance for those requiring refreshment.

CROFT CASTLE   8
Leominster, Hereford and Worcester. Tel: (056885) 246

The National Trust ✱ *5m NW of Leominster off B4362* ✱ *Parking* ✱
Refreshments: in restaurant at Berrington Hall nearby. Picnics in parkland ✱
Toilet facilities ✱ *Partly suitable for wheelchairs* ✱ *Dogs in park only on lead* ✱
House open ✱ *Garden open April and Oct, Sat and Sun, 2 – 5pm, Easter Sat,*
Sun, Mon, 2 – 6pm, May to Sept, Wed – Sun and Bank Holiday Mon, 2 – 6pm
(last admission ¹/₂ hour before closing) ✱ *Entrance: £2.70, family £7.40. Parkland*
and Croft Ambrey open all year.

This is a traditional estate garden with formal beds around the house which
dates from the fourteenth century. It is well-kept and pleasant to walk through
but lacks specific interest for the specialist except perhaps for the walled garden
which is in good condition and the fine avenue of Spanish chestnuts. There are
charming walks in the Fishpool valley. Berrington Hall is nearby (see entry).

DINMORE MANOR   9
Dinmore, Leominster, Hereford and Worcester. Tel: (043271) 322

Mr R.G. Murray ✱ *6m N of Hereford on A49. 1m driveway signposted* ✱ *Best*
season: summer ✱ *Parking* ✱ *Teas most afternoons* ✱ *Toilet facilities* ✱
Suitable for wheelchairs ✱ *Open daily, 9.30am – 5.30pm* ✱ *Entrance: £2, OAP*
£1, accompanied children under 14 free. Party bookings by arrangement.

The site includes the twelfth to fourteenth-century church of the Knights
Hospitaller. An unusual garden centred around the small church, its
outstanding feature is the rock garden with some excellent specimens of *Acer*
palmatum. This part of the garden is bordered on two sides by modern cloisters
linking the house to a small tower which help to evoke a medieval atmosphere.
The house and garden are built on high ground with surrounding stone wall
giving way to lower ground and some fine views.

EASTGROVE COTTAGE GARDEN NURSERY   10
Sankyns Green, Nr Shrawley, Little Witley, Hereford and Worcester.
Tel: (0299) 896389

Mr and Mrs J. Malcolm Skinner ✱ *8m NW of Worcester between Shrawley*
(B4196) and Great Witley (A443) ✱ *Best season: June/July* ✱ *Parking* ✱
Toilet facilities ✱ *Plants for sale* ✱ *Open April to July, Sept to Nov, daily except*
Tues and Wed, 2 – 5pm. Closed Aug ✱ *Entrance: £1, children 20p*

This delightful cottage garden with a superb range of hardy plants has been
created and maintained by the present owners since 1970. The garden is full of
colour, spring to autumn. It has the benefit of being connected with a
commercial nursery developed by the owners and is highly recommended to
plantspersons and others.

EASTNOR CASTLE   11
Eastnor, Ledbury, Hereford and Worcester. Tel: (0684) 567103/(0531)
3160

Eastnor Estates ✱ *2m E of Ledbury on A438* ✱ *Best seasons: spring and early autumn* ✳ *Parking* ✳ *Refreshments on Castle open days* ✳ *Toilet facilities* ✳ *Dogs on lead* ✳ *Shop* ✳ *Castle open selected days for collections of armour and tapestries. Parties of 20 or more by appointment any day* ✳ *Garden open Easter Sun and Bank Holiday Mons, May to mid-Oct, Sun, July and Aug, Tues, Wed and Thurs, 2 – 5pm. Parties by appointment at other times* ✳ *Entrance: £1.50 (house and garden £3)*

Essentially an arboretum, Eastnor has one of the best nineteenth-century plantings in the country with many mature specimens. It is worth visiting early in the year for the display of spring bulbs. The house is an early nineteenth-century castle in medieval style surrounded by a deer park now, alas, much overgrown. Maintenance is largely confined to the vicinity of the Castle and the trees rise, and, in some cases, lie fallen amid a jungle of saplings and weeds. The view of the Castle from the far end of the large lake is still striking although a considerable area of the latter is covered in summer with a thick growth of 'Pattypans', *Nuphar lutea*, the common yellow water lily, and around the edges are clumps of khaki shelters which, by day, partially conceal the coke cans of the common white fisherman. To judge by the number of tractors, the estate is not without staff, and it is sad to see such a noble and extensive park degenerating. Despite the great variety of both conifers and broad-leaved trees there are no labels. However, some replanting has been undertaken in parts of the estate and paths have been kept clear, and the keen tree enthusiast will enjoy the long walks in the woodland.

HERGEST CROFT GARDEN ★   12
Kington, Hereford and Worcester. Tel: (0544) 230160

W.L. Banks and R.A. Banks ✳ *¹/₂m W of Kington off A44* ✳ *Parking* ✳ *Teas* ✳ *Toilet facilities* ✳ *Partly suitable for wheelchairs* ✳ *Dogs on lead* ✳ *Plants for sale* ✳ *Shop* ✳ *Open 17th April to 25th Oct, daily, 1.30 – 6.30pm* ✳ *Entrance: £2, children under 15 free, season ticket £8, parties of 20 or more £1.50 per person*

This has been the family home of the Banks family since 1896, and the garden design was much influenced by the writings of William Robinson and Gertrude Jekyll. There is an interesting collection of plants including huge rhododendrons in delightful woodland setting which extends to 50 acres and has general appeal as well as to the plantsperson. Formal garden. Half a mile through the park is a wood containing vast sheets of rhododendrons quite 30 feet high. By following the path at the top of the dingle you can look down on a scene not far removed from those in their native habitat. In late May, wellington boots are usually necessary not least in crossing the park in which many sheep graze.

THE HILL COURT   13
Hom Green, Ross-on-Wye, Hereford and Worcester. Tel: (0989) 763123

Mr C. Rowley ✳ *2³/₄m SW of Ross-on-Wye. Take B4228 towards Walford, after ¹/₂m bear right and follow garden signs for 1¹/₂m to lodge gates on right* ✳ *Best season: summer* ✳ *Parking* ✳ *Refreshments: tearoom open daily April to Sept* ✳ *Toilet facilities* ✳ *Suitable for wheelchairs* ✳ *Dogs on lead* ✳ *Plants for sale at garden centre open daily* ✳ *Walled garden, Yew walk and water garden open daily without charge. Private gardens open for charity on certain Sundays, 2 – 5.30pm* ✳ *Entrance: £1.50, OAP and children 75p*

An eighteenth-century Grade I listed house (not open), The Hill Court is set in a park, the house itself being approached by a splendid avenue. A large walled garden has been set out with symmetrical beds, clipped low hedges and garden furniture, the borders being arranged to highlight in turn those plants at their best in each of the twelve months. Old pear trees, carefully trained, a large glasshouse and well-kept paths preserve the image of what was, presumably, the kitchen garden while at the same time offering an elegant and educational place in which to walk. Another smaller walled garden of great charm is used for teas with accomodation under cover if it is wet. Large outbuildings and an area surrounded by hedges house a small garden centre with well-grown, if slightly pricey, general stock. The private gardens include a bronze and silver fountain garden.

28 HILLGROVE CRESCENT ★   14
Kidderminster, Hereford and Worcester. Tel: (0562) 751957

Mr and Mrs D. Terry ✳ *Hillgrove Crescent is a short semicircle linking A449 and A448 near their junction, the three roads enclosing a school* ✳ *Limited parking in road* ✳ *Plants for sale* ✳ *Open 17th May, 21st June, 9th Aug, 2 – 6pm and by appointment* ✳ *Entrance: 80p, children free*

Mrs Terry has transformed the area behind her semi-detached house into a miniature Paradise Garden. An immense variety of material, much of it uncommon, has been expertly grown and cunningly combined to form contrasts of shape, texture and colour which blend into a whole which is much more than the sum of the parts. An object lesson for every gardener with restricted space, it has the appearance of being three times its actual size without the least impression of crowding. It is, quite simply, a masterpiece.

HOW CAPLE COURT   15
How Caple, Hereford, Hereford and Worcester. Tel: (0989) 86626

Mr and Mrs Peter Lee ✳ *10m SE of Hereford on B4224, turn right at How Caple crossroads* ✳ *Best season: summer* ✳ *Parking* ✳ *Refreshments on Sun and Bank Holidays. Parties by appointment* ✳ *Toilet facilities* ✳ *Dogs on leads* ✳ *Plants for sale* ✳ *Shop* ✳ *Open April to Oct, Mon – Sat, 9.30am – 5pm, also May to Sept, Sun 10am – 5pm* ✳ *Entrance: £2, children £1*

A large house and medieval church set in 11 acres of grounds with fine trees lining a valley which flows down to a bend in the River Wye. Much of the Edwardian planting is being re-established, there are good formal terraces, and a big pool surrounded by a curious pergola. A large ruined Florentine garden is in the process of restoration and if the original water supply can be replaced the whole should be spectacular. There is a fabric shop on one side of the stable yard and a small area selling some unusual shrubs and old roses. Recent plantings in the valley are maturing well, but there is still a good deal of work to be done if the gardens' former glory is to be recaptured.

LAKESIDE 16
Gaines Road, Whitbourne, Nr Worcester, Hereford and Worcester.

Mr D. Gueroult and Mr C. Philip ✱ *9m W of Worcester off A44. Turn left at county boundary sign, signposted Linley Green (ignore sign to Whitbourne)* ✱ *Teas* ✱ *Plants for sale* ✱ *Open 19th April, 17th May, 14th June, 2 – 6pm* ✱ *Entrance: £1.50, children free*

The first glimpse of this six-acre garden is a moment of sheer delight: a dramatic vista of the lake at the bottom of a steep grassy slope. The main part of the garden is situated within the walls of what was the fruit garden of Gaines House nearby and consists of mixed beds and borders with many unusual shrubs and plants, bulbs and climbers. It has been created by the present owners since 1984 and is now well-established, with continuing expansion, particularly the newly-planted bog garden. At least one plant of every variety in the garden is labelled. The main lake – complete with fountain – is the largest of three medieval stewponds which are thought to have provided fish for the Bishop of Hereford's palace nearby at Whitbourne Court. There is a short woodland walk bordered with ferns and different varieties of holly, leading to the very attractive lakeside walk, where there are various kinds of daffodil in spring. An exceptionally-situated garden, with great variety and interest. Don't miss the view from the top of the heather garden.

LOWER HOPE 17
Ullingswick, Hereford and Worcester.

Mr and Mrs Clive Richards ✱ *At the roundabout on the A465 near Burley Gate take the A417 towards Leominster. After 2m turn right. Lower Hope is about ¹/₂m on left. Signposted* ✱ *Parking* ✱ *Refreshments* ✱ *Toilet facilities* ✱ *Suitable for wheelchairs* ✱ *Open 13th April, 5th July, 2 – 6pm* ✱ *Entrance: £1.50, children 50p*

On entering this five-acre garden through a gate in the hedge which largely conceals it from the road, the effect is of finding the south banks of the Chelsea Flower Show transported bodily to Herefordshire. Artfully contrived streams meander, crossed by Japanese-type bridges under which swim Koi carp; beds backed with shrubs and filled with perennials and annuals in profusion; serried masses of roses; herbaceous borders; a laburnum tunnel; fruit and vegetable gardens; two conservatories full of giant begonias, ferns and the grander kind of indoor pot display, a swimming pool surrounded by fashionable garden furniture, a paved yard with a weather-vaned stable block. There are some interesting shrubs and everything is a great tribute to the Richards' gardeners.

MARLEY BANK 18
Bottom Lane, Whitbourne, Hereford and Worcester. Tel: (0886) 21576

Mr and Mrs R. Norman ✱ *10m W of Worcester on A44. Turn right to*

Whitbourne. At T junction by church after 1m turn left for 600 yards ✻ *Restricted parking* ✻ *Plants for sale* ✻ *Open 4th April to 10th Oct, Sat, 10am – 5.30pm and all year by appointment. Closed 30th May, and 8th to 15th Aug* ✻ *Entrance: £1*

Sue and Roger Norman are experts and the garden not only contains a great variety of plants in terraced beds but has been created with a designer's eye for form and texture. Very few of these plants are at all common, unusual cultivars are the norm, and rare treasures, particularly alpines, abound. The many paths are carefully constructed of different materials to complement the plantings and the whole looks out over a very fine view. All plants for sale are propagated at Marley Bank and purchasers need have no qualms about nomenclature and provenance – factors not always found in sales from private gardens.

OVERBURY COURT ★ 19
Overbury, Hereford and Worcester.

Mr and Mrs Bruce Bossom ✻ *5m NE of Tewkesbury. 2¹/₂m N of Teddington Hands roundabout (A435 and A438 crossing)* ✻ *Parking in field off lane by church* ✻ *Teas nearby* ✻ *Suitable for wheelchairs* ✻ *Plants usually for sale* ✻ *Open 5th April, 28th June, 2 – 6pm* ✻ *Entrance: £1, children free*

The south side of this magnificent Georgian house boasts a fine stone terrace overlooking a great sweep of formal lawned garden with hundreds of yards of clipped hedges, specimen clipped yews and a formal pool. To the east the lawn is framed by a silver and gold border with a crinkle-crankle edging of golden gravel leading to a gazebo overlooking the road and the country to the south. On the west the frame is completed by more hedging and a sunken garden of attractively-underplanted species roses leading to the west side of the house where, under enormous plane trees a stream winds its way from a grotto over vast lawns, falling gently into pools before it disappears underground. Elsewhere, shrub and flower borders and aged cherries merge and blend into the adjacent Norman churchyard. Everything, from the family totempole near the grotto to the polished plate on the Estate Office door speaks of a continuity that is rare today. An exceptionally restful garden. Nevertheless, visitors with children should note that there is an unguarded opening in the south hedge which is immediately above a considerable drop to the road beneath.

PERSHORE COLLEGE OF HORTICULTURE 20
Avonbank, Pershore, Hereford and Worcester. Tel: (0386) 552443

Hereford and Worcester County Council ✻ *1m S of Pershore on A44. 7m from M5 junction 7* ✻ *Best season: summer* ✻ *Parking* ✻ *Toilet facilities* ✻ *Suitable for wheelchairs* ✻ *Dogs on lead* ✻ *Plants for sale* ✻ *Open 6th June for College Open Day and weekdays for RHS members, with garden centre open Thurs and Fri pm* ✻ *Entrance: free to RHS members*

The gardens are designed with a definite bias towards education so although not picturesque they are worth visiting. Extensive ornamental grounds include an arborctum, orchard, vegetables, automated glasshouses and a large commercial nursery. The RHS Centre at Pershore and Alpine Garden Society Headquarters are situated on the College estate.

THE PICTON GARDEN   21
Old Court Nurseries, Colwall, Malvern, Hereford and Worcester. Tel: (0684) 40416

*Mr and Mrs P. Picton * 3m W of Malvern on B4218 * Best seasons: June to Oct * Limited parking * Suitable for wheelchairs * Plants for sale * Open April to Oct, daily except Mon and Tues, 10am – 1pm, 2.15 – 5.30pm * Entrance: £1*

This small garden has been created on the site of the Old Court Nurseries. It retains a nursery atmosphere (old frames now contain alpine beds) and plants for sale in neat rows. Herbaceous borders and shrubs create diversity. Holds the NCCPG Michaelmas daisy collection, a genus on which the owner, Paul Picton, the son of the late Percy Picton, is an acknowledged expert.

THE PRIORY   22
Kemerton, Tewkesbury, Gloucestershire. Tel: (038689) 258

*The Hon. Mrs Healing * 5m NE of Tewkesbury off B4080 * Parking * Suitable for wheelchairs * Dogs on lead * Plants for sale at small nursery * Open 24th May, 14th June, 12th July, 9th, 30th Aug, 20th Sept and June to Sept, Thurs, 2 – 7pm * Entrance: £1, children free*

A garden of herbaceous borders, planted in colour groups with many unusual trees and shrubs. A stream garden, sunken garden and fern garden add diversity and the careful use of colours and textures using a wide range of plants, many of them unusual, make the borders outstanding.

SPETCHLEY PARK   23
Spetchley, Nr Worcester, Hereford and Worcester. Tel: (090565) 224/213

*Mr J. Berkeley * 3m E of Worcester on A422 * Parking * Refreshments on Sun and Bank Holidays * Toilet facilities * Suitable for wheelchairs * Plant centre * Open April to Sept, Tues – Fri, weekdays 11am – 5pm, Suns, 2 – 5pm, Bank Holidays 11am – 5pm. Closed all other Mons and all Sats * Entrance: £1.80, children 90p*

Rose Berkeley was sister of the great Ellen Willmott and in her day the garden was one of the wonders of England. Now, this formal garden provides many vistas along borders and walls, through clipped yew hedges and open arches. Combined with the successive planning and planting it has a rich and abundant feel. The old kitchen garden is now surrounded by splendid borders although the beds within the walls would be improved by thinning out. There are large drifts of naturalised Turk's Cap lilies in early July, and the new rock beds near the entrance are maturing well. As one would expect, fine specimen trees abound and the wooden rusticated arbour must be one of the best examples of Victorian taste in garden furniture still standing..

STAUNTON PARK 24
**Staunton-on-Arrow, Leominster, Hereford and Worcester.
Tel: (05447) 474**

*Mr E.J.L. and Miss A. Savage * 3m from Pembridge, 6m from Kington on the Titley road. Signposted * Best season: spring/summer * Parking inside garden * Teas * Toilet facilities * Suitable for wheelchairs * Dogs on lead * Plants for sale * Shop * Norman church adjoining open * Garden open April to mid-Oct, Wed and Sun, 2 – 6pm * Entrance: £1, children 50p*

A 14-acre setting for some fine trees, mixed borders, a lake and a herb garden laid out on traditional lines. If the heavy Victorian planting of *Rhododendron ponticum* and the rampant bracken could be eliminated from the far side of the lake the effect would be much enhanced.

STONE HOUSE COTTAGE GARDENS ★ 25
Stone, Kidderminster, Hereford and Worcester. Tel: (0562) 69902

*Major and the Hon. Mrs Arbuthnott * 2m SE of Kidderminster via A448 * Parking * Toilet facilities * Suitable for wheelchairs * Plants for sale * Open March to Oct, Wed – Sat and May and June, Suns, 10am – 6pm * Entrance: £1.50, children free*

This garden has been created since 1974 and looking round it now it is difficult to believe that the whole area was once flat and bare. The owners have skilfully built towers and follies to create small intimate areas in the garden and at the same time provide homes for very many unusual climbers and shrubs. Yew hedges break up the area to give a vista with a tower at the end, covered with wisteria, roses and clematis. Hardly anywhere is a climber growing in isolation – something will be scrambling up it, usually a small late-flowering clematis. Raised beds are full to overflowing, shrubs and unusual herbaceous plants mingle happily. In a grassed area shrubs are making good specimens. All plants are labelled so the visitor knows what to looks for in the adjacent nursery (but buy with care. Many of the plants are tender, and this is a very sheltered garden.) During the annual local music festival the towers have a secondary purpose as platforms for the wind ensembles. You are invited to picnic in the garden for a modest fee. The effect is akin to non-pretentious Glyndebourne transplanted to San Gimignano. At other times you may ascend the towers to view the garden as a whole for the price of a donation to the Mother Theresa charity.

THE WEIR GARDEN 26
Swainshill, Hereford and Worcester.

*The National Trust * 5m W of Hereford on A438 * Best season: spring * Parking. No coaches * Open 14th Feb to Oct, Wed-Sun and Bank Holiday Mon, 11am – 6pm. Open Good Fri * Entrance: £1.50*

This garden offers a pleasant walk along the banks of the Wye. The main interest is to visit in the spring since the chief charm resides in the drifts of bulbs. It is terraced in an informal way on a cliffside and would be improved by extensive re-planting. Features include a small Japanese-style garden.

WHITE COTTAGE (Cranesbill Nursery)   27
Earls Common Road, Stock Green, Nr Redditch, Hereford and Worcester. Tel: (0386) 792414

*Mr and Mrs S.M. Bates * 7m E of Worcester off A422 * Best season: May/ June * Limited parking * Teas at Jinny Ring Craft Centre, Hanbury (approx 5m) * Toilet facilities * Suitable for wheelchairs * Plants for sale * Open Easter to Oct, daily except Thurs, 10am – 5pm but by appointment only in Aug and Oct * Entrance: 75p for charity, children free*

A two-acre garden with large lawns bordered by interesting shrub and herbaceous borders. Artificial stream bordered by peat blocks creates good conditions for primula collection. Extensive collection of hardy geraniums. Part of the garden has been set aside for a small nursery selling many of the plants featured in the garden.

WHITFIELD ★   28
Wormbridge, Hereford and Worcester.

*Mr G.M. Clive * 8m SW of Hereford on A465 to Abergavenny * Picnic parties welcome * Suitable for wheelchairs * Open 14th June, 2 – 6pm and occasionally for local charities (see local press for details) * Entrance: £1, children 50p*

Within this large park, the owner has created one of the largest private gardens made in Britain in the last half-century. The park itself has some fine old trees which may be seen on the one-and-a-half-mile woodland walk, including an 1851 redwood grove and what is said to be the tallest oak in Britain. Near the house, a new terrace with fine planting and statuary was the first step towards developing the grand garden which expands across the lawn to the south of the house. To the east a large cedar dominates an area now managed as a wildflower meadow, cut only twice a year. To the north, Mr Clive has created superb water features, including a lake and, rare in this century, a folly ruin. Attractive planting too, for the plantsperson.

CUTTINGS
Readers may wish to be reminded that the taking of cuttings without the owners' permission can lead to embarrassment and, if it continues on a large scale, may cause the owners to close their gardens to the public. This has to be seen in the context of an increasing number of thefts from gardens. At Nymans, the famous Sussex garden, thefts have reached such a level that the gardener will not now plant out any shrub until it is semi-mature and of such a size that its theft would be very difficult. Other owners have reported the theft of artifacts as well as plants.

HERTFORDSHIRE

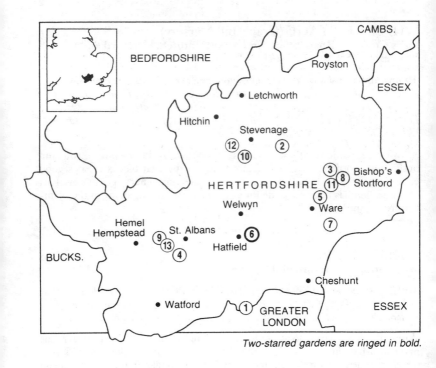

Two-starred gardens are ringed in bold.

THE BEALE ARBORETUM 1
West Lodge Park, Hadley Wood, Hertfordshire. Tel: (081) 440 8311

Mr T. Edward Beale ✳ *Leave M25 at junction 24 and take road marked Cockfosters (A111). West Lodge Park 1m further on left* ✳ *Parking* ✳ *Light refreshments are available in the gardens on open days. Set teas and dinner in the adjoining hotel if booked in advance* ✳ *Suitable for wheelchairs but gravel paths undulating* ✳ *Dogs on lead* ✳ *Open all year by appointment for organised groups and for charity 7th June, 2 – 6pm and 25th Oct, 12 noon – 4pm* ✳ *Entrance: by donation, and on charity days £1*

Mr Beale bought the West Lodge Park Hotel in 1945 with the intention of enriching its fine eighteenth-century park with many more trees to turn it into the important arboretum which it has now become. To help him he enlisted the professional advice of Frank Knight, a former director of Kew, Derek Honour and Frank Hillier, the famous Winchester nurseryman. Today, there are 18 acres of arboretum with some fine rare trees and now, with the help of his head gardener, the Wisley-trained Michael Helliwell, Edward Beale plans to add a further 16 acres to the arboretum. The trees at West Lodge Park plus the three acres of more formal garden, many azaleas, rhododendrons and a lake, coupled with the fine food in the hotel dining room can make a visit to this little-known gem, only 13 miles from central London, memorable. And certainly if he was to visit the property today, as he did in 1675, the diarist John Evelyn would still be able to say that it was 'a very pretty place – the garden handsome'. He would, however, fail to recognise the strawberry tree which was believed to be there at the time of his visit and which has become one of the largest in England.

BENINGTON LORDSHIP ★ 2
Benington, Nr Stevenage, Hertfordshire. Tel: (043885) 668

Mr and Mrs C.H.A. Bott ✳ *5m E of Stevenage* ✳ *Parking* ✳ *Refreshments* ✳ *Toilet facilities* ✳ *Plants and pots for sale* ✳ *Open Easter, Spring and Summer Bank Holiday, 12 noon – 5pm, April to Sept, Wed, 12 noon – 5pm, April to Aug, Sun, 2 – 5pm* ✳ *Entrance: £2, OAP £2, children free*

Here is a garden that has almost everything: wonderful views, lakes to wander round, a Victorian folly and a Norman keep and moat, as well as a colourful rockery and big double herbaceous borders. Borders in the kitchen garden, one in shades of gold and silver, another full of penstemons.

BROMLEY HALL 3
Standon, Ware, Hertfordshire. Tel: (027984) 2422

Mr and Mrs A.J. Robarts ✳ *6m W of Bishop's Stortford near A120 and A10 on Standon – Much Hadham road* ✳ *Parking* ✳ *Suitable for wheelchairs* ✳ *Open 7th, 14th June, 2.30 – 5.30pm (dates unconfirmed at time of going to press – please check by phone)* ✳ *Entrance: £1, children 50p*

Mrs Robarts has created this garden entirely herself over the last 20 years. Improvements and alterations are going on all the time. It is both an architectural garden making good use of walls and hedges, statuary and seats, and also a plantsman's garden. Mr Robarts looks after the vegetable garden, and it is immaculate. The wide border on the edge of the drive is backed by a tall hedge and is a well-designed mixture of shrub and foliage planting with unusual and elegant perennials.

CAPEL MANOR Horticultural and Environmental Centre
(see LONDON (Greater))

DOCWRA'S MANOR
(see CAMBRIDGESHIRE)

GARDENS OF THE ROSE ★ 4
Chiswell Green, St Albans, Hertfordshire. Tel: (0727) 50461

Royal National Rose Society ✳ *2m S of St Albans on B4630 (signposted)* ✳

Parking ✳ *Refreshments: licensed cafeteria* ✳ *Toilet facilities* ✳ *Suitable for wheelchairs with good facilities for disabled* ✳ *Dogs on lead* ✳ *Miniature rose plants for sale, growers' catalogues available* ✳ *Open 13th June to 18th Oct, Mon – Sat, 9am – 5pm, Suns and Bank Holidays, 10am – 6pm* ✳ *Entrance: £3, OAP and disabled £2, groups £2.50 per person. Members and children free*

The Royal National Rose Gardens provide a wonderful display of one of the best and most important collections of roses in the world. There are some 30,000 rose trees and at least 1700 varieties including hybrid teas, floribundas and climbing roses of every kind, miniature roses and ground-cover roses. Some of the roses are thought to differ little from the roses admired in the classical world. Part of the gardens is the trial grounds for roses from all over the world. The Society is now trying to introduce other plants which harmonize with roses and enhance the planting schemes to give a more natural effect. Already there is a touch of blue from a bank of geraniums and an edging of golden *Alchemilla mollis*. H.M. The Queen Mother is particularly fond of old roses and the garden named for her contains a fascinating collection of Gallicas, Albas, Damasks, Centifolias, Portlands and Moss roses. Here can be seen what is thought to be the original red rose of Lancaster and white rose of York. Among the Gallicas is the 'Rosa Mundi' said to have been named for Fair Rosamond, the mistress of Henry II. This is an historic wonderland which could be explored indefinitely by rose lovers and will have interest for all gardeners. (Note: for those who wish to be up-to-date, hybrid teas and floribundas are now known as large-flowered and cluster-flowered roses respectively.) The garden is being enlarged over the next ten years from its current 12 to some 60 acres.

GREAT MUNDEN HOUSE   5
Nr Dane End, Ware, Hertfordshire. Tel: (0920) 244

Mr and Mrs D. Wentworth Stanley ✳ *W off A10. Turn off N of Puckeridge roundabout* ✳ *Best season: May/June* ✳ *Parking* ✳ *Refreshments* ✳ *Suitable for wheelchairs* ✳ *Plants for sale* ✳ *Open 26th April, 14th June, 2 – 5.30pm* ✳ *Entrance: £1.50, children 50p*

A charming garden, beautifully planned and immaculately kept. It is situated down the side of a valley with a backdrop of wheat fields and trees. Good windbreaks of beech hedges as the wind funnels down the valley. Kitchen garden with vegetables planted in patterns. Good mixed border imaginatively planted with shrubs, shrub roses and excellent foliage plants. Intimate secret corners and a paved area surrounded by silver plants and a *Juniperus virginiana* 'Skyrocket' in each corner. A rather less successful island bed on the other side of the garden, but on the whole a most satisfactory small garden.

HATFIELD HOUSE ★★   6
Hatfield, Hertfordshire. Tel: (0707) 262823

The Marquess and Marchioness of Salisbury ✳ *Opposite Hatfield railway station on A1000, 2m from A1(M) junction 4* ✳ *Parking* ✳ *Refreshments: light meals and teas, 11am – 5pm* ✳ *Toilet facilities* ✳ *Suitable for wheelchairs* ✳ *Plants*

for sale ✳ *Garden and other shops* ✳ *House open* ✳ *Garden open 25th March
to 11th Oct. West Gardens, daily except Good Friday, 11am – 6pm. East Garden
(Lord and Lady Salisbury's private garden) Mon except Bank Holidays, 2 – 5pm*
✳ *Entrance: £2.40, OAP £2.20, children £1.80 (house supplement £1.90, children
£1.10). Enquire for party rates and garden guide*

Originally laid out in the early seventeenth century by Robert Cecil and planted
by John Tradescant the Elder. Nothing new can be written about this
fascinating garden with its presiding genius the Marchioness of Salisbury,
except to say do visit it. Try to choose a time when the private gardens in front of
the house are open for it is here that some of the most beautiful plants are to be
seen. See the mop-headed *Quercus ilex* imported especially for the garden and
the great double anemone said to have been given to Tradescant, now reintroduced and growing. Amongst the many features are the varied knot
gardens, the wilderness and the scented gardens. There is an annual
midsummer festival at Hatfield, part country fair, part garden party and part
flower show, which gives an opportunity to visit the gardens, including the
splendid East Garden, normally only open on Monday afternoons in season.
There is a lovely wild garden bank behind the old Palace, and a charming herb
garden.

HILL HOUSE ★   7
Stanstead Abbotts, Ware, Hertfordshire. Tel: (0920) 870013

Mr and Mrs R. Pilkington ✳ *Halfway between Hertford and Harlow. From A10
turn E on to A414, and at roundabout take B181 for Stanstead Abbots, left at end of
High Street and first right past church* ✳ *Parking* ✳ *Teas* ✳ *Toilet facilities* ✳
Dogs on lead ✳ *Unusual plants for sale* ✳ *Picture gallery* ✳ *Open 3rd May, 7th,
14th June, 2 – 5.30pm* ✳ *Entrance: £1.50, children 50p*

Six acres of very varied garden including woodland, a bog garden, a fine
herbaceous border and a highly recommended conservatory. The owners tend
the immaculate borders themselves and employ help to mow the extensive
lawns. A delightful cottage garden. A magnificent conservatory. The position is
an interesting one, on a south-facing slope overlooking Stanstead Abbotts and
as a bonus, ospreys have been seen in the valley.

HOPLEYS ★   8
Much Hadham, Hertfordshire. Tel: (027984) 2509

Mr A. Barker ✳ *50 yards N of Bull public house in centre of Much Hadham* ✳
Parking ✳ *Toilet facilities* ✳ *Suitable for wheelchairs* ✳ *Plants for sale* ✳ *Open
all year except Jan and Aug; Sun, 2 – 5pm, Mon, Wed – Sat, 9am – 5pm and also
on special days for charities* ✳ *Entrance: £1, children 50p on charity days. Other
days free*

The owner and his parents have been working on this garden for many years
and it has been expanding yearly. The relatively new pool and bog area look well
established. There are numerous borders filled with shrubs and hardy plants,
most of which are for sale in the nursery. The long-established conifer bed

illustrates the different sizes and shapes of mature conifers. There is also a border for tender plants which have come through the last few winters well. Not far from Hopleys is the headquarters of Andrew Crace who designs and sells a wide range of fine garden furniture and bronze and stone ornaments. He is planning to open on a regular basis and visitors to Much Hadham would be well advised to watch the press for details.

KING CHARLES II COTTAGE 9
Leverstock Green, Hemel Hempstead, Hertfordshire. Tel: (0442) 64233

Mr and Mrs F.S. Cadman * *Via A4147, midway between Hemel Hempstead and St Albans* * *Parking* * *Teas at Westwick Cottage nearby* * *Suitable for wheelchairs* * *Plants for sale elsewhere in village on charity days* * *Open 28th June, 11am – 5pm* * *Entrance: £2, children free*

This one-acre garden has evolved over 30 years from an overgrown orchard. A huge gnarled apple tree and a yew hedge are survivors from a former garden. The roses are a special feature, planted in long beds and following the curve of the drive, with some splendid shrub roses in island beds. One remembers especially a rock pool beneath the willows planted with foliage plants; the terrace with cushions of pinks and small bedding plants between the York paving stones; climbers on the black and white cottage walls, mainly roses and clematis; and a vista across the lawn through the beech hedge to a mixed border beyond planted with a successful mixture of unusual shrubs, herbaceous plants, azaleas in late spring, providing a succession of good colour and foliage. Other gardens in this village and Gorhambury also open, including Westwick Cottage (see entry).

KNEBWORTH HOUSE 10
Knebworth, Nr Stevenage, Hertfordshire. Tel: (0438) 812661

The Lord Cobbold * *30m N of London, 2m from Stevenage. Direct access from A1(M) junction 7* * *Parking* * *Refreshments: In sixteenth-century tithe barn* * *Toilet facilities* * *Open 4th April to 17th May, 12th Sept to 4th Oct, weekends, school holidays and Bank Holidays, 23rd May to 6th Sept, daily except Mon but open Bank Holiday Mons), 12 noon – 5pm. Closed 31st July to 3rd Aug* * *Entrance: £3.50, OAP and children £3 (house and garden) (1991 prices)*

As the historic home of the Lytton family, the garden evolved from a simple Tudor green and orchard to Sir Edward Bulwer Lytton's elaborate design of the mid-1800's. Edwin Lutyens made alterations and simplified the main central area. His twin pollarded lime avenues lead to an upper lawn of rose beds and herbaceous borders, with tall yew hedges behind. There are mixed borders of blues and mauves with old-fashioned roses of yellows and creams. A recent addition is the restoration of the unique Quincunx pattern herb garden designed for Knebworth in 1907 by Gertrude Jekyll and containing a delightful mixture of unusual herbs. Other features are a vast 300-year old oak tree, a large Wellingtonia and small dogs' graveyard. *Clematis montana* and *Rosa* 'The Garland' are draped over Lutyens' garden bothy. The 'Wilderness', laid out in

1887, is currently undergoing new developments, including restoration of the pond.

ST PAUL'S WALDEN BURY ★ 11
Whitwell, Nr Hitchin, Hertfordshire. Tel: (0438) 871218

Mr and Mrs Simon Bowes Lyon ✳ *5m S of Hitchin, ¹/₂m N of Whitwell on B651* ✳ *Best season: April to July* ✳ *Parking* ✳ *Teas* ✳ *Suitable for wheelchairs* ✳ *Dogs on lead* ✳ *Open 26th April, 10th May, 7th June, 19th July, 2 – 7pm. Other times by appointment* ✳ *Entrance: £1.50, children 75p*

This is a formal landscape garden, laid out about 1730, and influenced by French tastes, and one of the few to survive the landscape movement. Long rides (or *allées*) lined with hedges fan out from the north-east through about 40 acres of woodland, leading to temples, lakes and ponds; the way this area has been treated has been described as evocative of Versailles. One temple was designed by Sir William Chambers, another by Wyatt. The views to distant features make the garden seem larger than its actual area. The Bowes-Lyons, a family which has lived here for over 150 years, has created more recent flower gardens, and a woodland garden planted with rhododendrons, azaleas and magnolias, some rare, as well as bluebells in season. An important garden, in addition to its connection with the Queen Mother.

WESTWICK COTTAGE 12
Leverstock Green, Hemel Hempstead, Hertfordshire. Tel: (0442) 2521291

Mrs Sheila MacQueen ✳ *On A4147, midway between Hemel Hempstead and St Albans* ✳ *Parking* ✳ *Teas, coffees and light refreshments* ✳ *Suitable for wheelchairs* ✳ *Plants for sale* ✳ *Open 28th June, 11am – 5pm* ✳ *Entrance: £2 (combined admission to four gardens), children free*

Created by the owner 40 years ago, and planted with the idea of picking for flower arranging. A large border designed to be viewed end on from the house is full of colour and interest, with mixed perennials and annuals, white delphiniums, *Alchemilla mollis*, phlox and interesting shrubs to give it body and texture. Staddle stones under a big flowering cherry, *Prunus* 'Kanzan', catch the eye, as does a stone trough in front of the house. A stone urn filled with nicotiana, pelargoniums, etc. shows Mrs MacQueen's skills as a flower arranger. Other Leverstock Green gardens are open on the same day (see entry for King Charles II Cottage).

HUMBERSIDE

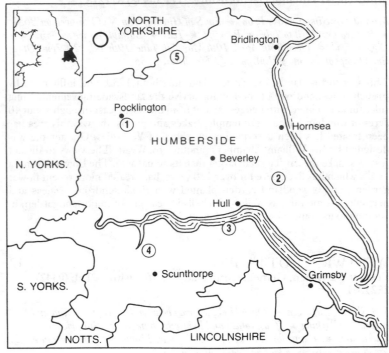

Two-starred gardens are ringed in bold.

BURNBY HALL GARDENS AND MUSEUM ★ 1
Pocklington, Humberside. Tel: (0759) 302068

*Stewart's Burnby Hall Gardens and Museum Trust ＊ 13m E of York on B1247
in Pocklington ＊ Best season: June to Sept ＊ Parking, inc. coaches ＊
Refreshments: cafeteria for teas in garden ＊ Toilet facilities ＊ Suitable for
wheelchairs ＊ Shop ＊ Open Easter to mid-Oct, daily, 10am – 6pm ＊
Entrance: £1.50, OAP £1, children 5 – 16 50p, under 5 free. Parties of 20 or more
£1 per person (1991 prices)*

The gardens were established on open farmland in 1904 by Major Stewart, the
original ponds being constructed for fishing and swimming, but in 1935 they
were converted to water lily cultivation. They are now one of the finest water

gardens in Europe covering two acres. A large collection of hardy water lilies forms a subsidiary of the National collection. Lilies may be seen from May to mid-September in a normal year and in July there are some 5000 blooms of 60 different varieties.

BURTON CONSTABLE HALL   2
Nr Hull, Humberside. Tel: (0964) 562400

Mr J. Chichester Constable ✳ 7¹/₂m NE of Hull. Take A165 between Hull and Skirlaugh and follow signs ✳ Parking ✳ Cafeteria ✳ Toilet facilities ✳ Suitable for wheelchairs ✳ Shop ✳ House open as garden, 1 – 4.30pm ✳ Garden open Easter, May and Spring Bank Holiday Suns and Mons. Also Suns in June and July and 19th July to 6th Sept, Sun – Thurs, 12 noon – 5pm. Parties at any time by arrangement with administrator ✳ Entrance: £2 (house and grounds) (1991 prices)

A fine Elizabethan house surrounded by parkland which 'Capability' Brown, whose plans can still be seen, laid out in the 1770s. His 20 acres of lakes are spanned by a good stone bridge, and while his trees have not all survived they are being replaced by new plantings, still in their infancy. Around the house is a four-acre garden with handsome eighteenth-century orangery, statuary and borders.

THE COTTAGES   3
Ferry Road, Barrow-Haven, Nr Barton-on-Humber, South Humberside. Tel: (0469) 31614

Mr and Mrs E.C. Walsh ✳ 4m E of Barton-on-Humber off A1077 adjacent to Barrow-Haven railway station ✳ Parking ✳ Teas ✳ Partly suitable for wheelchairs ✳ Plants for sale ✳ Open 3rd, 4th May, 30th, 31st Aug, 11am – 5pm and by appointment ✳ Entrance: £1, OAP and children 50p

Situated on a disused tile works near the River Humber this one and a quarter-acre garden is on a direct flight path for many migratory birds. By careful management the owners have maximised the number of food sources, nest sites and habitats for visiting and resident species. There are bird-watching hides for the enthusiast. The result is a pastoral haven of old thorn trees intermingled with more recently-planted trees, shrubs and herbaceous plants. Grassy paths meander to a dyke planted with bog plants, a pond and reed bed and an organic vegetable plot on raised beds. In contrast, the well-manicured area around the house has beds, borders and trellises brimming with plants providing year-round colour.

NORMANBY HALL   4
Normanby Hall Country Park, Nr Scunthorpe, South Humberside. Tel: (0742) 720588

Run by Scunthorpe Borough Council ✳ 4m N of Scunthorpe on B1430 ✳ Best season: June/July ✳ Parking ✳ Refreshments ✳ Toilet facilities ✳ Suitable for wheelchairs ✻ *Dogs on lead* ✻ *Shop* ✻ *House open April to Nov, Mon – Fri, 11am – 5pm, Sat and Sun, 1 – 5pm, Bank Holiday Mon, 11am – 5pm* ✻ *Farm Museum open April to Nov, daily, 1 – 5pm* ✻ *Park open all year, dawn – dusk* ✻ *Entrance: small fee to car park*

Although the parkland and woodland at Normanby is extensive, with superb nature trails, rhododendron walks, lakes and accessible deer park, the actual pleasure gardens are rather limited. They are, however, well-maintained and as an addition to the many attractions here are worth seeing. Next to the Regency house are formal rose beds and a lavender-edged sunken garden with a fish pond. Further away, and easily missed, is a lovely, walled 'secret garden'. Enclosed by mellow brick walls, holly and conifer hedges are double-sided herbaceous borders, grass paths and good wall shrubs and climbers, a peaceful retreat from the often busy park. Within the grounds is a small farm museum which, like the house, has no entry charge and allows all the family to find something of interest at a minimal cost.

SLEDMERE HOUSE   5
Sledmere, Great Driffield, Humberside. Tel: (0377) 86208

Sir Tatton Sykes, Bart. ✻ *9m NW of Great Driffield, signposted off A166* ✻ *Parking* ✻ *Teas* ✻ *Toilet facilities* ✻ *Suitable for wheelchairs* ✻ *Shop* ✻ *House open* ✻ *Garden open 4th May to Sept, daily except Mon and Fri (but open Bank Holiday Mons), 1.30 – 5pm* ✻ *Entrance: £1, children 60p (house and garden)*

A listed garden, Sledmere is among the most well-preserved of 'Capability' Brown's landscape schemes. Dating from the 1770s it clearly reveals his characteristic belting and clumping of trees and carefully controlled diagonal vistas to distant 'eye-catchers'. His use of a ha-ha allows the park to flow up to the windows of the house (whence it is best seen) across extensive tree-planted lawns. To the rear of the house are a well-stocked herbaceous border, a newly planted knot garden and an interesting Italian paved sculpture court (1911) which is undergoing restoration. The eighteenth-century walled gardens are now grassed over and planted with mainly spring-flowering shrubs and are entered through a small but attractive rose garden set off by garden urns.

KENT

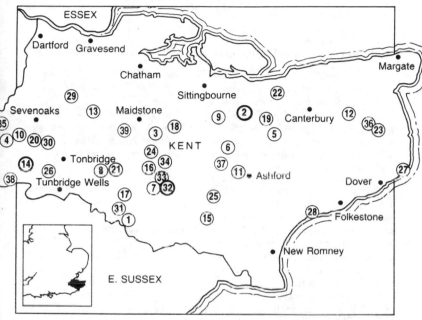

Two-starred gardens are ringed in bold.

BEDGEBURY NATIONAL PINETUM ★   1
Nr Goudhurst, Cranbrook, Kent. Tel: (0580) 211044 (Curator)

Forestry Commission ✳ *On B2079 Goudhurst – Flimwell road off the A21* ✳
Parking. Disabled persons may be brought to and collected from lake ✳
*Refreshments: ice creams available in car park. Light refreshments available at shop
in garden Easter to Oct, daily* ✳ *Toilet facilities* ✳ *Suitable for wheelchairs* ✳
Dogs on lead ✳ *Shop open Easter to Sept, 11am – 5pm and Oct, 12 noon – 4pm
* ✳ *Arboretum open daily, 10am – 8pm or dusk if earlier, winter months, 10am –
4pm* ✳ *Entrance: £1.50, OAP £1, children 50p. Exact money required at certain
times*

The Pinetum lies on sandy soil too infertile for sustained agriculture, being
silty, very acid and deficient in phosphates. Specimen trees were initially
cultivated with the addition of essential nutrients. However, although the size

of some of the conifers is inevitably limited, the variety of species is not, and the Pinetum offers a comprehensive collection of the conifers that can be grown in Britain. It has been planted so that the form, colour and texture of the mature trees can readily be seen. As well as being a valuable educational resource for schools and students of forestry and related subjects, it is also a place for quiet enjoyment.

BELMONT ★★ 2
Belmont Park, Throwley, Faversham, Kent. Tel: (079589) 202

Harris (Belmont) Charity ✳ 4m SW of Faversham, 1¹/₂m W of A251 Faversham – Ashford road. From A2 or M2 junction 6, take the A251 S towards Ashford. At Badlesmere follow brown Tourist signs ✳ Best season: May/June ✳ Parking ✳ Teas June to Sept, 3 – 5pm. Suitable for picnics ✳ Toilet facilities ✳ Suitable for wheelchairs ✳ Dogs on lead ✳ Plants usually for sale ✳ Shop ✳ House open ✳ Garden open Easter Sun to Sept, Sat, Sun and Bank Holiday Mons, 2 – 5pm ✳ Entrance: £1.50, children 50p (house, clock museum and gardens £3.50, children £2)

The eighteenth-century house by Samual Wyatt has been the seat of the Harris family since 1801 and though somewhat off the beaten track down winding lanes, it is well worth a visit. It was built at a time when beautiful country house architecture was required to blend in with equally beautiful and well-planned surroundings; well exemplified here by 40 acres of formal and informal gardens blending with the 150 acres of parkland to give marvellous vistas of aged and noble trees. There is a yew walk and a pinetum. The pleasure gardens were conceived as a series of walled 'rooms', each with its own individuality and recording the interests of various members of the family who have lived here for generations. These include borders, a pool, a rockery and note also the shell grotto and folly. There is a touching pets' cemetery for those who like that kind of thing. The present administrators of the property have done much to restore the gardens, which had become overgrown, but now look pristine.

BOUGHTON MONCHELSEA PLACE 3
Nr Maidstone, Kent. Tel: (0622) 743120

Mr Charles Gooch ✳ On B2163 5m S of Maidstone, off A229 ✳ Parking ✳ Refreshments: tearoom ✳ Toilet facilities ✳ Shop ✳ Open Easter to early Oct, Suns and Bank Holidays, and Weds in July and Aug, 2.15 – 6pm ✳ Entrance: £2, children £1.50 (house and gardens £3, children £1.75). Parties welcome by appointment

This is an attractive walled garden built and established behind the main house, full of roses and herbaceous plants in season. It is not a plantsman's garden but is very peaceful in the wider context of the old ragstone walls and the rooftops of Boughton Monchelsea Place. This is situated on the greensand ridge and the lawn in front of the house gives fine views over the Weald, with a steep drop almost immediately below. It is said that the herd of deer in the park has been there for at least 300 years. The old church nearby is also well worth a visit.

CHARTWELL 4
Westerham, Kent. Tel: (0732) 866368

*The National Trust ✳ 2m S of Westerham off B2026 ✳ Parking ✳
Refreshments: licensed self-service restaurant ✳ Toilet facilities ✳ Partly suitable
for wheelchairs ✳ Dogs on lead ✳ Shop ✳ House open but entry by timed ticket
✳ Garden open April to 1st Nov, Tues, Wed and Thurs, 12 noon – 5.30pm, Sat,
Sun and Bank Holiday Mon, 11am – 5.30pm. Closed Good Fri and Tues following
Bank Holiday Mon ✳ Entrance: £1.60 (house and garden £3.80)*

The lawns to the front of the house slope down to two large lakes and a
swimming pool (constructed by Sir Winston Churchill). A walled rose garden
at the side of the house leads to a loggia, with grapevine, adjoining the
Marlborough Pavilion which contains bas reliefs of the Battle of Marlborough.
Another main feature, adjoining an orchard, is the Golden Rose Garden and
Walk – extending to the kitchen garden, where Sir Winston built the summer
house and part of the brick wall. Lady Churchill had a good deal to do with the
original design of the garden. This is a garden worth exploring and enjoying the
sense of space and history, but it is not of particular interest to the plantsperson.

CHILHAM CASTLE 5
Chilham, Nr Canterbury, Kent. Tel: (0227) 730319

*The Viscount Massereene and Ferrard ✳ S side of A252, just W Chilham village
✳ Best season: spring, summer ✳ Parking ✳ Occasional refreshments ✳ Toilet
facilities ✳ Dogs on lead ✳ Shop ✳ Open week before Easter to mid-Oct, Sun –
Sat, 11am – 5pm ✳ Entrance: Mon and Fri, £2.60, other weekdays with birds of
prey display £3*

Considerable work over the last year has brought about many improvements.
The lake has been restored as a central feature. A new rose bed has been started
and herbaceous beds show signs of renewed vigour. Above all one visits
Chilham to see the outstanding view down to the Stour Valley and the terracing
supposedly designed by John Tradescant. This was later destroyed by
'Capability' Brown in the interests of naturalism, then restored in the 1920s. All
the elements of garden history are here – Jacobean terracing, mid-eighteenth-
century deer park, viewing mound, formal Victorian garden, lake garden. Old
trees include a fine *Quercus ilex* planted to mark the completion of the house,
and a splendid cedar of Lebanon. Some say this garden looks rather tired, but
shut your eyes and think of Old England while others in your party enjoy the
tourist attractions at the side.

CHURCH HILL COTTAGE GARDENS 6
Charing Heath, Ashford, Kent. Tel: (023371) 2522

*Mr and Mrs M. Metianu ✳ Leave M20 at junction 8 from Maidstone or junction
9 from Folkestone to join A20. Follow sign S from dual-carriageway section of A20,
¹/₂m W of Charing, to Charing Heath and Egerton. Fork right at Red Lion pub after
1 mile, take next right and 250 yards on right ✳ Best season: May to July ✳
Parking ✳ Toilet facilities ✳ Suitable for wheelchairs ✳ Plants for sale ✳*

Garden and nursery open March to May, daily, June to Nov and Feb, daily except Mon and Tues. Closed 1st to 15th Sept, Dec and Jan ✳ Entrance: £1, children free

In spite of current works for the M20 in the vicinity, Church Hill Cottage Gardens have an air of peace and tranquillity rarely equalled in much larger gardens. There is a strong sense of design in the curves of borders and island beds but these are so well matched by the fine and well-developed planting that the whole seems natural and much more established than one normally expects after only eight years. Established birches form a central point. Beds are varied, some with colour themes, others with shrubs heavily underplanted with a wide range of unusual hardy plants, bulbs in season, foliage plants, etc. One point of plantsman's interest is the large collection of dianthus, which includes between 30 and 40 types of old forms dating from the sixteenth to eighteenth centuries. This garden is always evolving and the new woodland area is developing well.

THE COACH HOUSE 7
Sissinghurst, Kent. Tel: (0580) 712007

Mr & Mrs Michael Sykes ✳ 2m N of Cranbrook, E of the village of Sissinghurst on the A262 ✳ Parking ✳ Suitable for wheelchairs ✳ Plants for sale ✳ Open 20th, 21st June, 12 noon – 6pm and by appointment ✳ Entrance: £1 combined charge for this garden and Sissinghurst Place next door

This garden was created from a derelict site in 1983, bordered by established yew hedges. There is a *Ribes speciosum* on the house, which was originally part of Sissinghurst Place. The garden has areas with many unusual trees, shrubs and plants, including a small 'secret' garden.

CRITTENDEN HOUSE ★ 8
Crittenden Road, Matfield, Nr Tonbridge, Kent. Tel: (0892) 832554

Mr B.P. Tompsett ✳ 6m SE of Tonbridge on B2160. Turn left in village along Chestnut Lane, house on right after 1m ✳ Best seasons: spring and early summer ✳ Parking ✳ Refreshments: at Cherrytrees on Matfield Green ✳ Toilet facilities ✳ Partly suitable for wheelchairs ✳ Open 29th March, 5th, 19th, 20th April, 4th, 17th, 25th May, 7th, 21st June, 2 – 6pm ✳ Entrance: £1.25, children under 12 25p. Parties by appointment

An extraordinary range of soil types has led to a wide variety of species blending within the labour-saving concept of the owner's design; with spring bulbs, rhododendrons, roses, lilies, waterside plantings and autumn colours, this garden teems with interest throughout the year. Curved lawns sweep to island beds and interestingly-planted water fringes within a framework of trees. The local native flora, such as *Primula vulgaris* and *Dactylorhiza fuchsii*, mingle strikingly with more rarified species such as *Paeonia lutea ludlowii* ('Sherriff's Variety'), a gift from George Sherriff, and *Malus* 'Crittenden' (awarded First Class Certificate in 1971). *Crataegus* varieties, such as *monogyna* 'Pink May', x *lavallei* and *laciniata*, contrast with *Davidia involucrata* var. *involucrata* (with its outstanding autumn colours) and *Rhododendron* 'Elizabeth', *R.* 'Unique', *R. yakushimanum* 'Exbury' and *R. auriculatum* 'Lady Chamberlain'. Several trees have been raised from seeds collected by the owner – *Pinus ayacahuite* from Popacatapetl, Mexico, and *Hippophae salicifolia* from Nepal, for example. The local stone used in the garden has many fossil sand-ripples and even a fossil footprint of a dinosaur – possibly Iguanodon.

DODDINGTON PLACE 9
Doddington, Nr Sittingbourne, Kent. Tel: (079586) 385

*Mr R. and the Hon. Mrs Oldfield * 6m S of Sittingbourne. From A20 turn N at Lenham. From A2 turn S at Teynham. Signposted * Best season: May/June * Parking * Refreshments: morning coffee, light lunch, afternoon tea * Toilet facilities * Suitable for wheelchairs * Dogs on lead * Plants for sale when available * Shop * Open Easter Mon to Sept, Weds and Bank Holidays, 11am – 6pm. Also Suns in May * Entrance: £1.50, children 25p*

Created in the nineteenth century by Nessfield and developed in the 1910s with woodland garden added in the 1960s by Mr and Mrs Oldfield, the gardens are set in open countryside in 10 acres of landscaped grounds surrounding a Victorian country house. They include lawns with established oaks, a Wellingtonia walk, a sunken garden, rock garden and much fine yew hedging. The main feature for the plantsman is the well-designed woodland garden set, in the 1960s, on acid soil to the side of the main garden. Here are rhododendrons and azaleas, numerous acers and a variety of other trees and shrubs, some rare. The ideal time for this is spring and early summer, but there is year round interest – the rest of the garden has a sense of space and fine views. Plans for redevelopment in rockery and sunken garden should bear fruit in a few years. This garden continues to develop, with new planting throughout.

EMMETTS GARDEN ★ 10
Ide Hill, Sevenoaks, Kent. Tel: (073275) 429

*The National Trust * 1¹/₂m S of A25 on Sundridge to Ide Hill road. 1¹/₂m N of Ide Hill off B2042 * Best season: spring to midsummer * Parking. Buggy available from car park to entrance * Teas 2 – 5pm * Partly suitable for wheelchairs * Dogs on lead * Open April to Oct, Wed – Sun and Bank Holiday Mon, 2 – 6pm (last admission 5pm) * Entrance: £2.20, children £1.10. Pre-booked parties £1.70, children 90p*

Set on the top of Ide Hill, Emmetts Garden gives a superb view over the Weald of Kent and provides an impressive setting for this plantsman's collection of trees and shrubs. This is a garden to visit at any time of the year, but is particularly fine in spring, with its bluebell woods and flowering shrubs. First planted by Frederick Lubbock, the owner, from about 1890 until his death in 1926, it is specially noted for its rhododendrons and azaleas. It follows the late nineteenth-century style of combining exotics with conifers to provide a 'wild' garden, all well listed in the Trust guide. Recent additions to extend the interest throughout the season include a rose garden, a rock garden and extensive planting of acers for autumn colour. The enforced clearance of some trees and shrubs after the gales of 1987 has enabled new planting to keep the traditions of the garden but also to expand it. Recent planting is continuing to develop well.

The new rock garden in particular has grown on and is becoming established. Sadly the general upkeep seems to have deteriorated – the grassland in the shrub areas with azaleas was scruffy. Perhaps the recession is pinching here. It is still a wonderful site and a fascinating garden.

GODINTON PARK ★   11
Ashford, Kent. Tel: (0233) 620773

*Mr Alan Wyndham Green * 1¹/₂ W of Ashford on A20 at Potter's Corner * Best season: summer * Parking * Toilet facilities * Partly suitable for wheelchairs * Dogs on lead * Plants for sale sometimes * House open * Garden open Easter weekend Sat – Mon, other Bank Holidays Mons, and June to Sept, Sun, 2 – 5pm and parties by appointment * Entrance: 70p (house and garden £1.50, children 70p. Parties of 20 or more £1.20 per person)*

The key features of the formal areas are the water garden, well stocked with lilies and surrounded by shrubs and beds, and the small enclosed Italian garden; two statues, draped in wisteria, guard the entrance to this peaceful spot with its cruciform pool, statuary, loggia and summerhouse. There are also several shrubbed areas, a rose garden with triangular beds of annuals, and much statuary, reflecting the architectural interest of the designer. The layout was developed by Sir Reginald Blomfield when remodelling the house between 1902-6, and he used yew hedges to separate the gardens from the park, marking the different areas with lesser hedges and level changes, evolving a happy mix of balance and order. Much of the topiary reflects the outlines of the Jacobean house, although some of the symmetry has been lost with time. The garden is important evidence of Blomfield's formal style which was so much at variance with Robinson's. Round the house and gardens is an ancient park, of some 240 acres, containing some of the oldest trees in England. Unfortunately all the grey poplars (*Populus canescens*) which lined the avenue in the park were lost in the winds of Jan 1990.

GOODNESTONE PARK ★   12
Nr Wingham, Canterbury, Kent. Tel: (0304) 840218

*The Lord and Lady FitzWalter * 5m E of Canterbury on A257 turn S onto B2046, after 1m turn E * Parking * Teas May to Aug * Toilet facilities * Suitable for wheelchairs * Plants for sale * Shop * Open 30th March to 30th Oct, weekdays 11am – 5pm, 5th April to 27th Sept, Sun, 2 – 6pm and July to Aug only, Sat, 2 – 6pm * Entrance: £1.50, OAP £1.30, Disabled in wheelchairs £1, children under 12 20p, parties over 25 or more £1.30 per person (£1.50 per person for guided tour)*

Goodnestone (pronounced Gunston) Park is a 14-acre garden in rural setting round the eighteenth-century house. First built in 1700, by Brook Bridges, this Palladian-style house was rebuilt and enlarged by his great-grandson, Sir Brook Bridges, 3rd Bart. whose daughter Elizabeth, married Jane Austen's brother, Edward. Jane Austen refers frequently to Goodnestone and her Bridges cousins in her letters. There are pleasant vistas within the garden and good views out to open countryside. The garden ranges in planting from the mid-eighteenth-century parkland with fine trees and cedars to the walled area behind the house which dates back to the sixteenth and seventeenth centuries. The garden tour leads along a broad terrace in front of the house, planted with an abundance of roses and mixed shrubs. Behind the house a small woodland garden, laid out in the 1920s, gives pleasant walks and welcome shade. Here are rhododendrons, camellias, magnolias and hydrangeas among many others. A cedar walk leads between spring borders on the left and more roses on the right, to a new walled garden overlooked by the church tower. Old roses mingle with mixed underplanting. Walls bear clematis, jasmine, climbing roses. New planting in the woodland area shows continued development of this fine garden.

GREAT COMP ★   13
Borough Green, Sevenoaks, Kent. Tel: (0732) 882669

*Great Comp Charitable Trust * 2m E of Borough Green. Take B2016 S from A20 at Wrotham Heath, right at first crossroads, then ¹/₂m ahead on left * Best season: July and Aug * Parking * Teas by arrangement for parties * Toilet facilities, but not adapted for wheelchairs * Suitable for wheelchairs * Plants for sale * Open April to Oct, 11am – 6pm * Entrance: £2, children £1*

Great Comp consists of seven acres of mature gardens round a seventeenth-century house and an original Edwardian-style garden created by Mr and Mrs Roderick Cameron since 1957. This is a delightful garden with semi-woodland walks, changing vistas and plantsman's interest. Extended from an original four and a half acres of garden, rough woodland and paddock, Great Comp now contains 3,000 named plants. Each area or walk makes a separate entity yet is designed to lead on to another part. Some stonework gives added interest at focal points, and there have been some cement additions to mock ruins. Carefully mixed deciduous and evergreen planting provides all-year round variety, including magnolias, rhododendrons, azaleas, maples, underplanted with heathers, hostas and geraniums. Good herbaceous planting. The recent stonework is looking more established. When visited in July it seemed in fine order. A guide book is available at the gate. Not far away is the National Trust property Ightham Mote, a small gem of a house with a pleasant enough garden.

HEVER CASTLE ★★   14
Hever, Edenbridge, Kent. Tel: (0732) 865224

*Broadlands Properties Ltd * 3m SE of Edenbridge, midway between Sevenoaks and East Grinstead between B2026 and B2027 * Refreshments * Toilet facilities * Suitable for wheelchairs * Plants for sale * Shop * Castle open 17th March to 8th Nov, 12 noon – 6pm (last admission 5pm) * Garden open 17th March to 8th Nov, 11am – 6pm (last admission 5pm) * Entrance: £3.05, OAP £2.65, children 5 – 16 £1.85, family ticket £8. Groups per person: £2.65, students £2.35, children £1.65 (castle and gardens, £4.50, OAP £4.10, children £2.25) (1991 prices)*

The gardens were laid out between 1904-8 to William Waldorf Astor's designs. One thousand men were employed, 800 of whom dug out the 35-acre lake;

steam engines moved rock and soil to create apparently natural new features and teams of horses moved mature trees from the Ashdown forest. Today the gardens have reached their maturity and are teeming with colour and interest throughout the year. Amongst the many superb features is an outstanding four-acre Italian garden, the setting for a large collection of classical statuary. Opposite, there is a magnificent pergola, supporting camellias, wisteria, crab apple, Virginia creeper and roses. It fuses into the hillside beyond which has shaded grottos of cool damp-loving species such as hostas, astilbes and polygonum. Less formal areas include the rhododendron walks, Anne Boleyn's orchard and her walk, which extends along the full length of the grounds and is particularly attractive in autumn.

HOLE PARK   15
Rolvenden, Near Cranbrook, Kent, Tel: (0580) 241251

Mr D.G.W. Barham ✳ On B2086 between Cranbrook and Rolvenden ✳ Parking ✳ Toilet facilities ✳ Suitable for wheelchairs ✳ Open 5th, 12th, 26th April, 3rd, 17th, 24th May, 3rd June, 2 – 7pm, 11th, 18th Oct, 2 – 6pm; also a Garden Fair with plants on 9th May, 11.30am – 5.30pm ✳ Entrance: £1.50, children under 12 50p

The present owner inherited the house and gardens in 1959 and used the existing framework of fine trees to develop his scheme to provide interest throughout the year. The yews, dating from just after World War I, are closely planted and the resultant topiary is excellent. There are several walled areas and other distinctly individual parts within the garden. A particular interest in euphorbias shows in the variety of these plants, which include *E. wulfenii*, *E. polychroma* and *E. griffithii*. The borders and beds are full of colour; the long east border contains yellow and white helianthemum 'Wisley Primrose', *Cistus corbariensis* and lonicera 'Baggesen's Gold', while the sunken garden consists mainly of greys and blues. The rose garden has especially fine examples of the giant Scotch thistle *Onopordum giganteum*. The wooded areas contain many rhododendrons and azaleas and in spring burgeon with daffodils and bluebells. The autumn colours too are developing well, and there is continuous colour and variety for the whole of the opening season.

IDEN CROFT HERBS   16
Frittenden Road, Staplehurst, Kent. Tel: (0580) 891432

Rosemary and David Titterington ✳ Sign from A229 S of Staplehurst. Turn down Frittenden Road at Elf garage and follow signposts ✳ Parking ✳ Light refreshments ✳ Toilet facilities ✳ Suitable for wheelchairs ✳ Plants for sale ✳ Shop ✳ Open all year, Mon – Sat, 9am – 5pm, additional opening from April to Sept, Sun and Bank Holidays, 11am – 5pm ✳ Entrance: by donation box

Gardens situated in quiet backwater near Staplehurst. There are acres of herbs bordered by grass paths and a large walled garden. A variety of demonstration gardens help the garden planner and over 600 varieties of herbs are available in pots for planting according to seasonal variations. The origanums here were designated as The National collection in 1983. The latest garden is specially designed for the enjoyment of blind and disabled visitors.

LADHAM HOUSE ★ 17
Goudhurst, Kent. Tel: (0580) 211203

Betty Lady Jessel ✻ *NE of village off A262* ✻ *Best seasons: April/May and July*
✻ *Parking* ✻ *Toilet facilities* ✻ *Dogs on lead* ✻ *Open 3rd, 10th May, and 19th*
July, 11am – 6pm. Open at other times by appointment and for coaches ✻
Entrance: £1.50, children 50p on charity days. £2 at other times

This Georgian farmhouse with additional French features has been in the
family for over 100 years and the garden developed over that period. Interesting
features are the newly-planted bog garden, replacing a leaking pond, and the
arboretum, in an early stage of development, with the outlines of the old kitchen
garden still much in evidence. The mixed shrub borders are attractive; notable
are the magnolias – two *watsonii* over 30ft and a deep red flowering 'Betty
Jessel'. Amongst the other rarer trees and shrubs are American oaks, *Aesculus
parviflora* and *Carpenteria californica*. The newly-planted arboretum replaces
over 250 trees and shrubs lost in the 1987 storm and the Fountain Garden has
been completely reconstructed.

LEEDS CASTLE AND CULPEPER GARDENS 18
Maidstone, Kent. Tel: (0622) 765400

Leeds Castle Foundation ✻ *On B2163 off junction 8 of M20* ✻ *Best season:*
Culpeper Gardens in spring, rose season and high summer, Castle grounds, spring
and autumn ✻ *Refreshments* ✻ *Toilet facilities* ✻ *Suitable for wheelchairs with*
transport from car park to castle ✻ *Dogs in car park only* ✻ *Shop* ✻ *House open*
✻ *Gardens open 16th March to Oct, daily, 11am – 5pm and winter weekends,*
11am – 4pm ✻ *Entrance: £4.70 (park and gardens), OAP and students £3.70,*
children £2.70, family ticket £12.50

Visit Leeds Castle and grounds for its romantic, wooded setting, designed by
'Capability' Brown. The woodland walk with old and new plantings of shrubs is
especially beautiful in daffodil time. The atmosphere is also much enhanced by
wildfowl. The Culpeper Garden alone, in a secluded area beyond the Castle,
provides the main interest for the keen gardener. This is not the herb garden as
often thought, though a small area does include some herbs, but is named after
a seventeenth-century owner of Leeds Castle, distantly related to the herbalist.
Started in 1980 by Russell Page on a slope overlooking the River Len, and
surrounded by high brick walls of stabling and old cottages, the garden already
gives an established feel of old world charm. A simple pattern of paths lined
with box contains areas full of old roses (40 varieties), riotously underplanted
with herbaceous perennials. The National collection of bergamots (nepetas
and monardas) is situated in one corner. The new grotto has been much
publicised. There is also a maze, duckery and aviary.

LONGACRE 19
Perry Wood, Selling, Nr Faversham, Kent. Tel: (0227) 752254

Dr and Mrs G. Thomas ✻ *5m SE of Faversham. From A2 (M2) take A251 S*
then follow signs for Selling. Pass White Lion on left, 2nd right, then left, continue

*for ¹/₄m. From A252 at Chilham, take road to Selling at Badgers Hill Fruit Farm, turn left at 2nd crossroads, first right, next left, then right. * Best season: spring and summer * Parking * Teas * Suitable for wheelchairs * Plants for sale from own nursery * Open by appointment, 2 – 5pm * Entrance: 90p*

Longacre remains a first-class small garden. Whatever the weather, it continues to delight. Created entirely by the present owners, it provides year-round plantsman's interest with a wide variety of unusual hardy plants. Woodland section, alpine section and pleasantly designed beds stand out for their colour themes with attractive foliage base. Numerous spring bulbs and flowers give way to summer herbaceous plants. Nearby Perry Woods give good opportunity for walking dogs and children.

LONG BARN 20
Long Barn Road, Weald, Nr Sevenoaks, Kent.

*Brandon and Sarah Gough * 3m S of Sevenoaks. Follow signs to Weald from junction of A21 and B245. Continue through village * Best season: summer * Parking * Toilet facilities * Open 21st June, 19th July, 2 – 5pm * Entrance: £1, children 30p*

Three acres of sloping garden round a fourteenth-century Wealden hall house are being restored by the owners following the basic design by Harold Nicolson and Vita Sackville-West when they lived here before buying Sissinghurst. The main feature is a Dutch knot garden, said to have been designed by Lutyens. This contains in season a fine display of mixed herbaceous planting. New features include a small rhododendron glade, rose walk, pergola and herb gardens. Well situated with fine views over the Weald, this is a garden to watch as it develops further.

MARLE PLACE 21
Brenchley, Nr Tonbridge, Kent. Tel: (089272) 2304

*Mr and Mrs G. Williams * 8m SE of Tonbridge on B2162. 1m NW of Horsmonden and 1¹/₂m N of Lamberhurst, turn W on Marle Place road * Best season: May to July * Parking * Refreshments * Toilet facilities * Suitable for wheelchairs * Plants for sale * Shop * Open April to Oct (but closed on Suns and Bank Holidays), 10am – 5pm and also by appointment * Entrance: £2, OAP and children £1.50*

The present owners have worked for over 30 years on the soil and with constant digging in of compost, the unyielding clay has become productive. Despite the fact that the garden is made on the site of old farm buildings, there are many attractions surrounding the seventeenth-century listed house. The owners particularly favour the aromatic, culinary and medicinal herbs (the National collections of santolina and catmint are here) and the wild flower garden; other features include the walled fragrant garden, ornamental ponds and a Victorian gazebo. For the plantsman, there are shrub borders, and for general interest there are family pets and a variety of bantams which wander throughout what is described by the owners as a 'family garden'.

MOUNT EPHRAIM 22
Hernhill, Nr Faversham, Kent. Tel: (0227) 751496

Mrs M.N. Dawes and Mr and Mrs E.S. Dawes ✳ *Take A299 N from A2/M2,
then right to Hernhill at Duke of York pub, through village on left* ✳ *Parking* ✳
*Refreshments: homemade teas on Sun and Bank Holidays only. Licensed to sell wine
from own vineyard* ✳ *Toilet facilities* ✳ *Partly suitable for wheelchairs* ✳ *Dogs
on lead* ✳ *Craft centre shop on Suns only* ✳ *Open 19th April to Sept, daily,
11am – 6pm* ✳ *Entrance: £1.50, children 25p*

Mount Ephraim is remarkable for its variety on seven sloping acres with distant
views of the Thames Estuary, surrounding fruit orchards and new vineyard.
With a backdrop of trees of outstanding shapes and contrasts, it includes rose
gardens, rock garden, a small Japanese garden and a lake. Restored, from 1950
onwards after years of neglect, it retains much of the original design of the
1800s, laid out again in 1912 by William Dawes, including topiary effects and
the original rock garden. It has continuously evolved and a new water garden is
now established. Spring bulbs, prunus in blossom, and rhododendrons make
spring to early June an ideal time to visit but herbaceous borders and shrubs
extend the interest through the season. A three quarters of a mile orchard walk
on Sundays gives extra interest, explaining growth, development and types of
fruit farming. Kent Countryside Productions produce Shakespeare in grounds
at the end of June.

NORTHBOURNE COURT 23
**Northbourne, Deal, Kent. Tel: (0304) 360813 (evenings and
weekends), (0304) 611281 (office hours)**

The Hon. Charles James ✳ *1¹/₂m W of Deal. From A258 at W of Deal take
turning W towards Great Mongeham and Northbourne* ✳ *Best season: June and
July* ✳ *Parking* ✳ *Refreshments sometimes* ✳ *Toilet facilities: unisex* ✳ *Partly
suitable for wheelchairs* ✳ *Plants for sale* ✳ *Open 3rd, 24th May, 6th, 21st June,
5th, 19th July, 6th, 16th, 30th Aug, 13th Sept, 2 – 5pm* ✳ *Entrance: £2.50,
OAP and children £1.50. Coach parties by arrangement. Enquiries to the Hon.
Charles James, Betteshanger Home Farm Office, Northbourne, Deal, Kent.*

Originally created in Tudor times, with Jacobean structure providing the basis,
the garden in its present form was the creation of the father of the present Lord
Northbourne. The main feature of this delightful garden, set within high walls
to protect it from easterly winds, is the series of small and enclosed gardens with
profuse and colourful, cottage-style planting. The old tiered terraces give
further character and a distinctive setting for chalk-loving plants. Specially
noticeable are grey-foliage plants, including lavender and dianthus. Also
distinctive fuchsias and geraniums. Numerous pots and urns.

THE OLD PARSONAGE 24
Sutton Valence, Kent. Tel: (0622) 842286

Dr and Mrs Richard Perks ✳ *From A274 Maidstone – Headcorn road, turn E into
Sutton Valence. At King's Head Inn take upper road up hill. House is at the top on*

right with clearing by tree at gate ✳ *Best season: late June* ✳ *Parking at entrance* ✳ *Toilet facilities* ✳ *Partly suitable for wheelchairs* ✳ *Plants for sale* ✳ *Open 21st, 23rd, 25th, 27th June, 2 – 6pm and by appointment* ✳ *Entrance: £1, children 50p*

This is a delightful garden, set on the steep slopes of the greensand ridge with remarkable views southwards over the Weald of Kent. Shrub roses, an exceptional tree peony (*Paeonia delavayi*) and a wide variety of foliage plants feature strongly and provide a profusion of contrast and interest along the well-kept paths that lead along the various levels of the hillside. There is strong emphasis on ground cover, with hostas, geraniums and hellebores a special feature, presumably a gesture towards labour-saving maintenance claimed modestly by Dr Perks.

PEDDAR'S WOOD 25
14 Orchard Road, St Michael's, Tenterden, Kent. Tel: (05806) 3994

Mr and Mrs B.J. Honeysett ✳ *From A28 1m N of Tenterden turn W to Grange Road at Crown Hotel, 2nd right Orchard Road* ✳ *Refreshments* ✳ *Open 9th May, 6th, 27th June, 15th July, 8th Aug, 2 – 6pm and by appointment* ✳ *Entrance: £1, children 20p*

This plantsman's garden of exceptional opulence and interest is approximately a quarter of an acre behind a typical small semi-detached town house. Great imagination and expertise have been used to develop it over the last six years into a garden of many delights. Other than potash only the usual organic composts are used but a two inch mulch of peat has been laid over the loamy soil. Amongst the clematis which trail rampantly are 'Victoria' and 'Margo Kosta'. Pink abutilon, solanum, vines, wisterias and roses vie for space while specimens such as cannas, the unusual red rose 'Baron Giro de l'Aln' and impatiens 'Congo Cockatoo' are evident. There are in fact over 100 varieties of clematis including some of the owner's own seedlings as well as 40 varieties of lilies, 50 varieties of climbing roses and ferns in abundance.

PENSHURST PLACE ★ 26
Penshurst, Tonbridge, Kent. Tel: (0892) 870307

Lord De L'Isle ✳ *S of Tonbridge on B2176, N of Tunbridge Wells on A26* ✳ *Parking* ✳ *Refreshments: 12.30 – 5pm* ✳ *Toilet facilities* ✳ *Suitable for wheelchairs in grounds* ✳ *Guide dogs only* ✳ *Shop* ✳ *House open April to 4th Oct* ✳ *Garden open March to Oct, daily, 12.30 – 6pm (last admission 5pm). Open Bank Holidays* ✳ *Entrance: £4, OAP £3.50, children under 16 £2.25, inc. entrance to house, toy museum and venture playground*

The 600-year-old gardens, contemporary with the house, reflect their development under their Tudor owner Sir Henry Sidney and the restoration by the present owner and his grandfather Lord De L'Isle. The many separate enclosures, surrounded by trim tall yew hedges, offer a wide variety of interesting planting, with continuous displays from spring to early autumn. The Italian garden with its oval fountain and century-old gingko dominates the front of the magnificent house. The herbaceous border is teeming with colour from irises, phlox, anemones, anchusa, coreopsis and yuccas amongst others. Contrast is made by the nut trees and over a dozen different crab apples underplanted with daffodils, myosotis, tulips, bluebells, Lenten lilies and a magnificent bed of peonies which borders the orchard. Even in late summer the rose garden is colourful with 'King Arthur' and 'Elizabeth Glamis' and their perfumes mingle with that from mature lavender bushes. A new lake and nature trail are being developed so that the style of design so much enjoyed here by Gertrude Jekyll and Beatrix Farrand is fully recaptured. Numerous seats make it easy to enjoy the garden and the views. Two medieval fish ponds have been reclaimed and are to be stocked with fish. The nature trail has been restored.

THE PINES GARDEN 27
Beach Road, St Margaret's Bay, Kent. Tel: (0304) 852764

*St Margaret's Bay Trust * 3m NE of Dover off B2058, S of the village of St Margaret's at Cliffe * Best seasons: spring and summer * Parking nearby in road * Toilet facilities * Suitable for wheelchairs * Plants for sale when available * Open daily except 25th Dec, from 10am * Entrance: small admission charge*

It is hard to believe that this well-stocked and perfectly maintained garden was a rubbish dump until 1970. Fred Cleary, founder of St Margaret's Bay Trust, and his wife transformed the original three acres, with a second three-acre site known as the Barrack Field, once home and training ground for soldiers during the Napoleonic Wars. Now the garden is established, with a good variety of trees, including conifers, flowering shrubs, bulbs and bog plants. An avenue of elms is an encouraging sight. A lake, well-stocked with fish, and a rockery provides further interest. A huge bronze statue of Sir Winston Churchill seems intrusive but is understandable in this cliff-top situation near to Dover cliffs.

PORT LYMPNE 28
Lympne, Nr Hythe, Kent. Tel: (0303) 264646/7

*Mr J. Aspinall * 3m W of Hythe, 3m S of Canterbury * Parking * Refreshments: restaurant * Shop * Mansion open. A Lutyens-style house with Rex Whistler and Spencer Roberts murals * Garden open daily, 10am – 5pm (summer) and to 1 hour before dusk (winter) * Entrance: £6, OAP and children £4 (house and garden)*

This is one of those gardens which some people enjoy very much and leaves others pretty cold. It stands in a 300-acre zoo park with views across the Channel. Before World War I Sir Philip Sassoon began building a new house and garden with the help of Sir Herbert Baker and Ernest Willmote and, after the war, with much assistance from the architect Philip Tilden. After a period of distinction in the 1920s and 30s it fell into decay until it was rescued in the 1970s by John Aspinall who wanted the surrounding land for his private zoo. He has reconstructed the 15-acre garden to something like its original design with advice from experts like the late Russell Page. Visitors enter down a great stone stairway of 125 steps, flanked by clipped Leyland cypress, to the paved

KENT

West Court with lily pool. Beyond is the Magnolia Walk and a series of terraces planted with standard fig trees and vines. Everywhere there is fine stone paving and walls with appropriately-placed urns, statues from Stowe, etc. There is extensive bedding and use of bedding-out. Arthur Hellyer admits that 'for years it has been fashionable to denigrate Port Lympne' but he admires it. Others, however, feel that it lacks 'soul' – that vital element that every great garden must have, however extensive the resources that have been poured into it. Arthur Hellyer waxes lyrical about the beautiful wrought ironwork by Bainbridge Reynolds.

THE RECTORY, FAIRSEAT 29
The Rectory, Vigo Lane, Fairseat, Sevenoaks, Kent. Tel: (0732) 822494

The Reverend and Mrs David Clark ✳ *¹/₂m W A227 at the Vigo pub, 1¹/₂m N of Wrotham* ✳ *Parking in village* ✳ *Refreshments: tea and biscuits for June opening* ✳ *Toilet facilities* ✳ *Suitable for wheelchairs* ✳ *Plants for sale* ✳ *Open 28th June, 19th, 22nd July, 2 – 5.30pm* ✳ *Entrance: £1, children 50p*

This is a delightful garden in the grounds of the only weather-boarded rectory in Kent. Though still on the North Downs, there is a good layer of soil (Bagshot clay) over the chalk, permitting pieris and magnolia to flourish. The present incumbent and his wife have created the garden over the last 20 years. With 14 island beds set in and around a large lawn, the plant succession is excellent, giving colour in all seasons. Individual beds have different colour themes, combining shrubs and herbaceous plants. It is worth visiting to see how to bring a sense of garden design into a relatively small space. The garden is only open three days a year, in its best seasons, thus enabling the owners to have ready a plant description written for each occasion in minute and lively detail.

RIVERHILL GARDENS 30
Sevenoaks, Kent. Tel: (0732) 452557

Mr John Rogers (correspondence to Mrs David Rogers) ✳ *On A225 left-hand side of road, 2m S of Sevenoaks* ✳ *Best season: spring and early summer* ✳ *Parking. Coaches by appointment* ✳ *Home-made teas* ✳ *Toilet facilities* ✳ *Plants for sale* ✳ *Shop* ✳ *House open only to bona fide booked parties* ✳ *Garden open April to June, Sun and Bank Holidays, 12 noon – 6pm* ✳ *Entrance: £1.50, children 50p (house and garden £2 per person for parties of 20 or more, but no children inside house)*

This was originally one of the great smaller country-house gardens, housing a plantsman's collection of trees and species shrubs as introduced by John Rogers, a keen horticulturist, in the mid-1800s. Massive rhododendrons, many of them species, topped by cedar of Lebanon planted in 1815, also azaleas, and outstanding underplanting of bulbs make Riverhill a fine sight in early summer. Other features include wood garden, rose walk and old orchard with Wellingtonia (planted in 1815), magnolias etc.

SCOTNEY CASTLE ★ 31
Lamberhurst, Tunbridge Wells, Kent. Tel: (0892) 890651

The National Trust ✳ *1¹/₂m S of Lamberhurst on E side of A21, 8m SE of*

218

Tunbridge Wells ✱ *Best season: spring and autumn* ✱ *Parking* ✱ *Toilet facilities* ✱ *Partly suitable for wheelchairs but hilly approach* ✱ *Shop* ✱ *Castle open May to Aug Bank Holiday Mon same times as garden* ✱ *Open April to 8th Nov, Wed – Fri, 11am – 6pm, Sat, Sun and Bank Holidays, 2 – 6pm or sunset if earlier (last admission 1 hour before closing)* ✱ *Entrance: Wed – Sat, £2.40. Sun and Bank Holidays, £3. Pre-booked parties, £1.80, children £1*

This is an unusual garden designed in the romantic manner by the Hussey family following the tradition established by William Kent. The sloping grounds include many smaller garden layouts in the overall area. A formal garden overlooks a quarry garden. The grounds of the old castle enclose a rose garden. Herb garden. Lakeside planting adds an air of informality. Evergreens and deciduous trees provide the mature planting. They link shrubs and plants to give something in flower at every season. Daffodils, magnolias, rhododendrons and azaleas are the most spectacular. Also notable are the kalmias and hydrangeas. In a good autumn, the colours are spectacular. In some ways the planting seems occasional and haphazard, but visit this garden for its setting on a slope that gives fine views of open countryside, and for the romantic eighteenth to nineteenth-century theme uniting it. The old castle beside the lake gives added interest. At the end of August a Shakespeare play will be performed in the grounds.

SISSINGHURST CASTLE ★★   32
Sissinghurst, Nr Cranbrook, Kent. Tel: (0580) 712850

The National Trust ✱ *2m NE of Cranbrook, 1m E of Sissinghurst on A262, 13m S of Maidstone* ✱ *Parking but parties by appointment only and no coaches at weekends* ✱ *Refreshments: Tues – Fri, 12 noon – 6pm, Sat and Sun, 10am – 6pm. Picnics in car park and grass field in front of castle only* ✱ *Toilet facilities* ✱ *Wheelchairs restricted to two chairs at one time because of narrow uneven paths* ✱ *Shop* ✱ *Tower and library open* ✱ *Garden open April to 15th Oct, Tues-Fri, 1 – 6.30pm, Sat, Sun and Good Fri, 10am – 6.30pm (last admission 6pm). Closed Mons, inc. Bank Holidays* ✱ *Entrance: Tues-Sat: £1.50, Sun: £5*

'Profusion, even extravagance and exuberance within the confines of the utmost linear severity' is Vita Sackville-West's description of her design when creating Sissinghurst with her husband Harold Nicolson. It is a romantic garden with seasonal features throughout the year. Certain colour schemes have been followed, as in the purple border, the orange and yellow cottage garden, and the white garden, which is probably the most beautiful garden at Sissinghurst, itself one of the outstanding gardens in the world. The Nicolsons added little to, but saved much of the Elizabethan mansion. The site was first occupied in the twelfth century, when a moated manor was built where the orchard now stands. The library and tower are open and the latter is well worth climbing in order to see the perspective of the whole garden and surrounding area. The garden is in immaculate condition, well-labelled, well-restored after the gales of 1987, with changing vistas at every turn of the winding paths or more formal walks. The rose garden contains many old-fashioned roses as well as flowering shrubs such as *Ceanothus impressus, Hydrangea villosa* which together with yuccas, clematis and pansies fill the area. There is a thyme lawn leading to the herb garden filled with fragrance and charm. It is a truly magnificent example of Englishness and has had immense influence on garden design because of its structure of separate 'gardens' within the garden – but be warned that it is liable to be very crowded at weekends and afternoons. See also Long Barn entry.

SISSINGHURST PLACE   33
Sissinghurst, Kent.

Mr and Mrs Simon MacLachan ✳ *2m N of Cranbrook, E of the village of Sissinghurst on the A262* ✳ *Parking* ✳ *Teas* ✳ *Toilet facilities* ✳ *Suitable for wheelchairs* ✳ *Open 20th, 21st June, 12 noon – 6pm* ✳ *Entrance: £1 combined charge for this garden and The Coach House next door*

The original house was destroyed by fire in 1948, watched by Vita Sackville-West and then described in 'The Easter Party'. The servants' wing is now the house and the ruins are a garden with climbers, a pool and a very large fig tree. The large garden has lawns, fine trees, shrubs, roses and herbaceous plants in a tranquil country setting.

SOUTHFARTHING   34
Hawkenbury, Staplehurst, Kent. Tel: (0580) 892140

Mr and Mrs Ivan Smith ✳ *From A229 Staplehurst crossroads, turn E for 2m, or from A274 1m S of Sutton Valance turn W following signposts for Hawkenbury for 1m* ✳ *Best season: spring* ✳ *Parking on road* ✳ *Plants for sale* ✳ *Open 15th March, 2 – 5.30pm, 19th April, 2 – 3.30pm, 20th April, 4th May, 2 – 5.30pm, and March to June by appointment* ✳ *Entrance: 75p, accompanied children free*

The small garden of approximately a quarter of an acre is divided into three equal areas. Nearest the house are the alpines with a wide variety of plants, bulbs and dwarf conifers – some inspired from a visit to Russia and Afghanistan, another third is a small orchard of old apples; the final part is an organic 'no dig' area. The house itself has several interesting climbers including a good-sized fig.

SQUERRYES COURT   35
Westerham, Kent. Tel: (0959) 562345/563118

Mr and Mrs John Warde ✳ *¹/₂m W of Westerham on A25, 10 minutes from M25 junctions 5 or 6* ✳ *Parking* ✳ *Teas* ✳ *Toilet facilities* ✳ *Partly suitable for wheelchairs* ✳ *Dogs on lead* ✳ *House open. £2.80, children £1.40* ✳ *Garden open March, Suns only, April to Sept, Wed, Sat, Sun and Bank Holiday Mons, 2 – 6pm* ✳ *Entrance: £1.60, children 80p. Parties of 20 or more by appointment*

The gardens are divided into about 20 acres of formal areas and 200 of parkland. Lime groves, which are the oldest in the country, lead to a gazebo, built around 1740, from where a former member of the family used to watch his racehorses in training; nearby is a fine old dovecote. The main feature is the newly restored formal area to the rear of the house; a 1719 print has been used as an outline on which to base the ongoing developments, which reflect the mellowed brickwork of this handsome house. Beds, edged with box, contain lavender, rue, purple sage and *Nicotiana affinis*, with contrasting magenta and pink of penstemon and verbena; all are framed by well-kept yew hedges. There are several rose gardens, heather beds and azalea and rhododendron shrubberies and fine examples of topiary, which, together with a broad variety of spring bulbs, make this a garden for all seasons. Many fine magnolias around the house, a cenotaph in memory of General Wolfe (a close family friend), and a large lake complete this most attractive garden, which even when viewed towards the end of its opening period at the end of a difficult summer, was colourful and well-kept. The house is worth a visit, too, for its collection of paintings.

UPDOWN FARM   36
Betteshanger, Deal, Kent. Tel: (0304) 611895

Mr and the Hon. Mrs Willis-Fleming   ✳   3m S of Sandwich. From A256 Sandwich – Dover road, turn S off the Eastry bypass signposted Northbourne. Turn first left and into first house on the right   ✳   Parking   ✳   Refreshments   ✳   Toilet facilities   ✳   Suitable for wheelchairs   ✳   Open 3rd, 24th May, 2 – 6pm   ✳   Entrance: £1, OAP 70p, children 30p

Standing on chalk downland in open country, this is a delightful garden with many facets. A mixture of formal, enclosed areas lead on to open and informal gardens with a good variety of shrubs and with quiet woodland area. The present owners have created it over the last fifteen years and it is continually developing. Shrub and climber roses are a special feature. Well worth visiting in conjunction with nearby Northbourne Court (see entry).

WALNUT TREE FARM GARDENS   37
Swan Lane, Little Chart, Nr Ashford, Kent. Tel: (023384) 214

Mr and Mrs M. Oldaker   ✳   3m NW of Ashford off A20 Ashford – Maidstone road. From Little Chart by The Swan Inn take road towards Pluckley. The gardens are 500 yards on left   ✳   Best season: late spring to mid-summer   ✳   Parking   ✳   Teas subject to weather   ✳   Suitable for wheelchairs   ✳   Plants for sale in nursery   ✳   Open 24th May to 9th Aug, Suns only, 2 – 5pm and 27th June, 4th July, 5 – 7pm   ✳   Entrance: £1.50

Already well-developed, this six-acre garden is one to watch over the years as it has promise of more delights to come. Carefully-selected herbaceous plants combine with shrubs in island beds. A walled garden beside the house provides the setting for a wide variety of climbing roses. A bog garden created in the last three years contains a mixture of moisture-loving plants. Views to the North Downs take in shrub roses and also young trees planted with care – native trees on the garden edge and ornamental trees further in. Mrs Oldaker has searched hard for rare plants. It is worth a search in her small but growing nursery for some of these on sale there. Open twice on summer evenings so that visitors can appreciate the fragrance of the gardens.

WAYSTRODE MANOR 38
Cowden, Kent. Tel: (0342) 850695

Mr and Mrs Peter Wright ✳ *4¹/₂m S of Edenbridge, off B2026 Edenbridge –
Hartfield road* ✳ *Parking in road* ✳ *Teas* ✳ *Toilet facilities* ✳ *Partly suitable
for wheelchairs* ✳ *Plants for sale* ✳ *Open by appointment for groups and 27th
May, 1.30 – 5.30pm, 31st May, 2 – 6pm, 10th June, 1.30 – 5.30pm and 28th
June, 2 – 6pm (last admission ¹/₂ hour before closing)* ✳ *Entrance: £1.50, children
50p*

The half-timbered sixteenth-century house and its surrounding gardens,
developed by the present owners over the past 25 years, are set deep in the
wooded Kentish countryside on Wealden clay. Plants tumble over the paving
stones around the house and borders of shrubs and perennials, the wisteria
walk and the laburnum tunnel all make more formal contrasts. Clipped yew
hedges surround the island beds which are arranged in varying colour schemes;
for example the oranges and reds of dahlias and roses in one and grey-foliage
plants in another. The plants are well-labelled and there is also an interesting
small collection of garden statuary.

WEST FARLEIGH HALL 39
West Farleigh, Maidstone, Kent.

Mr and Mrs Stephen Norman ✳ *4¹/₂m W of Maidstone, turn S off A26
Maidstone – Tonbridge road at Teston Bridge. Turn right at T-junction. Garden on
left, opposite 'Tickled Trout' pub* ✳ *Parking* ✳ *Teas* ✳ *Toilet facilities* ✳
Partly suitable for wheelchairs ✳ *Open 28th June, 2 – 6pm* ✳ *Entrance: £1.50,
children free*

This large garden was created by the present owner's grandmother and apart
from making the original vegetable garden considerably smaller, the garden
layout is unchanged. There are many fine trees, shrubs, lawns, a rose garden,
an old rose walk, a wild garden, spring, iris and peony borders and four
herbaceous borders each with a different colour scheme.

HOW TO FIND THE GARDENS
Directions to each garden are included in the entry. This information has been
supplied by the garden inspectors and is aimed to be the best available to those
travelling by car. However, it has been compiled to be used in conjunction with
a road atlas. The unreliability of train and bus services makes it unrewarding to
include details, particularly as many garden visits are made on Sundays.
However, many properties can be reached by public transport, and National
Trust guides and the Yellow Book [NGS] sometimes give details. Future
editions of the *Guide* may include a special list of gardens easily reached by
public transport if readers indicate that this would be helpful. *The Maps*: The
numbers on the maps correspond to the numbers of the gardens in each county.
The maps show the proximity of one garden to another so that visits to several
gardens can be planned for the same day. It is worthwhile referring to the maps
of bordering counties to see if another garden visit can be included in the
itinerary.

LANCASHIRE

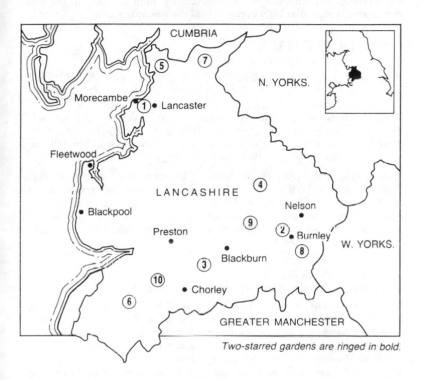

Two-starred gardens are ringed in bold.

ASHTON MEMORIAL 1
Williamson Park, Lancaster, Lancashire. Tel: (0524) 33318

Lancashire County Council ✳ *E of Lancaster town centre. Signposted* ✳ *Best season: spring* ✳ *Parking* ✳ *Refreshments: tea shop* ✳ *Toilet facilities inc. disabled* ✳ *Suitable for wheelchairs* ✳ *Dogs* ✳ *Shop* ✳ *Memorial open. Entrance to viewing gallery 50p, ground floor with exhibition free. Butterfly house £2.25* ✳ *Garden open daily except 25th, 26th Dec and 1st Jan, Easter to Sept, 10am – 5pm, Oct to Easter, 11am – 4pm* ✳ *Entrance: free to gardens*

Ashton Memorial was described by Pevsner as 'the grandest monument in England'. It stands at the highest point of Williamson Park looking down on the town of Lancaster. There are many views of the surrounding country from various points in the superbly landscaped park. Broad paths run through the grounds much of which is woodland with an underplanting of rhododendrons

223

and other shrubs. There is a small lake spanned by a stone bridge, and from near here is a large stairway that leads to the huge domed monument. Behind the monument across a cobbled area and mosaic is the palm house which now houses a collection of tropical butterflies. To the rear is a small garden containing plants attractive to local butterflies. Both monument and palm house were designed in 1906 in the style of the Baroque revival.

GAWTHORPE HALL   2
Padiham, Nr Burnley, Lancashire. Tel: (0282) 78511

Lancashire County Council (on lease from The National Trust) ✳ *N of A671 just E of Padiham town centre* ✳ *Best season: spring* ✳ *Parking* ✳ *Refreshments: Tues – Fri, 11am – 5pm, Sat and Sun, 1 – 5pm* ✳ *Toilet facilities inc. disabled* ✳ *Partly suitable for wheelchairs* ✳ *Dogs on lead* ✳ *Craft gallery and shop* ✳ *House open 29th March to Oct, daily except Mon and Fri but open Good Friday and Bank Holiday Mon, 1 – 5pm (last admission 4.15pm)* ✳ *Open all year 10am – 6pm* ✳ *No charge for gardens (house and gardens £2)*

This garden, though not particularly special in botanical terms, does set off the Elizabethan Hall. To the front is a formal layout of lawns and gravel paths, to the rear a parterre by Barry in the form of a sunburst overlooks the River Calder. The woodlands that surround the formal garden are planted with rhododendrons and azaleas. Through them are many walks with views back to the house and across the valley.

HOGHTON TOWER   3
Hoghton, Nr Preston, Lancashire. Tel: (025485) 2986

Sir Bernard de Hoghton ✳ *5m SE of Preston N of A675 midway between Preston and Blackburn* ✳ *Best season: summer* ✳ *Parking* ✳ *Refreshments: tearooms* ✳ *Toilet facilities* ✳ *Partly suitable for wheelchairs* ✳ *Dogs on lead in grounds but not garden* ✳ *Shop* ✳ *House open* ✳ *Garden open 18th April to Oct, Suns and Bank Holidays, 2 – 5pm. Also Sats in July and Aug, and Weds in June, July and Aug, 11.30am – 4.30pm* ✳ *Entrance: £1 (house and garden £2.50, children £1)*

Hoghton Tower, a sixteenth-century house built of stone, occupies a hilltop position with good views to all sides. The house and outbuildings are built around two courtyards which although not qualifying as gardens are fine areas. Surrounding the house are three walled gardens; the first contains a large lawn and herbaceous borders. The second has a smaller rectangular lawn at the centre of which is a raised square pond with an elaborate stone fountain; to one end is a statue and at the other a sundial on a stone pedestal; clipped yews flank two sides of the lawn. The third is mainly lawn with access to the tops of two small crenellated towers. Around the walled gardens runs 'the long walk' which passes under some large beech trees and is newly planted with shrubs, mainly rhododendrons and azaleas. Good views of the surrounding countryside.

HOLDEN CLOUGH NURSERY   4
Holden, Nr Bolton by Bowland, Clitheroe, Lancashire. Tel: (02007) 615

Peter Foley ✳ *7m N of Clitheroe turn N off A59 to Sawley and follow road*

towards Bolton by Bowland, turn left to Holden before Bolton and fork left in village
✳ *Parking in road* ✳ *Toilet facilities* ✳ *Plants for sale* ✳ *Open all year except
25th Dec to 1st Jan, Mon – Thurs, 1 – 5pm, Sat, 9am – 5pm, Bank Holidays 9am
– 5pm, and Suns in April and May only, 2 – 5pm* ✳ *Entrance: free*

It is refreshing after visiting so many modern garden centres to find a nursery
that is dedicated simply to plants. Much of this two-acre site is given to display
areas where a large range of perennials, shrubs, heathers, rhododendrons and
conifers are grown. Alpines are also prominent with areas of raised beds and
sink and trough gardens on show. Astilbes, hostas, primulas and saxifrages are
amongst the nursery's specialities, and many other plants are available in great
variety, too. The beautiful local countryside is another attraction to visiting this
garden.

LEIGHTON HALL   5
Carnforth, Lancashire. Tel: (0524) 734474

Mr R.G. Reynolds ✳ *2m W of Yealand Conyers, signposted from M6 junction 35*
✳ *Parking* ✳ *Teas* ✳ *Toilet facilities* ✳ *Suitable for wheelchairs* ✳ *Dogs on
lead in park only* ✳ *Shop* ✳ *House open* ✳ *Open May to Sept, daily except Sat
and Mon, 2 – 5pm* ✳ *Entrance: £2.80, OAP £2.30, children £1.80, parties of 25
or more £2.30 per person, schools £1.50 per child (house and grounds)*

Very striking when first seen from the entrance gates, the white stone facade (*c.*
1800) shines out in its parkland setting with the hills of the Lake District visible
beyond. The most interesting area of the gardens, which lie to the west of the
house, is the walled garden with its unusual labyrinth in the form of a gravel
path that runs under an old cherry orchard. Opposite is a vegetable garden
made in a geometric design with grass paths. There are also herbaceous
borders and a very aromatic herb garden containing a wide variety of perennials
with climbing roses on the wall behind.

RUFFORD OLD HALL   6
Rufford, Nr Ormskirk, Lancashire. Tel: (0704) 821254

The National Trust ✳ *7m N of Ormskirk, N of Rufford village on E of A59* ✳
Best season: spring ✳ *Parking* ✳ *Refreshments: lunches and teas, teas only on
Sun* ✳ *Toilet facilities* ✳ *Suitable for wheelchairs* ✳ *Dogs on lead* ✳ *Shop* ✳
House open as garden (last admission 4.30pm) ✳ *Garden open April to 1st Nov,
daily except Fri, 1 – 5pm, Sun, 2 – 5pm* ✳ *Entrance: £1.30 (house and garden
£2.60)*

Rufford Old Hall is an exceptional fifteenth-century timber-framed house
whose gardens complement it perfectly, having been laid out by the Trust in the
style of the 1820 period. On the south are lawns and gravel paths laid out in a
formal manner. The many island beds are formal in layout, too, but the shrubs,
small trees and herbaceous plants they contain are planted in a more relaxed
way. In the centre a path leads from two large topiary squirrels to a beech
avenue that goes beyond the garden towards Rufford. There are many mature
trees and rhododendrons in this area. To the east of the house by the stables is

an attractive cobbled area with climbing plants on the surrounding walls. When visiting, look for the gardener's own garden to the north side of the house, in which grow many old-fashioned plants enclosed by a rustic wooden fence.

SELLET HALL GARDENS 7
Kirkby Lonsdale, via Carnforth, Lancashire. Tel: (05242) 71865

Mrs J. Gray ✳ *1m SW of Kirkby Lonsdale, signposted from B6254* ✳ *Best seasons: spring and summer* ✳ *Parking* ✳ *Toilet facilities* ✳ *Partly suitable for wheelchairs* ✳ *Plants for sale. Nursery open daily except winter Bank Holidays* ✳ *Shop* ✳ *Garden open March to Oct, 10am – 5pm* ✳ *Entrance: 50p, children free*

Created over the last 20 years, this garden is set around an old and attractive grey stone house in a beautiful part of North Lancashire. A fairly large herb garden is its best feature, formal in layout and surrounded by a high yew hedge. The symmetrical beds contain a great number of herbs and other perennials; there are good collections of lavenders, thymes and artemisias. Behind the herb garden is a wild-flower garden and to one side a bee garden. Also a small Japanese garden and other areas of shrubs, perennials, dwarf conifers and heathers. The small courtyard has been attractively planted. Some areas are still being developed, and the results are impressive for this exposed part of the country.

TOWNELEY PARK 8
Todmorden Road, Burnley, Lancashire. Tel: (0282) 24213

Burnley Borough Council ✳ *1¹/₂m SE of Burnley town centre on A671* ✳ *Best season: spring* ✳ *Refreshments: cafeteria* ✳ *Toilet facilities* ✳ *Suitable for wheelchairs* ✳ *Dogs on lead* ✳ *Gift shop in Hall* ✳ *Hall open daily except Sat, weekdays 10am – 5pm, Sun, 12 noon – 5pm. Closed Christmas week* ✳ *Park open all year during daylight hours* ✳ *Entrance: free*

The Hall dates from 1500 but its exterior is largely the work of 1816 – 20. The gardens are not its main attraction but are pleasantly grassed and contain many mature trees. Parkland laid out in the late eighteenth century forms the basis of today's gardens. The front of the house looks out over a pond and beyond a ha-ha to open parkland. There are some formal beds to the east of the house planted with bright arrangements of annuals. Further to the east as well as to the south and west are extensive woodlands containing many large rhododendrons and long walks. There is also a craft museum and a nature centre.

WHALLEY ABBEY 9
Whalley, Blackburn, Lancashire. Tel: (025482) 2268

Diocese of Blackburn ✳ *8m NNW of Burnley, Whalley is S of A59 between Clitheroe and Blackburn* ✳ *Best season: summer* ✳ *Refreshments: in coffee shop. Picnic area* ✳ *Toilet facilities* ✳ *Partly suitable for wheelchairs* ✳ *Dogs on lead* ✳ *Shop and exhibition area* ✳ *Open all year, dawn – dusk* ✳ *Entrance: £1, OAP 50p*

Whalley Abbey is visited mainly by those wishing to see the ruins of the fourteenth-century abbey, and the gardens run round their periphery. These gardens are of recent creation and consist mainly of herbaceous borders and shrubs; in one area there are conifers and heathers. The stone terraces that have been made against the north outer wall of the garden are perhaps its most attractive feature. To the south of the ruins is an avenue of mixed trees flanking the River Calder that runs behind them. Development of the gardens is continuing.

WORDEN PARK   10
Leyland, Lancashire. Tel: (0772) 421109

Borough of South Ribble ✳ *Take B5248 S from Leyland and at Leyland Cross follow signs to Worden Park* ✳ *Parking* ✳ *Refreshments: coffee shop and snacks at Craft Centre* ✳ *Toilet facilities, inc. one adapted on RADAR key scheme* ✳ *Partly suitable for wheelchairs* ✳ *Dogs* ✳ *Craft centre* ✳ *Open daily, 8am – sunset* ✳ *Entrance: free, except first Sat in June when a charge is made*

These gardens are set around part of an old house and a stable block that now contains a craft workshop (the rest of the house was burnt down in the 1950s). There are formal gardens with brightly planted beds amongst cobbled paths and a garden for the blind with scented plants grown in raised beds. The maze is quite unusual being made of hornbeam hedges in a circular pattern. A little distance away is a large conservatory with a rockery to one side and a herbaceous border to the other. They face a formal lawned area that is enclosed by a low balustrade and some fine ironwork gates. On occasions a walled garden can be entered; this has a mulberry tree and a greenhouse with a vine. Large areas of open parkland surround the gardens.

WHEELCHAIR USERS
Please note that entries which describe a garden as 'suitable for wheelchairs' refer to the garden only. If there is a house open, it may or may not be suitable.

LEICESTERSHIRE

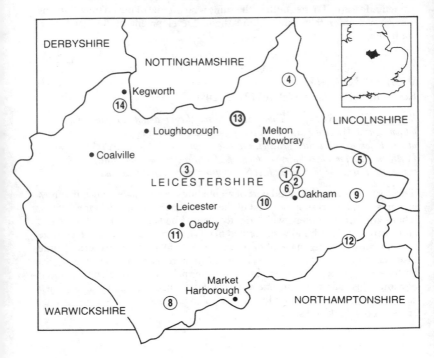

Two-starred gardens are ringed in bold.

ASHWELL HOUSE 1
Ashwell, Leicestershire. Tel: (0572) 722833

Mr and Mrs S.D. Pettifer ✳ 3m N of Oakham via B668 towards Cottesmore, turn left to Ashwell ✳ Parking ✳ Toilet facilities ✳ Suitable for wheelchairs ✳ Plants sometimes for sale ✳ Open for parties by appointment ✳ Entrance: £1 per person

An old garden, well-planned with colour combinations to provide all year colour, and golden plants to light up the various borders. There are peaches, plums, pears and blackberries on the old walls and soft fruits in the garden along with a range of vegetables, and some nut trees. A wide range of shrubs and perennials in the borders, and a large variety of flowers grown for drying.

ASHWELL LODGE ★ 2
Ashwell, Nr Oakham, Leicestershire. Tel: (0572) 722825

Mrs B.V. Eve ✳ 3m N of Oakham between A606 to Melton Mowbray and B668 Oakham – Cottesmore road ✳ Parking in street ✳ Teas ✳ Toilet facilities ✳ Suitable for wheelchairs ✳ Plants for sale ✳ Open 26th April, 2.30 – 6pm ✳ Entrance: £1, children free

A one and a half-acre garden redesigned by Percy Cane about 1973 and divided up into little gardens by hedges of beech and yew. A paved rose garden with shrub and pillar roses and a crown-shaped trellis with roses, as well as clematis with roses on arches provide masses of colour. A border of peony. A good range of cottage-garden plants in the herbaceous borders and also shrubs and acers. Water and a greenhouse are other features in this very pleasant garden which in spring is colourful with bulbs. There are fruit trees, and smaller plants on the patio.

BARKBY HALL ★ 3
Barkby, Nr Syston, Leicestershire.

Mr and Mrs J. Pochin ✳ 5m NE of Leicester off A46 ✳ Parking ✳ Suitable for wheelchairs ✳ Open 5th July, 3 – 6pm and by written appointment ✳ Entrance: £1, children 50p

A beautiful varied eight-acre garden, containing many rare and unusual plants, within a surrounding framework of parkland and a fine house that has been in the same family for centuries. As seen today, the garden is wholly the inspiration of the late owner, Mrs Elizabeth Pochin, and is maintained to her standards by her son. There is a rose garden, with shrub, patio and modern roses, a woodland garden massed with rhododendrons, hellebores, erythroniums and trilliums, an exquisite scented garden in memorium to the late owner, walled gardens containing orchards, vegetables and flowers for cutting, and newly-restored glasshouses massed with fuchsias. A herb garden is being planned. Many secluded sitting areas.

BELVOIR CASTLE 4
Belvoir, Grantham, Leicestershire. Tel: (0476) 870262

The Duke of Rutland ✳ 6m from Grantham, S of A52 Nottingham – Grantham road and N of Melton Mowbray road. By Belvoir village. Signposted ✳ Parking ✳ Refreshments: lunches and teas. Picnics in car park ✳ Toilet facilities ✳ Partly suitable for wheelchairs ✳ Shop ✳ Castle open ✳ Garden open April to Sept, Tues, Wed, Thurs, Sat and Sun, Oct, Sun only, 11am – 5pm (last admission to house 4.30pm). Open Bank Holiday Mons. Groups at other times by appointment ✳ Entrance: £3.20, OAP and children £2.20 (house and garden)

From a distance this castle (pronounced Beaver) has all the appearance of a medieval fortress, although on arrival it is clearly a more solid eighteenth-century erection. The house is famous for its rooms by James Wyatt. The mid-nineteenth century garden descends from the castle in a series of terraces and slopes with some small gardens created by hedging. Bulbs, early-flowering shrubs, roses and arbours. Some seating. Good views of Belvoir Vale. Friendly peacocks.

CLIPSHAM HOUSE 5
Clipsam, Leicestershire. Tel: (0780) 410238

*Mr and Mrs R. Wheatley * 10m NE of Oakham, E of A1 on B668 * Parking in grounds or nearby lane * Teas on charity day * Toilet facilities * Suitable for wheelchairs * Dogs on lead * Plants for sale on charity day * Open by appointment and one day in June for charity * Entrance: by donation when open for charity*

This garden is set in parkland with some good trees and various conifers and acers. There is a lovely walled garden with island beds and grass paths and a pool and fountain. Herbaceous borders contain a wide range of shrubs, ground-cover plants and roses, and on the walls are climbers and fruit trees. A conservatory houses more tender plants and there is a vegetable garden and orchard. Designed to give pleasure and colour throughout the summer.

LANGHAM LODGE 6
Langham, Nr Oakham, Leicestershire. Tel: (0572) 722912

*Mr and Mrs H.N. Hemsley * ^{1}/$_2$m out of Langham on Burley Road. Go up farm drive beside pair of cottages * Best season: June/July * Parking * Suitable for wheelchairs * Dogs on lead * Plants for sale * Open by appointment * Entrance: £1, children free*

This one-acre garden, with rich soil, should be of interest to plantspersons for its imaginative foliage combinations and good sense of shape and colour contrasts. Old-fashioned roses, a peony border, iris, azaleas, hebes, sedums, berberis, dogwoods, eucalyptus, elaeagnus and hostas. There is a hot-coloured bed, an evergreen border, and bulbs in spring. A delightful walled garden with water and a wide range of cottage-garden plants together with a greenhouse and vegetable garden are other features to enjoy.

OLD HALL 7
Ashwell, Leicestershire. Tel: (0572) 722823

*Mrs N.L. McRoberts * 3m N of Oakham via B668 towards Cottesmore, turn left to Ashwell * Best season: mid-June to late July * Parking * Toilet facilities * Open for parties by arrangement * Entrance: £1 per person*

Fine old garden with some good colour combinations both with shrubs and in the herbaceous borders, and a range of variegated foliage specimens. A large yew hedge forms a screen and the church provides a backcloth to the raised border of shrubs and trees. In the walled garden is a good range of cottage-garden plants and perennials and climbers on the wall add further colour. A pleasant garden with a peaceful atmosphere.

ORCHARDS 8
Hall Lane, Walton, Nr Lutterworth, Leicestershire. Tel: (0455) 556958

Mr and Mrs G. Cousins ∗ *8m S of Leicester. Take A50, turn right for Bruntingthorpe then follow signs for Walton* ∗ *Best season: summer* ∗ *Parking in nearby roads* ∗ *Toilet facilities* ∗ *Suitable for wheelchairs* ∗ *Dogs on lead* ∗ *Plants for sale* ∗ *Open by appointment* ∗ *Entrance: £1, children free*

A fine example of how to create variety in a small area round a village bungalow. There are raised beds around a pool, old brick paths, troughs with alpines, island beds, a cottage garden with shrub roses, lavender, verbascum and geraniums. Full of ideas and original plant combinations in foliage and colour.

PREBENDAL HOUSE 9
Empingham, Leicestershire.

Mr and Mrs J. Partridge ∗ *4m from Stamford, just off A606 in Empingham behind the church* ∗ *Parking* ∗ *Teas in Audit Hall* ∗ *Toilet facilities* ∗ *Suitable for wheelchairs* ∗ *Open 30th Aug, 2 – 6pm* ∗ *Entrance: £1, children 50p (1991 prices)*

The medium-sized garden of the old bishop's palace has yew hedges dividing the garden into smaller areas and forming backing to herbaceous borders. The walled kitchen garden has a wide range of vegetables, fruit trees and bushes as well as herbaceous borders with masses of dahlias and peonies. Also in this area are greenhouses and a fig on the wall. The sunken garden contains three pools with fish and water lilies and a beautiful beech tree. There are several large trees in the garden and drive which blend the garden into the adjacent parkland. Many shrub roses along with cottage-garden plants give the garden a great feeling of peace. The yews are an attractive feature.

ROCKINGHAM CASTLE
(see Northamptonshire)

ROSE COTTAGE 10
Owston, Nr Oakham, Leicestershire. Tel: (066477) 545

Mr J.D. Buchanan ∗ *6m W of Oakham via Knossington, 2m S of Somerby* ∗ *Parking outside village hall* ∗ *Home-made teas* ∗ *Toilet facilities* ∗ *Suitable for wheelchairs* ∗ *Open 10th May, 21st June, 2 – 6pm. Also by appointment* ∗ *Entrance: £1, children free*

This one and three quarter-acre garden made from an old sand quarry over the past 12 years on clay and lime conditions has a wide range of plants and the design features are very good. There is a beautiful hedge of *Rosa rugosa*, island beds, a raised bed with conifers and heathers, ground-cover plants, collections of hollies, roses, hardy geraniums, hebes, ferns, alpines and potentillas. In addition a peat bed, scree border and a good vegetable garden. Pool. A garden full of interesting ideas.

UNIVERSITY OF LEICESTER BOTANIC GARDEN ★   11
Stoughton Drive South, Oadby, Leicestershire. Tel: (0533) 717725

Leicester University ✳ *3m SE of city centre, just off the A6 opposite Oadby race course* ✳ *Parking in nearby roads* ✳ *Toilet facilities* ✳ *Suitable for wheelchairs* ✳ *Plants for sale when available* ✳ *Open all year, Mon – Fri (except Bank Holidays), 10am – 4.30pm (3.30pm on Fri) or dusk if earlier* ✳ *Entrance: free*

A 16-acre garden founded in the early 1900s incorporating the gardens of four large houses with many interesting features ranging from the large trees of *Pinus nigra*, *Sequoiadendron giganteum*, *Fraxinus excelsior* and *Juglans regia* to the alpine houses' lewisias and drabas. A cactus house, shrub borders with a wide range of acers and conifers, a fern house, fuchsias and herbaceous borders. Borders of ericas, climbers on the wall and on a stone pergola, a formal pool and a raised-bed garden. National collections of aubretias, hardy fuchsias and skimmias. A typical Leicestershire meadow has been recreated. Visitors can learn much botanically.

WAKERLEY MANOR   12
Wakerley, Nr Uppingham, Leicestershire. Tel: (057287) 511

Mr and Mrs A.D.A.W. Forbes ✳ *6m from Uppingham. Turn right off A47 through Barrowden to Wakerley* ✳ *Best season: July* ✳ *Parking* ✳ *Refreshments* ✳ *Suitable for wheelchairs* ✳ *Dogs on lead* ✳ *Plants for sale when available* ✳ *Open by appointment and 28th June, 2 – 6pm. For weekdays March to Nov, telephone Stuart Baines on the above number evenings only* ✳ *Entrance: £1, OAP 50p, children 10p*

A four and a half-acre garden landscaped 15 years ago and being developed by the present owners with large areas of lawn and mature trees – weeping ash, *Cedrus atlantica* and sequoiadendron. Autumn colour is provided by several acers, sorbus and fagus and new trees and shrubs are being planted to provide shelter. Herbaceous borders with perennials, shrubs and shrub roses provide summer colour. Climbers adorn the house walls and there is a pool with fish and plants. A hedge of lavatera gives a splash of colour and in the greenhouses are a range of good pot plants. Vegetable garden.

WARTNABY GARDENS ★★   13
Wartnaby, Nr Melton Mowbray, Leicestershire.

Lord and Lady King ✳ *4m NW of Melton Mowbray. From A606 turn W in Ab Kettleby for Wartnaby* ✳ *Best season: end May to mid-Aug* ✳ *Parking* ✳ *Refreshments* ✳ *Toilet facilities* ✳ *Partly suitable for wheelchairs* ✳ *Dogs on lead* ✳ *Plants for sale* ✳ *Open 14th June, 12th July, 2 – 6pm* ✳ *Entrance: £1, children 20p (1991 prices)*

This garden has delightful little gardens within it, including a grey garden, a sunken garden and a purple border of shrubs and roses, and there are good herbaceous borders, climbers and old-fashioned roses. A large pool has an adjacent bog garden with primulas, ferns and astilbe and several varieties of willow. There is an arboretum with a good collection of trees and shrub roses, and alongside the drive is a beech hedge in a Grecian pattern. Greenhouses contain peaches, orchids and a vine and there is a new fruit garden with fruit arches and cordon trees. Fine views.

WHATTON HOUSE ★   14
Nr Kegworth, Leicestershire. Tel: (0509) 842268

Lord Crawshaw   ✶   4m NE of Loughborough on A6 between Kegworth and Hathern. 1m from M1 junction 24   ✶   Best season: spring   ✶   Parking in grounds ✶ Refreshments in tea room ✶ Toilet facilities ✶ Partly suitable for wheelchairs ✶ Dogs on lead ✶ Plants for sale ✶ Open Easter to Sept, Sun and Bank Holiday Mons, 2 – 6pm. Weekdays by appointment ✶ Entrance: £1, OAP 50p, children 40p

This 15-acre garden created by Lord Crawshaw and developed over the years contains wide interest with the lovely herbaceous border, the unusual Chinese garden and the many large trees and more recently-planted arboretum. Note the Art Nouveau gate. There is an ice-house, a dog cemetery, rose garden, woodland garden and the Canyon garden. Water adds to the beauty with pools and there are brick channels that can be filled with water. There is a large walled kitchen garden and in the early part of the year masses of wild flowers. Some areas are somewhat overgrown but an air of peace surrounds the whole.

CUTTINGS
Readers may wish to be reminded that the taking of cuttings without the owners' permission can lead to embarassment and, if it continues on a large scale, may cause the owners to close their gardens to the public. This has to be seen in the context of an increasing number of thefts from gardens. At Nymans, the famous Sussex garden, thefts have reached such a level that the gardener will not now plant out any shrub until it is semi-mature and of such a size that its theft would be very difficult. Other owners have reported the theft of artifacts as well as plants.

LINCOLNSHIRE

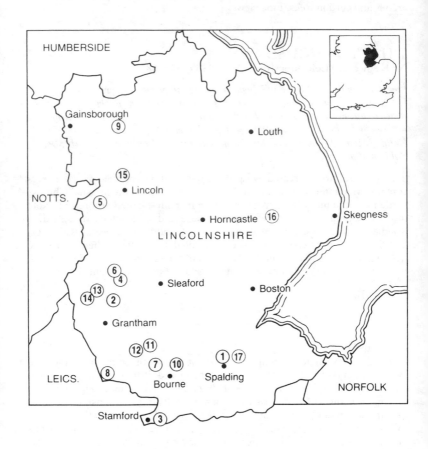

AYSCOUGHFEE HALL AND GARDENS 1
Churchgate, Spalding, Lincolnshire. Tel: (0775) 725468

*South Holland District Council ✻ Centre of Spalding ✻ Parking on Churchgate
✻ Refreshments: café open seasonally ✻ Toilet facilities inc. disabled ✻ Suitable
for wheelchairs ✻ Dogs on lead ✻ Hall open daily, 9am – 5pm (4.30pm on Fri).
Closed weekends Oct to Feb ✻ Gardens open weekdays, 8am – dusk, Sun 10am –
dusk. Closed 25th Dec ✻ Entrance: free*

Next to the River Welland the gardens of this public park are in a beautiful setting. Entirely enclosed by lovely old walls, they are worth visiting for the bizarrely-shaped, clipped yew walks, its old rectangular fish pond with fountains and the fascinating medieval red-brick hall now housing the museum of South Holland. In addition there are good bedding displays, lawns, formal rose garden, pergola, and wall shrubs including a fruiting vine.

BELTON HOUSE ★ 2
Belton, Nr Grantham, Lincolnshire. Tel: (0476) 66116

The National Trust ✱ *3m N of Grantham off A607* ✱ *Parking* ✱ *Refreshments: light lunches, teas, etc., 12 noon – 5.30pm* ✱ *Toilet facilities inc. disabled* ✱ *Suitable for wheelchairs* ✱ *Dogs on lead* ✱ *Gift shop* ✱ *House open April to Oct, Wed – Sun and Bank Holiday Mons, 1 – 5.30pm. Closed Good Friday* ✱ *Gardens open April to Oct, Wed – Sun and Bank Holiday Mons, 11am – 5.30pm (last admission 5pm). Free access to park on foot from Lion Lodge gates all year but this does not give admittance to house, garden or adventure playground* ✱ *Entrance: £3.80 (house and gardens)*

The gardens at Belton are large and impressive. The extensive woodland area has two lakes, a small canal and good cedars; a children's adventure playground makes it ideal for families. However, it is the formal area to the north of the house, completed with the superbly restored and replanted Jeffrey Wyatville orangery, that makes the garden memorable. The 'Dutch garden' has clipped yew hedging, formal beds with lavender edging, standard 'Iceberg' roses and well-planted stone urns. The earlier Italian garden has a large central pond with fountain, a lion-headed exhedra, lawns and clipped yews. The gradual but extensive restoration of the garden, including the reforming of herbaceous borders and the old statue walk, ensures a garden of great merit and authenticity. 200 trees were blown down during recent gales in the park, 29 of which were in the garden, including six cedars of Lebanon and two large beeches.

BURGHLEY HOUSE 3
Stamford, Lincolnshire. Tel: (0780) 52451

Burghley House Preservation Trust. Custodian: Lady Victoria Leatham (née Cecil) ✱ *¹/₂m E of Stamford on Barnack Road, close to A1. Well signposted* ✱ *Parking* ✱ *Refreshments* ✱ *Toilet facilities* ✱ *Limited access for wheelchairs* ✱ *Dogs on lead in park* ✱ *Shop* ✱ *House open* ✱ *Garden open 17th April to early Oct, daily, 11am – 5pm. Avoid Burghley Horse Trials 3rd to 6th Sept* ✱ *Entrance: £3.80, OAP £3.50, children £2.30, family ticket £10 (inc. guided tour of house and entrance to special exhibition)*

The main attraction at Burghley is the magnificent Elizabethan house with its immense collection of art treasures, built by Richard Cecil, created Lord Burghley by his Queen. Both the house and its custodian, Lady Victoria Leatham, have appeared on many television antiques programmes. The parkland, landscaped by 'Capability' Brown, is delightful and extensive. There is only a small area of formal rose garden with oval pond, lavender, fountain and urns so Burghley is of limited interest to visitors with more botanical leanings. In addition to creating a large serpentine lake, Brown built a new stable block, an orangery, a gamekeeper's lodge, a dairy and an ice-house. The finest surviving small building is a lakeside summer house.

CAYTHORPE COURT 4
Lincolnshire College of Agriculture and Horticulture, Caythorpe, Grantham, Lincolnshire. Tel: (0400) 72521

Lincolnshire County Council ✳ *10m N of Grantham off A607* ✳ *Parking* ✳ *Refreshments on open day* ✳ *Toilet facilities* ✳ *Partly suitable for wheelchairs* ✳ *Plants and produce for sale* ✳ *Open 6th June, 1.30 – 5pm for College Open Day and 6th, 14th, 19th May by appointment for evening guided tours at 7 and 7.15pm* ✳ *Entrance: £2 per car on open day, £5 per party for evening guided tours*

One of three centres for the Lincolnshire College of Agriculture and Horticulture, this is reflected in its glasshouses and display beds of roses, shrubs, bedding and herbaceous plants. However, it is the original garden around the 1899 hunting lodge that makes a visit worthwhile. Three large terraces built on a west-facing slope are wonderfully romantic with Ancaster stone walls, balustrades and stairways. For ease of maintenance all are quite simply planted. The upper terrace has a good shrub border and lawn with a specimen monkey-puzzle tree. The middle terrace, a delight in spring, has walls covered in aubretia, and a row of flowering cherries. The third has Virginia creeper and wisteria swathing the balustraded stairs, and a wide rose border underplanted with flag irises and backed by clematis-covered walls from the upper terrace; walks lead through the surrounding woodland. To the east of the house, from the central lavender-edged bed, shrub-lined drives lead to other parts of the college.

DODDINGTON HALL 5
Doddington, Nr Lincoln, Lincolnshire. Tel: (0522) 694308

Mr and Mrs A.G. Jarvis ✳ *5m W of Lincoln on B1190* ✳ *Parking* ✳ *Refreshment: restaurant open from 12 noon* ✳ *Toilet facilities inc. disabled* ✳ *Suitable for wheelchairs* ✳ *Dogs on lead* ✳ *Shop* ✳ *House open* ✳ *Garden open Easter Mon and May to Sept, Wed and Sun inc. Bank Holiday Mons, 2 – 6pm. Parties at other times by arrangement* ✳ *Entrance: £1.65, children 85p (house and garden £3.30, children £1.65), special rates for disabled in wheelchairs and parties of 20 or more*

The romantic gardens of the Elizabethan house successfully combine many different styles and moods. The simplicity of the gravel, box and lawned courtyard, the formal croquet lawn and the gravel walk along the kitchen garden wall contrasts with the walled west garden with its elaborate parterres of roses, iris and clipped box edging with borders of herbaceous plants and old roses. (The parterres were restored in Elizabethan style in 1900.) Fine eighteenth-century Italian gates open from here on to a formal yew alley, more old roses and a good wild garden. Here the meandering walks take in a turf maze, stream, ancient specimens of sweet chestnut, cedar, yew and holly, and the Temple of the Winds built by the present owner. The more recently-planted herb garden, pleached hornbeams and dwarf box-edging continue to harmonize the different areas and create more interest in this peaceful garden.

FULBECK HALL 6
Fulbeck, Nr Grantham, Lincolnshire. Tel: (0400) 72205

*Mr and Mrs Fry * On A607 Lincoln – Grantham road * Parking * Picnic area * Toilet facilities * Suitable for wheelchairs * Dogs on lead * Plants for sale * House open Easter, 4th, 25th May, 1st to 26th July, daily, and 31st Aug, 2 – 5pm. Extra charge * Garden open Easter, 4th May to 26th June, Mon-Fri, 29th June to 26th July, daily, and 31st Aug, 2 – 5pm * Entrance: £1.50, children £1*

The 11-acre garden at Fulbeck is varied and interesting with newly-planted informal areas together with a formal Victorian terrace. Many of the trees here are as old as the house (1733). The top terrace with a gravel walk is backed by a superbly-shaped clipped yew hedge. The bottom lawn has shrubs, roses, unusual clematis and ramblers climbing into the surrounding trees. Against a lime-stone wall at the south of the house is a herbaceous border with many choice plants. Beyond the immediate garden is a pleasant wild garden and nature trail. In 1990, 500 native trees and shrubs around the north and western edge of the garden were planted, and a pond was constructed near the northern boundary by the nature trail. Planting plans available for the whole formal area of the garden which visitors may buy or borrow.

GRIMSTHORPE CASTLE 7
Grimsthorpe, Nr Bourne, Lincolnshire. Tel: (0778) 32205

*Grimsthorpe and Drummond Castle Trust Ltd * 4m NW of Bourne on A151 Colsterworth Bourne road * Parking * Teas * Toilet facilities inc. disabled * Suitable for wheelchairs * Castle open 30th May to 13th Sept, Suns and Bank Holidays, 2 – 6pm (last admission 5pm) * Home Park and Gardens open 19th, 20th April, and 2nd May to 13th Sept, Sats, Suns and Bank Holidays, 12 noon – 6pm (last admission 5pm) * Entrance: £1, children under 16 50p (house and garden £3, OAP £2 and children under 16 £1.50)*

The impressive house, part-medieval, part-Tudor and part-eighteenth-century, of Vanbrugh design, is surrounded on three sides by good pleasure gardens in which 'Capability' Brown had a hand. The Victorian knot garden to the east of the house has beds of lavender, roses and catmint with edges of clipped box. To the south are two yew-hedged rose gardens with topiary, a yew 'broad walk' and a retreat. Leading to the west terrace is a double yew walk with classic herbaceous borders and beyond a shrub rose border and row of 70-year-old cedars. The yew hedging throughout the garden is superbly maintained and differs in design from one area to another. Beyond the pleasure gardens are the arboretum, wild garden, an unusual geometrically-designed kitchen garden with clipped box and bean pergola, and extensive parkland. Views of old oak and chestnut avenues and the parkland, its lake and Vanbrugh summer house are provided by cleverly positioned vistas and terraces.

GUNBY HALL ★ 8
Gunby, Nr Spilsby, Lincolnshire.

The National Trust ✳ *2¹/₂m NW of Burgh-le-Marsh on S of A158* ✳ *Parking*
✳ *Toilet facilities* ✳ *Suitable for wheelchairs* ✳ *Dogs on lead* ✳ *Plants for sale*
✳ *House and garden open April to Sept, Wed only, 2 – 6pm (last admission*
5.30pm). Garden also open Thurs, 2 – 6pm. Also Tues, Thurs and Fri by written
appointment to Mr and Mrs J.D. Wrisdale ✳ *Entrance: £1.50 (house and garden*
£2.30)

The early eighteenth-century house, with its walls smothered in fine plants, is
set in parkland with avenues of lime and horse chestnut. The shrub borders,
wild garden, lawns with old cedars and the restrained formal front garden of
catmint and lavender beds backed by clipped yew provide a startling contrast to
the main attraction of Gunby – its walled gardens. The dazzling pergola garden
with its apple-tree walkway has a maze of paths leading to beds of old roses,
herb garden and brimming herbaceous and annual borders. The second walled
area houses an impressive kitchen garden reached after passing more borders
of perfectly-arranged herbaceous plants and hybrid musk roses. Backing on to
its wall is another wonderfully classic herbaceous border and beyond an early
nineteenth-century long fish pond and orchard completing an altogether
enchanting garden. It is fitting that it was the subject of Tennyson's 'Haunt of
Ancient Peace'.

HALL FARM AND NURSERY 9
Harpswell, Gainsborough, Lincolnshire. Tel: (042773) 412

Mr and Mrs M Tatam ✳ *7m E of Gainsborough on A631* ✳ *Best season:*
summer ✳ *Parking* ✳ *Teas* ✳ *Toilet facilities* ✳ *Partly suitable for wheelchairs*
✳ *Dogs on lead* ✳ *Plants for sale* ✳ *Open daily, except 25th Dec to 1st Jan,*
10am – 6pm ✳ *Entrance: donation to charity*

This garden has been carefully planned and exuberantly planted. The owners'
sheer delight in plants, satisfied by their adjoining nursery, is evident
everywhere. A santolina-edged rose pergola leads down the side of the farm
house to two large terraced lawns. The wide borders here are of mainly shrub
roses (there are 84 rose varieties in the garden) underplanted with herbaceous
plants. From the top terrace old stone pillars make an imposing entrance to a
round sunken garden with miniature box edging and seasonal bedding. A short
walk away is an interesting medieval moat. In their short time here, the owners
have achieved a great deal and still have ambitious plans for the future.

32 MAIN STREET 10
Dyke, Nr Bourne, Lincolnshire. Tel: (0778) 422241

Mr and Mrs D. Sellars ✳ *1m N of Bourne, off A15* ✳ *Parking* ✳ *Teas* ✳
Toilet facilities at nearby village hall ✳ *Dogs on lead* ✳ *Plants for sale* ✳ *Open*
May Bank Holiday and some Suns in April and Aug. Also by appointment ✳
Entrance: 80p, children 20p

This small area of 100 x 50 feet is subdivided into tiny compartments allowing
an astonishing number of planting schemes. Every available space is crammed

with a choice plant, ornament, trough or architectural feature and by careful planning and underplanting overflows with a continuous display of colour. Such is the enthusiasm of the owners that the garden is constantly changing and may well vary significantly from year to year; it is daunting to recall that it has been developed over a period of only six years.

MANOR FARM   11
Keisby, Nr Lenton, Bourne, Lincolnshire.

Mr and Mrs C.A. Richardson ✳ *9m NW of Bourne, N of A151* ✳ *Parking* ✳ *Teas* ✳ *Toilet facilities on ground floor* ✳ *Suitable for wheelchairs* ✳ *Dogs on lead* ✳ *Plants for sale* ✳ *Open 24th May, 28th June, 2 – 6pm* ✳ *Entrance: £1, children free*

This pretty, informal garden is a delight with its artistic planning and colour harmonization. The tiny paths to the vegetable plot, pergola and stream meander through the beds and so allow close inspection of the many choice plants, including shrub roses, ramblers and clematis. The garden was featured on *Gardener's World*.

MANOR HOUSE   12
Bitchfield, Grantham, Lincolnshire. Tel: (047685) 261

Mr John Richardson ✳ *Centre of Bitchfield village on B1176 SE of Grantham* ✳ *Best season: mid-June to mid-July* ✳ *Parking* ✳ *Toilet facilities* ✳ *Open for parties of 20 or more by appointment only. No children* ✳ *Entrance: donations to charity. £2 per person*

The restrained courtyard entrance has walls of soft apricot-pink, perfectly matching the gravel, and is decorated merely with clipped box in French-style planters. Just south of the house is a formal box-edged garden with a central armillary sphere, planted with the grey-foliaged, white-flowering *Cerastium tomentosum* var. *columnae* that gives a welcome winter colour and interest for this is a summer garden, magnificent in June and July. There are 94 rose varieties mixed with herbaceous plants in formal and informal borders. Roses also provide colour round the pond and ramble happily through old apple trees in the lawn and over the house walls. By careful design, views over a ha-ha to the paddock are never lost, even with the owner's generous planting schemes. Much recommended for lovers of shrub roses and summer-flowering herbaceous plants. Robin Lane Fox helped with the design.

MARSTON HALL   13
Marston, Nr Grantham, Lincolnshire. Tel: (0400) 50225

Reverend Henry Thorold ✳ *6m NW of Grantham, 1¹/₂m off A1* ✳ *Teas* ✳ *Toilet facilities* ✳ *Suitable for wheelchairs* ✳ *Dogs on lead* ✳ *Plants for sale when available* ✳ *House open* ✳ *Garden open 14th, 21st June, 14th July, 9th Aug, 2 – 6pm. Other times by appointment* ✳ *Entrance: £1.50, children 75p*

The gardens reflect the intimate nature of the beautiful and ancient Ancaster stone house. A series of small, walled and high-hedged gardens, courtyards and walks house formal rose beds, cottage garden, knot garden planted with herbs, and vegetables screened by herbaceous borders and trellising. To the south of the house are lawns, clipped yews and walks through the newly-planted laburnum avenue and ancient trees including an enormous laburnum and a 400-year-old wych elm. The Lancing avenue of Lombardy poplars stretches from the orchard to the nearby River Witham and perfectly unites the garden with the parkland beyond.

ORCHARD NURSERIES   14
Tow Lane, Foston, Grantham, Lincolnshire.

Janet and Richard Blenkinship ＊ 7m NW of Grantham off A1 ＊ Parking ＊ Refreshments when open for charity ＊ Toilet facilities ＊ Suitable for wheelchairs ＊ Plants for sale ＊ Open March to Sept, daily, 10am – 5pm ＊ Entrance: on certain days 50p, otherwise voluntary donation to charity

Set around the owners' nursery and propagating areas, the one-acre garden offers an ideal opportunity for viewing the many herbaceous plants in which they specialise. The small areas of lawns and grassy paths, separated by hedges and plant-laden arches, provide a foil for the many borders. Varying from shady shrub-backed borders to bright and cottagy beds, they are filled with labelled, choice plants. A small meadow, bog garden and a pond are additional features of especial interest to the plantsperson.

RISEHOLME HALL   15
Lincolnshire College of Agriculture and Horticulture,Riseholme, Lincoln. Tel: (0522) 522252

Lincolnshire County Council ＊ 5m N of Lincoln off A15 ＊ Parking ＊ Refreshments on Open Day and in evenings if booked ＊ Toilet facilities ＊ Suitable for wheelchairs ＊ Plants for sale ＊ Farm shop ＊ Open 13th June, 1.30 – 5pm for College Open Day and 10th, 23rd, 24th June, 7th July by appointment for evening guided tours at 7, 7.15 and 7.30pm ＊ Entrance: £2 per car on Open Day, £5 per party for evening guided tours

Typically eighteenth-century landscaped parkland, with a picturesque lake, surrounds the house and gardens. Reflecting its educational as well as decorative function the garden provides a rare opportunity to view a vast selection of labelled plants. The horticultural department's demonstration plots show rock, water, low maintenance and heather gardens as well as demonstration hedges, genus beds, bedding, vegetables and glasshouses. The long Bishop's Walk has a yew hedge to the north and a warm brick wall to the south allowing the cultivation of many tender wall shrubs and climbers normally only found in more southerly districts. Along the walk is a herbaceous border and island beds of flowering shrubs. Also a newly restored, walled organic vegetable garden, an arboretum planted in 1971, mixed borders, rose beds and conservation areas.

SAUSTHORPE OLD HALL   16
Sausthorpe, Nr Spilsby, Lincolnshire. Tel: (0790) 53275

Mrs W.F. Kochan ＊ 8m E of Horncastle on A158 ＊ Parking ＊ Refreshments

Toilet facilities ✳ *Suitable for wheelchairs* ✳ *Dogs on lead* ✳ *Open for charity probably in Sept but date unavailable at time of going to press*

Sadly overgrown and damaged by rabbits, this garden still manages to look lovely. It is designed as a series of interconnecting lawns, borders and beds divided by tall hedges and arches, with a long straight walk from the house, through the old kitchen garden with its rose pergola and flowers, which eventually reaches a pond and summerhouse. The planting is informal with good shrubs and conifers and some beautiful old trees, including a grand cut-leaf beech, reputedly one of the best in Lincolnshire. The borders, rockery, retaining walls and steps spill over with border geraniums, roses, foxgloves and *Alchemilla mollis*. It is perhaps this unrestrained neglect that instils the atmosphere with such peace and romance.

SPRINGFIELDS GARDENS   17
Springfield, Spalding, Lincolnshire. Tel: (0775) 724843

Springfields Horticultural Society ✳ *1¹/₂m from Spalding on A151* ✳ *Best season: April and Sept* ✳ *Parking* ✳ *Refreshments: café, tea shop and licensed restaurant* ✳ *Toilet facilities* ✳ *Suitable for wheelchairs* ✳ *Plants for sale* ✳ *Shop* ✳ *Open 29th March to 29th Sept, daily, 10am – 6pm* ✳ *Entrance: £2, children free (£3, OAP £2, children 5 – 16, £1 special events)*

The 25 acres of gardens have been designed to maximize areas of show bedding – whether of the colourful spring displays of thousands of bulb varieties or of the later roses and annuals. Subdivided into smaller areas by shrub borders and small copses, the garden boasts many different features all easily accessible for wheelchairs. However, with the exception of an excellent herbaceous border, with its bold plantings, the gardens and glasshouses can be monotonous. The colour schemes are dazzling but wearing and the gardens themselves – the lake, the pergolas and the architecture – are all somewhat dated.

DOGS, TOILETS & OTHER FACILITIES
If these are *not* mentioned in the text, then facilities are not available. For example, if dogs are not mentioned, owners will probably not permit entry, even on a lead.

LONDON (Greater)

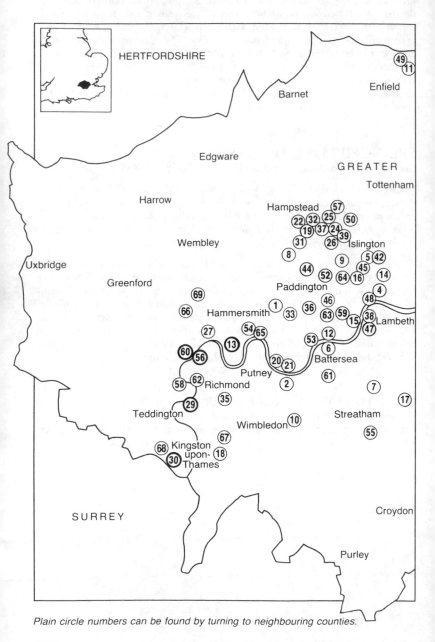

HERTFORDSHIRE

Barnet

Enfield

Edgware

GREATER

Tottenham

Hampstead

Harrow

Wembley

Uxbridge

Greenford

Paddington

Islington

Hammersmith

Lambeth

Putney

Battersea

Richmond

Streatham

Teddington

Wimbledon

Kingston
upon-
Thames

SURREY

Croydon

Purley

Plain circle numbers can be found by turning to neighbouring counties.

242

ESSEX
LONDON
Romford
41
Ilford
Dagenham
Stepney
Erith
23
28
Crayford
Lowicham
3
34
Bromley
51
Orpington
40
KENT
SURREY

Two-starred gardens are ringed in bold.

29 ADDISON AVENUE 1
London W11. Tel: (071) 603 2450

Mr and Mrs D.B. Nicholson ✳ *Off Holland Park Avenue, W of tube station. Cars must enter via Norland Square and Queensdale Road* ✳ *Best season: summer* ✳ *Parking* ✳ *Open 26th July, 2 – 6pm (but telephone to check)* ✳ *Entrance: £1*

Meticulously kept and well-designed small town walled garden (about 30 x 40 feet) with a profusion of plants on every surface. It makes the best use of every inch of space. A tiny lawn is dominated by two venerable pear trees. Beyond them are perennial borders, slightly raised, and formally laid out but informally planted with an emphasis on phlox and hardy geraniums. To one side of the studio workshop at the end of the garden is a small shade garden, complete with statue. In late summer *Solanum jasminoides* blossoms profusely on one of the walls. The colour themes of the borders (pink, blue and white) and the variegated foliage help to unify the garden, which is an excellent balance between design and planting. Interestingly 'everything is used to being moved and hardly ever sulks.'

32 ATNEY ROAD 2
Putney, London SW15. Tel: (081) 785 9355

Mrs Sally Tamplin ✳ *Off Putney Bridge Road* ✳ *Parking in street* ✳ *☆Teas* ✳ *Open by appointment and 26th April, 7th June, 12th July, 20th Sept, 2 – 6pm* ✳ *Entrance: £1*

A spacious London garden with attractively planted terrace and wide lawn beyond, which has been described as 'brilliant'. Wide borders along the boundaries are packed with herbaceous plants, roses, hydrangeas and other shrubs to ensure a long season of interest. A central rose arch leads to the rear of the garden where young hedges are establishing, and a scree garden has been recently created. A tiny 'woodland dell'. Nearby is 17 Fulham Park Gardens.

AVERY HILL PARK 3
Eltham, London SE9. Tel: (081) 850 3217

London Borough of Greenwich ✳ *Off Bexley Road and Avery Hill Road* ✳ *Parking* ✳ *Refreshments: small café* ✳ *Toilet facilities* ✳ *Suitable for wheelchairs* ✳ *Some restrictions on dogs* ✳ *Open 7.30am – dusk. The winter garden open Mon – Thurs, 1 – 4pm, Fri, 1 – 3pm, Sat and Sun, 10am – 4pm. Closed 24th, 25th Dec and 1st Jan* ✳ *Entrance: free*

More remains of the gardens at Avery Hill Park than the 50-room mansion, which was badly damaged in the Blitz. The house, built by Colonel John North, otherwise known as The Nitrate King because he made a fortune from Chilean nitrates which were much in demand as fertiliser, was the perfect example of the excesses of the Victorian nouveaux-riches. Since 1906 it has been used as a teachers' training college, while the gardens are enjoyed by the local inhabitants. There are rose gardens and three giant conservatories which look like icebergs which have come to a halt on the southern slope of Shooter's Hill.

The domed temperate house is bursting with bougainvillaea and staghorn ferns. The tropical house attracts school parties to see bananas, coffee and ginger while the camellias draw the crowds to the cold house in the spring. There is also an aviary.

BARBICAN CONSERVATORY ★   4
The Barbican, London EC2. Tel: (071) 638 6114

*City of London * In the Barbican Centre, on the 8th floor * Parking * Refreshments at Waterside Café in Barbican Centre * Toilet facilities * Partly suitable for wheelchairs * Shop in Barbican Centre * Open weekends and Bank Holidays only, 12 noon – 5pm. Ring to confirm opening times as the conservatory is sometimes used for conferences * Entrance: 75p, OAP and children 50p, family ticket (2 adults and up to 4 children) £2*

The lift to the eighth floor of the Barbican transports you from a concrete jungle to a lush jungle of temperate and semi-tropical plants. Planted in the autumn of 1980-81, using 1,600 cubic metres of soil, the conservatory was opened in 1984. Twin *Cupressus cashmeriana* grace the main entrance while a vast banyan tree (*Ficus bengalensis*) in the eastern section is in need of pruning before it goes through the roof. Many familiar houseplants, like *Ficus benjamina* have reached giant proportions and a colossal Swiss Cheese plant (*Monstera deliciosa*) produces edible fruits after flowering. The Arid House on the second level, added in 1986, contains epiphyllum and cacti, including the largest *Carnegiea gigantea* in Europe. Fred, as it is affectionately known, was a gift from the Mayor of Salt Lake City. There are finches in the aviary and the ponds are alive with fish and terrapins. There is a fresh stock of chameleons, which live in tanks rather than the trees. Natural predators and pathogens are used to keep down pests, and the hard Thames water is softened to stop nutrients becoming locked in the soil. Floodlighting has recently been installed, but the limited winter opening hours don't allow visitors to take full advantage of it.

28 BARNSBURY SQUARE   5
London N1. Tel: (071) 607 2001

*Mr F.T. Gardner * Off Thornhill Road * Parking in road * Refreshments * Open 14th June, 2 – 6pm * Entrance: £1 (£1.50 for combined entry with 338 Liverpool Road N7 – see entry)*

A real period piece! For the most part, an un-reconstructed Victorian garden, cared for by the third and fourth generation of owners. There is a re-discovered grotto dating from the nineteenth century, linked with a pool (exceptionally full of frogs), waterfall and fountain, all previously run with rationed mains water but now pumped in the conventional manner. There is a traditional 1930s wooden greenhouse and a Victorian gazebo of real distinction, though slightly askew. Magnificent trees lent by surrounding gardens create the London oasis effect. Planting reflects changing fashions and styles giving year round interest.

BATTERSEA PARK   6
Battersea, London SW11. Tel: (081) 871 7530/1

*Wandsworth Borough Council * S side of Thames, from Chelsea Bridge to Albert*

LONDON (Greater)

Bridge ✳ *Parking free in car park* ✳ *Refreshments* ✳ *Toilet facilities* ✳
Suitable for wheelchairs ✳ *Dogs* ✳ *Open daily, 7am – dusk* ✳ *Entrance: free*

Laid out 1852-8 on Battersea Fields, an old duelling rendezvous. It had been much improved by the late-lamented GLC and contains many interesting features such as the Buddhist temple, zoo, aviary, sculptures, large boating lake and also frequent entertainments in tented accommodation. The plantsperson should make a point of visiting the glasshouses near Albert Bridge. Interesting sub-tropical garden, water garden and modern wooden arbourwork. It is to be hoped that the improvements will continue under the new regime.

BROCKWELL PARK 7
Tulse Hill, London SE24. Tel: (081) 674 6141

Lambeth Council ✳ *Take A205 then A215, entrances at Herne Hill Gate, Norwood Road, Brockwell Gardens Road etc.* ✳ *Best season: summer (July)* ✳
Parking: Herne Hill Gate, Norwood Road, Brockwell Gardens Road ✳
Refreshments ✳ *Toilet facilities inc. disabled* ✳ *Partly suitable for wheelchairs* ✳
Dogs, except in walled garden ✳ *Open daily, 9am – dusk* ✳ *Entrance: free*

A peaceful and attractive refuge from nearby Brixton shopping centre, within a surprisingly large park, Brockwell has both a pretty and secluded old English walled garden, with rose beds, and a delightful mixture of herbaceous bedding, providing almost year-round interest. (Radios, cassettes, and dogs are banned from the walled garden – and children under 14 have to be accompanied by an adult.) On the hilltop surrounding the clock-tower are a variety of shrubs and trees and formal bedding. Both park and gardens are very well-maintained. The parkland is well provided with benches. Ground staff are helpful and informative. There are three ponds. Good views to the north over a London of many towers and a few spires which looks surprisingly attractive and even romantic.

15A BUCKLAND CRESCENT ★ 8
London NW3.

Lady Barbirolli ✳ *Near Fitzjohn's Avenue at Swiss Cottage end. 5 minutes from Swiss Cottage tube station and various buses* ✳ *Parking in neighbouring streets* ✳
Suitable for wheelchairs ✳ *Plants for sale* ✳ *Open 12th July, 2.30 – 6.30pm* ✳
Entrance: £1

The strong sense of space and line that musicians often possess is expressed in this dignified third-of-an-acre town garden. The ground plan combines flowing unfussy lines and ingenious geometry. Planting ranges from a functional but decorative vegetable patch to some remarkable mature tree specimens, such as *Cornus alternifolia* 'Variegata' and *Metasequoia glyptostroboides*; it is everywhere discriminating. A generous terrace is enhanced by boldly planted urns.

CAMLEY STREET NATURAL PARK 9
12 Camley Street, London NW1. Tel: (071) 833 2311

London Borough of Camden; managed by the London Wildlife Trust ✳ *Behind*

*King's Cross gasometers, turn off Goods Way or Pancras Way   *   Parking in nearby streets   *   Toilet facilities   *   Partly suitable for wheelchairs   *   Open daily, Mon – Fri, 9.30am – 5pm, Sat and Sun, 11am – 5pm   *   Entrance: free. Donations welcome*

Now threatened by the King's Cross Development scheme, this is an example of an extremely successful urban wild garden created against all the odds. Plants, wildlife and people thrive in it. In two and a fifth acres set between the Regent's Canal, imposing black and red gasometers and a noisy skipyard, it has been landscaped with a large pond at its centre. This tranquil space has a fine record of sighted birds and other wildlife. A simple pergola next to a small area of flower beds frames a view of the canal and passing long boats; the whole is somewhat romantically framed by relics of Victorian industry.

CANNIZARO PARK   10
Westside, Wimbledon, London SW19. Tel: (081) 946 7349

*London Borough of Merton   *   Westside, Wimbledon   *   Best season: March to May   *   Parking: Westside Common and surrounding side roads   *   Teas on Summer Suns only, 2 – 6pm, provided by Wimbledon Guides and Brownies   *   Toilet facilities   *   Wheelchairs have reasonable access to top gardens   *   Dogs on lead   *   Open daily, Mon – Fri, 8am – sunset, Sat, Sun and Bank Holidays, 9am – sunset   *   Entrance: free*

Formerly the grounds of Cannizaro House, the approach is through imposing gates and a formal drive, lined with beautifully-kept seasonal bedding. Cannizaro's trees are its principal attraction: cork oaks, mulberry and sassafras (until a few years ago it had the oldest sassafras in England). Some enormous and beautiful beeches have been slightly damaged. In the midst of the trees a secluded picnic area, set with tables, contains – somewhat unexpectedly – a bust of the Emperor Haile Selassie of Ethiopia, who sought refuge in Wimbledon. There is a small aviary, a pretty walled rose garden, an azalea and rhododendron collection and a heather garden. The old garden, the rather disappointing formal Italian garden and the pool are found down a steep slope directly in front of Cannizaro House. A wild garden is being created in the same location. Sculpture exhibitions are sometimes held in the park.

CAPEL MANOR Horticultural and Environmental Centre   11
Bullsmoor Lane, Enfield, Middlesex. Tel: (0992) 763849

*London Borough of Enfield   *   From the M25 junction with the A10, it is AA signposted via Turkey Street/Bullsmoor Lane   *   Parking   *   Teas   *   Toilet facilities   *   Suitable for wheelchairs   *   Dogs on lead   *   Plants for sale sometimes at weekends, special events and shows   *   Open April to Oct, daily, weekdays 10am – 4.30pm, weekends 10am – 5.30pm, Nov to March, weekdays, 10am – 4.30pm   *   Entrance: £1.50, OAP and children 75p (1991 prices for non-show days)*

These gardens are intended to show the history of gardening from the sixteenth century to the present. They also function as a design centre for the garden industry. The contrast with Myddelton House, along the road, could not be stronger: at Capel, maintenance is excellent but a unifying sensibility completely lacking. The gardens here are from first to last a curate's egg; good areas, such as the garden for the disabled, jostle with aberrations and queasy inventions, such as 'A Lover's Garden'. Detailing is mixed; jagged rocks are sunk in the middle of smooth, rounded pebbles. But there is lots of interest for the family outing, enhanced by an adjoining 'educational farm'. In 1990 the *Sunday Times* Beginner's Garden, featured at Chelsea, was moved here for display, and funds are being collected for further development.

CHELSEA PHYSIC GARDEN ★ 12
66 Royal Hospital Road, Chelsea, London SW3. Tel: (071) 352 5646

Trustees of Chelsea Physic Garden ＊ *One entrance in Swan Walk, off Chelsea Embankment and another in Royal Hospital Road* ＊ *Parking: meters in side street and in Battersea Park on opposite side of river* ＊ *Teas* ＊ *Toilet facilities* ＊ *Partly suitable for wheelchairs* ＊ *Plants for sale* ＊ *Open 22nd March to 18th Oct, Wed, Sun, 2 – 5pm, also during Chelsea Flower Show, 12 noon – 5pm Entrance: £2.50, students, children and unemployed £1.30*

Founded to train London's apothecaries in herbal medicine in the seventeenth century, the Chelsea Physic Garden is still actively involved in research into herbal medicine, as well as playing an important botanical role. Its three and a half acres, tucked between Cheyne Walk and Swan Walk, are well worth visiting, not only for the fascinating range of medicinal plants grown there, but also for their rare and interesting ones, including beautiful trees like the magnificent golden rain tree (*Koelreuteria paniculata*). The gardens also house what is believed to be the earliest rock garden in Europe, created on basaltic lava brought back by the botanist Joseph Banks from Iceland in 1772. The main part of the garden is devoted to systematic-order beds of plants, but there are also displays associated with the plant hunters and botanists who have played their part in the development of the garden, including Banks, Philip Miller, William Hudson and Robert Fortune, as well as an attractive woodland garden. The National collection of cistus is housed here. You can become a Friend of the Chelsea Physic Garden for a smallish sum, entitling you and a guest to free entry on all public open days and to entry at other times in office hours.

CHISWICK HOUSE ★★ 13
Burlington Lane, Chiswick, London W4. Tel: (081) 742 1225

London Borough of Hounslow ＊ *5m W of central London, just off A4* ＊ *Parking. Entrance on A4* ＊ *Refreshments* ＊ *Toilet facilities* ＊ *Suitable for wheelchairs* ＊ *Dogs on lead, not admitted in Italian garden* ＊ *House open* ＊ *Garden open April to Sept, daily, 10am – 6pm, Oct to March, 10am – 4pm. Closed 24th, 25th Dec* ＊ *Entrance: £1.90, concessions £1.50, children 95p*

Handsome, semi-classical gardens, stretching over many acres, with lakes, statues, monuments and magnificent trees. Created by William Kent to complement the Palladian villa built by Lord Burlington in 1729, the gardens are full of splendid vistas, avenues and changes of contour. There is a formal Italian garden with parterres filled with technicolour bedding plants in front of the handsome conservatory (both introduced after Kent's day) and a large canal-shaped lake, with informal woodland planting around it. The gardens are well worth visiting at any time of the year, but particularly in autumn and winter when many other gardens have lost their charm. Mature cedars and gingkos were felled as part of the restoration programme to recreate the original gardens, causing much local outrage.

CITY OF LONDON PARKS AND GARDENS   14

Although there is inevitably a certain similarity in the design and planning of any group of gardens administered by a public body, those within the City of London, being principally located on bomb sites, churchyards and former churchyards, perhaps have more variety than might be expected. For tourists and workers they provide a welcome respite from the dirt and noise of the City and almost all have lots of benches. They are open 8am – 7pm or dusk, 7 days a week unless otherwise stated.

EC1: *Postman's Park*, St Martins Le Grand. [Open Mon – Fri, 7am – dusk. Closed weekends and Bank Holidays] Close to St Paul's Cathedral. An area of formal bedding in the centre with mature trees, bushes and shrubs and a fine sculpture by Michael Ayrton. There is also a small fountain with goldfish, and tombs and headstones from the time when it was a churchyard. An arcade protects a tiled wall commemorating the deeds of those who died in their efforts to save others. *Greyfriars Rose Garden*, Newgate Street. [Not open, but visible from the road] A collection of hybrid teas and climbing roses trained up wooden pillars with rope linking them.

EC2: *Bunhill Fields Graveyard*. Between Bunhill Row and City Road. [Open Mon – Fri, 7.30am – 7pm (4pm Oct to March), weekends 9.30am – $^1/_4$ hour before dusk] A former burial ground containing many fine tombs and memorials, including those of William Blake and John Bunyan. Most of the tombs are behind railings, but part of the grounds which were bomb-damaged have been planted with grass, trees and shrubs. *Finsbury Circus*. The largest open space in the City and London's first public park (1606). Apart from the ubiquitous London plane trees, it also boasts the only bowling green in the City, surrounded by low box hedges, bedding plants, shrubs, a drinking fountain and a small bandstand. *St Agnes and St Anne Churchyard*, Gresham Street. [Permanently open] Here the church still stands, alongside the remains of part of London Wall and those of a Roman fort, surrounded by trees and shrubs. *St Botolphs Bishopgate Churchyard*, Wormwood Street. [Permanently open] Apart from the usual planting, there is also a tennis court and a former school house, restored in 1952 by the Worshipful Company of Fan Makers to serve as a church hall. *St Mary Aldermanbury*, Love Lane. [Permanently open] Made within the low ruined walls of a Wren church destroyed in the Blitz, the stumps of remaining pillars mark different levels of the garden. A shrubbery encloses a monument to Shakespeare's pals, John Heminge and Henry Condell. There is also a small knot garden. *St Mary Staining*. [Permanently open] Another patch of grass surrounded by shrubs, roses and benches.

EC3: *Pepys Garden*, Seething Lane. [Open weekdays only, 9am – 5.30pm] A splinter of garden on the site of the Navy Office, where Samuel Pepys lived and worked. A surprising number of trees in a tiny area. *St Dunstans Church Garden*, St Dunstans Hill. The most romantic garden in the City, it has been created within the walls of a Victorian Gothic church which was bombed during World

War II. Only the Wren tower survived and was restored. The remaining walls, containing arched windows and doorways, are covered with creepers and climbing plants and the spaces between planted with small trees and shrubs. There is a small fountain surrounded by benches and large tubs planted with standard fuchsias and bedding plants.

EC4: *St Laurence Pountney*, Laurence Pountney Hill. [Closed weekends] Two pocket-handkerchief patches of greenery with benches on the site of St Laurence Pountney Church and Corpus Christi College, destroyed in the Great Fire, 1666. *St Paul's Churchyard*. [Open 6am – 7.30pm, 7 days a week] Winding paths surround the back of the Cathedral with welcome shade and a resting place for the weary tourist. Apart from the usual municipal planting, there is a rose garden in the SE corner with hybrid teas and climbing roses on the fine early wrought-iron railings.

E1: *Portsoken Street Garden*, between Portsoken Street and Goodman's Yard. A tiny oasis with a bubbling fountain, brick walls, small trees and shrubs in raised beds behind low brick walls.

COLLEGE GARDEN AND LITTLE CLOISTER   15
Westminster Abbey, London SW1. Tel: (071) 222 5152

*Dean and Chapter of Westminster * ✳ * Off Dean's Yard, next to Abbey shop * ✳ * Best season: spring * ✳ * Suitable for wheelchairs * ✳ * Abbey shop * ✳ * Abbey open and band concerts 12.30 – 2.30pm in Aug * ✳ * Garden open April to Sept, Thurs, 10am – 6pm, Oct to March, Thurs, 10am – 4pm. Closed Maundy Thurs * ✳ * Entrance: free*

The eleventh-century college garden has been under cultivation for more than 900 years making it possibly the oldest garden in England. Whereas it was once tended by monks who would have produced herbs for the kitchen and infirmary it is now a communal garden for members of the Abbey staff whose houses overlook it. The garden has a utilitarian atmosphere and uninspired planting. Large plane trees, a large fig, propped up and underplanted with laurel, rose beds and beds of canna lilies. There are brass band concerts during August and September. The tiny Little Cloister garden has far more atmosphere with a gentle fountain just catching the sun at its centre. More figs are trained against the walls and the beds beneath a curtain of Virginia creeper are filled with acanthus, rosemary and hostas. Overlooking the Thames, across Millbank, is the Victoria Tower Garden, with a replica of Rodin's *Burghers of Calais*. Lovers of sculpture should also cross the road to look at Henry Moore's bronze *Knife Edge*.

COLVILLE PLACE   16
London W1

*London Borough of Camden * ✳ * Between Charlotte Street and Whitfield Street, near Tottenham Court Road * ✳ * Parking very difficult * ✳ * Suitable for wheelchairs * ✳ * Open 7.30am – dusk * ✳ * Entrance: free*

Fortunate houses in Colville Place look across a paved path on to what is a cross between a *hortus conclusus* and a small piazza. This imaginative tiny public garden was created a few years ago on a bomb site. There is a lawn, a pleasing pergola, fruit trees, and slightly tucked away, a children's play area. Planting is bold, simple and pleasing, with lots of lavender. This seems to be London's nearest equivalent to modern garden design in the public arena, and the result has enormous charm. A haven from Oxford Street.

CRYSTAL PALACE PARK   17
Crystal Palace Road, London SE22.

London Borough of Bromley ✳ Entrance at junction of Thicket Road and Crystal Palace Road ✳ Parking ✳ Refreshments ✳ Toilet facilities ✳ Partly suitable for wheelchairs ✳ Open all year ✳ Entrance: free

After the success of his Crystal Palace at the Great Exhibition Sir Joseph Paxton was asked to re-erect it in Sydenham in what has become known as Crystal Palace Park. He was also responsible for creating the fine terraces which surrounded his 'glass cathedral'. Sadly the Crystal Palace was burnt down in the 1930s but the terraces remain and they have recently been refurbished and are worth walking to gain a true impression of the massive scale of the former building. There are also interesting garden features which make a visit to Crystal Palace Park worthwhile. Among them are a maze built in 1870, a tree trail and a unique series of astonishing reproductions of huge pre-historic creatures.

THE ELMS   18
13 Wolverton Avenue, Kingston-on-Thames, Surrey. Tel: (081) 546 7624

Dr and Mrs R. Rawlings ✳ 1m E of Kingston on A308, 100 yards from Norbiton station. Entry opposite Manorgate flats in Manorgate Road ✳ Parking in street ✳ Teas by Home Farm Trust/Princess Alice Hospice ✳ Seeds and plants for sale ✳ Open 14th, 15th March, 11th, 12th April, 9th, 10th May, 13th, 14th June, 11th, 12th July, 2 – 5pm and groups by appointment ✳ Entrance: 80p

Recently re-designed by the owners (Mrs Rawlings is a professional landscape gardener), this is a true collector's garden with some rare and unusual plants, featuring rhododendrons, magnolias, camellias, dwarf conifers and a wide range of evergreen and deciduous shrubs. Small trees, ground cover (herbaceous), a two-level pool with geyser and well planted margins, also interesting alpine trays featured. This very small garden (only 55 x 25 feet) even has fruit, plum, pears and soft fruit.

FENTON HOUSE   19
Hampstead Grove, London NW3. Tel: (071) 435 3471

The National Trust ✳ Centre of Hampstead in area known as Holly Hill behind Heath Street ✳ Parking difficult ✳ Toilet facilities only if house is also visited ✳ Partly suitable for wheelchairs ✳ House open ✳ Garden open March, Sat and Sun, 2 – 6pm; April to Oct, Sat, Sun and Bank Holiday Mon, 11am – 6pm and Mon – Wed, 1 – 7pm (last admission ¹/₂ hour before closing). Parties on weekdays by appointment ✳ Entrance: free (house £3)

Handsome seventeenth-century house and walled garden (about half an acre).
The formal south garden is seen through an impressive iron gate (not open) and
can be approached from the house. The entrance to the house is via the side
door. Directly behind the house the walled garden is formal with standard
Prunus lusitanica in tubs, gravel walks and herbaceous borders edged with
neatly-clipped box. Standard lavenders are an unusual feature, and here as in
the rest of the garden the walls are particularly well-planted. There is an
interesting collection of varieties of *Clematis viticella*. The garden is terraced on
several levels with yew hedges (eight years old) dividing the areas, which
become less formal further from the house. There is a sunken rose garden with
secluded seating, good vistas and many scented plants. The far wall hosts a
beautifully-trained *Magnolia grandiflora*. Adjacent to the main garden below
another wall is an old orchard, carefully cut at three mower heights, and a small
kitchen/cottage garden. The garden is surprisingly peaceful and has the
delightful, unhurried atmosphere of the traditional old-world garden. Particularly good views of it are to be had from the attic floor of the house.

FULHAM PALACE   20
Bishops Avenue, Off Fulham Palace Road, London SW6.
Tel: (071) 736 5821

*London Borough of Hammersmith and Fulham * Fulham Palace Road and
Bishop's Avenue to the N * Parking * Suitable for wheelchairs * Plants for
sale in nearby nursery * Small Artefacts Museum open * Garden open daily
except 25th Dec, 1st Jan, 8am – dusk. Tours of Botanic Garden by arrangement
with Museum Curator * Entrance: free*

The palace, surrounded by a moat in its prime, was the former home of the
Bishops of London where in the sixteenth century Bishop Compton used his
missionaries to help him establish here a collection of shrubs and trees sent
back from America. Today it is rather sad in a faded way, like an overgrown
country house garden, but it is a charming place for a peaceful walk, far
superior to many other open spaces in London, and the two gardeners are
doing their best in the impossible position in which they are placed by the
Borough Council's financial problems. The 37-acre area to wander round is
seldom crowded. The south front of the house looks over lawns with enormous
cedars and other trees. The remains of the old walled garden contains a very
long ruined glasshouse built along a curved wall, and a box-edged herb garden.
Another part has order beds. A large rough area with beech hedges. The small
courtyard at the front of the house (part Henry VII, part Victorian) has
euphorbias, some climbers and other plants and a fountain. It must be said that
some visitors find the overall atmosphere depressing but that is not the general
view. Do not mistake this for Bishop's Park which extends to the south as far as
the river. There are rumours that this garden, which is of great historical
importance, will shortly be refurbished, and it has also been proposed as a
potential site for a national museum of garden history.

17 FULHAM PARK GARDENS   21
London SW6. Tel: (071) 736 4890

*Anthony Noel * From Putney Bridge underground station, turn along Kings Road*

and left at Threshers off-licence, then right into Fulham Park Gardens ✳ *Parking*
✳ *Open 7th June, 12th July, 20th Sept, 2.30 – 6pm* ✳ *Entrance: £1*

This tiny garden measuring 40ft by 17ft was awarded Best Garden by the
Chelsea Gardeners' Guild in 1991. Each year Anthony Noel, actor turned
landscape designer, experiments with new colour schemes in this romantic
stage set of a garden. Plants are usually grown in tiers for maximum decorative
effect in a small space. Great emphasis is placed on foliage and colour
combinations with rare clematis, ferns and hostas. There is a small water
feature and a wonderful array of pots including what must be the most
immaculate lawn in town. On open days this garden is usually open for charity
at the same time as 32 Atney Road (see entry), and queues of visitors have been
known to stretch down the street.

GOLDERS HILL PARK   22
North End Way, Hampstead, London NW3. Tel: (081) 455 5183

Corporation of London ✳ *From Hampstead, past Jack Straw's Castle on road to
Golders Green, opposite Bull and Bush pub. The flower garden is on right of park,
past café* ✳ *Refreshments: North End Way entrance, March to Oct* ✳ *Toilet
facilities* ✳ *Partly suitable for wheelchairs* ✳ *Dogs on lead* ✳ *Greenhouses open
weekends, 2 – 4pm* ✳ *Open daily, 7.30am – dusk* ✳ *Entrance: free*

The manicured 39-acre park was created in 1899 in the grounds of a manor
house (bombed in World War II). The two-acre dazzling flower garden on the
north side is designed in a series of garden rooms, with a mixture of perennial
and bedding plants. It has an almost Victorian feel with its neat, brilliantly
coloured displays of flowers, although the colour schemes can appear on the
vulgar side. On a less strident note is the canal feature planted with water-
loving and woodland plants, leading down to the ornamental pool with its ducks
and flamboyant flamingos. Plenty of seats at strategic points ensure that the
garden is much used by elderly local residents. (The park itself has a large
menagerie with deer, goats, wallabies, oryx and many birds.)

GREENWICH PARK   23
Greenwich, London SE10. Tel: (081) 858 2608

Department of the Environment ✳ *Entrances in Greenwich (Romney Road) and in
Blackheath (Charlton Way). Good service to Greenwich by river, tel: (071) 376
3676 or (081) 305 0300 for winter timetables* ✳ *Parking easier at Blackheath
entrance* ✳ *Refreshments* ✳ *Toilet facilities* ✳ *Suitable for wheelchairs but quite
steep in places* ✳ *Dogs* ✳ *Observatory and Maritime Museum, Greenwich Theatre
and Ranger's House. Ships at Greenwich pier. Thames Barrier Visitors' Centre* ✳
Open dawn – dusk ✳ *Entrance: free*

Henry VIII was born at Greenwich and he planted The Queen's Oak in the
park to commemorate his young daughter Elizabeth. The ancient Lizzie Oak,
as it is affectionately known, became hollow and was used as a jail for anyone
found drunk and disorderly in the park. For years the tree was held together
with ivy but after a wet night in July 1991 it toppled over. Some say that when

the Lizzie Oak goes, the park goes. At about the same time that the old tree fell, employees of the Royal Parks were made redundant and the upkeep of the parks put out for private tender. Visitors going to Greenwich Park to enjoy the panoramic view from The Observatory, overlooking the Naval College, will notice that the new Dockland development has altered the City skyscape, but hopefully the high standard of horticulture seen in the park will remain the same under privatisation.

4 THE GROVE ★ 24
Highgate, London N6.

Mr Cob Stenham ＊ *In Highgate village, off Hampstead Lane* ＊ *Parking in street* ＊ *Open 21st June, 2 – 5pm* ＊ *Entrance: 50p*

The seventeenth-century house sits behind a dignified front courtyard, beautifully paved with brick (as is the rear terrace) with restrained planting of skimmias and other evergreens. A side passage brings the visitor through to an outstanding vista; the terrace, with a formal pool surrounded by dramatic planting, is the foreground to an immaculate lawn with well-planted, mixed borders. Beyond this is an extensive backdrop to the wooded slopes of Hampstead Heath. An arbour of silver pears overlooks this stunning view and a ceanothus arch leads one down, through a tunnel of *Vitis coignetiae*, to the lower garden. This comprises an orchard with an old mulberry tree and some good statuary. One yew hedge conceals the well-ordered compost/bonfire area, and another balances this to enclose a tiny secret garden dominated by a *Cladrastis lutea*. *Rosa laevigata* 'Cooperi' flourishes on the south wall of the house, and the whole garden, which is beautifully designed and maintained, has exceptional charm.

7 THE GROVE ★ 25
Highgate, London N6. Tel: (081) 340 7205

The Hon. Mrs Judith Lyttelton ＊ *In Highgate village* ＊ *Best season: summer* ＊ *Parking in street* ＊ *Suitable for wheelchairs* ＊ *Open 31st May, 2 – 5pm* ＊ *Entrance: £1*

A huge half-acre London walled town garden behind a very handsome Georgian house *c*.1815, splendidly designed by the owner for low-mainte-nance, but with bags of interest. Tunnels, arbours, screens abound. A series of brick built arches across the width of the garden separate it into two compartments. The area near the house is formal with a lawn, the area beyond the screen much less so, with many fine compartments and features. Full of secret paths and unexpected views. A magic garden for children. Much use is made of evergreens and there are some exquisite shrubs, including a row of camellias down one wall and a massive *Hydrangea petiolaris* with a trunk as thick as a boxer's biceps! There are many species and varieties of a particular genus – five varieties of box and even more of ivies for example. The owner describes it as a gold, green and red garden. The canal feature, planted with yellow irises, and the allées and tunnels provide inspiration for busy garden-owners who would still like to have an interesting garden. Several other gardens in The Grove are open on charity days.

24 GROVE TERRACE 26
London NW5.

Lucy Gent ✻ *Off Highgate Road* ✻ *Parking in street* ✻ *Open 24th May, 19th July, 2 – 6pm and by written appointment* ✻ *Entrance: £1, children 50p*

An extra long, narrow garden crammed with plants arranged in such a way as to create an illusion of greater space and to forget that one is in a crowded London terrace. Different areas of interest and many unusual plants including a *Cercis* 'Forrest Pansey' and *Gleditsia* 'Ruby Lace'. Imaginative use is made of pots, the most interesting and handsome of them made by Jeni Jones, to establish points of focus and differing heights. One large pot contains a robust *Lonicera* 'Reflexa' trained into a standard. The small garden at the front of the house contains an unusual rosemary 'Benenden Blue', lavenders and wild roses. It is very much the plantsman's garden, with expert guidance for visitors from the owner.

GUNNERSBURY PARK 27
London W3. Tel: (081) 992 1612

London Borough of Ealing and Hounslow ✻ *¹/₂m N of Chiswick roundabout turn left off A406* ✻ *Parking: entrance from Popes Lane, no coaches* ✻ *Refreshments* ✻ *Toilet facilities* ✻ *Suitable for wheelchairs* ✻ *Dogs* ✻ *Museum open Mon – Fri, 1 – 5pm, winter, 1 – 4pm, Bank Holidays, March and Sept, 2 – 6pm, winter, 2 – 6pm. Closed Christmas* ✻ *Park open daily, 7.30am – dusk* ✻ *Entrance: free*

Little remains of the grandiose gardens of the Rothschild days except the rose gardens in the traditional 'Clock' pattern. Formal flower beds near the museum are well kept and colourfully planted, with a background of parkland. Beyond the trees the sports grounds, golf course and tennis courts are hidden from view from the terrace where it is difficult to realize one is only a few miles from Marble Arch. Amongst the gardeners who have toiled here were William Kent and J.C. Loudon. For children, there is a boating pool.

HALL PLACE 28
Bexley, London. Tel: (081) 310 2777

London Borough of Bexley ✻ *Just N of A2 near junction of A2 and A223* ✻ *Parking* ✻ *Restaurant* ✻ *Toilet facilities* ✻ *Garden and parts of glasshouses open daily, Mon – Fri, 7.30am – dusk, weekends and Bank Holidays, 9am – dusk* ✻ *Entrance: free*

Surrounding a splendid Jacobean mansion, this is arguably the most interesting and best-kept public garden in South East London. Although there is a strong emphasis on municipal annual bedding plants, like ageratum, *Senecio* x *hybrida* and African marigolds to provide summer colour, they are used with great restraint and good taste as are the roses in the large classical rose garden. So, too, are the herbaceous plants in two splendid borders separated by a turf allée and backed by a characterful old brick wall on one side and a tightly-clipped yew hedge on the other. Features include a raised walk overlooking one of

Britain's finest topiary gardens, several rich shrubberies, a large and beautifully designed patterned herb garden, a rock garden, canals and meandering stretches of the River Cray, a heather garden and acres of lawn studded with an interesting mixture of evergreen and deciduous trees to provide vistas.

HAM HOUSE ★★   29
Ham Street, Richmond, Surrey. Tel: (081) 940 1950

The National Trust ✳ *On S bank of Thames, W of A307 at Petersham* ✳ *Parking 400 yards by river, disabled on terrace* ✳ *Refreshments: teas* ✳ *Toilet facilities inc. disabled* ✳ *Partly suitable for wheelchairs* ✳ *House closed throughout 1992 for major works* ✳ *Gardens open daily, 10.30am – 6pm (or dusk if earlier)* ✳ *Entrance: free*

Relatively recently restored by the National Trust, the gardens at Ham House now retain their seventeenth-century appearance in which formality predominates. In the south garden, below a wide gravel terrace, are eight square lawns divided by paths. The strong architectural nature of the hornbeam avenues, gravel terraces and parterres of box and cotton lavender mean that the garden looks good in any season, and the authenticity of the restoration, down to replicas of the seventeenth-century garden furniture, adds to its charm. Even the tea room, in part of the old orangery, with tables and chairs on the lawns in summer, has a stately elegance.

HAMPTON COURT PALACE ★★   30
East Molesey, Surrey. Tel: (081) 977 8441

Historic Royal Palaces Agency ✳ *On A308 at junction of A309 on N side of Kingston bridge over Thames* ✳ *Limited parking* ✳ *Toilet facilities* ✳ *Mostly suitable for wheelchairs* ✳ *Dogs on lead* ✳ *Shop* ✳ *Palace open (admission charge)* ✳ *Open daily, dawn – dusk* ✳ *Entrance: free*

Hampton Court Palace is worth a visit to study the activities of British monarchs from Henry VIII onwards, and the gardens are an exciting and eclectic mixture of styles and taste, with many different areas of interest. Most famous for its Great Vine, planted in 1796, which still produces hundreds of 'Black Hamburg' grapes each year (on sale to the public when harvested in September or October) and its maze, replanted in 1690, with half-a-mile of densely hedged paths. The pond gardens offer a magnificent display of bedding plants (best seen in summer), and there is a Tudor knot garden with interlocking bands of dwarf box, thyme, lavender and cotton lavender, infilled with bedding plants. On a truly grand scale, the great fountain gardens, an immense semi-circle of grass and flower beds with a central fountain, is probably the most impressive element, but the wilderness garden in spring, with its mass of daffodils and spring-flowering trees – principally cherry and crab – has the most charm. The laburnum walk off the wilderness garden – a tunnel of trained trees with butter-coloured rivulets of flowers in May – is another great attraction. The former kitchen garden now houses a rose garden, mainly comprising old-fashioned roses. The 40p guide book gives an excellent potted history of the gardens and a much-needed map. Too much to see in one day – plan at least two trips; one in spring and one in summer. 1990 saw the launch of a major flower show here which is intended to become an annual event. It was well-attended in its first and second years and though not as stylish as Chelsea, visitors do at least benefit from being able to see the exhibits, unlike at the more famous show, which the RHS seem determined to make too crowded for comfort.

37 HEATH DRIVE   31
London NW3. Tel: (071) 435 2419

*Mr and Mrs C. Caplin * Off Finchley Road * Best season: late spring and summer * Parking * Refreshments * Suitable for wheelchairs * Plants for sale * Open 17th May, 16th Aug, 2.30 – 6pm * Entrance: £1.50*

Largish, square garden (about one fifth of an acre) with a vast number of plants packed into it. There is an attractive pergola walk and unusual and interesting plants. Lots of lavatera, tree peonies, rhododendrons, palms (*Trachycarpus*), broom trees, a tamarisk tree, a fig and a mulberry tree. Other features of the garden include a pool and rockeries, a fruit tree tunnel (apples, pears and plums), raised beds and a greenhouse and conservatory for exotics. The garden has a very effective compost heap hidden behind a hedge of delightful cut-leaved alder. In the front garden there is a particularly good semi-evergreen *Buddleia colvillei* with magenta hanging flowers in June and July. The Caplins have won the Frankland Moore Trophy (for gardens with help) seven times and are well featured in Arabella Lennox-Boyd's book *Private Gardens of London*.

THE HILL   32
Inverforth Close, North End Way, London NW3. Tel: (081) 455 5183

*Corporation of London * From Hampstead past Jack Straw's Castle on road to Golders Green, on left hand side * Partly suitable for wheelchairs * Open daily, 9am – dusk * Entrance: free*

Created by Lord Leverhulme in the 1920s, the garden was designed by Thomas Mawson, an architect. Overgrown in parts, its chief charm lies in its secluded setting and the romantic pergola walk, festooned in unchecked climbers, although part of this is now closed. Wonderful views across the heath from many points in the garden. There is a large formal lily pond (slightly unkempt) as well as herbaceous borders, undulating lawns, and many shrubs and trees.

HOLLAND PARK   33
Kensington, London W8. Tel: (071) 602 9483

*Royal Borough of Kensington and Chelsea * Between Kensington High Street A31 and Holland Park Avenue, with several entrances * Parking from Abbotsbury Road entrance * Refreshments: light lunches etc. Restaurant (rather expensive) * Toilet facilities * Dogs on lead * Open daily, 8am – sunset * Entrance: free*

Most of the famous Holland House was destroyed by bombs in World War II. The formal gardens, created in 1812 by Lord Holland, have been maintained.

The small park contains some rare (unlabelled) trees such as Pyrenean oak, Chinese sweet gum, Himalayan birch, violet willow and the snowdrop tree which flowers in May. The rose walk has now been replanted with a variety of azaleas. There is a small iris garden round a fountain. Peacocks strut the lawns and drape the walls with their tail feathers and in the woodland section birds and squirrels find sanctuary from London's noise and traffic. There is a children's play area. One of the nicest small London parks. In September 1991, a one-acre Kyoto Garden was opened in Holland Park as a permanent souvenir of the Japanese Festival. It is to be maintained on a regular basis by a commercial sponsor and is well worth a visit.

HORNIMAN GARDENS 34
London Rd, Forest Hill, London SE23. Tel: (081) 699 8924

Private charity ∗ Refreshments: at tearoom in Museum. Picnics allowed ∗ Toilet facilities ∗ Horticultural demonstrations March to Sept, first Wed in the month at 2.30pm ∗ Open all year except 25th Dec, Mon – Sat, 7.15am – dusk, Sun, 8am – dusk ∗ Entrance: free

Charming, rather old-fashioned park in fine situation with extensive views over alas, rather hideous south London, on three sides. Formal bedding, rose pergola, bandstand (with band on summer Sunday afternoons), steep hill garden with rocks, stream, conifers, etc. Large and impressive Victorian conservatory rebuilt recently behind the Horniman Museum which does not contain any plants but is used for functions from time to time.

ISABELLA PLANTATION ★ 35
Richmond Park, Richmond, Surrey. Tel: (081) 948 3209

Department of the Environment, Royal Parks ∗ Richmond Park, Broomfield Hill ∗ Best season: late spring ∗ Parking: Broomfield Hill car park, Pembroke Lodge (Roehampton Gate), disabled at north entrance by way of Ham Gate ∗ Refreshments (Pembroke Lodge) ∗ Toilet facilities (summer only) ∗ Suitable with care for wheelchairs ∗ Dogs on lead ∗ Open daily, dawn – dusk ∗ Entrance: free

A wooded enclosure, this features many fine indigenous forest trees – oaks, beeches and birch – as well as more exotic specimens like the pocket handkerchief tree (*Davidia involucrata*) and many species of magnolia. The principal glory, however, is the collection of rhododendrons and azaleas, the earliest rhododendron 'Christmas Cheer' blossoming in the New Year, but the garden is at its best from April until June, when the dwarf azaleas and the waterside primulas around the pond are also in flower. The garden is a notable bird sanctuary – nuthatches, treecreepers, kingfishers, woodpeckers and owls have all been spotted here, and badgers have their own entrance to the gardens. The Waterhouse Plantations in neighbouring Bushy Park are also very fine (see entry).

KENSINGTON GARDENS 36
London W2. Tel: (071) 724 2826

Royal Parks ∗ Entrances off Bayswater Road, Kensington High Street and West

Carriage Drive, Hyde Park ✳ *Best seasons: spring and summer* ✳ *Refreshments: Orangery Tea Room and Broadwalk Kiosk* ✳ *Toilet facilities, all suitable for disabled* ✳ *Suitable for wheelchairs* ✳ *Dogs* ✳ *Palace State Apartments open Mon – Sat, 9am – 5pm, Sun, 11 am – 5pm. Outdoor sculpture sometimes on display at Serpentine Art Gallery open weekly, 10am – 6pm (dusk in winter)* ✳ *Open daily, 5am – dusk* ✳ *Entrance: free*

This 274 acres of the finest park, adjoining Hyde Park, have their own pleasures, including sculpture by Henry Moore and G.F. Watts and, for children and older enthusiasts, the Peter Pan statue. The orangery, probably by Hawksmoor with decoration by Grinling Gibbons, is well worth a visit. So, too, is the sunken water garden surrounded by beds of bright seasonal flowers which can be viewed from 'windows' in a beech walk. From the Broad Walk south to the Albert Memorial, semi-circular flower beds are kept planted against a background of flowering shrubs. Many different species of nannies and prams are in evidence along the Flower Walk at the South side near the Albert Memorial.

KENWOOD 37
Hampstead Lane, London NW3. Tel: (081) 348 1286

English Heritage ✳ *N side of Hampstead Heath, on Highgate to Hampstead Road* ✳ *Parking at West Lodge car park, Hampstead Lane* ✳ *Refreshments: hours as house* ✳ *Toilet facilities* ✳ *Suitable for wheelchairs* ✳ *Dogs on lead* ✳ *House open April (or Maundy Thurs if earlier) to 1st Oct, 10am – 6pm, Oct to April (or Maundy Thurs), 10am – 4pm* ✳ *Park open daily, dawn – dusk* ✳ *Entrance: free*

Vistas, sweeping lawns from the terrace of Kenwood House and views over Hampstead Heath (and London) predominate. Magnificent mature trees, mainly oak and beech. Large-scale shrubberies, dominated by rhododendrons – among which nestles Dr Johnson's summer house (used by the great man on visits to his friends, the Thrales, in Streatham). There is also some magnificent modern sculpture including a Henry Moore. The garden slopes down towards two large lakes known as the Lily pond (the largest) and the Concert pond (where open air concerts are held in summer). Woods fringe the heath side of the gardens, with several gates onto the heath itself. A good place to walk at any season, but particularly when the trees are turning in autumn.

LAMBETH PALACE GARDENS 38
Lambeth Palace Road, London SE1. Tel: (071) 928 8282

Church of England ✳ *S side of the Thames, next to Lambeth Bridge* ✳ *Best season: spring and summer* ✳ *Suitable for wheelchairs* ✳ *Open 11th April, 13th June, 19th Sept, 2 – 5.30pm* ✳ *Entrance: £2*

Only Buckingham Palace, apparently, has bigger grounds in central London. Lambeth Palace stands in 10½ acres, roughly nine of them devoted to the gardens. There is a magnificent fig tree in the entrance garden to the palace. Behind the palace, and facing it, is a restored rose terrace, fronted by a perennial border designed by Beth Chatto. Beyond, more or less around the walled perimeter of the garden, is what will eventually be a woodland walkway that will encompass at various points a scented garden, a wild garden (with lily pond) and a Chinese garden. Close to the house is a relatively newly commissioned herb garden (by Faith and Geoff Whitten) the design of which, though attractive, seems at odds with the nearby rose terrace. The occupants have undertaken much restoration work in the garden over the last few years and over 2000 trees and shrubs have been planted. Despite the attractive setting, the gardens have a curiously bitty and disconnected feel to them, although some of that may be due to the newness of a lot of the planting which needs a good five or six years before its impact begins to be felt. Not far from Lambeth Palace, towards Waterloo is St Thomas's Hospital. Inside one of the large courtyards is a pleasant garden, abutting the foot of Westminster Bridge, which contains one of the most spectacular modern sculpture water fountains in the world. This is the stainless steel *Revolving Torsion* by Naum Gabo.

15 LANGBOURNE AVENUE   39
Holly Lodge Estate, London N6. Tel: (081) 340 5806

Mr R. Partridge ✳ Off Swain's Lane, which is off Highgate Road ✳ Parking in neighbouring roads ✳ Open 19th July, 2.30 – 5.30pm ✳ Entrance: £1

A front garden with a large hamamelis and other striking shrubs tell that this is no ordinary town garden. Behind the semi-detached house the ground rises steeply. Starting with a chamaerops and *Bergenia ciliata*, there are many interesting plants in excellent associations: *Brunnera* 'Langtrees', *Melianthus major*, *Rosa glauca*, *Acer negundo* 'Flamingo' and, behind, *Phormium tenax*. At the top of the garden sits a wide terrace with pond. Foliage, dramatic throughout, is especially good here: gunneras, lysichitums, rodgersias and *Peltiphyllum peltatum*. Trees include a tulip tree and a corkscrew willow so large as to be positively statuesque in its central position.

43 LAYHAMS ROAD   40
West Wickham, Croydon, Surrey. Tel: (081) 462 4196

Mrs Dolly Robertson ✳ Layhams Road is off Addiscombe Road, West Wickham ✳ Best season: June/July ✳ Limited parking ✳ Toilet facilities ✳ Suitable for wheelchairs ✳ Open all year by appointment ✳ Entrance: by donation to charity

In front of this semi-detached house is a sunken garden. Behind it large paving slabs have been used to create raised beds for vegetable and salad crops, plus fruits such as yellow raspberries. The garden is designed for maintenance from a wheelchair, and Mrs Robertson is happy to pass on her experience as a disabled gardener.

1 LISTER ROAD ★   41
London E11. Tel: (081) 556 8962

Mr Myles Challis ✳ Off High Road, Leytonstone about 10 minutes walk from the tube station ✳ Parking on Lister Road ✳ Toilet facilities ✳ Plant exchanges ✳ Open June to Sept by appointment

This is one of London's great surprises; a 40 ft x 20 ft garden of subtropical and bold foliage hidden away in Leytonstone. An Abyssinian palm, canna lilies, daturas, gingers and tree ferns, all wintered under cover, flourish in a matrix of hardy plants, such as bamboos, gunneras, phormiums and euphorbias. A narrow path leads past a screen of bamboos to a pond. This garden strikes a note of rich fantasy, not least in the wind's sound in the giant leaves. It is also a unique store of ideas easily adapted to more conventional gardens, and as Myles Challis is a garden designer, this is in effect his showroom.

338 LIVERPOOL ROAD   42
London N7.

Mr and Mrs Simon Relph ✳ *The house is on the corner of Furlong Road. 5 minutes walk from Highbury and Islington tube station* ✳ *Parking in side streets* ✳ *Teas* ✳ *Open 14th June, 2 – 6pm* ✳ *Entrance: £1 (£1.50 for combined admission with 28 Barnsbury Square, N1 – see entry)*

A densely-planted front garden of mainly grey and silver plants, with a basement area of ivy and ferns, is entered from Liverpool Road, while the entrance to the back garden is round the corner in Furlong Road. Although small, this is beautifully designed to show many interesting plants. An unusual and very successful water feature comprises a narrow canal right across the garden.

LONDON SQUARES   43

Many other cities have squares but probably none has more than London. They were mostly built in the eighteenth and nineteenth centuries to provide an outlook for the fashionable houses which surrounded them and in not so fashionable areas like Pimlico so that the lesser classes could imitate the behaviour of their betters. A few squares still remain the joint property of the owners of houses (and today, flats) round them, the grandest being Belgrave Square built by Basevi in 1825, Eaton Square and Cadogan Square. Other private squares, hardly less grand, include Montpelier, Brompton, Carlyle, Lowndes, Onslow and others to the west of Hyde Park Corner. Since they so rarely appear to be occupied by the residents, particularly at weekends when they have gone to their houses in the country, it is surprising that there has been no movement to agitate for their occasional unlocking to admit the public at large. However, some squares (and 'gardens' as other areas are called) have over the years become places where the public may be admitted and these include the following:

Central area: *Berkeley Square, Cavendish Square, Grosvenor Square*, and *St James's Square* (this is the earliest, begun 1665, and the quietest). Eastern area: *Gray's Inn* (where Field Court is open to the public during weekday lunchtimes in the summer), *Inner and Middle Temple Gardens*, with entrance in Fleet Street, *Lincoln's Inn*, with one of its 'squares' New Hall open to the public Mon – Fri, 12 noon – 1 .30pm only. Northern area: *Fitzroy Square*, the work of Geoffrey Jellicoe, not open but viewable, *Gordon Square*, closed weekends, *Russell Square*, and *Soho Square*.

At least one London Square has begun limited opening to the public, *Eccleston Square* in Pimlico. This four and a half-acre square, run by a committee of residents and normally reserved for the use of the residents, has something for everyone – a tennis court, areas for children to play and a paved area where the fortunate residents can have a barbeque. (Open for charity 26th April, 14th June).

The newest square in London is surrounded by offices, not houses. This is Arundel Great Court which may be viewed from The Strand, south of Aldwych, and entered from Arundel and Norfolk Streets. To the south is the luxurious courtyard garden of the Norfolk Hotel.

22 LOUDOUN ROAD   44
London NW8.

*Mrs Ruth Barclay * Less than 5 minutes walk from St John's Wood tube station, between Abbey Road and Finchley Road. Also near bus stop * Parking in street * Teas * Open 31st May, 2 – 6.30pm * Entrance: £1, children 25p*

In this small front garden maximum use of the space is achieved by good design and interesting plant associations. There is a charming sheltered courtyard at the back where peaches and grapes ripen annually and passion flowers romp. Some statuary is well-positioned and one's eye is raised by a glowing canopy of golden acacia cascading at the boundary.

1-8 AND 10 MALVERN TERRACE   45
London N1

*Off Thornhill Road * Best season: April to Aug * Parking in neighbouring streets * Refreshments and music on open day * Suitable for wheelchairs * Open 10th May, 2 – 5.30pm * Entrance: £1, children free*

This is a touch of Edinburgh's Ann Street: fair-sized – and south-facing – front gardens come right down to the cobbled cul-de-sac. Across it in Thornhill Gardens mature trees complete the illusion of remoteness from London. Generous planting plays against well-tended grass and paths. All is in scale with the pleasing 1830s housing; the occasional vast pot or shrub adds a bit of piquancy. There is a nice flow through these front patches; a detour to see them if you're in the neighbourhood is well worthwhile.

MOUNT STREET GARDENS   46
Mount Street, London W1. Tel: (071) 798 2063/4

*Westminster City Council * Access from Mount Street, South Audley Street near the Public Library and South Street, Mayfair * Dogs on lead * Open spring and summer, weekdays, 8am – up to 9.30pm; autumn and winter, 8am – 4.30pm. Sun and Public Holidays, open from 9am * Entrance: free*

This well-hidden leafy retreat is much loved by locals while the throng of the city seems to pass it by. Tasteful planting and lofty trees make it the perfect spot to take your ease after shopping. Versailles tubs planted with palms, beds of sugar pink and white geraniums can be enjoyed from dozens of wooden benches donated by those who have enjoyed this garden's charm.

MUSEUM OF GARDEN HISTORY   47
St Mary-at-Lambeth, Lambeth Palace Road, London SE1. Tel: (071) 261 1891

The Tradescant Trust ✱ *Lambeth Palace Road, parallel to River Thames on S bank, hard by Lambeth Bridge* ✱ *Best season: spring and summer* ✱ *Refreshments* ✱ *Toilet facilities* ✱ *Suitable for wheelchairs* ✱ *Plants for sale* ✱ *Shop* ✱ *Antique collection of garden tools and artefacts which include Gertrude Jekyll's desk, lectures, exhibitions and concerts* ✱ *Open Mon – Fri, 11am – 3pm, Sun, 10.30am – 5pm. Closed Sat* ✱ *Entrance: free, donations appreciated*

A small formal knot garden in the churchyard of St Mary-at-Lambeth features the plants originally collected by the John Tradescants (Elder and Younger) on their plant-hunting trips to America and Asia in the sixteenth and seventeenth centuries, many of them now so familiar we think of them as indigenous to this country. The knot garden designed by Lady Salisbury has 32 compartments of dwarf box, densely infilled with herbs and perennials. The centrepiece of the knot is a handsome clipped holly, *Ilex* 'Silver King'. Plants are all labelled. Although small the garden has a few well-placed benches. Part of its charm are the old brick and stone paths and the tombs and tombstones. A detailed planting plan of the knot is available (price 25p) in the museum shop, and some of the plants featured in the knot are on sale as well. Lambeth Palace (see entry) is next door.

MUSEUM OF LONDON GARDEN COURT   48
The Museum of London, London Wall, London EC2. Tel: (071) 600 3699

Museum of London ✱ *Underground: St Paul's, Barbican or Moorgate* ✱ *Best season: summer* ✱ *Refreshments, licensed restaurant* ✱ *Toilet facilities* ✱ *Suitable for wheelchairs but steps make assistance necessary* ✱ *Museum shop* ✱ *Open May to Oct, Tues – Sat, 10am – 6pm, Sun, 2 – 6pm (last admission 5.30pm). Closed Mon* ✱ *Entrance: £3, concessions £1.50 (museum)*

In 1990 the Museum of London put on a much welcomed exhibition called 'London's Pride' which traced the history of the capital's gardens. The exhibition was an excuse to bring in garden designers Colson and Stone and totally revamp the internal courtyard. The team transformed an almost lifeless area into a living history of plantsmanship in the City from medieval times to the present day. Legendary names like Henry Russell, who sold striped roses in Westminster, to James Veitch, who sold exotica like the monkey puzzle tree from his nursery in Chelsea, are represented. This tiny roof garden is flanked on four sides by high buildings yet the designers have still managed to incorporate a tumbling rill and a rock garden. A visit here should be combined with the Barbican Conservatory (see entry).

MYDDELTON HOUSE ★ 49
Bulls Cross, Enfield, Middlesex. Tel: (0992) 717711

Lea Valley Regional Park Authority ✳ *From M25/A10 junction 25, turn W from A10 on Bulls Moor Lane, bear left into Bulls Cross and Myddelton House is on the right at the junction with Turkey Street* ✳ *Parking* ✳ *Toilet facilities* ✳ *Suitable for wheelchairs* ✳ *Plants for sale occasionally* ✳ *Open weekdays, 10am – 3.30pm. Closed weekends and Bank Holidays except special open days which are usually last Sun in the months Feb to Oct* ✳ *Entrance: £1, concessions 50p*

A magnificent diverse plant collection set in four acres built up by the famous E.A. Bowles and now restored. Splendid spring bulbs, followed by iris, followed by autumn crocus and impressive varieties of autumn-remontant iris make this garden a joy all year round. Zephyranthus, nerines, belladonna lilies, acidantheras are but a few of the autumn bulbs and there is a fine *Crinum moorei* near the conservatory. This is by no means a municipal garden and the impressive plant collection is displayed attractively, in a well-designed garden surrounding the impressive Regency house of mellow golden brick. Serious understaffing has resulted in some untidiness but the garden is still unified by Bowles's plants and vision.

NOEL-BAKER PEACE GARDEN 50
Elthorne Park, Hazelville Road, London N19.

London Borough of Islington ✳ *There are several entrances to Elthorne Park, including those in Beaumont Road and Sunnyside Road* ✳ *Best season: summer* ✳ *Parking in adjacent roads* ✳ *Toilet facilities in adjacent playground* ✳ *Suitable for wheelchairs* ✳ *Open daily, Mon – Fri, 8am – dusk, Sat, 9am – dusk, Sun, 10am – dusk* ✳ *Entrance: free*

This is a small well-designed formal garden within a London park, created in 1984 in memory of Philip Noel-Baker, winner of the Nobel Peace Prize in 1959. It is a lovely example of late twentieth-century garden design and planting, centering on an interesting water feature and a striking bronze figure (with horizontal bronze reflection). Much use is made of brick and York stone paving, and raised beds together with lawns; the overall effect is softened and enlivened by the excellent planting, with many unusual species (e.g. *Feijoa sellowiana*, *Clerodendrum bungei* and *C. trichotomum*). The emphasis is on green, grey and white, lifted here and there by splashes of colour and linked by the strong lines of the asymmetric design which creates several secluded sitting areas. It receives extensive use and support from the local community and although the results of limited maintenance are sometimes apparent, the overall impression is of well-loved amenity. There is a good children's playground and a fitness trail in adjacent Elthorne Park.

PRIORY GARDENS 51
Orpington, London. Tel: (081) 313 1113

London Borough of Bromley ✳ *Behind library, Church Hill off Orpington High Street* ✳ *Toilet facilities* ✳ *Separate area for dogs* ✳ *Open daily, 8am – dusk (9pm in summer)* ✳ *Entrance: free*

Skirting the Old Priory which is now the Orpington Public Library, this is one of the most tastefully-gardened public spaces in outer London. It has an excellent example of patterned annual bedding, a recently-replanted herbaceous garden, a rich rose garden, fine mature trees and shrubs and a refurbished lake. Considering the recent cutbacks in public spending, the level of husbandry and maintenance in these gardens is exemplary.

QUEEN MARY'S ROSE GARDEN   52
Inner Circle, Regent's Park, London NW1. Tel: (071) 486 7905

Department of the Environment ✳ *Off Marylebone Road. Many other entrances to the park* ✳ *Best season: June, July and Aug* ✳ *Parking: Inner Circle, weekdays, from 11am, Sat and Sun, all day* ✳ *Refreshments* ✳ *Toilet facilities* ✳ *Suitable for wheelchairs* ✳ *Open daily, dawn – dusk* ✳ *Entrance: free*

These sedate, well-laid out and beautifully manicured gardens are justly famous. Playing host to more than 60,000 roses – dominated by Hybrid Teas and floribundas, although also including old-fashioned, shrub and species roses – the sight and scent of the gardens in high summer is a magnet for thousands of visitors. It must be said, however, that this style of rose garden is not to everyone's taste. The roses are grown with almost military precision and are in perfect condition. Swagged and garlanded climbers surround the circular rose garden, but the herbaceous borders are also worth visiting, particularly in late July and August, as is the large ornamental lake with its central island. It attracts many varieties of waterfowl, including herons which nest on the island. The Broad Walk (five minutes from the Rose Gardens) between the Inner and Outer circle towards Cambridge Gate is another exquisitely-maintained Victorian-style area of planting. St John's Lodge, on the north side of the Inner Circle and now part of what was Bedford College, has a secluded garden including a rose garden. The park as a whole is one of the most pleasant in London.

RANELAGH GARDENS ★   53
London SW3. Tel: (071) 730 0161

Royal Hospital Chelsea ✳ *Chelsea Bridge Road. Through Chelsea Hospital London Gate in Royal Hospital Road, and through next gate into the South Gardens, then through small gate on left* ✳ *Parking difficult in street* ✳ *Suitable for wheelchairs* ✳ *Open daily (except 25th Dec and during the Chelsea Flower Show period), Mon – Sat, 10am – 1pm, 2pm – sunset, Sun, 2pm – sunset* ✳ *Entrance: free*

Elegant and attractive gardens with over a mile of wide walkways through undulating park-like grass and handsome tree and shrub planting, with a few perennial and shrub borders. Formerly the pleasure grounds of Ranelagh, complete with a large rotunda (now demolished) and laid out in formal style, they were redesigned by Gibson in the nineteenth century, but turned into allotments for pensioners between the World Wars. They were later reconstructed according to Gibson's plan. A summerhouse by Sir John Soane, near the entrance to the garden, houses several seats plus glass cases with a history and a map of the gardens with the major trees marked on it. These include many species of poplar, birch, beech, holly, cherry, chestnuts, lime, oak and so on, with a couple of more exotic ones – the tree of heaven and the maidenhair tree. The serenity of the gardens is slightly marred by traffic in Chelsea Bridge Road. To one side of the park is the area used to house the Chelsea Flower Show. A long avenue of plane trees marks the western edge of the gardens.

RAVENSCOURT PARK   54
King Street, London W6.

*Hammersmith and Fulham Borough Council * Near junction of King Street and Chiswick High Street * Best season: June/July * Parking outside * Refreshments: summer, 10am – 7pm, winter, 10am – 5pm * Toilet facilities * Suitable for wheelchairs * Dogs in dog exercise areas * Plants for sale Wed – Sat, 10.30am – 4.45pm, Sun 10.30am – 5.45pm * Open daily, 7.30am – dusk * Entrance: free*

A delightful park, with dog exercise areas and dog-free zones, and a variety of trees and shrubs relatively unscathed by recent gale damage. A scented garden, a pond with Canada geese and other waterfowl, a bowling green, an impressive cactus house and extensive playing facilities for children. One of the best park cafeterias in London in a former coach house.

THE ROOKERY   55
Streatham Common South, London SE25. Tel: (081) 764 5478

*Lambeth Council * Streatham High Road, then Streatham Common South * Best season: July * Parking top of Streatham High Road * Light refreshments * Toilet facilities * Partly suitable for wheelchairs * Dogs on lead on top terrace only * Open daily, 10am – dusk. Closed 25th Dec * Entrance: free*

This secluded and once beautifully-kept mixed garden is struggling to survive. Formerly the walled garden of a private house and the surrounding hillside – with sloping lawns and terraces. Views over Streatham Vale. Walled garden, the beautiful white garden best seen in July, extensive rock garden with a small stream and goldfish pond. Orchard. Delightful old English garden, beautifully scented, with large variety of annual and perennial plants. An orchard picnic area with tables. Abundance of benches donated by grateful Streatham residents for this peaceful and pretty garden a quarter of a mile (uphill) off the busy High Road. Plenty of litter bins. Children enjoy the orchard area (no ball games), the dense shrubbery and hidden, winding paths leading up through the rock garden area and stream.

ROYAL BOTANIC GARDENS ★★   56
Kew, Richmond, Surrey. Tel: (081) 940 1171

*Trustees * Kew Green, S of Kew Bridge * Parking Kew Green/Queen*

Elizabeth's Lawn car park (Brentford Gate) ✳ *Refreshments: Orangery restaurant, pavillion and tea bar* ✳ *Toilet facilities inc. disabled* ✳ *Suitable for wheelchairs which may be reserved in advance free of charge* ✳ *Shop* ✳ *Kew Palace open summer, Queen Charlotte's cottage open summer weekends and public holidays (April to Sept)* ✳ *Open daily, 9.30am – 4/6pm depending on season, glasshouses, 10am – 4pm* ✳ *Entrance: £3, OAP and students £1.50, children £1, season ticket (for Kew and Wakehurst Place) £12, family season (2 adults and 3 children) £23*

Internationally renowned, and primarily a botanic institution, collecting, conserving and exchanging plants from all over the world, Kew's delightful and varied gardens and grounds of more than 300 acres have something for everyone. In spring, the flowering cherries, crocuses, daffodils, and tulips and the lovely rock garden, in May and June, the bluebell wood, its lilacs (made famous by the song) and the water-lily house, in summer the herbaceous garden, the rose and cottage gardens, in the autumn bulbs and trees, and in the winter, the heath garden, the winter flowering cherries and (indoors) the alpine house, as well as the year-round pleasure of Decimus Burton's Palm house, the temperate and arid houses, and the Princess of Wales Conservatory with its computer-controlled micro-climates. The recently-opened Sir Joseph Banks building houses seasonal exhibitions on economic botany.

Kew's grounds also contain four temples, the famous Pagoda, Japanese Gateway, a campanile, the wood museum, the Marianne North gallery, (filled with 832 oil paintings of plants) besides Kew Palace itself, and the charming Queen Charlotte's cottage. The grass garden has over 600 grasses – besides those of the bamboo garden. About fifty per cent of the herbaceous garden's 2000 species are of wild origin. There is a somewhat formal rose garden, a delightful rock garden – originally of limestone, but completely replaced by sandstone. The Cambridge cottage gardens, the Queen's garden (in the style of a seventeenth-century garden) and the heather garden should not be missed.

The huge glasshouses, some of which are kept at tropical temperatures, are well worth visiting in winter, with their unique collections of exotic and unusual plants, ranging from banana trees to giant water lilies. In the Princess of Wales Conservatory are imaginative mangrove swamps and deserts, carnivorous plants and orchids.

The trees range from ash and birch collections, through conifers, eucalyptus and mulberry to walnut. The wood museum contains not only specimens of different woods but also inlay work, a history of the manufacture of paper, etc. The lake, once a disused gravel pit, has an abundance of wildfowl. The orangery does not contain oranges – which are to be found in the Citrus Walk (the orangery now has a bookshop, exhibition area and waiter-service restaurant).

It is well worth buying the souvenir guide and planning a route for the elderly or unenergetic. The disabled will find most parts of Kew very accessible. Children will particularly enjoy the Princess of Wales Conservatory, with its Namib deserts and carnivorous plants, as well as the Palm House to see 'real' bananas. Tree-climbing, ball-games, and other sports are not allowed. Neither are radios, cassettes, etc.

SOUTHWOOD LODGE 57
33 Kingsley Place, Highgate, London N6.

Mr and Mrs Christopher Whittington ✳ *Off Southwood Lane, Highgate village*

Parking in street ✳ *Plants for sale* ✳ *Open 10th May, 21st June, 2 – 6pm* ✳
Entrance: 80p

An imaginatively-designed garden created in 1963 from a much larger, older garden, set at the highest part of London with a magnificent view to the east 'as far as the Urals'. In approximately a third of an acre of a fairly steep site, there is much variety of mood and planting. By the house, which is clad in many fine clematis, a densely-planted paved area is enclosed on two sides by a high beech hedge through which steps lead down to a grassy walk planted with bushes, shrubs, more clematis and herbaceous plants. A wooded area in the lowest part of the garden, with many shade-loving plants leads one up past two pools with the soothing sound of trickling water and suitable bog plants. Alpines growing in troughs on a low wall.

7 ST GEORGE'S ROAD ★   58
St Margaret's, Twickenham, Middlesex. Tel: (081) 892 3713

Mr and Mrs R. Raworth ✳ *Off A316 between Twickenham Bridge and St Margaret's roundabout* ✳ *Best season: May to July* ✳ *Parking in road* ✳ *Teas on open day* ✳ *Plants for sale* ✳ *Open by appointment and 14th, 28th June, 2 – 6pm* ✳ *Entrance: £1, children free*

A most successful result of garden design inspired by Hidcote and Tintinhull, on a miniature scale, nearly a generation ago. Mature garden of grace and peacefulness only yards from one of London's main routes to the west. The various rooms, Italianate patio, herb garden and knot garden lead through to an emerald carpet of grass and flower borders backing onto old trees in a private park. There are honeysuckles, old roses and many rare shrubs to interest the plantsperson and also the contents of a large elegant greenhouse on the north-facing wall of the wisteria-covered house. A recent addition is a Mediterranean and scree garden.

ST JAMES'S PARK ★   59
Horse Guards Parade, London SW1. Tel: (071) 930 1793

Department of the Environment, Royal Parks ✳ *From Buckingham Palace on the W to Horse Guards Parade on the E, the Mall on the N and on the S by Birdcage Walk* ✳ *Parking difficult* ✳ *Refreshments in park* ✳ *Toilet facilities* ✳ *Suitable for wheelchairs* ✳ *Dogs allowed but must be on lead in certain areas* ✳ *Open daily* ✳ *Entrance: free*

One of the smaller royal parks but one of the prettiest. It was Henry VIII who turned this swampy field into a pleasure ground and nursery for deer. After the Restoration, in 1660, Charles II employed the French garden designer Le Nôtre, who planned the gardens at Versailles, to refashion the park into a garden. Le Nôtre drew up plans for the lake and islands and included an aviary along Birdcage Walk. He also incorporated a 600-yard pitch for King Charles to play the old French game of Paille Maille (a crude form of croquet). The game gave its name to Pall Mall. Nash remodelled the lake in 1827-29 but the islands are still home to a wide variety of birds from ducks to pelicans. The park is also a sanctuary for politicians and civil servants as well as weary sightseers who can doze on deckchairs.

SYON PARK ★★ 60
Brentford, Middlesex. Tel: (081) 560 0881

His Grace the Duke of Northumberland ✳ *2m W of Kew Bridge, road marked from A315/310 at Bush Corner* ✳ *Parking* ✳ *Refreshments* ✳ *Toilet facilities* ✳ *Suitable for wheelchairs* ✳ *Plants for sale* ✳ *Shop* ✳ *House open Easter to Sept, daily, 12 noon – 5pm* ✳ *Garden open daily, 10am – 6pm* ✳ *Entrance: £1.75, OAP and children £1.25 (house and gardens £3.30, OAP and children £2.25)*

The house built by Robert Adam *c.*1760 was the London seat of the Percy family which also employed 'Capability' Brown. From woodland garden to Charles Fowler's Great Conservatory (1830), Syon Park shows British gardening on a grand scale. The lakeside walk is of great interest; specimen trees planted in the eighteenth century by Brown still survive, supplemented by irises, day lilies and clumps of Chilian rhubarb. The six-acre rose garden, separated from the park (entrance 10p coin) created on the raised terrace that was constructed by the Protector Duke of Somerset in the sixteenth century, is well worth the extra effort of visiting, especially in June.

TRINITY HOSPICE ★ 61
30 Clapham Common North Side, London SW4. Tel: (071) 622 9481

Trustees of the Hospice ✳ *Off N side of the Common* ✳ *Best season: spring, mid-summer* ✳ *Parking on Common* ✳ *Refreshments* ✳ *Toilet facilities* ✳ *Suitable for wheelchairs* ✳ *Plants for sale* ✳ *Open 25th, 26th April, 6th, 7th June, 18th, 19th July, 19th, 20th Sept, 2 – 5pm* ✳ *Entrance: 50p, children free*

The gardens at Trinity Hospice were designed primarily for the benefit of patients, their families and the staff. Stretching over nearly two acres, the gardens are set out on slightly rolling park-like terrain and designed by John Medhurst and David Foreman of London Landscape Consortium on the principles adhered to by Lanning Roper. The latter had originally been asked by the Sainsbury Family Charity Trust to design these gardens on a dilapidated site but his illness caught up with him before he could do much. The gardens were finished because of donations made by his friends and called the Lanning Roper Memorial Garden. Perennials and shrubs predominate but there is also a wild garden at one end and a large pool with a mobile sculpture.

TRUMPETER'S HOUSE AND LODGE GARDEN ★ 62
Old Palace Yard, Richmond, Surrey.

Mrs Pamela and Miss Sarah Franklyn ✳ *On Richmond Green* ✳ *Best season: summer* ✳ *Parking* ✳ *Refreshments* ✳ *Toilet facilities* ✳ *Suitable for wheelchairs* ✳ *Plants for sale, inc. old-fashioned pinks* ✳ *Open 12th July, 2.30 – 5.30pm* ✳ *Entrance: £1.50, OAP £1, children 50p*

Three acres of garden stand on the site of the former Richmond Palace. The gardens feature ponds, many varieties of roses, Judas and mulberry trees and extensive lawns. Behind ironwork gates lies a 'secret garden' where Queen Elizabeth I walked and where a raised Georgian gazebo overlooks one of the loveliest stretches of the river. Here the garden has been laid out with plants of the Elizabethan period and the eye is drawn to a fine white aviary housing white doves. Very well maintained, this is one of the most interesting middle-sized gardens in the London region.

VICTORIA AND ALBERT MUSEUM   63
Cromwell Road, London SW7.

Board of Trustees of the Victoria and Albert Museum ✳ *Cromwell Road, close to South Kensington tube station and in walking distance of Harrods* ✳ *Parking difficult* ✳ *Toilet facilities* ✳ *Suitable for wheelchairs* ✳ *Open daily, Mon – Sat, 10am – 5.50pm, Sun, 2.30 – 5.50pm* ✳ *Entrance: £3 (OAP, students and children 50p, Friends of tthe V&A free) suggested voluntary donation for museum and garden*

Only rarely does the owner of a run-down garden find himself in the position of being offered vast sums by a sponsor who will foot the bill for a complete redesign. This was the case with Sir Roy Strong, then director of the V & A, and his benefactor Pirelli. It is strange that Sir Roy, who is a distinguished writer on gardening and has developed a beautiful garden of his own, should have approved a scheme which is so dessicated, although perhaps he was influenced by the desire to acknowledge his debt to the Italians by making this large open space at the heart of the museum a classic geometry which would shine under a blue Roman sky of the kind rarely prevailing in South Kensington. Whatever the reason, what was done was done with elegance and is maintained to a high standard.

WALLACE COLLECTION   64
Manchester Square, London W1. Tel: (071) 935 0687

Trustees of the Wallace Collection ✳ *N of Wigmore Street, behind Selfridges* ✳ *Parking difficult* ✳ *Toilet facilities (most elegantly tiled in London)* ✳ *Suitable for wheelchairs* ✳ *Shop* ✳ *Gallery open* ✳ *Garden open daily, weekdays, 10am – 5pm, Sun, 2 – 5pm. Closed Good Fri, May Day Bank Holiday and 24th to 26th Dec* ✳ *Entrance: free*

A secluded paved courtyard in the centre of Hertford House, a mansion built in 1776-88 for the then Duke of Manchester. When this storehouse of paintings, china and other treasures, collected by the Marquis of Hertford, was bequeathed to the nation, the government bought this mansion to display them. This stylish courtyard is like a stage set, dramatised by four magnificent bronze urns, two of which once stood in the Chateau de Bagatelle, the home of the Marquis and his son, Sir Richard Wallace. The centrepiece is an elegant fountain with a golden snake recoiling from the fish in the pool. The planting is kept simple with beds edged with clipped box and filled with santolina.

WALPOLE HOUSE ★   65
Chiswick Mall, London W4.

Mr and Mrs Jeremy Benson ✳ *S of Great West Road (M4) between Hammersmith*

flyover and Hogarth roundabout. Approached from Eyot Gardens South or Church
Street ✳ *Parking in adjacent roads* ✳ *Seeds for sale from excellent lists, packed*
with information and from 10p a packet ✳ *Open for parties April, 2 – 6pm, May,*
2 – 7pm ✳ *Entrance: £1, children 20p*

This is one of the beautiful old houses on the Mall with two thirds of an acre of
formally-designed and informally-planted garden whose sheer size (for
London) takes your breath away as you come out into it from the house. A large
paved area leading up steps to wide lawns with mature and handsome trees
including two poplars, a tulip tree, several large ornamental cherries, acers and
a magnolia. A strawberry grape from which cuttings are sometimes for sale.
Beyond a yew hedge is a woodland area, heavily shaded, and intersected with
old brick paths. A formal lily pond (larger than many town gardens) is
surrounded by borders and a fence covered with climbers. Many varieties of
peonies, irises, climbing roses, clematis, etc. Other borders and further small
pool. Much self-seeding in the borders which accounts for the informality
within the mostly formal lay-out. Note the 'front' gardens across the road (other
owners) which are regularly flooded by the river. The nearby Strawberry
House, splendidly developed by Lady Rothes, is alas up for sale and closed to
the public. One hopes temporarily.

WALPOLE PARK 66
Ealing, London W5. Tel: (081) 579 2424

London Borough of Ealing ✳ *Centre of Ealing, access from Uxbridge Road and*
High Street ✳ *Parking in surrounding residential roads* ✳ *Toilet facilities* ✳
Suitable for wheelchairs ✳ *Dogs on lead* ✳ *Open daily, 8am – dusk* ✳
Entrance: free

The gardens were acquired by the Borough Council and opened to the public
in 1901. Large walled rose garden with a pergola. Formal beds set in lawn
framed by old cedar trees. Centrepiece of topiary in the shape of a peacock but
its tail is a bed of suitably-coloured flowering plants. There is also a water
garden in Oriental style.

THE WATER GARDENS ★ 67
Warren Road, Kingston Hill, Kingston, Surrey.

Octagon Developments Ltd ✳ *From Kingston take the A308 (Kingston Hill)*
towards London. About $^1/_2$m on right, turn right into Warren Road ✳ *Parking on*
street ✳ *Partly suitable for wheelchairs* ✳ *Open 10th May, 4th Oct, 2 – 5pm* ✳
Entrance: £1, children 50p

A new development of luxury apartments has been built on part of the site,
overlooking what is thought to be the oldest Japanese-style garden in Britain.
An idyllic woodland setting of azaleas, acers, rhododendrons and magnolias
among mature broadleaf trees and conifers. Gravel paths and stepping stones
wind through these magnificent gardens, and you are never far from the sound
of water, which runs in streams and cascades into tranquil ponds. Part of the
original nineteenth-century Veitch nurseries.

WATERHOUSE PLANTATION (also known as Woodland Garden) ★ 68
Bushy Park, Hampton, London. Tel: (081) 979 1586

Department of the Environment ✳ *On A308 Hampton Court road, ¹/₄m W of Hampton Court roundabout. Short walk from car park, gate on main road alongside* ✳ *Best season: spring* ✳ *Parking* ✳ *Suitable for wheelchairs* ✳ *Open daily, 9am – dusk* ✳ *Entrance: free*

There are two Plantations, both in Bushy Park, adjoining Hampton Court. Planting similar to the Isabella Plantation in Richmond Park (see entry) concentrating on masses of shrubs – rhododendrons, azaleas and camellias. The artificial river, the Longford, is a dramatic feature with many small bridges. Waterhouse suffered in the 1987 gales but has recovered well and there is something to see at all times of the year, such as a heather garden and wild flowers in season.

42 WOODVILLE GARDENS 69
Ealing, London W5. Tel: (081) 998 4134

J. Welfare ✳ *Off Hanger Lane (off A40)* ✳ *Best season: early summer* ✳ *Parking in street* ✳ *Open by appointment only* ✳ *Entrance: by donation to charity*

Larger than average town garden laid out predominantly to accommodate the owner's love of plants. The beds surrounding the lawn have grown in size as the need for more plant space demanded. There are a number of interesting and unusual ones, including a *Cestrum parqui* on the house wall, a small bed under an apple tree with four different pulmonarias and a large number of silver-leaved and variegated perennials and shrubs. The small raised terrace by the house is interplanted with low-growing silver-foliage plants and geraniums. Below it is a densely planted bed of dwarf alpines. At the bottom is a small bog garden.

GREATER LONDON AND SURREY
A few gardens with Surrey addresses are included in the Greater London section for convenience, but check the Surrey section as another beautiful garden may be nearby.

MANCHESTER (Greater)

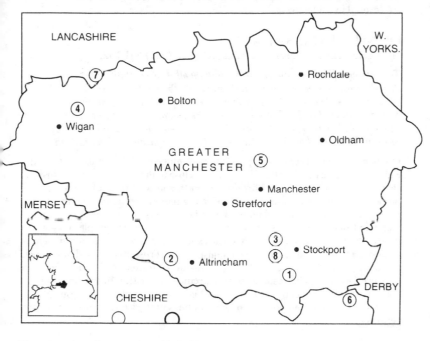

LANCASHIRE

W. YORKS.

⑦

● Rochdale

④

● Bolton

● Wigan

● Oldham

GREATER
MANCHESTER ⑤

● Manchester

MERSEY

● Stretford

③

⑧

● Stockport

② ● Altrincham

①

DERBY

CHESHIRE

⑥

Two-starred gardens are ringed in bold.

BRAMALL HALL   1

Bramhall Park, Bramhall, Stockport, Greater Manchester. Tel. (061) 485 3708

Stockport Metropolitan Borough Council ✳ 2m S of Stockport on A5102 between Bramhall and Stockport, follow signposts ✳ Best season: late spring/early summer ✳ Parking ✳ Refreshments in tea shop in converted stables ✳ Toilet facilities ✳ Partly suitable for wheelchairs ✳ Dogs on leads in some areas ✳ Shop in Hall ✳ House open April to Sept, daily, 1 – 5pm, Oct to Dec, Feb to March, daily except Mon, 1 – 4pm. Closed Jan and 25th, 26th Dec. Entrance £2, OAP and children £1 ✳ Open daily all day ✳ Entrance: free (to gardens only)

The gardens of Bramall Hall are a missed opportunity. At the front of this magnificent black and white timber-framed house is a courtyard covered in tarmac. To the back a slope down from the house has been terraced using brick retaining walls. These are in bad repair and of an unfortunate choice of brick. The best parts of the gardens are a little distance to the front of the house where, in a narrow strip of land, are some formal beds containing bright annuals and a herbaceous border enclosed by a hedge. The parkland is another matter. In the valley of a small river are broad areas of grassland and a number of small lakes. Woods, which contain some very large beech trees, surround the park and hide all sign of the suburbs of Stockport. Along the river there is a walk, the banks of which are covered in wild flowers.

DUNHAM MASSEY ★ 2
Nr Altrincham, Greater Manchester. Tel: (061) 941 1025

The National Trust ✳ *3m SW of Altrincham off A56* ✳ *Parking* ✳ *Refreshments: licensed self-service restaurant* ✳ *Toilet facilities* ✳ *Suitable for wheelchairs* ✳ *Dogs on lead in park only* ✳ *Shop* ✳ *House open April to 1st Nov, daily except Fri, 1 – 5pm, Sun and Bank Holiday Mons, 12 noon – 5pm (last admission 4.30pm)* ✳ *Garden open April to 1st Nov, daily, 12 noon – 5.30pm, Sun and Bank Holiday Mons, 11am – 5.30pm* ✳ *Entrance: £2 garden only*

Dunham Massey has extensive parkland with much of its layout dating from the eighteenth century and earlier. The gardens close to the house have many historic elements, too. The lake that borders the north and west sides of the house was formerly part of a moat and overlooking it is a mount that dates from the Tudor period, now grassed over and planted with false acacias. On the north side of the house, in front of the lake, is an Edwardian parterre planted in purple and gold; to the east is a large lawn bordered by shrubs and trees where there is an eighteenth-century orangery and an old well house. The Trust has carried out much replanting with the aim of restoring it 'in the character of the late-Victorian Pleasure Ground'. The result appears extremely successful. In the centre of the house is an attractive courtyard with four beds of shrubs and herbaceous plants. One of the rooms of the house contains paintings of the gardens made at various periods in history.

FLETCHER MOSS BOTANICAL GARDENS AND PARSONAGE GARDENS ★ 3
Mill Gate Lane, Didsbury, Greater Manchester. Tel: (061) 434 1877

Manchester City Council (Recreational Services) ✳ *5m S of Manchester city centre on Mill Gate Lane which runs S of the A5145 close to the centre of the village of Didsbury* ✳ *Limited parking* ✳ *Refreshments: in small café (the building where the first meeting of the RSPB took place) but opening times uncertain* ✳ *Toilet facilities inc. disabled* ✳ *Partly suitable for wheelchairs* ✳ *Dogs allowed in certain areas only* ✳ *Open all year, 9am – dusk* ✳ *Entrance: free*

Much of this garden is set on a steep south-facing bank that is planted with a great variety of shrubs, heathers, bulbs, alpines, azaleas and small trees. Amongst them are rocky streams running down to a water garden and lawned area where there are moisture-loving plants including a large clump of gunneras. Across some tennis courts is a large grassed area containing specimen trees. Within a short walking distance are the Parsonage Gardens which are the grounds of the Fletcher Moss Museum. They were laid out in Victorian times and are more formal, containing lawns, good herbaceous borders, camellias and rhododendrons. There is also an Orchid House and some fine trees, notably a swamp cypress and a mulberry. Excellent well-maintained gardens.

HAIGH HALL GARDENS 4
Haigh Country Park, Haigh, Nr Wigan, Greater Manchester.   Tel: (0942) 832895

Metropolitan Borough of Wigan (Department of Leisure) ✳ 2m NE of Wigan on N side of B5238. Signposted ✳ Parking (50p during peak summer season) ✳ Refreshments: café ✳ Toilet facilities ✳ Suitable for wheelchairs which are available from the information centre ✳ Dogs on lead ✳ Shop ✳ Parkland open all year, daily during daylight hours. Zoo open, daily except 25th, 26th Dec and 1st Jan ✳ Entrance: mainly free, but some areas of the gardens are entered through the zoo for which there is a charge

Haigh Hall is surrounded by mature parkland, and a short distance to the east of the hall are some formal gardens probably of Victorian and Edwardian origin. In an open area of lawn there is an oval pool around which are rose beds and specimen shrubs. Close by are three adjoining walled gardens, the middle one containing a good herbaceous border and a well-stocked shrub border. The second, to the south, has shrubs around the walls and young specimen trees planted in a lawn in the centre; the wall to the south is low and gives a view across a wild garden with a pond. The third walled garden at the northern end can only be entered from the zoo, and here against the south facing wall is a cactus house and a butterfly house. On the west side is a landscaped area with heathers and conifers. The rest is a formal layout with roses, yew hedges and lawns and, against the east wall, a border of shrub roses. The arboretum set in woodlands is into its fifth year, with new specimens being planted every year.

HEATON HALL 5
Heaton Park, Prestwich, Greater Manchester.   Tel: (061) 236 5244 (Hall enquiries); (061) 773 1085 (Park enquiries)

Manchester City Council ✳ 4m N of the city centre on A576 just S of junction with M66 ✳ Best season: spring/early summer ✳ Parking ✳ Refreshments: café ✳ Toilet facilities ✳ Some areas suitable for wheelchairs, but ring for advice before visiting ✳ Dogs ✳ Shop ✳ House open summer months only ✳ Garden open all year during daylight hours ✳ Entrance: free

Heaton Hall, built in 1772 by Wyatt, was described by Pevsner as 'the finest house of its period in Lancashire'. To the front of the lovely Hall is an area of formal, brightly planted gardens that would perhaps go better in front of a Victorian house. To the rear are some stables, with a small heather garden at their front and behind a large formal rose garden. A path leads through a tunnel to an attractive dell planted with a variety of mature trees and many rhododendrons. From here a path follows a stream through a series of pools and waterfalls with many new plantings on its surrounding banks leading to a large boating lake. On the Prestwich side of the park is an old walled garden where small demonstration gardens have been created, including a low-maintenance garden, a cottage garden and an alpine garden. A large greenhouse is also open to view.

LYME PARK ★ 6
Disley, Stockport, Greater Manchester. Tel: (0663) 62023
The National Trust ✳ 6m SE of Stockport just W of Disley on A6 ✳ Parking ✳

Refreshments: teas sometimes available in hall, kiosk in car park ✳ *Toilet facilities* ✳ *Special help is available with wheelchairs. Phone in advance* ✳ *Dogs on leads* ✳ *Shop* ✳ *House open at different times and at extra charge* ✳ *Garden open all year, daily except 25th and 26th Dec: summer 11am – 5pm, winter 11am – 4pm. Guided tours at special times* ✳ *Entrance: pedestrians free, car £3 to include occupants. This charge applies to National Trust members*

Lyme Park has immense character and the gardens contrast well with the rugged hills (and usually clouds) that surround it. A lawn at the front of the house leads down to a lake beyond which is a woodland garden underplanted with rhododendrons and other shade-loving plants. To the east is a fine orangery and below the terrace to the west is a well-kept geometric Dutch garden. An extensive programme to restore the gardens to their original design is nearly complete.

RIVINGTON TERRACED GARDENS   7
Rivington, Greater Manchester. Tel: (0204) 691549 (Rivington Information Centre)

North West Water ✳ *2m NW of Horwich. Follow the signposts to Rivington from the A673 in Horwich or in Grimeford village. The gardens are reached by a 10-minute walk from Rivington Hall and Hall Barn* ✳ *Best season: June* ✳ *Parking, refreshments, toilet facilities at Hall Barn and refreshments, toilet facilities and information at Great House Barn* ✳ *Dogs* ✳ *Open at all times* ✳ *Entrance: free*

These are not gardens as such but the remains of gardens that were built by Lord Leverhulme in the early part of this century. They are set mainly in woodland on a steep west-facing hillside and have fine views across Rivington reservoirs. It is worth buying the guide which leads the visitor round and explains the various features. Particularly impressive is a rocky ravine, the remains of a Japanese garden and the restored pigeon tower. There are a variety of mature trees and many rhododendrons and once this must have been a very grand estate. When visiting be prepared for a stiff walk and beware of the paths which can be slippery in some areas.

WYTHENSHAWE HORTICULTURAL CENTRE   8
Wythenshawe Park, Wythenshawe Road, Baguley, Greater Manchester. Tel: (061) 945 1768

Manchester City Council ✳ *7m S of Manchester city centre, ¹/₄m from M63 junction 9, ¹/₂m from M56 junction 3, S of B5167* ✳ *Parking* ✳ *Refreshments: cafeteria at hall, open weekends only 10am – 5pm* ✳ *Toilet facilities inc. disabled* ✳ *Partly suitable for wheelchairs* ✳ *Plants for sale Wed, 1 – 4pm, also Sat and Sun 10am – 4pm* ✳ *Open daily, 10am – 4pm* ✳ *Entrance: free*

Set on the site of an old vegetable garden, this centre is now the nursery that provides most of the bedding stock for the city's parks. It also houses many surprisingly large collections of plants. Outside are herbaceous beds, vegetable plots, heather beds and an area of small trees and conifers. Among the many greenhouses is a cactus house containing many large specimens, a temperate house, a fern and orchid house, an alpine house and a chrysanthemum house. There is also a Visitors' Centre where the staff are always willing to help with advice. To the east of the Centre is the Hall, with some formal garden, including a large bed devoted to spiraeas.

MERSEYSIDE

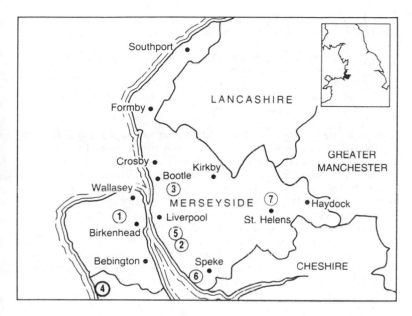

Two-starred gardens are ringed in bold.

BIRKENHEAD PARK ★
Birkenhead, Wirral, Merseyside. Tel: (051) 647 2366

Metropolitan Borough of Wirral * *1m from the centre of Birkenhead on S of A553* * *Best season: autumn* * *Parking around park* * *Refreshments: tea kiosk sometimes open* * *Partly suitable for wheelchairs* * *Code of practice for dog owners and poop scoop byelaws introduced* * *Open during daylight hours* * *Entrance: free*

Birkenhead Park is rich in history. Opened in 1847, it was the world's first park to be built at public expense. Joseph Paxton produced its design which was highly influential in the creation of New York's Central Park. It is split into two by a road; on the eastern side is a lake with well-landscaped banks planted with trees and shrubs. A Swiss-style bridge links two islands and to one end is a fine stone boathouse that has been recently restored. In the west part is another lake with weeping willows and rhododendrons planted round its edge. There is also an enclosed area of more ornamental plants. This park is so well landscaped and planted that it is possible to overlook the litter and vandalism from which it suffers.

CALDERSTONE PARK ★   2
Liverpool, Merseyside. Tel: (051) 225 4835

Liverpool City Council, Environmental Services ✳ 4m SE of Liverpool city centre, S of A562 ✳ Parking ✳ Refreshments in teashop ✳ Toilet facilities ✳ Suitable for wheelchairs ✳ Dogs in park only ✳ Park open at all times. Old English Garden and Japanese Garden open April to Sept, 8am – 7.30pm, Oct to March, 8am – 4pm. Closed 25th Dec ✳ Entrance: free

This is a large landscaped park with mature trees, shrubs, a lake and rhododendron walk. In its centre are three gardens set around an old walled garden which are a credit to the city council gardener here. The first is the Flower garden which has semiformal beds of perennials and grasses, formal beds of annuals and a long greenhouse. Next is the Old English garden, where amongst a formal layout of paths are beds containing a huge range of perennials, bulbs and shrubs. There is a circular pond at the centre and pergolas carrying clematis, vines and other climbers cross the paths at various points. Finally the Japanese garden has a chain of rocky streams and pools around which are pines, acers and clumps of bamboo. A greenhouse contains the National Collection of the genus *Aechmea*. Altogether this must be one of the best 'free' gardens in the country.

CROXTETH HALL AND COUNTRY PARK   3
Liverpool, Merseyside. Tel: (051) 228 5311

Liverpool City Council, Environmental Services ✳ Turn N off A5058 Liverpool ring road into Muirhead Avenue on NE side of city. Croxteth Park is well signposted ✳ Best season: summer ✳ Parking ✳ Restaurant ✳ Toilet facilities ✳ Partly suitable for wheelchairs ✳ Dogs in outer park only ✳ Shop in house ✳ House and Victorian Farm also open ✳ Garden open Good Fri to Sept, daily, 11am – 5pm, winter times on request ✳ Entrance: 50p for walled garden (all facilities £2). Reductions for OAP and children

Croxteth Hall stands in 500 acres of parkland in which there are large areas of woodland and many rhododendrons. The centre of interest to gardeners is the large walled garden to the north of the house. Divided up by gravel paths, this garden contains areas growing a great variety of fruit, vegetables and decorative plants; fruit espaliers are grown against the walls and trained on wire fences and the south-facing wall has a broad herbaceous border containing a good variety of perennials and ornamental grasses. In the north east corner several greenhouses and a mushroom house are all open to the visitor. To the south end is a small weather station surrounded by herb beds, and, close by, some working beehives.

ISLE OF MAN
(see Cumbria)

NESS GARDENS ★★   4
University of Liverpool Botanic Gardens, Ness, South Wirral, Merseyside. Tel: (051) 336 2135

University of Liverpool ✳ *2m off A540 on Neston Road between Ness and Burton* ✳ *Parking* ✳ *Refreshments* ✳ *Toilet facilities* ✳ *Partly suitable for wheelchairs* ✳ *Plants for sale* ✳ *Shop* ✳ *Open daily except 25th Dec, March to Oct, 9.30am – dusk, Nov to Feb, 9.30am – 4pm* ✳ *Entrance: £2.80, OAP and children 10 – 18 years £1.80, family ticket £7*

A Mr Bulley began gardening on this site in 1898 using plants collected for him by George Forrest, the noted plant hunter. His daughter gave the gardens to the University in 1948. They extend to over 60 acres. Those who have experience of the north west winds blowing off the Irish Sea will marvel at the variety and exotic nature of the plant life. The secret is in the Lombardy poplars, holm oaks and Scots pines which have been planted as shelter belts shielding the specialist areas. The aim has been to provide all-year round interest from the spring, through the herbaceous and rose gardens of the summer to the heather and sorbus collections of the autumn. There are in addition areas of specialist interest such as the Nature Plant Garden which houses plants raised from seed or cuttings from wild plants and used for propagation or the re-stocking of natural habitats. For all its specialist and academic background the labelling of plants is somewhat inadequate and though there are a number of signed 'walks' of varying distances (including one suitable for wheelchairs) here again the signs could be clearer without being obtrusive. The coloured illustrated guide is therefore a must.

SEFTON PARK   5
Liverpool, Merseyside. Tel: (051) 724 2371

Liverpool City Council (controlled by Environmental Services, Calderstone Park) ✳ *3m SE of Liverpool city centre, N of A561* ✳ *Best season: spring* ✳ *Parking at various points around park* ✳ *Refreshments at café in centre of park* ✳ *Suitable for wheelchairs* ✳ *Dogs* ✳ *Open at all times* ✳ *Entrance: free*

Although this large park suffers badly from litter and vandalism it remains an extremely fine Victorian park, with many of its monuments, gateways and shelters as well as the large houses surrounding it built in the Gothic style of the late 1800s. A large serpentine boating lake has two small streams entering at its northern end. One stream flows from the east through a lightly wooded valley that has been landscaped with large rocks and planted with rhododendrons. The other flows from the north through a series of small lakes passing a replica of Piccadilly's Eros, a statue of Peter Pan and an ornate bandstand. In the centre of the park is a magnificent palm house now in bad repair but a restoration scheme is soon to be undertaken.

SPEKE HALL 6
The Walk, Liverpool, Merseyside. Tel: (051) 427 7231

*The National Trust * 8m SE of Liverpool city centre, S of A561. Signposted *
Best season: spring * Refreshments in teashop from 12 noon. Picnics in orchard *
Toilet facilities inc. disabled * Partly suitable for wheelchairs * Shop * Hall
open April to Oct, daily except Mon. £2.40, children £1.20. Reductions for parties
* Garden open April to 1st Nov, daily except Mon, 1 – 5.30pm, 30th Oct to 13th
Dec, daily except Mon, 12 noon – 4.30pm. Closed 1st Jan, 17th April, 24th to
26th, 31st Dec * Entrance: 60p (hall and gardens £3)*

The gardens at Speke are neither as old nor as impressive as the Elizabethan
Hall. They are remarkable, however, for although they are situated amidst the
industrial areas of south Liverpool they seem to be set in the heart of the
countryside, despite their proximity to Liverpool airport. In front of the house is
a large lawn with shrub borders to the sides containing mainly rhododendrons
and hollies. On the side opposite the house is a ha-ha allowing views to the
fields and woodland. A stone bridge leads over a drained moat to the ornate
stone entrance of the hall. The moat continues to the west where there is a
herbaceous border with a variety of perennials; a large holm oak stands
opposite. To the south is a formal rose garden containing fragrant varieties of
old-fashioned roses. In the centre of the house is a large cobbled courtyard in
which grow two enormous yews. The Trust is continuing to develop many areas
of the gardens.

WINDLE HALL 7
St Helens, Merseyside.

*The Lady Pilkington * 1¹/₂m NE of St Helens, N of A570 * Parking *
Refreshments * Toilet facilities * Partly suitable for wheelchairs * Dogs on
leads * Open 5th July, 6th Sept, 2 – 5.30pm * Entrance: 70p, children 30p
(1991 prices)*

A large part of these gardens is set in a 200-year old walled garden where there
is a complex layout of well-tended lawns, paths and flower beds. The latter
contains many bright annuals and modern roses. There are also herbaceous
borders, rose trellises and fruit trees. At one end is a small greenhouse and
close by a pool with a fountain. To the east of the walled garden in an area that is
mainly lawned is a small rock garden, water garden and stone grotto. The east
front of the hall looks down on a pool that is surrounded by azaleas and backed
by high conifers. In an area of woodland around the garden are spring-
flowering plants.

MIDLANDS (West)

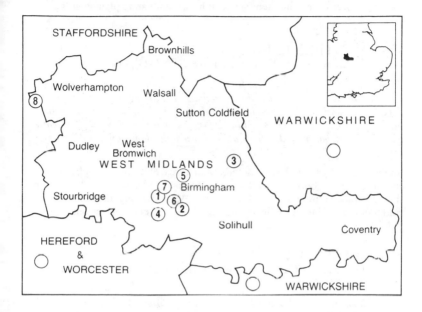

BIRMINGHAM BOTANICAL GARDENS AND
GLASSHOUSES ★   1
**Westbourne Road, Edgbaston, Birmingham, West Midlands. Tel:
(021) 454 1860**

2m from city centre. Approach from Hagley Road or Calthorpe Road ∗ *Parking* ∗
Refreshments: restaurant. Picnics allowed ∗ *Toilet facilities* ∗ *Suitable for
wheelchairs. Two chairs available for use free of charge* ∗ *Plants for sale* ∗ *Shop*
∗ *Open daily, 9am (10am on Suns) – 7.30pm (or dusk if earlier)* ∗ *Entrance:
£2.70 (£3 on summer Suns), OAP, disabled, students and children £1.40. Parties
£2.30 per person (£1.20 for concessions)*

This garden will appeal to the keen plantsperson and also to the everyday
gardener. In addition to the unusual plants in the Tropical house and the
orangery, there is a cactus and succulent house, and cages with parrots and also
guinea fowl, ducks, peacocks, geese and other birds. Some beautiful old trees, a
border for E.H. Wilson plants, a raised alpine bed and a raised garden area to
give ideas and enjoyment to disabled visitors. Good colour foliage contrasts and

a small area laid out with model domestic gardens. The rock garden contains rhododendrons, primulas, astilbes and azaleas and there are also herbaceous borders and a rose garden. There is a small display of carnivorous plants. A children's playground and adventure trail makes the garden a pleasant place for a family outing. The model domestic gardens perhaps should be called theme gardens, covering low maintenance, children, colour and a plantsman's garden.

CANNON HILL PARK 2
Moseley, Birmingham, West Midlands. Tel: (021) 449 0238

*Birmingham City Council * 2m from Birmingham city centre opposite Edgbaston Cricket Ground * Best season: spring/summer * Parking * Refreshments: lunches and snacks in park restaurant. Picnic area * Toilet facilities in Midlands Art Centre open 9am – 9pm * Suitable for wheelchairs * Dogs * Art Centre in park, bookshop, gallery and restaurant * Open daily, 8am – dusk * Entrance: free*

Eighty acres of park with formal beds, wide range of herbaceous plants, shrubs and trees. Glasshouse with collection of tropical and sub-tropical plants open 10am – 4pm. Nature trails. Children's area. Also boating, miniature golf, bowls and tennis available. A model of the Elan Valley is set in the garden area.

CASTLE BROMWICH HALL ★ 3
Old Chester Road, Castle Bromwich, Birmingham, West Midlands. Tel: (021) 749 4100

*Castle Bromwich Hall Gardens Trust * 4m E of Birmingham city centre. 1m from junction 5 of M6 northbound * Parking * Refreshments * Toilet facilities * Suitable for wheelchairs * Seeds for sale * Shop * Open Easter to Sept, Mon – Thurs, 1.30 – 4.30pm. Sat, Sun and Bank Holidays, 2 – 6pm. Guided tours Wed, Sat, Sun and Bank Holidays * Entrance: £2 with concessions for OAPs and children*

The hall, built at the end of the sixteenth century, was sold to Sir John Bridgman in 1657 and his wife created the garden with expert help. It fell into decay, and now a series of formal connecting gardens is being restored to give them the appearance and content of a garden of 1680/1740. The perimeter wall and orangery have been rebuilt. There are fan- and espalier-trained fruit trees and orchard, a kitchen garden, ponds, cold bath, archery ground, maze, wilderness, and historic borders. New orchards of period varieties were planted winter 1990/91. Wild flower meadow, nut grounds. Visitors have the rare opportunity to see a period garden being restored year-by-year.

MARTINEAU ENVIRONMENTAL STUDIES CENTRE 4
Priory Road, Edgbaston, Birmingham, West Midlands. Tel: (021) 440 4883

*City of Birmingham Education Department * Turn off A38 road into Priory Road* *and entrance is 100 yards on right opposite Priory Hospital ∗ Parking ∗ Tea on open day ∗ Toilet facilities ∗ Suitable for wheelchairs ∗ Plants for sale ∗ Open three times a year (contact Centre for dates), 10.30am – 6pm ∗ Entrance: £1, children 50p*

This is a two-acre educational garden designed for teachers and children but the wide range of features make it interesting for all, and a good place for the family with children interested in gardening. There are annuals, herbaceous and shrub borders, roses, raised beds, herbs, alpines, bulbs, miscanthus and the greenhouse with a collection of cactus, tomatoes and peppers along with tropical things such as a banana, fig and coffee plant. In the woodland area there are native plants and a pool with plenty of wildlife. The vegetable plots contain brassicas, root crops and legumes and the fruit trees and soft fruit include a medlar, greengage, apricot, blueberry and tayberry. The children work on some of the plots – so with school holidays everything cannot always be weed free. There are now some sheep, ducks and hens.

26 SUNNYBANK ROAD   5
Wylde Green, Sutton Coldfield, Birmingham, West Midlands. Tel: (021) 384 8474

Chris and Margaret Jones ∗ From S take A5127, turn left on to A452 Chester road, right at next traffic lights, B4531. The third right is Sunnybank Road. From N follow signs through Sutton Coldfield for Birmingham, turn right for Wylde Green station into Station Road and left under bridge into Sunnybank Road ∗ Parking in road ∗ Refreshments ∗ Plants for sale ∗ Open 31st May, 2 – 6pm, 26th July, 2.30 – 5.30pm, 2nd Aug, 2 – 6pm ∗ Entrance: 50p, accompanied children free

This garden has been made in six years from a sandy lawn filled with a large amount of builder's rubbish and one silver birch tree. A terrace outside the house is bordered by beds with all-year interest, and tubs of annuals. Winding paths lead down to a pool and a bog garden beyond which is a lawn. Beds and borders contain a good variety of shrubs and plants, many raised from seed by the owners, and are full of attractive different shapes and colours. It shows what can be created from an unpromising, rectangular town back garden and will be interesting to plantspersons or just to enjoy for its surprises and its colours.

THE UNIVERSITY OF BIRMINGHAM BOTANIC GARDEN ★   6
Winterbourne, 58 Edgbaston Park Road, Edgbaston, Birmingham. Tel: (021) 414 5590

The University of Birmingham School of Continuing Studies ∗ Off A38 Bristol Road leading out of the city, adjacent to the University campus ∗ Parking ∗ Toilet facilities ∗ Suitable for wheelchairs ∗ Plants sometimes for sale on open days ∗ Open all year except during university terms and Bank Holidays, 8am – 5pm and for parties by arrangement. Also for charity 12th April, 21st June, 2 – 6pm ∗ Entrance £1, children 50p

About seven acres of garden originally belonging to a large house owing much to the landscape style developed by Edward Lutyens and Gertrude Jekyll.

Because of its wide range of plants and different features it should be of interest to the botanist as well as the ordinary gardener. There are geographical beds showing typical trees and shrubs from Europe, Australasia, the Americas, China and Japan. The pergola is covered with clematis and roses and there are herbaceous borders backed by brick walls covered with climbers. A miniature arboretum contains interesting specimens including giant oaks, acers, conifers and a *Gingko biloba* along with hedges of yew, *Taxus baccata* and copper beech. In a fairly new Commemorative Garden is a Black Mulberry planted to mark the 100th anniversary of the City of Birmingham. The range of plants continues with the sandstone rock garden, troughs, rhododendrons, heathers and alpines. There is an unusual nut walk containing several varieties of *Corylus avellana* trained over an iron framework. A special feature is the walled garden laid out with beds of roses showing the History of the Rose, and elsewhere are more recent plantings of roses. Clearing of old shrubs at one side of the house has opened up the small paved garden attractively. Friends of Winterbourne can take advantage of visits and lectures by annual subscription.

8 VICARAGE ROAD 7
Edgbaston, Birmingham, West Midlands. Tel: (021) 455 0902

Charles and Tessa King-Farlow ✱ *1¹/₂m W of city centre off A456 Hagley road. Going out of the city, turn left into Vicarage Road* ✱ *Best season: May to early July and Sept/Oct* ✱ *Parking in local roads* ✱ *Teas on June open day only* ✱ *Suitable for wheelchairs* ✱ *Plants for sale at certain times* ✱ *Open 28th June, 2 – 6pm and by appointment* ✱ *Entrance: £1, OAP and children 50p*

A visit to this garden should give pleasure to most gardeners as there is a sense of mystery as one moves from one area to the next. Plenty of good planting ideas can be seen with the clever use of colour and foliage combinations – a range of grey and variegated foliage. Roses and clematis scramble through old fruit trees and other shrubs. There is a bank of shrub roses, and the herbaceous border consists of three tiers and contains a wide range and some rare plants. There is a conservatory, pool and 1920s rock garden providing year-round colour. The walled kitchen garden has fruit and vegetables, and improvements are planned for this area. It is hard to believe that one is walking through a garden so near the centre of a large city.

WIGHTWICK MANOR 8
Wightwick Bank, Wolverhampton, West Midlands. Tel: (0902) 761108

The National Trust ✱ *3m W of Wolverhampton off A454. Turn by the Mermaid Inn up Wightwick Bank* ✱ *Parking* ✱ *Minimal refreshments* ✱ *Toilet facilities* ✱ *Suitable for wheelchairs* ✱ *Dogs on lead* ✱ *Shop* ✱ *House open same days as garden, 2.30 – 5.30pm. Timed tickets* ✱ *Garden open March to Dec, Thurs and Sat, Bank Holiday Sun and Mon, 2 – 6pm. Closed 25th, 26th Dec. Pre-booked parties accepted Wed and Thurs* ✱ *Entrance: £1.50 (house £3.50)*

This 10-acre garden, designed by the engineer Alfred Parsons, surrounds an 1887 house strongly influenced in its design by William Morris and his movement; it contains a collection of pre-Raphaelite paintings. Large trees form a delightful framework to the garden with a central octagonal arbour with climbing roses and clematis. Through an old orchard is a less formal area with pools surrounded by shrubs and rhododendrons. There are herbaceous borders, two rows of barrel-shaped yews and beds containing plants from gardens of famous men. As a surprise round a corner one comes across a line of boulders from Scotland and the Lake District which were left when the great glaciers melted in the last Ice Age.

TELEPHONE NUMBERS

Except where owners have specifically requested that they be excluded, telephone numbers to which enquiries may be directed are given for each property. To maintain the support and cooperation of private owners' it is suggested that the telephone be used with discretion. Where visits are by appointment, the telephone can of course be used except where written application, particularly for parties, is specifically requested. Code numbers are given in brackets. For the Republic of Ireland phone 010353 followed by the code (Dublin is 1) followed by the subscriber's number. In all cases where visits by parties are proposed, owners should be advised in advance and arrangements preferably confirmed in writing.

NORFOLK

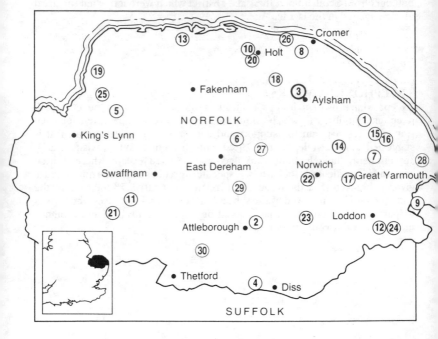

Two-starred gardens are ringed in bold.

BEESTON HALL 1
Beeston St Lawrence, Wroxham, Norfolk. Tel: (0692) 630771

Sir Ronald and Lady Preston ∗ 2¹/₄m NE of Wroxham on road to Stalham off A1151 ∗ Best season: early summer ∗ Parking ∗ Refreshments: tearoom ∗ Toilet facilities ∗ Suitable for wheelchairs ∗ Shop ∗ House open ∗ Garden open Easter Sun to mid-Sept, Fri, Sun, Bank Holiday Mon, also Wed in Aug, 2 – 5.30pm ∗ Entrance: £2, children £1, grounds only 50p

The Gothic house of 1786 stands on rising ground overlooking a long serpentine lake. The gardens to the south of the house are pretty although not extensive. There is a brick orangery, herbaceous and shrub borders, and some mature trees of early nineteenth-century planting. The park originally laid out by Richmond (a contemporary of 'Capability' Brown) is now largely given over to farming and a broad path winds down through corn fields to woodland where there is an ice-house and a lakeside walk.

BESTHORPE HALL ★   2
Besthorpe, Attleborough, Norfolk. Tel: (0953) 452138

Mr J.A. Alston ✳ *1m E of Attleborough on Bunwell Road. Entrance on right, past church* ✳ *Best season: June* ✳ *Parking* ✳ *Refreshments* ✳ *Toilet facilities* ✳ *Suitable for wheelchairs* ✳ *Plants for sale* ✳ *Open 14th June, 12th July, 2 – 5pm* ✳ *Entrance: £1*

A pool and fountain occupy the centre of the entrance forecourt. Beyond the house, more pools and fountains are set among lawns skirted by high clematis-hung walls of Tudor brick which form a backdrop to long herbaceous borders. The largest lawn, believed to have once been a tilt yard, has developing topiary, while on another is an enormous and shapely Wellingtonia. There are many other fine trees among which are paulownia, and a variety of birches, acers and magnolias including the sumptuous *M. delavayi*. There are walled kitchen gardens, a nuttery, a herb garden, and a small lake with wildfowl. On another lushly planted pool live a pair of black swans.

BLICKLING HALL ★★   3
Aylsham, Norfolk. Tel: (0263) 733084

The National Trust ✳ *1¹/2m NW of Aylsham on N side of B1354* ✳ *Best seasons: spring and summer* ✳ *Parking* ✳ *Refreshments 11am – 5pm. Picnic area in walled garden* ✳ *Toilet facilities* ✳ *Suitable for wheelchairs* ✳ *Dogs in park on leads* ✳ *Plant Centre open 10am – 5pm* ✳ *Shop* ✳ *House open 1 – 5pm* ✳ *Cycle hire on house open days* ✳ *Garden open 28th March to 1st Nov, daily except Mon and Thurs, 12 noon – 5pm and daily in July and Aug. Open Bank Holiday Mons. Closed Good Fri* ✳ *Entrance: £2.30 (house and gardens £4.90)*

Although the gardens of Blickling Hall seem so suited to the style and beauty of the Jacobean house, they consist of a blend of features from the seventeenth to the twentieth centuries. From the earliest period come the massive yew hedges flanking the south approach. To the east is the parterre planned by Nesfield and Wyatt in 1870 with its topiary pillars and blocks of yew shaped like grand pianos. Complicated flower beds were replaced in 1938 with Norah Lindsay's four large square beds of herbaceous plants in selected colours with surrounding borders of roses edged with catmint. The central pool has a seventeenth-century fountain bought from nearby Oxnead Hall. A high retaining wall bounds the southern side while in the centre of the eastern side flights of steps mount up to the highest terrace with a central vista through blocks of woodland to the Doric temple of 1730 raised above parkland beyond. The two blocks are intersected by allées in seventeenth-century style although planted in 1861-64. Recent gales have done much damage but replanting has been undertaken using Turkey oak, lime and beech. On the southern side is the Orangery of 1782 by Samuel Wyatt which houses half-hardy plants and a statue of Hercules by Nicholas Stone made for Oxnead in the 1640s. In the corner of the northern block is the secret garden, a remnant of a larger eighteenth-century garden for which Repton made recommendations. It now consists of a lawn with a central sundial surrounded by high beech hedges. The shrub border through which it is approached is by Norah Lindsay who was also responsible for the planting of the dry moat around the house. North of the parterre is a raised grassy area, possibly a remnant of the Jacobean mount; here grow enormous, sprawling Oriental planes. To the north-west is landscaped parkland where woods descend to the curving lake formed before 1729 and later extended. West of the house are cedars of Lebanon and a collection of magnolias around a nineteenth-century fountain. Elsewhere in the park are the Gothic Tower of 1773 and the Mausoleum of 1796, a pyramid 45 ft square by Joseph Bonomi.

BRESSINGHAM GARDENS ★   4
Bressingham, Diss, Norfolk. Tel: (037988) 386/382

Mr Alan Bloom and Mr Adrian Bloom ✳ *3m W of Diss on A1066* ✳ *Parking* ✳ *Refreshments* ✳ *Toilet facilities* ✳ *Suitable for wheelchairs* ✳ *Plants for sale* ✳ *Shop* ✳ *Open Easter to Oct, daily, 10am – 5.30pm. Adrian Bloom's garden open 8th March, 19th July, 5th, 6th Sept, 11th Oct* ✳ *Entrance: £3.50, children £2 (joint entrance to both gardens £3.50)*

The six acres of this garden are chiefly occupied by island beds, a scheme which allows for the display of over 5000 kinds of hardy perennials, and the beds are full of colours and interest throughout the spring, summer and autumn. Although a miniature railway runs through to one side of the garden, the owners believe that it and the associated steam museum are not a distraction, particularly as they run only on Sun, Wed and Thurs, leaving four days for those who prefer to come solely for the garden. This is of a very high standard and comparisons have been made with Wisley. The large plant centre offers a wide range of trees, shrubs and herbaceous plants. The adjoining garden of Adrian Bloom contains over 300 varieties of conifers, some 50 different heathers and at least 1000 shrubs and perennials.

CONGHAM HALL HOTEL   5
Lynn Road, Grimston, Nr King's Lynn, Norfolk. Tel: (0485) 600250

Mr and Mrs T. Forecast ✳ *NE of King's Lynn. Go to A149/A148 interchange, then follow A148 signed Sandringham/Fakenham/Cromer for 100 yards. Turn right for Grimston. Hotel is 2¹/₂m on left hand side of road* ✳ *Parking* ✳ *Suitable for wheelchairs* ✳ *Open April to Sept, daily except Sat, 2 – 4pm. Small parties by arrangement at other times. No coaches* ✳ *Entrance: free*

Herb garden. Over 300 varieties grown in about two acres of hedged *jardinière* set near the Georgian manor house, now a hotel, which is itself surrounded by 40 acres of parkland. Mrs Forecast began the herb garden a few years ago as part of a vegetable and soft fruit supply for the kitchen. Now it has become an obsession, and includes medicinal herbs which, it goes without saying, are rarely if ever required by diners. Anyone interested in herbs should certainly visit. *Bon viveurs* will find the hotel in the *Good Food Guide*.

ELSING HALL ★ 6
Elsing, Nr East Dereham, Norfolk. Tel: (0362) 83224

Mr and Mrs D.H. Cargill ✳ 5m NE of East Dereham. Elsing signposted off A47 and B1067 ✳ Parking ✳ Refreshments ✳ Dogs on lead ✳ Open 21st June and 28th June to 5th July, all 2 – 6pm and by appointment ✳ Entrance: £1.50, children free

The romantic appearance of this garden is in complete harmony with the moated flint and half-timbered house which it surrounds. The garden, although mostly of recent planting, is rich, lush and unrestrained and in mid-summer is filled with the scent of the old garden roses which cover the walls and fill the borders. The lawn between the house and the moat has been abandoned to wild orchids; wildfowl nest among the reeds. Both the moat and a nearby stewpond are encircled by moist borders supporting luxuriant growth. On the walls of the kitchen garden grow old roses many of which seem unique to this place. A large variety of new trees has been planted, a knot garden is being developed, and an avenue of gingkos has been established.

FAIRHAVEN GARDEN TRUST ★ 7
South Walsham, Norwich, Norfolk. Tel: (060549) 449

Fairhaven Garden Trust ✳ 9m NE of Norwich off B1140 ✳ Best season: May/ June ✳ Parking ✳ Refreshments ✳ Toilet facilities ✳ Suitable for wheelchairs ✳ Dogs on lead ✳ Plants for sale ✳ Open 12th April to 4th May, Sun and Bank Holidays. 6th May to 13th Sept, Wed – Sun and Bank Holiday Mons, also Suns 20th, 27th Sept, all 11am – 6pm, except Sats 2 – 6pm. 1st Nov, 10am – dusk ✳ Entrance: £1.80, OAP £1.30, children 80p. Season tickets £6

A garden created in natural woods of oak and alder extending to about 230 acres surrounding the unspoiled South Walsham Broad. Paths wind among banks of azaleas and large-leaved rhododendrons and lead to the edge of the broad itself. Much of the area is wet and supports a rich variety of primulas, with lysichitons, astilbes, ligularias and gunneras of exceptional size, merging into the natural vegetation among which are many Royal ferns and some majestic oaks. Although particularly colourful during the flowering of the azaleas in the spring, this garden gives pleasure at all times of the year when natural beauty is preferred to man-made sophistication.

FELBRIGG HALL ★ 8
Roughton, Norwich, Norfolk. Tel: (026375) 444

The National Trust ✳ 3m SW of Cromer off A148. Main entrance on B1436 ✳ Best season: summer ✳ Parking ✳ Refreshments: April to 1st Nov, 11am – 5pm. 2nd Nov to 20th Dec, 11am – 3.30pm, 4th Jan to March, Sat and Sun only, 11am to 3.30pm ✳ Toilet facilities ✳ Suitable for wheelchairs ✳ Dogs in park only on leads ✳ Shop ✳ House open as garden, 1.30 – 5.30pm ✳ Garden open 28th March to 1st Nov, daily except Tues and Fri, 11am – 5.30pm. Woodland walks all year except 25th Dec, daily, dawn – dusk ✳ Entrance: £1.60 (house and gardens £4.30)

The house faces south across the park which is notable for its fine woods and lakeside walk. A ha-ha separates the park from the lawns of the house where there is an orangery planted with camellias. To the north the ground rises and there are specimen trees and shrubs. At some distance to the east there is a large walled kitchen garden now richly planted with a combination of fruit, vegetables and flowers in a formal design behind clipped hedges. There is also a vine house and a great brick dovecote. In early autumn there is a display of many varieties of colchicums: the National collection is kept here. The gardens are kept in immaculate order. Sheringham Park is nearby (see entry).

FRITTON LAKE 9
Fritton, Great Yarmouth, Norfolk. Tel: (0493) 488208

Lord and Lady Somerleyton ✳ *5m SW of Great Yarmouth off the A143* ✳ *Best season: summer* ✳ *Parking* ✳ *Refreshments* ✳ *Toilet facilities* ✳ *Suitable for wheelchairs* ✳ *Shop* ✳ *Golf, putting, boat hire and craft workshops* ✳ *Garden open Good Fri to 1st Oct, daily, 10am – 6pm* ✳ *Entrance: £3, OAP and children £2.20*

Visitors should not be put off at the entrance by the paraphernalia associated with the development of Fritton Lake as a country park. The large lake remains almost unspoilt and separate from the tea rooms and other commercial attractions. An unusual feature is a Victorian garden of about half an acre in the gardenesque style with irregular beds surrounded by clipped box hedges and filled with shrubs and herbaceous perennials that give a colourful display in the summer.

GLAVENSIDE 10
Letheringsett, Nr Holt, Norfolk. Tel: (0263) 713181

John Cozens-Hardy ✳ *1m W of Holt on A148* ✳ *Best seasons: spring and summer* ✳ *Parking* ✳ *Toilet facilities* ✳ *Suitable for wheelchairs* ✳ *Mill shop* ✳ *Working water mill overlooking the garden is open* ✳ *Garden open daily, 10am – 6pm* ✳ *Entrance: £1, children 50p. Group discounts with tea and coffee facilities*

A three-acre garden on the banks of the River Glaven which is crossed by a high arched bridge. Sloping lawns flank the river and there are further streams and pools, a small rock garden, rose garden and kitchen garden. Turn-of-the-century working hydraulic ram. In spite of the number of recently established trees and shrubs, this could not be described as a plantsman's garden but the flower beds are colourful and well-maintained. Five other gardens are open in Letheringsett usually for one day in April.

GOODERSTONE WATER GARDENS 11
Crow Hall, Gooderstone, King's Lynn, Norfolk. Tel: (0366) 21208

Mr and Mrs W.H. Knights ✳ *4m SW of Swaffham. E of Gooderstone village. Signposted. Gardens on opposite side of road to car park* ✳ *Best season: summer* ✳ *Parking* ✳ *Tea and biscuits* ✳ *Toilet facilities* ✳ *Suitable for wheelchairs* ✳ *Open weekdays, 10.30am – 6pm, Sun, 1.30 – 6pm* ✳ *Entrance: £1, children 30p*

Somewhat difficult to find, the entrance to these gardens is along a concreted path between modern industrial buildings. A series of broad streams with many recently added trees and shrubs have been excavated in open woodland. These are bordered by a variety of aquatic plants and crossed by numerous wooden bridges connecting wide grassy paths. No great variety of design and one part of this extensive garden is very much like another but the effect is pleasing.

HALES HALL   12
Hales, Loddon, Norfolk. Tel: (050846) 395

*Mr and Mrs T.E. Read * 14m SE of Norwich, signposted off A146 * Parking
* Plants for sale in nursery * Fifteenth-century Great Barn open * Garden
open Tues – Sat, 10am – 5pm (closed 1 – 2pm) and at other times by appointment.
Party visits by arrangement * Entrance: collection box*

A moat surrounds the remaining wing of a vast house of the early sixteenth century and a central lawn with well-planted borders backed by high brick walls. Work is continuing on the restoration of the garden after centuries of neglect. The owners specialise in growing rare and unusual perennial plants, and look after the National collection of citrus, figs and greenhouse grapes. The associated nurseries offer an extensive range of conservatory plants, vines, figs and mulberries.

HOLKHAM HALL ★   13
Holkham, Wells-next-the-Sea, Norfolk. Tel: (0328) 710374 (garden centre number)

*The Viscount Coke * 2m W of Wells on A149 * Parking * Refreshments *
Toilet facilities * Suitable for wheelchairs * Plants for sale in garden centre *
Pottery and gift shop * House open * Terrace gardens open 19th, 20th April and
3rd, 4th May, 11.30am – 5pm; end May to Sept, daily except Fri and Sat, 1.30 –
5pm, Sun, 2 – 5pm. Garden centre gardens open throughout the year Mon-Sat,
10am – 1pm, 2 – 5pm * Entrance: £2, OAP £1.75, children 75p (State rooms
and terrace gardens). Discounts for pre-paid parties of 20 or more. Parking 50p.
Garden centre gardens free (1991 prices)*

The vast park at Holkham was laid out originally by William Kent and later worked on by both Brown and Repton. The park is famous for its holm oaks and contains an arboretum with many rare trees and shrubs. On the west side of the house, lawns sweep down to the great lake. The terrace which fronts the south facade was added in 1854 but the scale of the house and park is so large that, from a distance at least, this does not seriously disrupt the vision of the two, in spite of the garish and inappropriate beds of polyantha roses. These formal beds flank a great fountain representing Perseus and Andromeda. The garden centre walled gardens in the grounds extend to over six acres, subdivided into six areas with perennial borders and the original greenhouses. Alpines, shrubs, perennials, herbs, roses, bedding and house plants for sale.

HOVETON HALL   14
Nr Wroxham, Norfolk. Tel: (0603) 782798

*Mr and Mrs Andrew Buxton * 1m N of Wroxham Bridge on A1151 * Best* *season: May/June* ✳ *Parking* ✳ *Teas* ✳ *Toilet facilities* ✳ *Suitable for wheelchairs* ✳ *Plants for sale* ✳ *Open Easter Sun to 15th Sept, Wed, Fri, Sun and Bank Holidays, 2 – 5.30pm. Coach parties and tours by arrangement* ✳ *Entrance: £1.75, children 25p*

Set in the Norfolk Broads area, the gardens are amply supplied with water and streams. At the end of May and beginning of June the rhododendrons and azaleas, many rare varieties, are spectacular, dominating and scenting the woodland walks. The formal walled garden, originally planted in 1936, with herbaceous borders of the period, is now in the process of additional planting. A delightful gardener's cottage is set picturesquely in one corner, covered in roses. The adjoining walled kitchen garden is a good example of traditional vegetable planting, with herbaceous plants from the garden for sale. The entrance to the two walled gardens has an intriguing iron gate in the shape of a spider, hence the formal garden is called the spider garden. A water garden, leading to the lake, has good water plants, vast examples of *Gunnera manicata*, peltiphyllums, hostas and good stands of bamboos. The whole area is laced with streams and interesting bridges, adding calm and reflection at every corner. Birds, both migratory and native, abound – the garden map lists 50 species seen in 1988.

HOW HILL FARM ★   15
Ludham, Norfolk. Tel: (069262) 558

Mr P.D.S. Boardman ✳ *2m W of Ludham. Follow signs to How Hill, Farm Garden S of How Hill* ✳ *Parking* ✳ *Refreshments* ✳ *Toilet facilities* ✳ *Partly suitable for wheelchairs* ✳ *Open 10th May, 2 – 5pm. Party visits at other times by arrangement* ✳ *Entrance: £1.50, children free*

This garden adjoins that of the How Hill Trust but is not open at the same time for fear of being overwhelmed. The garden around the farm is comparatively conventional except for a large Chusan palm planted in a dog cage from which it threatens to escape. Here, too, is a collection of over 50 varieties of *Ilex aquifolium* as well as many rare species of the holly genus. Over the road in the river valley is a rich combination of exotics mingled with native vegetation. Around a series of pools, banks of azaleas merge into reed beds, rhododendron species rise over thickets of fern and bramble, wild grasses skirt groves of the giant *Arundo donax*, with birches and conifers against a background of a recently-created three-acre broad, thick with water lilies. The soil in places is exceptionally acid, as low as pH 2.8, other parts vary up to pH 7.5 supporting a wide variety of trees and shrubs.

HOW HILL GARDEN ★   16
Ludham, Norwich, Norfolk. Tel: (069262) 555

How Hill Trust ✳ *2m W of Ludham, signposted from village* ✳ *Parking* ✳ *Refreshments* ✳ *Toilet facilities* ✳ *Suitable for wheelchairs* ✳ *Shop* ✳ *House open* ✳ *Garden open 24th, 31st May, 7th June, 2 – 6pm* ✳ *Entrance: £1.70, children 50p*

There are two gardens here, a formal Edwardian garden terraced into rising ground overlooking the valley of the River Ant, and a separate water and woodland garden. The formal garden has herbaceous borders surrounded by high yew hedges forming a series of linked enclosures and backed by a great brick wall above which rises the dramatically-positioned house. Unfortunately the borders have lost much of their Edwardian character and a white border has gone entirely. Some informal planting leads towards the woodland in which the water garden is set, where quiet waterways, crossed by wooden bridges, are lined with native and exotic aquatic plants. This area is thickly planted with azaleas, highly colourful at the time of the spring open days.

LAKE HOUSE WATER GARDENS   17
Brundall, Norwich, Norfolk.

Mr and Mrs Garry Muter ✳ *5m E of Norwich. From A47 roundabout take Brundall turn and turn right at T-junction into Postwick Lane* ✳ *Best season: May* ✳ *Limited parking* ✳ *Refreshments: tea and biscuits* ✳ *Dogs on lead* ✳ *Unusual plants for sale* ✳ *Open 19th, 20th April, 3rd, 4th May, 11am – 5pm* ✳ *Entrance: £1*

An acre of water gardens set in a steep cleft in the river escarpment. From the top of the hill the gardens fall away to a lily-covered lake at the bottom. They were once part of a 76-acre private estate and arboretum planted about 1880. The fascinating history has been researched and written by the owners and can be purchased by visitors. A magnificent *Clematis armandii* hits the eye at the garden entrance, set off by clever and interesting plant associations. This is a feature throughout the whole garden, reflecting Mrs Muter's talent as a flower arranger. Surrounding the formal gardens are drifts of primroses, bluebells and daffodils in season; wild flowers abound. The formal planting has many rare and interesting species. *Zantedeschia* 'Green Goddess' and 'Crowborough' in a large clump cool down a flamboyant *Hemerocallis* 'Frans Hals'. A pale blue galega blends with *Hydrangea* 'Quadricolor' – a combination of lettuce-green edged leaves and pink and blue flowers. A plantsman's garden.

MANNINGTON HALL ★   18
Nr Saxthorpe, Norfolk. Tel: (026387) 4175

Lord and Lady Walpole ✳ *18m NW of Norwich, signposted at Saxthorpe off B1149* ✳ *Best season: June/July* ✳ *Parking* ✳ *Refreshments* ✳ *Toilet facilities* ✳ *Suitable for wheelchairs* ✳ *Plants for sale* ✳ *Shop* ✳ *Open Easter Sun to Oct, Sun, 12 noon – 5pm, also June to Aug, Wed – Fri, 11am – 5pm* ✳ *Entrance: £2, OAP and students £1.50, children free*

The romantic appearance of this garden of 20 acres is only matched in Norfolk by Elsing Hall where the house is also of the fifteenth century. Lawns run down to the moat which is crossed by a drawbridge to herbaceous borders backed by high walls of brick and flint. The moat also encloses a secret, scented garden in a design derived from one of the ceilings of the house. Outside the moat are borders of flowering shrubs flanking a Doric temple, and beyond are woodlands containing the ruins of a Saxon church. Within the walls of the former kitchen garden, a series of rose gardens has been planted following the design of gardens from medieval to modern times and featuring roses popular at each period. A lake, woods and meadowland with extensive walls are other features.

NORFOLK LAVENDER 19
Caley Mill, Heacham, King's Lynn, Norfolk. Tel: (0485) 70384

Norfolk Lavender Ltd ✳ 13m N of King's Lynn on A149 ✳ Best season: June to Sept ✳ Parking ✳ Refreshments ✳ Toilet facilities ✳ Suitable for wheelchairs ✳ Plants for sale ✳ Shop ✳ Open all year except two-week Christmas holiday ✳ Entrance: free

Here is the National collection of lavenders, displaying many of the species and varieties which can be grown in this country, set in two acres around a nineteenth-century watermill on the banks of the Heacham river. The fields of lavender are a fine sight in July and August, and there is also a rose garden and a herb garden.

THE OLD RECTORY 20
Holt, Norfolk. Tel: (0263) 712204

Lady Harrod ✳ ¹/₂m W of Holt on A148 ✳ Parking ✳ Refreshments ✳ Partly suitable for wheelchairs ✳ Plants for sale ✳ Open 25th Feb, 1st, 3rd March, 10.30am – 1pm ✳ Entrance: £1.50 inc. coffee

As Lucinda Lambton remarks, 'the countryside has been woven into this garden in the most wild and wonderful way'. A meadow full of wild orchids is by the gate, laurels have grown into shady groves, a fast-flowing stream emerges from a rushy pool to make its way into the heart of the garden and then to disappear into a mysterious long-hidden moat. Banks of cow parsley rise above it. There is a walled garden where old roses and vegetables mingle. But it is in late winter that this garden should be seen when a carpet of snowdrops spreads over the wooded hillside which rises above the stream.

OXBURGH HALL 21
Oxborough, Nr King's Lynn, Norfolk. Tel: (036621) 258

The National Trust ✳ 7m SW of Swaffham off A134 ✳ Parking ✳ Refreshments ✳ Toilet facilities ✳ Suitable for wheelchairs ✳ Shop ✳ House open 28th March to 1st Nov, daily except Thurs and Fri, 1.30 – 5.30pm, Bank Holiday Mons, 11am – 5.30pm ✳ Garden open 28th March to 1st Nov, daily except Thurs and Fri, 12 noon – 5.30pm ✳ Entrance: £3.50

The neat gardens of this fine moated house, carefully tended by the National Trust, lack the romantic appeal of Elsing or Rainthorpe. There are some good trees, pleasant lawns, and well-stocked herbaceous borders. On the north side of the house is a parterre with bedding plants in colour masses, said to be of French design but somewhat modest by French standards and, while worth inspecting, somehow seeming inappropriate here.

THE PLANTATION GARDEN 22
4 Earlham Road, Norwich, Norfolk. Tel: (0603) 616025 (Tony Eggleston)

Plantation Garden Preservation Trust ✳ Entrance off Earlham Road, shared with

Beeches Hotel immediately to W of R.C. cathedral ✳ *Best season: summer* ✳
Suitable for wheelchairs ✳ *Open by appointment* ✳ *Entrance: donations welcome*

Designed by the architect Edward Boardman in the 1850s this garden shows
the possible influence of Sir Charles Barry's 'Shrublands' near Ipswich. It was
formed in a narrow steep-sided chalk quarry not far from the centre of
Norwich. Now crowded around with mature trees, lawns cover the quarry floor
reached by an extraordinary series of terraces constructed of a jumble of
architectural fragments and slag, and other industrial waste. The centrepiece is
a tall, multi-tiered fountain. Flower beds with typical Victorian bedding have
been reinstated although more, now covered by grass, have yet to be recovered.
Dedicated volunteers have made themselves responsible for restoration and
although there is still much to do, this has been revealed as a most remarkable
garden which will merit a ★ rating in due course.

RAINTHORPE HALL GARDENS ★   23
Tasburgh, Norwich, Norfolk. Tel: (0508) 470618

Mr G.F. Hastings ✳ *8m S of Norwich off A140. At Newton Flotman fork right on
Flordon Road by garage, on 1m to red brick gates on left* ✳ *Best season: May to
Sept* ✳ *Parking* ✳ *Refreshments* ✳ *Toilet facilities* ✳ *Suitable for wheelchairs*
✳ *Plants for sale* ✳ *House open by appointment only* ✳ *Gardens open Easter to
Oct, Wed, Sat, Sun and Bank Holiday Mon, 10am – 5pm* ✳ *Entrance: £1.50,
OAP and children 75p*

The gardens here at one of the most beautiful houses in Norfolk extend to five
acres. Of the sixteenth-century garden there are some remains in the knot
garden, the nuttery, and an ancient yew tree. The lawn runs down to the River
Tas and there is a recently developed conservation lake. There are many fine
and rare trees and a collection of bamboos. What this garden lacks in overall
cohesion of design, it makes up for in the peace and beauty of its setting.

RAVENINGHAM HALL ★   24
Raveningham, Norwich, Norfolk. Tel: (050846) 222

Sir Nicholas Bacon ✳ *14m SE of Norwich off A146, left at Hales on B1136, then
first right* ✳ *Parking* ✳ *Refreshments* ✳ *Toilet facilities* ✳ *Suitable for
wheelchairs* ✳ *Plants for sale* ✳ *Open April to Sept, Suns and Bank Holidays, 2
– 5.30pm. Nursery open weekdays all year, Sats Feb to Nov, and Suns and Bank
Holidays Easter to mid-Sept* ✳ *Entrance: £1.70, children free*

This garden, in a fine landscaped park, has a rich variety of trees, shrubs and
herbaceous plants dating from the eighteenth century to the present day. There
is a large collection of galanthus species and varieties. The walled kitchen
garden and greenhouses are still in use, and the associated nurseries offer an
exceptional range of shrubs, climbers and herbaceous plants, many rarely
available elsewhere. An arboretum is being developed.

SANDRINGHAM HOUSE ★   25
Sandringham, King's Lynn, Norfolk. Tel: (0553) 772675

H.M. The Queen ✳ *9m NE of King's Lynn on B1440 near Sandringham*

Church ✳ Best seasons: spring and autumn ✳ Parking ✳ Refreshments in restaurant and cafeteria ✳ Toilet facilities ✳ Suitable for wheelchairs ✳ Plants for sale ✳ Shop ✳ House open as garden but closed 20th July to 8th Aug ✳ Ranger's Interpretation Centre and country park ✳ Garden open 19th April to 1st Oct (except 24th July to 5th Aug), Sun – Thurs, 11am (12 noon on Sun) – 4.45pm. Also open Good Fri and Easter weekend ✳ Entrance: £2, OAP £1.50, children £1 (house and grounds £2.50, OAP £2, children £1.50)

The house stands among broad lawns with an outer belt of woodland through which a path runs past plantings of camellias, hydrangeas, cornus, magnolias and rhododendrons with some fine specimen trees including *Davidia involucrata* and *Cercidiphyllum japonicum*. The path passes the magnificent cast and wrought iron 'Norwich Gates' of 1862. In the open lawn are specimen oaks planted by Queen Victoria and other members of the royal family. To the south-west of the house is the upper lake whose eastern side is built up into a massive rock garden using blocks of the local carstone, and now largely planted with dwarf conifers. Below the rock garden, opening onto the lake, is a cavernous grotto, intended as a boathouse, while above is a small summerhouse built for Queen Alexandra. There are thick plantings of hostas, agapanthus and various moisture-loving plants around the margin of the lake. The path passes between the upper and largest lower lake set in wooded surroundings. To the north of the house is a garden designed by Sir Geoffrey Jellicoe for King George VI. A long series of beds is surrounded by box hedges and divided by gravel and grass paths and flanked by avenues of pleached lime, one of which is centred on a gold-plated statue of a Buddhist divinity.

SHERINGHAM PARK ★   26
Upper Sheringham, Norfolk. Tel: (0263) 823778

The National Trust ✳ 4m NE of Holt off A148 ✳ Best season: May/June ✳ Parking: £2.10 per car to include all occupants ✳ Refreshments at Felbrigg Hall (also NT) during their opening hours (see entry) ✳ Partly suitable for wheelchairs ✳ Dogs on lead in park ✳ House occupied, but limited access to some rooms by appointment with the leaseholder in writing, April to Sept only ✳ Garden open daily, dawn – dusk ✳ Entrance: £2.10 per car inc. parking

Sheringham Park stands in a secluded valley at the edge of the Cromer/Holt ridge, close to the sea but protected from its winds by steep wooded hills. Both house and park are now the property of the National Trust although the house remains in private occupation. The park is remarkable not only for its great beauty and spectacular views but also for an extensive collection of rhododendrons which thrive in the acid soil. Crowning an eminence is a classical temple based on a design by Repton and erected to mark the 60th birthday of Mr Thomas Upcher, the last descendant of the original owner to live at Sheringham. Since coming into its ownership the Trust has begun to remove some inappropriate twentieth-century planting and to restore the original form of the garden, the favourite and best-preserved work of Repton.

SWANINGTON MANOR   27
Swanington, Nr Reepham, Norfolk.

Mr and Mrs David Prior ✳ NW of Norwich. Take A1067 to Attlebridge and from

there take the road signposted to Swanington ✳ *Best season: June to Aug* ✳
Parking ✳ *Toilet facilities* ✳ *Partly suitable for wheelchairs* ✳ *Open by
appointment for tours* ✳ *Entrance: £1.50*

The first thing which strikes the visitor are the enormous yew hedges cut into
chimneys and puddings and other curious shapes evolved over the 300 years of
their lives. The imaginative eye can see engines, animals and much more, all
toppling into each other. A knot garden recently planted but already mature has
yellow and green box interlacing with standard box balls. The herbaceous
borders have been planted to provide colour all the year round and contain
many interesting and rare plants with clever colour schemes. These are true
plantsmen's borders. A stream with interesting water plants – ligularias, lilies,
peltiphyllums – all jostling for a place along the meandering path.

THRIGBY HALL WILDLIFE GARDENS 28
Filby, Great Yarmouth, Norfolk. Tel: (0493) 369477

Mr K.J. Sims ✳ *6m NW of Great Yarmouth, signposted at Filby on A1064* ✳
Best season: summer ✳ *Parking* ✳ *Refreshments* ✳ *Toilet facilities* ✳ *Suitable
for wheelchairs* ✳ *Shop* ✳ *Open daily, 10am – 5pm or dusk* ✳ *Entrance: £3.30,
OAP, £2.80, children £2*

The chief attraction of these gardens is a collection of Chinese plants arranged
to form the landscape of the Willow Pattern plate, complete with pagodas and
bridges across a small lake. Complementing a collection of Asiatic animals, the
plants are those particularly associated with temple gardens and include *Gingko
biloba*, *Pinus parviflora*, *Paeonia suffruticosa*, *Nandina domestica* and *Chimonobam-
busa quadrangularis*, set against a background of willows of many species.
Planted 1989 but interesting even in an immature state.

WELL HOUSE 29
Market Place, Hingham, Norfolk. Tel: (0953) 850280

Mrs Maureen Watson ✳ *12m from Norwich, 5m N of Wymondham, on B1108
Norwich – Watton road. In Hingham market place next to chemist. Pedestrian
entrance at back* ✳ *Best season: May to July* ✳ *Parking* ✳ *Refreshments: on
request or in village* ✳ *Toilet facilities in village* ✳ *Suitable for wheelchairs* ✳
Plants sometimes for sale ✳ *Open by appointment weekdays except Tues, and some
Suns, 2 – 5pm* ✳ *Entrance: £1.50*

Situated in a conservation village with Abraham Lincoln connections, the
mellow red-brick house is a perfect example of a Georgian town residence. The
garden is a typical walled town garden in two rooms. The walls are covered in
rare and choice climbers; several felicias hide the base of an enormous
honeysuckle which scents the long border. The eye is then arrested by a
magnificent liquidambar. Further on is a sink garden, full of choice plants, and
a hosta corner surrounding a charming statue. Two box pyramids lead on to a
lawn and a series of herbaceous borders full of interesting and rare plants. A
splendid white abutilon has a variegated pink jasmine and pink ceanothus on
either side. The garden is full of scents.

WRETHAM LODGE ★ 30
East Wretham, Thetford, Norfolk. Tel: (0953) 498366

Mrs A. Hoellering ✳ *6m NE of Thetford off A1075. Left by village sign, right at crossroads then bear left* ✳ *Best season: May to July* ✳ *Parking* ✳ *Refreshments* ✳ *Toilet facilities* ✳ *Suitable for wheelchairs* ✳ *Plants for sale* ✳ *Open 3rd, 17th May, 28th June, 5th July, 2.30 – 5.30pm and by appointment. Parties by appointment* ✳ *Entrance: £1, children 50p*

Extensive lawns surround the handsome flint-faced former rectory set in its own walled park. There are herbaceous borders and hundreds of old, species and climbing roses massed in informal beds or covering high flint walls. Walls surround the kitchen garden supporting espalier and fan-trained fruit trees – pears, cherries and apricots. There is a vine house and a variety of figs. Roses and herbaceous plants are mixed with the vegetables and in the spring there is a display of many species of tulip. A wide grassy walk runs round the park through a range of mature and recently established trees where spring-flowering bulbs are naturalised, with a mass display of bluebells in May.

OPENING DATES AND TIMES
Times of access given are the best available at the moment of going to press, but some may have been changed subsequently. In the entries, the times given are inclusive – that is, an entry such as May to Sept means that the garden is open from 1st May to 30th Sept inclusive and 2 – 5pm also means that entry will be effective during that period. Please note that many owners will open their gardens to visitors by appointment. They will often arrange to give a personally-conducted tour on these occasions.

NORTHAMPTONSHIRE

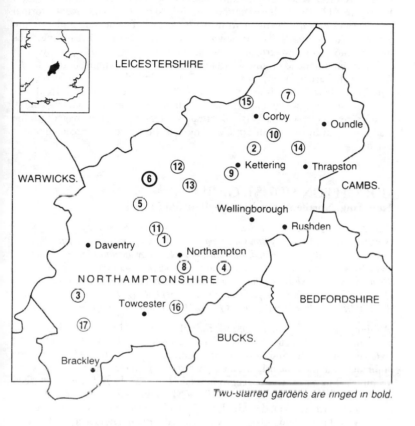

LEICESTERSHIRE

⑮ ⑦

● Corby   ● Oundle

⑩

② ⑭

⑫ ● Kettering   ● Thrapston

WARWICKS.   ⑥ ⑨

⑬   CAMBS.

⑤

Wellingborough
●

⑪   ● Rushden
① ●

● Daventry   Northampton

⑧ ④

N O R T H A M P T O N S H I R E

③   BEDFORDSHIRE

Towcester ⑯
●

⑰   BUCKS.

Brackley
●

Two-starred gardens are ringed in bold.

ALTHORP HALL   1
Althorp, Northampton, Northamptonshire. Tel: (0604) 770209

*Earl and Countess Spencer ✳ W of Northampton on A428 Northampton – Rugby
road ✳ Parking ✳ Refreshments: light snacks, teas and cakes ✳ Toilet facilities
✳ Suitable for wheelchairs ✳ Shop ✳ House open ✳ Gardens open Sept to
June, 1 – 6pm, July and Aug, 11am – 6pm ✳ Entrance: £2.95, children £1.95*

The main attraction of Althorp, the family home of the Princess of Wales, is the
fine house (largely remodelled after 1786 from the original Elizabethan
building) with its collections of pictures, furniture and china brought together

over the centuries by the Spencer family. Early prints suggest that the original formal gardens were swept away during the fashionable eighteenth-century improvements by the architect Henry Holland, helped by Samuel Lapidge, 'Capability' Brown's assistant. The present gardens were laid out in the 1860s by the architect W.M. Teulon and enclosed by stone walls and balustrades. Blue-painted Versailles boxes containing clipped bay trees enhance the formal gravel walks and the lawns in front of the house. To the side and rear the gardens are also mainly laid to lawn, apart from the somewhat incongruous beds planted with low-growing, low-maintenance plants. Beyond, pleasant walks through wooded grounds lead to the lake and the Temple, bought for £3 by the fifth Earl Spencer, First Lord of the Admiralty, from the garden of Admiralty House. Here is an interesting collection of conifers and deciduous trees and shrubs (sadly not all labelled), with new specimens still being added. The large well-treed park is an attractive feature; still managed in the traditional way by sheep and cattle grazing, it is the venue for occasional public events.

BOUGHTON HOUSE GARDEN 2
Kettering, Northamptonshire. Tel: (0536) 515731

*The Duke and Duchess of Buccleuch and Queensberry * Signposted off A43, N of Kettering, between Weekley and Geddington * Parking * Refreshments: light snacks and teas during weekends and Aug, other times by appointment * Toilet facilities * Partly suitable for wheelchairs * Dogs on lead in park only * Plants for sale * Shop * House open Aug to 1st Sept, * Grounds open 25th April to 27th Sept, daily except Fri, (Aug to 1st Sept, daily) 1 – 5pm * Entrance: £1, children 50p (house and grounds £3, OAP and children £2) (1991 prices)*

Although with only very limited formal gardens, Boughton House will nonetheless be attractive to garden enthusiasts and the whole family. The extensive sixteenth- and seventeenth-century house, with a strong French influence and monastic origins, contains extensive collections of paintings and furniture. The magnificent park, with its lakes and canals, and avenues of trees, was originally laid out by the first Duke of Montagu before 1700 with the help of a Dutch gardener, Van der Meulen, who had experience of reclamation work in the fens. The second Duke, known as John the Planter, added a pond and the network of rides and avenues of elms and limes in the 1720s. These avenues originally extended to 70 miles before Dutch elm disease took its toll. The limited planting close to the house includes an herbaceous border and some fine planted vases. Behind the house a small circular rose garden leads on to the outstanding rectangular lily pond, beyond which the walled garden houses a long herbaceous border and the well-stocked nursery and plant shop. In the 350-acre park, there are walks and trails, including one for the disabled, and a woodland adventure play area for children.

CANONS ASHBY HOUSE ★ 3
Canons Ashby, Nr Daventry, Northamptonshire. Tel: (0327) 860044

*The National Trust * 6m S of Daventry. Easy access from either M40/M1/A5* *(please phone for details)* ✳ *Parking 200 yards from house. Disabled ring in advance and park near house* ✳ *Refreshments: light lunches and teas* ✳ *Toilet facilities* ✳ *Wheelchairs available. Taped guide for visually handicapped visitors* ✳ *Dogs on lead in home paddock only* ✳ *House open as garden, 1 – 5.30pm or dusk if earlier (last admission 5pm)* ✳ *Garden open April to Oct, Wed – Sun and Bank Holiday Mon, 12 noon – 5.30pm or dusk if earlier (last admission 5pm)* ✳ *Entrance: garden free (house and garden £2.80, children £1.40)*

This well-maintained garden is being extensively restored by the National Trust. Formal with axial arrangements of paths and terraces, high stone walls, lawns and gateways, it dates almost entirely from the beginning of the eighteenth century. Borders with majestic plants such as acanthus and giant thistles. Yew court with fine topiary. Old varieties of pear, apple, plum trees and soft fruit. Cedar planted in 1715. Espaliers grown from original stock planted by Edward Dryden whose family owned the house from the sixteenth century.

CASTLE ASHBY GARDENS ★ 4
Castle Ashby, Northamptonshire. Tel: (060129) 234

The Marquess of Northampton ✳ *5m E of Northampton, between A45 Northampton to Wellingborough road and A428 Northampton – Bedford road* ✳ *Best seasons: March to May, July to Sept* ✳ *Parking* ✳ *Refreshments at tea rooms in village, 400 yards* ✳ *Suitable for wheelchairs, paths not very smooth* ✳ *Dogs on lead* ✳ *Plants rarely for sale* ✳ *Farm shop and Rural Craft Centre in village* ✳ *House open and tours for parties by appointment during 'Country Fair', 1st week July, check by phone* ✳ *Gardens open daily, 10am – 6pm, with occasional closures for events* ✳ *Entrance: £1, OAP and children 50p. (Tickets from machine when car park unattended)*

Originally Elizabethan, then a park landscaped by 'Capability' Brown, and later a Matthew Digby Wyatt Terrace, Italian garden and arboretum, Castle Ashby is now primarily an 'all function centre' for company and private events. There is public access to most of the gardens (except East terrace although good views from near the church) which present a glorious combination of views. A nature walk past mature trees leads over a terracotta bridge and to the 'knucklebone arbour', a summerhouse with what are probably sheep or deer knuckles set in the floor. Among the wild and naturalised plants are carpets of aconites and snowdrops, winter heliotrope, butterbur, daffodils, bluebells, wood anemones, celandines, bush vetch, wood buttercups and a wide selection of lake and pondside plants. Features include an orangery and archway greenhouses, topiary and well-planted large vases. Restoration of the garden and its architectural features is continuing.

COTON MANOR GARDENS 5
Ravensthorpe, Northamptonshire. Tel: (0604) 740219

Cdr and Mrs Ian Pasley-Tyler ✳ *10m N of Northampton, signposted on A428 and A50* ✳ *Parking* ✳ *Home-made teas* ✳ *Toilet facilities* ✳ *Partly suitable for wheelchairs* ✳ *Dogs on lead* ✳ *Unusual plants and shrubs for sale* ✳ *Shop* ✳ *Open Easter to Sept, Wed, Sun and Bank Holidays, also Thurs in July and Aug, 2 – 6pm* ✳ *Entrance: £2.50, OAP £2, children 50p*

A carefully planned and tended garden on several sloped acres which provide colour and interest throughout the year. There is an excellent variety of foliage plants, herbaceous borders, lawns and hedges plus lakes with ornamental waterfowl. It is a garden which will appeal most to those seeking inspiration for their own medium-sized gardens, and those who enjoy waterfowl.

COTTESBROOKE HALL ★★ 6
Cottesbrooke, Northampton, Northamptonshire. Tel: (060124) 808

Captain and Mrs J. Macdonald-Buchanan ✳ *10m N of Northampton between A50 and A508* ✳ *Parking* ✳ *Teas* ✳ *Toilet facilities* ✳ *Unusual plants for sale* ✳ *House open* ✳ *Gardens open 23rd April to 24th Sept, Thurs only. Also Bank Holiday Mons Easter to Aug, 2 – 5.30pm (last admission 5pm)* ✳ *Entrance: £1.50, children 75p (£3.50 house and gardens). Parties by appointment when possible*

An excellently-maintained formal garden surrounding a fine Queen Anne house, set in a large park (also open) with lakes and a stream, vistas and avenues. Design and planting work by Edward Schultz, Geoffrey Jellicoe, Sylvia Crowe and the late Hon. Lady Macdonald-Buchanan is being continued by the present owners and their head gardener, Mrs Daw. The result is a series of delightful enclosed courtyards and gardens around the house with superb borders, urns and statues. The spinney garden is at its best in spring with bulbs and azaleas. New trees, borders, yew hedges, walls, gates and vistas have only recently been added. Beyond the thatched Wendy house the wild garden surrounds a series of small lakes and cascades, with azaleas, rhodendrons, acers, cherries, spring bulbs and wild flowers. The magnolia, cherry and acer collections are notable. The house (possibly the model for Jane Austen's *Mansfield Park*) and garden were only opened to the public for the first time in 1991, and are expected to become increasingly popular with visitors.

DEENE PARK 7
Corby, Northamptonshire. Tel: (078085) 278/223

Mr Edmund Brudenell ✳ *6m N of Corby off A43 Kettering to Stamford road* ✳ *Parking* ✳ *Teas* ✳ *Toilet facilities* ✳ *Partly suitable for wheelchairs* ✳ *Dogs in car park only* ✳ *Shop* ✳ *House open* ✳ *Park open June to Aug, Sun, 2 – 5pm and Bank Holiday Suns and Mons, Easter to Aug. Groups by appointment* ✳ *Entrance: £3, children £1, inc. house*

The glory of Deene, which was created by generations of the Brudenell family, is its trees. Fine mature specimens and groups fringe the formal areas and frame tranquil and enchanting views of the parkland and countryside. Main features of its garden are the long borders, old-fashioned roses and the lake. The gardens, parkland, church and house together provide a delightful, interesting and relaxing afternoon for visitors in what was the home of the Earl of Cardigan who led the Charge of the Light Brigade in 1854.

DELAPRE ABBEY 8
London Road, Northampton, Northamptonshire. Tel: (0604) 761074

Northampton Borough Council Leisure Department ✳ *1m S of Northampton on*

A508 ✳ Best season: summer ✳ Parking ✳ Toilet facilities ✳ Suitable for wheelchairs ✳ Dogs on lead ✳ Open March to Sept, daily, 10am – sunset. Park open all year ✳ Entrance: free

Largely rebuilt in the seventeenth century, the house on the site of the former nunnery of St Mary of the Meadow, together with 500 acres of land, passed into public ownership in 1946. With improving standards of maintenance (although some associated buildings are in need of repair) it is still possible to glimpse the hey-day of a lovely garden. Beyond the walled former kitchen garden well-tended lawns, perennial, annual and rose beds and an eighteenth-century thatched game larder are walks through the wilderness garden with fine trees, shrubberies and lily ponds. There are lakes and a golf course in the park, and at the roadside close to the entrance, one of the country's Queen Eleanor Crosses commemorates the funeral procession in 1290 of Edward I's queen.

31 DERWENT CRESCENT 9
Kettering, Northamptonshire. Tel: (0536) 520070

Mr and Mrs B.J. Mitchell ✳ W side of Kettering, off A43 to Northampton. Travelling away from Kettering town centre, turn right along Bowhill after going under railway bridge, then 1st right, 1st right, 1st left or phone for instructions ✳ Parking on street ✳ Open by appointment ✳ Entrance: by donation

Strictly for the plantsperson, but an absolute jewel for herbaceous, bulb, alpine and fern enthusiasts. Owners' knowledge of their plants and propagation methods (over 33 years experience here) is enormous and enthusiastically passed on to satisfy the curiosity of visitors.

HILL FARM HERBS 10
Park Walk, Brigstock, Northamptonshire. Tel: (0536) 373694

Eileen and Mike Simpson ✳ 8m from Kettering via A43. 5m from Corby, 6m from Thrapston. Signposted in Brigstock, just off A6116 ✳ Best season: summer ✳ Parking ✳ Refreshments: during summer ✳ Toilet facilities ✳ Suitable for wheelchairs ✳ Plants for sale ✳ Shop with wide range of herbs, dried flowers and pots ✳ Open March to Dec. daily except 25th, 26th Dec, 10.30am – 5.30pm. Evening parties by arrangement May to July ✳ Entrance: free

Hill Farm Herbs is set at the back of an old stone village farmhouse. Many herbs and cottage garden plants are grown in a number of garden areas, some in informal cottage mixtures, others laid out with specific themes, such as dyers' herbs, medicinal herbs and aromatic herbs. Garden owners planning a new or remodelled cottage or herb garden will find these areas a great inspiration. Many of the plants are available for sale.

HOLDENBY HOUSE GARDENS 11
Holdenby, Northampton, Northamptonshire. Tel: (0604) 770241

Mr and Mrs James Lowther ✳ 7m W of Northampton, signposted A50 and A428

* Parking * Refreshments: teas. Meals by appointment * Toilet facilities *
Partly suitable for wheelchairs * Dogs on lead * Plants and herbs for sale *
Shop inc. croquet mallet hire * House open Bank Holiday Mons * Garden open
July to Aug, Thurs, 2 – 6pm, Sun, Bank Holidays, Easter to Sept, 2 – 6pm. Groups
by appointment * Entrance: £2.30, children £1.20

Only grassed terraces and a fish pond remain of the extensive Elizabethan
garden which surrounded the vast mansion built by Elizabeth I's chancellor, Sir
Christopher Hatton, in the late sixteenth century. The recent gardens still link
the surviving remnant of the house (only one eighth of its former size) to its past,
especially the delightful Elizabethan garden, planted in 1980 by Rosemary
Verey as a miniature replica of Hatton's original centrepiece, using only plants
available in the 1580s. Other features include the fragrant border, part of the
nineteenth-century garden also replanted by Mrs Verey. The rare breeds and
falcons displayed in the old kitchen garden, and occasional events in the
gardens, attract school and family visits.

KELMARSH HALL   12
Kelmarsh, Northamptonshire. Tel: (060128) 276

Miss C.V. Lancaster * On A508 5m S of Market Harborough, 11m N of
Northampton * Best season: spring * Parking * Refreshments * Toilet
facilities * Dogs on lead * Plants and produce for sale occasionally * James
Gibb's Palladian house open with escorted visits * Garden open Easter to Aug,
Sun and Bank Holidays, 2.15 – 5pm, April and Sept, by appointment (minimum
12 persons) * Entrance £1.50, OAP and children over 12 £1, children under 12
free (house and gardens)

The drive is an avenue of lime trees bordering the park of 20 acres where a herd
of rare British white cattle graze. Maze-like close-clipped box and yew hedges
and colonnades lead to secret and quiet gardens with views of a lake. There are
herbaceous borders and a rose garden. Seats are provided at vantage points and
spring flowers and rhododendrons are special features. Keen gardeners will
probably wish to visit only if they are combining it with a tour of the house.

LAMPORT HALL GARDEN   13
Lamport Hall, Northampton, Northamptonshire. Tel: (060128) 272

Lamport Hall Trust * 8m N of Northampton on A508 * Parking *
Refreshments * Toilet facilities * Suitable for wheelchairs * Dogs on lead in
picnic area only * Shop * House open * Garden open Easter to Sept, Sun and
Bank Holidays, July and Aug also Thurs, 2.15 – 5.15pm. Coach parties/groups at
any time by arrangement * Entrance: £2.50, OAP £2, children £1 (house and
gardens) (1991 prices)

The main attraction here is Lamport Hall itself, now essentially an event (dog
shows, antique fairs) and school study centre. Grounds initially laid out by
Gilbert Clarke in 1655 are in the process of restoration and provide a pleasant
setting, but at this stage will mainly interest those who want to follow the
progress of restoration. Ultimately the local ironstone rock garden and the

refurbished nineteenth-century Italian garden with its fine urns should be most attractive. Also public access to the attractive park.

THE OLD RECTORY ★ 14
Sudborough, Northamptonshire. Tel: (08012) 3247

*Mr and Mrs Anthony Huntington * Off A6116 Corby – Thrapston road * Best season: April and June/July * Teas by prior request * Toilet facilities * Suitable for wheelchairs * Plants for sale occasionally * Open by appointment and 28th June, 2 – 6pm for charity * Entrance: £1*

Delightful three-acre rectory garden in beautiful stone and thatch village. Much has been accomplished in recent years to develop a garden of interest to all. Copious planting in the mixed borders, around the pond and with climbers. Vegetable garden fascinating, small beds with brick paths leading to a central wrought-iron arbour. Standard roses and gooseberries and tents of runner beans provide vertical features. A wilder garden along the stream completes the picture, while excellent labelling throughout will help visitors keen to improve their knowledge of plants.

ROCKINGHAM CASTLE GARDENS 15
Corby, Northamptonshire. Tel: (0536) 770240

*Commander Michael Saunders Watson and family * 2m N of Corby on A6003. Signposted * Best season: June * Parking. Disabled may park near entrance * Teas * Toilet facilities * Partly suitable for wheelchairs * Dogs on lead * Shop * House open * Garden open Easter Sun to Sept, Sun and Thurs, Bank Holiday Mons and the Tues following, also Tues in Aug, 1.30 – 5.30pm. Groups by appointment at other times * Entrance: £3.30, children £2 (castle and gardens)*

Rockingham sits on a hilltop fortress site with stunning views of three counties. Features remain from all periods of its 800-year history, ranging from formal seventeenth-century terraces and yew hedges to the romantic wild garden of the nineteenth century. There is a circular rose garden surrounded by a yew hedge and also good herbaceous borders. The wild garden was replanted with advice from Kew Gardens in the late 1960s and it includes over 200 species of trees and shrubs. The result is a delightful blend of form, colour, light and shade. Recommended for group/family outings and for those who combine interest in horticulture with history.

STOKE PARK 16
Stoke Bruerne, Towcester, Northampton, Northamptonshire. Tel: (0604) 862172

*Mr R.E. Chancellor * Clearly signposted from A5, N of Milton Keynes. ¹/₄m W of village, opposite junction to Blisworth * Best season: summer * Parking * Suitable for wheelchairs * Dogs on lead * Pavilion open * Garden open June to Aug, weekends and Aug Bank Holiday, 2 – 6pm, rest of year by appointment * Entrance: £1*

Stoke Park was the first house to display the Palladian plan in Britain but now (due to a fire) only the splendid pavilions with colonnaded walls remain. The outline of the original Italianate garden by Inigo Jones can be seen below the lawn so the site is of particular interest to students of historical gardens. However, the svelte lawns, herbaceous borders and a large fountain basin with water lilies are the features at Stoke Park which will be enjoyed by all who visit.

SULGRAVE MANOR   17
Sulgrave, Northamptonshire. Tel: (029576) 205

Trustees, endowed by Colonial Dames of America ✳ 7m NE of Banbury, 5m from M40 junction 11, 1m off B4525 ✳ Parking ✳ Refreshments sometimes available, otherwise at Thatched House Hotel opposite ✳ Toilet facilities ✳ House open ✳ Garden open Feb only to pre-booked parties of 12 or more, March, daily except Wed, 10.30am – 1pm, 2 – 4pm, April to Sept, daily except Wed, 10.30am – 1pm, 2 – 5.30pm, Oct to Dec, daily except Wed, 10.30am – 1pm, 2 – 4pm. Closed 25th and 26th Dec ✳ Entrance: £2.50, children £1.25 (house and garden). Discounts for parties of 12 or more

American visitors are in the majority here, as the house was built in 1560 by a distant ancestor of George Washington. It was acquired in 1914 and restored after World War I, with the benefit of U.S. generosity. The gardens, like the house, bear little relation to their sixteenth-century condition, but the rose garden, herb garden, herbaceous borders and kitchen garden are attractive examples of their kind.

NORTHUMBERLAND

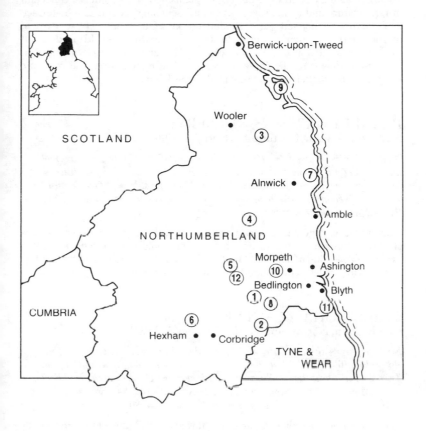

BELSAY HALL ★

Belsay, Nr Newcastle-upon-Tyne, Northumberland. Tel: (0661) 881636

*Sir Stephen Middleton * 14m NW of Newcastle on A696 * Parking. Coaches please notify in advance * Refreshments: drinks machine, picnic area * Toilet facilities inc. disabled * Suitable for wheelchairs (available on loan) * Dogs on lead * Shop * House open * Gardens open Easter to Sept, daily, 10am – 6pm, Oct to Easter, daily except Mons, 10am – 4pm * Entrance: £1.90, OAP £1.50, children 95p (1991 prices)*

The gardens are the creation of two men who between them owned the Hall in succession from 1795 to 1933. Sir Charles Monck built a severe neo-classical mansion with formal terraces leading through woods to a 'garden' inside the quarry from which the house was built. His grandson took over in 1867, adding Victorian features. Both were discerning plantsmen. The result is a collection of rare, mature and exotic specimens in a fascinating sequence. The terrace looks across to massed early rhododendrons. Other areas (rose garden, magnolia terrace, winter-flowering heathers) lead to woods, a wild meadow and the quarry garden itself. Reminiscent of the ancient Greek quarries in Syracuse, it was carefully contrived and stocked to achieve a wild romantic effect and give shelter to some remarkable specimens.

BRADLEY GARDENS NURSERY   2
Sled Lane, Wylam, Northumberland. Tel: (0661) 852176

Bradley Gardens Nursery ∗ 10m W of Newcastle off A695 between Crawcrook and Wylam (well signposted) ∗ Parking ∗ Picnic area ∗ Toilet facilities ∗ Suitable for wheelchairs ∗ Dogs on lead ∗ Plants for sale ∗ Shop planned for 1992 ∗ Open mid-March to mid-Oct, Mon – Fri, 10am – 4pm, Sat and Sun, 9am – 5pm ∗ Entrance: free

This walled cottage garden has particular appeal for the plantsperson. It is stocked at present with a variety of Victorian apple trees, lavenders and an extensive collection of some 200 herbs. Fresh cut herbs are sold to both public and catering trades. The scented garden is a new feature.

CHILLINGHAM CASTLE   3
Chillingham, Northumberland. Tel: (06685) 359/390

Sir Humphry Wakefield, Bart ∗ 12m NNW of Alnwick between A1 (signposted), A697, B6346 and B6348 ∗ Best seasons: spring, midsummer ∗ Parking ∗ Teas ∗ Toilet facilities ∗ Shop ∗ House open ∗ Gardens open Good Fri to Easter Mon and May to Sept, daily except Tues, 1.30 – 5pm ∗ Entrance: £2.50, OAP £2, children over 5 £1.80, parties of 20 or more £1.80 per person

Not easy to find but well worth an effort, this one-time home of the Grey family and their relations since the 1200s is being vigorously restored along with the grounds landscaped by Wyatville (of Hampton Court fame). The Elizabethan-style walled garden has been virtually excavated by Isobel Murray to expose its intricate pattern of clipped yew and box (enlivened by scarlet tropaeolum), a central avenue and flourishing borders around the walls. Outside are lawns and a rock garden, delightful woodland and lakeside walks through drifts of snowdrops and spring displays of daffodils, bluebells and, later, rhododendrons.

CRAGSIDE HOUSE AND COUNTRY PARK   4
Rothbury, Morpeth, Northumberland. Tel: (0669) 20333

The National Trust ∗ 14m SW of Alnwick off A697 between B6341 and B6344

Best season: early summer ✳ *Parking* ✳ *Refreshments in Visitor Centre.*
Picnics by Nelly's Moss Lakes ✳ *Toilet facilities inc. disabled* ✳ *Partly suitable for*
wheelchairs ✳ *Dogs on lead in grounds only* ✳ *Visitor Centre inc. shop* ✳
House open as Country Park, 1 – 5.30pm (last admission 5pm) ✳ *Country Park*
open April to Oct, daily except Mon (but open Bank Holiday Mons), 10.30am –
7pm, Nov to Dec, Tues, Sat and Sun, 10.30am – 4pm ✳ *Entrance: £2.20 (house*
and park £4.20), party rate £1.80 (house and park £3.80)

Lord Armstrong, the greatest of Victorian engineers, clothed this hillside above
the Coquet Valley with millions of trees and shrubs as the setting for a house
designed by R Norman Shaw (the first ever lit by hydro-electricity) that was
then the wonder of the world. Now properly managed, the 900-acre park with
its 40 miles of driveways and rambling paths is a mass of rhododendrons in
June. Higher up there are enclaves of bare rock and heather, a reminder of the
original state of the land, with lovely views over wooded valleys under broad
Northumbrian skies. The man-made lakes, hydro-electric and hydraulic
systems (also on view) add another dimension and a tribute to Victorian vigour
and ingenuity at its peak. In 1991 The National Trust acquired a further 40
acres of parkland at Crayside, containing 10 buildings including a house,
glazed orchard house, stone terraces and formal gardens, thus bringing
together the whole Armstrong estate.

HERTERTON HOUSE 5
Hartington, Cambo, Morpeth, Northumberland. Tel: **(067074) 278**

Frank and Marjorie Lawley ✳ *2m N of Cambo on B6342* ✳ *Best season:*
summer ✳ *Parking* ✳ *Toilet facilities* ✳ *Plants for sale* ✳ *Open April to Oct,*
daily except Tues and Thurs, 1.30 – 5.30pm ✳ *Entrance: 75p (1991 price)*

The Lawleys took over this land and near-derelict Elizabethan building, with
commanding views over picturesque upland Northumberland, in 1976. With
vision and skill they have created three distinct areas. In front, a winter garden
with tranquil vistas; alongside, a cloistered 'monastic' knot garden of mainly
medicinal, occult and dye-producing herbs; and to the rear, their most
impressive achievement, a flower garden. This is a carefully designed Persian
carpet, with perceptively mingled hardy flowers chosen with an artist's eye.
Many are unusual traditional plants (including many species from the wild) that
flourish within the newly-built sheltering walls. A gem of a place, of great
interest to the plantsperson.

HEXHAM HERBS ★ 6
The Chesters Walled Garden, Humshaugh, Nr Hexham,
Northumberland. Tel: **(0434) 681483**

Kevin and Susie White ✳ *5m N of Hexham, ¹/₂m W of Chollerford on B6318* ✳
Best season: March to Sept ✳ *Parking* ✳ *Refreshments: planned* ✳ *Toilet*
facilities: planned ✳ *Suitable for wheelchairs* ✳ *Plants for sale* ✳ *Shop* ✳ *Open*
March to Oct, daily, 10am – 5pm, reduced hours in winter. Also by appointment ✳
Entrance: 80p

The tall brick walls of the old kitchen garden slope gently south from the very
line of Hadrian's Wall, echoing the Roman forts that lie to east and west. Within

these ramparts, still with vestiges of the Victorian glasshouses and heating system, the Whites have fashioned a superb herb collection, including most fittingly a unique Roman garden with plants (myrtle, etc.) identified by archaeologists through pollen analysis. A major feature is the national NCCPG thyme bank. A rose garden (over 60 species), extensive herbaceous sections (some 800 varieties) and terraced lawns against an architectural backdrop (Norman Shaw's Chesters mansion) fill out this splendid intriguing 'fort'. A labelled wildflower meadow and woodland walk with pond are also open.

HOWICK HALL ★   7
Howick, Northumberland. Tel: (066577) 285

Lord Howick of Glendale (Howick Trustees Ltd) ✳ *5m NE of Alnwick off B1339* ✳ *Best season: spring/summer* ✳ *Parking* ✳ *Toilet facilities* ✳ *Partly suitable for wheelchairs* ✳ *Open Easter to Oct, 1 – 6pm* ✳ *Entrance: £1, children and concessions 50p*

Acquired by the Grey family in 1301, Howick was enriched with an avenue by Prime Minister Grey in the 1820s. The accident of woodland which sheltered this site from the blasts of the North Sea enabled Lord and Lady Grey to come here during World War I and start building an amazing collection of tender plants which would do credit to a Scottish west coast garden. The central terrace has a pool and excellent borders and the lawns run down through feature shrubs to a stream. Winding paths lead through shrubbery or parkland to the 'silver wood', under whose magnificent trees one passes among numerous fine shrubs and woodland flowers given to Earl and Countess Grey for their silver wedding in the 1930s. There are good varieties of rhododendron and azalea, and outstanding species hydrangea (*H. villosa*) apart from unusual flower varieties. A large pond-side garden is developing and an arboretum. Labelling is scarce but a catalogue is in preparation. This is a plantsperson's garden but there are many delights for the aesthete such as the agapanthus of varying blues on the terrace.

KIRKLEY HALL COLLEGE   8
Ponteland, Northumberland. Tel: (0661) 860808

Northumberland County Council ✳ *11m NW of Newcastle off A696, right at Ponteland on C151 for 2¹/₂m. RAC signposted* ✳ *Parking* ✳ *Refreshments* ✳ *Toilet facilities* ✳ *Suitable for wheelchairs* ✳ *Plants for sale* ✳ *Open daily, 10am – dusk* ✳ *Entrance: £1.20, OAP and children 8 – 16 60p, family ticket £3, parties of 13 or more (no guide) £1 per person, guided tours of 13 or more by prior arrangement £2.50 per person.*

The 10-acre grounds with their three-acre walled garden form a showcase for all the gardening arts from propagation onwards. Inside the walls are climbers, borders and bedding plants in profusion, all pleasingly grouped and labelled. The grounds contain a succession of beds, skilfully shaped to follow the rolling contours of the land, each carefully composed for variety of profile and continuity of colour – the heathers being spectacular. Then to the Hall with its outstanding array of beautifully-planted containers on terraces down to a most attractive sunken garden and a wildlife pond. National collections include beech, ivy and willow. The whole is thoroughly professional. Permanent exhibition of modern sculpture. Series of evening talks for Friends of Kirkley Hall.

LINDISFARNE CASTLE 9
Holy Island, Berwick-upon-Tweed, Northumberland. Tel: (0289) 89244

The National Trust ✳ *On Holy Island, 6m E of the A1 across a causeway at low tide only. Tide tables printed in local papers and displayed at causeway. Access to garden on foot only, ¹/₂m from parking area* ✳ *Parking by castle ¹/₂m from garden* ✳ *Refreshments in village* ✳ *Dogs on lead as far as Lower Battery only* ✳ *National Trust shop in village* ✳ *Castle open. Visitors must leave bulky objects inc. back-packs in entrance* ✳ *Open April to Sept, daily except Fri; Oct, Wed, Sat and Sun, 1 – 5.30pm (last admission 5pm). Admission to the garden is only permitted when a gardener is in attendance.* ✳ *Entrance: £3 (inc. castle)*

This garden must be unique both in design and setting. Its existence on Holy Island off the coast of Northumberland came about like this: in 1901 Edward Hudson, owner and founder of *Country Life*, on holiday saw the ruins of the castle, rapidly purchased them from their owner, the Crown, and invited the young architect Lutyens to rebuild. Lutyens had been introduced to Hudson by his friend Gertrude Jekyll. The latter advised Hudson to have a low walled garden built to the north of the castle approached by a walk across the fields. This was done in 1911. In the patterned paving, a selection of Jekyll's favourite plants were planted in gradations of colour. The original plans were recently discovered in a Californian collection and recreated by the Trust and the University of Durham. The result is not entirely entrancing. The garden is at its best in summer, as was Hudson's intention, since he asked Jekyll to design a holiday garden for August.

MELDON PARK 10
Morpeth, Northumberland. Tel: (0670) 72661

Mr and Mrs M.J.B. Cookson ✳ *6m W of Morpeth on B6343* ✳ *Best season: early June* ✳ *Parking* ✳ *Light refreshments at weekends and Bank Holidays only* ✳ *Toilet facilities* ✳ *Suitable for wheelchairs* ✳ *House open* ✳ *Garden open 23rd May, 21st June, 31st Aug, 2 – 5pm* ✳ *Entrance: £2, children 50p*

When, in 1832, Newcastle glassmaster Isaac Cookson purchased a 700-acre estate enclosing a stretch of the steep Hartburn dene, he simply asked John Dobson to pick his spot and design the house. His trust was rewarded. Dobson built a broad plateau on which he planted a fine neo-classical house facing squarely south over terrace and ha-ha to the dene below. This was flanked by shrubberies and mature imported trees of which at least one fine cedar still survives – as does the serene charm of the original vision, a tribute to the continuing care of the Cookson family. Attractions include rose beds, a small orangery, woodland and wild meadow walks, and in particular the walled garden, quartered by pathways in part apple-hedged, where kitchen beds and venerable plums are accompanied by much innovative planting.

SEATON DELAVAL HALL   11
Seaton Sluice, Near Whitley Bay, Northumberland. Tel: (091) 2373040/2371493

Lord Hastings ✳ *10m NE of Newcastle, ¹/₂m inland from Seaton Sluice on A190* ✳ *Best season: June to Aug* ✳ *Parking* ✳ *Toilet facilities* ✳ *Partly suitable for wheelchairs* ✳ *Souvenir stall* ✳ *Parts of house open* ✳ *Garden open May to Sept, Wed, Sun and Bank Holidays, 2 – 6pm* ✳ *Entrance: £1.50, children 50p*

The original grounds of this architectural masterpiece by Vanbrugh no doubt matched its magnificence, but little is known save for an early painting showing a swan lake. A notable weeping ash survives from that time, and there is a venerable rose garden. Since 1950 an excellent parterre has been laid out, now embellished by a large Italianate pond and fountains. An attractive shrubbery (rhododendron, azalea, etc.) and herbaceous borders have also been established on the south side towards the fine Norman chapel. Replanting continues and the garden is obviously in good hands.

WALLINGTON ★   12
Cambo, Morpeth, Northumberland. Tel: (067074) 283

The National Trust ✳ *20m W of Newcastle off A696 (signed on B6342)* ✳ *Best season: spring – autumn* ✳ *Parking* ✳ *Refreshments: coffee, lunch and teas in Clock Tower Restaurant (067074) 274. Picnics in car park* ✳ *Toilet facilities inc. disabled* ✳ *Suitable for wheelchairs* ✳ *Dogs on lead in garden, free in grounds* ✳ *Shop* ✳ *House and children's museum open April to Oct, daily, except Tues, 1 – 5.30pm (last admission 5pm)* ✳ *Walled garden open April to Sept, daily, 10.30am – 7pm, Oct to March 1993, daily, 10.30am – 4pm. Grounds open all year round during daylight hours* ✳ *Entrance: £1.80 (house and grounds £3.80)*

The superb house in a 100-acre landscape of lawns, terraces and flower beds has an excellent walled garden, with a great variety of climbers and an impressive summer house designed in Tuscan style by 'Capability' Brown who was a local man. The conservatory plants include a great tree fuchsia. Outside, the walks step down from a classical fountain past beds re-designed by Lady Trevelyan in the 1930s, including notable heathers and many herbaceous varieties, through to the water meadow. Trees include two larches by the China Pond planted by the Duke of Argyll in 1738. The Hall is steeped in the history of the Trevelyan family and is associated with Ruskin and the pre-Raphaelite painters who decorated it. New circular walk.

NOTTINGHAMSHIRE

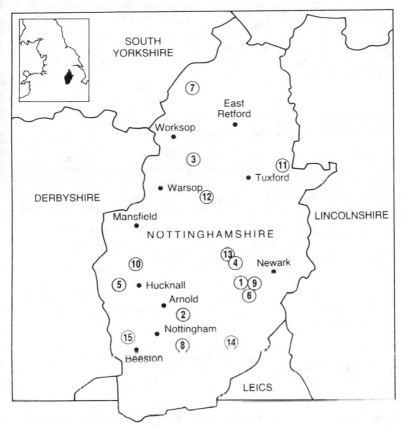

SOUTH
YORKSHIRE

⑦

East
Retford

Worksop

③

⑪

Tuxford

Warsop
⑫

DERBYSHIRE

Mansfield

N O T T I N G H A M S H I R E

LINCOLNSHIRE

⑬
④

Newark

⑩

① ⑨

⑤ Hucknall

⑥

Arnold

②

⑮ Nottingham

⑧

⑭

Beeston

LEICS.

Two-starred gardens are ringed in bold.

BRACKENHURST COLLEGE   1
Southwell, Nottinghamshire. Tel: (0636) 812252

*Nottinghamshire Education Committee * 1m S of Southwell on A612 *
Parking by arrangement * Refreshments: tea, cakes and sandwiches * Toilet
facilities * Partly suitable for wheelchairs * Dogs * Plants for sale * Careers*

*information * Farm museum open * Open 5th July, 2 – 6pm * Entrance: £1, children 20p for charity*

This was once a wealthy estate with gardens to match, and fine views of the surrounding countryside. Ornamental shrubs, rose and sunken gardens, walled garden, glasshouses, mature trees, especially fine cedars of Lebanon, experimental trial beds. The artificial lake constructed on the dewpond principle is carefully managed with wildlife in mind. The garden is in the process of being rehabilitated, and some areas are now less impressive; more labelling would be helpful. The college already has an extensive range of lilies and it will hold the National lily collection. A farm museum is open and a farm institute is established on the estate.

17 BRIDLE ROAD 2
Burton Joyce, Nottingham. Tel: (0602) 313725

*Mr and Mrs Bates * Turn N off A612 Nottingham to Southwell Road up Lambley Lane. After ¹/₂m fork right down impassable-looking Bridle Road, and the property is on the left * Best season: spring/summer * Parking very restricted in lane by the gates to the house * Partly suitable for wheelchairs * Open Sats throughout the year by appointment * Entrance: 75p, children 25p (1991 prices)*

The one-acre garden is situated on a slope, mainly facing south and west. The mixed border is of the highest standard combining extremely well a variety of plants including dahlias and grasses. Worth looking at is the way the very steep slope on the garden's southern border has been utilized with zigzagging gravel paths. Common and unusual bulbous plants abound – those such as acidanthera and nerines are in the hot, sunny spots near the house, others in the grass, woodland and mixed border. There is a stream with naturalized ferns, primulas and the like.

CLUMBER PARK 3
Clumber Estate Office, Clumber Park, Worksop, Nottinghamshire. Tel: (0909) 476592

*The National Trust * 4¹/₂m SE of Worksop off A1 and A57, 11m from junction 30 off M1 * Parking * Refreshments: cafeteria and restaurant, daily, 10.30am – 5pm and in summer to 6pm * Toilet facilities * Partly suitable for wheelchairs (wheelchairs inc. those for children available) * Dogs * Plant sales centre open 29th March to 24th Oct, 10.30am – 6pm * National Trust shop * Chapel open except 25th Dec, 10 – 4pm * Park always open during daylight hours. Garden, Vineries and Tools exhibition open April to Sept, Sat, Sun, Bank Holiday Mons and some weekdays during summer school holidays, 10am – 5pm (last admission 4.30pm) * Entrance: pedestrians free, cars £2.30, coaches £6 (£12 at weekends and Bank Holidays). Bicycle hire*

In 1707 the Park was enclosed from Sherwood Forest and the Dukes of Newcastle had their seat here. Only the stable block, chapel and entrance gates remain as the great house was demolished in 1938. The National Trust purchased the park in 1946. The Lincoln terrace and pleasure gardens were laid out by William Sawrey Gilpin in the early nineteenth century. Twenty-five acres out of the 3,800 acres of parkland are managed by just two gardeners. The vinery and palm house survive (being restocked) and the extensive glass-houses (450 feet) are the best and longest in the National Trust's properties. The kitchen garden exhibition of late nineteenth-century and early twentieth-century tools is fascinating and reminds us that modern powered-garden tools have taken much of the heavy work out of gardening. The walled kitchen garden has some fruit bushes, a herb garden in the making and a few young fruit trees in the grassy centre but is otherwise a disappointment. The Lincoln terrace reached its height of excellence in the 1920s and after years of neglect is being restored. The cedar avenue has cedars and sweet chestnut trees of breath-taking size.

CLYDE HOUSE 4
Westgate, Southwell, Nottinghamshire.

Mr and Mrs G. Edwards ✳ *In Southwell on A612 a few hundred yards before the Minster on the right* ✳ *Restricted roadside parking* ✳ *Toilet facilities* ✳ *Suitable for wheelchairs* ✳ *Plants for sale* ✳ *Open 10th May, 2 – 6pm* ✳ *Entrance: £1.25 (1991 price)*

Totally organically-managed private gardens are regrettably rare but this example will convince visitors that it is possible to 'go organic' and still have a beautifully healthy garden. The immaculate green lawn on closer inspection was full of clover – but so what if it looked and felt luxurious underfoot? The composting area (the secret of success?) is an education in itself and Mr Edwards will explain its workings.

FELLEY PRIORY ★ 5
Underwood, Jacksdale, Nottinghamshire. Tel: (0773) 810230

Major and The Hon. Mrs Chaworth Musters ✳ *From M1 junction 27, take A608 for Heanor and Derby and the garden is on the left, ¹/₂m W of M1* ✳ *Parking on open days in field adjacent* ✳ *Teas on open days* ✳ *Toilet facilities* ✳ *Suitable for wheelchairs* ✳ *Plants for sale* ✳ *Open 25th March, 12th April, 27th May, 7th, 24th June, 22nd July, 23rd Sept, 28th Oct, 2 – 5.30pm and by appointment for parties* ✳ *Entrance: £1, children 25p*

Despite the M1 being only half a mile away, above the house, but out of sight, the first impression is of a garden with quiet English countryside as a backdrop. The owners have, with the use of hedging, created several gardens within the one, the original ancient walls unifying the separate parts as well as providing shelter and support for many unusual and slightly tender shrubs and climbers. The new rose garden will be glorious when more mature – at present domed pergolas add instant height.

FLINTHAM HALL ★ 6
Flintham, Nottinghamshire.

Mr Miles Thoroton Hildyard ✳ *6m SW of Newark on A46* ✳ *Parking in*

adjacent field ✳ *Toilet facilities* ✳ *Suitable for wheelchairs* ✳ *Dogs on lead* ✳
Open for charity and at other times by written appointment ✳ *Entrance: £1.50,*
OAP £1, children 50p

Do set aside plenty of time to visit this garden; it will not be wasted. The hall
and extensive gardens are obviously loved and lavish amounts of time and effort
are spent on them. It is therefore remarkable to learn that Michael Blagg is the
sole gardener, though Mr Hildyard regularly attends to the gardens and lawns
himself. The unique Victorian conservatory is a heady experience; the exotic
plants and ornate architecture vying with each other for attention. In the *Shell
Guide to Nottinghamshire* it is described as the most spectacular in the country. It
is only one of many surprises; the Regency pheasantry, recently imaginatively
restored, has been frescoed by Ricardo Cinalli. The gardens were featured in
Country Life in Sept 1989.

HODSOCK PRIORY ★ 7
Blyth, Worksop, Nottinghamshire. Tel: (0909) 591204

Sir Andrew and Lady Buchanan ✳ *1m from A1 at Blyth off B6045 Blyth –
Worksop road* ✳ *Parking. Coaches must book* ✳ ☆*Teas in the conservatory* ✳
Toilet facilities, inc. disabled ✳ *Dogs in car park only* ✳ *Plants for sale* ✳ *Open
Easter Sun, then May, Spring and Aug Bank Holiday Suns and Mons, also mid-
June to mid-July, Wed and Thurs, 12 noon to 5pm plus 'Special Spectaculars'
(10am to 5pm) for 'Snowdrops' (Feb/Mar), 'Daffodils' (April), 'Blossom and
Bluebells' (May) and 'Autumn Colours' (Oct/Nov)(ring for further details, dates and
group bookings)* ✳ *Entrance: £1.50, disabled persons in wheelchairs free, children
25p. Discount for prebooked groups of 50 or more.*

Historic site including a Grade I listed gatehouse *c.* 1500 and a moat. There are
fine trees including a huge cornus, a very old catalpa (Indian bean), tulip tree
and swamp cypress, and much replanting is going on. In the spring there are the
bulbs, and later, mixed borders with perennials and old roses, the latter much
admired. Interesting holly hedges. Good walks, mainly grass, beyond the small
lake and bog garden and into the old moat, which is accessible to the disabled.

HOLME PIERREPONT HALL 8
Radcliffe-on-Trent, Nottinghamshire. Tel: (0602) 332371

Mr and Mrs R. Brackenbury ✳ *5m SE of Nottingham off A52. Approach past the
National Water Sports Centre and continue for 1¹/₂m* ✳ *Parking* ✳ *Teas. Other
refreshments by prior arrangement* ✳ *Toilet facilities* ✳ *Suitable for wheelchairs*
✳ *Dogs on lead* ✳ *Shop* ✳ *House open* ✳ *Garden open Easter Sun – Tues, May
Day Bank Holiday Mon, Spring Bank Holiday Sun – Tues. Also June to Aug, Sun,
Tues, Thurs, Fri, 2 – 6pm. Groups by appointment all year* ✳ *Entrance: courtyard
garden £1 (house and garden £2.50, children £1)*

The Hall is a medieval brick manor house but the garden and parterre have
been restored by the present owners. The box parterre is the outstanding
feature of the gardens and the newly created herbaceous borders next to the
York stone path (replacing old rose beds) once matured will enhance the

courtyard garden further. (The Jacob sheep are very friendly lawnmowers.) Mr and Mrs Brackenbury work hard with improvements to this peaceful house and garden and willingly provide ample information. Their improvements include a winter garden.

MILL HILL HOUSE 9
Elston Lane, East Stoke, Newark, Nottinghamshire. Tel: (0636) 525460

*Mr and Mrs R.J. Gregory * 5m S of Newark. Take A46, turn left into Elston Lane (signposted to Elston) and the house is the first on the right * Parking 100 yards past the house * Toilet facilities * Suitable for wheelchairs * Dogs on lead * Plants for sale * Open April to Sept, Wed – Sun, 10am – 6pm and by appointment. Groups welcome by appointment * Entrance: 75p, children 20p*

Ignoring the electricity pylons, the heavy clay and exposed position, the owners have created a cottage garden from a mere half-acre field. If you have similar obstacles, a visit to this garden will uplift the spirits and show how such adversities can be overcome. Much of the propagating material for the nursery comes from the wealth of hardy plants within the garden.

NEWSTEAD ABBEY ★ 10
Linby, Nottinghamshire. Tel: (0623) 793557

*Nottingham City Council * 11m N of Nottingham on A60 * Parking * Refreshments: tea room in grounds open Good Friday to Sept * Toilet facilities * Partly suitable for wheelchairs * Dogs on lead * Shop * House open at extra charge, Good Friday to Sept, 12 noon – 6pm (last admission 5pm). Contains Byron memorabilia and period rooms * Gardens open daily, 10am – dusk * Entrance: £1.35, children 65p (1991 prices)*

Water predominates in this estate that the poet Byron inherited but could rarely afford to live in. In most of the extensive and immaculate gardens there is much of interest. The Japanese gardens are justly famous and the rock and fern gardens worth visiting. Indeed the waterfalls, wildfowl, passageways, grottos and bridges provide plenty of fun for children, but in addition there is an excellent, imaginatively-equipped play area with bark mulch for safety. The tropical garden and the monks' stew pond are visually uninteresting but they are of laudable age. It is a pity that the large walled kitchen garden is now a rose garden – rose gardens however pretty are commonplace, but large kitchen gardens to the great houses are rare now and of more interest. The old rose garden is now the iris garden – an insipid area with gladioli planted in the regular plots in an effort to liven up the place.

PURELAND JAPANESE GARDEN 11
North Clifton, Nr Newark, Nottinghamshire. Tel: (0777) 228567

*Maitreya * 9m N of Newark, 1m from A57. Take A1133 from Newark and turn left to North Clifton. At end of High Street, turn right * Parking in field * Teas*

Toilet facilities ✳ *Open May to Sept (Oct Suns only), Tues – Sat, 1 – 5.30pm, Sun and Bank Holidays 10.30am – 5.30pm* ✳ *Entrance: £2, OAP, students and unemployed £1.50, children over 5 £1*

The Japanese owner, though originally lacking gardening experience or knowledge, has fashioned a charming Japanese garden in the middle of the Nottinghamshire farming community since he began work on it in 1980. Its one and a half acres contain all the features expected in a traditional water garden. For those who enjoy 'meditation and relaxation' in the Japanese way, there is also a garden at Newstead Abbey (see entry).

RUFFORD COUNTRY PARK 12
Nottinghamshire. Tel: (0623) 824153

Nottinghamshire County Council ✳ *2m S of Ollerton on A614* ✳ *Parking* ✳ *Refreshments: main meals – the Buttery, Mon – Sat, 12 noon – 2.30pm, Sun, 12 noon – 3.30pm, snacks at the Coach House daily, 10am – 5pm* ✳ *Partly suitable for wheelchairs, four available which can be booked in advance* ✳ *Dogs (guide dogs only in shops and restaurants)* ✳ *Shops* ✳ *Rufford Abbey Cistercian area open* ✳ *Park open daily, dawn – dusk* ✳ *Entrance: free*

Rufford Country Park contains almost everything that might be expected of an important country park, e.g. lakes, lime avenues, mature cedars, etc. The promise has been fulfilled – a visit to the newly established eight theme gardens within the sculpture garden is well worthwhile. Large areas are managed with wildlife in mind hence plenty of birdlife. Ball games are allowed on the lawns beneath cut-leaved beeches and cedars. Ample picnic areas. Conducted walks arranged during the week and weekends. Telephone for dates and times. The Reg Hookway Arboretum, established in 1983, shows promise with a good collection of oaks and birches – all well-labelled. There is a new rose garden in front of the abbey ruins which are now open to the public.

ST HELEN'S CROFT 13
Halam, Nr Southwell, Nottinghamshire. Tel: (0636) 813219

Mrs E. Ninnis ✳ *Take A614 Nottingham – Doncaster road and turn off at White Post roundabout to Southwell and Halam* ✳ *Parking in adjacent field* ✳ *Suitable for wheelchairs* ✳ *Plants for sale* ✳ *Open for charity first Tues in each month March to Oct, 2 – 5pm and by appointment* ✳ *Entrance: £1, children 25p during April*

A lovely three quarter-acre garden which is an inspiration for all elderly gardeners as it is still cared for by its creator despite her being in her seventies. Undaunted by the heavy clay soil she constantly introduces changes and has grand plans for future plantings. Featured in *Gardener's World* programme. An informative leaflet is provided at the entrance. A six-acre conservation meadow adjoins the garden planted with 20,000 fritillaries and other wildlings and trees, wild violets, cowslips, primroses, honeysuckles and bluebells. The meadow only is open every afternoon in April, 2 – 5pm (other times by appointment). There is access to the meadow for wheelchairs (and cars for severely disabled) on mown paths.

THE WILLOWS 14
5 Rockley Avenue, Radcliffe-on-Trent, Nottinghamshire. Tel: (0602) 333621

Mr and Mrs R.A. Grout ✳ *6m E of Nottingham N of A52. From Radcliffe-on-Trent High Street P.O. turn into Shelford Road, over railway bridge, 300 yards opposite bus shelter turn left into Cliff Way, then 2nd right* ✳ *Limited parking on street. Coaches strictly by appointment* ✳ *Tea and biscuits on charity open days* ✳ *Open 1st April, 6th May, 3rd June, 1st July, 5th Aug, 2nd Sept, 2 – 5.30pm* ✳ *Entrance: £1, children free*

This small private garden, designed by the owners in 1982, is of greatest appeal to those interested in rare hardy herbaceous plants. Because of its size, trees and shrubs are limited but are unusual or handled in such a way as to fit the area, e.g. pollarding. Excellent labelling. Collections of hostas, hellebores, pulmonarias, snowdrops, crocus and peonies.

WOLLATON HALL 15
Nottingham. Tel: (0602) 281333

Nottingham City Council ✳ *2¹/₂m from the city centre on A609. From M1 junction 25 take A52, turn left onto A614 and left onto A609* ✳ *Parking* ✳ *Refreshments: snacks near Wollaton Road car park* ✳ *Toilet facilities* ✳ *Partly suitable for wheelchairs* ✳ *Dogs on lead because of deer* ✳ *Shop* ✳ *Natural history museum in hall open April to Sept, Mon – Sat, 10am – 7pm, Sun, 2 – 5pm, Oct to March, Mon – Sat, 10am – dusk, Sun, 1.30 – 4.30pm. Closed 25th Dec. Free except small charge on Sun and Bank Holidays* ✳ *Garden open daily all year* ✳ *Entrance: free*

This large park and garden is surrounded by the city but because of its size the visitor feels deep in the country – unfortunately near the park periphery the roar of traffic dispels that illusion. The polyanthus in spring are spectacular as is the summer bedding where castor-oil plants and ornamental cabbages have their place in the schemes. The formal gardens at the top of the hill give onto views of huge cedars and holm oaks and thence on to the lime avenues and the deer in the park.

OXFORDSHIRE

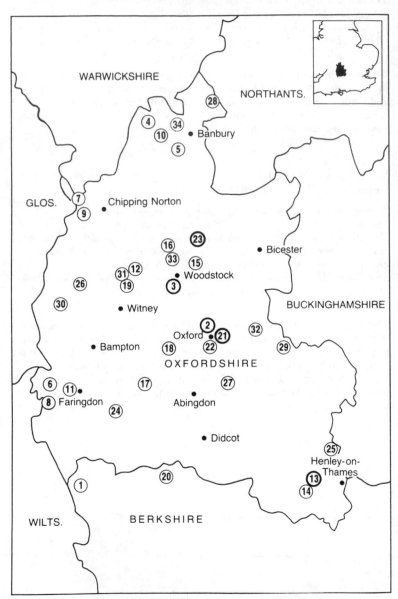

Two-starred gardens are ringed in bold.

ASHDOWN HOUSE   1
Lambourn, Newbury, Berkshire. Tel: (0488) 72584

The National Trust ✻ 2¹/₂m S od Ashbury, 3¹/₂m N of Lambourn on W side of B4000 ✻ Parking 250 yards from house ✻ Grounds suitable for wheelchairs ✻ Dogs on lead ✻ House open ✻ Woodlands open all year, Sat – Thurs, dawn – dusk ✻ Grounds free

Seen from the main road, Ashdown House appears to have a tall central section replete with cupola flanked by two lower wings. It is only when the visitor approaches the front entrance that it becomes obvious that the wings are quite separate from the central block – one was the kitchen and the other the servants' quarters of this fine hunting lodge built by the first Lord Craven for Elizabeth of Bohemia. The remains of a large formal park are present in a western lime avenue. A complementary lime avenue planted in 1970, to the north of the house, is now maturing well. Also an appropriately intricate parterre, designed by A.H. Brookholding-Jones, was planted by The National Trust in the 1950s. The garden is best enjoyed in spring when thousands of snowdrops, naturalised in the avenue and woodland, are at their showiest.

23 BEECH CROFT ROAD ★★   2
Summertown, Oxford. Tel: (0865) 56020

Mrs A. Dexter ✻ Summertown, 2m from centre of Oxford. Beech Croft Road runs between the Banbury and Woodstock roads which connect Oxford centre to ring road ✻ Parking limited in Beechcroft Road. Advisable to use public parking in Summertown ✻ Open by appointment only from June to Sept ✻ Entrance: £1.50 for charity

Clever use of perspective creates the effect of a much larger garden than would seem possible in an area of 23 x 7 yards. Foliage of different colours, textures, sizes and shapes is planted and pruned to form a backdrop to a variety of well-chosen plants. Ramondas and ferns are given room in the lower, damper end of the garden, alpines in stone troughs are placed in a sunnier position near the house. This is a tapestry garden, every inch contains unusual and interesting plants displayed with great skill.

BLENHEIM PALACE ★★   3
Woodstock, Oxfordshire. Tel: (0993) 811325

The Duke of Marlborough ✻ 8m NW of Oxford on A44 at Woodstock. Entrances off A44 and through the town of Woodstock ✻ Parking ✻ Refreshments: cafeterias, Indian Room Restaurant on Water Terraces ✻ Toilet facilities, inc. disabled ✻ Partly suitable for wheelchairs ✻ Dogs on lead in Park only ✻ Good garden centre open daily, 9.30am – 5.30pm, with refund on entrance charge for purchases ✻ House open, mid-March to Oct, 10.30am – 5.30pm (last admission 4.45pm) £5.50, OAP £4.50, children £2.80 ✻ Park open daily except 25th Dec, 9am – 5pm ✻ Entrance: park only, pedestrians 70p, children 40p. Cars including occupants £3 (includes admission to park, butterfly house, train, adventure play area, nature trail and car parking. Optional but extra: the Marlborough Maze and rowing boat hire) (1991 prices)

The visitor who walks through Hawksmoor's Triumphal Arch into Blenheim Park sees one of the greatest contrived landscapes in Britain. The architect Vanbrugh employed Bridgeman and Henry Wise, Queen Anne's master gardener and the last of the British formalists, to contrast a bastion-walled 'military' garden and kitchen gardens. Wise also planted immense elm avenues and linked Vanbrugh's bridge to the sides of the valley. However, the garden was far from ready when the first Duke of Marlborough moved into the palace in 1719. Major alterations were made by the 4th, 5th and 9th Dukes, one of the earliest of which was the grassing over of Wise's formal gardens by 'Capability' Brown after 1764. Brown also developed the two huge lakes. It is possible to spend several hours walking through the grounds, for which no charge is made. The gardens (entrance only with £2.50 garden ticket) include formal areas restored by Achille Duchêne in the 1920s from those grassed by Brown in the North forecourt. He made formal gardens on the east and west, the latter two water terraces in the Versailles style. To the east of the elaborate Italian garden is a sunken garden of patterned box and golden yew, interspersed with various seasonal plantings. To the west from the terraces are the rose garden and arboretum (1984). From the vast south lawn 'one passes through a magnificent grove of cedars and on towards Wise's walled garden, part shrubberies of laurel and an Exedra of box and yew, the whole exemplifying the Victorian pleasure grounds' in the words of the *Oxford Companion*. As a contribution to the celebration of the 300th anniversary of the replanting of the maze at Hampton Court, the Duke of Marlborough planted a maze here which is maturing well. In a few years time it should provide visitors with a puzzling and pleasurable experience.

BROOK COTTAGE ★   4
Well Lane, Alkerton, Nr Banbury, Oxfordshire. Tel: (029587) 303/590

Mr and Mrs D. Hodges ∗ 6m W of Banbury. From A422 Banbury – Stratford road, turn W at sign for Alkerton. Soon after entering village, small war memorial on right. Turn left into Well Lane and right at fork ∗ Partly suitable for wheelchairs ∗ Teas on June weekend and DIY tea or coffee every weekday ∗ Plants for sale ∗ Open April to Oct, Mon – Fri, 9am – 6pm. Open at other times and for group visits by appointment and on 20th, 21st June, 2 – 7pm ∗ Entrance: £1.50, OAP £1, children free for charity

This garden, designed and planted since 1964, is on a steeply-sloping, west-facing site of four acres. The owners have used the natural features in an interesting way. For example by planting large species, old-fashioned and modern shrub roses in the grass on a steep slope. Good use is made of water and there is a large unusual-shaped pond. Indeed shape is a feature of the overall effect, such as in a sweeping crimson copper beech hedge. Note the interesting grouping of hollies and conifers. There is something here for everyone in all seasons, from the alpine scree to the small 'cottage' and vegetable gardens above the house. Most plants are labelled. On charity open days, the owner next door at Alkerton House unlocks the connecting gate to show off his two and a half acres of trees, shrubs and conifers. Upton House (see Warwickshire entry) nearby shows an earlier and more formal use of slopes.

BROUGHTON CASTLE ★ 5
Broughton, Nr Banbury, Oxfordshire. Tel: (0295) 262624

The Lord Saye and Sele ✻ 2¹/₂m SW of Banbury on B4035 ✻ Parking ✻ Teas on open days, refreshments for parties by arrangement ✻ Toilet facilities ✻ Suitable for wheelchairs ✻ House open ✻ Garden open 18th May to 14th September, Wed and Sun, also Thurs in July and Aug and Bank Holiday Sun and Mon, inc. Easter, 2 – 5pm. Also by appointment for groups throughout year ✻ Entrance: £2.80, children £1.50

More of a house than a castle, the gardens are unexpectedly domestic within the confines of the moat. In 1900 there were 14 gardeners but the present owner and his inspired gardener have reduced the workload somewhat while retaining the overall splendour. The most important changes were made after 1969 following a visit from Lanning Roper who suggested opening up the views across the park. There are now two magnificent borders. The west-facing one, backed by the battlement wall, has a colour scheme of blues and yellows, greys and whites. The other long border is based on reds, mauves and blues. Great planting skill is evident in the serpentine flows of colour. On the south side is the walled 'ladies garden' with box-edged fleur-de-lys-shaped beds holding floribunda roses. Another wonderful border rises up to the house wall. Everywhere is a profusion of old-fashioned roses and original planting.

BUSCOT PARK ★ 6
Faringdon, Oxfordshire. Tel: (0367) 240786 (not weekends)

The National Trust ✻ On A417 between Lechlade and Faringdon ✻ Parking ✻ Teas and light refreshments. Lunches for parties by prior arrangement ✻ Toilet facilities ✻ Plants for sale ✻ House open ✻ Garden open April to Sept, Wed – Fri and every 2nd and 4th Sat and Sun immediately following, 2 – 6pm (last admission 5.30pm). Closed Bank Holiday Mon ✻ Entrance: £2.50, (house and garden £3.50)

Although the house was built in 1780, this garden has been developed during the twentieth century. The water garden was created by Harold Peto in 1912, though the avenues linking lake to house were added later using a goose foot plan from the house, with fastigiate and weeping varieties of oak, beech and lime. The Egyptian avenue created by Lord Faringdon in 1969 is guarded by sphinxes and embellished with Coade stone statues copied from an original from Hadrian's Villa. The large walled kitchen garden was redesigned by Tim Rees using pleached hedges of Judas trees (which should grow into a tunnel) and hornbeam underplanted with hemerocallis. Deep borders under walls with unusual, and skilful, mixture of old roses and vegetables (gourds, marrows, red chard, parsley, etc.) Walkway outside kitchen garden between two wide borders using exterior wall and trellis as screens. Exceptionally effective planting by the late Peter Coats three years ago and, over the years, imaginative development by Lord Faringdon. The planting of the kitchen garden and the double borders is so skilful that even in drought conditions none of the effect is lost.

CHASTLETON GLEBE 7
Chastleton, Oxfordshire.

Mr and Mrs C.R. Kruger ✻ 3m SE of Moreton-in-Marsh off A44 ✻ Parking in field ✳ ☆*Teas* ✳ *Toilet facilities* ✳ *Suitable for wheelchairs* ✳ *Dogs on lead* ✳ *Plants and jams for sale* ✳ *Open 28th June, 2 – 6pm* ✳ *Entrance: £1*

A Cotswold house surrounded by lawns and fine old trees on three sides, and open on the south side to views across the lake and island with its enchanting Chinese bridge and pagoda. Enjoy this view from the red planted terrace. A border of cream, blue and yellow plants is sheltered by hedges of beech and yew. Croquet lawn is bordered with old shrub roses, and the kitchen garden is very attractively planted with flowers for picking and drying, vegetables and herbs. Other gardens in the village are open on the same days, and are well worth visiting. The future of Chastleton House hangs in the balance at the moment, but look over the churchyard wall at the charming topiary garden. Another fine Chastleton garden which has just changed hands is The Old Post Office. This may be opened when others in the village do so for charity.

CLOCK HOUSE ★   8
Coleshill, Faringdon, Oxfordshire. Tel: (079376) 2476

Michael and Denny Wickham ✳ *3¹/₂m SW of Faringdon on B4019* ✳ *Best season: June/July* ✳ *Parking* ✳ *Teas in courtyard in fine weather* ✳ *Toilet facilities* ✳ *Suitable for wheelchairs* ✳ *Dogs on lead* ✳ *Plants for sale* ✳ *Open 28th June, 4th Oct, 2 – 6pm* ✳ *Entrance: 70p, children free*

Situated on a hillside with inspiring views over the Vale of the White Horse, this exuberant, delightful garden was created by the present owners in the last thirty years in the grounds of Coleshill House, burned then demolished in the 1950s. The groundplan of the original house is being planted out in box, to show layout of walls and windows. Courtyard with collection of plants in pots, and a sunny walled garden in the old laundry-yard with roses and mixed planting and a fine greenhouse. Lime avenue at the front of the house sweeps you down to the views, and a pond and terrace are sheltered by tall shrubs. Mixed herbaceous borders with interesting and unusual plants. This is an original garden, designed by an artist, with a large collection of plants in imaginative settings, the atmosphere being prolific rather than tidy.

CORNWELL MANOR ★   9
Cornwell, Nr Kingham, Oxfordshire. Tel: (0608) 658 555

The Hon Peter Ward ✳ *2m from Chipping Norton, S off A44* ✳ *Parking* ✳ *Teas on charity days* ✳ *Toilet facilities* ✳ *Plants for sale* ✳ *Open for parties by appointment in June and July only at £2 per person. Tel: (0608) 658 671 and 3rd May, 10th June, 16th July, 2 – 6pm* ✳ *Entrance: £1.50*

Looking at this house and garden through the wrought-iron gates on the road frontage, it seems all-year-round the quintessence of seventeenth-century gracious living. Inside, the garden has been modernised without losing any of its charm. Begin by standing on the south-facing terrace in front of the house and looking down over the croquet lawn and up to the roadside gates and the view beyond; it is as good as anything in Italy. To the east is the spring garden and a formal garden on three levels with interesting plantings such as box-edged beds of peonies. Everywhere there are trained trees and clever plantings to emphasise leaf colouring. On the other side of the house is the original one and a quarter-acre walled kitchen garden, organically cultivated and, in the owner's words 'maintained in the traditional manner, now rarely seen.' Note also the children's garden, with an early form of Wendy house, and peek in the indoor games-room window to see the mass of amazing trophies of the chase. The swimming pool area is attractively arranged. Returning to the main house, the visitor descends the south terraces to the water pools below and turns east along the woodland walk, passing on the way the rock and bog gardens. The wild garden surrounds vast and unspoilt lakes. Everywhere there is evidence of sensitive new planting. The plant sales are amongst the best. The small village nearby was refurbished by the architect of Portmeirion, Sir Clough Williams Ellis (see entry under Wales).

EPWELL MILL 10
Epwell, Nr Banbury, Oxfordshire. Tel: (029578) 327 8242

Mr R.A. Withers ✳ 7m W of Banbury off B4035. The Mill is about ¹/₂m on the right after leaving Epwell village ✳ Parking in road at top of drive ✳ Teas ✳ Open 5th April, 17th May, 13th Sept, 2 – 6pm ✳ Entrance: £1, children free

Set in attractive countryside, the garden of this old mill has interesting water-garden features, and steps made from old mill wheels. Masses of bulbs down the drive and in the orchard in spring, azaleas and old roses in early summer, and autumn colours for the September opening. Don't miss the enchanting sculpture under the willow tree.

FARINGDON HOUSE 11
Faringdon, Oxfordshire. Tel: (0367) 240240

Miss S. Zinovieff ✳ Entered from centre of town which is off the A420 between Oxford and Swindon ✳ Parking ✳ Teas on charity days ✳ Partly suitable for wheelchairs ✳ Open by appointment and 29th March, 18th April, 24th May, 6th Sept, 2 – 5pm ✳ Entrance: £1, accompanied children free

Medium-sized apparently conventional park with fine terrace, views and trees. Its main charm lies in its eccentric features such as the coloured doves introduced by a previous owner, the dilettanti musician Lord Berners. In the orangery pool, half-submerged and looking as though he might have lunched rather too well, is a bust of General Havelock, of the Indian Mutiny. The swimming pool has a medieval influence, with lovely views over the top of old apple and pear trees, and a rare fruit walk, between two high sheltering walls. Good autumn border, lined in box, and massed bulbs down the drive in spring.

GOTHIC HOUSE 12
Gothic House, Charlbury, Oxfordshire.

Mr and Mrs Andrew Lawson ✳ In centre of Charlbury village on B4022 Witney – Enstone road ✳ Parking in street ✳ Teas ✳ Toilet facilities ✳ Suitable for

*wheelchairs * Plants for sale * Open 10th May, 13th Sept, 2 – 6pm *
Entrance: £1*

Gothic House, a third of an acre walled town garden, recently designed by one
of the country's leading garden photographers and his sculptress wife. Artistic
flair is evident everywhere, from the entrance through a fine Gothic glass
structure to the tour round the many gems picked out in miniature. The
planting is highly imaginative. So is the clever use of green wood structures in
treillage style including a romantic seat, and the railway sleepers which define
the pond. Note the *trompe l'oeil* painting on wood by Briony Lawson. Her
sculptures are everywhere, numbered and for sale. *Objets trouvée* amid the
foliage. The whole effect delightful.

GREYS COURT ★★ 13
Rotherfield Greys, Henley-on-Thames, Oxfordshire. Tel: (04917) 529

*The National Trust * 3m W of Henley-on-Thames E of B481 * Best season:
April to June * Parking * Teas Wed and Sat only in April and May, and Mon,
Wed, Fri and Sat from June to Sept * Toilet facilities * House open April to
Sept, Mon, Wed, Fri (but closed Good Fri, 2 – 6pm * Garden open April to Sept,
daily except Thurs and Sun, 2 – 6pm (last admission 5.30pm) * Entrance: £2.50
(house and garden £3.50)*

The statue of St Fiacre, the protector of gardeners, stands modestly in this
beautiful garden, or several gardens, set against the ruins of a fourteenth-
century fortified house. The largest area, an orchard, is divided by lines of
morello cherries and parallel hedges of 'Rosa Mundi'. An ancient wisteria
forms a canopy over a walled area, approached on one side through a tunnel of
younger wisterias in pinks and blues. Impeccably kept peony bed and rose
garden glow against the ancient walls. Beyond the kitchen garden, across the
nut avenue, is the maze, designed by Randoll Coate and inspired by one seen in
a dream by the then Archbishop of Canterbury.

GREYSTONE COTTAGE ★ 14
**Colmore Lane, Kingwood Common, Henley-on-Thames,
Oxfordshire. Tel: (04917) 559**

*Mr and Mrs W. Roxburgh * 5m N of Reading between B481 Nettlebed – Reading
road, and Sonning Common – Stoke Row road. 1m down Colmore Lane, next to
Unicorn pub * Best season: spring/summer * Parking in lane and field on open
day * Refreshments on special opening days * Suitable for wheelchairs * Plants
for sale * Open by appointment March to Sept and 10th May, 2 – 6pm *
Entrance: £1, children free*

The owners have created this garden over the past 18 years. Sunny courtyard in
front of house contains beds planted with white-flowered regale lilies, mallows
and perennial stock following on from spring bulbs. A large border is partly
Mediterranean, with *Cistus* species, myrtle, yuccas, etc., and white and blue
harebells. Pots of *Lilium longiflorum* and non-hardy plants by the door. Pear-
tree allée (80 years old) leading away from house, with vegetable garden to

right, hedges of beech beyond; lawns and woodland with long border to the west, full of unusual plants, especially a large number of hostas. Woodland with primroses, primulas and fritillaries, hellebores, azaleas, bilberries and blueberries. Golden garden behind house with wildlife pond.

HILL COURT   15
Tackley, Oxfordshire.

*Mr and Mrs Andrew C. Peake * 9m N of Oxford, just E of A423. Coming from Oxford turn opposite Sturdy's Castle; if driving south turn off at earlier sign marked Tackley * Parking * Teas * Suitable for wheelchairs * Plants for sale * Open 3rd weekend in June, 2 – 6pm * Entrance: £1, children free*

A two-acre, sixteenth-century walled garden, no longer physically attached to the house which was demolished c. 1960. Remains of the manor house, also demolished, can be seen across the park which dates from 1787. The garden, whose design was influenced by Russell Page, is unusual because it is terraced uphill from the entrance. The rose beds had to be removed about five years ago and the sensitive and original new planting is the work of Rupert Golby. Designers will find it pleasurable.

KIDDINGTON HALL   16
Kiddington, Nr Woodstock, Oxfordshire.

*Hon. Maurice and Mrs Robson * E of A44 N of Woodstock. Turn right at . crossroads in Kiddington village and turn down hill * Parking * Teas * Toilet facilities * Partly suitable for wheelchairs * Open for charity 14th June, 2 – 6pm * Entrance: £1, children free*

This is a curious timewarp. The Hall, incorporating a house of 1673 no longer visible, is by Sir Charles Barry (c. 1850) architect of the House of Commons, Cliveden, etc. Very Italianate. But earlier owners are reputed to have brought in 'Capability' Brown so the view from the terrace is of a fine park of a century earlier. Grazing horses appear to be in the garden, although in fact they are on the other side of the ha-ha. This south-facing terrace is an excellently-maintained parterre of rose beds with good stone urns, etc. Connected to the house is the former orangery now an open loggia, from which the owners can walk through the adjacent churchyard to their devotions. Descending from the terrace is a fine lake, developing from the River Glymp, and a walk along the river bank allows a view of the house and of a rustic boathouse (which it is hoped the owners will restore). Large walled garden (well-maintained), and espaliered fruit up the walls. Interesting two-tier greenhouse. Pleasing teas in the stables, also by Barry, described by Pevsner as pioneering design.

KINGSTON HOUSE   17
Kingston Bagpuize, Oxfordshire. Tel: (0865) 820259

*Lord and Lady Tweedsmuir * 5¹/₂m W of Abingdon at entry to Kingston Bagpuize where the A415 meets the A420 * Parking * Teas * Toilet facilities **

Suitable for wheelchairs (garden only) ✳ *Plants for sale* ✳ *Shop* ✳ *House open* ✳ *Garden open April to Sept, Sun and Bank Holiday Mons, 2.30 – 5.30pm* ✳ *Entrance: 50p, children under 5 free (house and garden £2.50, OAP £2, children £1. Children under 5 not admitted to the house.) Groups by written appointment only – special rates*

This Charles II manor house was owned in the pre-war years by Miss Marlie Raphael, a friend of Sir Harold Hillier, the great tree and shrub plantsman; accordingly she planted a woodland garden crossed by narrow curving earth paths and featuring plants from all over the world. This can be reached by an original green walk, which is to the left of the entrance. Miss Raphael's niece, Lady Tweedsmuir, continued the good work by planting the so-called Leap Wood begun on 29 February 1984. It has many rare and interesting plants although their arrangement is in some cases incongruous. A useful notated map can be purchased at the gate. Perhaps the garden should be visited in the late spring to see the best effect.

MANOR HOUSE ★   18
Stanton Harcourt, Oxfordshire. Tel: (0865) 881928

Mr and The Hon Mrs Gascoigne ✳ *9m W of Oxford, 5m SE of Witney on B4449* ✳ *Best season: late spring/early summer* ✳ *Parking* ✳ *☆Teas* ✳ *Toilet facilities* ✳ *Suitable for wheelchairs* ✳ *Dogs on lead* ✳ *Plants for sale* ✳ *House open* ✳ *Garden open 5th, 16th, 19th, 20th, 30th April, 3rd, 4th, 14th, 17th, 21st, 24th, 25th May, 4th, 7th, 18th, 21st June, 2nd, 5th, 16th, 19th, 30th July, 2nd, 13th, 16th, 27th, 30th, 31st Aug, 10th, 13th, 24th, 27th Sept, 2 – 6pm* ✳ *Entrance: £1.50, OAP and children £1 (house and garden £3, OAP and children £2)*

Twelve acres of gardens incorporated in and around ruins of a fourteenth- and fifteenth-century manor house. An avenue of clipped yew leads from the house to the chapel, and there are herbaceous and rose borders, with clematis, hydrangeas and roses clambering up the magnificent old walls. The kitchen garden is still in the process of redesign as a formal rose garden using David Austin's New English roses, espaliered apple trees, and a fountain in the middle. The stew ponds are sadly low in water, but covered with water lilies in high summer, and fringed with water-loving plants, and are crossed by some enchanting old bridges. It would take an army of gardeners to keep this garden immaculate, so enjoy it for its nostalgic atmosphere and history, magnificent walls and urns, and romantic paths winding through nut-walks which are underplanted with bulbs and primulas in the spring. Don't miss the delicious teas in the medieval kitchens.

MOUNT SKIPPET ★   19
Ramsden, Oxfordshire. Tel: (0993) 868253

Dr and Mrs M.A.T. Rogers ✳ *4m N of Witney off B4022 to Charlbury. At crossroads marked to Finstock turn E and almost immediately turn right. Then after 400 yards turn left up No Through Way Lane* ✳ *Parking* ✳ *Refreshments by arrangement. Picnic area available* ✳ *Suitable for wheelchairs* ✳ *Plants usually for sale* ✳ *Open April to Sept by appointment* ✳ *Entrance: £1 to charity*

Dr Rogers, now retired after a career as a research chemist, is a dedicated plantsman, preferring to grow everything from seeds or cuttings. He took over this family house of two acres and has developed a very attractive garden in a beautiful Cotswold setting. Plants are his love and there are many rare ones, including several that Wisley cannot identify. He has two rock gardens, an alpine house, interesting shrubs and trees and a bog garden adjoining the village pond. Everywhere there are collections of pots with rare treasures, some of which are sometimes for sale. Almost everything in the garden is labelled, and if you are lucky, Dr Rogers will delight in giving you an enthusiastic and highly informative tour of his garden. Swot up on your Latin names and plant origins before you go!

THE OLD RECTORY ★   20
Farnborough, Wantage, Oxfordshire. Tel: (04882) 298

Mrs Michael Todhunter ✻ *4m SE of Wantage off B4494* ✻ *Best season: June/ July* ✻ *Parking* ✻ *Teas sometimes* ✻ *Suitable for wheelchairs* ✻ *Plants for sale* ✻ *Open for charity 26th April, 17th May, 28th June, 2 – 6pm and by written appointment* ✻ *Entrance: £1, Children free*

Outstanding four-acre garden created over 25 years on good original structure of large trees and hedges with magnificent views over the Downs. Deep, parallel herbaceous borders, backed by yew hedges. Subtle and effective planting next to front of house; smaller areas laid out for sun or shade-loving plants; woodland and shrubs, lawns; swimming pool surrounded by large *Hydrangea sargentiana*, potted lilies, agapanthus, with mixed roses around outside walls. Collection of old roses and small-flowered clematis. Wild flowers at edge of front lawn by ha-ha. Incidentally, those who like John Betjeman's poetry will be interested to know that he lived here 1945-50 and can look for the ghost of Miss Joan Hunter Dunn in the shrubberies. One of Oxfordshire's highest gardens, 600 feet, prey to winds from the Downs.

OXFORD BOTANIC GARDEN ★★   21
Oxford. Tel: (0865) 276920

University of Oxford ✻ *In centre of Oxford opposite Magdalen College near bridge* ✻ *Parking difficult* ✻ *Picnics, while not specifically authorised, could be taken overlooking river* ✻ *Suitable for wheelchairs* ✻ *Professional photography and music prohibited* ✻ *Open daily, 9am – 5pm (4.30pm during GMT). Greenhouses 2 – 4pm. Closed 25th Dec and Good Fri* ✻ *Entrance: free except during July and August £1 (half to charity)*

This is the oldest botanic garden in Britain and one of the most attractive to the general visitor. Founded in 1621, it is surrounded by a high wall and entered through a splendid gateway by Inigo Jones's master mason. Two yews survive from the early plantings and there are a series of beds containing herbaceous plants in systematic and labelled groups. The old walls back beds with tender plants, including roses and clematis. To the left is the greenhouse area, modern ones replacing those built in 1670. There is also a rock garden. Outside the front entrance is a large rose garden donated by Americans in memory of those university staff who developed penicillin. Several miles away at Nuneham Courtenay (south of the A423) is the University Arboretum opened in 1968 (see entry).

OXFORD COLLEGE GARDENS 22

Most colleges are helpful about free access to their gardens although the more private ones, such as the Master's or Fellows', are rarely open. Specific viewing times are difficult to rely on because some colleges prefer not to have visitors in term time or on days when a function is taking place. The best course is to ask at the Porter's Lodge or to telephone ahead of visit. However, it is fair to say that some Oxford college gardens will always be open to the visitor, by arrangement with porters, even if others are closed on that particular day.

Amongst the college gardens of particular interest are the following: *Christ Church*; famous for Lewis Carroll's reference to the Cheshire Cat's chestnut tree in the Deanery garden. Also an Oriental plane planted 1636. Visitors in May should see the Meadow with its fritillaries. Memorial garden on St Aldates [Memorial garden open winter 8am – 4.30pm, summer 8am – 8pm. Deanery and Master's garden only open once a year for charity. Meadow open daily]. *Corpus Christi*; the smallest college [Open term time 1.30 – 4pm, vacations 10am – 4pm]. *Green College* near the Radcliffe Observatory's Tower of the Seven Winds which visitors may ascend for an aerial view, and the small gardens, part labelled, may be seen by appointment only. *Holywell Manor*; part of Balliol, a restful, well-maintained garden of one acre [Open 10.30am – 6.30pm]. *Lady Margaret Hall*; eight acres of formal and informal, mainly designed by the Victorian architect Blomfield, also responsible for the building [Open 2 – 6pm or dusk if earlier. All visitors are requested to call at the Porter's Lodge.] *New College*; admirers of the writings of Robin Lane Fox will be able to see examples of his plantings. [Open term time 2 – 5pm, vacation 11am – 5pm. There is an admission charge of £1 during parts of the Easter and summer vacations, but this includes entry to chapel, hall, quadrangles and cloisters as well as gardens]. *Nuffield College*; small formal garden with water features [Open 9am – 7pm]. *The Queen's College*; a garden with a fourteenth-century history, today pleasantly modernised. Good herbaceous borders in Fellows' garden and statues in Provost's garden [Open 2 – 5pm]. *Rewley House*, Wellington Square, has an interesting roof garden, opened in 1986, which can be seen by appointment and on one afternoon in July for charity. *Rhodes House*, not a college and not a pretty building but an unexpectedly pleasant garden behind [9am – 5pm weekdays only]. *St Hugh's College*; an interesting 10-acre garden largely created by Annie Rogers, a Fellow, and open only by appointment. *St John's College*; landscaped in the eighteenth century and immaculately kept still. Striking in spring when bulbs in flower [Open daily, 1 – 5.30pm or dusk if earlier]. *Wadham College*; fine old trees [Open 1 – 4.30pm]. *Wolfson College*; nine acres designed around modern college buildings by Powell and Moya, open daily subject to college commitments. *Worcester College*; the only true landscaped garden in Oxford, including a lake, made from a swampy area in 1817. Brightly-coloured beds in front quad [Open term time 2 – 6pm, vacation 9am – 12 noon and 2 – 6pm].

The *University Parks*, laid out in 1864, are the perfect place for walking in all weathers and across the bridge and into Mesopotamia next to the nature reserve and woodland. The gardens near South Lodge Gate, one Edwardian with brilliant and startling colours and the other with Jekyllian subtleties of grey and silver, are well worth seeking out. [Open daily, except St Giles Fair, dawn – dusk]

ROUSHAM HOUSE ★★   23
Steeple Aston, Oxfordshire. Tel: (0869) 47110 or (0860) 360407

Cottrell-Dormer family ✻ *Not in Steeple Aston but 2m S off A4260 Oxford – Banbury road and B4030* ✻ *Parking* ✻ *Toilet facilities* ✻ *House open April to Sept, Wed, Sun and Bank Holidays, 2 – 4.30pm* ✻ *Garden open all year, daily, 10am – 4.30pm* ✻ *Entrance: £2, no children under 15*

This is much admired because William Kent's design of 1738 is effectively frozen in time. Historical enlightenment can be combined with the enchantment of the setting and the use he made of it. In fact, before Kent it was already a famous garden described by the poet Pope as 'the prettiest place for waterfalls, jetts, ponds, inclosed with beautiful scenes of green and hanging wood, that ever I saw.' Kent's design, influenced perhaps by stage scenery, created a series of effects, and the best way to view the garden is to follow these one by one, rather than to attempt to grasp the design as a whole, although it is important to follow the various effects in the order Kent intended, and for this a guidebook is necessary. By taking the effects one-by-one, a feeling for the whole will then gradually emerge. In fact this was one of the first places where the garden took in the whole estate, also 'calling-in' the surrounding countryside, to use Pope's words. There are splendid small buildings and follies, fine sculpture, water and many seats and vantage points. The walled gardens next to the house are earlier than Kent. Allow plenty of time for a visit and plan to return another year, unless you are one of those who think a garden must be a mass of multi-coloured flowers, in which case Rousham will not be your cup of tea, except in the spring when it is mass of bulbs, including noteworthy daffodils.

STANSFIELD ★   24
49 High Street, Stanford-in-the-Vale, Oxfordshire. Tel: (0367) 710340

Mr and Mrs D. Keeble ✻ *3¹/₂m SE of Faringdon, turn off A417 opposite Vale Garage* ✻ *Best season: June to Aug* ✻ *Parking in street* ✻ *Suitable for wheelchairs by consultation with owners* ✻ *Plants for sale* ✻ *Open 14th April to 22nd Sept, Tues, 10am – 4pm. Also by appointment* ✻ *Entrance: £1*

A one-acre plus plantsman's garden, not yet finished, with many island beds and borders. Large collection of plants, both for damp and dry conditions. All-year round interest in wide use of foliage and seasonal flowers, starting with species spring bulbs. Many shrubs interplanted and a new woodland area is planned. Alpines in sinks and troughs. A new scree garden has been made. Attention is focused on number and variety of plants rather than layout and design.

STONOR PARK   25
Henley-on-Thames, Oxfordshire. Tel: (049163) 587

Lord Camoys ✻ *5m N of Henley-on-Thames on B480* ✻ *Best season: June/July*

❋ Parking ❋ Teas. Party lunches by arrangement ❋ Toilet facilities ❋ Suitable for wheelchairs by special arrangement ❋ Dogs on leads ❋ Shop ❋ House open ❋ Garden open April: Sun and Bank Holiday Mon only. May, June and Sept: Wed and Sun and Bank Holiday Mons. July and Aug: Wed, Thurs, Sat (Aug only), Sun and Bank Holiday Mon, 2 – 5.30pm. Parties by arrangement, Tues, Wed or Thurs (am and pm) and Sun pm ❋ Entrance: £3, OAP £2.40, children under 14 in family parties free. Party rates on application (1991 prices)

The house, a red-brick Tudor E-shaped building, is the main attraction at Stonor Park. It is set in a bowl on the side of a hill with open parkland and large trees in front, and with flower and vegetable garden behind and to the side sheltered against the hill. Lawns behind the house lead up to a terrace with pools, stone urns and planting along the steps. Orchard with cypresses and espaliered fruit trees, lavender hedges.

SWINBROOK HOUSE   26
Swinbrook, Nr Burford, Oxfordshire.

Mr J.D. Mackinnon ❋ 2m NE of Burford on road between Swinbrook and Shipton-under-Wychwood ❋ Parking ❋ Suitable for wheelchairs ❋ Open 19th July, 2 – 6pm ❋ Entrance: £1

Here on the edge of the Wychwood Forest is a beautifully-preserved example of how the other half lived in the years between the wars. Old-fashioned shrub roses in immaculate beds, greenhouses full of peaches and vast beds of asparagus presumably reigned over by 'Uncle Matthew' with his entrenching tools. It was to Swinbrook House that the Mitfords moved after leaving Batsford. A substantial area is put over to breeding pheasants for the shoot. There is a fine walled garden and pleached fruit trees alongside the croquet lawn and everywhere ancient trees, presumably from the forest, as the house itself was not built until the late 1920s. A mile or two nearer Burford is Fulbrook, probably opening its smaller 'village' gardens on the same day and providing tea.

UNIVERSITY ARBORETUM   27
Nuneham Courtenay, Nr Oxford, Oxfordshire.

Oxford University ❋ S of Oxford on A423 ❋ Best season: May to Oct ❋ Parking ❋ Open May to Oct, Mon – Sat, 9am – 5pm, Sun, 2 – 6pm ❋ Entrance: free

The village and church of Nuneham were demolished in the 1670s in order to construct a classical landscape to be seen from the house; Oliver Goldsmith's poem 'The Deserted Village', written in 1770, may be based on that upheaval. Horace Walpole, in 1780, described the gardens, designed by 'Capability' Brown and William Mason (the poet gardener) as the most beautiful in the world. Most of those gardens were destroyed in the 1830s, and subsequently, with the house, became part of Nuneham Park Conference Centre. The remaining 55 acres of garden, now with the Botanic Garden under the University's care, include rhododendron walks, camellia, bamboo and heather collections under magnificent conifers.

WARDINGTON MANOR 28
Wardington, Nr Banbury, Oxfordshire. Tel: (0295) 750202/758481

The Lord Wardington ✳ *5m NE of Banbury off A361* ✳ *Parking* ✳ *Teas* ✳
Toilet facilities ✳ *Suitable for wheelchairs* ✳ *Plants for sale* ✳ *Open 12th April,
17th May, 16th Aug* ✳ *Entrance: £1, children free*

One of the great lawns of England spreads itself in front of this Jacobean manor
house with its wisteria-covered walls. The topiary is impeccable too, and there
are attractive borders. Away from the house, the owners have created a
flowering shrub walk leading down to a pond.

WATERPERRY GARDENS ★ 29
Nr Wheatley, Oxfordshire. Tel: (0844) 339226/339254

9m E of Oxford, 2^1/$_2$m N of Wheatley. Turn off M40 junction 8 and follow signs ✳
Parking ✳ *Refreshments: Tea shop open 10am to* ^{1}/$_2$ *hour before closing. Light
lunches, wine licence* ✳ *Toilet facilities* ✳ *Suitable for wheelchairs* ✳ *Plants for
sale in large nursery* ✳ *Shop* ✳ *Church open (Saxon origins) all year round* ✳
*Garden open daily, April to Sept, 10am – 5.30pm or 6pm at weekends; Oct to
March, 10am – 4.30pm. Closed Christmas and New Year holidays. During the
three days 16th to 19th July open only to visitors to Art in Action (enquiries (071)
381 3192)* ✳ *Entrance: Nov to Feb, 60p. March to Oct, £1.85, OAP £1.40,
children 90p, coach parties (of 15 or more) by appointment only, £1.30 per person*

Waterperry has to be included in this guide although its 20 acres are difficult to
categorize. There is a strong institutionalised/ education atmosphere going
back to the 1930s when a Miss Havergal opened up a small horticultural school.
There is also a commercial garden centre which occupies large areas of the so-
called garden, with row upon row of flowers and shrubs being grown from seeds
or cuttings. Intermixed with all this are major features of the old garden, lawns
and a substantial herbaceous border; also new beds containing collections of
alpines, dwarf conifers and other shrubs. The South Field is a growing area for
soft fruit. The Clay Bank is planted with shade lovers. Almost all the plants are
labelled and the owners describe the place as one where 'the ornamental and
the utilitarian live side by side'. The greenhouses in the nursery are interesting
too: containing a good stock of houseplants for sale, usually including orchids
and tall ficus; another, in the old walled garden, has an enormous citrus tree
(it's worth the detour just to catch the scent of blossom) and other
Mediterranean specimens, which are not for sale. Several hours need to be
spent here to do it justice and if the visitor is overpowered by the 'utilitarian'
aspect, he or she can stroll down the shady path by the little River Thame. A
guide is sold at the shop. Several Wheatley gardens are also open in May for
charity, together with Shotover House.

WESTWELL MANOR ★ 30
Nr Burford, Oxfordshire.

Mr and Mrs T.H. Gibson ✳ *2m SW of Burford off A40* ✳ *Parking in village* ✳
Teas ✳ *Plants for sale on open days* ✳ *Open for charity 19th April, 12th July
only, 2 – 6.30pm* ✳ *Entrance: £1, children 50p*

Six acres of garden divided into different 'rooms' by stone walls and topiary in yew and box surround a large house with a sixteenth-century centre, and later additions. Stone terraces with steps to different levels shelter many stone-carpeting plants, and interesting bulbs. Good potager with box and lavender hedges, and pear trees trained over hoops make you feel as if you are standing in a Kate Greenaway painting. Wild garden, herbaceous and rose gardens, and a calm lily pool flanked by peonies, and a wonderful wisteria-clad pergola.

WILCOTE HOUSE ★ 31
Wilcote, Finstock, Oxfordshire. Tel: (0993) 868606

*The Hon. Charles Cecil * 3m S of Charlbury E off B4022 * Best season: May to July * Parking * Teas on Suns and Bank Holidays only * Toilet facilities * Suitable for wheelchairs * Plants for sale on Suns and Bank Holidays only * Open 25th May to 5th June. Also 26th April, 5th July, 11th Oct, 1 – 5.30pm * Entrance: £1, children free. Conducted tours by arrangement £2 per person*

It is worth visiting this garden in May/June in order to walk down the laburnum tunnel planted as recently as 1984. The house is a splendid seventeenth/nineteenth-century copy in Cotswold stone of earlier periods and the large garden is also a period piece with extensive beds of old-fashioned roses and mixed borders. An unusual feature is the vast wild garden planted with an interesting selection of trees and intersected by grass paths. Very fine setting in this beautiful part of England. Arrive early for best plant sales. Mount Skippet (see entry) is nearby.

WOODPERRY HOUSE 32
Nr Stanton St John, Oxfordshire.

*Mr and Mrs Robert Lush * 4m E of Oxford. From Headington roundabout on ring road, take turning to Horton-cum-Studley. After 1¹/2m cross over B4027. Road is signed to Horton-cum-Studley. Woodperry House is 1/3m down this road on right * Parking * Refreshments in aid of charity * Toilet facilities * Plants for sale * Open 17th May, 21st June, 23rd Aug, 2 – 5pm. Also open to special interest groups by prior appointment * Entrance: £1, children free*

There is something here for most visitors, particularly those who want to see a five-acre garden built more or less from scratch (started c. 1987) in a style suited to the early eighteenth-century country house (not open), which Pevsner rightly described as 'strikingly beautiful'. A large formal lawned area at the back of the house looks out over Otmoor. Lime tree avenue. Elaborate beds. Stone summer houses. Beyond is a well-planted herbaceous border on one side, presumably eventually to be matched by the one opposite. Below is a very large walled vegetable garden.

WOOTTON PLACE 33
Wootton, Nr Woodstock, Oxfordshire. Tel: (0993) 811485

*Mr and Mrs H. Dyer * 3m N of Woodstock, turn E off the A34 * Parking *

Teas ✳ *Suitable for wheelchairs* ✳ *Plants for sale* ✳ *Open 12th April, 2 – 5.30pm* ✳ *Entrance: £1, children free*

A venerable mulberry tree leans to welcome you by the front door, and huge cedars and beeches dominate the lawns to the east of the house. Over 150 varieties of daffodils and spring bulbs are the great attraction here. The old walled kitchen garden has quiet charm and nostalgic atmosphere, with ancient fruit trees, roses, herbs, peonies and romneyas, mixed with vegetables, bulbs and picking borders of annuals. A warm terrace shelters a fine plumbago, passion flower, scented geraniums and agapanthus. The park to the north of the house has more fine trees. These gardens were thought to have been laid out by 'Capability' Brown. (See cover picture.)

WROXTON ABBEY   34
Wroxton, Nr Banbury, Oxfordshire. Tel: (0295) 730551

Wroxton College of Fairleigh Dickinson University of New Jersey USA ✳ *3m W of Banbury off A422* ✳ *Parking in village* ✳ *Suitable for wheelchairs* ✳ *Dogs on lead* ✳ *House (now used for academic purposes) open only by appointment* ✳ *Grounds open all year, dawn to dusk* ✳ *Entrance: free*

The historical interest of this garden and park is that in 1727 Tilleman Bobart (a pupil of Wise) was commissioned to construct a Renaissance-style garden with canals by the owners of the large Jacobean manor house, the 2nd Baron of Guildford. But by the late 1730s his son had this grassed over to convert it to the then fashionable landscape-style. Sanderson Miller designed some of the garden buildings c. 1740. The present American owners have restored much of this early landscape garden since 1978. On entering the long drive up to the house, it appears to be a conventional park, but beyond are interesting features including a serpentine river, lake, cascade which can be seen from a viewing mount, Chinese bridge, Doric temple, Gothic dovecote, obelisk, ruined arch and ice-house all restored from their derelict state. There is a rose garden and a newly-created knot garden which still needs further development. In all, the grounds cover 56 acres and offer many hours of pleasant walks. Unfortunately there is no map readily available and sign-posting is minimal.

WHEELCHAIR USERS
Please note that entries which describe a garden as 'suitable for wheelchairs' refer to the garden only. If there is a house open, it may or may not be suitable for wheelchairs.

SHROPSHIRE

Two-starred gardens are ringed in bold.

ATTINGHAM PARK   1
Attingham, Nr Shrewsbury, Shropshire. Tel: (074377) 203

*The National Trust ✱ 4m SE of Shrewsbury. Turn off A5 at Atcham ✱ Parking
✱ Licensed tearoom, 12.30 – 5pm. Picnics allowed along Mile Walk ✱ Toilet
facilities ✱ Partly suitable for wheelchairs. Electric scooter available but prior
booking essential ✱ Dogs on lead in grounds (not allowed in deer park) ✱ Shop
✱ House open 18th April to 6th Sept, Sat – Wed, 1.30 – 5pm (last admission*

4.30pm) ✳ *Grounds and park open daily except 25th Dec during daylight hours*
✳ *Entrance: £1 (house and park £3)*

The house is really the main attraction, but after a tour of it one can enjoy a half-mile walk by the River Tern with daffodils in the spring followed by azaleas and rhododendrons. In autumn, colour is provided by dogwoods and American thorns. Foundations of the old mill can be seen below the upper weir. A few perennials near the house but this is a garden mainly of large trees and shrubs.

BENTHALL HALL   2
Broseley, Shropshire. Tel: (0952) 882159

The National Trust ✳ *1m SW of Broseley off B4375, 4m NE of Much Wenlock, 8m S of Wellington* ✳ *Best season: spring and summer* ✳ *Parking 150 yards down road* ✳ *Toilet facilities* ✳ *Partly suitable for wheelchairs* ✳ *Part of house open same times as garden* ✳ *Garden open April to Sept, Wed, Sun and Bank Holiday Mon, 1.30 – 5.30pm (last admission 5pm). Parties at other times by arrangement* ✳ *Entrance: £1 (£2.20 house and gardens)*

A small garden containing some interesting plants and features and some nice topiary. George Maw and Robert Bateman both lived in the house and contributed to the garden design and plant collection. Graham Stuart Thomas was involved in the restoration work. The rose garden has some lovely plants and a small pool and there is a delightful raised scree bed. A good collection of geraniums and ground-cover plants together with a peony bed, clematis and roses through trees and shrubs create a pleasant garden to stroll through. The crocus introduced by George Maw and daffodils in spring provide interest, and the many large trees of Scots pine, beech and oak are stunning features. A monument to botanical history. Visitors should also view the house and other properties in the area.

BROWNHILL HOUSE   3
Ruyton XI Towns, Shropshire. Tel: (0939) 260626

Roger and Yolande Brown ✳ *10m NW of Shrewsbury on B4397 in the village* ✳ *Best season: end May/mid-July* ✳ *Parking at the Bridge Inn 100 yards away* ✳ *Teas* ✳ *Toilet facilities* ✳ *Plants for sale* ✳ *Open 17th, 30th, 31st May, 21st June, 18th, 19th July, 2 – 6pm and by appointment May to Aug* ✳ *Entrance: £1, children free*

This garden is a great credit to the owners who have incorporated a wide range of design features in a most difficult sloping site of one and a half acres. There are about 300 steps through the garden which includes a laburnum walk, patio with a pond, riverside beds with polygonum, astilbe and wild flowers, a bog garden with iris and primulas. Herbaceous borders, a rock garden with shrubs, a range of shrubs and conifers and a good vegetable garden and soft fruit as well as 16 different types of fruit and nut trees; also grape vines and a peach tree. The variety of features is remarkable in a garden started from scratch in 1972 but improvements are constantly being made.

BURFORD HOUSE GARDENS
(See Hereford and Worcester)

DAVID AUSTIN ROSES   4
**Bowling Green Lane, Albrighton, Nr Wolverhampton, Shropshire.
Tel: (0902) 373931**

Mr and Mrs David Austin ✳ *8m NW of Wolverhampton, 4m from Shifnal,
between the A41 and A464. Take junction 3 off M54 towards Albrighton. Turn
right at sign 'Roses and Shrubs' then take the second right (Bowling Green Lane)* ✳
Best season: late June/July ✳ *Parking* ✳ *Refreshments: teas, coffee and biscuits*
✳ *Toilet facilities* ✳ *Suitable for wheelchairs* ✳ *Dogs on leads* ✳ *Plant centre*
✳ *Garden open Feb to Nov, Mon-Fri, 9am – 5pm, Sat and Sun, 10am – 6pm,
Dec and Jan, Mon-Fri, 9am – 5pm, Sat and Sun, 10am – dusk. Closed 25th, 26th
Dec and 1st Jan*

David Austin is one of the country's leading rose breeders so this is an ideal
place for inspecting roses. There are about 700 varieties, including shrub, old
roses, climbing and species. At flowering time there is a riot of colour. They are
well displayed and elsewhere there are iris, a peony garden and hardy plants.
The nursery stocks a good range of plants other than roses. David Austin's
private garden is occasionally open to the public and a charge is made for this.

THE DOROTHY CLIVE GARDEN
(see Staffordshire)

DUDMASTON   5
Quatt, Nr Bridgnorth, Shropshire. Tel: (0746) 780866

The National Trust ✳ *4m SE of Bridgnorth on A442* ✳ *Best season: late May
but planted for spring, summer and autumn colour* ✳ *Parking* ✳ *Teas* ✳ *Toilet
facilities* ✳ *Partly suitable for wheelchairs* ✳ *Dogs on lead in garden and Dingle
only* ✳ *Plants for sale* ✳ *Shop* ✳ *House open* ✳ *Garden open 31st March to
Sept, Wed and Sun, 2.30 – 6pm (last admission 5.30pm. Special opening for pre-
booked parties only Thurs, 2.30 – 6pm* ✳ *Entrance: £1.80 (house and garden
£2.80)*

An eight-acre garden of appeal and interest with its large pool and bog garden
and the associated plants along with island beds with shrubs, azaleas,
rhododendrons, viburnum and lovely old roses. Some large specimen trees
bring an air of peace to the garden, and there are old fruit trees including
mulberry and medlars to add to the interest of old shrubs. Alas, there are no
plant labels to help identify the specimens.

ERWAY FARM HOUSE   6
Nr Ellesmere, Shropshire. Tel: (069175) 479

Mr and Mrs Alan Palmer ✳ *3m N of Ellesmere, 2m S of Overton on Dee. On*

B5068 Ellesmere – St Martins road after Dudleston Heath, turn right then second left ✳ Best season: late May ✳ Parking ✳ Toilet facilities ✳ Rare plants for sale ✳ Open Easter Sun and Mon, and last Sun of every month following until Sept, 2 – 6pm ✳ Entrance: £1, children free. Parties by appointment

It is difficult to describe adequately the wonderful range of plants this garden contains. Starting early in the year are masses of galanthus, hellebores, aconites, and Sprengeri tulips, followed by hostas, iris, peonies and roses. There are many shrubs and trees, including rare willows, under which grow lilies, alliums, hardy cyclamen and fritillarias. Other rare specimens include *Ulmus* x *hollandica* 'Wredei' and *Abutilon vitifolium*. A charming cottage garden is being made to add summer interest; other plants provide autumn colour. A true plantsperson's garden.

FARLEY HOUSE 7
Nr Much Wenlock, Shropshire. Tel: (0952) 727017

Mr and Mrs R.W. Collingwood ✳ In Much Wenlock on the A458, turn left by garage on to A4169 signed Ironbridge, garden is 1m on left ✳ Parking very limited on main road ✳ Toilet facilities ✳ Plants for sale ✳ Open by arrangement April to Oct. Coach parties welcome ✳ Entrance: £1

This one-acre garden has been created on a hillside since 1980 by the present owners, and it is interesting to see how they have gradually cleared land to create island beds containing a wide variety of plants. The garden is not yet finished. It has a cottage-garden feel and this is reflected in the plants. Paved area with alpines and raised beds and a peat bed. Small vegetable garden. Nice troughs and range of conifers. There is something of interest in this garden over many months.

FOUR WINDS
(see Wales)

GATACRE PARK 8
Six Ashes, Nr Bridgnorth, Shropshire. Tel: (038488) 211

Lady Thompson ✳ 6m SE of Bridgnorth on A58 Stourbridge – Bridgnorth road ✳ Parking ✳ Teas ✳ Toilet facilities ✳ Plants for sale ✳ Open 10th, 17th May, 2 – 6pm ✳ Entrance: £1, OAP 50p, children free. Parties by arrangement

This eight-acre garden has a wide range of features and plants. Vast rhododendrons and azaleas in the woodland area contrast with the Italianate sunken garden with a rectangular lily pool, and columnar trees and a yew arch. Island beds of shrubs and herbaceous plants provide good colour and foliage contrasts and include a vast yucca. Nearby on the lawn is a wonderful specimen of *Liriodendron tulipifera* and a large mulberry tree. Elsewhere is fascinating topiary, ranging from teapots, teddy bears and a corkscrew to the Gatacre monster. There are roses, acers, herbaceous borders, an excellent walled garden and good climbers around the house.

GLAZELEY OLD RECTORY 9
Glazeley, Nr Bridgnorth, Shropshire. Tel: (074635) 221

Mr and Mrs J.A. Goodall ∗ 3¹/₂m S of Bridgnorth on B4363 ∗ Best season: spring and July ∗ Parking by church ∗ Teas. Teas and lunch for parties by arrangement ∗ Toilet facilities ∗ Suitable for wheelchairs ∗ Plants for sale ∗ Open for parties by appointment and 5th July, 2 – 6pm ∗ Entrance: £1, children 25p

This two-acre garden was for many years a nursery and is well designed, leading from one interesting area to another, with a wonderful collection of plants. There is a heather border, paved garden, bed of potentillas, a glade garden with hellebores, hostas, alliums and agapanthus, scree bed, a bog area with primulas and rodgersias, a fern collection and several good herbaceous borders. There are imaginative colour and foliage combinations and many unusual plants; in spring masses of bulbs.

HAWKSTONE HALL 10
Weston-under-Redcastle, Nr Shrewsbury, Shropshire. Tel: (063084) 242

Redemptorists ∗ 13m NE of Shrewsbury, 6m SW of Market Drayton on A442. Enter from Marchamley ∗ Teas ∗ Toilet facilities ∗ Principal rooms of house open ∗ Garden open Spring Bank Holiday Mon and 5th to 31st Aug, 2 – 5pm. Coach parties by arrangement ∗ Entrance: £2, children 75p (house and gardens)

Fine formal gardens surrounding a Grade I Georgian mansion which is undergoing restoration. At the Hall is a colourful indoor winter garden and also a courtyard garden with ideas for those with restricted space. Set in extensive parkland, the terraced gardens include a lily pool with adjacent rockery and some beautiful old trees including a monkey puzzle. Rhododendrons provide spring colour. The owners are proud of their garden antiquities which include a large temple, an arbour (decorative iron construction soon to be thatched), a collection of stone statues depicting Our Lady of Fatima appearing to children, an ornamental sundial, and a metal mermaid on a stone rescued from the lily pool. A huge stone frog near the water basin feeds the lily pool. There are extensive woodland walks and views to the Welsh mountains.

HAYE HOUSE 11
Eardington, Nr. Bridgnorth, Shropshire. Tel: (0746) 764884

Mrs Eileen Paradise ∗ 2¹/₂m S of Bridgnorth on the B4555 Highley road. Through village of Eardington, then farmhouse 1m on left ∗ Best season: July ∗ Parking in courtyard ∗ Teas with home-made cakes by prior arrangement ∗ Toilet facilities ∗ Partly suitable for wheelchairs ∗ Plants possibly for sale ∗ Open by appointment May to 20th Sept ∗ Entrance: £1

The owner is a National Flower Demonstrator and accepts parties for demonstrations. The garden is planned to provide appropriate material and specimens. Half the vegetable garden contains foliage material. The old tennis court on the outskirts is being planted up with trailing plants. Of particular interest to flower arrangers but also to keen gardeners.

HODNET HALL ★★ 12
Hodnet, Shropshire. Tel: (063084) 202

Mr A.E.H. and The Hon. Mrs Heber-Percy ✻ *5¹/₂m SW of Market Drayton, 12m NE of Shrewsbury at junction of A53 and A442* ✻ *Best season: early summer* ✻ *Parking for cars and coaches* ✻ *Refreshments: snacks and teas* ✻ *Toilet facilities* ✻ *Partly suitable for wheelchairs* ✻ *Dogs on lead* ✻ *Plants for sale* ✻ *Shop* ✻ *Open April to Sept, Mon – Sat, 2 – 5 pm, Sun and Bank Holidays, 12 noon – 5.30pm* ✻ *Entrance: £2.25, OAP and parties per person £2, children £1*

This garden has been superbly planted to give interest through the seasons – daffodils and blossom in spring, then primulas, rhododendrons, azaleas, laburnums and lilacs, followed by roses, peonies and astilbes merging in summer with the hydrangeas and shrubs that continue until the autumn foliage and berries round off the year. There are great trees on the estate and a magnolia walk along with many unusual plants. One of the oak trees is mentioned in the Domesday Book. Arranged around a chain of lakes which comprise one of the largest water gardens in England, it is the home of a romantic bevy of black swans. Magnificent at all seasons. The walled kitchen garden is set aside for the sale of shrubs, fruit, flowers and vegetables.

LIMEBURNERS ★ 13
Lincoln Hill, Ironbridge, Shropshire. Tel: (0952) 433715

Mr and Mrs J.E. Derry ✻ *Turn off B4380 W of Ironbridge up Lincoln Hill and garden is on left at top* ✻ *Toilet facilities* ✻ *Partly suitable for wheelchairs* ✻ *Open April to Sept by appointment* ✻ *Entrance: £1, children 25p*

Walking round this delightful garden there are always surprises in store and a wealth of interesting plants to see. The wildlife garden has a wide range of trees and shrubs and the use of ground cover plants must help to reduce maintenance. Nice to see roses climbing through shrubs; the planting combinations throughout the garden are excellent. The owners have even managed to provide colour on a limestone bank. Further developments keep taking place, including an area of trees with colourful bark.

LLANYFELIN HOUSE 14
Dudleston, Nr Ellesmere, Shropshire. Tel: (069) 175 279

Martin and Pat Mundy ✻ *5m from Ellesmere, 2m from Overton on Dee. Signposted off B5068 Ellesmere – St Martins road and off B5069 Overton – St Martins road* ✻ *Parking nearby* ✻ *Teas* ✻ *Plants for sale* ✻ *Open 21st June, 12 noon – 6pm. Other times by appointment* ✻ *Entrance: £1, children 25p*

Before and after photographs show the conversion from a house perched on top of a steep empty grassy slope to one settled at the crown of terraces and areas of ground cover, which include a juniper bank. Effective use is made of surrounding trees as a background to a variety of island beds, unusual specimen trees, shrub and prostate roses and, at the top of the garden, colourful beds of flowers, shrubs and herbs. Decorative vegetable garden. Interesting and clever use of a difficult site to make an alternative garden set in beautiful countryside.

LOWER HALL ★ 15
Worfield, Nr Bridgnorth, Shropshire. Tel: (07464) 607

Mr and Mrs C.F. Dumbell ✳ *A454 Wolverhampton/Bridgnorth road, turn right to Worfield and after passing village stores and pub turn right* ✳ *Best season: May to July* ✳ *Parking in driveway or nearby roads* ✳ *Tea and biscuits for parties. Garden room available for coach party picnics. Catered events can be arranged* ✳ *Toilet facilities* ✳ *Suitable for wheelchairs* ✳ *Dogs on lead* ✳ *Plants for sale* ✳ *Open by appointment and for charity 31st May, 21st June* ✳ *Entrance: £1.50*

This modern plantsman's garden has been created by the present owners since 1964 with help from the designer Lanning Roper. The walled garden has old brick paths and fruit trees through which climb roses and clematis; over the walls the village cottages and the Tudor house provide a fine backcloth to the garden. Everywhere the use of colour combinations and plant associations is good – a red border, another of white and green, giving a cool effect. The water garden contains two weirs and the woodland garden includes rare magnolias, a collection of birch to provide bark interest, conifers, acers, amelanchiers – everything to provide all-year variety and colour.

MILLICHOPE PARK 16
Munslow, Craven Arms, Shropshire. Tel: (058476) 234

Mr and Mrs L. Bury ✳ *8m NE of Craven Arms, 11m from Ludlow on B4368 Craven Arms road* ✳ *Parking* ✳ *Refreshments for June opening date. Picnics allowed in woodland* ✳ *Toilet facilities* ✳ *Dogs on lead* ✳ *Plants for sale when available* ✳ *Open 26th April, 5th July, 2 – 6pm* ✳ *Entrance: £1.50, children 50p*

This 13-acre garden stands on the slopes of Wenlock Edge looking across to the Brown Clee Hill, and the view from the house includes a splendid artificial lake and vast trees, including a cedar of Lebanon, Douglas firs, copper beeches, Californian redwoods and an 140-foot *Abies procera*. Wandering through the woodland in spring, visitors enjoy masses of wild flowers – primroses, violets, bluebells and rhododendrons. The herbaceous borders are in the form of several small gardens surrounded by yew hedges. There is a series of small lakes and a pool surrounded by bog plants. Good pieces of sculpture and a fine old temple.

OLDFIELD 17
Nr Long Meadow End, Craven Arms, Shropshire. Tel: (0588) 672733

Mr and Mrs P. Housden ✳ *From Craven Arms take B4368 towards Clun. After 1*

*¹/₂m turn right at telephone box, then after 200 yards, turn left over cattle grid and continue on 1m * Best season: June to Oct * Parking * Teas on open day and for pre-booked parties * Toilet facilities * Partly suitable for wheelchairs * Open 5th July and parties by arrangement * Entrance: £1, children 50p*

The owners have worked hard since 1980 to create this three-acre garden with its pool and bog garden. Roses surround the house and are also used for ground cover. A range of soft fruits and fan and espalier-trained trees, a vegetable garden and old and new woodland areas. Other attractions include bee hives and bonsai trees. A new shrubbery contains some fine specimens including golden birch and there are five different oaks, *Quercus rubra*, alder and acers in the Oak Wood. The walls of an old ruin edge a delightful paved area with iris and euphorbias amongst other lovely plants. The garden continues to be developed with the aim of all year round colour.

OTELEY   18
Ellesmere, Shropshire.

*Mr and Mrs R.K. Mainwaring * From S entrance opposite convent. Near A528/495 junction 1m E of Ellesmere From N past The Mere turn left opposite convent. Drive through park to house * Best seasons: spring/summer * Parking * Refreshments * Toilet facilities * Suitable for wheelchairs if dry * Dogs * Plants for sale * Open 20th April, 25th May, 28th June, 2 – 6pm * Entrance: £1, children 50p*

A magnificent 10-acre garden set in park and farmland with glimpses of The Mere beyond surrounding trees. Extensive lawns with architectural features, interesting and old handsome trees set about the lawns. Herbaceous borders backed by high walls covered with roses, clematis and other climbing plants. White border. Walled kitchen garden. Decorative island beds. Rhododendrons, azaleas, roses, shrubs in a gracious setting. Collection of peonies flowering simultaneously. Large selection of plants for sale.

THE PADDOCKS   19
Chelmarsh Common, Chelmarsh, Nr Bridgnorth, Shropshire. Tel: (0746) 861271

*Mr and Mrs P. Hales * 3m S of Bridgnorth on Highley Road * Best season: late spring/early summer * Parking 300 yards away at The Bulls Head, Chelmarsh * Open by appointment * Entrance: £1 for charity, children free*

A contrast to the more formal garden next door, with good use of old materials to make paths, pergolas and a rockery. Typical cottage plants have been used and the garden is divided into 'room' areas. There is a stream garden with a bog area with good ideas for the amateur gardener. With the nursery attached to Dingle Bank next door, the two gardens contain a vast range of plants. A charming small rose garden has been added and a lightly-wooded wild garden is being created. Winner of the Spring Garden of the Year 1990 and 1991.

PREEN MANOR ★   20
Church Preen, Nr Church Stretton, Shropshire. Tel: (06943) 207

*Mr and Mrs P. Trevor-Jones * 5m SW of Much Wenlock on B4371, 3m turn* *right for Church Preen and Hughley and after 1¹/₂m turn left for Church Preen, over crossroads and drive ¹/₂m on right * Parking * Teas * Plants for sale if available * Open to parties by arrangement in June and July only * Entrance: £1.50, children 25p*

An exceptional garden designed by Norman Shaw with many features, and set in a park with fine old trees. The present owners have restored and replanned it and round every corner or through a gateway there is always a surprise. The gravel garden has a yellow and white border and elsewhere is a silver border. The chess garden has replaced the swimming pool and there is a pot garden filling a corner. The vegetable garden has a parterre design and each bed has variety. The bog garden is attractive, and the unusual fernery is sited amongst some ruins. One could spend a day here trying to absorb the design features and superb planting and enjoying the setting.

RUTHALL MANOR ★   21
Ditton Priors, Bridgnorth, Shropshire. Tel: (074634) 608

*Mr and Mrs G.T. Clarke * From Morville take B4368 and turn off for Ditton Priors. Weston Road from village church and take 2nd left road * Best season: Easter to Oct * Parking in adjacent field * Tea shop in village from 11am – 5pm * Toilet facilities * Suitable for wheelchairs * Plants possibly for sale * Open by appointment and for parties * Entrance: £1.20*

This one-acre garden has been cleverly designed since 1972 for ease of maintenance and planted to give pleasure to keen plant lovers. There are some unusual specimens and a collection of daphnes and birches and a group of sorbus, ilex, robinia and willows. By the pool is a collection of primulas, astilbes and iris. Good foliage and colour contrasts and something of interest all through the year. There is also a small vegetable garden and a collection of ferns.

SWALLOW HAYES ★   22
Rectory Road, Albrighton, Nr Wolverhampton, Shropshire. Tel: (0902) 372624

*Mrs Michael Edwards * 7m NW of Wolverhampton. Use M54 junction 3. Turn off A41 into Rectory Road after Garden Centre * Best seasons: May/June and autumn * Parking in drive and nearby road * Teas on open days * Toilet facilities * Suitable for wheelchairs * Dogs on lead * Plants for sale when available * Open 5th January (for National collection of witch hazel), 12 noon – 4pm, 29th April, 13th, 17th, 27th May, 7th June, 7th Oct, 2 – 6pm and for parties by arrangement * Entrance: £1, children 10p*

A delightful two-acre modern garden with many design features and a beautiful display of plants, shrubs and trees. Although planted for easy maintenance, it contains 2000 different types of plants and provides all-year interest. Alpine border divided into various soil conditions, Mediterranean wall with tender plants. Small pools, herbs, a woodland area, colour and foliage contrasts. The National collection of witch hazels and lupins and an interesting area of small gardens for one to copy at home. Vegetables and fruit trees; further developments in hand.

WESTON PARK ★ 23
Weston-under-Lizard, Nr Shifnal, Shropshire. Tel: (095276) 207

Weston Park Foundation ✳ On A5 7m W of junction 12 on M6 and 3m N of junction 3 on M54 ✳ Best season: May/June ✳ Parking ✳ Stable Tea Rooms providing home baking and estate produce. Also picnic teas ✳ Toilet facilities ✳ Partly suitable for wheelchairs ✳ Dogs ✳ Shop ✳ House open on certain occasions at additional entrance fee ✳ Garden open Easter to Sept (please enquire for dates and times) ✳ Entrance: £3, OAP and children £2

A distinctive 'Capability' Brown creation covering almost 1000 acres of delightful woodland planted with rhododendrons and azaleas, together with beautiful pools. Some magnificent trees form a handsome backcloth to many shrubs. A rose walk leads to the deer park and there is a walled garden. The rose garden by the house and the Italian parterre garden have been restored. There are many architectural features – The Temple of Diana, Roman bridge and the orangery all designed by James Paine. For children there is an adventure playground, the Weston Park Railway, a pets corner, pottery, aquarium and museum.

WOLLERTON OLD HALL 24
Wollerton, Hodnet, Shropshire. Tel: (0630) 84769, or (0630) 84756 during office hours

Mr and Mrs John Jenkins ✳ From Shrewsbury take A53 to Hodnet. Turn right towards Market Drayton, then right just after Wollerton sign. Keep right at red brick animal shelter. The garden is the third drive on left ✳ Parking ✳ Teas ✳ Toilet facilities ✳ Plants for sale ✳ Open June to Sept, Fri, 2 – 6pm and 3rd July, 2nd Aug, 2 – 6pm ✳ Entrance: £1.25, children 50p

Mrs Jenkins has returned to her childhood home and has redesigned the garden. Small gardens with individual characters have been created using brick walls, beech and yew hedges with paths made of a variety of materials. Roses and clematis scramble over arches, and the white garden is charming. A wide variety of shrubs and perennials have been cleverly planted to give foliage and colour associations, and there are many rare and unusual plants throughout the one and a half-acres.

SOMERSET

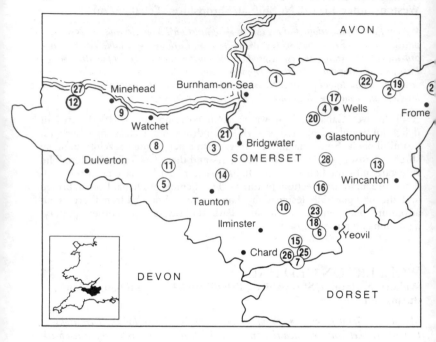

Two-starred gardens are ringed in bold.

AMBLESIDE AVIARIES AND GARDENS 1
Lower Weare, Nr Axbridge, Somerset. Tel: (0934) 732362

Mrs T.K. Pickford ✳ 1¹/₂m SW of Axbridge on A38 ✳ Best season: May ✳ Parking ✳ Coaches by appointment ✳ Refreshments: licensed restaurant, cream teas, ice-creams ✳ Toilet facilities ✳ Suitable for wheelchairs ✳ Souvenir and gift shop ✳ Open March to Oct, daily, 10am – 5pm ✳ Entrance: £1.75, OAP 90p, children over 3 75p

The trees around the large pool, which is bisected by a bridge, are really all that remain of the original plan by the owner of some 40 years ago who conceived the idea of a water garden as depicted on the 'Willow Pattern' plate. The cherry blossom reflected in the lily pond, silhouetted by willows of different varieties, give an oriental effect. The aviaries do not intrude on the water garden and the variety of ducks adds to the atmosphere of rural peace in spite of the busy road running alongside a high hedge.

AMMERDOWN HOUSE ★ 2
Kilmersdon, Radstock, Somerset.

*Lord Hylton * On the B3139, ¹/₂m off A362 Radstock to Frome road *
Parking * Open Bank Holiday Mons only: 20th April, 4th, 25th May, 31st Aug,
11am – 5pm * Entrance: £1.50*

A Bath-stone house perched on the crest of a hill with panoramic views on one side and a Lutyens garden on the other. This garden was a brilliant conception by Lutyens who wanted to link the house with the orangery. When one walks through the Italianate 'rooms' of yew and sculpture and parterre, one is unaware of the tricks of space that are being played. Massive yew planting, now mature and fully 12 foot high, creates enclosed formal areas which lead irresistably one from another – the awkward-shaped spaces between being almost entirely filled with hedging. Upkeep seems to have been pared to a minimum but the originality and grandeur remain as do some particularly nice details such as the clipped Portuguese laurels, honeysuckles trained over nice umbrellas and ancient lemon verbenas in pots in the orangery.

BARFORD PARK ★ 3
Enmore, Nr Bridgwater, Somerset. Tel: (0278) 67269

*Mr and Mrs M. Stancombe * 5m W of Bridgwater. Turn left to Enmore off the
Spaxton road from Bridgwater * Best season: May to July * Parking * Teas by
arrangement * Partly suitable for wheelchairs * Dogs on lead * House open *
Garden open May to Sept, Wed, Thurs and Bank Holidays, 2 – 6pm. Parties by
arrangement at any time * Entrance: 50p (£2 house and garden), children free*

This is a garden in the eighteenth-century style developed over the last 32 years. Set in parkland and protected by a ha-ha on three sides, it has many features. After watching the golden orfe darting around the lily pond, stroll down a sweep of lawn to a stand of tall trees. There, in the woodland glade is a carpet of many shades of primulas. The eighteenth-century walled garden is unusually situated in view of the terrace – a sweep of lawn with deep herbaceous borders on each side make a colourful vista.

THE BISHOPS PALACE 4
Wells, Somerset. Tel: (0749) 78691

*The Church Commissioners * In centre of Wells, adjacent to Cathedral * Public
parking in city car parks nearby * Light refreshments * Toilet facilities *
Bishop's Chapel open * Garden open Easter Sun to Oct, Sun, Thurs and Bank
Holidays, 2 – 5.30pm. Also 22nd July to 1st Aug, daily, 2 – 5.30pm * Entrance:
prices vary but usually minimum £1*

The ruins of the banqueting hall have been 'room scaped' with shrubs and herbaceous plants. A shrub rose garden has been planted near the water (from the wells). An unusual garden ornament has been carved from the root of a very old yew tree, depicting Adam and Eve being expelled from the Garden of Eden by an angel with a flaming sword. There are fine mature trees from plantings in the mid-nineteenth century, e.g. black walnut, gingko; and an acre of the walled garden was laid out as an arboretum to commemorate the Queen's Silver Jubilee in 1977. An interesting collection includes the Chinese foxglove tree and a European hornbeam. Allow time to enter the Cathedral.

BITTESCOMBE MANOR 5
Upton, Nr Wiveliscombe, Taunton, Somerset. Tel: (039) 87240

Mr and Mrs D. Wood ✳ *6m W of Wiveliscombe. Leave M5 at junction 25. Take B3227 Wiveliscombe road* ✳ *Parking* ✳ *Teas* ✳ *Toilet facilities* ✳ *Partly suitable for wheelchairs* ✳ *Dogs on lead* ✳ *Plants for sale* ✳ *Open Late Spring Bank Holiday Sun and Mon, 2 – 5.30pm* ✳ *Entrance: £1.50, children free*

A formal walled rose garden surrounded by shrubs – brilliant rhododendrons in tall clumps glow against the foliage of the trees growing up the hillside. The water garden is formed from a series of large pools, with water falling gently down the hillside to a small lake in a grassy setting.

BRYMPTON D'EVERCY ★ 6
Yeovil, Somerset. Tel: (0935) 862528

Mr and Mrs Charles Clive-Ponsonby-Fane ✳ *Just W of Yeovil, signposted off A30 and A3088* ✳ *Best seasons: spring and June/July* ✳ *Parking* ✳ *Home-made teas* ✳ *Toilet facilities* ✳ *Suitable for wheelchairs* ✳ *Plants for sale* ✳ *Shop* ✳ *House, vineyard, distillery, museum and parish church open* ✳ *Garden open Easter, then May to Sept, Sat – Wed, 2 – 6pm* ✳ *Entrance: £3.50 (house and gardens). Discounts for OAPs and NT members*

The quiet elegance of the forecourt, a smooth lawn edged with yellow and white herbaceous plants, hardly prepares one for the wealth of colour on which the door of the south terrace opens. Shrub roses, escallonias, hibiscus and cistus flourish in the narrow bed along the many-windowed stone wall up which climb 'Albertine' roses, wisteria, *Robinia hispida* 'Rosea', abutilons, and a creamy, variegated euonymus. On the lower terrace lilies, alstroemerias and erigerons have been planted between roses. Across the sweep of lawn the pond, fringed with iris and gunneras, shimmers with water lilies and is backed by an interesting grouping of oaks, yews, acacias, golden-leaved poplars contrasting with copper beech and *Liriodendron tulipifera*. On the north side of the house the vineyard is planted on the south-facing slope of a small hill protected from the wind by the surrounding arboretum which is now developing.

CLAPTON COURT GARDENS ★ 7
Clapton, Crewkerne, Somerset. Tel: (0460) 73220/72200

Captain S.J. Loder ✳ *3m S of Crewkerne on B3165* ✳ *Parking* ✳ *Coaches and private parties by arrangement only* ✳ *Refreshments: light lunches and teas* ✳ *Toilet facilities* ✳ *Partly suitable for wheelchairs* ✳ *Unusual plants for sale March to Oct in large centre* ✳ *Open March to Oct, Mon – Fri, 10.30am – 5pm, Sun, 2 – 5pm and Easter Sat only, 2 – 5pm* ✳ *Entrance: £3, children under 14 £1, groups of 20 or more £2.40 per person*

A very well-kept formal garden, with rare plants and shrubs clearly labelled, rubbing shoulders with some homely indigenous varieties. The woodland garden developed by the present owner on a steep slope set amongst some mature trees has a stream controlled by a series of small brooks that provides the conditions required for rarer wild plants. Many of the plants are 'Loderi' varieties and hybrids of rhododendrons which were introduced by Captain Loder's great uncle who developed the famous Leonardslee garden in Sussex. Captain Loder has completely redesigned and replanted the rose garden in a new formal design.

COMBE SYDENHAM HALL 8
Monksilver, Taunton, Somerset. Tel: (0984) 56284

Mr and Mrs W. Theed ✳ *5m S of Watchet on B3188 between Monksilver and Wiveliscombe* ✳ *Parking inc. coaches* ✳ *Refreshments: home-made lunches, cream teas* ✳ *Toilet facilities* ✳ *Plants for sale* ✳ *Shop (inc. trout from estate)* ✳ *Hall (west wing) open as garden, Mon – Fri, 11am – 4pm* ✳ *Country Park open Easter to Oct, Mon – Fri, 10am – 5pm* ✳ *Entrance: £2.80, OAP/children £1.80 (garden and country park)*

Set in a deer park, the small formal Elizabethan parterre-garden is being restored and restocked with old types of roses. The pink lavender is a source of pride to Mrs Theed who also cultivates the old herb garden. Quince trees and a peacock house create the atmosphere of a domestic garden in Tudor times.

DUNSTER CASTLE ★ 9
Dunster, Nr Minehead, Somerset. Tel: (0643) 821314

The National Trust ✳ *3m SE of Minehead on A39* ✳ *Best season: May/June* ✳ *Parking* ✳ *Refreshments in Dunster* ✳ *Toilet facilities* ✳ *Electrically-operated self-drive Batricar available for disabled and infirm* ✳ *Dogs in park only* ✳ *Shop* ✳ *Castle open April to 4th Oct, Sat – Wed, 11am – 5pm (closed Good Fri), 5th Oct to 1st Nov, Sat – Wed, 11am – 4pm* ✳ *Garden and park open Feb to mid-Dec, daily, 11am – 5pm (closes 4pm Feb and March, and Oct to Dec). Garden and park open Good Fri* ✳ *Entrance: £2.20, children under 16 £1.10 (castle, garden and park £4.30, children under 16 £2.10, pre-arranged parties £3.80 per person)*

The family which had lived here since the fourteenth century gave it to the National Trust in 1976. A very fine herbaceous border backed by rare shrubs surrounds a lawn by the keep and is well worth the steep climb to view. On the formal terraces below thrive a variety of sub-tropical plants, camellias and azaleas. There are views across to Exmoor, the Quantocks and the Bristol Channel. The park totals 28 acres in all.

EAST LAMBROOK MANOR ★ 10
Nr South Petherton, Somerset. Tel: (0460) 40328

Mr and Mrs A. Norton ✳ *2m NE of South Petherton off A303* ✳ *Parking* ✳ *Coaches by arrangement* ✳ *Refreshments: coffee and biscuits only but parties by arrangement* ✳ *Toilet facility* ✳ *Plants for sale (mailing list)* ✳ *Shop for Margery Fish publications* ✳ *Open March to Oct, Mon – Sat and Bank Holiday Sun and Mon, 10am – 5pm* ✳ *Entrance: £1.90, OAP £1.70, school age children 50p*

Margery Fish established these gardens for endangered species and the present owners have carried on her tradition. The result is an impression of luxuriant growth. The garden's ring paths are half-hidden by the profusion of plants and its controlled wilderness of colour and scent give the discerning a chance to find rare plants and shrubs.

FORDE ABBEY
(see Dorset)

GAULDEN MANOR ★   11
Tolland, Nr Lydeard St Lawrence, Somerset. Tel: (09847) 213

Mr J.H.N. Starkie ✳ *9m NW of Taunton off A358* ✳ *Parking* ✳ *Teas by arrangement for parties* ✳ *Toilet facilities* ✳ *Shop* ✳ *House open* ✳ *Open Easter Sun and Mon, and 3rd May to 6th Sept, Sun, Thurs and Bank Holidays, 2 – 5.30pm* ✳ *Entrance: £1 (house and gardens £2.50)*

Garden seats at vantage points give the visitor a chance to appreciate the many different vistas provided in this country garden which includes a bog garden, herb garden, butterfly garden and herbaceous borders of selected colour. A short walk through a woodland glade leads to a secret garden of white flowering plants. Visitors should not miss the small duck garden with carvings on the fence posts, which is near the tea house.

GREENCOMBE ★★   12
Porlock, Somerset. Tel: (0643) 862363

Greencombe Garden Trust (Miss Joan Loraine) ✳ *¹/₂m W of Porlock off B3225* ✳ *Parking* ✳ *Coaches by arrangement* ✳ *Toilet facility* ✳ *Partly suitable for wheelchairs* ✳ *Plants for sale* ✳ *Open April to July, Sat – Tues, 2 – 6pm or by appointment* ✳ *Entrance: £2, children 50p*

Created in 1946 by Horace Stroud, this garden was extended by the present owner over the last 21 years. Overlooking the Severn, set on a hillside where the sun cannot penetrate for nearly two months in the winter, it glows with colour. The formal lawns and beds round the house are immaculate and by contrast the woodland area, terraced on the hillside, provides a nature walk of great interest. A wide variety of rhododendrons and azaleas flower in the shelter of mature trees, where ferns and woodland plants flourish. No sprays or chemicals are used in the cultivation of this completely 'organic' garden which contains the National collection of polystichum.

HADSPEN GARDEN AND NURSERY ★   13
Castle Cary, Somerset. Tel: (0963) 50939

Mr N.A. Hobhouse ✳ *2m SE of Castle Cary on A371* ✳ *Parking* ✳ *Coaches by arrangement* ✳ *Teas on Sun and Bank Holidays* ✳ *Toilet facilities* ✳ *Partly suitable for wheelchairs* ✳ *Plants for sale* ✳ *Open March to 1st Oct, Thurs – Sun but open Bank Holiday Mon, 9am – 6pm* ✳ *Entrance: £2, children 50p*

The basic plan in this garden was created by Margaret Hobhouse in the Victorian gardening 'boom' days to provide a setting for the eighteenth-century hamstone Hobhouse home. Over the years the garden became overgrown and formless with an interval in the 1960s when Penelope Hobhouse endeavoured to restore some order. In the last few years the present owners have reclaimed the garden, retaining the best of the original plan and embellishing it with a variety of planting to provide colour, shape and interest. It is now a classic country house garden, with carefully colour-schemed herbaceous borders, a lily pond in a formal setting, shrub walks, a curved walled garden contrasted by wild flowers in the meadow, all framed in parkland.

HESTERCOMBE HOUSE GARDENS 14
Cheddon Fitzpaine, Taunton, Somerset. Tel: (0823) 337222

Somerset County Council ✳ *Close to the village of Cheddon Fitzpaine just N of Taunton, follow the 'Daisy' sign to the garden* ✳ *Best season: midsummer* ✳ *Parking* ✳ *Coaches by arrangement only* ✳ *Picnics on lawn* ✳ *Toilet facilities in house* ✳ *Wheelchairs limited to four main areas* ✳ *Open all year, Mon – Fri, 9am – 5pm, also May to Sept, Sat and Sun, 2 – 5pm* ✳ *Entrance: £1.50, OAP and children £1. Garden plan and guide available 50p*

This is a superb product of the collaboration between Edwin Lutyens and Gertrude Jekyll, blending the formal art of architecture with the art of plants. On a limited budget the Somerset County Council has endeavoured to maintain the gardens, respecting the colour groupings of the original designs and keeping the water courses flowing as they would have in Edwardian days. The *Oxford Companion* describes this as Lutyens at his best in the detailed design of steps, pools, walls, paving and seating. The canal, pergola and orangery are fine examples of his work. The Council's programme to restore the gardens to Gertrude Jekyll's original plant design, which they have discovered, is proceeding well. The Eastern Terrace is completed and is a good example.

LOWER SEVERALLS 15
Haselbury Road, Crewkerne, Somerset. Tel: (0460) 73234

Audrey and Mary Pring ✳ *1¹/₂m NE of Crewkerne off B3165* ✳ *Parking on road* ✳ *Teas on charity open days* ✳ *Suitable for wheelchairs* ✳ *Plants for sale* ✳ *Open March to Oct, weekdays except Thurs, 10am – 5pm, Sun, 2 – 5pm and 14th June, 12th July for charity* ✳ *Entrance: by collecting box, 50p for charity*

A typical cottage garden with herbaceous border against stone-walled house. The garden is being enlarged through stone pillars which make a frame for the view of the valley over lawn and varied shrubs, a bank of hostas and a bog garden. Specialists in herbs, geraniums and salvias.

LYTES CARY MANOR 16
Nr Somerton, Somerset. Tel: (045822) 3297

The National Trust ✳ *2¹/₂m NE of Ilchester, signposted from large roudabout on*

A303 ✳ *Best season: late June/early July* ✳ *Parking* ✳ *Suitable for wheelchairs* ✳ *Plants for sale inc. good selection of perennials* ✳ *Open April to Oct, Mon, Wed and Sat, 2 – 6pm or dusk if earlier (last admission 5.30pm)* ✳ *Entrance: £3, children £1.50*

This garden was revived by its former owner with advice from Graham Stuart Thomas. Pleasing lawns with hedges in Elizabethan style and some topiary. A wide herbaceous border along the length of a stone wall. A large orchard with naturalised bulbs and mown walks adds to the peaceful ambience. Regretfully there is no trace of the original herb garden for which Lytes Cary was famed in the sixteenth century, but a border along the south front is stocked with species of plants cultivated in those days.

MILTON LODGE ★   17
Wells, Somerset. Tel: (0749) 672168

Mr D.C. Tudway Quilter ✳ *¹/₂m N of Wells. From A39 to Bristol turn N up Old Bristol Road* ✳ *Best season: midsummer* ✳ *Car park on left before reaching drive to house but no coaches* ✳ *Teas on Sun* ✳ *Toilet facilities* ✳ *Open Easter to Oct, daily except Sat, 2 – 6pm* ✳ *Entrance: £1, children 50p. Private parties by special arrangement but no coaches*

The garden, replanted by the present owners in the 1960s, is cultivated down the side of a hill overlooking the Vale of Avalon, affording a magnificent view of Wells Cathedral. A wide variety of plants all suitable for the alkaline soil provide a succession of colours and interest during the summer season, interspersed with ancient oak, cedar and established gingko trees.

MONTACUTE HOUSE ★   18
Montacute, Yeovil, Somerset. Tel: (0935) 823289

The National Trust ✳ *4m W of Yeovil. NT signs off A3088 and A303 near Ilchester* ✳ *Best season: June to Sept* ✳ *Parking* ✳ *Refreshments: light lunches and teas* ✳ *Toilet facilities* ✳ *Suitable for wheelchairs* ✳ *Dogs on lead in park only* ✳ *Plants for sale March to mid-Dec* ✳ *National Trust shop* ✳ *House open April to 1st Nov* ✳ *Park and garden open throughout year, daily except Tues, 12 noon – 5pm. Other times by arrangement with administrator* ✳ *Entrance: £2.20 (2nd Nov to April 1993 £1) (house and garden £4.30)*

This Elizabethan garden of grass lawns surrounded by clipped yews set in terraces is a triumph of formality. Colours are provided by herbaceous borders from mid-summer. The arboretum of rare trees is so far not labelled. The gardens are surrounded by graceful parklands giving vistas and an impression of space. The house provided a backcloth for George Curzon's affair with Elinor Glyn though the tiger skin he gave her is no longer in evidence.

THE OLD RECTORY (Seaborough)
(see Dorset)

R.T. HERBS AND GARDEN   19
Kilmersdon, Radstock, Somerset. Tel: (0761) 35470

Mr and Mrs R. Taylor ✳ *6m NE of Shepton Mallet on B3139* ✳ *Best season:*

spring/summer ✻ *Public car park adjacent* ✻ *Refreshments in local pub* ✻ *Plants for sale* ✻ *Open daily, 9am – 6pm or dusk* ✻ *Entrance: donation box for charity*

This is a working garden far removed from the gracious lawns of a stately home but demonstrating the potential of a narrow plot to become a graceful and attractive garden. The wide variety of herbs mingled with herbaceous plants and wild flowers attracts bees, butterflies and insects during the summer and provides feeding grounds for wildlife during the winter months.

SEITHE 20
Godney, Wells, Somerset. Tel: (0934) 712278

John and Renata White ✻ *5m W of Wells on B3139. Turn left at Panborough* ✻ *Parking* ✻ *Teas* ✻ *Toilet facility* ✻ *Suitable for wheelchairs* ✻ *Organic plants, vegetables and dried flowers for sale* ✻ *Etching exhibition* ✻ *Open 3rd May, 16th Aug, 2 – 6pm* ✻ *Entrance: £1, children free*

From house and pond area surrounded by a distinctive range of bamboos, an arch in a towering hedge of clipped x *Cupressocyparis leylandii* leads to a garden of rich organically-grown vegetables surrounded by cologne shrubs and herbaceous plants. This unusual combination has been developed by the owners over the last 25 years from abandoned peat diggings. There have been many changes in the garden recently including pergola arches through the middle of the vegetable raised beds and a new round pond in the shape of a well head.

SHERBORNE GARDEN
(See Avon)

SOMERSET COLLEGE OF AGRICULTURE AND HORTICULTURE ★ 21
Cannington, Somerset. Tel: (0278) 652226

Somerset County Council ✻ *3m NW of Bridgwater on A39* ✻ *Parking* ✻ *Teas for parties by arrangement* ✻ *Toilet facilities* ✻ *Suitable for wheelchairs* ✻ *Plant centre* ✻ *Open daily except Mon, 2 –5pm* ✻ *Entrance: £1. Groups contact Mr Ruddle (ext. 234)*

The College was founded in 1922 in the grounds of an old Benedictine priory. Plant specialists may find here the fulfillment of their wildest expectations: the National collection of ceanothus, fremontia, wisteria, osteospermum, abutilon, phormium, cordyline and yucca. Various greenhouses reproduce the conditions – Mediterranean, alpine etc. – for house plants of a different clime. Younger gardeners will be interested in the documented development over the last few years of a butterfly garden. On the other side of the A39 from the College buildings an open area has been landscaped to include a nine-hole golf course and a putting green as well as science plots.

STON EASTON PARK ★ 22
Ston Easton, Somerset. Tel: (076121) 631

Peter and Christine Smedley ✻ *11m from Bath, 6m from Wells on A37* ✻

*Parking * Teas at hotel * Toilet facilities in hotel * Open by appointment only * Entrance: free*

Ston Easton Park is a listed Grade I Palladian house and park. The grounds were laid out and planned by Humphry Repton in 1792/3. Penelope Hobhouse is working with the Smedleys on the restoration of the park, now the grounds of their hotel. For the opportunity to study the restoration of a great eighteenth-century park in progress it is worth making an appointment to visit. A suitably impressive drive winds past old stables to the plain Palladian magnificence of the house. As always Humphry Repton made a Red Book with his proposals for improvements. There is a terrace, wide lawns, woods, cedars, beeches, oaks, willows and some new yew hedges. The glory is the view from the great Saloon – or the terrace – over the River Norr which has a bridge and cascades for the correct romantic effect. Vast kitchen garden with glasshouses, a cutting garden and yards of beautifully presented fruit and vegetables. As an example of the dedication of the restoration it took seven years to repair the kitchen garden walls, three and a half years for either side.

TINTINHULL HOUSE GARDEN ★ 23
Tintinhull, Yeovil, Somerset.

*The National Trust * 5m NW of Yeovil, 1/2m S of A303 * Parking * Teas in courtyard * Suitable for wheelchairs and special parking by arrangement * Open April to Sept, Wed, Thurs, Sat and Bank Holiday Mons, 2 – 6pm * Entrance: £2.80*

A relatively small modern garden, barely one acre, which achieves an impression of greater size with a series of vistas created under the influence of Gertrude Jekyll and Hidcote. The wide variety of plants are not labelled in order to retain the charm of a private garden but an inventory is available for interested visitors.

THE TROPICAL BIRD GARDENS 24
Rode, Nr Bath, Somerset. Tel: (0373) 830326

*Mr and Mrs D. Risdon * 5m NE of Frome, signed off A361 * Parking * Refreshments: licensed cafeteria in summer, light refreshments in winter * Toilet facilities * Suitable for wheelchairs * Clematis for sale in season * Shop * Clematis collection open all year except 25th Dec, summer 10am – 6.30pm, winter 10am – dusk (last admission 1 hour before closing) * Entrance: £3.20, OAP £2.70, children £1.60 (1991 prices)*

The gardens have been developed to provide the background and natural habitat, as far as possible, for the birds. The clematis collection was started in 1985 and is now established. Mrs Risdon is the membership secretary of the International Clematis Society (GB and Ireland Branch). The tree trail was badly damaged in the 1990 gales and had to be closed for the time being. It is expected to be open again in 1991 when a detailed guide will name the wide variety of trees.

WATER MEADOWS 25
Clapton, Nr Crewkerne, Somerset. Tel: (0460) 74421

*Mr and Mrs R. Gawen * 3m SW of Crewkerne on B3165 * Best season: May* *to June* ✳ *Parking. No coaches* ✳ *Suitable for wheelchairs when dry* ✳ *Dogs on lead* ✳ *Plants for sale* ✳ *Open Easter to Sept, daily, 9am – 5pm* ✳ *Entrance: 75p*

This garden beside a busy country road is sheltered by a very long rugosa hedge and slopes gently towards an open view across a stream. One hundred and fifty old-fashioned roses rub shoulders with vegetables and herbs providing food both for the eye and the palate. Many interesting plants and shrubs, from the dwarf *Viola cornuta* to the willow-leaved pear, will intrigue the plantsperson. The water garden, a recent development but well established, runs along the lower boundary path.

WAYFORD MANOR ★   26
Crewkerne, Somerset. Tel: (0460) 73253

Mr and Mrs R.L. Goffe ✳ *3m SW of Crewkerne off B3165 at Clapton* ✳ *Parking* ✳ *Teas for parties* ✳ *Dogs on lead* ✳ *Plants for sale* ✳ *Open 26th April, 17th, 31st May, 2 – 6pm. Parties by appointment* ✳ *Entrance: £1.50, children 50p*

A very well-maintained garden of flowering shrubs and trees, rhododendrons and spring bulbs, against the stonework of an Elizabethan house. This is a fine example of the work of Harold Peto who redesigned the garden in 1902 and whose original plans are being restored by the present owners and their dedicated gardener, 'Old' Michael. The loss of 16 mature trees and larger shrubs in the 1990 gale opened up an area which led to the discovery of a waterway previously buried. This has been cleared and now runs from the lower of a series of small pools down to a very much larger pool whose original shape had been lost by the force of peltiphyllum rhizomes pushing out the retaining stonework. Order has now been restored. Restoration of the winter garden is one of the new projects, with the introduction of more reliable dwarf trees than were available in Peto's day (such as *Cupressus sempervirens* 'Stricta'). The garden has also some rare and colourful maples.

WOODBOROUGH   27
Porlock Weir, Somerset. Tel: (0643) 862406

Mr and Mrs R.D. Milne ✳ *From A39 take B3226 towards Porlock Weir. At Porlock Vale House on right, take left tarmac lane uphill. Garden is the first on right* ✳ *Best season: May* ✳ *Limited parking. No coaches* ✳ *Dogs on lead* ✳ *Open Bank Holiday weekends in May for charity, 11am – 5.30pm and at other times by appointment* ✳ *Entrance: £1, children under 10 free*

Sturdy footwear is recommended when visiting this fascinating garden created on a steep (1 in 4) hillside with magnificent views over Porlock Bay. The wide variety of shrubs include some of the lesser-known hybrid rhododendrons and a number of Ghent azaleas. A bog garden and two pools add interest over a longer season. Mr and Mrs Milne are hoping to share with visitors their hard-won experience in garden restoration and battle with the dreaded honey fungus.

WOOTTON HOUSE ★ 28
Butleigh Wootton, Nr Glastonbury, Somerset. Tel: (0458) 42348

The Hon. Mrs J. Acland-Hood ✳ 3m S of Glastonbury. Minor road to Butleigh from Glastonbury, turn right to Butleigh Wootton. Continue through the village to house ✳ Parking in road ✳ Teas on charity day ✳ Suitable for wheelchairs ✳ Dogs on lead ✳ Open for charity and by appointment ✳ Entrance: £1 (1991 price)

The present garden design has been developed since 1900. It is a beautiful example of a private country-house garden. A terrace with a view to the Beacon Hill in the Mendips framed by herbaceous beds set in a sweep of lawn. The old-fashioned rose garden against a stone wall leads to the woodland area where anemones and fritillaries grow as well as cyclamen. In the park is a monument to Admiral Hood, a family ancestor.

STAFFORDSHIRE

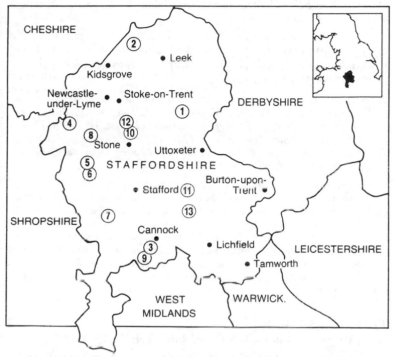

Two starred gardens are ringed in bold.

ALTON TOWERS ★   1
Alton, Staffordshire. Tel: (0538) 702200

Alton Towers ✳ From N take M6 junction 16 or M1 junction 28, from S take M6 junction 15 or M1 junction 23A. Signposted ✳ Best season: spring/summer ✳ Parking ✳ Refreshments: restaurants, kiosks, picnic areas ✳ Toilet facilities ✳ Suitable for wheelchairs ✳ Dogs on lead ✳ Shops ✳ Ruin open. Theme park open Easter to early Nov ✳ Garden open all year ✳ Entrance: end March to early Nov £10.50, OAP £4.99, children 4 – 14 £7.99, children under 4 free (theme park and gardens). Early Nov to end March £2, children £1 (theme park closed)

This fantastic garden of ornamental architecture was one of the last great follies, created in the early nineteenth century. It contains many beautiful and unusual features including the Chinese Pagoda fountain, a copy of the To Ho pagoda in Canton. The enormous rock garden is planted with a range of conifers, acers and sedums. The fine conservatory houses geraniums and other colour according to the season and the terraces have rose and herbaceous borders. There is a Dutch garden, Her Ladyship's Garden featuring yew and rose beds, the Italian garden, a yew arch walkway and woodland walks. There is water to add further beauty and interest. In addition, there are all the attractions of the pleasure park in season.

BIDDULPH GRANGE GARDEN ★ 2
Biddulph Grange, Biddulph, Stoke-on-Trent, Staffordshire. Tel: (0782) 517999 (Head gardener)

The National Trust ✳ *5m SE of Congleton, 7m N of Stoke-on-Trent. Access from A527 Tunstall road* ✳ *Best season: May/June* ✳ *Parking* ✳ *Refreshments* ✳ *Access for disabled difficult* ✳ *Shop* ✳ *Open April to 1st Nov, Wed – Fri, 12 noon – 6pm, Sat, Sun and Bank Holiday Mon, 11am – 6pm (last admission 5.30pm or dusk if earlier). 7th Nov to 20th Dec, Sat and Sun, 12 noon – 4pm* ✳ *Entrance: £3.50, children £1.75, family ticket £8.75*

One of the most remarkable and innovative gardens of the nineteenth century. Designed by James Bateman and Edward Cooke, it contains a series of smaller gardens separated by rocky outcrops, tunnels, walls and tree-lined banks. An Egyptian Garden contains a pyramid of clipped yews and stone sphinx and a stone monster. In the Chinese Garden is a pagoda, joss house and water buffalo and a fine pool. Masses of rhododendrons reflect in the waters of a lily pool, and elsewhere is a rocky glen and sunken dahlia walk. Beautiful trees form a backcloth to this most interesting garden of about 15 acres. Alton Towers (see entry) is nearby.

12 DARGES LANE 3
Great Worthy, Nr Cannock, Staffordshire. Tel: (0922) 415 064

Mrs A. Hackett ✳ *2m SW of Cannock. From A5 (Churchbridge junction) take A34 towards Walsall. First turning on right over brow of hill. House on right on the corner of Cherrington Drive* ✳ *Best seasons: spring/summer* ✳ *Parking in road* ✳ *Refreshments* ✳ *Plants for sale* ✳ *Shop selling dried flower arrangements* ✳ *Open 24th May, 14th June, 12th July, 2nd Aug, 2 – 6pm* ✳ *Entrance: £1*

Quarter-acre garden on two levels, well-stocked and of great interest to plantsmen. Attractive trees and large variety of shrubs and foliage plants as background to comprehensive collection of flowering plants and small shrubs, some unusual, even rare. Borders and island beds. Small water garden. Every inch is used to grow or set off the collection which has year-round appeal to flower-arrangers. The overall effect is attractive as well as enticing to the plant lover. Plants for sale include some more unusual ones. Mrs Hackett was West Midlands Gardener of the Year 1990.

THE DOROTHY CLIVE GARDEN ★ 4
Willoughbridge, Nr Market Drayton, Shropshire. Tel: (0630) 647237

Willoughbridge Garden Trust ✳ *7m N of Market Drayton, 1m E of Woore on A51*

between Nantwich and Stone ✱ *Parking inc. car park for disabled* ✱
Refreshments in tea room ✱ *Toilet facilities* ✱ *Partly suitable for wheelchairs* ✱
Plants for sale in certain seasons ✱ *Open April to Oct, daily, 10am – 5.30pm* ✱
Entrance: £2, children 50p

Created by the late Colonel Clive in memory of his wife with the help of distinguished gardeners including John Codrington, this garden has wide appeal because of both its design and inspired planting. The coloured guide identifies the highlights season by season. These include the rhododendrons and azaleas in the quarry garden and the pool with the scree garden rising on the hillside above it. In spring there are unusual bulbs and primulas, in summer colourful shrubs, unusual perennials and many conifers; other trees provide autumn colour. The scree garden must give gardeners many good ideas. Additional gardens to the left of the quarry garden are under construction which should be interesting to inspect next season.

ECCLESHALL CASTLE GARDENS 5
Eccleshall, Staffordshire. Tel: (0785) 850204

Mr and Mrs Mark Carter ✱ *¹/₂m N of Eccleshall on A519. 6m from M6 junction 14 or 10m from M6 junction 15* ✱ *Best season: April/May and July* ✱ *Parking* ✱ *Dogs on lead* ✱ *Open 19th April; June to Aug, Weds, and other times by prior arrangement. Also for charity 31st May, 2 – 5.30pm* ✱ *Entrance: by donation*

The entrance is along the lime avenue, probably over 200 years old; there are many other old trees in the grounds, and new ones are being planted. The 650-year-old walls of the moat garden and the beautiful arches of the bridge and the renovated fourteenth-century tower are features of this old-world garden. The rose garden, espalier pear trees, rows of indigenous hornbeam, herbaceous borders and masses of rhododendrons create a sense of tranquillity. At present there is some disruption as work goes on to restore the garden to its former glory, but with a visit to the William and Mary mansion included one can enjoy its charm nonetheless.

HEATH HOUSE 6
Nr Eccleshall, Staffordshire. Tel: (0785) 280318

Dr and Mrs D.W. Eyre-Walker ✱ *3m W of Eccleshall. Take B5026 towards Woore. At Sugnall turn left and after 1¹/₂m turn right immediately by stone garden wall. After 1m straight across crossroads and the garden is on right in few yards* ✱ *Limited parking* ✱ *Teas* ✱ *Toilet facilities* ✱ *Plants for sale when available* ✱ *Open 17th May, 9th Aug, 2 – 5pm* ✱ *Entrance: £1.50, children free*

A one and a half-acre garden round a country house with varied features, including a delightful bog garden and wide herbaceous borders with good plantings to provide a succession of colour. A fruit and vegetable garden, an old mulberry tree, and rose border. The woodland area with various ground-cover plants make a good contrast to the formal front garden. There are large shrubs and a good selection of unusual plants.

LITTLE ONN HALL 7
Church Eaton, Near Stafford, Staffordshire. Tel: (0785) 840154

Mr and Mrs I.H. Kidson ✱ *6m SW of Stafford, 2m S of Church Eaton, midway*

between the A5 and A518 ✳ *Parking* ✳ *Teas* ✳ *Partly suitable for wheelchairs*
✳ *Open 17th May, 14th June, 2 – 6pm* ✳ *Entrance: £1.50, children 50p*

Entering this six-acre garden the driveway is flanked with long herbaceous borders backed by yew hedges and elsewhere are more herbaceous borders. The large rose garden has standards, shrub and hybrid teas. An unusual-shaped pool known as the 'Dog Bone' has water lilies and elsewhere in the garden are bog plants. Since 1971 the present owners have been planting new trees and are trying to maintain the original design by Thomas H. Mawson of Windermere. There are many rhododendrons, spring bulbs and large beeches and conifers thus ensuring colour for quite a long season. Some areas are somewhat overgrown, but the moat garden gives the garden a sense of mystery and charm.

MANOR COTTAGE 8
Chapel Chorlton, Nr Newcastle-under-Lyme, Staffordshire. Tel: (0782) 680206

Mrs Joyce Heywood ✳ *From A51 Nantwich – Stone road turn behind Cock Inn at Stableford. House on village green* ✳ *Parking on road around the village green* ✳ *Toilet facilities* ✳ *Suitable for wheelchairs* ✳ *Plants for sale* ✳ *Open May to Sept by appointment* ✳ *Entrance: £1.25, children 50p*

This two-thirds of an acre garden has been created by the present owner over several years and is beautifully designed with excellent colour combinations and varieties of foliage, including many variegated forms. It is a flower arranger's paradise with a wide range including collections of ferns, geraniums, hellebores, grasses and hostas. Small paths lead one to find beauty round each corner, and there are roses climbing through old fruit trees and a good range of conifers and a lovely alpine area. All year round colour and interest.

MOSELEY OLD HALL 9
Moseley Old Hall Lane, Fordhouses, Wolverhampton, Staffordshire. Tel: (0902) 782808

The National Trust ✳ *4m N of Wolverhampton. Traffic from S on M6 and M54 take junction 1 to Wolverhampton. Traffic from N on M6 leave motorway at junction 11 then take A460. Coaches must go on A460* ✳ *Best season: June/July* ✳ *Refreshments: in tearoom. Lunches for parties if pre-booked* ✳ *Shop* ✳ *House open (Elizabethan house where Charles II hid after the Battle of Worcester)* ✳ *Garden open April to Oct, Wed, Sat and Sun (and Tues in July and Aug), 2 – 5.30pm. Also Bank Holiday Mons, 11am – 5pm* ✳ *Entrance: £2.80, children £1.40, family ticket £7 (house and garden)*

A garden mainly for the specialist interested in old plants as all specimens are seventeenth-century except for a few fruit trees. The knot garden is from a design of 1640 by the Reverend Walter Stonehouse. A wooden arbour is covered with clematis and *Vitis vinifera* 'Purpurea'. The fruit trees include a mulberry, medlars and a morello cherry. The walled garden has topiary and herbaceous borders, and fritillaries grow in the nut walk. There is a small herb garden and boles for bees. Interesting to see plants grown in former days to provide dyes and for cleansing and medicinal purposes.

OULTON HOUSE 10
Oulton, Nr Stone, Staffordshire. Tel: (0785) 813556

Mr and Mrs J.E. Bridger ✻ ¹/₂m NE of Stone. From Stone take the Oulton road and after the Oulton village sign turn left. After passing a few houses turn right up a long drive ✻ Parking ✻ Teas ✻ Toilet facilities ✻ Plants for sale ✻ Open 5th July, 2 – 6pm and by appointment during first two weeks of July ✻ Entrance: £1.60, children 75p

This three-acre garden with fine views has been developed by the present owners over 15 years and is surrounded by parkland; a range of large trees provides shelter for the garden. A conservatory contains vines, camellias and roses, and large greenhouses have nectarines, figs and peaches. There is a rhododendron walk, large rockery, herbaceous borders containing interesting colour combinations and a wide range of plants including geraniums, delphiniums, euphorbias and astrantias. There are masses of old shrub roses, a grey and silver border by the house, which has clematis and roses climbing its walls. There is a patio area, a golden corner, white area and a large vegetable and fruit garden. Although not a weed-free garden, there is plenty to delight the eye and it is hoped it may be open more often as spring bulbs must be a delight to see. Something of interest all summer.

SHUGBOROUGH ★ 11
Great Haywood, Milford, Staffordshire. Tel: (0889) 881388

The National Trust ✻ 6m E of Stafford on A513 ✻ Best season: July ✻ Parking ✻ Refreshments: lunches and snacks in tea room, also picnic areas ✻ Toilet facilities ✻ Suitable for wheelchairs ✻ Dogs on lead in park only ✻ Shop ✻ House, museum and adjacent farm open at same time as gardens ✻ Garden open 27th March to 30th Oct, daily, 11am – 5pm. Open for pre-booked parties all year round from 10.30am ✻ Entrance: £1 per vehicle to parkland. House, museum and farm £7.50 (OAP £5)

Of interest to garden historians because Thomas Wright of Durham worked here, and because there are many buildings and monuments ascribed to James 'Athenian' Stuart and built for Admiral Anson from the 1740s onwards. These are some of the earliest examples of English neo-classicism and there is also an early example of chinoiserie based on a sketch made by one of the officers on Admiral Anson's voyage round the world. However, the buildings are 'somewhat randomly scattered rather than sited according to a programme' as at Stourhead, according to the *Oxford Companion*. As for the garden, the Victorian layout was revitalized for the Trust in the mid-1960s by Graham Stuart Thomas who designed a rose garden with various elements in the French style, with roses appropriate to the period. There is also a woodland walk.

TRENTHAM PARK GARDENS 12
Trentham, Stoke-on-Trent, Staffordshire. Tel: (0782) 657341

Country Sports International ✻ On A34 S of Stoke-on-Trent. 2m from M6 *junction 15 * Best season: summer * Parking * Refreshments * Toilet facilities * Suitable for wheelchairs * Dogs on lead * Garden centre and conference centre with restaurant facilities adjacent * Open 17th April to 4th Oct, 11am – 7pm * Entrance: £2.50, OAP and children £1.50. Half price after 6pm (1991 prices)*

These 400 acres of parkland were designed by 'Capability' Brown. Nesfield added a large Italian garden and Sir Charles Barry laid out formal gardens for the Duke of Sutherland. The gardens have been greatly simplified but still retain many features such as Brown's large lake on which one can now water sport or go boating. Rose garden and displays of bedding plants, a good selection of shrubs including hebes, potentillas and buddleias. Magnificent trees both alongside the River Trent, which flows through the gardens, and in the woodland area by the lake. The Italian garden has masses of colour from annuals and also some yew trees. A clematis walk has been replanted, but the rock garden needs some attention. A good place for a family day-out as there are picnic areas, a riding school with pony rides, a children's play area, wildfowl pens and a Shire and Craft Centre. There is a Video Gallery along with a newly opened Nature Trail and Heritage Trail.

WOLSELEY GARDEN PARK ★ 13
Wolseley Bridge, Stafford, Staffordshire. Tel: (0889) 574888; 24 hour information line (0889) 574766

*Sir Charles and Lady Wolseley * At junction of A51 with A513 between Rugeley and Stafford * Parking * Refreshments * Toilet facilities * Suitable for wheelchairs * Plants for sale at Cramphorn garden centre adjacent * Open daily. Times vary seasonally but 10am – 6pm in summer * Entrance: charges seasonally variable, advertised*

An outstanding new 50-acre garden development as part of the owners' plan to make the site a major leisure and educational centre. Important features include a two-acre walled rose garden, a water bog garden with broad walk, rockery, a collection of willows, a large new lake set in a water meadow, a woodland spring garden with flowering shrubs and bulbs. There is a scented garden for the particular enjoyment of the blind and partially sighted and a winter garden aimed at giving colour Nov – March. Similar 'theme' gardens are being developed by the team of designers. Summer visitors will also be intrigued by the sight of the archaeologists excavating the remains of the twelfth-century castle.

SUFFOLK

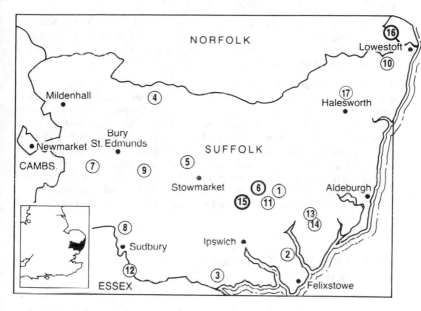

Two-starred gardens are ringed in bold.

AKENFIELD
1 Park Lane, Charsfield, Woodbridge, Suffolk. Tel: (047337) 402

*Mrs Peggy Cole ✱ 3m W of Wickham Market on B1078 ✱ Plants for sale ✱
Open end May to Sept, daily, 10.30am – 7pm ✱ Entrance: £1, OAP 75p*

Akenfield, formerly a council house, has a quarter of an acre cottage garden full of charm, and overflowing with flowers and vegetables. To one side the front garden is planted with roses and bedding plants, to the other a small honeysuckle arch leads to a patio with containers of flowers, hanging baskets – and a shed full of home-made wines which is an irresistible attraction to robins who nest among the bottles. Opposite the patio is a tiny water garden complete with waterfall and wishing well. The back garden is divided in two; to one side is a vegetable garden with about 30 different kinds of vegetables and a hen house at the far end. On the other side there are two large greenhouses, overflowing with pot plants, tomatoes and cucumbers. Beyond are small gardens connected

1

by archways, apple trees and a grape vine; hanging baskets and even bottles hold more plants.

BUCKLESHAM HALL ★ 2
Bucklesham, Ipswich, Suffolk. Tel: (0473) 659263

Mr and Mrs P.A. Ravenshear ✳ *6m E of Ipswich, ¹/₂m E of Bucklesham village.*
Entrance opposite and just N of Bucklesham primary school ✳ *Parking. Coaches by appointment* ✳ *Refreshments by special arrangement* ✳ *Plants for sale* ✳ *Shop*
✳ *Open by appointment* ✳ *Entrance: £2, OAP and children £1.50*

The great interest of Bucklesham is how these five acres of interlocking gardens, terraces and lakes have been created from scratch by the present owners since 1973. Round the house are secret gardens so packed with flowers that no weed could survive; newly planted beds of old-fashioned roses overflow their borders, and a courtyard garden has been created with the use of every kind of container. Descending terraces of lawns, ponds and streams lead to the woodland and beyond; round each corner is a new vista. Skill, wide horticultural knowledge and imagination have enabled Mr and Mrs Ravenshear to achieve their aim of displaying plants, shrubs and trees of interest to the plantsman in tranquil surroundings appealing to the layman, all with minimum maintenance.

EAST BERGHOLT LODGE 3
Via Colchester, Suffolk. Tel: (0206) 298278

Captain C. Wake-Walker RN ✳ *Halfway between Colchester and Ipswich on A12. Take B1070, first right and through white gate at crossroads* ✳ *Parking* ✳ *Teas and picnic area* ✳ *Toilet facilities* ✳ *Partly suitable for wheelchairs* ✳ *Dogs on lead* ✳ *Plants for sale* ✳ *Open by appointment and some Suns in May and June, 2 – 6pm or as arranged* ✳ *Entrance: £1, OAP 50p, children under 12 free*

The gardens at East Bergholt are rather wild and informal but beautiful, with terraced, semi-formal areas developed by the family since 1912, full of old-fashioned roses. Snowdrops, daffodils, bluebells and many wild flowers lead to woodland where damage by the 1987 gales is still being cleared. Walking is quite an adventure but the paths and rides lead the visitor to discover over 350 different varieties of trees and shrubs grown in a natural setting teeming with wildlife.

EUSTON HALL ★ 4
Euston, Thetford, Suffolk. Tel: (0842) 766366

The Duke and Duchess of Grafton ✳ *3m S of Thetford on A1088* ✳ *Best season: June and July* ✳ *Parking* ✳ *Refreshments* ✳ *Toilet facilities* ✳ *Suitable for wheelchairs (garden, shop and tearoom only)* ✳ *Plants for sale* ✳ *Shop* ✳ *House open* ✳ *Garden open 4th June to 24th Sept, Thurs, 2.30 – 5pm, and 28th June and 6th Sept, 2.30 – 5pm* ✳ *Entrance: £2.25, OAP £1.50, children 50p, parties of 12 or more £1.50 per person*

Fronted by terraces, the Hall stands among extensive lawns and parkland along a winding river, the work of William Kent in the 1740s, (followed by 'Capability' Brown) as is the splendid domed temple isolated on an eminence to the east, and also the pretty garden house in the formal garden by the house, developed by the present Duke. The pleasure grounds, laid out in the seventeenth century by John Evelyn, have grown into a forest of yew but straight rides trace out the original formal layout. Also from this period are the stone gate piers which, together with the remnants of a great avenue, mark the original approach to the house. A small lake reflects the house across the park, and there are many fine specimen trees and a wealth of shrub roses.

HAUGHLEY PARK ★   5
Nr Stowmarket, Suffolk. Tel: (0359) 40205

Mr A.J. Williams ✳ *4m NW of Stowmarket, signposted Haughley Park (not Haughley) off A45* ✳ *Parking. Coaches by appointment* ✳ *Picnics in grounds* ✳ *Toilet facilities inc. disabled* ✳ *Suitable for wheelchairs* ✳ *Dogs on lead* ✳ *House open* ✳ *Garden open May to Sept, Tues, 3 – 6pm* ✳ *Entrance: £2, children £1*

A hundred acres of rolling parkland edged by 50 more acres of woodland surround the seventeenth-century Jacobean mansion. Unexpected secret gardens edged by clipped hedges or flint and brick walls hide their immaculate flower beds, climbers and flowering shrubs; each garden has its own character. The main lawn is surrounded by herbaceous borders, with, at the end, a splendid lime avenue drawing the eye across many miles of open countryside. Rhododendrons, azaleas and camellias grow on soil which is, unexpectedly for Suffolk, lime-free. The trees include a splendid *Davidia involucrata*, a 40 foot-wide magnolia and a flourishing oak, over 30 foot in girth, reputed to be 1000 years old. Beyond is the walled kitchen garden, the greenhouses and the shrubbery. In spring the broad rides and walks through the ancient woodland reveal not only the newly planted trees, specimen rhododendrons and other ornamental shrubs but 10 acres of bluebells and, more remarkably, two acres of lilies-of-the-valley.

HELMINGHAM HALL ★★   6
Stowmarket, Suffolk. Tel: (047339) 217/363 (Contact Mrs McGregor)

Lord Tollemache ✳ *9m NE of Ipswich on B1077. 6m E of A45 on B1078 then signposted* ✳ *Parking* ✳ *Teas in coach house, picnic facilities* ✳ *Toilet facilities* ✳ *Suitable for wheelchairs (garden but not coach house)* ✳ *Dogs on lead* ✳ *Plants for sale* ✳ *Gift shop. Safari rides to see deer, Highland cattle and Soay sheep* ✳ *Open 3rd May to 13th Sept, Sun, 2 – 6pm* ✳ *Entrance: £2, OAP £1.80, children £1.10, parties of 30 or more £1.60 per person*

The double-moated Tudor mansion house of great splendour and charm, built of warm red brick, stands in a 400-acre deer park. A nineteenth-century parterre, edged with a magnificent spring border, leads to the Elizabethan kitchen garden which is surrounded by the Saxon moat with banks covered in daffodils. Within the walls the kitchen garden has been transformed into an enchanting garden most subtly planted; the meticulously maintained herb-aceous borders and old-fashioned roses surround beds of vegetables separated by arched tunnels of sweet peas and runner beans. Beyond is a meadow garden with, leading from it, a yew walk with philadelphus and shade-loving plants. On the other side of the Hall is a newly created garden dating from 1982. Designed by Lady Salisbury and planted by the Tollemaches, it is an historical knot garden and herb garden, with a magnificent collection of shrub roses underplanted with campanulas and geraniums, framed by a yew hedge. All the plants are chosen to be contemporary with the house.

ICKWORTH   7
The Rotunda, Horringer, Bury St Edmunds, Suffolk. Tel: (0284) 735270

*The National Trust * 3m SW of Bury St Edmunds, W of A143 * Car and coach park. Disabled drivers may park near house * Refreshments: restaurant in house when open * Toilet facilities in house * Suitable for wheelchairs but paths are gravel and access to shop and restaurant via steps * Shop * House open * Garden open 28th March to April, Sat, Sun and Bank Holidays, 1.30 – 5.30pm (last admission 5pm). May to Sept, daily except Mon and Thurs, 1.30 – 5.30pm (last admission 5pm). Oct, Sat and Sun, 1.30 – 5.30pm. Park all year, daily, 7am – 7pm * Entrance: £1.50 (house and garden £4.10), parties of 15 or more £3.50 per person*

Until recently the gardens at Ickworth were disappointing but over the last few years there have been some exciting changes. Research has shown that the earliest plantings appear to have been an unusual attempt to re-create a realistic Italian landscape to complement the emphatically Italian building. Much of what the visitor sees today is the recent restoration of this theme. Cypress and other sharp Mediterranean trees punctuate secret gardens surrounded by newly planted hedges and the main path to the south terrace is bordered with the evergreen shrub phillyrea, which will be clipped to window height. The south garden is further enclosed by a fine terrace which has a wonderful view of the garden and surrounding parkland. The north gardens, to the front of the house as you drive up, were largely planted in the 1870s and have now been considerably re-planted following general neglect and the 1987 gales. Although many of the great trees still remain, there has been an impressive planting of cedars to restore a unique feature – the cedar woodland as well as a small arboretum. The north gardens are at their best in the spring months with lawns of spring bulbs and wild flowers.

MELFORD HALL ★   8
Long Melford, Sudbury, Suffolk. Tel: (0787) 880286

*The National Trust. Sir Richard Hyde Parker, Bart * E side of A134, 14m S of Bury St Edmunds, 3m N of Sudbury * Parking * Refreshments in Long Melford, picnics in car park * Toilet facilities by main entrance * Mostly suitable for wheelchairs, one wheelchair provided. Disabled driven to Hall * House open with special Beatrix Potter exhibition * Garden open April to Sept, Wed, Thurs,*

Sat, Sun and Bank Holidays, 2 – 5.30pm; Oct, Sat and Sun only ＊ *Entrance: £2.40 (principal rooms and garden) (1991 price)*

This magnificent sixteenth-century Hall of mellow red brick is set in a park and formal gardens. A plan by Samuel Pierse of 1613 shows that the park was separated from the Hall by a walled enclosure outside which was the moat. Part of this is now the sunken garden. The avenue at side of the house is currently being replanted with oak grown from acorns taken from the existing trees. The octagonal brick pavilion, a rare and beautiful example of Tudor architecture, on the north side of the path, overlooks the village green and the herbaceous borders inside the garden which are being restored to their original Victorian and Edwardian design and planting. Outside the pavilion are clipped box hedges and a bowling green terrace which lead past dense shrubbery. The garden has many good specimen trees including the rare Oriental tree *Xanthoceras sorbifolium*. Great domes of box punctuate the lawns and an interesting detail is the arrangement of yew hedges and golden yew to the north of the house. Outside the walls are topiary figures. Round the pond and fountain are beds originally planted with herbs in 1937 and now being gradually improved. Kentwell, also near Long Melford, is open at specified times in the summer, and has a range of 'period' gardens.

NETHERFIELD HERBS 9
37 Nether Street, Rougham, Nr Bury St Edmunds, Suffolk. Tel: (0359) 70452

Ms L. Bremness and J.R. Lowe ＊ *Extremely difficult to find. 4m SE of Bury St Edmunds between the A45 and the A134. Aim for Rougham Post Office and ask for directions* ＊ *Parking. No coaches* ＊ *Plants for sale* ＊ *Open daily, 10.30am – 5.30pm (best to telephone first)* ＊ *Entrance: free*

Twisting lanes through beautiful unspoilt countryside eventually bring the visitor to a small, early cottage, charmingly restored, buried in a garden full of specialist herbs. Box hedges outline the beds in which culinary, medicinal, cosmetic, aromatic and decorative herbs and perennials grow in exotic confusion. Over 100 varieties of herb plants are for sale – as well as books on how to use and grow them; herb pillows, sachets and pot pourri, essential oils and herbal teas.

NORTH COVE HALL 10
North Cove, Beccles, Suffolk. Tel: (050276) 631

Mr and Mrs B. Blower ＊ *3¹/₂m E of Beccles, 50 yards off A146 Lowestoft road* ＊ *Best season: summer* ＊ *Parking* ＊ *Teas* ＊ *Toilet facilities* ＊ *Suitable for wheelchairs* ＊ *Dogs on lead* ＊ *Plants for sale* ＊ *Open 28th June and probably 5th July, 2.30 – 6pm and by appointment* ＊ *Entrance: £1, OAP 70p, children free*

Climbing roses adorn the eighteenth-century house which is set in lawns with parkland beyond. Belts of trees and shrubs, including shrub roses, hide a large deep pool with steeply-sloping grassy banks. There are many conifers here, ranging from a border of dwarf forms to ancient yews and cedars. Beyond the pool are herbaceous borders and kitchen garden, backed by high brick walls. A woodland walk runs outside the walls – a mature davidia is among the trees to be seen here.

OTLEY HALL 11
Otley, Ipswich, Suffolk. Tel: (0473) 890264

*Mr and Mrs J.G. Mosesson * 8m NE of Ipswich, 1/2m from centre of Otley * Parking * Refreshments * Toilet facilities * Suitable for wheelchairs * Dogs on lead * House open * Garden open Bank Holiday Suns and Mons April to Sept (except May Day Bank Holiday), 2 – 6pm and all year by appointment for parties of 30 or more * Entrance: £3, children £2*

One of the most remarkable small houses in Suffolk, the romantic fifteenth-century Otley Hall, a Grade I listed building, is surrounded by 10 acres of formal and informal gardens. The house is moated; flowers tumble down the banks edged with flowering shrubs and ancient trees; behind is a grassy walk widening here and there into formal and informal gardens, an orchard and two romantic nutteries. Elegant black swans enhance the beauty of two medieval fish ponds, linked by a formal canal, which face the south entrance of the house. On the far side is a large mound with views over woodland and surrounding countryside. The gardens were originally designed by Frederick Inigo Thomas in 1915 and were influenced by the French eighteenth-century style; today the layout and planting, which dates only from the 1960s, provide an authentic and enchanting setting for the ancient manor house.

TELEPHONE NUMBERS
Except where owners have specifically requested that they be excluded, telephone numbers to which enquiries may be directed are given for each property. To maintain the support and cooperation of private owners' it is suggested that the telephone be used with discretion. Where visits are by appointment, the telephone can of course be used except where written application, particularly for parties, is specifically requested. Code numbers are given in brackets. For the Republic of Ireland phone 010353 followed by the code (Dublin is 1) followed by the subscriber's number. In all cases where visits by parties are proposed, owners should be advised in advance and arrangements preferably confirmed in writing.

PARADISE CENTRE 12
Lamarsh Bures, Suffolk. Tel: (0787) 269449

*Hedy and Cees Stapel-Valk * Through village of Lamarsh, lane opposite white Georgian house, on right up lane * Parking * Refreshments and picnic area * Toilet facilities * Plants for sale * A paddock with unusual pets will amuse the children * Open Easter to Nov 1st on Bank Holidays, Sats and Suns, 10am – 5pm, and by appointment * Entrance: £1, children 80p*

A nursery specialising in unusual plants and bulbs, especially those which are shade-loving, naturalizing in a sloping five-acre garden, attractively laid out amongst the trees and hills of the lovely Stour Valley. In autumn the garden is carpeted with autumn crocus, including the double variety and sweeps of cyclamen leading down to three ponds full of golden orfe and Koi carp. The banks are edged with bog plants and giant gunnera. Children will particularly enjoy the many ornamental duck, the African pygmy goats and other wildlife.

THE ROOKERY 13
Eyke, Woodbridge, Suffolk. Tel: (0394) 460226

*Captain and Mrs R. Sheepshanks * 5m E of Woodbridge. Turn N off B1084 Woodbridge – Orford road when sign says Rendlesham 2 * Parking * Refreshments on charity days * Suitable for wheelchairs * Plants for sale on charity days * Open by appointment and 3rd, 31st May, 28th June, 2 – 6pm * Entrance: £1*

The gales which devastated so many fine gardens had occasionally the unexpected advantage of opening up large areas which were subsequently, as at the Rookery, planted as an arboretum with many rare specimen trees. Captain and Mrs Sheepshanks have designed a garden which is landscaped on differing levels, providing views and vistas; the visitors' curiosity is constantly aroused as to what is round the next corner. A small pond, a bog garden, shrubbery and evergreen walk, spring bulbs and large collection of cornus add to the general interest. The old vegetable garden is now a flourishing vineyard of one acre.

RUMAH KITA 14
Church Lane, Bedfield, Woodbridge, Suffolk. Tel: (0728) 76401

*Mr and Mrs Dickings * 2¹/₂m NW of A1120 between Earl Soham and Saxtead * Parking * Teas * Suitable for wheelchairs * Open 28th June, 3rd Aug, 6th Sept, 2 6pm * Entrance: £1*

A garden full of unusual plants and unusual features. The two-acre site is divided into many different styles of garden, bordered by mixed formal/informal hedges. Unusual knot garden using pots to give added height. Formal water garden is a surprising feature in an otherwise informal setting. Beautiful use of half-hardy perennials. A recent bed is planted with osteospermums and verbenas giving a marvellously colourful display. Some interesting plant combinations – a garden to inspire the amateur plant-hunter.

SHRUBLAND HALL ★★ 15
Coddenham, Suffolk. Tel: (0473) 830404

*Lord de Saumarez * 4m N of Ipswich. Turn off A45 to B1113 at Claydon * Parking * Refreshments and picnic area in car park * Toilet facilities * Suitable for wheelchairs * Plants for sale * Open 19th July, 2 – 6pm * Entrance: £1.50*

The magnificence of Shrubland Hall is reflected in the Victorian gardens, laid out by Sir Charles Barry and later modified by William Robinson. They are amongst the most important of their type remaining in England. From the upper terrace outside the house one descends by a stunning cascade of a hundred steps and descending terraces to a garden of formal beds, fountain and eye-catcher arch. Beyond is the wild garden which merges into the woods and is bordered by the park with its many fine trees, some reputed to be 800 years old. The gardens are punctuated by a series of enchanting follies ranging from a Swiss cottage to an alpine garden and magnificent conservatory. Lord and Lady de Saumarez have an extensive programme of restoration which includes the box maze and the old dell garden. Many trees blown down in the gales are being cleared and replaced.

SOMERLEYTON HALL ★★ 16
Nr Lowestoft, Suffolk. Tel: (0502) 730224/730308

Lord and Lady Somerleyton ✳ *8m from Yarmouth, 6m NW of Lowestoft off B1074 signposted* ✳ *Parking* ✳ *Teas and picnics* ✳ *Toilet facilities inc. disabled* ✳ *Suitable for wheelchairs* ✳ *Gift shop* ✳ *House open. On certain days the miniature railway runs* ✳ *Open Easter Sun to 27th Sept, Thurs, Sun and Bank Holidays, July and Aug, Tues – Thurs and Sun, 2 – 5.30pm* ✳ *Entrance: £3.40, OAP £2.70, children £1.80, parties of 15 or more £2.70 per person, children £1.50*

An Elizabethan house extensively rebuilt in the mid-nineteenth century as a grand Italianate palace and the gardens splendidly reflect this magnificence with 12 acres of formal gardens, a beautiful walled garden, an aviary and a loggia surrounding a sunken garden displaying statues from the old, now demolished, winter garden. A major programme of replanting and restoration has included replacing many of the great trees in the park which were lost in the gales and cutting back the overgrown yews of the maze, originally laid out by William Nesfield in 1846. Not to be missed are the extraordinary peach cases and ridge-and-furrow greenhouse, designed by Sir Joseph Paxton, and now containing peaches, grapes and a rich variety of tender plants. The Victorian kitchen garden and a museum of gardening are being developed.

ST STEPHENS COTTAGE 17
Spexhall, Nr Halesworth, Suffolk. Tel: (0986) 873394

Mr and Mrs D. Gibbs ✳ *2m N of Halesworth. From the A144 Bungay – Halesworth road take the crossroad at Spexhall marked 'To Spexhall Church and village hall'. St Stephens is the first cottage on the left* ✳ *Best seasons: spring and summer* ✳ *Parking* ✳ *Teas* ✳ *Suitable for wheelchairs* ✳ *Plants for sale* ✳ *Open 19th, 20th April, 3rd, 4th, 10th, 23rd, 24th, 25th May, 6th, 7th, 27th, 28th June, 25th, 26th July, 5th, 6th, 27th Sept, 10am – 5pm* ✳ *Entrance: 50p*

This informal garden of one acre, with mixture of mature trees and newly-planted island beds, is full of surprises and very different styles. The island beds are packed with unusual plants, including some exceptionally rare specimens; the natural pond leads to a new bog garden surrounded by a small woodland area. There is a more formal area overlooking the bog garden. The plants thrive – some in very extreme conditions.

SURREY

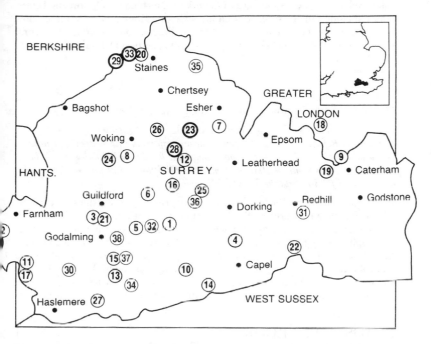

Two-starred gardens are ringed in bold.

ALBURY PARK MANSION 1
Albury, Guildford, Surrey. Tel: (048641) 2964 (Administrator)

Country Houses Association Ltd ✱ *Turn off A25 onto A248 (signposted Albury).*
Turn left just before village and entrance is immediately left ✱ *Best season: spring,*
early summer ✱ *Parking* ✱ *Toilet facilities* ✱ *House open (Pugin) also old*
Saxon church ✱ *Garden open May to Sept, Wed, Thurs, 2 – 5pm* ✱ *Entrance:*
£1.50

The gardens remaining around the house are mainly under grass with gravel
walks, a ha-ha and stream providing the boundaries. A small formal rose
garden, azaleas and rhododendrons are to be seen and an herbaceous border.
However, it is the trees that are most impressive – several oaks, a tulip tree and a
very old London plane amongst them. There is a tree chart of the estate in the

house. Although not open to visitors, the azaleas and rhododendrons on the estate are visible from the garden in spring and are a beautiful sight when in bloom. The pleasure grounds which lie north of the Tillingbourne remain in the ownership of the Trustees of the Albury Estate and are not open to the public. This is unfortunate as the layout owes much to the assistance given by John Evelyn to his neighbour, later 6th Duke of Norfolk, in or before the 1660s. These included the terraces, one in the style of a Roman bath, a tunnel, now walled in at one end, and a canal. In 1882 William Cobbett on one of his rural rides described them as 'without exception the prettiest in England; that is to say, that I ever saw in England.'

BIRDWORLD 2
Holt Pound, Nr Farnham, Surrey. Tel: (0420) 22140

*The Harvey family * 3m S of Farnham on A325 * Best season: Aug * Parking * Refreshments: café for light lunches, coffee and teas * Toilet facilities * Suitable for wheelchairs. Wheelchairs available for hire * Shop * Open daily except 25th Dec, summer 9.30am – 6pm, winter 9.30am – 3.30pm * Entrance: £2.95, OAP £2.30, children £1.60 (1991 prices)*

First-time visitors to Birdworld will be surprised by the extensive gardens which provide a backdrop to the bird sanctuary. With its wide flat paths and ample seating there is plenty of space to enjoy the variety of planting on show. Although lacking a unifying theme (and the family disagree over which comes first, the birds or the gardens), the variety ensures that the gardens are attractive and colourful on all of the 364 days a year that they are open. Features include summer bedding, hanging baskets, wall baskets, rose garden, heather bed, ornamental grasses border, pergola and climbing roses, pond and white garden.

BRADSTONE BROOK 3
Shalford, Guildford, Surrey. Tel: (0483) 68686

*Scott, Brownrigg & Turner * 3m S of Guildford on A281 towards Horsham then A248 to Dorking. Sign on left past the Common * Parking * Teas * Open for charity 17th May, 2 – 6pm * Entrance: £1.50, children 50p*

The layout for this 20-acre garden was Gertrude Jekyll's, particularly the water garden, but the area was derelict for 25 years until discovered by the present owners 10 years ago. Set against the background of the Surrey hills, the Edwardian house is framed by lawns and an ornamental rose garden with lavender and box hedges. Other features include an alpine garden, a lily tank and several woodland walks to a variegated beech and the snowdrop tree, *Halesia carolina*, that flowers in late spring/early summer, and swamp cypresses. Over 150,000 bulbs and some trees under preservation orders including a *Betula nigra* said to be the largest in the country. A video showing the gardens in all their former glory is shown in the tea room.

BROOK LODGE FARM COTTAGE 4
Blackbrook, Dorking, Surrey. Tel: (0306) 888368

*Mrs Basil Kingham * 3m S of Dorking off A24 * Parking on farm field*

*opposite * Soup and sandwiches in April and Oct. Teas * Toilet facilities *
Suitable for wheelchairs * Plants for sale * Open 8th April, 11am – 3pm; 20th,
21st June, 6th Sept, 2 – 6pm; 7th Oct, 11am – 3pm * Entrance: £1.50*

This plantsman's pleasure garden was begun by the present owners 50 years
ago in what had been fields. The entrance is through the gardens of a pair of
cottages, which have a formal and an informal pond. A pineapple-scented
Cytisus battandieri reaches the eaves on the end cottage wall. Beyond, the
spacious lawns of the main house are framed by curving borders of shrubs and
flowering trees, shrub roses and interesting and unusual plants.

CHILWORTH MANOR   5
Chilworth, Surrey. Tel: (0483) 61414

*Lady Heald * 3^1/2m SE of Guildford on A248. Turn off in village centre up
Blacksmiths Lane * Best season: spring and June * Parking * Refreshments:
teas in house on Sat and Sun. Picnicking from 12.30pm * Toilet facilities *
Partly suitable for wheelchairs * Dogs on lead * House open Sat and Sun *
Garden open 4th, 5th April, 9th, 10th May, 13th, 14th June, 18th, 19th July,
15th, 16th Aug, 2 – 6pm and by appointment * Entrance: £1.00 (house £1.00),
children free*

A lovely old garden, particularly in spring and autumn, but something to see all
the year round. Laid out in the seventeenth century, a walled garden was carved
in three tiers out of the side of the hill early in the next century by Sarah,
Duchess of Marlborough before she moved to Blenheim. The high walls,
backed by wisteria, shelter many fine plants, a herbaceous border, lavender
walks and shrubs. There is also a rock garden and a woodland area with
magnolias, rhododendrons, azaleas, an oak tree reputed to be 400 years old and
a Judas tree. Our visitor, there in spring, was impressed by the candelabra
primulas along the stream and golden carp in the monastic stewponds. At
weekends, the house is decorated by various Surrey flower clubs in turn.

CLANDON PARK   6
West Clandon, Guildford, Surrey. Tel: (0483) 222482

*The National Trust * 3m E of Guildford. Take A247 or A3 to Ripley and join
A247 via B2215 * Parking. Disabled drivers only near front of house *
Refreshments: licensed restaurant when house is open, lunches 12.30 – 2pm, teas for
visitors to the house only. Picnic area * Toilet facilities inc. disabled * Suitable
for wheelchairs * Dogs on lead in picnic area and car park only * Shop *
House open * Garden open April to Oct, daily except Thurs and Fri, 1.30 – 5pm,
but open Good Fri, Bank Holiday Suns and Mons, 11am – 5pm * Entrance:
£3.30*

Built by a Venetian architect in the early 1730s for the 2nd Lord Onslow, whose
family still owns the park, although the house and seven-acre garden are owned
by the Trust. It is a pleasant garden to visit and look around. An interesting
feature is the Maori meeting house, known as Hinemihi, brought from New
Zealand by Lord Onslow, which is said to be one of the oldest in existence. Also

note the grotto and parterre. The garden is on a hillside and gives a fine view of the lake which is in the private park. Nearby garden centre (not NT).

CLAREMONT LANDSCAPE GARDEN ★ 7
Portsmouth Road, Esher, Surrey. Tel: (0372) 69421

The National Trust ✳ *E of A307, S of Esher just out of the town* ✳ *Parking* ✳ *Refreshments in tea room 12th Jan to March, Sat and Sun, 11am – 4pm, April to Oct, daily except Mon, 11am – 5.30pm, Nov to 15th Dec, daily except Mon, 11am – 4.30pm. 11th Jan – March 1993, Sat and Sun, 11am – 4pm* ✳ *Toilet facilities* ✳ *Partly suitable for wheelchairs* ✳ *Dogs, Nov to March only, on lead* ✳ *Shop* ✳ *House, not NT, not open* ✳ *Garden open all year, daily, March, 9am – 5pm, April to Oct, 9am – 7pm (15th to 19th July garden closes 4pm), Nov to March 1993, 9am – 5pm or sunset if earlier (last admission 1/2 hour before closing). Closed 25th Dec and 1st Jan* ✳ *Entrance: Mon – Sat £1.50, Sun and Bank Holiday Mon £2.50. Guided tours for 15 or more £1.10 extra by prior booking*

The *Oxford Companion* describes this as one of the most significant historic landscapes in the country. The 50 acres being restored by the Trust is only part of the original estate which was broken up in 1922 and part became a school. The great landscape designers of the eighteenth century each adapted it in turn for the owner, the immensely wealthy man who eventually became Duke of Newcastle. First he retained Vanbrugh, then Bridgeman, then Kent. Later, when Clive of India purchased the estate he brought in 'Capability' Brown who also designed the house, now the school and, in typical form, diverted the London-Portsmouth road to improve the viewpoints, the most striking of which is the grass amphitheatre. In the nineteenth century it was a favourite retreat of Queen Victoria and her younger son. A useful leaflet describes the various contributions to the park, which will appeal to everyone by its sensitive reconstruction of the eighteenth-century English style, even if it has nothing specific to offer the plantsperson, except perhaps the magnolia walk. The garden is a very popular recreation park for local families, sunbathers and picnickers.

2 THE COTTAGE 8
Maybourne Rise, Mayford, Woking, Surrey. Tel: (0483) 764958

Mr Trevor Bath ✳ *3m S of Woking off A320. Along track at top of Maybourne Rise* ✳ *Parking in Maybourne Rise* ✳ *Teas* ✳ *Plants for sale* ✳ *Open 22nd April, 20th May, 17th June, 10am – 5pm and by appointment mid-April to mid-July* ✳ *Entrance: 50p*

Mr Bath began this delightful garden 25 years ago. There is a profusion of fascinating and unusual varieties of cottage plants: granny's bonnets (*Aquilegia vulgaris*), hardy geraniums, pulmonarias, comfreys and roses. Intersecting paths lead to an arbour; a curving lawn; an unexpectedly formal water garden, a black mulberry and a gravel scree. Although compact, there is much to see.

2 COURT AVENUE 9
Old Coulsdon, Surrey. Tel: (07375) 54721

Dr K. Heber ✳ *In Old Coulsdon, opposite the Tudor Rose pub* ✳ *Best season:*

summer * *Parking in Court Avenue* * *Teas* * *Suitable for wheelchairs* *
Plants for sale * *Open 25th July, 1st Aug, 10am – 5pm* * *Entrance: £1,*
children 50p

From the corner of a busy road, visitors step into a colourful oasis. Dr Heber began this garden 25 years ago and now grows around 3000 different plants in a level third of an acre. Against a background of shrubs, roses and clematis are many unusual varieties of herbaceous and foliage plants. The design is open and informal, with every inch of earth covered by plants, leaving no room for weeds. Knightsmead (see entry) is nearby.

COVERWOOD LAKES AND GARDEN 10
Peaslake Road, Ewhurst, Surrey. Tel: (0306) 731103

Mr and Mrs C.G. Metson * *7m SW of Dorking. Off A25 ¹/₂m S of Peaslake* *
Parking * *Home-made teas, and for 25th Oct, hot soup and sandwiches* * *Toilet*
facilities * *Suitable for wheelchairs* * *Plants for sale* * *Open 10th, 17th May*
(gardens only), 24th, 27th, 31st May, 7th, 14th June (gardens and farm), 2 –
6.30pm. Also 25th Oct, 11am – 4.30pm (gardens and farm) * *Entrance: £1.50,*
children 75p (£2, children 75p gardens and farm). Reductions for large parties by
prior arrangement

The original gardens were designed in 1910 by a rich Edwardian businessman. Now it is a woodland estate surrounding four lakes the water for which arises from the natural springs in the bog garden. Each lake has a different character, from the towering rhododendrons reflecting in the calm water of the highest to the largest alongside the arboretum. This was planted early in 1990 and contains 100 different kinds of trees which prospered through the baking summer of 1990. Bordering the paths are a great many varieties of hostas, trilliums and candelabra primulas. Lilies of the valley form a green and white carpet below a wide variety of rhododrons and azaleas. The farm specialises in pedigree Poll Hereford cattle.

CROSSWATER FARM 11
Crosswater Lane, Churt, Farnham, Surrey. Tel: (025125) 2698

Mr and Mrs E.G. Millais * *6m from Farnham and Haslemere. ¹/₂m N of Churt.*
Follow signs for Millais Nurseries * *Parking in field beside garden* * *Teas*
available on charity days which are 23rd to 25th, 30th, 31st May and 6th, 7th
June * *Toilet facilities* * *Suitable for wheelchairs* * *Plants for sale in specialist*
rhododendron nursery * *Open 16th May to 14th June, daily, 10am – 5pm* *
Entrance: £1, children free

These six acres of woodland gardens were begun in 1946 by Mr and Mrs Millais who specialise in rhodendrons and azaleas. Among the mature and some more recent plantings are rare species collected in the Himalayas, and hybrids raised by the owners, including 'High Summer' which won an Award of Merit in 1989. All the work in the gardens and the nursery, which produces more than 500 different varieties of rhododendron, is done by the owners and their two sons. The top soil is very shallow and exceptionally acidic, with pH 4.0 in places.

DUNSBOROUGH PARK ★   12
Ripley, Surrey. Tel: (0483) 224348 (evenings)

Mr C.F. Hughesdon ✳ *Entrance in the village through lych gate. Drive crosses Ripley Green* ✳ *Parking outside garden* ✳ *Teas* ✳ *Dogs* ✳ *Toilet facilities* ✳ *Partly suitable for wheelchairs* ✳ *Open 23rd Aug and possibly two other dates for charity, 2 – 6pm* ✳ *Entrance: £1, children 50p*

The house is seventeenth- and eighteenth-century. The Onslow family, who lived here from 1785 to 1895, built the Georgian extension. Mr Hughesdon has been here since 1948. Around the house are terraces with beds of pansies; lawns and ha-has allow uninterrupted views over meadowland. Beyond the lawns, paths fan out, leading to rose gardens enclosed by yew hedges, to herbaceous borders and a sunken garden with an ancient black mulberry. In the glasshouses are tropical plants, while extensive walled fruit and vegetable gardens shelter clipped boxes of gingko, the maidenhair tree. A water garden ends in a spectacular ornamental bridge with a belvedere.

FEATHERCOMBE GARDENS   13
Feathercombe, Hambledon, Nr Godalming, Surrey. Tel: (0483) 860257

Miss Parker ✳ *5m S of Godalming, E of A283 between Hydestile and Hambledon* ✳ *Parking* ✳ *Picnic area available* ✳ *Toilet facilities* ✳ *Partly suitable for wheelchairs* ✳ *Dogs on lead* ✳ *Plants for sale* ✳ *Open 3rd, 4th, 24th, 25th May, 2 – 6pm* ✳ *Entrance: £1, children 10p*

Although mainly worth visiting for the good display of rhododendrons and azaleas, there are fine views across three counties framed by larches and some tree heaths which are now 20 to 30 feet high. Now that the garden is maintained solely by the family, some of the features in the original design of 1910 by Eric and Ruth Parker have had to be changed through lack of labour. Ruth Parker was one of Leonard Messel's daughters and there must have been strong connections between her garden at Feathercombe and his at Nymans (see entry).

HAMPTON COURT
(see LONDON)

HANNAH PESCHAR GALLERY AND SCULPTURE GARDEN   14
Black and White Cottage, Standon Lane, Ockley, Surrey. Tel: (030679) 269

Hannah Peschar ✳ *1m SW of Ockley. Signposted from Cat Hill Lane onwards as Black and White Cottage* ✳ *Parking* ✳ *Refreshments for group visits by arrangement* ✳ *Toilet facilities* ✳ *Suitable for wheelchairs (but not the indoor gallery)* ✳ *Open May to Oct, Fri and Sat, 11am – 6pm, Suns and Bank Holidays,*

*2 – 5pm. Any other day, except Mons, by appointment for buyers and group visits only * Entrance: £3, children £1.50. Guided tours for parties £5 per person, group picnics £4 per person. Special leaflet on request*

This delightful Surrey woodland garden is of primary interest to those who enjoy contemporary outdoor sculpture, as Mrs Peschar represents a wide range of artists whose work is displayed in natural settings, including water. The exhibits change, of course, as they are sold, and anyone planning to place objects of art outdoors will find a study of the sculptures here a source of inspiration. Note too the way art contributes to function as in the bridge made by landscape designer Anthony Paul.

HASCOMBE COURT ★   15
Hascombe, Godalming, Surrey. Tel: (048632) 254

*Mr and Mrs O. Poulsen * 3¹/₂m S of Godalming. Entrance to drive is on a bend on B2130 * Parking in paddock * Teas * Toilet facilities * Open 12th April, 10th May, 14th, 17th June, 2 – 5pm * Entrance: £1*

Gertrude Jekyll advised on the original design of these extensive gardens, and Percy Cane later planned further areas; over the past 12 years they have been beautifully restored after a period of decline. There is a double herbaceous border, a rectangular sunken garden planted in white, pale blue and silver, and a curved shrubbery walk with a belvedere giving wonderful views. A woodland area leads to two further viewing points. Around the house, fine stone terraces with balustrades, walls with a recessed lily pool and steps drop down to the delightful Japanese rock and water gardens with stone lanterns, rills and pools.

HATCHLANDS   16
East Clandon, Guildford, Surrey. Tel: (0483) 222787

*The National Trust * E of East Clandon, N of A246 * Best season: spring and summer * Parking. Disabled visitors may be set down at house * Home-made teas * Toilet facilities * Suitable for wheelchairs * House open * Garden open April to 18th Oct, Tues, Wed, Thurs, Sun and Bank Holiday Mon, also Sats in Aug, 2 – 5.30pm (last admission 5pm) * Entrance: garden free, house £3.20*

The main interest is in the Gertrude Jekyll garden which is being returned to its original dimensions and being replanted to her original plans (1914 revision). It will be one to two years before completion as plants are coming from abroad and some have to be propagated. There is a wild meadow featuring cowslips and many wild flowers. It is never cut until July. Mature London plane and cedar trees. Further improvements will include regrading to Humphry Repton's original design.

HIGH MEADOW   17
Tilford Road, Churt, Surrey. Tel: (0428) 606129

*Mr and Mrs John Humphries * 3m N of Hindhead. Take A287 from Hindhead* *then fork left to Tilford. House is nearly 2m on right* ✻ *Parking at Avalon PYO farm on left past turning to house. Disabled may park in drive to house* ✻ *Teas* ✻ *Toilet facilities* ✻ *Plants for sale* ✻ *Open 24th, 25th May, 5th, 6th July, 30th, 31st Aug, 2 – 6pm* ✻ *Entrance: £1, children free*

As the name suggests this garden is situated high on a meadowside protected by a series of hedges of beech, holly and cupressus. A small terrace is overlooked by a pergola with a variety of climbers. Unusually-shaped beds surround grass of putting-green quality and contain a wealth of colour co-ordinated shrubs, roses and herbaceous plants which are cleverly graded by height. There is a small pool set in a rock garden, a bog plant section, rockery and small peat garden. A plantsman's garden.

HILEY NURSERY   18
25 Little Woodcote Estate, Wallington, Surrey. Tel: (081) 647 9679

Mr and Mrs Brian Hiley ✻ *Off Woodmansterne Lane which links B278 and A237. Signposted SCC Smallholding* ✻ *Best season: summer* ✻ *Parking in field beside garden* ✻ *Toilet facilities* ✻ *Suitable for wheelchairs* ✻ *Plants for sale in nursery* ✻ *Open April to Sept, Wed and Sat, 9am – 5pm, also 20th April, 4th, 25th May* ✻ *Entrance: £1.20 for charity*

Twenty years ago Brian and Heather Hiley came here to market garden. Now they specialise in rare and tender perennials and display them in a chalky acre divided into a series of small gardens. There are herbaceous borders, a rockery and an alpine house all packed with rare and unusual plants. There are also hardy perennials, a blaze of annuals and many varieties of penstemons, diascias and osteospermums, as well as some plants which the Hileys have saved from near extinction.

KNIGHTSMEAD   19
Rickman Hill Road, Chipstead, Surrey. Tel: (0737) 551694

Mrs C. Jones and Miss C. Collins ✻ *1m SW of Coulsdon, 3m SE of Banstead, off the B2032* ✻ *Parking in Bouverie Road/Rickman Hill Road* ✻ *Teas* ✻ *Plants for sale* ✻ *Open 20th, 21st June, 2 – 5.30pm and by appointment* ✻ *Entrance: £1, accompanied children 50p*

When the present owners came here 10 years ago, the half-acre garden was overshadowed by vast Lawson's cypresses. Now the tall stumps support shrub roses and clematis. A graceful 50ft Deodar cedar dominates this well-designed plantsman's garden. A lily pond, a rose arch and beds of shrubs and perennials give year-round interest. On heavy clay soil, a bog garden, peat bed and limestone scree provide ideal conditions for choice plants. 2 Court Avenue (see entry) is nearby.

LONDON UNIVERSITY BOTANIC GARDENS   20
Egham Hill, Egham, Surrey. Tel: (0784) 433303

University of London ✻ *On A30, 2m SW of M25 junction 13. Opposite Royal*

*Holloway and Bedford New College ✳ Best seasons: spring and autumn ✳
Parking in surrounding streets ✳ Teas on open days ✳ Toilet facilities ✳
Suitable for wheelchairs ✳ Plants for sale when available ✳ Guided tours of
Gardens and College on open days ✳ Open by appointment all year, 9am – 4pm
and 26th April, 4th Oct, 2 – 6pm for charity ✳ Entrance: £2*

Founded in 1950 to grow plant material for teaching and research work at the
University, and much involved in the conservation of plants that are threatened
in the wild. There are around 4000 different species of plants (all labelled) and
11 plant-houses, (two of which are tropical). Here, rarities include an unusual
succulent from Hawaii (*Brighamia citrina*) and the New Zealand *Elingamita
johnsonii*. Many beds of unusual plants, (naturally occuring forms rather than
cultivars). Unusual plants are grouped in family beds. Some of these plants may
be on sale, but a request to the Curator on availability of others and their cost
may be made. Some are rarely on sale elsewhere. There is an arboretum, which
is considered one of the finest post-war British plantings, including an
extensive collection of Southern beech species and rarities like golden larch
and American plane. Unique Memorial Walk of dawn redwoods. Ferns,
mosses, liverworts and carnivorous plants. On open days there are guided
lecture tours by expert botanists at extra charge. Resulting from what are
politely called 'financial restraints' the botanic garden area, having grown, is
now being reduced, and the surplus areas handed over to Royal Holloway and
Bedford New College private grounds. No wonder Britain's advanced
education, once second to none, is becoming second to a good many. Visitors
can slow, if not reverse, this decline by becoming 'Friends' of LUBG.

LOSELEY PARK 21
Nr Guildford, Surrey. Tel: (0483) 304440

*Mr and Mrs J. More-Molyneux ✳ 3m SE of Guildford off B3000 ✳ Parking
✳ Refreshments: wholefood restaurant offering organic lunches, snacks and teas.
Open 11am – 5pm in season ✳ Toilet facilities ✳ Shop selling own organic
produce. Open 11am – 5pm in season, Fri, 10am – 1pm in closed season ✳ House
open ✳ Garden open 27th May to 26th Sept, Wed – Sat, 2 – 5pm. Also Bank
Holidays 25th May and 31st Aug ✳ Entrance: £1, children 50p*

The house, garden and farm provide interest and entertainment for all the
family by offering such attractions as farm tours and trailer rides. The
Elizabethan house is set in a sweep of lawn surrounded by parkland. The
secluded garden to the side of the house has yew hedges creating 'rooms', an
herbaceous bed with familiar plants and a moat walk. Through the hedge to the
vegetable garden catch a glimpse of the organically-grown vegetables, a very
good advertisement for the system.

THE MOORINGS 22
14 Russells Crescent, Horley, Surrey.

*Dr and Mrs C.J.F.I. Williamson ✳ Near town centre, 400 yards from railway
station ✳ Parking in Russells Crescent ✳ Teas ✳ Suitable for wheelchairs ✳
Dogs on lead ✳ Plants for sale ✳ Open 27th to 29th June, 2 – 6pm ✳
Entrance: £1, children 25p*

Here is a retreat, a secret garden, close to the bustle of a town centre, full of rare and interesting plants, with rocks, pools and ornaments hidden amongst them. There are lawns, too, with unusual specimen trees and wide borders of roses. Long paths make the garden seem bigger than its one acre.

PAINSHILL PARK ★★   23
Portsmouth Road, Cobham, Surrey. Tel: (0932) 868113

*Elmbridge Borough Council on lease to Painshill Park Trust * 1m W of Cobham on A245. Entrance on right, 200 yards E of A3/A245 roundabout * Limited parking * Teas and light refreshments * Toilet facilities inc. disabled * Partly suitable for wheelchairs * Shop in Visitor Centre * Open 12th April to 18th Oct, Suns only, 11am – 6pm (last admission 5pm). Also all year by appointment for parties of 10 or more * Entrance: £3, concessions £2, parties £2.50 per person inc. refreshments*

Painshill was developed by Charles Hamilton (1704 – 86), a great English landscape designer who acquired the lease in 1738 and got severely into debt by his ambitious plans. He should be better known and is described by the *Oxford Companion* as 'a brilliant and subtle designer (who) could create illusion and vary scene and mood. His work strikes a delicate balance between art and nature, between the artist and the plantsman'. His work was nearly lost to posterity but after 30 years of neglect and delay it was rescued at the eleventh hour when it was bought by Elmbridge Borough Council and an independent Trust was established in 1981. There are now 158 acres of which 14 are taken up by the lake. A great deal of work has already been done, and Charles Hamilton's garden is coming to life again. There are about 100 trees surviving at Painshill that were planted between 1738–1773, including the great cedar of Lebanon, the largest in England (120 x 32 feet) and the pencil cedar (*Juniperus virginiana*) approx 60 x 6½ feet – the tallest in England, with a mountain ash growing from the trunk seven feet from the ground. Another unusual sight is a beech and London plane with branches apparently fused together. Features include Gothic temple, water wheel, grotto island and ruined abbey.

PINEWOOD HOUSE   24
Heath House Road, Worplesdon Hill, Woking, Surrey. Tel: (04867) 3241

*Mr and Mrs Van Zwanenberg * 5m NW of Guildford. Turn off A322 opposite Brookwood Cemetery wall * Parking * ☆Teas * Toilet facilities * Specially planned for wheelchairs * House open * Garden open March to Oct by appointment * Entrance: £1*

In 1986, Mr and Mrs Van Zwanenberg built a new house in four acres of their original garden. They retained the water garden and rhododendrons massed against a backdrop of Scots pines. There is a young arboretum and a charming new circular walled garden with a fountain. An automated conservatory with exotic plants built into the house is open and also displays fine embroideries worked by Mrs Van Zwanenberg.

POLESDEN LACEY ★   25
Great Bookham, Nr Dorking, Surrey. Tel: (0372) 458203

*The National Trust   ✳   5m NW of Dorking, 2m S of Great Bookham off A246
Leatherhead – Guildford road   ✳   Parking 150 yards away   ✳   Refreshments:
coffee, lunches, and teas in licensed restaurant in courtyard. Picnic site in grounds
(not in formal areas)   ✳   Toilet facilities inc. disabled   ✳   Partly suitable for
wheelchairs   ✳   Dogs on lead in estate grounds only   ✳   Shop   ✳   House open
March and Nov, Sat and Sun, 1.30 – 4.30pm, April to Oct, Wed – Sun (inc. Good
Fri), 1.30 – 5.30pm and Bank Holiday Mon and preceeding Sun, 11am – 5.30pm
✳   Grounds open all year, 11am – dusk   ✳   Entrance: April to Oct, £2, Nov to
March 1993, £1.50. House, Sun and Bank Holiday Mons £3.20 extra, other open
days £2.50 extra. Parties £4 per person (house and garden) weekdays only by prior
arrangement with the Administrator*

This 17-acre garden has grown up over several centuries. Richard Brinsley
Sheridan, the dramatist who owned the house for over 20 years, lengthened the
Long Walk before he died here in 1816. The present house was built a few
years later by Cubitt in the Greek classical manner for an owner who made
extensive alterations and planted over 20,000 trees. The garden was further
developed early this century and given to the Trust in 1944. The walled rose
garden is in four square areas divided by paths and covered by wooden pergolas
and the area is dominated by a well-head covered by an ancient Chinese
wisteria. There are small gardens of peonies, bearded irises, beds of different
kinds of lavender. A winter garden overshadowed by four iron trees. A long
border of herbaceous plants is a colourful sight in summer. There is also a
sunken garden. A fully detailed garden guide is available giving numbered lists
of plants, shrubs and flowers.

PYRFORD COURT   26
Pyrford Common Road, Pyrford, Woking, Surrey. Tel: (0483) 765880

*Mr C. Laikin   ✳   2m W of Woking. M25 Junction 10. B367 junction with Upshott
Lane   ✳   Parking   ✳   Teas   ✳   Toilet facilities   ✳   Suitable for wheelchairs   ✳
Dogs on lead   ✳   Open by appointment and 24th, 31st May, 2 – 6.30pm, 18th Oct,
12 noon – 4pm   ✳   Entrance: £1.50, children 50p*

Transformed at the turn of the century by Lord and Lady Iveagh with advice
from Gertrude Jekyll, this varied garden covers about 20 acres, both formal and
woodland. The wild garden to the South is a blaze of colour in the autumn,
especially the Japanese maples. The north lawn of around four acres is
bordered by a high brick wall with a pillared loggia and features several pear-
shaped Irish yews. Noticeable on the wall is a loquat, *Eriobotrya japonica*. The
wisterias on the pergola walk are from Japanese raised seedlings imported
about 70 years ago from Yokohama and are remarkable for their extremely long
flower panicles. The ornamental grape, *Vitis coignetiae*, is a fine sight at the end
of the pergola walk, brilliant when in autumn colours. By the stream is a rare
flowering camellia (*C.* x *williamsii* 'Hiraethlyn') which flowers in October.
There are views to the North Downs and to Guildford cathedral.

RAMSTER 27
Chiddingfold, Surrey. Tel: (0428) 644422

Mr and Mrs P. Gunn ✳ *1¹/₂m S of Chiddingfold on A283* ✳ *Best season: spring* ✳ *Parking* ✳ *Refreshments: teas on Sat, Sun and Bank Holiday Mon. Lunches for pre-booked coach parties* ✳ *Toilet facilities* ✳ *Suitable for wheelchairs* ✳ *Dogs on lead* ✳ *Plants for sale* ✳ *Open 25th April to 7th June, 2 – 6pm and parties by appointment* ✳ *Entrance: £1.50, children free*

Laid out in 1904 by Gauntlett Nurseries of Chiddingfold and owned by the same family for close to 70 years. Twenty acres of peaceful woodland with views of lakes and hillsides filled with colour and interest. Planting includes Californian redwoods, cedars, firs, camellias, rhododendrons and azaleas plus the rarer *Styrax obassia*, *Tetracentron sinense*, and *Kalopanax pictus*. A camellia garden, magnolia bed and widespread bluebells and daffodils ensure flowers are on view throughout the spring. Especially notable is an avenue of *Acer palmatum* 'Dissectum'.

ROYAL HORTICULTURAL SOCIETY'S GARDEN ★★ 28
Wisley, Woking, Surrey. Tel: (0483) 224234

Royal Horticultural Society ✳ *7m from Guildford, 4m from Cobham, 1m from Ripley, W of London on A3 and M25 (junction 10)* ✳ *Parking* ✳ *Refreshments: licensed restaurant and self service cafeteria* ✳ *Toilet facilities inc. disabled* ✳ *Suitable for wheelchairs* ✳ *Plants for sale* ✳ *Shop* ✳ *Open to non-members of the RHS Feb to Oct, Mon-Sat, 10am – 7pm or dusk if earlier, Nov to Jan, 10am – 4.30pm (Sun for RHS members only)* ✳ *Entrance: by membership or £3.95, children 6–14 £1.75, under 6 free*

George Fox Wilson, a former treasurer of the RHS, established a famous woodland garden here *c.* 1880. After his death it was purchased by Sir Thomas Hanbury (owner of the famous La Mortola garden in Italy) and together with surrounding land became the site of the fourth RHS garden. In common with a number of gardens in the South East, Wisley was devastated by the storms of 1987 and 1990. This presented the opportunity for redevelopment and rejuvenation including a collection of Mediterranean plants on the southern side of Battleston Hill. Wisley fulfills its teaching role so splendidly that it warrants a two star classification. Impeccably planted and tended, the garden thrills the thousands of visitors it attracts each year who are understandably impressed by one of the finest alpine rock gardens in Europe, a fine range of plants in the glasshouse range and yards of quintessentially English, deep and richly-appealing herbaceous border. Bonuses available from a Wisley visit are that it is possible to browse among what is arguably the best selection of modern gardening books available anywhere in the world and to buy very well grown plants in the sales area after obtaining informed advice upon their performance.

THE SAVILL GARDEN ★★ 29
Wick Lane, Englefield Green, Surrey. Tel: (0753) 860222

Administered by the Crown Estate Commissioners ✳ *5m from Windsor. From*

A30, turn into Wick Road and follow signs, or follow signs from Englefield Green ✳ *Parking* ✳ *Refreshments: licensed self-service restaurant open Feb to 20th Dec (0784) 432326. Picnics allowed in car park area* ✳ *Toilet facilities inc. disabled* ✳ *Suitable for wheelchairs* ✳ *Plants for sale* ✳ *Gift and book shop* ✳ *Open daily, 10am – 6pm (7pm at weekends) or sunset if earlier. Closed 25th to 28th Dec* ✳ *Entrance: £2.50, OAP £2.30, accompanied children under 16 free. Parties of 20 or more £2.30 per person. Guided tours are available – apply to Keeper of the Garden*

The violent storms of recent years have taken such a toll of the tall trees that much of the high canopy has been reduced and the garden has lost some of its former more enclosed woodland feel. Nevertheless covering some 35 acres of woodland, it contains a fine range of rhododendrons, camellias, magnolias, hydrangeas and a great variety of other trees and shrubs producing a wealth of colour throughout the seasons, particularly in spring and summer – meconopsis and primulas in June especially. In the shadier areas a wonderful collection of hostas and ferns flourishes. Daffodils in impressive drifts dominate in the spring while lilies are the highlight of high summer. The tweedy autumn colours in the Savill Garden are almost as satisfying in their mellowness as its jauntier spring hues. A more formal area is devoted to modern roses, herbaceous borders, a range of alpines and a very interesting and attractive dry garden. Windsor Castle gardens nearby (admission free, 10am – 7.15pm, 4.15pm in winter) retain the formal gardens designed by W.J. Aiton for George IV. The Valley Gardens are also nearby (see entry).

STREET HOUSE   30
Thursley, Godalming, Surrey. Tel: (0252) 703216

Mr and Mrs B.M. Francis ✳ *W of A3 between Milford and Hindhead, near road junction in village* ✳ *Best seasons: spring and summer* ✳ *Parking on village recreation ground. From A3, beyond the house* ✳ *Teas* ✳ *Toilet facilities* ✳ *Dogs on lead* ✳ *Plants for sale* ✳ *Open 26th April, 31st May, 28th June, 26th July, 30th Aug, 27th Sept, 11am – 5pm* ✳ *Entrance: £1.50, children 50p*

Sir Edwin Lutyens spent his early years at this listed Regency house, and it was here that he first met Gertrude Jekyll. There are three separate gardens around the house. A walled garden is full of interesting and unusual plants, trees and shrubs, including *Rubus* x *tridel* and an immense acacia (*Robinia pseudoacacia*). The main lawn is surrounded by shrubs with a curving backdrop of fine limes, while the lower lawn is framed by dazzling rhododendrons and azaleas and has splendid views. There is an astrological feature constructed with Bargate stone unearthed from the garden, and local ironstone.

TILGATES   31
Little Common Lane, Redhill, Surrey. Tel: (0883) 742402

Mr David Clulow ✳ *3m E of Redhill. From Redhill take A25. Immediately after crossing motorway bridge, turn left into Big Common Lane, then first right into Little Common Lane* ✳ *Parking in car park opposite* ✳ *Plants for sale* ✳ *Open from March 1992, daily except 25th Dec, 10am – 5pm* ✳ *Entrance: £1*

This valley garden was created in 1912 though very little planting was done until the present owner came here 17 years ago. A seven-acre garden with views of the Downs, it has over 4000 different trees and shrubs, including a National collection of magnolias. Trees with interesting bark are planted in a curving avenue, with massed daffodils. There are collections of birches (*Betula*), maples (*Acer*), rhododendrons and conifers. A large pond, recorded in the Domesday Book, feeds a stream which runs through the garden. A recent feature is the raised alpine bed. Labelling is exceptionally clear and complete.

VALE END   32
Albury, Surrey. Tel: (048641) 2594

*Mr and Mrs J. Foulsham * 4¹/₂m SE of Guildford. From Albury take A248 W for ¹/₂m * Best season: summer/autumn * Limited parking * Refreshments * Toilet facilities * Dogs on lead * Plants for sale when available * Open 28th June, 2 – 6pm, 2nd Aug, 10am – 5pm * Entrance: £1*

A one-acre walled cottage garden surrounding an eighteenth to twentieth-century house. Fine views from terrace across sloping lawns to mill pond and woodlands with a wide variety of herbaceous plants and roses, ornamental pond. This garden is entirely maintained by its owners and as well as being in a beautiful setting will interest plantsmen because on a light, well-watered soil, the owners have interspersed old favourites with 'little gems' such as diascia. There is a fine magnolia with a spread of over 40 feet and a small fruit and vegetable garden.

THE VALLEY GARDENS (Windsor Great Park) ★★   33
Wick Road, Englefield Green, Surrey. Tel: (0753) 860222

*Administered by the Crown Estate Commissioners * 5m from Windsor. From A30 turn into Wick Road and follow signs for Savill Garden (¹/₂m to W) and drive to car park adjoining Valley Gardens, avoiding a 2m round walk * Parking * Refreshments at Savill Garden * Plants for sale at Savill Garden * Open all year, 8am – 7pm or sunset if earlier. Possible closure if weather inclement * Entrance: £2 car and occupants (10p, 50p and £1 coins only)*

One of Britain's most discriminating and experienced garden visitors, Arthur Hellyer suggests that The Valley Gardens are among the best examples of the 'natural' gardening style in England. With hardly any artefacts or attempts to introduce architectural features they are merely a tract of undulating grassland (on the north side of Virginia Water) which is divided by several shallow valleys, that has been enriched by the introduction of a fine collection of trees and shrubs. It was started by the royal gardener Sir Eric Savill when he ran out of room in the Savill Garden to continue making 'natural' landscapes. One of the valleys is filled with deciduous azaleas. In another, 'The Punchbowl', evergreen azaleas rise in tiers below a canopy of maples. Notable too are collections of flowering cherries, a heather garden which amply demonstrates the ability to provide colour during all seasons, and one of the world's most extensive collection of hollies. Lovers of formal gardening might be forgiven for suggesting that the Valley Gardens have something of the rather too open, amorphous, scrupulously-kept, American golf-course feel.

Virginia Water Lake, off the A30, adjacent to the junction with the A329, was a grand eighteenth-century ornamental addition to Windsor Great Park by the Duke of Cumberland who became its ranger in 1746. It had dams, rockwork, a cascade and grotto. There was a fake 'Mandarin Yacht', a Chinese pavilion and a Gothic belvedere with a mighty single arch bridge spanning the water. Alas, almost all have disappeared but the woodland and the lovely one and a half mile lake, full of fish and wildfowl, survive, and there is still a colonnade of pillars.

VANN 34
Hambledon, Surrey. Tel: (042868) 3413

*Mr and Mrs M.B. Caröe * 6m S of Godalming, E of A283 at Chiddingfold * Best season: spring * Parking as indicated * Refreshments: home-made teas in 'Barn' on Bank Holiday Mons and 7th June. Lunches and teas bookable for parties by arrangement * Limited toilet facilities * Limited access for wheelchairs * Dogs on lead * Plants for sale if available * Open 20th April, 4th May, 7th June, 2 – 7pm and 21st to 26th April, 5th to 10th May, 8th to 13th June, 10am – 6pm * Entrance: £1.30, children 30p*

The six different areas within this garden will provide some interest for most types of gardener. From the student of garden design viewing the water garden still containing plants selected by Gertrude Jekyll, to the admirer of the formal garden complete with clipped yews and regular brick paths, there is something for everyone. Of particular interest is the yew walk now planted with deer-resistant plants providing foliage of all year interest. Colourful annuals are introduced when the spring bulbs are over.

THE WALLED GARDEN 35
Sunbury Park, Thames Street, Sunbury-on-Thames, Surrey. Tel: (0784) 451499 (Community Services)

*Surrey County Council; maintained by Spelthorne Borough Council * In Sunbury-on-Thames via B375 Thames Street. Entrance through car park * Best seasons: spring and summer * Parking * Toilet facilities * Suitable for wheelchairs * Open daily except 25th Dec, 8am – dusk * Entrance: free*

Although no house remains, this eighteenth-century walled garden has been developed since 1985 into a pleasant open space of about two acres designed to include garden styles from past centuries. Also four large areas of island beds display collections of plants from all parts of the world. The rose garden is composed entirely of species roses and varieties which were either introduced or widely planted during the reign of Queen Victoria. During the summer exhibitions of sculpture, paintings, etc, are on view and a band plays at published times.

WALTON POOR 36
Ranmore, Dorking, Surrey. Tel: (04865) 2273

*Mr and Mrs N. Calvert * 5m WNW of Dorking, on road to Ranmore and East*

Horsley ✳ *Parking in adjacent field* ✳ *Teas in The Old Cartlodge, Ranmore Common* ✳ *Suitable for wheelchairs* ✳ *Plants for sale* ✳ *Garden open by appointment 17th May, 7th June, 11th Oct. Herb garden and nursery open April to Sept, Wed – Sun and Bank Holidays, 10am – 5pm* ✳ *Entrance: £1, children 50p*

A number of the mature trees were planted when the house was built in 1925, but the present three-acre garden has been created by the Calverts who came here 20 years ago. Grass paths wander among a wide variety of interesting and unusual shrubs (which sadly lack labels). There is a sheltered bowl-shaped dell and a herb garden. A small specialist nursery sells herbs and plants grown for scent and foliage.

THE WATER GARDENS, Kingston upon Thames
(see LONDON)

WINKWORTH ARBORETUM   37
Hascombe, Nr Godalming, Surrey. Tel: (048632) 477

The National Trust ✳ *2m SE of Godalming, E of B2130* ✳ *Best season: spring/ autumn* ✳ *Parking inc. disabled. Coaches must book in advance* ✳ *Refreshments: teashop open April to Oct, Tues – Sun, 2 – 6pm or dusk if earlier. March, Nov, Dec, Sat and Sun only* ✳ *Toilet facilities* ✳ *Dogs on lead* ✳ *Shop (048632) 265* ✳ *Open all year, daily, dawn – dusk* ✳ *Entrance: £2 donation*

The public footpath through Winkworth ensures access 365 days of the year, so it's a great place to take the family for a walk on Christmas Day or any other! The 60 plant families and 150 genera grown here provide variety and interest throughout the year. In the spring there are the azaleas, rhododendrons, cherries and maples and in the autumn sorbus, liquidambar, acers and *Cotinus coggygria*. Its hillside setting and two lakes give pleasing views from almost all of the site. Clearer labelling would help the enthusiast to identify the more unusual species. Contains the National whitebeam collection. Some 262 trees were damaged in the 1990 gales.

WINTERSHALL MANOR   38
Bramley, Surrey. Tel: (0483) 892167 [Mrs Willoughby]

Mr and Mrs Peter Hutley ✳ *2¹/₂m S of Bramley on A281 from Guildford towards Horsham. Right turn to Selhurst Common, fork right and the Manor is on the left* ✳ *Parking* ✳ *Teas from 3.30pm* ✳ *Toilet facilities* ✳ *Suitable for wheelchairs* ✳ *Open 10th May, 19th July, 2 – 5.30pm* ✳ *Entrance: £1, OAP 50p, children 25p*

This formal garden with roses and colourful herbaceous walk is steeped in history. The old mulberry tree planted by James II was badly damaged by the January 1990 gale but has fruited later. Garden railings were put up to celebrate the Battle of Waterloo. Walks through 100 acres of park and woodland with bluebells, rhododendrons and daffodils. Suitable areas for picnics are provided and there is a small chapel to St Francis for the contemplative. A path leads uphill past Stations of the Cross which are marked by the works of 15 contemporary sculptors.

WISLEY
(see Royal Horticultural Society's Garden)

SURREY AND GREATER LONDON
We have included some gardens with Surrey postal addresses in the Greater London section for convenience. So before planning a day out in Surrey it is worthwhile consulting the Greater London section.

SUSSEX (East)

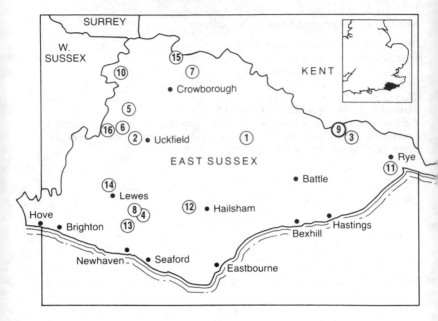

Two-starred gardens are ringed in bold.

BATEMAN'S 1
Burwash, Etchingham, East Sussex. Tel: (0435) 882302

The National Trust ✳ ¹/₂m S of Burwash off A265 towards Lewes ✳ Parking ✳ Refreshments: light lunches, coffees, teas. Picnics in Quarry Garden and Copse ✳ Toilet facilities, inc disabled ✳ Suitable for wheelchairs ✳ Shop ✳ House open and mill which grinds flour on Sats in season ✳ Gardens open April to Oct, daily except Thurs and Fri but open Good Fri, 11am – 5.30pm (last admission 4.30pm) ✳ Entrance: weekdays £3.20, weekends, Good Fri and Bank Holidays £3.70. Pre-booked parties reduced rates. All prices inc. house and mill

Kipling may not be widely read these days, but his home from 1902-36 is much visited. The house was built in 1634 and the rooms and study remain as they were during the period when Kipling wrote many of his best-known works. Much of the garden was his doing and contains formal lawns with yew hedges, a rose garden and pond, a wild garden, and, on the right as you descend from the car park, an exceptional herb garden.

BEECHES FARM 2
Buckham Hill, Nr Uckfield, East Sussex. Tel: (0825) 762391

Mrs V. Thomas ✴ *1¹/₂m W of Uckfield on Isfield road off A2102* ✴ *Parking* ✴ *Teas on charity open days* ✴ *Dogs on lead* ✴ *Vegetables for sale when in season* ✴ *House open by appointment with seven days notice. £1 extra* ✴ *Garden open all year, daily, 10am – 5pm and for charity* ✴ *Entrance: 50p, children 25p*

One wall of this sixteenth-century tile-hung farmhouse is covered by a *Magnolia grandiflora* and it is surrounded by a dozen or more enormous and very attractive containers, once used for cooling the local smelted iron ore. The circular rose garden has mainly old French, musk and moss roses. There are beds of lilies near the house and various borders of annuals add colour to the lawned areas. There is a newly planted 'glade' and *Eucalyptus niphophila* and *dalrympleana* are settling in well. The garden has been cleverly planted for winter colour and is one of the few in Sussex open between October and February.

BRICKWALL 3
Northiam, East Sussex. Tel: (0797) 223329

The Frewen Educational Trust ✴ *On B2088 Rye road* ✴ *Best season: July* ✴ *Parking* ✴ *Suitable for wheelchairs* ✴ *Dogs on lead* ✴ *House open* ✴ *Garden open Easter to Sept, Sat and Bank Holiday Mons, 2 – 5pm* ✴ *Entrance: £1.50, children under 10 free. Coach parties by arrangement*

Brickwall is an interesting example of a Stuart garden, and care has been taken to use the plants chosen by Jane Frewen when she was making and planting it between 1680-1720, such as day lilies, bergamot, *Lychnis chalcedonica*, Cheddar pinks and columbines. There are large lavender beds, a number of ancient mulberries, groups of clipped yew, and a superb pleached beech walk. A striking modern addition is the Chess Garden with green and golden yew chessmen in iron frames, set in squares of white and black limestone chips. This garden is not far from Great Dixter (see entry) and a visit to both would make an excellent day out.

CHARLESTON FARMHOUSE ★ 4
Nr Firle, Lewes, East Sussex. Tel: (0323) 811626

The Charleston Trust ✴ *6m E of Lewes on A27* ✴ *Best season: spring and midsummer* ✴ *Parking 50p* ✴ *Refreshments* ✴ *Toilet facilities* ✴ *Plants for sale* ✴ *Shop* ✴ *House open* ✴ *Garden open April to Oct, Wed, Thurs, Sat (guided tours of house), Sun and Bank Holiday Mons, 2 – 6pm (last admission 5pm)* ✴ *Entrance: £3.50, children £2.75 (house and garden)*

In terms of pure gardening this does not deserve a grading, but it is of national interest because it was created by leaders of the Bloomsbury movement. The walled garden has been meticulously restored through painstaking research and the memories of people who visited when Vanessa Bell and Duncan Grant lived at the farmhouse and of those like Angelica Garnett and Quentin Bell who spent their childhood there. It is a delightful example of a garden created during the 1920s by an idiosyncratic group of highly creative people, and might be called an artist's garden. The crush of visitors may result in limitation on access.

CHELWOOD VACHERY ★   5
Nutley, Nr Uckfield, East Sussex. Tel: (082571) 2293

BAT Industries ✳ *Between Wych Cross and Nutley on A22* ✳ *Best season: spring* ✳ *Parking* ✳ *Refreshments* ✳ *Toilet facilities* ✳ *Dogs on lead* ✳ *Plants for sale* ✳ *Open 17th May, 12 noon – 5pm* ✳ *Entrance: £1.50, OAP £1, children 50p*

The house built in 1906 was bought by a Mr Nettlefold in 1925 and bought by BAT as a conference centre in 1955. Nearly 103 acres of woodland and formal garden offer a wide variety of plantings and interest. Even the well-preserved tea room rewards careful inspection of its kingpost and mouldings. Over 280 varieties of heathers are to be found either in their own areas or as underplanting for acer, azalea or dwarf conifer collections. The rock garden is shingled over polythene for practical purposes, and among the myriad plants are more than 20 varieties of gentians. A Zen garden is a simple yet dominant feature, as is the nearby grave of Mr Nettlefold's retriever. Ten varieties of magnolias mingle with rhododendrons. A substantial broad-leaved planting scheme is under way to replace the damage from the 1987 gales, and wildlife conservation is much in mind, with bird and bat boxes and wild flowers. There are three large lakes, two smaller ones, bog gardens, and several small ponds and waterfalls. Amongst the variety of interesting species are *Stransvaesia davidiana* 'Palette', *Viburnum opulus* 'Fructuluteo', *Salix hyptilloides* 'Pink Tassel', *Populus* x *candicans* 'Aurora', *Magnolia* x *thompsoniana* (60 feet tall). There is careful, ample labelling.

CLINTON LODGE ★   6
Fletching, Nr Uckfield, East Sussex. Tel: (0825) 722952

Mr and Mrs Cullum ✳ *4m W of Uckfield from A272. Turn N at Piltdown from Fletching, 1¹/₂m in main village street surrounded by a yew hedge* ✳ *Parking on street* ✳ *Refreshments* ✳ *Toilet facilities* ✳ *Suitable for wheelchairs* ✳ *Dogs on lead* ✳ *Open 14th, 15th June, 2 – 6pm* ✳ *Entrance: £1.50*

This Queen Anne house was built for the first Lord Sheffield's daughter who married Henry Clinton. The garden of about four acres of clay soil is basically divided into areas by period. There is an Elizabethan herb garden with well-tended camomile paths and turf seats, and four knot gardens are being developed. A lawn and ha-ha at the rear of the house with views to distant woods create an eighteenth-century atmosphere; a white, yellow and blue Victorian herbaceous border with its 'hot' colours purposely absent, and a pre-Raphaelite alley of white roses, purple vines and lilies; the twentieth century is represented in the area surrounding the swimming pool. There are also various walks of quince, vines and white cherry underplanted with white bluebells, and a rose garden of musk and English roses complete with fully-occupied dovecote. Pillars of ceanothus and roses cover the walls in early summer, and less formal areas of orchard and wild flowers complete a garden of outstanding imagination and charm. All minor storm damage has been repaired and trees staked.

CROWN HOUSE 7
Eridge Green, Nr Tunbridge Wells, East Sussex. Tel: (0892) 864389

Major and Mrs L. Cave ✳ *3m SW of Tunbridge Wells. Take A26 Tunbridge Wells – Crowborough road. In Eridge take the Rotherfield turn S. House is first on the right* ✳ *Parking on road* ✳ *Home-made teas* ✳ *Toilet facilities* ✳ *Suitable for wheelchairs* ✳ *Plants for sale* ✳ *Shop for home-made produce* ✳ *Open 11th, 12th July, 2 – 6.30pm and by appointment* ✳ *Entrance: £1.25, children 25p for charity*

This gently sloping one and a half-acre garden contains several different areas of interest. Dominating the side of the house is a colourful umbrella of old-fashioned musk roses above astilbes, golden flame spiraea and catmint. At the front of the house the alpine garden is to be extended and a further pond added. The rose garden is underplanted with cranesbill and is surrounded by a yew hedge and *Clematis montana* 'Rubens'. The heather bed, herb garden and herbaceous borders are all carefully tended, giving a great variety of colour and interest which extend to the aviary, with budgerigars, cockatiels and green parrots.

FIRLE PLACE 8
Lewes, East Sussex. Tel: (0273) 858335

Viscount Gage ✳ *On A27 Lewes – Eastbourne road. Entrance 1m from house* ✳ *Best season: summer* ✳ *Parking* ✳ *Refreshments: cold buffet, licensed 12.30 – 2pm, Sussex cream teas 3pm onwards on days when house is open* ✳ *Toilet facilities* ✳ *Parkland suitable for wheelchairs* ✳ *Dogs on leads* ✳ *Small selection of plants for sale* ✳ *Shop* ✳ *House open May to Sept, Wed, Thurs, Sun and unguided Connoisseurs Days first Wed of every month* ✳ *Garden open May to Sept, Wed, Thurs, Sun and Bank Holiday Mons, 12.30 – 5.30pm* ✳ *Entrance: £3.25, children £1 (house and garden). Parties of 25 or more by appointment £2.85 per person. Connoisseurs Day £3.75 per person. No charge for terrace*

The accessible part of the garden is nowadays small although attractive. The house, with its honey-coloured Normandy stonework, lies at the foot of the South Downs and has long views over the parkland and a nearby lake. Immediately below the Georgian facade, a terrace (where tea can be taken on house open days) overlooks the formal area of Italianate terraces and balustrades, a fountain and a ha-ha. There are several seats from which to enjoy the surroundings.

GREAT DIXTER ★★ 9
Dixter Road, Northiam, East Sussex. Tel: (0797) 253160

The Lloyd family ✳ *¹/₂m N of Northiam. Turn off A28 at Northiam post office* ✳

*Parking * Refreshments * Toilet facilities * Plants for sale at nursery. Extensive choice of clematis * Shop * House open * Garden open April to 11th Oct, daily except Mon, 2 – 5pm. Open all Bank Holiday Mons and 17th, 18th and 24th, 25th Oct. Open from 11am on 23rd to 25th May, Suns in July and Aug and 31st Aug * Entrance: £2, children 25p (house and garden £3.20, children 50p. Concessionary rates for OAP and National Trust members on Fridays only when house and garden £2.50)*

Probably too well-known to need describing, Great Dixter was bought by Nathaniel Lloyd in 1910. The fifteenth-century house was restored by Lutyens. The sunken garden was designed and constructed by Mr Nathaniel Lloyd. His son Christopher has continued his family's fine gardening tradition, striving to maintain the garden with a dwindling labour force. Composed of a series of gardens, these include fine topiary, a magnificent long mixed border, and enchanting rose garden, gardens where vegetables and flowers mingle, and throughout the complex of gardens are pockets of wild flowers. The spring at Great Dixter is famous for the huge drifts of naturalised bulbs. Truly a plantsman's garden, but a joy for anyone who enjoys gardening in the finest tradition.

KIDBROOK PARK   10
Forest Row, East Sussex. Tel: (0342) 822275

*Rudolph Steiner Trust * At Forest Row 1m W of A22. Entrance in Priory Road * Best season: summer * Parking * Toilet facilities (not disabled) * Suitable for wheelchairs * Dogs on lead * Open Aug, daily, 11am – 6pm * Entrance: £1, family £2*

A sandstone house built in 1725, now used as Michael Hall School, and its park lies on the northern boundary of the Ashdown Forest. Work is in progress to restore the main elements of Repton's design, though this was hampered by the loss of 1500 trees during the 1987 gales. 'Swallow' spring, cascades, stepping stones, a pond and a twentieth-century weir add interest, together with wild and bog gardens. The parkland is obviously a shadow of its former glory. Maps available showing recommended walks through the 125 acres.

LAMB HOUSE   11
West Street, Rye, East Sussex.

*The National Trust * In centre of Rye, in West Street, near the church * Parking difficult * House open. Home of Henry James, American novelist, 1898-1916. Later, the brothers Benson, now televised writers, lived there * Garden open April to Oct, Wed and Sat, 2 – 6pm. (last admission 5.30pm) * Entrance: £1.50 (house and garden) (1991 prices). No reductions for children or parties*

Americans are frequent visitors to this house where Henry James wrote some of his best books and studied the English character including its passion for gardening. Although not of considerable botanic interest, the high-walled garden has great charm and it is surprising to find it so big – one acre in the middle of overcrowded Rye. It is well-maintained by the Trust's tenants.

MICHELHAM PRIORY ★   12
Upper Dicker, Hailsham, East Sussex. Tel: (0323) 844224

The Sussex Archaeological Society ✳ *10m N of Eastbourne off the A22 and A27. Signposted* ✳ *Best season: spring/summer* ✳ *Parking* ✳ *Refreshments and picnic area* ✳ *Toilet facilities inc. disabled* ✳ *Suitable for wheelchairs* ✳ *Dogs on lead in car park* ✳ *Herbs and some herbaceous plants for sale* ✳ *Shop* ✳ *House and working watermill open. Blacksmiths and Rope museum* ✳ *Garden open 25th March to Oct, daily, 11am – 5.30pm, Nov and March, Sun, 11am – 4pm* ✳ *Entrance: £3, OAP £2.70, children £1.70*

A major feature is the Physic Garden, a reconstruction of a monastic physic garden, based on that at ninth-century St Gall, which was regarded as the ideal. The 11 beds contain medicinal plants for specific complaints. Many of them are the herbs of the hedgerows. A serpentine moatside border has been planted and there are plans to extend it. The monastery stewponds are also being planted up. A large herbaceous border, backed by a shrubbery, was designed and planted by local horticultural students.

MONK'S HOUSE ★   13
Rodmell, Lewes, East Sussex.

The National Trust ✳ *4m SE of Lewes off former A275 now C7. In Rodmell village follow signs to Church. Sign is 400 yards from the house* ✳ *Parking further down narrow road* ✳ *Toilet facilities* ✳ *House open* ✳ *Garden open April to Oct, Wed and Sat, 2 – 5.30pm (last admission 5pm)* ✳ *Entrance: £2. No reduction for children or parties*

The cottage home of Virginia and Leonard Woolf from 1919 until his death in 1969. In autumn 1989 work commenced on redesigning the garden on the basis of the Woolf's notebooks and writings. Leonard Woolf had kept the village self-sufficient in vegetables, as well as showing them, and the original vegetable area is still thriving. There are two ponds, one in dewpond style. An orchard, underplanted with spring and autumn bulbs, contains a comprehensive collection of daffodils. The one and three quarter acre garden is a mixture of chalk and clay, nurturing a wide variety of species. Flint stone walls and yew hedges frame the more formal herbaceous areas, leading to a typical Sussex flint church at the bottom of the garden. Among the interesting specimen trees are *Salix hastata* 'Wehrhahnii', Chinese lantern (20 feet tall), *Magnolia liliflora*, walnut, mulberry, and *Catalpa bignonioides* (Indian bean). Literary folk will want to campare and contrast this garden with the other Bloomsbury lot's house at Charleston Farmhouse (see entry).

OFFHAM HOUSE   14
Offham, Nr Lewes, East Sussex. Tel: (0273) 474824

Mr and Mrs H.N.A. Goodman ✳ *2m N of Lewes on A275, ¹/₂m from Cooksbridge Station* ✳ *Best season: late spring, high summer* ✳ *Limited parking on property, more on road* ✳ *Refreshments* ✳ *Toilet facilities* ✳ *Suitable for wheelchairs* ✳ *Dogs on lead* ✳ *Plants for sale* ✳ *Open 3rd May, 7th June, 2 – 6pm* ✳ *Entrance: £1, children 25p*

This garden offers a wide variety of interest and perspectives. Lawns sweep from the extremely attractive house (with its well-blended, lush conservatory) to a colourful shrubbery, which contains shrub roses and a variety of trees, including an evergreen or holm oak, a tulip tree underplanted with bulbs, and a weeping mulberry; beyond is an arboretum with a weeping elm and collections of acers and sorbus. The colourful well-stocked herbaceous borders contain a variety of penstemons, euphorbias and salvias as well as an unusual sundial, contemporary with the house. Other features include a spring path with early purple orchids and fritillaries, a collection of lilacs, a cherry orchard (with several Japanese varieties), and an unusually long bed of peonies and aquilegias. A fine new addition is the herb garden, which is bursting with life: bergamots, alpine strawberries and marjorams, mixed with *Tricyrtis stolonifera*, *Phygelius aequalis* 'Yellow Trumpet', euphorbias and verbenas, are framed by box, lavenders and thymes. At the front of the house is a fountain and a splendid example of davidia (pocket handkerchief tree). A particularly large and well-kept greenhouse is the backbone to this fine, well-tended garden.

PENNS IN THE ROCKS   15
Groombridge, East Sussex. Tel: (0892) 864244

Lord and Lady Gibson ＊ 7m SW of Tunbridge Wells on Groombridge – Crowborough road just S of Plumeyfeather Corner ＊ Parking ＊ Refreshments ＊ Toilet facilities ＊ Suitable for wheelchairs ＊ Dogs in park only ＊ Open 20th April, one day in early July, 31st Aug, 2.30 – 5.30pm ＊ Entrance: £1.50, first 2 children 50p, further children free

The name comes from the distinguished American Quaker whose family owned the property from 1672 to 1762 and from the Tunbridge Wells rock formations in the garden. It has emerged over the years into a happy combination of formality and informality within a lovely setting. Lady Dorothy Wellesley developed it extensively and built the temple on the slope facing the Georgian house. The present owners have much developed the grounds since purchasing the house in 1956. It is approached by a long drive through parkland full of wild daffodils and other spring flowers. Pleached limes, a walled garden, a stream and pools, a clipped yew hedge, statuary, old roses and extensive borders provide more formal features, and many well-placed seats help visitors enjoy its beauties.

SHEFFIELD PARK GARDEN ★★   16
Nr Uckfield, East Sussex. Tel: (0825) 790655

The National Trust ＊ 5m NW of Uckfield, midway between East Grinstead and Lewes on E of A275 ＊ Teas at Oak Hall (not National Trust) ＊ Toilet facilities ＊ Partly suitable for wheelchairs. Wheelchairs available ＊ Shop ＊ House under separate ownership ＊ Garden open daily except Mon, 11am – dusk (Sun 1pm – dusk) ＊ Entrance: £3.70, children £1.80

One hundred-acre garden and arboretum with two lakes installed by 'Capability' Brown for the Earl of Sheffield in 1776. Repton also worked here in 1789 and was responsible for the string of lakes up to the mansion. Later still, the lakes were extended and cascades added. Between 1909 and 1934 a collection of trees and shrubs notable for their autumn colour was added, including many specimens of *Nyssa sylvatica*. These and other fine specimen trees, particularly North American varieties, provide good all-year-round interest. Features include good water lilies in the lakes, the Victorian Queen's Walk and, in autumn, two borders of the Chinese *Gentiana sino-ornata* of amazing colour. The Trust is continuing to open up new areas.

HOW TO FIND THE GARDENS

Directions to each garden are included in the entry. This information has been supplied by the garden inspectors and is aimed to be the best available to those travelling by car. However, it has been compiled to be used in conjunction with a road atlas. The unreliability of train and bus services makes it unrewarding to include details, particularly as many garden visits are made on Sundays. However, many properties can be reached by public transport, and National Trust guides and the Yellow Book [NGS] sometimes give details. Future editions of the *Guide* may include a special list of gardens easily reached by public transport if readers indicate that this would be helpful. *The Maps*: The numbers on the maps correspond to the numbers of the gardens in each county. The maps show the proximity of one garden to another so that visits to several gardens can be planned for the same day. It is worthwhile referring to the maps of bordering counties to see if another garden visit can be included in the itinerary.

SUSSEX (West)

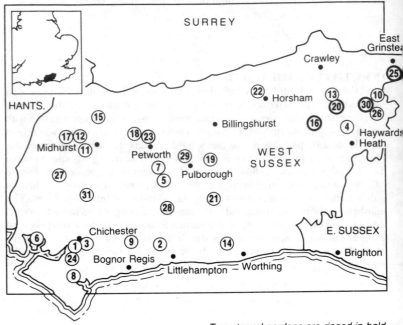

SURREY

East Grinstead

Crawley

HANTS.

22 • Horsham

13
20

10
30 26
25

15

• Billingshurst

16

4

Haywards Heath

17 12
Midhurst 11

18 23

Petworth

WEST SUSSEX

27

29 19
7
5 Pulborough

31

28

21

Chichester 9

2

14

E. SUSSEX

6

1 3
24

Bognor Regis

Littlehampton — Worthing

• Brighton

8

Two-starred gardens are ringed in bold.

APULDRAM ROSES   1
Apuldram Lane, Dell Quay, Chichester, West Sussex. Tel: (0243) 785769

Di Sawday ∗ Turn off A259 (old A27) at signpost to Dell Quay, Apuldram ∗ Best season: midsummer ∗ Parking ∗ Suitable for wheelchairs ∗ Dogs on lead ∗ Shop ∗ Open daily, except 24th Dec to 7th Jan. Mon – Sat, 9am – 5pm, Sun and Bank Holidays, 10.30am – 4.30pm ∗ Entrance: charity collection box

The garden has the brightest and latest HTs, floribundas, miniature and patio roses, as well as climbers, several old roses, modern shrubs and standards. Every rose sold in the nursery is grown in a delightful enclosed garden with grass paths. Vistors can also wander through the rose field, a sheet of fragrance and colour in July. Catalogue available for 50p plus 1st class stamp.

BERRI COURT ★ 2
Yapton, Arundel, West Sussex. Tel: (0243) 551663

Mr and Mrs J.C. Turner ✳ *5m SW of Arundel, on A2024 Chichester/
Littlehampton road in centre of village between Black Dog pub and Post Office* ✳
Parking by Baptist Church opposite ✳ *Suitable for wheelchairs* ✳ *Dogs on lead*
✳ *Open 5th, 6th April, 10th, 11th May, 28th, 29th June, 2 – 5pm, 18th, 19th
Oct, 12 noon – 4pm* ✳ *Entrance: £1, children 30p (1991 prices)*

A series of sheltered gardens within a three-acre garden of great interest to
plant enthusiasts, created over a period of 20 years. There is a mass of daffodils
in spring with azaleas and rhododendrons. The borders have an impressive
display of shrubs and herbaceous plants and many varieties of shrub and
climbing roses. Around the house are magnificent *Magnolia grandiflora*, *Drimys
winteri* and *Clematis rehderiana*. Eucalyptus grove.

BISHOP'S PALACE 3
Chichester, West Sussex.

Diocese of Chichester ✳ *From South Street, turn into Canon Lane, left through the
Palace Gatehouse* ✳ *Parking in public car parks* ✳ *Refreshments: refectory in
Cathedral cloisters* ✳ *Toilet facilities in Cathedral cloisters* ✳ *Suitable for
wheelchairs* ✳ *Cathedral shop* ✳ *Open daily, 8am to 9pm or sunset* ✳
Entrance: free

After roaming the Cathedral pass down St Richard's Walk from the cloisters,
turn right in the close, through the Palace gatehouse and follow the path to the
gardens. These lie just within the city walls and have many tall ilex and bay
trees. Well kept herbaceous borders and shrubs. A place to linger in the shadow
of the Cathedral with a view of the medieval palace. On the way out along
Canon Lane, the houses and gardens should not be passed in a hurry.

BORDE HILL GARDEN ★ 4
**Haywards Heath, West Sussex. Tel: (0444) 450326 or weekends (0444)
412151**

Borde Hill Gardens Ltd ✳ *1¹/₂m N of Haywards Heath on Balcombe – Haywards
Heath road* ✳ *Best season: March to May* ✳ *Parking* ✳ *Refreshments* ✳ *Toilet
facilities* ✳ *Suitable for wheelchairs* ✳ *Dogs on lead* ✳ *Plants for sale* ✳ *Shop*
✳ *Open 28th March to 25th Oct, daily, and weekends in March, 10am – 6pm* ✳
*Entrance: £2, OAP £1.25, children 75p, parties of 20 or more £1.25 per person,
individual season tickets £8, family season tickets £15*

The garden was started by Col. Stephenson Clarke when he bought the Borde
Hill property in 1893. Many of the trees, shrubs and particularly the
rhododendrons were grown from seed collected by great plant hunters like
Reginald Farrer, George Forrest, Frank Kingdon-Ward and Joseph Rock.
There is a sad lack of labels on the plants, and parts of the garden, especially the
bog and bamboo garden, show signs of neglect. However, the garden is
important for its collection of exotics.

CHAMPS HILL 5
Coldwaltham, Pulborough, West Sussex. Tel: (0798) 831868

Mr and Mrs D. Bowerman ✳ *From A29 at Coldwaltham turn W towards Fittleworth. Champs Hill is 300 yards up on right* ✳ *Parking* ✳ *Refreshments: coffees and teas (but not in March)* ✳ *Open 29th March, 3rd, 15th to 17th, 24th May, 7th June, 16th, 21st to 23rd Aug, 11am – 5pm, Sun, 1 – 5pm* ✳ *Entrance: £1, children free*

Champs Hill house is approached by a long drive through the 27-acre garden with one of the most interesting collections of heathers in the area. The current owners plan to plant parts of the garden with something different. The sandy soil and high woodland walks make this a pleasant place for a country walk with views over the Arun, while keeping the plantsperson in the family occupied provided he or she likes heathers.

CHIDMERE HOUSE 6
Chidham, Chichester, West Sussex. Tel: (0243) 572287/573096

Mr T. Baxendale ✳ *E of Emsworth, W of Chichester, S off A259. Turn right at southern end of Chidham village* ✳ *Best season: spring* ✳ *Parking in road* ✳ *Toilet facilities* ✳ *Suitable for wheelchairs* ✳ *Dogs on lead* ✳ *Open 19th, 20th April, 24th, 25th May, 28th, 29th June, 30th, 31st Aug, 2 – 7pm* ✳ *Entrance: £1, children 40p*

Chidmere gardens were laid out in 1930-36 by the present owner's father on the site of a farm and orchard. Modelled on Hidcote they incorporate impressive allées bordered by tall yew and hornbeam hedges together with a sizeable lake. The house (not open) is medieval in origin and, together with the outbuildings, it has been blended into a setting which looks far older than the 1930s. Trees include *Gingko biloba*, *Prunus serrula* and *Davidia involucrata*. There is a good collection of flowering shrubs and interesting French statues from the nineteenth century. In spring the daffodils in the orchard and plantation make a spectacular display.

COATES MANOR ★ 7
Fittleworth, Pulborough, West Sussex. Tel: (0798) 82356

Mrs G.H. Thorp ✳ *¹/₂m S of Fittleworth off B2138* ✳ *Suitable for wheelchairs* ✳ *Plants for sale* ✳ *Open 14th, 15th, 16th June, 11am – 6pm and by appointment* ✳ *Entrance: £1, children 20p*

An unusual garden, which, Mrs Thorp modestly explains, has been planned for ease of maintenance using only plants which respond to local conditions. As an experienced flower arranger, she uses trees and shrubs which give long-term pleasure in the form of interesting foliage, berries and autumn colour. The front border running along the road blends a fine copper beech with *Elaeagnus pungens* and a purple-leaved *Cotinus coggygria*. The house is covered with a large-leaved variegated ivy and, particularly on the back lawn, there are some fine specimen trees, including a dramatically-sited *Liquidambar styraciflua*

'Worplesden', giving autumn colour. In addition to the two main gardens there is a delightful small walled garden to the side of the house with ceanothus, clematis and a host of scented honeysuckles and borders containing *Choisya ternata* and *Philadelphus coronarius*. This is a truly inspiring one-acre garden.

DANESACRE ★   8
Mill Lane, Sidlesham, Nr Chichester, West Sussex. Tel: (0243) 641322

Captain and Mrs A.J. Petrie-Hay ✳ From B2145 Selsey road, turn E 300 yards after petrol station at Sidlesham down Rookery Lane. Enter Mill Lane and house is second on right ✳ Parking in road ✳ Teas ✳ Plants for sale ✳ Open 31st May, 2 – 5.30pm ✳ Entrance: £1 (inc. tea), children 50p

A rather special plantsman's garden, taking full advantage of the south coast climate to grow an unusual variety of hardy and semi-hardy plants. There is a sizeable pond and marsh area, playing host to many different species of exotic waterfowl, which make an idyllic backdrop to the colourful display of plants seen at their best in May and June. These include lapageria, schisandra, mitraria, erythrina and feijoa, and some herbaceous plants not commonly seen, such as adelocaryum, anemonopsis, dianella, eomecon, jeffersonia, *Trifolium pannonicum*, and vancouveria, etc.

DENMANS ★   9
Denmans Lane, Fontwell, West Sussex. Tel: (0243) 542808

Mrs J.H. Robinson/ Mr J. Brookes ✳ 5m E of Chichester. Turn S off A27, W of Fontwell racecourse ✳ Best season: late May/early June ✳ Parking ✳ Refreshments☆: dairy tea shop offering coffee, light lunches and teas from 10am – 5pm ✳ Toilet facilities ✳ Plants for sale ✳ Shop ✳ The Clock House is home to John Brookes' school of garden design running day courses on a variety of horticultural topics ✳ Open daily except 25th, 26th Dec, 9am – 5pm ✳ Entrance: £1.95, OAP £1.70, children £1, groups of 12 or more £1.55 per person

A small walled garden of approximately three and a half acres purchased originally as a vegetable garden by the Robinsons in 1946 and gradually extended and redesigned by Mrs Robinson who retired in 1984 when John Brookes took over. With so much colour and variety, one does not at first realize that there are relatively few flowers. Use is made of groups of trees and shrubs with matching foliage to provide background colour for low-growing and ground cover plants of similar shades that self-seed and naturalize at the front of borders and through gravel paths. For example *Robinia pseudoacacia* 'Frisia', a variegated holly, *Elaeagnus pungens* 'Maculata', marjoram 'Aureum', and *Alchemilla mollis* provide yellow accents in one border, whilst in another *Berberis thunbergii* 'Atropurpurea', *Cotinus coggygria* 'Foliis Purpureis', *Sedum spectabile* and *Anemone* x *hybrida* 'Max Vogel' are all toning shades of pink. The idea of growing in gravel beds came to Mrs Robinson when visiting Greece and has been skilfully extended by John Brookes to include a lake.

DUCKYLS   10
Sharpthorne, Nr East Grinstead, West Sussex. Tel: (0342) 801352
Lady Taylor ✳ 4m SW of East Grinstead, 6m E of Crawley. Take B2028 S at

Turners Hill and fork left after 1m to W Hoathly. Left at sign to Gravetye Manor garden on right ✻ *Parking* ✻ *Toilet facilities* ✻ *Partly suitable for wheelchairs* ✻ *Dogs on lead* ✻ *Plants for sale if available* ✻ *Open 24th, 25th May, 2 – 6pm. Also parties by appointment* ✻ *Entrance: £2, children 50p*

These 14 acres of terraced and hilly grounds, established with rhododendrons and azaleas, are gradually being developed into many interesting individual areas without any loss of the overall grandeur. Carpets of bluebells, daffodils, fritillaries, common primroses and violets burgeon. A *Clethra alnifolia* (sweet pepper bush) has reappeared from beneath brambles, and many of the old paths lead through colourful pink pearls, griersonianum and chaetomallum to two ponds and a bog garden. Dogwoods and *Kalmia latifolia* are benefitting from a hard cut-back. The orchard has several wild orchids – early purple, green-winged and common-spotted – and the undisturbed areas nurture a wide variety of butterflies and birds. The more formal areas reflect the present owners' keen interest in auriculas and double primroses, in particular 'Duckyls Red' (which received an R.H.S. Award of Merit). Among other features, the restored rose garden and several newly planted alpine areas, rare poultry and magnificent views across to Wierwood Reservoir make this an ever-inviting garden.

FITZHALL   11
Iping, Nr Midhurst, West Sussex. Tel: (073081) 3634

Mr and Mrs Bridger ✻ *W of Midhurst off A272. Turn S opposite Iping turnoff* ✻ *Parking* ✻ *Teas* ✻ *Toilet facilities April to Sept* ✻ *Plants for sale* ✻ *Shop* ✻ *Open daily, 2 – 6pm* ✻ *Entrance: £1.25, children 60p*

Three generations of the Bridger family work together to restore and maintain the nine-acre garden on a high South Down site. Surrounded by high rhododendron and yew hedges, the lawns south of the house include fine herbaceous borders, shrubs and heathers, but perhaps the best surprise is the hidden herb garden, enclosed by fine spruce hedges. This in turn gives onto a flagstone walk between two large herbaceous borders. A short woodland walk, carpeted in April with bulbs and in September with cyclamen, leads to a highly productive vegetable garden with produce on sale. Children will be interested in the farm animals.

HAMMERWOOD HOUSE GARDEN   12
Iping, Midhurst, West Sussex. Tel: (0730) 813635

The Hon Mrs Lakin ✻ *3m W of Midhurst, 1m N of A272* ✻ *Best season: spring* ✻ *Parking* ✻ *Refreshments* ✻ *Toilet facilities* ✻ *Suitable for wheelchairs* ✻ *Dogs on lead* ✻ *Plants for sale* ✻ *Open 10th, 17th May, 2 – 6.30pm* ✻ *Entrance: £1.20, children 50p*

This is a peaceful country garden formerly part of a Regency vicarage that has been planted with care and a fine eye for good plants. Although the rhododendrons and azaleas give it its most spectacular flowering season, there are some good seedling abutilons and specimen trees. Across a meadow from the main garden is the semi-wild garden set in a small wood.

HIGH BEECHES GARDENS ★ 13
Handcross, West Sussex. Tel: (0444) 400589

High Beeches Gardens Conservation Trust ＊ 1m E of Handcross, S of B2110 ＊ Best seasons: spring and autumn ＊ Parking ＊ Refreshments on Spring Bank Holidays and for Autumn Event on 18th Oct ＊ Toilet facilities inc. disabled ＊ Spring plant sale 25th May ＊ Open Easter to June and 5th Sept to Oct, daily except Sun and Wed, 1 – 5pm. Also Spring Bank Holidays and Event days, 10am – 5pm ＊ Entrance: £2 (accompanied children under 14 free). Guided parties of 10 or more by appointment, £3 per person with lunches etc. by arrangement any day or time

A garden bearing the mark of the Loder family, which is now being maintained by the Boscawen family as Col. Loder designed it in 1906. The early planting was influenced by John Millais, son of the pre-Raphaelite artist; by Arthur Soames of Sheffield Park, Sussex; and by William Robinson whose philosophy of allowing plants to grow naturally has greatly influenced the development of the garden. A series of valleys or ghylls, the garden has a superb collection of rhododendrons and specimen trees. Willow gentians grow wild, and the front meadow, which has not been ploughed in living memory, is filled with native grasses and wild flowers. The woodland garden is also a haven for wild flowers. Autumn colouring is outstanding.

HIGHDOWN 14
Littlehampton Road, Goring-by-Sea, West Sussex. Tel: (0903) 48067

Worthing Borough Council ＊ 3m W of Worthing, N of A259 ＊ Best season: April ＊ Parking ＊ Refreshments at peak times ＊ Toilet facilities inc. disabled ＊ Open all year, Mon – Fri, 10am – 4.30pm, and first weekend in April to last weekend in Sept, weekends and Bank Holidays, 10am – 8pm ＊ Entrance: free – donation box

Created by Sir Frederick Stern from a bare chalk pit in 1910, Highdown was donated to Worthing Corporation in 1968. Without a rhododendron or camellia in sight, Highdown makes a refreshing change for those used to gardening on acid soil. From such an unpromising site a garden has been created illustrating the scope and possibilities of a garden of chalk-loving plants. These include buddleia, mahonia, paulownia, althaea and paeonia, as well as rarities such as *Itea ilicifolia* and *Clerodendron trichotomum fargesii*.

CUTTINGS
Readers may wish to be reminded that the taking of cuttings without the owners' permission can lead to embarassment and, if it continues on a large scale, may cause the owners to close their gardens to the public. This has to be seen in the context of an increasing number of thefts from gardens. At Nymans, the famous Sussex garden, thefts have reached such a level that the gardener will not now plant out any shrub until it is semi-mature and of such a size that its theft would be very difficult. Other owners have reported the theft of artifacts as well as plants.

DOGS, TOILETS & OTHER FACILITIES

If these are *not* mentioned in the text, then facilities are not available. For example, if dogs are not mentioned, owners will probably not permit entry, even on a lead.

KING EDWARD VII HOSPITAL 15
Midhurst, West Sussex. Tel: (0730) 812341

King Edward VII Hospital Trust ✳ *3m NW of Midhurst on A286. Well signed down a 1m drive* ✳ *Parking* ✳ *Refreshments* ✳ *Toilet facilities* ✳ *Suitable for wheelchairs* ✳ *Dogs on lead* ✳ *Open 9th May, 2 – 5pm* ✳ *Entrance: by donation*

Gertrude Jekyll laid out a series of fine herbaceous borders on terraces immediately south of the large hospital opened for officers after World War I The terraces overlook extensive parkland and playing fields with an elevated view towards the South Downs Way. There are good woodland walks to the north of the hospital which stands in parkland of 152 acres. Also good beds of chrysanthemums etc. grown for the hospital shop.

LEONARDSLEE GARDENS ★★ 16
Lower Beeding, Nr Horsham, West Sussex. Tel: (0403) 891212

The Loder family ✳ *3m SW of Handcross and M23 on the A279/A281* ✳ *Best season: mid-April to mid-June and autumn* ✳ *Parking* ✳ *Refreshments: café and licensed restaurant* ✳ *Toilet facilities* ✳ *Large selection of plants, esp. rhododendrons, for sale* ✳ *Shop* ✳ *Open 17th April to June, daily, 10am – 6pm (May, 10am – 8pm), July to Oct, Mon – Fri, 2 – 6pm, Sat and Sun, 10am – 6pm* ✳ *Entrance: £2.50 – £4 (depending on season), children £1 – £2*

This famous garden was started by Sir Edmund Loder, a member of the family which has left its mark on a number of great gardens in West Sussex. Sir Edmund raised the famous Rhododendron Loderi hybrids, with their enormous scented flowers. The gardens, with their seven lakes, contain a superb collection of rhododendrons, azaleas, acers, two magnificent dawn redwoods (*Metasequoia glyptostroboides*), as well as a wide variety of shrubs. Far from being depressed by the hurricane damage of 1987, Mr Robin Loder, who runs the gardens, is using the natural clearance to develop and replant and eventually extend the gardens and parklands to over 200 acres. A great deal of money and care has been expended on the excellent facilities for visitors. New features include a bonsai exhibition and an alpine house.

MALT HOUSE 17
Chithurst, Rogate, West Sussex. Tel: (0730) 433

Mr and Mrs Graham Ferguson ✳ *From A272, 3¹/₂m W of Midhurst, turn N* *signposted Chithurst, then 1¹/₂m or from A3, 2m S of Liphook, turn SE to Milland then follow signs to Chithurst for 1¹/₂m* * *Best season: early summer* * *Parking* * *Refreshments* * *Toilet facilities* * *Plants for sale* * *Open 26th April, 3rd, 10th, 17th, 24th, 25th, 31st May, 2 – 6pm* * *Entrance: £1, children 50p*

Four acres of flowering shrubs and trees, including fine *Cornus nuttallii*, *Caragana arborescens*, rhododendrons and azaleas on slopes surrounding a picturesque house in a valley.

THE MANOR OF DEAN   18
Tillingworth, Petworth, West Sussex.

Miss S.M. Mitford * *Turn N from A272 ¹/₄m W of Tillington* * *Best season: spring* * *Parking nearby* * *Tea and biscuits 50p* * *Shop for produce* * *Open for charity on 21st to 23rd March, 25th to 27th April, 16th to 18th May, 18th to 20th July, 15th to 17th Aug, 12th to 14th Sept, 3rd to 5th Oct, 2 – 6pm* * *Entrance: 50p, children 20p*

A charming garden, with old walls and terraces, some dating from the building of the house in 1615, also old sundial and other impressive stone ornaments. Some rare plants still survive from Captain Mitford's subscription to the Kingdon-Ward expeditions, the last of the great plant-hunting journeys. The one-acre walled kitchen garden is still used for growing vegetables and also houses a greenhouse containing a fine yellow rose, grown from a cutting from the wedding bouquet of the present owner's great-grandmother. Throughout the garden there are fine lilies and dense banks of the wild Swiss mauve crocus.

MILL HOUSE   19
Nutbourne, Nr Pulborough, West Sussex. Tel: (0798) 813314

Sir Francis and Lady Avery Jones * *At far end of cul de sac immediately to the left of the Nutbourne Manor Vineyard (signposted)* * *Open by appointment and 28th, 29th June, 2 – 6pm* * *Entrance: £1.50, combined with other Nutbourne gardens*

Mill House garden slopes steeply to a fast-running stream surrounded by bamboo thickets and a water garden. The steep banks are a profusion of wild flowers in June/July and the house itself is surrounded by a cottage garden. There is a fine walled herb garden containing about 140 different species to the side. Other gardens open in Nutbourne include Ebbsworth and Manor Farm and you can also visit the neighbouring Nutbourne Manor Vineyard, of 14 acres, predominantly vines imported from Germany.

NYMANS ★★   20
Handcross, Nr Haywards Heath, West Sussex. Tel: (0444) 400321

The National Trust * *At the southern end of Handcross village, off M23 and A279. Well signposted* * *Best season: spring and summer* * *Parking* * *Teahouse* * *Toilet facilities* * *Suitable for wheelchairs* * *Plants for sale* * *Shop* * *Open April to Oct, daily except Mon and Fri (but open Good Fri and Bank*

Holiday Mon), 11am – 7pm or sunset if earlier. Last admission 1 hour before closing ✳ *Entrance: £3, pre-booked parties £2.50 per person*

For 100 years the Messel family have developed Nymans gardens to accommodate a very wide collection of plants, of which rhododendrons, magnolias, camellias and eucryphias are outstanding. The large circular rose garden has been restored and replanted with the old-fashioned roses for which the garden is also famous. Wild and woodland gardening, influenced by William Robinson, dominate Nymans, but there are fine examples of more formal gardening, such as the circular garden sheltered by camellias, and planted with annuals, and the walled garden with its fine double borders of perennial and annual herbaceous plants. Lord and Lady Ross made a fine decision when leaving the relics of a nineteenth-century Gothic portion of the house standing after it was gutted by fire in the 1950s as it provides the garden with a wonderfully romantic backdrop. Leaflets for sale.

PARHAM HOUSE AND GARDENS ★ 21
Pulborough, West Sussex. Tel: (0903) 742021

Mrs P.A. Tritton ✳ *4m SE of Pulborough on A283* ✳ *Parking* ✳ *Refreshments in big kitchen 2.30 – 5.30pm. Picnic area* ✳ *Toilet facilities* ✳ *Suitable for wheelchairs (garden only)* ✳ *Plants for sale* ✳ *Shop* ✳ *House open as garden but 2 – 6pm* ✳ *Garden open Easter Sun to 1st Sun in Oct, Wed, Thurs, Sun and Bank Holidays, 1 – 6pm. Last admission 5.30pm* ✳ *Entrance: £1.60, children 75p (house and garden £3.20, OAP £2.50, children £1.50). Pre-booked guided groups of 20 or more £3.50 per person. Pre-booked unguided groups £2.50 per person (1991 prices)*

The gardens of this Elizabethan house are approached through the Fountain Court. A broad gravelled path leads down a slope through a wrought-iron gate guarded by a pair of Istrian stone lions to the walled garden of about four acres. This retains its original quadrant layout divided by broad walks and includes an orchard. In 1982 it was redesigned retaining its character and atmosphere; the borders were replanted to give interest for many months, with shrubs as well as herbaceous plants. In one corner is the enchanting miniature house, a delight for both children and adults. The pleasure grounds of about seven acres provide lawns and walks under stately trees to the lake, with views over the cricket ground to the South Downs. Veronica's brick and turf maze is new.

PARK HOUSE GARDEN 22
North Street, Horsham, West Sussex.

Horsham District Council ✳ *Behind Park House in North Street* ✳ *Parking nearby* ✳ *Refreshments in tea room* ✳ *Toilet facilities* ✳ *Suitable for wheelchairs* ✳ *Open all year round during daylight hours* ✳ *Entrance: free*

This new garden opened in 1991 and financed by Horsham District Council and Sun Alliance has been very subtly designed to cater principally for the needs of disabled people. It is unashamedly a flower-packed summer garden which in its first season has become a much-appreciated calm and beautiful retreat only minutes from the centre of a busy town. Its pathways are broad to allow prams and wheelchairs to pass easily. Their surface material has been chosen to avoid glare on bright days which people who are partially-sighted can find baffling. And while there are red flowers, that end of the colour spectrum is chiefly served by pinks because as people lose their visual acuity, it is the ability to see red which is lost first. All the turnings of the paths are set at either 90 degrees or 135 degrees so that blind people can easily become familiar with them and do not have to negotiate anything unexpected. An attractive and slightly corrugated band of tiles flanks the paths allowing them to be detected with sticks. Even the figures on the impressive central sundial are deeply incised to allow recognition with the finger tips, the shadow of a gnomon being fairly easily perceived by blind people. Stone-surround walls topped by very substantial wooden paling and climber-clad metal hoopwork supported by massive columns provide both a sense of security and screening from the wind which is vital for people who are likely to spend a lot of time sitting. Plenty of good benches are provided and sited in alcoves so that outstretched legs won't trip people moving along the paths. Benches are set inside arched arbours more than 7 feet high because guide dogs are trained not to pass under arches lower than that. This garden should serve as a model for similar gardens elsewhere.

PETWORTH HOUSE ★ 23
Petworth, West Sussex. Tel: (0798) 42207

The National Trust ∗ *6¹/2m E of Midhurst on A272 in the centre of Petworth* ∗ *Parking ¹/2m N of Petworth on A283* ∗ *Refreshments: lunch 12.30 – 2.30pm, teas 3 – 5pm* ∗ *Toilet facilities* ∗ *Suitable for wheelchairs. Disabled arrangements with administrator* ∗ *Dogs under control in deer park only* ∗ *Shop* ∗ *House open as park, 1 – 5.30pm (last admission 5pm). £3.80, children £1.90* ∗ *Deer park open all year, daily, 8am – sunset. Gardens and car park open April to Oct, daily except Mon and Fri (but open Good Friday and Bank Holiday Mon but closed Tues following), 12.30 – 6pm* ∗ *Entrance: park free*

The park grew from a small enclosure for fruit and vegetables in the sixteenth century to its present size of 705 acres over centuries, and is enclosed by an impressive 14-mile-long stone wall. George London worked here as did 'Capability' Brown. The latter toiled from 1753-63 for the 2nd Lord Egremont modifying the contours of the ground, planting cedars and many other trees and constructing the serpentine lake in front of the house. It was one of Brown's earliest designs, planned while he was still at Stowe. Turner painted fine views of the park (as well as the interior of the house) and it is interesting to see these and have them in one's mind as one strolls around the park as he must have done many times while staying at Petworth. This is not a garden for the botanist, but it is a very splendid experience, all year round, for any lover of man's improvements over nature, and individual trees and shrubs, including Japanese maples and rhododendrons, deserve close study. It is interesting to contemplate that at the turn of the century Petworth had over two dozen gardeners (they were always counted in dozens).

RYMANS 24
Apuldram, Chichester, West Sussex. Tel: (0243) 783147

Lord and Lady Phillimore ∗ *1¹/2m SW of Chichester. Turn right off A286*

signposted Apuldram and turn right again ✳ *Best season: spring* ✳ *Parking* ✳
Partly suitable for wheelchairs ✳ *House open sometimes for art exhibitions* ✳
Open 5th, 26th April, 21st June, 12th July, 30th Aug, 2 – 6pm ✳ *Entrance: £1,
children 30p*

Surrounding this fifteenth-century house are three pretty walled gardens laid
out by the owners, and containing ponds, rose borders and fine cherry trees;
past a huge ilex is the orchard which is a mass of bulbs in spring. The tennis
court has flowering shrub borders and the eighteenth-century walled kitchen
garden contains herbaceous borders, fruit trees and vegetables. The 200-yard
long poplar avenue leads near the church (not to be missed) and gives a good
view towards Chichester and the cathedral. Along another avenue is a wood of
mixed trees underplanted with varieties of narcissus. The owners have
specialised in unusual plants and shrubs, many from South Africa and New
Zealand.

STANDEN ★★   25
East Grinstead, West Sussex. Tel: (0342) 323029

The National Trust ✳ *2m N of East Grinstead signposted from A22 at Felbridge,
and also B2110* ✳ *Best season: May/June* ✳ *Parking* ✳ *Refreshments* ✳ *Toilet
facilities* ✳ *Partly suitable for wheelchairs* ✳ *Dogs in car park and woodland
walks only* ✳ *Shop* ✳ *House open 1.30 – 5.30pm* ✳ *Garden open April to Oct,
Wed – Sun and Bank Holiday Mon (closed Tues following), 12.30 – 5.30pm* ✳
Entrance: £2 (house and garden £3.50 (Sat, Sun and Bank Holiday Mon £4))

The house and estate have close connections with William Morris, and the late
Victorian garden reflects much of the romantic era of the latter part of the
nineteenth century. It is made up of a succession of small, very English gardens.
Perhaps the most outstanding is the little quarry, which has survived as a
Victorian fernery. Good views from this hillside-garden across the Medway
Valley. The house, designed by Philip Webb, will be of interest to architectural
pundits.

STONEHURST   26
Ardingly, West Sussex. Tel: (0444) 892488 (Estate Manager)

Mr and Mrs D.R. Strauss ✳ *On B2028, 800 yards N of South of England
Showground, Ardingly* ✳ *Best season: spring and early summer* ✳ *Parking* ✳
Refreshments ✳ *Toilet facilities* ✳ *On charity days the nursery is open to the
public for the sale of camellias, azaleas, rhododendrons and orchids only* ✳ *Garden
open two or three Suns for charity. Telephone (0444) 892 052 for dates and times.
The Druid's Rocks may be seen by appointment* ✳ *Entrance: £1.50, children 50p*

Thirty acres. Edwardian house set above valley, with contemporary brick
balustrading, terrace, gazebos, observatory and summerhouses. Nearby are
herbaceous border and lawns, with views of South Downs, valley and lakes.
Slopes below are informally landscaped with steps, paths, grotto, rock garden
and planted with shrubs, camellias, azaleas and specimen trees. Five lakes
constructed before World War I fall into each other by a series of waterfalls.

Black swans. Woodland walk to weird rock formations nearby, mentioned in the Domesday Book and Cobbett's *Rural Rides*. Woodland is a designated Site of Special Scientific Interest because of its lichens, liverworts and ferns.

TELEGRAPH HOUSE ★ 27
North Marden, Chichester, West Sussex. Tel: (0730 825) 206

Mr and Mrs D. Gault ✳ *Turn N on B2141 Chichester/South Harting road opposite North Marden* ✳ *Parking* ✳ *Teas on charity open days* ✳ *Toilet facilities* ✳ *Suitable for wheelchairs* ✳ *Open 20th, 21st June, 18th, 19th July and by appointment May to Aug, 2 – 5pm* ✳ *Entrance: £1.50, children 75p*

Originally a semaphore station used to convey news from Portsmouth to the Admiralty, Telegraph House is approached up a magnificent one-mile drive of copper beeches, and the gardens sit in a park which includes a yew wood with a 40-minute woodland walk. The views, as far as the Isle of Wight, are preserved while an impressive array of roses, autumn and spring crocuses, and herbaceous plants and shrubs are enclosed by immaculate yew and hornbeam hedges. It is very interesting to see what the owners have managed to develop from a chalky, windswept site, albeit in a magnificent setting, over a period of 20 years.

UPPER HOUSE 28
West Burton, Pulborough, West Sussex. Tel: (0798) 831604

Mr and Mrs C.M. Humber ✳ *5m SW of Pulborough. Turn right off A29 at Bury/ West Burton crossroads* ✳ *Teas* ✳ *Partly suitable for wheelchairs* ✳ *Plants for sale* ✳ *Open 6th, 7th, 27th, 28th, 29th June, 2 – 6pm* ✳ *Entrance: 75p, children 25p*

A large garden that incorporates several different 'rooms' each enclosed within yew hedges. One side of the house gives on to a paved garden with a wide variety of herbs. By the front door is a large *Magnolia grandiflora* and shrubs surrounding a gravelled drive. A large Victorian greenhouse in an immaculate state of preservation, in front of which you can see a rose garden which the owners have now replanted. Beyond this can be found a lawn enclosed by a close-clipped yew hedge. There is a new water garden and bog area at one end. This is a generous country-house garden, with a deceptive air of having happened by chance.

UPPER LODGE 29
Stopham, Pulborough, West Sussex. Tel: (079882) 532

Mr J.W. Harrington ✳ *From Pulborough take A283 westwards towards Fittleworth. At Stopham, the Lodge is on the left by the telephone box past the entrance to Stopham House* ✳ *Plants for sale* ✳ *Open 5th, 12th, 17th, 19th, 20th April, 2 – 5pm, 3rd, 4th, 10th, 17th, 24th, 25th May, 2 – 6pm* ✳ *Entrance: £1, children 30p*

By no means the cottage garden that the name Lodge might suggest. The acid soil has enabled Mr Harrington to concentrate on an impressive range of azaleas and rhododendrons within a comparatively small area, raised from the road and with views over the surrounding park and farmland. There is usually a good range of shrubs for sale and it is a particularly useful garden to visit for those with similar acid soil.

WAKEHURST PLACE GARDEN ★★   30
Ardingley, Nr Haywards Heath, West Sussex. Tel: (0444) 892701

The National Trust/The Royal Botanic Gardens Kew   ✳   From London take A(M)23, A272, B2028 or A22, B2110   ✳   Parking   ✳   Refreshments: self-service teas, Easter to mid-Oct   ✳   Toilet facilities   ✳   Partly suitable for wheelchairs   ✳ Bookshop   ✳   Part of house open   ✳   Garden open all year daily, except 25th Dec and 1st Jan. Nov to Jan, 10am – 4pm; Feb and Oct, 10am – 5pm; March, 10am – 6pm; April to Sept, 10am – 7pm. Last admission ¹/₂ hour before closing   ✳ Entrance: Prices and opening times subject to variation

Dating from Norman times, the estate was bought by Gerald W.E. Loder (Lord Wakehurst) in 1903. He spent 33 years developing the woodland and formal gardens, a work carried on by Sir Henry Price. The gardens are leased to the Ministry of Agriculture, Fisheries and Food to be used as an annexe of the Royal Botanic Gardens, Kew. It has a fine collection of rhododendrons, kalmias, camellias, corylopsis and viburnums. Unique is the Himalayan glade planted with species growing at 10,000 feet in the Himalayas. Many tender plants such as callistemon, olearias, crinodendron, leptospermums, mimosa and hoherias flourish. Wakehurst is a place for the botanist, plantsman and garden lover.

WEST DEAN GARDENS ★   31
West Dean, Nr Chichester, West Sussex. Tel: (024363) 303

Edward James Foundation   ✳   5m N of Chichester on A286   ✳   Best season: spring/early summer   ✳   Parking   ✳   Toilet facilities   ✳   Suitable for wheelchairs ✳   Open March to Oct, daily, 11am – 6pm (last admission 5pm)   ✳   Entrance: £2.25, OAP £2, children £1. Parties by appointment £1.70 per person

This estate was acquired in 1891 by William James who planted fine trees in the 30 acres of informal nineteenth-century gardens which surround an impressive flint house by Wyatt. Range of plants slightly limited by alkaline soil and severe frost pockets. There is a sunken garden, with a deep pond; 300-foot pergola built in 1911 by Harold Peto, leads to a gazebo, surrounded by rare evergreens (*Clematis armandii, Cupressus goveniana, Cryptomeria japonica*) and fine fern-leafed beeches (*Fagus sylvatica heterophylla*). In addition to the romantic water garden (designed by Gertrude Jekyll) and wild garden, there is a sizeable walled garden with lovingly restored greenhouses containing an amusing collection of antique lawnmowers. The garden borders the Weald and Downland Museum of traditional rural life from 1400 to 1900. The house is now a training college. The arboretum forms part of the gardens.

YEW TREE COTTAGE ★   32
Crawley Down, Turner's Hill, West Sussex. Tel: (0342) 714633

Mrs Hudson   ✳   1m S of A264. Down lane opposite Cretan Pottery shop on B2028, take right turn and the cottage is the second of semi-detached on left ✳ *Best season: spring/summer* ✳ *Parking* ✳ *Plants for sale* ✳ *House open for small groups 50p extra* ✳ *Garden open 27th, 28th June, 2 – 6pm and by appointment for small groups* ✳ *Entrance: 50p, children 20p*

A plantsman's delight and an encouragement to all with small gardens, it is not surprising that this third of an acre plot has been a prizewinner. Developments continue and the vegetable garden is now a small Jekyll-style masterpiece. The front garden is divided between a scree with alpines and herbs and a shrubbery with a golden area including *Hypericum aurea*, physocarpus, forsythia and *Philadelphus aurea*. To the rear of the house a mature quince, underplanted with campanulas and rue, stands over a well, while the borders are bursting with colour and unusual plants. 'Ballerina' and 'Felicia' geraniums, *Mertensia asiatica*, pink phlomis, *Baptisia australis*, toad lilies, and *Cheiranthus mutabilis* (*semperflorens*), sweet rocket and *Rhododendron impeditum* are but a few of the interesting plants in this exceptional garden.

TELEPHONE NUMBERS

Except where owners have specifically requested that they be excluded, telephone numbers to which enquiries may be directed are given for each property. To maintain the support and cooperation of private owners' it is suggested that the telephone be used with discretion. Where visits are by appointment, the telephone can of course be used except where written application, particularly for parties, is specifically requested. Code numbers are given in brackets. For the Republic of Ireland phone 010353 followed by the code (Dublin is 1) followed by the subscriber's number. In all cases where visits by parties are proposed, owners should be advised in advance and arrangements preferably confirmed in writing.

TYNE AND WEAR

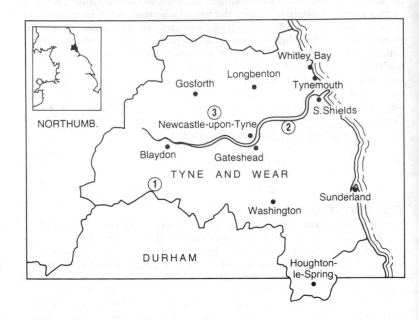

BEDE MONASTERY MUSEUM HERB GARDEN 1
Church Bank, Jarrow, Tyne and Wear. Tel: (091) 4892106

Bede Monastery Museum ✻ *6m E of Gateshead off A185* ✻ *Best season: June/ July* ✻ *Parking* ✻ *Refreshments* ✻ *Toilet facilities* ✻ *Suitable for wheelchairs* ✻ *Dogs on lead* ✻ *Plants for sale* ✻ *House open as garden. Entrance: 60p, student 40p, OAP and children 30p* ✻ *Garden open April to Oct, daily except Mon (but open Bank Holiday Mons), 10am – 5.30pm, Nov to Mar, 11am – 4.30pm, Suns, 2.30 – 5.30pm* ✻ *Entrance: free*

A nicely planted small herb garden with a wide range in four sections: culinary, Anglo-Saxon medicinal, aromatic and medicinal. Currently in need of attention but interesting to the herbalist.

GIBSIDE CHAPEL AND GROUNDS 2
Burnopfield, Newcastle-upon-Tyne, Tyne and Wear. Tel: (0207) 542255

The National Trust ✻ *6m SW of Gateshead, 20m NW of Durham from B6314,*

*off A694 Rowlands Gill ✳ Light teas and picnic area in car park ✳ Dogs on lead
✳ Shop ✳ Chapel open and service 1st Sun each month, 3pm. Concerts, guided
walks and events throughout the year ✳ Open April to Oct, daily except Mon (but
open Bank Holiday Mons), 11am – 5pm ✳ Entrance: £2, children £1*

The chapel is an outstanding example of English Palladian architecture by
James Paine. There is no 'real' garden but the fine avenue of Turkey oaks
leading to the derelict Gibside Hall is memorable. The chapel is surrounded by
woods managed by the Forestry Commission and has three Wellingtonia firs.
There is a Victorian walled kitchen garden which is an open space waiting to be
filled.

JESMOND DENE 3
Jesmond, Newcastle-upon-Tyne, Tyne and Wear. Tel: (091) 2810973

*Newcastle City Leisure Services Department ✳ 1m E of city centre along Jesmond
Road ✳ Best season: summer ✳ Parking in Freeman Road ✳ Refreshments: in
café ✳ Toilet facilities ✳ Partly suitable for wheelchairs ✳ Dogs on lead ✳
Visitor Centre open ✳ Garden open all year ✳ Entrance: free*

Presented to the city by Lord Armstrong, the famous engineer, in 1883 and
only a mile from the city centre, this steep-sided thickly-wooded dene provides
extensive walks in an entirely natural setting, complete with a waterfall, a ruined
mill and some fine old buildings (and even a well-run pets' corner). From
Freeman Road the upper park has a play pond and good bedding plants. Quite
exceptional condition for a city park.

WARWICKSHIRE

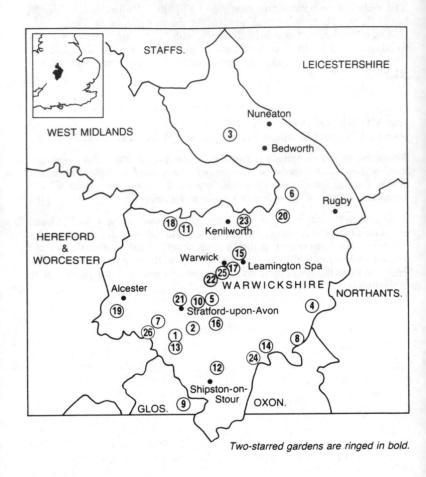

Two-starred gardens are ringed in bold.

ADMINGTON HALL 1
Admington, Nr Lower Quinton, Warwickshire. Tel: (0789) 450279

*Mr and Mrs J.P. Wilkerson ✳ 6¹/₂m S of Stratford-upon-Avon between A34 and
A46 ✳ Best season: June to Aug ✳ Parking in road and field opposite ✳ Teas
✳ Toilet facilities ✳ Partly suitable for wheelchairs ✳ Dogs on lead ✳ Plants for
sale ✳ Open 14th, 24th May, 15th, 16th Aug, 2 – 6pm ✳ Entrance: £1,
children 50p*

This recently-made garden contains a 1620 dovecote which is older than the house. There are 12 clipped yews, eleven inside the garden and one outside the gate, which may represent the apostles. A pool with fish and ducks is surrounded with a range of water-loving plants, and a stream meanders through the garden. The walled garden contains a wide range of vegetables and fruit, and old trees of chestnut, oak, beech and cedar provide a backcloth to the herbaceous borders. Peaceful walks through the woodland area.

ALSCOT PARK   2
Alscot, Warwickshire.

*Mrs James West * 2¹/₂m S of Stratford-upon-Avon on A34 * Parking *
Teas * Toilet facilities * Suitable for wheelchairs * Dogs * Plants for sale *
Open 14th June, 5th July, 2 – 6pm * Entrance: £1, children 20p*

A typical eighteenth-century park with one of the earliest mock-Gothic houses (not open), this has all the requisite main features – extensive lawns, fine trees, orangery, deer park, river and lakes. There is a small garden round the house but the main interest lies in the new garden developed by Mrs West near the orangery, now the site of a pool area. Around it a large semi-formal garden features old-fashioned roses, a mixed flower and vegetable garden and strong lines of hedging. Note the fine quality of the seats, urns, ornaments etc.

ARBURY HALL ★   3
Arbury, Nr Nuneaton, Warwickshire. Tel: (0203) 382804

*Viscount and Viscountess Daventry * 10m from Coventry, 7m from Meriden at
Astley off the B4102 Fillongley/Nuneaton road * Best season: spring/summer *
Parking in adjoining field * Teas * Toilet facilities * Suitable for wheelchairs
* Dogs on lead * Shop * House open * Garden open Easter to Sept, Sun and
Bank Holidays, 2 – 5.30pm * Entrance: £1.60, children 80p (park and gardens),
£3, children £1.60 (hall, park and gardens)*

A delightful garden with a sense of peace. Bulbs at the start of the season followed by rhododendrons and azaleas, then roses in June and autumn colour from trees and shrubs. Formal rose garden and climbing roses. Lakes with wildfowl, parkland, the drive and bluebell woods. A canal system was installed years ago as a method of transport. Pleached limes and the old walled garden are some of the features of this pleasant garden, along with the beautiful old trees. There is a museum in the old stables containing a collection of veteran cycles, motor cycles, sewing machines and some old farm implements. Gift and craft shop in the Old Dairy.

THE BUTCHERS ARMS   4
Priors Hardwick, Warwickshire. Tel: (0327) 60504

*Mr and Mrs L. Pires * 6m SE of Southam. From Southam take A425 Welsh
Road E towards Priors Hardwick * Parking * Teas on charity open day *
Toilet facilities * Plants for sale when available * Open 28th June, but also*

available at other times to clients dining in the restaurant ✳ *Entrance: 70p, children 30p*

This attractive four-acre garden stimulates design ideas. There are good colour combinations of plants, shrubs and trees and the island beds provide colour through most of the year. The pool is crossed by a pleasing bridge and surrounded by a collection of bog plants. Roses have been planted to climb through old trees, and there is a rockery. A pleasant garden to stroll round either before or after lunch, tea or dinner.

CHARLECOTE PARK 5
Charlecote, Warwickshire. Tel: (0789) 470277

The National Trust ✳ *1m W of Wellesbourne, 5m E of Stratford-upon-Avon on road immediately S of bridge* ✳ *Parking* ✳ *Refreshments: morning coffee, lunches, afternoon teas in Orangery. Picnics in deer park* ✳ *Toilet facilities* ✳ *Partly suitable for wheelchairs* ✳ *Large commercial plant nursery opposite main gate* ✳ *Shop* ✳ *House open (last admission 5pm)* ✳ *Garden open April to Oct, daily except Mon and Thurs but open Bank Holiday Mon, 11am – 6pm. Closed Good Fri. Evening tours for pre-booked parties May to Sept, Tues, inc. house 7.30 – 9.30pm* ✳ *Entrance: £3.40 (house and garden)*

More of picturesque and historic than garden interest. Home of Lucy family since the thirteenth century. Shakespeare reputedly poached the deer, which still populate the park alongside Jacob sheep. Park laid out by 'Capability' Brown who was directed not to destroy the avenues of elms, later eliminated by Dutch elm disease. Orangery and wild garden. Of special interest is the Shakespeare border with 32 plants which feature in the plays, ranging from herbs to quince and medlar, and old roses and carnations.

COOMBE ABBEY COUNTRY PARK 6
Nr Coventry, Warwickshire. Tel: (0203) 453720 Ranger Service

Just outside Coventry on A427 ✳ *Best season: June/July* ✳ *Parking* ✳ *Refreshments: bar with snacks. Picnics allowed* ✳ *Toilet facilities* ✳ *Suitable for wheelchairs* ✳ *Dogs on lead* ✳ *Open daily, 9am – dusk* ✳ *Entrance: free but pay and display parking charge all year. Seasonal price fluctuations*

The great attraction is the wide range of activities to be enjoyed in the 150 acres. There is a courtyard with a pool, boating for children along with an adventure play area, a countryside centre, guided walks, a heron lake, pleasure cruises, a Victorian garden and a selection of beautiful old trees and shrubs. On the west front of the house is the terrace and parterre, and the grounds contain canals and woodland walks among oaks, chestnuts, conifers and copper beeches. A heather border, rhododendrons and herbaceous plants give further interest.

ELM CLOSE 7
Binton Road, Welford on Avon, Warwickshire. Tel: (0789) 750793

Mr and Mrs E.W. Dyer ✳ *5m W of Stratford-upon-Avon on A439. Turn left* *after 4¹/₂m to Welford * Parking in road or pub car park nearby * Teas on special days * Toilet facilities * Suitable for wheelchairs * Plants for sale * Open 5th April, 14th June, 2 – 6pm. Also by appointment * Entrance: £1, children free*

It is fascinating to see the wide range of plants in a relatively small garden. Clematis are trained over pergolas and climb through trees and shrubs, and there are dwarf conifers, a rock garden, hellebores, a pool, a fruit and vegetable garden, alpine troughs, raised beds and an excellent variety of bulbs; herbaceous plants and shrubs provide interest and colour throughout the year. All visitors are likely to be stimulated by new ideas.

FARNBOROUGH HALL 8
Farnborough, Warwickshire. Tel: (029589) 202

*The National Trust/Mr and Mrs Holbech * 5m N of Banbury, ¹/₂m W off A423 or E off A41 * Suitable for wheelchairs (grounds only) * Dogs on lead (grounds only) * House open * Grounds open April to Sept, Wed and Sat, also 3rd, 4th May for charity; Terrace Walk only Thurs and Fri, 2 – 6pm * Entrance: £1.50*

Grounds improved in the eighteenth century with aid of Sanderson Miller, an architect, landscape gardener and dilettante who lived at nearby Radway. The fine S-shaped terrace walk climbs gently along the ridge looking towards Edgehill. Legend has it that the owner, William Holbech, built the walk in order to see, in the distance, another landowning friend. The *Oxford Companion* describes it as a majestic concept marking the movement towards the great landscaped parks at the end of the eighteenth century. Two temples along the walk and an obelisk at the end. The trees are beeches, sycamores and limes. To the north, part of the site of the former orangery, now a rose garden, is a yew walk ending where formerly a cascade linked the oval pond (now woodland) with the remaining long lake across the road from the house. The atmosphere is affected by the hum of traffic on the M40 nearby.

FOXCOTE 9
Nr Shipston-on-Stour, Warwickshire. Tel: (060882) 240

*Mr C.B. and the Hon Mrs Holman * 4¹/₂m W of Shipston-on-Stour, 4m N of Moreton-in-Marsh. It can also be approached by forking left in Ilmington * Parking * Teas on Sat only * Toilet facilities * Partly suitable for wheelchairs * Dogs on lead * Plants for sale * Open 19th, 20th June, 2 – 6pm * Entrance: £1, children free*

When the owners came here nearly 30 years ago there were mature yew and beech hedges and from this basic structure they have created a strong design which takes advantage of the wonderful setting. The plantsperson would probably call this minimalist gardening although there are good borders on the terraces with roses, irises, lavender and selected annuals which contrast with the fifteenth-century monastery fish ponds below. The owners have rebuilt these, stocked them with trout and created a woodland walk around. Note also the walled kitchen garden, very orderly and highly productive.

GREENLANDS 10
Wellesbourne, Warwickshire.

*Mr Eric T. Bartlett * Leave Stratford-upon-Avon E on B4086. Garden is on the crossroads at Loxley/Charlecote by airfield * Parking in road * Teas * Toilet facilities * Suitable for wheelchairs * Dogs on lead * Plants for sale * Open 14th, 17th June, 11am – 5pm * Entrance: 60p, children 20p*

Although this one acre garden has some uncultivated areas it has a sense of peace. Many unusual containers provide good colour. There are several pools with a range of water plants and fish. Pergolas are planted with roses, clematis and fuchsia. A wide variety of perennials, grasses and variegated foliage. There are herbaceous borders, shaded areas with ferns and hellebores, and clematis and honeysuckle rambling through old trees. New areas being developed. This is a garden with many ideas for keen gardeners.

HICKECROFT 11
Mill Lane, Rowington, Warwickshire.

*Mr and Mrs J.M. Pitts * 6m NW of Warwick and 15m SE of Birmingham on B4439 between Hockley Heath and Hatton. Turn into Finwood Road (signposted Lowsonford) at Rowington crossroads and first left into Mill Lane * Parking in field opposite house * Tea and biscuits * Toilet facilities * Suitable for wheelchairs * Open 10th May, 27th, 28th June, 2 – 6pm * Entrance: £1, children 30p*

This well-designed garden uses hedges to divide the different sections and there are surprises round most of the corners. The National collection of digitalis (see also entry for The Mill Garden) is matched by a good range of euphorbias, grasses, ferns, geraniums and astrantias, and also hebes and potentillas. Colour contrasts, topiary, pools, trees planted at strategic points with roses growing up through them. Different materials are used for paths. There is an orchard with daffodils and a fruit and vegetable garden to enjoy. This garden should be open more regularly so that vistors could see it throughout the seasons.

HONINGTON HALL AND VILLAGE GARDENS 12
Honington, Nr Shipston-on-Stour, Warwickshire. Tel: (0608) 61434

*Sir John Wiggin, Bart * 1¹/₂m N of Shipston-on-Stour, ¹/₂m to E off A3400 * Parking * Teas in Honington Hall on 28th June only * Toilet facilities * Honington Hall open June to Aug, Wed and Bank Holiday Mons, 2.30 – 5pm. Parties at other times by appointment. Village gardens open for charity 28th June (Hall garden not open) * Entrance: £2, children 50p*

Honington is a well-kept village of up-market houses – some may think so well-kept as to have lost the village character. From the A3400, the approach is over a charming eighteenth-century bridge from which the Carolean house can be seen to the left. This is surrounded by extensive lawns and fine trees and, like most of the front gardens in the village, well-manicured flower beds. A popular afternoon out, particularly on the day the village gardens are open.

ILMINGTON MANOR 13
Ilmington, Nr Shipston-on-Stour, Warwickshire. Tel: (060882) 230

Mr D.L. Flower ✳ *4m NW of Shipston-on-Stour, 8m S of Stratford-upon-Avon* ✳ *Parking* ✳ *Teas on charity open days* ✳ *Toilet facilities* ✳ *Suitable for wheelchairs* ✳ *Plants for sale* ✳ *Open by appointment and 12th April, 10th May, 21st June, 12th July, 2 – 6pm* ✳ *Entrance: £1.50, OAP £1, children free (except 12th April when £2 for combined admission with other village gardens)*

Created from an orchard in 1919, this is now a mature garden with strong formal design which is full of surprises. There is also much to interest the plantsperson. To the right of the drive is a paved pond, with thyme of many varieties ornamenting the stones. Scented and aromatic climbers surround this area. Next, a walk up the pillar border presents an unusual combination of shrubs and herbaceous plants in colour groups. Then, up stone steps, is the formal rose garden and the long double border planted with old and modern shrub roses. The so-called Dutch garden is really an informal cottage garden with a profuse mixture of colour. There is much more – a trough garden, iris and foliage beds, a rock garden and, in the spring, plenty of daffodils and crocus. New plants and trees are still being added.

IVY LODGE 14
Radway, Warwickshire. Tel: (029587) 371

Mrs M.A. Willis ✳ *7m NW of Banbury via A41 and B4086. 14m SE of Stratford-upon-Avon via A422* ✳ *Parking in village* ✳ *Teas on open day* ✳ *Suitable for wheelchairs* ✳ *Open 26th April, 2 – 6pm and by arrangement for parties at other times* ✳ *Entrance: £1, children free*

Radway nestles below Edgehill, and the garden of Ivy Lodge runs back across the former battlefield. Above on the skyline can be seen the mock castle, now a pub. In spring there is a profusion of bulbs and blossom; in summer a fine collection of roses. The village contains many cottages with interesting gardens and every other year (including 1992) about a dozen are open to the public. Their attractions range from a good collection of garden gnomes to grander efforts such as pleached limes. Recently the village achieved the 'Best Kept Village' award but despite this it retains a marked villagey character.

JEPHSON GARDENS 15
Royal Leamington Spa, Warwickshire. Tel: (0926) 450000 ext 2053 (Nigel Bishop, Parks Manager)

Warwick District Council ✳ *In centre of Leamington, main entrance off Pump Rooms* ✳ *Parking* ✳ *Refreshments* ✳ *Toilet facilities* ✳ *Suitable for wheelchairs* ✳ *Dogs on lead/poop scoop* ✳ *Open 8am (9am Sun and Bank Holidays) to $^1/_2$ hour after dusk* ✳ *Entrance: free*

This Spa town has always made a great effort in the floral decoration of its streets, and this activity can be enjoyed at its peak in the intensive bedding out of the principal formal public garden. It is fine enough to be listed by English

Heritage, and besides flowers, contains a remarkable collection of trees. Leamington has a string of parks and gardens running along the River Leam right across the town – an almost unique piece of town planning of a century ago. It is possible to walk their length – Mill Gardens, Jephson Gardens, Pump Room Gardens, York Promenade and Victoria Park. There are some fine listed examples of Victorian iron bridges, as well as earlier stone ones.

LOXLEY HALL 16
Loxley, Nr Stratford-upon-Avon, Warwickshire. Tel: (0789) 840212

*Col. A. Gregory-Hood * 4m SE of Stratford-upon-Avon, N off A422 or W off A429 * Parking in orchard opposite lodge * Teas on charity open days * Suitable for wheelchairs * Dogs * House closed but church open * Open 31st May, 28th June, 2 – 7pm. The sculpture may be visited by appointment with Mr Roy Chandler (0789) 840 212 * Entrance: £1, children 20p*

Though not an immaculate garden, this will interest some. Two reasons for visiting are: first, the owner has designed it as a series of 'rooms' in the Sissinghurst tradition and it is interesting to evaluate his success; second, he has added to them examples of contemporary sculpture from a London gallery. One of our inspectors finds the result rather arid, with not much of interest except large areas of grass; others have enjoyed the sculpture. The church next door is said to be one of the oldest in Britain, founded AD761.

THE MILL GARDEN 17
Mill Street, Warwick, Warwickshire

*A.B. Measures * Mill Street is off the A425 to the west just before reaching the Castle * Open Easter to mid-Oct, Sun and other times when possible. Parties by arrangement * Collecting box for charities*

This garden has a great sense of peace, nestling below the great towers of Warwick Castle (see entry) and beside the River Avon. The toll stocks in the garden recall the history of days gone by, and one can see the old bridge across which Shakespeare is said to have ridden to London. Good use of roses and clematis climbing through trees and large shrubs and something of interest all year, including herbs and alpines. The garden contains part of the National collection of digitalis (see also Hickecroft).

PACKWOOD HOUSE ★ 18
Lapworth, Solihull, Warwickshire. Tel: (0564) 782024

*The National Trust * 2m E of Hockley Heath on A3400, 11m SE of central Birmingham * Parking * Picnic site here * Toilet facilities * Suitable for wheelchairs * Shop * House open as garden * Open April to Sept, Wed – Sun and Bank Holiday Mon (closed Good Fri), 2 – 6pm, Oct, Wed – Sun, 12.30 – 4.30pm (last admission ¹/₂ hour before closing) * Entrance: £1.90 (house and garden £2.80, children £1.40, family 7.70)*

Hidden away from a rather suburban part of Warwickshire this garden is notable for its intact layout with courtyards, terraces, brick gazebos and mount of the sixteenth and seventeenth centuries when the house was built. Even more remarkable is the almost surreal yew garden, unique in design. Tradition claims that it represents the Sermon on the Mount but in fact the 'Apostles' were planted in the 1850s as a four-square pattern round an orchard. Never mind, the result is now homogenous. There is a spiral 'mount' of yew and box, which is a delightful illusion. Note also the clever use made of brick. G. Baron Ash, who gave the property to the Trust, made a sunken garden in the 1930s and restored earlier design features. He also introduced colourful border planting, but the garden also looks splendid early and late in the year when there is scarcely a flower to be seen.

RAGLEY HALL 19
Alcester, Warwickshire. Tel: (0789) 762090

Earl and Countess of Yarmouth ✳ 1m from Alcester on A435 ✳ Best season: spring ✳ Parking ✳ Refreshments: tearooms (small café open from 10am) ✳ Toilet facilities inc. disabled ✳ Partly suitable for wheelchairs ✳ Shop ✳ House open 12 noon – 5pm ✳ Garden open Easter to Sept, 10am – 6pm ✳ Entrance: House, gardens & park £4, children and OAP £3

Not a well-cultivated garden but the climbers on the pillar by the house, the rose garden and some lovely old trees are worthy of a visit. There is also a beautiful lake surrounded by lawns with picnic tables, an adventure area with very good facilities and woodland walks and country trails. The house is very popular with visitors.

RYTON GARDENS (National Centre for Organic Gardening) 20
Ryton-on-Dunsmore, Coventry, Warwickshire. Tel: (0203) 303517

The Henry Doubleday Research Association ✳ 5m SE of Coventry. Turn off A45 onto B4029 ✳ Parking ✳ Refreshments: café serving organic food ✳ Toilet facilities ✳ Suitable for wheelchairs ✳ Guide dogs only ✳ Plants for sale ✳ Shop ✳ Open April to Sept, daily, 10am – 6pm, Oct to Mar, daily except Christmas period, 10am – 4pm ✳ Entrance: £3, concessions £2, children free, parties £2 per person

Six acres including conservation area with pond, native woodland, wild flower meadow, wildlife garden, bee garden, soft fruit garden and trained fruit trees, rose garden, herbaceous and shrub borders, herbs, large vegetable plots including old varieties together with examples of compost-making, raised beds, mulching, green manure crops, plants for drying, use of deep beds and methods of attracting beneficial wildlife into the garden. Also an alpine garden. A children's play area and picnic facilities make it somewhere for the family to visit and learn something for their own garden, even if not intending to use organic methods.

SHAKESPEARE GARDENS 21
Stratford-upon-Avon, Warwickshire. Tel: (0789) 204016
Shakespeare Birthplace Trust

Located in Stratford-upon-Avon and surrounding area ✳ Many tea shops in town

＊ *Toilet facilities in town* ＊ *Shops in properties* ＊ *Open at individual times for properties. The Great Garden of New Place open daily, 9am – dusk. Closed all day 24th to 26th Dec and mornings of 1st Jan and Good Fri* ＊ *Entrance: to Trust properties by individual charge or £6, children £2.50 inclusive (1991 prices).*

If it is true that little is known about Shakespeare, less is known about his gardens. The Trustees have done their best to make them an interesting adjunct to the properties, mostly with tourists in mind. They include *The Birthplace Garden*, a small informal collection of over 100 trees, herbs, plants and flowers mentioned by the Bard. *Mary Arden's House*, the front a mélange of box, roses and flowers, the rear a stretch of lawn with, beyond, a wild garden. Country Museum with tools, etc. Light refreshments and picnic area. *Anne Hathaway's Cottage*; a recreation of a typical English cottage garden of a period later than Shakespeare's and the Tree Garden with examples of those mentioned in the Works. *New Place/Nash's House*; the house Shakespeare bought for his retirement, but alas burnt down, and the foundations planted with a garden around which, it is suggested, his orchard and kitchen garden lay. Reconstructed Elizabethan knot garden with oak pallisade and 'tunnell' or 'pleached bower' of that time. *Hall's Croft*; walled garden with little resemblance to its probable form in the period when it was owned by the Bard's son-in-law. *All the above are Trust properties and fee-charged.* Beyond the knot garden is a large free garden with separate access. Also free are Bancroft Gardens in front of the Theatre and the long stretch owned by the Royal Shakespeare Theatre, along the River Avon between the Swan Theatre and the church where Shakespeare is buried. (See also Charlecote entry.)

SHERBOURNE PARK ★ 22
Sherbourne, Nr Warwick, Warwickshire. Tel: (0926) 624255

Lady Smith-Ryland ＊ *^{1}/$_2$m N of Barford, 3m S of Warwick on A429, close to junction 15 of the M40* ＊ *Parking* ＊ *Teas. Lunches and teas for parties by arrangement* ＊ *Open 3rd, 17th May, 14th June, 6th Sept, 2 – 6.30pm. Also by appointment* ＊ *Entrance: £1.50, OAP £1, children 12 and under free*

A fine park surrounds the early Georgian house (1730), and adjacent Gilbert Scott church (1863), in which Lady Smith-Ryland has developed a series of imaginative smaller gardens characterized by inspired planting. In particular, the 'square' garden at an angle shows great originality. All the conventional features of the English garden – shrubs, herbaceous borders, roses, lilies and so on – are combined in most pleasing and sometimes surprising congruity. There is a temple and a small lake beyond the church. More of the grounds are being developed, and this will ultimately be one of the most distinguished in an area full of gardens of distinction.

UNIVERSITY OF WARWICK 23
Coventry, Warwickshire. Tel: (0203) 523713

Warwick University ＊ *Nearer to Coventry than Warwick, the most direct access is off the A46 signposted University/Stoneleigh just S of the Coventry city turn-off* ＊ *Parking difficult in term although there are short-term pay-and-display spaces* ＊

Refreshments: restaurant ✳ Toilet facilities ✳ Most parts of campus suitable for wheelchairs ✳ Open all year except Christmas and Easter Bank Holidays. Term dates: 6th Jan to 14th March, 27th April to 4th July, 5th Oct to 12th Dec ✳ Entrance: free

The Oxbridge college gardens are much-publicised so it is interesting to see what a new university makes of its campus in botanical terms. The buildings here have been the subject of some controversy, but the landscaping of the surrounding area has done something to mellow their impact on the Warwickshire landscape. The continuing work includes the long lake and the use of trees in landscaping larger areas, and in the smaller spaces, a wisteria-covered pergola in the Social Sciences block, and a water feature (cascading is planned). Formal gardens are being considered for some of the new residences. The university now has two lakes with a wetlands environment nature reserve and footpaths which can be followed using the attractive leaflet 'Campus Walks'.

UPTON HOUSE ★ 24
Edgehill, Nr Banbury, Warwickshire. Tel: (029587) 266

The National Trust ✳ 7m NW of Banbury on A422 ✳ Parking. Coaches by arrangement with administrator ✳ Light refreshments in tearoom ✳ Toilet facilities ✳ Partly suitable for wheelchairs ✳ House open as garden but last admission ¹/₂ hour before closing ✳ Garden open April and Oct, Sat, Sun and Bank Holiday Mon (closed Good Fri), 2 – 6pm. May to Sept, Sat – Wed, 2 – 6pm ✳ Entrance: £2 (house £3.50)

The house itself, which dates from 1695, contains a fine collection of paintings including two super Stubbs. More interesting to the garden visitor is that it stands on sandstone, 700 feet above sea level, at the ridge of Edgehill, site of the famous battle. Below a great lawn, the garden descends in a series of long terraces, along one side of which is an impressive flight of stone steps, leading down to the large lake below. The grand scale of the plan is the main interest, but there are many unusual plants, particularly perennials and, along the lake, bog plants. About twice a year the Warwickshire Hunt meets at the house, and by following the hunt to the surrounding hills at the back, gardening enthusiasts who are also hunt supporters may enjoy a unique view of the descending terraces and lake.

WARWICK CASTLE ★ 25
Warwick, Warwickshire. Tel: (0926) 495421

The Tussaud's Group ✳ In the centre of Warwick, which is off the A46 bypass ✳ Parking ✳ Refreshments of all kinds in castle and town. Picnics in grounds ✳ Toilet facilities ✳ Shop ✳ Castle open ✳ Garden open all year round except 25th Dec, March to Oct, 10am – 5.30pm, Nov to Feb, 10am – 4.30pm ✳ Entrance: £5.75, OAP £4, children £3.50, family ticket (2 adults, 2 children) £16, (2 adults, 3 children) £18. Charges include castle and grounds to Feb 1992 after which increased charges apply

Despite its commercial nature (the previous owner sold 63 acres to Madame Tussauds and 1000 acres to a farmer) this is a pleasant place to visit. There is, however, no reduction in the entrance price for visiting the grounds alone. Some 30 acres of the medieval castle site were set out by 'Capability' Brown, the first work commisioned after he set up on his own. He removed the old formal garden outside the wall and shaped the grounds to frame a view, using great trees, notably cedars of Lebanon. The courtyard was levelled and made into lawns with Scots pines. It is worth climbing the eleventh-century mound to gain a view of the site and country beyond the River Avon – Brown later worked on Castle Park on the other side. The newly-restored conservatory houses tender plants including the *Grevillea* species from Australia, named after the family. From this conservatory, the visitor looks across the large parterre, peopled by shrieking peacocks. This was laid out in the late nineteenth century when the Pageant Field park beyond was also planted with rhododendrons which this visitor finds obtrusive. On the other side of the castle entrance is a formal Victorian rose garden which has been recreated from Robert Marnock's designs of 1868 and a rock garden and pool of *c.*1900. The present owner's intention is to restore the whole to its appearance in 1901, the period of the main interior rooms, now peopled with waxworks of former distinguished guests.

One interesting way to see the castle walls is to go first to The Mill Garden (see entry), in Mill Street, Warwick, south of the town. Later from the castle grounds, the visitor can view this area from the riverside by crossing the bridge near the boat house.

WOODPECKERS   26
The Bank, Marlcliff, Nr Bidford-on-Avon, Warwickshire. Tel: (0789) 773416

*Dr and Mrs A.J. Cox * 7m SW of Stratford-upon-Avon off B4085 between Bidford and Cleeve Prior * Best season: spring/summer * Parking in road and nearby car park * No refreshments but picnics allowed * Suitable for wheelchairs * Plants for sale * Open April to Sept, last Tues of each month, 2 – 5pm and by appointment * Entrance: £1*

This two and a half-acre garden contains many good ideas and blends in with the surrounding countryside. Island beds and the patio area with troughs provide all year round interest and colour and there are several borders of individual colours. There is a pool and bog garden, an ornamental vegetable garden or potager with standard currants and gooseberries, a knot garden and a round greenhouse containing tender plants.

WILTSHIRE

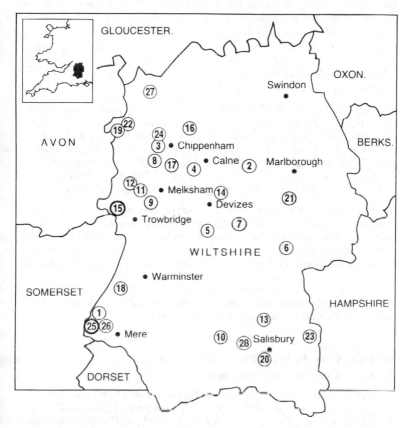

GLOUCESTER.

OXON.

Swindon

AVON

㉗

⑲ ㉒

⑯

㉔
③ • Chippenham

BERKS.

⑧ ⑰
⑧ ⑰   ④ • Calne   ②   Marlborough

⑫
⑪ • Melksham ⑭
⑨   • Devizes

⑮

• Trowbridge

⑤   ⑦

WILTSHIRE

⑥

• Warminster

⑱

SOMERSET

①
㉕ ㉖
• Mere

⑬

HAMPSHIRE

⑩ ㉘ Salisbury ㉓

⑳

DORSET

Two-starred gardens are ringed in bold.

ASHTREE COTTAGE ★   1
Kilmington Common, Warminster, Wiltshire. Tel: (0985) 844740

Wendy and Len Lauderdale ✳ 3m from Mere. Take B3092 from Mere, turn left beyond Stourton (signposted Kilmington) for 1m. The house is on the right, 200 yards beyond left turn to 'King Alfred's Tower' ✳ Parking ✳ Plants for sale in small nursery ✳ Open by appointment ✳ Entrance: £1

A densely-planted cottage garden built around a fine thatched house. A magnificent pergola covered with roses and clematis, and fringed with catmint, dominates the front, and a series of lawns, each enclosed by shrubs and herbaceous plants creates a riot of colour in summer. There are many unusual plants and some splendid and very varied phlox. The garden is kept immaculately. Plants propagated from those within the garden are available for sale in a small nursery adjacent and the stock seems very vigorous indeed. Stourhead and Stourton (see entries) are nearby.

AVEBURY MANOR 2
Marlborough, Wiltshire.

The National Trust ✳ 6m W of Marlborough, 1m N of A4 Bath road on A4361. The Manor is on the north side of the High Street, behind the church ✳ Parking outer village ✳ Refreshments adjacent ✳ Toilet facilities in village ✳ Suitable for wheelchairs ✳ Shop adjacent ✳ House open Sun pm only subject to restoration work. £1, no concessions ✳ Archaeological Museum and Great Barn adjacent ✳ Garden open daily, except Mon and Thurs, 11am – 5.30pm (last admission 5pm) ✳ Entrance: £2, children £1.30, parties £2.20 per person, children £1.10

House and gardens purchased by The National Trust in 1991 after recent chequered history. Fine eighteenth-century walls in need of repair. Well-maintained rose garden in the shadow of the church tower. Splendid lavender walk on main entrance to the house, which on the south and west is framed by lawns and much topiary. Herbaceous borders neatly behind low box hedges. Originally the garden was enhanced with statuary, but this has recently been sold. There is much conservation work to be done, trees to be replaced and substantial replanting of the herbaceous beds. This will be undertaken by The Trust over the next few years, a project well worth watching.

BOLEHYDE MANOR 3
Allington, Chippenham, Wiltshire.

Earl and Countess Cairns ✳ 1¹/₂m W of Chippenham on A420. Turn off to Allington then ¹/₂m on right ✳ Parking ✳ Toilet facilities ✳ Suitable for wheelchairs ✳ Plants for sale ✳ Open 12th, 13th July, 2.30 – 6pm or by written appointment (enclose SAE) ✳ Entrance: £1.50, children 50p

A sixteenth-century manor house with extensive gardens enclosed within high walls and topiary to form a series of garden rooms. Interesting variety of climbers, roses and shrubs. A new courtyard garden, vegetable and fruit gardens are the recent creations by the present owners and Melanie Chambers over the last five years.

BOWOOD ★ 4
Bowood House, Derry Hill, Calne, Wiltshire. Tel: (0249) 812102

The Earl and Countess of Shelburne ✳ 4¹/₂m W of Calne, 5m SE of Chippenham, 8m S of M4. On A342 ✳ Best seasons: spring and autumn ✳ Parking ✳

*Licensed restaurant and garden tea-rooms * Toilet facilities * Suitable for wheelchairs * Garden centre specialising in unusual plants * Shop * House open. Also adventure playground for children 12 and under * Garden open April to Oct, daily, 11am – 6pm or dusk if earlier * Entrance: £4.30, OAP £3.50, children £2.10*

Over 90 acres of 'Capability' Brown landscaped park with a very large lake. At the end of this, a cascade and grotto built by Josiah Lane (1785), and a classical temple. There is an arboretum and pinetum. Thousands of flowering bulbs bloom in spring. The Robert Adam orangery (converted into a gallery) is particularly fine and in front of it are formal Bath-stone terraces with rose beds, standard roses and fastigiate yews. *Fremontodendron californicum* flourishes on the Italianate terrace. The rhododendron walks are situated in a separate 50-acre area, which is only open when the rhododendrons are flowering. Robert Adam's mausoleum ('a little gem' well worth a visit) is in this area.

BROADLEAS GARDEN 5
Broadleas, Devizes, Wiltshire. Tel: (0380) 722035

*Lady Anne Cowdray/Broadleas Garden Charitable Trust * 1m S of Devizes. Entrance through Devizes (signposted from Long Street) * Parking * Teas on Sun until end of Aug * Toilet facilities * Own-propagated plants for sale * Open April to Oct, Sun, Wed, Thurs, 2 – 6pm * Entrance: £1.50, children under 12 50p*

This garden was bought just after World War II and started from nothing by Lady Anne Cowdray in a combe below Devizes. Mature and semi-mature magnolias grow on each side of a steep dell. As good as any Cornish garden, it is stuffed with fine things that one would think too tender for these parts. Large specimens of everything (much of it now forty years old), *Paulownia fargesii*, *Parrotia persica*, all manner of magnolias, azaleas, hydrangeas, hostas, lilies and trilliums of rare and notable species. It is a garden of tireless perfectionism, at its most stunning in spring when sheets of bulbs stretch out beneath the flowering trees. Rarely seen in such quantities for instance are the erythroniums or dog-tooth violets. Many of the more unusual plants, both shrubs and perennials, are grown at Broadleas. There is also a woodland walk, a sunken rose garden and a silver border. This is serious plantsmanship and dendrology.

CHIFFCHAFFS
(see Dorset)

CHISENBURY PRIORY ★ 6
Pewsey, Wiltshire.

*Mr and Mrs Alastair Robb * Off A345 Pewsey – Salisbury road. Turn E in Enford over the river Avon and then N on road to Upavon. Formal gate and avenue 1m on right * Best season: summer * Parking * Suitable for wheelchairs *

*Plants and wine for sale * Vineyard open * Garden open June to Aug, Wed and Sun; May and Sept, Wed only, 2 – 6pm * Entrance: £1.50*

A five-acre garden created in the last 15 years around a part-medieval and part-Georgian house. Fine herbaceous borders and series of more intimate walled gardens. Specimen trees rise from well-maintained lawns. Small stream with many damp-loving plants. Laburnum tunnel recently created. Many rare plants, some only semi-hardy and kept in pots. Many of these are from South Africa. A beautiful garden, full of light and shade and sudden vistas. Excellent use made of fine old walls. A recently-created vineyard is producing a dry white wine on sale at the house.

CONOCK MANOR 7
Devizes, Wiltshire.

*Mr and Mrs Bonar Sykes * 5m SE of Devizes off A342 * Parking * Teas * Suitable for wheelchairs * Open 17th May, 2 – 6pm * Entrance: £1, children 20p*

Set between distant views of Marlborough Downs and Salisbury Plain, the Georgian house looks on to the lawns with specimen trees, ha-has and a recently-planted arboretum. From a Reptonesque thatched dairy near the house, a long brick wall and mixed shrub border lead to the stable block, in style early Gothic Revival, with a copper-domed cupola. Beyond, yew and beech hedges and brick walls frame the meticulously-kept kitchen garden and 1930s shrub walk. Box forms attractive bays and clipped balls. Pleached limes, a magnolia garden including malus, sorbus and prunus, and a woodland walk are other features of this handsome garden.

CORSHAM COURT 8
Corsham, Wiltshire. Tel: (0249) 712214

*The Lord Methuen * 4m W of Chippenham on A4 * Best season: spring * Parking * Toilet facilities * Suitable for wheelchairs * Dogs on lead * House open * Garden open Jan to Nov, daily except Mon and Fri, 2 – 4.30pm and until 6pm from Good Fri to Sept, except Mon. Open all Bank Holidays * Entrance: £1.50*

Approaching from Chippenham, look out for a glimpse of this house on your left, once framed by an avenue of elms now replaced by some lime trees. Surrounded by a landscape of 'Capability' Brown's devising, finished off by Humphry Repton (the lake and boat-house particularly), it is an example of this kind of gardening at its best. Rare and exotic trees look entirely at home: black walnut, Californian redwood, cedars, Wellingtonias, and the most astonishing layered Oriental plane tree, shading beeches, oaks, sycamores and Spanish chestnuts. There are 340 species of trees and 75,000 daffodils in the 40-acre arboretum. The bath-house designed by Brown is a treat and one can get through it into a world of entirely different mood. The Bradford porch leads out into a small enclosed flower garden with catalpa trees. Repton's roses trained over metal arches encircling a round pond is a rare surviving example of the elegance of early nineteenth-century flower gardens. Here the flower borders contain the unusual *Clerodendrum trichotomum* and enormous iron supports for roses and *Clematis* x *jackmanii*. There is a box-edged garden, hornbeam allée, good urns and arbours and seats. In spring the park shines with flowers of countless bulbs under magnolia trees, and in August there are handsome hydrangeas and willow gentians.

THE COURTS 9
Holt, Trowbridge, Wiltshire. Tel: (0225) 782340

The National Trust ✳ *3m SW of Melksham, 3m N of Trowbridge, 2¹/₂m E of Bradford-on-Avon on B3107* ✳ *Best season: summer* ✳ *Parking at the village hall* ✳ *Suitable for wheelchairs* ✳ *Open April to 1st Nov, daily except Sat, 2 – 5pm. Out of season by appointment* ✳ *Entrance: £2, children £1*

Created by Sir George Hastings in 1900-1911, this has been an impressive garden and is still well worth visiting for both the plants and ideas. Extensive bog and water plants. The eighteenth-century house is set in formal areas of garden which give place to wild, bog and orchard gardens beyond. There are many lawns, much topiary, beguiling nooks and lots of good Edwardian features such as stone walls and paths, pergolas, hedges, lily ponds and terraces. A garden in the Hidcote mould, it is being substantially restored under the care of the present head gardener. The large terrace has been rebuilt and will be replanted for next year. Some superb specimen trees. A large part of the garden is given over to wild flowers, with close cut pathways winding through. A garden well worth seeing as it is being quietly restored.

FITZ HOUSE 10
Teffont Magna, Salisbury, Wiltshire. Tel: (0722) 716257

Major and Mrs Mordaunt-Hare ✳ *10m W of Salisbury on B3089* ✳ *Open May to Sept, Sat and Sun, 2 – 5.30pm* ✳ *Entrance: £2, children £1*

Teffont Magna is an exquisite village threaded along a chalk stream which runs also through the garden of Fitz House. What more could a gardener wish for than the beautiful stone of a sixteenth-century house as a backdrop for a garden and a stream to water it. Good hedges form the 'bones' of this scented garden infilled with massed spring bulbs and handsome shrub planting such as azaleas and roses. The garden is sloping and partly terraced, with large varied flowerbeds and handsome stone retaining walls. Delightfully peaceful.

GREAT CHALFIELD MANOR 11
Melksham, Wiltshire. Tel: (0985) 847777

The National Trust ✳ *3m SW of Melksham on B3107* ✳ *Parking* ✳ *House open* ✳ *Garden open April to Oct, Tues, Wed and Thurs, by guided tours only starting 12.15pm, 2.15pm, 3pm, 3.45pm and 4.30pm* ✳ *Entrance: £3*

This house and garden were rescued in the early 1900s by Mr Robert Fuller. The setting is extremely romantic, lost among tree-lined lanes and water meadows. One crosses a stream to enter the courtyard in front of the house with the parish church on the left. Behind the house and the inner court (replanted with pink roses in 1989), the land falls away to an orchard and to the lower moat which is spring-fed. The large lawn or pleasaunce has two topiary houses and a gazebo, all made by Mr Fuller, with a border below. The garden is not for plantsmen but its magic lies in the setting, the mill leat, nine hundred yards long, and in the fact that it is profoundly English and ancient.

HAZELBURY MANOR 12
Nr Box, Corsham, Wiltshire. Tel: (0225) 810715

Mr and Mrs I.D. Pollard ✳ *5m SW of Chippenham. From Box take A365 to Melksham, turn left onto B3109 , take the next left, and then turn right immediately into private drive* ✳ *Parking* ✳ *Tea rooms open daily* ✳ *Toilet facilities* ✳ *Plants for sale* ✳ *Open daily, 10am – 6pm. Coach parties welcome* ✳ *Entrance: £2.80, OAP £2, children £1*

Very extensive formal gardens about a sprawling Elizabethan house, immaculately restored and rejuvenated by its present owner. The massive rock garden at the front of the house is impressive although it couldn't be called in keeping with the house and makes as big a twentieth-century statement as the earlier Edwardian garden. This formal garden has a large lawn banked up on either side by high walks between clipped beeches. Every inch is extremely well looked after. In spring the alleys are all carpeted with brilliant polyanthus, cowslips and wallflowers. Mammoth herbaceous borders blaze in summer. There is a beautiful laburnum arched walk, and other notable features are a lime walk and – nearer the house – a terraced alpine garden. A more private and intimate garden nestles in the fortifications on the other side of the house. In this terraced area an old mulberry tree, irises, lavender and standard roses create an atmosphere appropriate to the genuine medieval archery walk. Beyond the fortifications is a new plantation of specimen trees, mostly conifers. There is a great deal to see and nothing is done by half measures. Very impressive.

HEALE GARDENS ★ 13
Middle Woodford, Salisbury, Wiltshire. Tel: (0722) 73504

Major David and Lady Anne Rasch ✳ *4m N of Salisbury between A360 and A345* ✳ *Parking* ✳ *Toilet facilities* ✳ *Suitable for wheelchairs* ✳ *Dogs on lead* ✳ *Extensive range of plants for sale, many home-grown* ✳ *Shop and plant centre open as gardens* ✳ *House not open except to groups of 20 or more booked in advance* ✳ *Gardens open all year, daily, 10am – 5pm* ✳ *Entrance: £2 (1991 prices)*

This is an idyllic garden with mature yew hedges. A tributary of the Avon meanders through it providing the perfect boundary and obvious site for the sealing-wax red Japanese bridge and the thatched tea-house which straddles the water. This was made with the help of four Japanese gardeners in 1910 and extends under the shade of *Magnolia* x *soulangiana* along the boggy banks planted with bog arums, *Rodgersia aesculifolia*, candelabra primulas and irises.

There are two terraces immediately beside the house, one rampant with alchemilla, spurges and irises. The other has two stone lily ponds, designed by Harold Peto, and two small borders given height by nine-foot high wooden pyramids bearing clematis and honeysuckle. The Long Border contains mostly hybrid musk roses backed by a simple but effective rustic trellis, and also many interesting herbaceous plants. The walled kitchen garden is possibly the most successful part of the garden – it achieves a very satisfying marriage between practicality and pleasure. It is not a regimented vegetable garden but the formal nature of rows of potatoes etc are made a feature and plots are divided by espaliered fruit trees forming an apple and pear tunnel, and by pergolas and hedges. The wonderful flint and brick wall provides protection for many plants including *Cytisus battandieri* and an ancient fig. This is a walled garden where one is encouraged to linger on the seats and in the shaded arbours and enjoy and admire the extraordinary tranquillity of the place. The plant centre is very comprehensive and the shop appeals to the discerning. Unique wrought-iron plant supports can be bought here. Look out for the ancient mulberry and the very old *Cercidiphyllum japonicum*, and *Magnolia grandiflora*. Winner of the Christies – HHA Garden of the Year Award 1984.

HOME COVERT ★ 14
Roundway, Devizes, Wiltshire. Tel: (0380) 723407

Mr and Mrs John Phillips ✻ *1m N of Devizes. Signposted to Roundway off A361 on edge of built-up area NE of town. Turn left towards Rowde in village. House is ¹/₄m beyond village, on left. Signposted* ✻ *Parking* ✻ *Refreshments on charity days* ✻ *Partly suitable for wheelchairs* ✻ *Open 15th July, 16th Aug, 2 – 6pm for charity and parties at all times by appointment* ✻ *Entrance: £1, children free*

Over the last 30 years this garden has been created by the present owners out of amenity woodlands of the now-demolished Roundway House. In front of the house there is a large lawn on a plateau edged with grasses, herbaceous plants and alpines producing much colour in August. Beyond this, grass pathways meander through an informal collection of trees and rare shrubs. A steep path drops from the plateau to a water garden, lake, waterfall and bog garden, rich with colour from bog primulas and other moisture-loving plants. This area is shaded by fine specimen trees. Excellent collections of hostas and hydrangeas are scattered informally throughout. Described as 'a botanical madhouse', this garden offers wonderful contrasts as well as enough richness and variety of planting to satisfy any enthusiast.

IFORD MANOR ★★ 15
Iford, Bradford-on-Avon, Wiltshire. Tel: (02216) 2364

Mr and Mrs J.J.W. Hignett ✻ *7m SE of Bath via A36* ✻ *Parking* ✻ *Teas May to Sept, Sun and Bank Holiday Mons* ✻ *Toilet facilities* ✻ *Open April and Oct, Sun, 2 – 5pm, May to Sept, Tues – Thurs, Sat and Sun and Summer Bank Holidays, 2 – 5pm. Other times and groups by appointment* ✻ *Entrance: £2, OAP, students £1*

It is always illuminating to see a famous architect and landscape gardener's own garden. Harold Peto found himself a near-ideal house in the steep valley through which the River Frome slides langorously towards Bath. The topography lent itself to the strong architectural framework favoured by Peto and the creation of areas of entirely differing moods. The overriding intention is Italianate with a preponderance of cypresses, juniper, box and yew, punctuated at every turn by sarcophagi, urns, terracotta, marble seats and statues, columns, fountains and loggias. In a different vein is a meadow of naturalised bulbs, most spectacularly martagon lilies. A path leads from here to the cloisters – an Italian-Romanesque building of Harold Peto's confection made with fragments collected from Italy. From here one can admire the whole, and the breath-taking valley and the walled kitchen garden on the other side.

KELLAWAYS   16
Chippenham, Wiltshire. Tel: (0249 74) 203

*Mrs D. Hoskins * 3m NE of Chippenham on the East Tytherton road * Parking * Teas * Toilet facilities * Partly suitable for wheelchairs * Plants for sale on 14th June * Open March to Nov by appointment and 14th June, 2 – 7pm * Entrance: £1.50, children 20p*

June is a very rewarding time to visit because of the old roses which, cleverly underplanted, predominate throughout. Winter is another outstanding time, because of the profusion of winter-flowering shrubs. The Cotswold-stone seventeenth-century house has a stone terrace on the walled garden side bursting with thyme and wild strawberries. The clemency of the walls mean that the owner can grow joyous things like sun roses, *Carpenteria californica* and other frailties. A serious cottage garden.

LACKHAM COLLEGE   17
Lacock, Chippenham, Wiltshire. Tel: (0249) 443111

*Wiltshire County Council * On A350 4m S of Chippenham, 4m N of Melksham. Signposted * Best season: June * Parking * Refreshments * Toilet facilities * Suitable for wheelchairs * Dogs (apart from guide dogs) in car park only * Plants for sale * Wiltshire Agricultural Museum on site * Open Easter to Oct, daily, 11am – 4pm and by arrangement * Entrance: £3, concessions £2, children £1, family ticket £8, season ticket £15*

The garden is divided into distinct halves. Around the original house, now the focus of the College, is an Italian garden of balustrades and rose terraces, absolutely magnificent in late June. Many of the roses are very old hybrids, some French, some German, all very clearly labelled. An indifferent long herbaceous border links the house to the walled garden which contains collections of vegetables (including ornamental cabbages), fruit and flowers all very neatly laid out and carefully labelled for instruction purposes. Fine greenhouses with a large citrus tree as well as a collection of poisonous plants. The Agricultural Museum is excellent, while there is also a collection of rare-breed sheep and pigs (very randomly labelled), pleasant but scruffy walks through the woodland and a well-placed bird hide perched above the River Avon. Not a great garden, but one with plenty to fill an afternoon.

LONGLEAT HOUSE ★   18
Warminster, Wiltshire. Tel: (09853) 551

The Marquess of Bath ✳ 4¹/₂m SE of Frome on A362 ✳ Parking ✳ Helicopter landing pad available by prior request ✳ Refreshments: café, licensed restaurant, kiosks ✳ Picnic area by lake ✳ Toilet facilities ✳ Suitable for wheelchairs ✳ Dogs on leads ✳ Shop ✳ House open ✳ Garden open daily except 25th Dec, Easter to Sept, 10am – 6pm, rest of the year, 10am – 4pm ✳ Entrance: £1.50, OAP £1, children free, coaches free (garden only)

This garden has been rearranged and tinkered with by most of the great names in English landscape history. There is nothing left to show today of the two earliest gardens here, the Elizabethan and that made by London and Wise in the 1680s which must have been one of the most elaborate ever made in England. Sadly it was barely half a century before 'Capability' Brown ironed out the formality and created a chain of lakes set amongst clumps of trees and hanging woods – best admired today from 'Heaven's Gate.' This was slightly altered by Repton in 1804 and added to in the 1870s when it became fashionable to collect exotic trees such as Wellingtonias and monkey puzzles and groves of rhododendrons and azaleas. In this century the fortunes of the garden came under the guiding hand of Russell Page. The park remains both beautiful and rewarding for all who delight in trees. The formal garden focused on the orangery to the south of the house was redeveloped in the nineteenth century. It was simplified and improved upon by Russell Page to great effect. The orangery itself is a dream of wisteria and lemon-scented verbenas. Near the house there is a small, trim rose garden, and a quarter of a mile to the south there is a pleasure walk in a developing arboretum, with many spring bulbs and wild flowers. Elsewhere, the safari park and other exhibitions are available to visitors.

MANOR FARM   19
West Kington, Chippenham, Wiltshire. Tel: (0249) 782671

Sir Michael and Lady Farquhar ✳ 2m NE of Marshfield ✳ Parking in village ✳ Teas ✳ Suitable for wheelchairs ✳ Open 31st May, 19th July, 6th Sept, 2 – 6pm ✳ Entrance: £1.50 combined with Pound Hill House (see entry)

Created since 1979 from a wilderness of concrete walks, horseradish and gooseberry bushes gone to seed, the garden of Manor Farm now offers suitably romantic views of rose-smothered arbours, pergolas and high walls dripping with old-fashioned climbers – the perfect foil to the square-cut classical villa *c.* 1820. A very personal garden and the labour of love of Lady Farquhar, the garden seems like an extension of the house with a new porch looking down the rose walk, planted with 'Iceberg' and silver plants. The herbaceous border is suitably Jekyllish in blues and pinks. A handsome wrought iron gate and posts topped with eagles offer views of the countryside. There is a ha-ha, a new wild garden and a domestic courtyard where tender plants flourish in tubs.

MOMPESSON HOUSE   20
The Close, Salisbury, Wiltshire. Tel: (0722) 335659

The National Trust ✳ In centre of Salisbury, N side of Chorister's Green in the

Cathedral Close ✻ *Parking charged for in Close* ✻ *Teas in Garden Room when house open* ✻ *Toilet facilities* ✻ *Suitable for wheelchairs in garden and ground floor of house* ✻ *House open* ✻ *Garden open April to Oct, daily except Thurs and Fri, 12 noon – 5.30pm (last admission 5pm)* ✻ *Entrance: £2.60 (house and garden)*

If visiting Salisbury, the Cathedral and the Close are a must, and if you have been fortunate enough to find a parking space, take time also to visit this small walled garden, which is in the old English style. Its reposeful atmosphere is very refreshing. Summer is best, with the old-fashioned roses in bloom, but it is attractive throughout the open season.

OARE HOUSE 21
Oare, Nr Pewsey, Wiltshire. Tel: (0672) 62613

Mr H. Keswick ✻ *2m N of Pewsey on A345* ✻ *Best season: spring/summer* ✻ *Parking* ✻ *Teas on charity open days* ✻ *Toilet facilities* ✻ *Partly suitable for wheelchairs* ✻ *Open 26th April, 26th July, 2 – 6pm* ✻ *Entrance: £1, children 20p*

The 1740 house was extended by Clough Williams Ellis in the 1920s and the garden created from 1920 to 1960 first by Sir Geoffrey Fry and now by Mr Henry Keswick. It is tantalising to glimpse this house from the road, set back as it is behind towering lime avenues and beech hedges – and when in spring magnolias flower and the grass is awash with narcissi you know the real garden must be something. To the south of the house is an intimate, formal 'library garden' of yew hedges reached by a wisteria covered pergola – a gap in the hedge leads the eye down a pleached lime walk to a loggia. Next to this is a narrow secret garden called 'the slip'. On the western side of the house is a long terrace which ends at the flower-bedded swimming pool garden. Far beyond is a wooded slope and a ride leading up into the hilly distance, forming a wonderful vista. The borders are necessarily substantial and planted as they should be with big shrubs and quantities of roses. The kitchen garden contains all the best things arranged in a purposeful manner, with Irish yews, espalier fruit trees, vegetables and an herbaceous border edged with lavender. All this is a model of maintenance on a large scale.

POUND HILL HOUSE 22
West Kington, Wiltshire. Tel: (0249) 782781

Mr and Mrs Philip Stockitt ✻ *2m NE of Marshfield* ✻ *Parking* ✻ *Teas* ✻ *Suitable for wheelchairs* ✻ *Wide range of rare plants for sale* ✻ *Open 31st May, 19th July, 6th Sept, 2 – 6pm* ✻ *Entrance: £1.50 combined with Manor Farm (see entry)*

An interesting update on the theme of the Cotswold garden, in two acres around a fifteenth-century stone house. It offers the visitor a series of gardening experiences that demonstrate the benefits of a well-trained eye and a professional knowledge of planting. Mrs Stockitt wanted a garden appropriate to the house. 'It's not contrived – gardening should be a refining process. And every year we have a new scheme.' There are lessons to be learned from the easy way the viewer takes in the effect from the yard through to an 'old-fashioned rose' garden (planted and labelled David Austin roses) leading to a Victorian vegetable garden with espaliered fruit trees, then through a clematis tunnel, culminating in a statue. Beyond there is an orchard, a Cotswold garden with topiary, pond, yew-screened tennis court, herbaceous border and drystone walls showing off 'Ballerina' roses, topiary and two trelliswork obelisks, designed by Mrs Stockitt. Extensive retail area adjacent to the garden selling progenies from 2000 varieties of rarer plants from the two nurseries.

ROCHE COURT SCULPTURE GARDEN 23
East Winterslow, Nr Salisbury, Wiltshire. Tel: (0980) 862204 and (071) 235 5844

*Mr and Mrs Arthur Ponsonby * 5m E of Salisbury off A30, S side, following the sign 'Roche Court, Winterslow' * Parking * Partly suitable for wheelchairs * Open April to Sept, Sat and Sun, 11am – 5pm, weekdays and Oct to March by appointment only * Entrance: free*

This is an exhibition of modern garden or 'public-place' sculpture by such noted practitioners as Armitage, Flanagan, Frink and by dead sculptors in the modern idiom: for example Gill and Hepworth. All works are for sale and information about them can be obtained from the New Art Centre, 41 Sloane Street, London SW1 (071) 235 5844. The garden itself, with pleasant views of Wiltshire downland, is eminently suited to its rôle as open air gallery. There is gorgeous lavender.

SHELDON MANOR 24
Chippenham, Wiltshire. Tel: (0249) 653120

*Major M.A. Gibbs * 1¹/₂m W of Chippenham, S off A420, signposted * Best season: June * Parking * Refreshments: home-made buffet lunches and teas * Toilet facilities * Suitable for wheelchairs * House open from 2pm * Garden open April to second week of Oct, Sun, Thurs and Bank Holidays, 12.30 – 6pm * Entrance: £1.75, OAP £1.50 (house and garden £3, OAP £2.75)*

The gardens of this ancient house are enclosed by barns and walls. The wonderful courts in front of the house have mostly been put to lawn but a whiff of formality remains in the form of yew hedges and lavender. It is best to visit in mid-June when the good collection of old-fashioned shrub roses, grown in grass, are blazing. The swimming pool is worth seeing as an example of the use of pleached trees and stone work to save it from looking as glaring as most do. Among the rare and interesting shrubs and plants look out for *Rosa gigantea* 'Cooperi', *Grevillea sulphurea*, *Carpenteria californica*, *Cytisus battandieri*, romneya, a white Judas tree and the Chilean fire bush.

STOURHEAD ★★ 25
Stourton, Wiltshire. Tel: (0747) 840348

*The National Trust * 3m NW of Mere at Stourton off the B3092 * Best season:*

May for rhododendrons – wonderful in winter when empty ✳ *Parking* ✳
Refreshments: tearoom (for further information please phone 0985 847777) ✳
Toilet facilities ✳ *Suitable for wheelchairs* ✳ *Shop* ✳ *House open April to 1st
Nov, daily except Thurs and Fri, 12 noon – 5.30pm or dusk if earlier (last
admission 5pm). Closed Good Fri* ✳ *Gardens open daily all year, 8am – 7pm (or
dusk if earlier, except 22nd to 25th July when gardens close at 5pm)* ✳ *Entrance:
Mar to Oct: £3.60, children £1.80, parties £3.20 per person; Nov to Feb: £2.60,
children £1.30 (house extra £4, children £2, parties £3.40 per person, children
£1.60)*

Many people go to Stourhead to see the rhododendrons, which are astonishing.
However they are not part of the original visionary design by Henry Hoare II in
1741-80, a paragon in its day and almost the greatest surviving garden of its
kind. The sequence of arcadian images is revealed gradually if one follows a
route anti-clockwise around the lake, having come from the house along the top
and seen the lake from above. Each experience is doubly inspiring in that one
enjoys the eye-catcher across the lake, almost unattainable and mirage-like,
and later when one reaches one's goal – and always some other vision lures one
on – the boat-house, the Temple of Flora, the bridge, Temple of Apollo, rock
bridge, cascade (these two are tucked away and very surprising) the pantheon,
thatched cottage and the grotto. The view from the Temple of Apollo (1765)
was described by Horace Walpole as 'one of the most picturesque scenes in the
world' by which he meant that it was as fine as a painting. To gain a better idea
of how these buildings would have looked had the surrounding planting
remained as it was originally, take a walk by Turner's Paddock Lake below the
cascade. Between 1791 and 1838 Richard Colt Hoare planted many new
species, particularly from America, tulip trees, swamp cypresses, Indian bean
trees – the beginning of an arboretum. He also introduced *Rhododendron
ponticum*. From 1894 the sixth Baronet replaced these with the latest kinds of
hybrid rhododendron and azaleas, and a large number of copper beeches and
conifers, such as the Japanese white pine, Sitka spruce and Californian nutmeg
– all are record-sized specimens now. In early summer the scent of azaleas is
delightful.

STOURTON HOUSE GARDEN ★   26
**Stourton House, Stourton, Nr Warminster, Wiltshire.   Tel: (0747)
840417**

Anthony and Elizabeth Bullivant ✳ *3m NW of Mere (on A303). Follow signposts
to Stourhead, then immediately before Stourhead car park, look out for blue sign
boards for Stourton House* ✳ *Parking in Stourhead (NT) car park. Free* ✳
*Refreshments: coffees and substantial home-made teas (The Bullivants provide a
guide leaflet to more elaborate catering)* ✳ *Toilet facilities. Disabled 300 yards
away in Stourton village* ✳ *Suitable for wheelchairs* ✳ *Unusual and rare plants
for sale* ✳ *Shop for dried flowers* ✳ *Open April to Nov, Wed, Thurs, Sun and
Bank Holiday Mons, 11am – 6pm or dusk if earlier. Also for groups of 15 or more
on other days by arrangement* ✳ *Entrance: £2, children 50p, groups £1.50 per
person on open days, £2 per person on other days. The owners have a series of special
days when they concentrate on specific plants; leaflet supplied on request.*

This colourful five-acre garden contains treasures in friendly, small spaces: a
wild garden, winter garden, secret garden, Apostles walk... seats abound. Rare

plants and imaginative designs are everywhere; 200 different varieties of hydrangea, many species of magnolia, unusual daffodils and camellias; euphorbias, chocolate plants and a profusion of flowers for drying. A switchback hedge of Leyland cypress encloses a herbaceous garden of island beds, lavishly planted, and a lily pond with many carnivorous plants and a great urn full of flowers.

THOMPSON'S HILL ★   27
Sherston, Nr Malmesbury, Wiltshire. Tel: (0666) 840766

Mr and Mrs J.C. Cooper ✳ On B4040. At Sherston turn left opposite church down hill, then bear right up Thompson's Hill until you come to house No 1 ✳ Best season: June ✳ Parking in road ✳ Plants for sale ✳ Open 29th June and by appointment ✳ Entrance: £1

Faultlessly-maintained half-acre garden created over the last ten years on derelict ground. Terraced area behind house, planted in grey colours, enclosed by clipped yew hedges and three Gothic arches with climbing roses and clematis. Beyond, set in lawns, are island beds with mixed herbaceous planting. Old roses and grouped prunus add height and colour. New conservatory. An example of what can be achieved with taste and energy on an unpropitious site.

WILTON HOUSE ★   28
Wilton, Salisbury, Wiltshire. Tel: (0722) 743115

The Earl of Pembroke ✳ 2¹/₂m W of Salisbury on A30 in the town centre ✳ Parking ✳ Refreshments: restaurant ✳ Toilet facilities ✳ Suitable for wheelchairs ✳ Plants for sale in garden centre separate from main house and garden area ✳ Shop (open all year) ✳ House open. Extra charge £5, concessions £4.50, children under 16 £3.50 ✳ Grounds open 7th April to 18th Oct, Mon to Sat, 11am – 6pm, Sun, 12 noon – 6pm (last admission 5pm) ✳ Entrance £2, children £1.50

The first garden that one sees at Wilton is almost the most recent. The front (north) courtyard of the house has been laid out to a design by David Vicary using formal pleached limes, lavender and a really torrential fountain which baffles the traffic noise on the A30. It has created a cool green place of immense style which manages to answer the architecture of the house. Dotted about this garden are statues, which along with the grotto facade (sadly not viewable), are the last vestiges of one of the earliest gardens here – the complex garden to the south front laid out by Isaac de Caus in 1633. Today it is almost impossible to imagine the elaborations of this garden when one sees only the stretch down to the River Nadder and the Palladian bridge of 1737. Beyond is the vista to Sir William Chambers's Pavilion. Visitors are not allowed into the nineteenth-century terraced garden on the west side, but a walk down the broad gravel near some cedars to the east of the house brings one to the recently established enclosed rose garden, which has a large collection of old-fashioned roses. Adjoining the rose garden, the New Japanese Water Garden opened in 1991. Beyond the rose garden is a summerhouse and a statue from the Arundel collection. For children there is a good adventure playground.

YORKSHIRE (North)

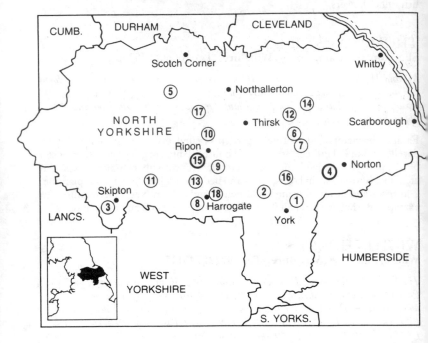

Two-starred gardens are ringed in bold.

ASKHAM BRYAN COLLEGE OF AGRICULTURE AND HORTICULTURE
1

York, North Yorkshire. Tel: (0904) 702121

North Yorkshire County Council ✳ 4m W of York on A64 ✳ Parking ✳ Toilet facilities ✳ Suitable for wheelchairs ✳ Plants for sale ✳ Open for College Open Day 6th June, 1.30 – 5.30pm, for charity 12th July, 2 –5pm. Also groups by appointment ✳ Entrance: £1, children 20p. Car parking charge

Although Askham Bryan is one of the prime centres for the teaching of practical amenity-horticulture and has hitherto maintained immaculate grounds and glasshouse collections, they are now showing signs of neglect following financial cutbacks. The outdoor collections have suffered least, the trees, shrubs and roses still being worth travelling to see. Almost all the plants are clearly labelled.

BENINGBROUGH HALL 2
Beningbrough, North Yorkshire. Tel: (0904) 470666

*The National Trust * 8m NW of York off A19 York – Thirsk road at Shipton *
Best season: spring and summer * Parking * Refreshments: restaurant. Picnics
in walled garden * Toilet facilities * Suitable for wheelchairs * House open
(last admission 4.30pm). Over 100 pictures on loan from National Portrait Gallery
* Gardens open 4th April to 1st Nov, Tues, Wed, Thurs, Sat, Sun, Good Fri and
Bank Holiday Mon; July and Aug, daily, 11am – 5.30pm (last admission 5pm) *
Entrance: gardens and exhibitions £2.50, children £1.20, family £6.60 (house,
gardens and exhibitions £4, children £2, family £10, parties £3.20 per adult, £1.60
per child)*

The main formal garden comprising geometrically-patterned parterres was
originally laid out at the time the house was constructed, but was replaced
during the late eighteenth century with sweeping lawns and specimen trees,
part of an estate of 365 acres. Although generally well-ordered, this is
essentially a pleasure garden with a historic framework amongst which
considerable recent planting has been integrated. The wilderness and two privy
gardens have been restored to eighteenth-century standards, and there is a
nineteenth-century American garden and a Victorian conservatory. In conjunction with the imposing Georgian house it is well worth a visit.

BROUGHTON HALL 3
Broughton, Nr Skipton, North Yorkshire. Tel: (0756) 799608

*Mr H.R. Tempest * 4m W of Skipton on the A59, take first left after the Bull Inn
* Parking * Toilet facilities * Hall open same times as garden. Tours on the
hour * Garden open Bank Holiday Mons only at Easter, May, Spring and Aug,
11am – 4pm and at other times by arrangement with the owner * Entrance: £3*

As well as being a pleasant country house in parklands, this is of interest to the
gardening historian as one of the best surviving examples of the Victorian
designer Nesfield who spent 30 years laying out the garden. He also sited
statues in the park and planted a semi-natural landscape, but it is the parterre
on the walled terrace which will most interest Nesfield fans. It has been
restored to his design, alas omitting the blue and white gravels he preferred.
Nesfield was successful in his time, working for Kew and submitting plans for
the forecourt of Buckingham Palace (which might have been rather fun in
coloured gravels) but in his later years his passion for parterres fell out of
favour.

CASTLE HOWARD ★★ 4
York, North Yorkshire. Tel: (065384) 333

*Castle Howard Estates Ltd * 5m SW of Malton off A64 York – Scarborough
road * Parking * Refreshments: cafeteria * Toilet facilities * Partly suitable
for wheelchairs * Plants for sale in large plant centre * Shop * House and
costume galleries open * Garden open 25th March to 1st Nov, daily, 10am –
4.30pm. Special tours of woodland garden available for pre-booked groups *

Entrance: £5.50, OAP £4.50, children £2.50, parties £4.50, OAP £4 (house and garden). Family tickets and gardens only tickets available

Described as one of the finest examples of 'The Heroic Age of English Landscape Architecture' the grounds were first designed by Sir John Vanbrugh assisted by Nicholas Hawksmoor to complement the castle designed by Vanbrugh. This layout still generally exists, although in recent times features have been added. Although known principally as a very fine landscape, there is also much for the enthusiastic garden lover. The rose garden developed during the past few years has one of the largest collections of old-fashioned and species roses in Europe. Way Wood and the adjacent area accommodate a very fine collection of rhododendrons, an adjunct to the newly extended arboretum which will soon be one of the largest and most important in the United Kingdom. Most of the plants are well labelled.

CONSTABLE BURTON HALL 5
Leyburn, North Yorkshire. Tel: (0677) 50428

*Mr Charles Wyvill * 3m E of Leyburn on A684 * Best seasons: spring and early summer * Parking * Partly suitable for wheelchairs * Open April to mid-Sept, daily, 9am – 6pm * Entrance: £1*

A pleasant garden to visit in beautiful countryside with large specimen trees in a parkland setting probably contemporary with the John Carr house. Essentially a strolling garden rather than one for the plantsperson. Despite obvious signs of labour shortage, it is holding its own.

DUNCOMBE PARK 6
Helmsley, North Yorkshire. Tel: (0439) 70213 (0439 71115 during open hours)

*Lord Feversham * 1m SW of Helmsley off A170 * Parking at Visitor Centre * Refreshments: at licensed tearoom. Picnic area * Toilet facilities * Shop * House open. Extra charge * Garden open 5th, 12th, 17th to 21st, 26th April, and 2nd May to 25th Oct, Sun – Thurs, 11am – 6pm. Also Bank Holiday Sats and all event Sats (13th, 20th June, 4th July and 26th Sept) * Entrance: £2.50. Discounts for pre-booked groups visiting house and grounds*

Home of the Duncombes for 300 years, the mansion has recently been restored to a family home by Lord Feversham. Its 35-acre garden, set in 300 acres of dramatic parkland, dates from c. 1715 and has been described as 'the supreme masterpiece of the art of the landscape gardener' by Sacheverell Sitwell. Tree-lined terraces, classical temples, statues, vast expanses of lawn and magnificent trees mostly dating from the original eighteenth-century planting. Tallest ash and lime trees according to the *Guinness Book of Records*. One of the earliest ha-has built. Views from terrace of River Rye and the Cascades. Yew walk. Orangery. Woodland and riverside walks.

FOUNTAINS ABBEY
(see STUDLEY ROYAL)

GILLING CASTLE   7
Gilling East, North Yorkshire. Tel: (04393) 207

The Right Reverend the Abbot of Ampleforth ✳ 18m N of York on B1363 York – Helmsley road ✳ Parking ✳ Open July and August, daily, 1pm – dusk ✳ Entrance: 70p, children free

A lovely garden in outstanding scenery. The terraces have been constructed on the south-facing side of the garden, four of them tumbling down the slope from an expansive lawn at the top. Many old-fashioned flowers grow in the borders with a backdrop of majestic trees.

HARLOW CARR BOTANICAL GARDENS ★   8
Crag Lane, Harrogate, North Yorkshire. Tel: (0423) 565418

Northern Horticultural Society ✳ 1¹/₂m W of centre of Harrogate on B6162 Otley road ✳ Parking ✳ Refreshments: licensed restaurant and refreshment kiosk (10am – 5pm) ✳ Toilet facilities ✳ Partly suitable for wheelchairs. Manual and electric wheelchairs available for loan ✳ Guide dogs only ✳ Plants for sale ✳ Gift shop ✳ Open all year, daily, 9am – 7.30pm or dusk if earlier ✳ Entrance: £3, OAP £2.40, accompanied children free. Groups of 20 or more £2.40, children under 16 free (subject to change)

A 60-acre site, formerly farmland, established in 1948 by the Northern Horticultural Society as a centre for garden plant trials in the north of England. Now also provides a wide range of horticultural courses for amateur gardeners. It is said that if a plant prospers at Harlow Carr it will grow anywhere in the north. Hosts the National collections of heather and rhubarb cultivars as well as those of hypericum, dryopteris and polypodium. Extensive streamside planting with one of the best collections of moisture-loving plants in the north of England. Large collections of rhododendrons, roses and alpines. Boasts a very fine alpine house and two extensive rock gardens. A new building programme has caused considerable disruption to the upper part of the gardens, but restoration of the area should be complete during 1992. The past year has seen maintenance problems, especially in the trials area which seems to have lost direction in terms of comparative trialling and interpretation. The arboretum regrettably shows some signs of neglect and some of the shrub borders are rather jaded.

NEWBY HALL AND GARDENS ★   9
Nr Ripon, North Yorkshire. Tel: (0423) 322583

4m SE of Ripon on B6265, 3m W of A1 ✳ Parking ✳ Refreshments: licensed restaurant. Picnic area ✳ Toilet facilities, inc. disabled ✳ Suitable for wheelchairs (provided) ✳ Dogs in area adjacent to picnic area only ✳ Plants for sale ✳ Shop

Open April to Sept, daily except Mon (but open Bank Holiday Mons), 11am – 5.30pm * *Entrance: £2.50, OAP £2.30, children £1.80 (house and gardens £4.50, OAP £3.60, children £2.50) (1991 prices). Reduced rate for parties by appointment, details from Administrator*

The family home of the owners who have set an exceptionally high standard of maintenance while retaining the atmosphere of an established and still lived-in country house. Newby Hall is seventeenth-century with additions and interior by Robert Adam, set in 25 acres of open parkland and some features remain from the eighteenth century, such as east to west walk marked by Venetian statuary, backed by yew and purple plum. The south face has long wide green slopes down to the River Ure, with herbaceous borders on either side backed by clipped hedges and flowering shrubs. Cross walks lead to smaller gardens full of interest. These include species roses, Tropical walled, rock and the stepped water gardens as well as a fine woodland area attributed to Ellen Willmott. National collection holder of genus *Cornus*. Facilities for children. Special events are held in June, July and September, such as craft fairs and historic car rallies, with special admission prices.

NORTON CONYERS   10
Ripon, North Yorkshire. Tel: (0765640) 333

Sir James Graham, Bart * *3¹/₂m N of Ripon, near Wath. 1¹/₂m from A1 turn off at the Baldersby flyover, take the A61 to Ripon, turn right to Wath* * *Parking* * *Teas on Bank Holiday Suns and Mons and on four charity open days. Buffet lunches, light refreshments and teas for booked parties by arrangement* * *Partly suitable for wheelchairs* * *Dogs on lead* * *Small garden centre specialising in unusual plants and Pick Your Own fruit in July and Aug* * *Shop* * *House open 17th May to 13th Sept, Suns. Also 27th July to 1st Aug, daily, and Bank Holiday Suns and Mons, 2 – 5.30pm. £2, OAP £1.50, children (4 – 14) £1, parties of 20 or more £1.50 per person. Enquiries to Beatrice, Lady Graham* * *Garden open all year, Mon – Fri, 9am – 5pm, 28th March to 3rd Oct, Sat and Sun, 2 – 5.30pm* * *Entrance: free*

The lure of the garden is very much with the past and particularly the association of the house with Charlotte Brontë who made it one of the models for Thornfield Hall in *Jane Eyre*. Norton Conyers has a historic feel that transcends the planting which is pleasant but modest. Most plantings are of the cottage-garden type, although the gardens themselves are quite extensive, including an eighteenth-century walled garden in full cultivation, with orangery and herbaceous borders.

PARCEVALL HALL GARDENS ★   11
Appletreewick, Skipton, North Yorkshire. Tel: (075672) 311

Walsingham College (Yorkshire Properties) Ltd * *1m NE of Appletreewick off B6265 Pateley Bridge – Skipton road* * *Parking* * *Picnics in orchard* * *Plants for sale* * *Open Easter to Oct, daily, 10am – 6pm and for charity* * *Entrance: £1.50, children 50p*

A garden of great interest to the plantsperson, many of Sir William Milner's treasures having survived years of neglect. The garden is currently being restored and is well worth a visit, if merely to enjoy the spectacular views from the terrace. A fine range of rhododendrons, many originally collected in China, still grow happily here. Fishponds. Rock garden.

RIEVAULX TERRACE AND TEMPLES ★   12
Rievaulx, Helmsley, North Yorkshire. Tel: (04396) 340

The National Trust ✳ *2¹/₂m NW of Helmsley on B1257* ✳ *Parking. Coach park 200 yards* ✳ *Picnics* ✳ *Toilet facilities* ✳ *Suitable for wheelchairs on terrace. Electric self-propelled chair available, free of charge. Steps to temples* ✳ *Dogs on lead* ✳ *Shop and information centre* ✳ *Two eighteenth-century temples and exhibition of landscape design in basement of Ionic temple* ✳ *Open April to Oct, daily, 10.30am – 5.30pm. Ionic Temple closed 1 – 2pm* ✳ *Entrance: £1.70, children 80p*

This is a unique example of the eighteenth-century passion for the romantic and the picturesque – that is, making landscape look like a picture. The work was done at the behest of Thomas Duncombe around 1754 and consists of a half-mile-long serpentine grass terrace high above Ryedale with fine views. At one end is a Palladian-style Ionic temple with furniture by William Kent and elaborate ceilings. At the other is a Tuscan temple with a raised platform from which are views to the Rye Valley. The concept is wonderfully achieved, but those who expect gardens to have flowers must prepare their minds for higher things.

RIPLEY CASTLE   13
Ripley, Harrogate, North Yorkshire. Tel: (0423) 770152

Sir Thomas Ingilby, Bart ✳ *3¹/₂m N of Harrogate off A61 Harrogate – Ripon road* ✳ *Best season: April/May and July/Aug* ✳ *Parking* ✳ *Refreshments: morning coffee and tea, picnics* ✳ *Toilet facilities* ✳ *Suitable for wheelchairs* ✳ *Guide dogs only* ✳ *Gift shop* ✳ *House open at extra charge* ✳ *Garden open Good Friday to Oct, 11am – 5pm* ✳ *Entrance: £2, OAP £1.50, children £1. Parties of 25 or more £1.50 per person*

A mid-eighteenth-century 'Capability' Brown landscape with formal gardens developed by Peter Aram for a family that has been here since the thirteenth century. A beautiful landscape, especially during spring at daffodil time. Magnificent specimen trees. The formal areas have seen better days, but the current owner is making considerable strides in their restoration. Lake with attractive Victorian iron bridge. Eighteenth-century orangery and summer houses. Vegetable garden. Woodland walk to a temple with fine views. Extensive new plantings of a rich variety of spring-flowering bulbs have been made to complement the National collection of hyacinths here. The tropical plant collection formerly owned by Hull University at Cottingham Botanical Gardens is now at Ripley and will be open to the public in newly-restored listed greenhouses in 1992.

SLEIGHTHOLME DALE LODGE   14
Fadmoor, Nr Kirbymoorside, North Yorkshire. Tel: (0751) 31942

Dr and Mrs O. James ✳ *3m N of Kirbymoorside. 1m from Fadmoor off A170* ✳

*Open by appointment and 7th June, 11.30am – 5pm, 18th, 19th July, 2 – 7pm ✳
Entrance: £1, children 40p (1991 prices)*

This garden occupies a unique position on the side of a wooded valley opening on to the moors. in the spring there is a blaze of blossom, wild daffodils and azaleas, and through the summer the walled garden, which runs steeply up the hill, is breathtaking in its colour and exuberance. As well as a mass of old-fashioned roses and delphiniums the owners have specialised in rare plants, notably meconopsis.

STUDLEY ROYAL AND FOUNTAINS ABBEY ★★   15
Ripon, North Yorkshire. Tel: (076586) 333

The National Trust ✳ 2m SW of Ripon, 9m N of Harrogate. Follow Studley Roger sign off B6265 Ripon – Pateley Bridge road ✳ Light lunches and teas at Studley Royal daily, and Abbey Easter to Oct. Picnic area ✳ Toilet facilities ✳ Suitable for wheelchairs. Powered runabouts available by prior booking ✳ Gift shop ✳ Deer park open all year during daylight hours. Abbey and garden open all year, daily except 24th, 25th Dec and Fri in Nov to Jan, as follows: Jan to March and Nov to Dec, 10am – 5pm or dusk if earlier. April to June and Sept, 10am – 7pm. July and Aug, 10am – 8pm. Oct, 10am – 6pm or dusk if earlier. Guided tours April to Oct, daily at 2.30pm ✳ Entrance: Deer park free. Gardens £2.70 to £3.50 depending on season, children £1.30 to £1.60, family rates available. Parking £1.50 at Studley Royal refundable if admission ticket purchased

The gardens were created by John Aislabie, who had been Chancellor of the Exchequer but whose finances were 'ruined' by the South Sea Bubble in 1720 and who retired here to his estate in 1722 and worked until his death in 1742 to make the finest water-garden in the country. The lakes, grotto springs, formal canal and water features plus buildings such as the Temple of Piety turn what is essentially a landscape with large trees and sweeping lawns into one of the most stunning of green gardens. Furthermore, there is the association with the largest and most complete Cistercian foundation in Europe described by the *Oxford Companion* as probably the noblest monastic ruin in Christendom. This can be seen in the distance from the 'surprise view', through a door in a small building. Nearby, at Grewelthorpe, is Hackfall Wood, an outstanding wood-land and water garden laid out in 1730s by William Aislabie (son of John). In the process of renovation, this has been listed by English Heritage as Grade I.

SUTTON PARK ★   16
Sutton-in-the-Forest, York, North Yorkshire. Tel: (0347) 810249

Mrs N.M.D. Sheffield ✳ 8m N of York on B1363 ✳ Parking. Coaches by appointment ✳ Refreshments: lunches, afternoon and high teas in tea room ✳ Toilet facilities ✳ Suitable for wheelchairs (gardens only ✳ Plants sometimes for sale ✳ Shop ✳ Georgian house open Easter weekend, and 6th May to 9th Sept, Bank Holiday Suns, Mons and Weds, 1.30 – 5pm and parties of 25 or more by appointment. Also ice-house and nature trail ✳ Gardens open Easter to 1st Oct, daily, 11am – 5.30pm. Parties at other times by appointment at reduced rates ✳ Entrance: £1, children 50p

One of the most distinguished English garden designers of recent times, Percy Cane, came to this Georgian house and its terraced site in 1962 with its views over parkland said to have been moulded by 'Capability' Brown. Cane was inspired to take up his profession after a visit to Harold Peto's Easton Lodge. He started the elegant planting which has been most carefully expanded by the present owners. There are several fine features on the terraces – a tall beech hedge curved to take a marble seat, ironwork gazebos and everywhere soft stone. The woodland walk leads to a temple.

THORP PERROW ARBORETUM ★   17
Bedale, North Yorkshire. Tel: (0677) 425323

Sir John Ropner, Bart ＊ 2m S of Bedale, signposted off B6268 Masham road ＊ Best season: spring and autumn ＊ Parking ＊ Picnic area ＊ Open all year, dawn – dusk ＊ Entrance: £2, OAP and children £1

The arboretum was established some 50 years ago on open farmland by Sir Leonard Ropner and is one of the finest collections of trees in the north of England, containing over 2000 species. Unfortunately the arboretum suffered some years of neglect, and the present owner is currently undertaking restoration. While many of the trees will never regain their natural habit owing to crowding and lack of pruning, the collection is still undisputedly one of the most comprehensive in the North. The arboretum is seeing a considerable revival and a number of new plantings have been made during the past year. Several National collections here include walnuts, oak, ash and lime. The fern walk down to the lake is a recent restoration. In the past year new interpretive signs and a small visitor information facility have greatly improved the pleasure of a visit.

VALLEY GARDENS ★   18
1 Valley Drive, Harrogate, North Yorkshire,. Tel: (0423) 500600

Harrogate Borough Council ＊ In centre of Harrogate, main entrance is near Pump Museum ＊ Best season: spring and summer ＊ Parking ＊ Refreshments: morning coffee, light lunches, teas ＊ Toilet facilities ＊ Suitable for wheelchairs ＊ Dogs ＊ Open daily during daylight hours ＊ Entrance: free

One of the best-known public gardens in the north of England, laid out earlier this century at the time Harrogate was fashionable as a spa. This is the site of the annual Great Spring Flower Show which sadly causes damage each year from which areas of the gardens are slow to recover. While the stream garden and rock features have gone into decline in recent years, the standard of formal bedding remains very high. A very fine dahlia display is an annual feature.

YORKSHIRE
(South & West)

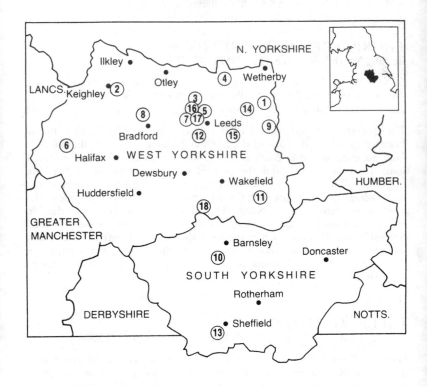

BRAMHAM PARK ★   1
Wetherby, West Yorkshire. Tel: (0937) 844265

Mr and Mrs G. Lane Fox ✳ *5m S of Wetherby just off northbound A1* ✳
Parking ✳ *Toilet facilities* ✳ *Partly suitable for wheelchairs* ✳ *House open at
extra charge* ✳ *Park open Easter and Spring Bank Holiday weekends and May
Day, and 14th June to 30th Aug, Sun, Tues, Wed, Thurs, 1.15 – 5.30pm (last
admission 5pm)* ✳ *Entrance: £1.50, OAP £1, children 50p (house and garden £2,
OAP £1.50, children £1) (1991 prices)*

Created by Robert Benson after the style of Le Nôtre some 250 years ago, this
is one of the few landscape gardens in the French style to survive in this

country. Although great storms have removed many specimen beeches and disrupted the layout of the avenues, the original concept has been maintained and is being perpetuated. Apart from its uniqueness of design, the gardens also have a substantial rose garden which provides summer-long colour, and an interesting herbaceous border. However, it is the splendid architectural features and the trees which would have been familiar to the garden's creator, in his day Chancellor of the Exchequer, that are outstanding; as visitors wonder at the beauty of this garden they may well muse how many Chancellors have left such a legacy to the nation. During restoration work in 1991 a massive eighteenth-century cascade was found. Apparently the family had tried to fill it in after it was put in place sometime in the late 1720s.

EAST RIDDLESDEN HALL 2
Bradford Road, Keighley, West Yorkshire. Tel: (0535) 607075

The National Trust ✳ 1m NE of Keighley on S side of A650 and 3m NW of Bingley ✳ Parking ✳ Teas ✳ Toilet facilities ✳ Suitable for wheelchairs: not in refreshment room ✳ Dogs on lead ✳ Shop ✳ House open ✳ Garden open 4th April to Oct, weekends and 17th to 22nd April, 12 noon – 5.30pm. May to Oct, Sat – Wed, 12 noon – 5.30pm (last admission 5pm) ✳ Entrance: £2.50, accompanied children £1.20

A traditional seventeenth-century Yorkshire manor house. Neglected through much of nineteenth and twentieth centuries and restored 1983 – 84 by The National Trust. The great barn is considered one of the finest in the north of England. A well-tended formal walled garden of modest size and a monastic fish pond in grounds running down to the river.

GOLDEN ACRE PARK ★ 3
Otley Road, Leeds, West Yorkshire. Tel: (0523) 463504

Leeds City Council ✳ Off A660 Leeds – Otley road at approach to Bramhope ✳ Parking ✳ Refreshments: morning coffee, teas, lunches ✳ Toilet facilities ✳ Suitable for wheelchairs ✳ Dogs ✳ Gift shop ✳ Open daily during daylight hours ✳ Entrance: free

Until 1945 when it was purchased by Leeds Corporation for £18,500, this was a privately-owned pleasure park. Since then it has been developed as an important public park and minor botanic garden. It is sited on a pleasant undulating site leading down to a lake. Extensively-planted tree collection with most specimens labelled. Rhododendrons are a feature in the spring, along with alpine plants both in the rock garden and in the alpine house. Golden Acre Park is noted for its very fine collection of houseleeks or sempervivums as well as its heather collection. Demonstration plots are maintained where instruction is provided for home gardeners. The quality of plantings and vegetables for these improves annually. Now one of the demonstration gardens for Fleuroselect award-winning flowers.

HAREWOOD HOUSE ★ 4
Harewood, Leeds, West Yorkshire. Tel: (0532) 886225

The Earl and Countess of Harewood ✳ 7m N of Leeds on A61 ✳ Best seasons:

YORKSHIRE (South & West)

April, early June and early Oct ✳ *Parking* ✳ *Refreshments: light lunches, teas, etc., restaurant and bar, picnic area* ✳ *Toilet facilities* ✳ *Partly suitable for wheelchairs* ✳ *Dogs on lead* ✳ *Shop* ✳ *House open* ✳ *Gardens open 5th April to 1st Nov, daily, 10am – 5pm* ✳ *Entrance: £2, children £1 (1991 prices)*

Originally laid out in the 1770s by 'Capability' Brown the gardens and park still retain many of his characteristic features, most notably a majestic lake and a well-wooded horizon although many of his trees have been lost. Nineteenth-century rhododendrons obscure the edge of his lake but afford a fine sight reflected on its surface when flowering in early June. Another feature in this woodland setting is a vaguely Japanese bog garden below the lake's cascade. Sir Charles Barry's terrace of the 1840s adds a formal contrast with its parterres and fountains, herbaceous border, bedding schemes and roses. Large quantities of trees and shrubs in these excellently maintained grounds ensure a long season of interest.

THE HOLLIES PARK ★   5
Weetwood Lane, Leeds, West Yorkshire. Tel: (0523) 782030

Leeds City Council ✳ *Entrance off Weetwood Lane, off A660 Leeds – Otley road* ✳ *Parking* ✳ *Toilet facilities* ✳ *Open daily during daylight hours* ✳ *Entrance: free*

The original layout is believed to be Victorian. The gardens were given to Leeds Corporation in 1921 by the Brown family in memory of a relative killed during World War I. The fine informal, largely woodland garden features woody plants, especially rhododendrons, many rarely seen growing in this part of the North. Ferns flourish throughout the gardens and a varied collection of hydrangeas provide late summer colour. Many slightly tender subjects, such as eucryphia, embothrium and drimys thrive in the pleasant micro-climate. The home of a number of National collections maintained by Leeds City Council, including probably the most comprehensive philadelphus collection in Europe, and also those of hemerocallis and deutzias.

LAND FARM   6
Colden, Nr Hebden Bridge, West Yorkshire. Tel: (0422) 842260

Mr and Mrs J. Williams ✳ *Off A646 between Sowerby Bridge and Todmorden. Call at the Visitors' Centre in Hebden Bridge for a map* ✳ *Best season: spring and summer* ✳ *Plants for sale* ✳ *Open May to Aug, Sat, Sun and Bank Holiday Mons, 10am – 5pm* ✳ *Entrance: £1*

A garden created by the owners on a north-facing one-acre site 1000 ft up in the Pennines. Designed as a low-maintenance garden, it nevertheless contains a wide diversity of shrubs, herbaceous plants and alpines. Featured on *Gardener's World*.

30 LATCHMERE ROAD   7
Leeds, West Yorkshire. Tel: (0532) 751261

Mr and Mrs Joe Brown ✳ *NW of Leeds off A6120 (ring road to Bradford), turn up Fillingfir Drive, right at pillar box, then left into Latchmere Road* ✻ *Plants for sale* ✻ *Open by appointment to horticultural societies and garden clubs, and every Sun from 28th June to 2nd Aug (note: open 5th July), 2.30 – 5.30pm* ✻ *Entrance: 75p, children 25p*

A garden of exceptional merit created from scratch over the last 20 years by Mr and Mrs Brown, this is now one of the finest examples of garden design in a small garden. Herbaceous plants, ferns, climbers and shrubs all contribute to a series of mini-features which the visitor passes through in a controlled circuit of the garden. These features include a clematis collection, camomile lawn, sink gardens, pools, patio and limestone garden.

LISTER PARK   8
Keighley Road, Bradford, West Yorkshire. Tel: (0274) 493313

City of Bradford Metropolitan Council ✻ *1¹/₂m N of Bradford centre (Forster Square) on A650 Bradford – Keighley road* ✻ *Best season: spring and summer* ✻ *Parking in surrounding streets* ✻ *Light refreshments: daily except Mon, 10am – 4pm* ✻ *Toilet facilities* ✻ *Suitable for wheelchairs* ✻ *Dogs on lead* ✻ *Cartwright Hall, City Art Gallery and Museum open, April to Sept, Tues – Sun, 10am – 6pm, Oct to Mar, Tues – Sun, 10am – 5pm* ✻ *Open daily during daylight hours* ✻ *Entrance: free*

This used to be a well-tended park with an excellent garden and botanical garden, including greenhouses with tropical plants. Recently there have been signs of improvement although the botanical garden, which still exists, appears untended, and the main reason for including the park in this guide is that there is a formal floral display in front of Cartwright Hall and an interesting floral clock, a rare example of Victorian ingenuity which is well worth seeing by those living in or passing through the city, perhaps to visit the National Museum of Photography, Film and TV.

LOTHERTON HALL   9
Aberford, West Yorkshire. Tel: (0532) 463510

Leeds City Council ✻ *3¹/₂m NE of Gosforth on B1217* ✻ *Best season: spring and summer* ✻ *Parking. Coaches by appointment* ✻ *Refreshments and picnics* ✻ *Toilet facilities* ✻ *Dogs except in bird garden* ✻ *Shop* ✻ *House open. Bird garden closed Mon. Working shire horses* ✻ *Garden open daily, 10.30am – dusk* ✻ *Entrance: free*

A 10-acre garden which grows surprisingly tender shrubs and climbers rare in this raw Northern climate but here protected by walls and tree shelters. The design is thought to owe something to Ellen Willmott and is rather an Edwardian period piece. Formal rose garden, an avenue of yews leading to a white summerhouse, walled garden, sunken garden with lily pond, a well-planted Japanese rockery glen of 1912 and a ha-ha now filled in and planted with primulas, astilbes and meconopsis. Sports lovers will be interested to see the tennis court, one of the earliest of brick construction, but some garden lovers have been disappointed at the lack of seasonal colour between spring and summer. Further restoration and improvement work is taking place and more period plants being introduced.

THE NORTHERN COLLEGE GARDENS ★ 10
Wentworth Castle, Stainborough, Barnsley, South Yorkshire. Tel: (0226) 285426

Barnsley Metropolitan Borough Council; leased and managed by the Northern College for Residential Adult Education ✳ *Off M1 at Junction 37, 2m down minor road signposted Stainborough/Dodworth* ✳ *Best season: spring* ✳ *Parking* ✳ *Refreshments* ✳ *Toilet facilities* ✳ *House and main buildings occupied by Northern College* ✳ *Gardens open Spring Bank Holiday (Sun and Mon) and 17th, 31st May, 7th, 14th June. Otherwise parties only catered for by conducted tours booked three weeks in advance* ✳ *Entrance: £2, OAP £1, accompanied children under 16 free*

One of the most exciting gardens in Yorkshire, laid out mainly under the direction of William Wentworth in 1740, it is currently undergoing a complete review of its activities. Contains one of the finest collections of rhododendrons in the North. These have been established during the past 15 years and form an invaluable educational resource. The owners and tenants at Wentworth are putting together an important development package which will preserve the fabric of the garden and yet enable its already valuable collections to be expanded. It has recently been designated the National collection for the *falconeri* rhododendrons and there are many new plantings. The gardens have recently twinned with the Kumming Botanical Gardens in China and many rare species of Asiatic plants are being introduced. Interpretive signs and a guide book have been produced during the past year greatly enhancing the enjoyment of a visit. There are extensive new plantings of magnolias, comprising one of the largest collections in northern England.

NOSTELL PRIORY 11
Nr Wakefield, West Yorkshire. Tel: (0924) 863892

The National Trust ✳ *6m SE of Wakefield on A638* ✳ *Best season: summer for rose garden* ✳ *Parking* ✳ *Light refreshments and teas. Picnic site* ✳ *Toilet facilities inc. disabled* ✳ *Suitable for wheelchairs* ✳ *Dogs on lead* ✳ *Gift shop* ✳ *House open from 12 noon* ✳ *Garden open 4th April to June, Sept to 1st Nov, Sats 12 noon – 5pm, Suns 11am – 5pm; July and Aug, daily except Fri, 12 noon – 5pm. Also Bank Holiday Mon, 11am – 5pm, Tues following 12 noon – 5pm* ✳ *Entrance: £2, children £1, (house and garden £3.30, children £1.70, parties £2.80 per adult, children £1.40)*

An eighteenth-century mansion set in open parkland with an attractive lake and a variety of well-established trees. A fine, well-tended and well-labelled rose garden is the main gardening feature. There is a children's playground and a picnic area. Special events and fairs are held during the season, some in marquees in front of the house, with a special admission charge (not applied if house and garden only visited).

ROUNDHAY PARK (Tropical World Canal Gardens) ★ 12
Roundhay Road, Leeds, West Yorkshire. Tel: (0523) 661850

Leeds City Council ✳ *Off A58 Roundhay Road from Leeds City centre* ✳ *Parking* ✳ *Refreshments: light snacks* ✳ *Toilet facilities* ✳ *Suitable for wheelchairs* ✳ *Dogs* ✳ *Open daily during daylight hours* ✳ *Entrance: free*

The intensively-cultivated canal gardens area was formerly the kitchen and ornamental gardens of the Nicholson family who sold the site to the Leeds Corporation in 1871. The extensive parkland with its fine trees is an excellent setting for the pure horticultural extravaganza of the canal gardens with their formal bedding and generous collections of Tropical plants in greenhouses. The collections are constantly being added to and are a mecca for enthusiastic gardeners.

SHEFFIELD BOTANICAL GARDENS 13
Sheffield, South Yorkshire. Tel: (0742) 671115

Sheffield Council ✳ *¹/₂m from A625, 1¹/₂m SW of Sheffield centre* ✳ *Parking in surrounding streets* ✳ *Toilet facilities inc. disabled* ✳ *Suitable for wheelchairs* ✳ *Dogs on lead* ✳ *Plants for sale occasionally, by Friends of Botanical Society* ✳ *Open daily during daylight hours* ✳ *Entrance: free*

An example of a botanical garden tended by a local authority, with support from and participation by local gardening societies and helpers. Flower displays are changed seasonally. All plants are well-labelled, including those in the special woodland area. A small aviary and an aquarium provide additional features. The gardens, though close to Sheffield centre, are secluded with good seating and grass areas suitable for children and recreation. However, recently the gardens were looking very downtrodden and seem sadly to be going into decline unless action is taken speedily.

SILVER BIRCHES 14
Ling Lane, Scarcroft, Leeds, West Yorkshire. Tel: (0532) 892335

Mr S.C. Thomson ✳ *7m NE of Leeds in Ling Lane, Scarcroft off A58 Leeds – Wetherby road* ✳ *Parking* ✳ *Refreshment: tea* ✳ *Partly suitable for wheelchairs* ✳ *Plants for sale* ✳ *Open 3rd, 17th May and by appointment June to Oct for parties* ✳ *Entrance: £1, children 50p*

A two and a half-acre garden with tastefully-added shrubs and conifers. Foliage plants are a significant component in the design. There are also good collections of roses, heathers and climbers as well as open water with a range of aquatic plants.

TEMPLE NEWSAM 15
Leeds, West Yorkshire. Tel: (0532) 645535

Leeds City Council ✳ *Signposted off junction of A63 and A6120 ring road E of*

Leeds ✳ *Best season: mid-May to early-Oct* ✳ *Parking* ✳ *Teas and snacks* ✳ *Toilet facilities* ✳ *Suitable for wheelchairs* ✳ *Shop* ✳ *House open daily except Mon, 10.30am – 6.15pm, 85p, OAP and children 35p (1991 prices)* ✳ *Park open daily, 9am – dusk* ✳ *Entrance: free*

A pleasant oasis surrounded by urban Leeds. Set in the remnants of a 'Capability' Brown landscape of the 1760s (much reduced by a golf course and open-cast mining) are a wide diversity of gardens. Around the house an Italian paved garden and a Jacobean-style parterre surrounded by pleached lime walks are poorly maintained. A rhododendron and azalea walk leads to small ponds with a bog garden and arboretum, beyond which is a large walled rose garden and greenhouses containing collections of ivies, cacti and some rather dashing climbing pelargoniums. Maintenance could be better.

5 WHARFE CLOSE 16
Adel, Leeds, West Yorkshire. Tel: (0532) 611363

Mr and Mrs C.V. Lightman ✳ *E of A660 Leeds – Skipton road and N of the north Leeds ring road (A6120). Turn off ring road into Adel along Long Causeway/ Sir George Martin's Drive to Derwent Drive* ✳ *Best season: spring and summer* ✳ *Parking between bus terminus and shop* ✳ *Teas* ✳ *Plants for sale* ✳ *Open 2nd, 16th Aug for charity, 2 – 5pm and also by appointment* ✳ *Entrance: 80p*

An interesting garden of about three quarters of an acre which includes two ponds, a Japanese feature and woodland glade. There are large collections of both ivies and conifers and an amazing array of planted sinks and troughs, a passion of the gardener responsible for laying out the site.

YORK GATE ★ 17
Church Lane, Leeds, West Yorkshire. Tel: (0532) 678240

Mrs Sybil B. Spencer ✳ *Off A660 Leeds – Otley road, behind Adel Church* ✳ *Parking, but no coaches* ✳ *Refreshments: tea and biscuits* ✳ *Plants for sale* ✳ *Open by appointment and 6th, 7th June, 2 – 6pm* ✳ *Entrance: £2, children free*

Bought by the owner and her late husband in 1951 this was a bleak farmhouse and an unpromising area of land. When her husband died, her son took over the design and in a tragically short life he achieved a garden of impeccable taste and style, using local stone, cobble stones and gravel to create a structure of taste and great interest. As to the design, Arthur Hellyer remarks on its debt to Hidcote, but notes that many of the ideas used there in 10 acres are here confined to barely one. He also comments on the clever use of eye-catching ornaments and topiary. 'This is a garden made for discovery' he says, as 'from no vantage point is it possible to see the whole... Nor is any route of exploration specially indicated'. This is also a plantsperson's garden maintaining a quality collection arranged in clearly defined model features. These include an extraordinary miniature pinetum as well as fern, peony and iris borders and an exquisite silver and white border. A garden of rare delight.

YORKSHIRE SCULPTURE PARK 18
Bretton Hall, West Bretton, Wakefield, West Yorkshire. Tel: (0924) 830302

Yorkshire Sculpture Park, Independent Charitable Trust ✳ *6m SW of Wakefield at*

West Bretton. Leave M1 at junction 38 ✳ Parking. Car parking charges operated seasonally. Coaches by prior arrangement ✳ Refreshments in Bothy Café ✳ Toilet facilities ✳ Access Sculpture Trail suitable for wheelchairs ✳ Dogs on lead ✳ Shop and Information Centre ✳ Open daily except 25th, 26th Dec and 1st Jan, summer, 10am – 6pm, winter, 10am – 4pm ✳ Entrance: free but donation requested

A lecturer at the college initiated this great project for Britain's first permanent sculpture park in 1977, which was the 25th anniversary of the famous Battersea Park exhibitions of sculpture. The Yorkshire Arts Association was set up by a permanent facility the same year. The Palladian-style house and its 260 acres of formal gardens, woods, lakes and parkland provide a fine setting for both temporary exhibitions and the permanent collection that is being built up from them. Work is not bought or given, but available on extended loan from artists, arts councils and, in a few cases from the Tate Gallery. The layout here makes it possible to view sculpture in 'garden' settings as well as the 'public' settings that demand a more monumental approach by the sculptor. Note also the imaginative use of colour on wooden fencing which leads to the Access Sculpture Trail designed by Don Rankin with emphasis on access for disabled visitors. The sculptures here are being worked upon *in situ*, evolving and growing with the gardens around them – a splendid example of the subtle relationship between art and nature.

IRELAND

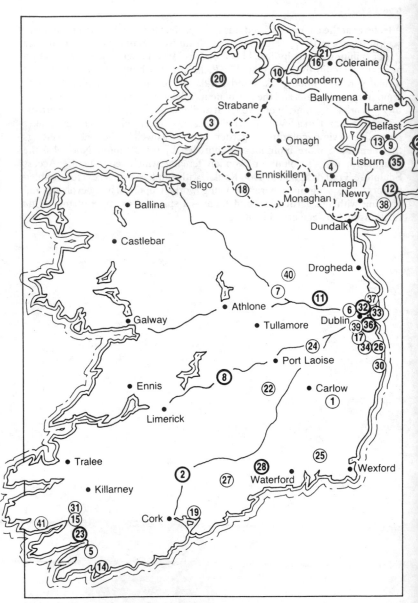

Two-starred gardens are ringed in bold.

ALTAMONT   1
Tullow, Co Carlow, Republic of Ireland. Tel: (0503) 59128

Mr and Mrs North ✳ 5m from Tullow, about 1m off main Tullow – Bunclody road (N80/81) ✳ Parking ✳ Home-made teas ✳ Partly suitable for wheelchairs ✳ Dogs on lead ✳ Plants for sale ✳ Open Easter to Oct, Suns, 2 – 6pm. Other times by appointment ✳ Entrance: IR£2, children under 10 free (1991 prices)

The lily-filled lake surrounded by fine, mature trees forms a backdrop for a gently sloping lawn. A central walkway formally planted with Irish yews and roses leads from the house to the lake. There is a beautiful fern-leaved beech, and some much more ancient beeches forming the 'Nun's walk'. A long walk through the demesne leads to the River Slaney with diversions to a bog garden, through a glen of ancient oaks undercarpeted with bluebells in spring. Mrs North's passion for trees is evident in the recent planting, and she has selected old-fashioned roses for her rose beds. She is also starting weekly residential gardening holidays.

ANNES GROVE ★★   2
Castletownroche, Co Cork, Republic of Ireland. Tel: (022) 26145

Mr and Mrs F.P. Grove Annesley ✳ 2m N of village of Castletownroche, between Fermoy and Mallow ✳ Parking ✳ Picnics ✳ Partly suitable for wheelchairs ✳ Dogs on lead ✳ Open April to Sept, Mon – Fri, 10am – 5pm, Sat and Sun, 1 – 6pm ✳ Entrance: IR£2, OAP and students IR£1.50, children IR£1

This is an archetypal 'Robinsonian' alias wild garden, but such tags are not helpful. Rhododendron species and cultivars arch over and spill towards the pathways, carpeting them with fallen blossoms. Steep paths descend at various places into the valley of the Awbeg river (which inspired Edmund Spenser). The statuesque conifers planted in the valley make a colourful tapestry behind the river garden, with *Primula florindae* and *P. japonica* cultivars in profusion. Perhaps least successful is the formal garden, maintained with bedding and a short herbaceous border. The glory of Annes Grove is the collection of rhododendron spp. wherein hidden, visitors may see surprises – a superb *Juniperus recurva* 'Castlewellan', a mature handkerchief tree (*Davidia involucrata*) and other exotic, flowering trees. Here is bird-song and the crystal-clear Awbeg, water-buttercups and primroses – peaceful groves.

ARDNAMONA ★★   3
Lough Eske, Donegal, Republic of Ireland. Tel: (073) 22650

Kieran and Amabel Clarke ✳ On NW shore of Lough Eske, approached from Donegal, following signs for Lough Eske ✳ Parking ✳ Open last week in Jan to last week in June by appointment ✳ Entrance: free

William Robinson would be proud of this garden created by the Wallaces 1880-1920. Ardnamona is 'Wild Gardening' at its most exuberant and refined. Imagine a Himalayan mountain slope cloaked with primeval rhododendron forest, 60 feet tall, with a carpet of fallen leaves underfoot embroidered in discarded flowers – you are close to imagining Ardnamona. The rhododendrons are mainly over 100 years old, and they proclaim their age with proud clean trunks, coloured from cinnamon to purple, and canopies well beyond reach. For the first time, in 1992 this garden (once neglected, now again cared for) will welcome visitors; rhododendron enthusiasts will need little more encouragement than the prospect of being in paradise.

ARMAGH OBSERVATORY 4
College Hill, Armagh, Northern Ireland. Tel: (0861) 522928

*Trustees of Armagh Observatory * In Armagh city at western end of Mall * Parking * Suitable for wheelchairs * Open Mon – Fri, 9.30am – 4.30pm * Entrance: free*

Founded over 200 years ago, the grounds of Archbishop Robinson's observatory have in recent years been tidied, and the plantings renewed. Of note is a 'sun-burst' parterre, the segments planted with shrubs for foliage and blossom effects. The sundial (designed by Mr Storm Dunlop) is fascinating and well worth a visit. It is a paved area and there is no gnomon – each viewer serves as the gnomon by walking to an allotted date stone. Highly entertaining – a place to bring the whole family, easily combined with a visit to the nearby planetarium.

BANTRY HOUSE 5
Bantry, Co Cork, Republic of Ireland. Tel: (027) 50047

*Mr and Mrs Egerton Shelwell-White * In Bantry town, a short distance from town centre * Parking * Refreshments * Toilet facilities * Partly suitable for wheelchairs * Shop * House open * Garden open all year, 9am – 6pm (8pm in summer) * Entrance: IR£2.50 (house and garden)*

Once upon a time there was a famous garden at Bantry House. Now, the stupendous terraces that rise steeply behind the house are infested with weedy shrubs – they would look much better after a little clearing up and be infinitely easier to maintain. Only the parterres encircling the house are carefully maintained, but too much attention is paid to indifferent bedding even in the well-executed new 'Italian Garden'. The information leaflet claims that the place has 'a vigorous, multiform and delicate variety of vegetation' – fanciful words to describe mediocrity. Having said that, the view from the steps is wonderful, the 'Grotesque' fountain is weird, and there is a good sculpture *Draped Georgian figure 1987* by Alexander Sokolov.

BEECH PARK ★ 6
Clonsilla, Co Dublin, Republic of Ireland. Tel: (01) 212216

*Jonathan and Daphne Shackleton * 1m from Clonsilla village on road to Lucan, 10m W of Dublin * Parking * Home-made teas * Toilet facilities * Suitable for wheelchairs * Plants for sale * Open March to Oct, first Sat and Sun of each month, and also Bank Holidays and every Sun in July and Aug, 2 – 6pm. Groups and overseas visitors by arrangement * Entrance: IR£2*

In an old walled garden of a Regency house, once bedded with vegetables in season, are raised beds and herbaceous borders brim-full of the choicest perennials and dwarf shrubs. The gems of this highly personal, indeed eclectic, collection begun about 1960 are celmisias (New Zealand mountain daisies), yet the raised beds contain many unusual and uncommon plants, all deliberately selected and superbly cultivated. The herbaceous borders which encircle the walled garden and line its intersecting pathways are planted with as great attention to excellence, and the collection of perennials is outstanding – meconopsis (esp. *M.* x *sheldonii*) phlox, papaver and iris cultivars are striking in season, and a listing of the entire assemblage would occupy a small book. The plants range from old-fashioned, cottage-garden types, some forgotten elsewhere, to the newest and best. David Shackleton, who created this garden, garnering cultivars from Ireland and Britain, died in 1988; his idiosyncratic garden is a wonderfully vivid memorial.

BELVEDERE 7
Mullingar, Co Westmeath, Republic of Ireland. Tel: (044) 40861 and (044) 42820

Westmeath County Council ✳ *4m from Mullingar town, on Tullamore road* ✳ *Parking* ✳ *Refreshments in house on Suns* ✳ *Toilet facilities* ✳ *Gardens and walks suitable for wheelchairs* ✳ *Dogs on lead* ✳ *House open* ✳ *Garden open May to Sept, 12 noon – 6pm* ✳ *Entrance: IR£1, children 50p*

The Jealous Wall is one of those typically Gothic-Irish follies, built in 1760 to separate two squabbling brothers. It looks antique and is impressive. Otherwise this garden does not abound in interest, but there are some fine trees and a large walled garden, containing some mundane bedding displays, and it is pleasant to be on the terraces dropping in steps to the shores of Lough Ennel, with views of its waters and islands.

BIRR CASTLE DEMESNE ★★ 8
Birr, Co Offaly, Republic of Ireland. Tel: (0509) 20056

Earl and Countess of Rosse ✳ *In town of Birr, 82m W of Dublin* ✳ *Parking outside castle gates* ✳ *Refreshments outside castle gate, picnics in walled garden* ✳ *Toilet facilities* ✳ *Suitable for wheelchairs* ✳ *Dogs on lead* ✳ *Plants for sale* ✳ *Shop* ✳ *Exhibitions featuring some aspect of the history of Birr Castle or the Earls of Rosse in gallery open 13th April to 19th May and 25th May to 29th Sept* ✳ *Castle not open* ✳ *Park open (?1992 dates and times)* ✳ *Entrance: (?1992 prices)*

The Victorian Gothic castle dominates vistas which strike through the park and at whose centre is the slumbering 'Leviathan' (a giant telescope which made Birr famous last century). Around, in profusion, are rare trees and shrubs especially many raised from seed received from central China in the mid-1900s. Over one of the rivers is a beautiful suspension bridge, and hidden amongst laurels is a Victorian fernery with recently restored water-works. Evergreen conifers, golden willows, carpets of daffodils, and world-record box hedges, magnolias in the river garden, a new cherry avenue and the original plant of *Paeonia* 'Anne Rosse' are mere selections of the many attractions. It is invigorating to walk around the lake, glimpsing the castle, examining the shrubs and trees (some of which are specially labelled), and revelling in the peace and quiet of central Ireland – three counties can be visited in one brief walk. It is fair to add that the beauties of this garden, which owe so much to Anne, Countess of Rosse, have given her international fame as a gardener.

THE BOTANIC GARDEN PARK   9
Stranmillis Road, Belfast, Co Antrim, Northern Ireland. Tel: (0232) 324902

Belfast City Council Parks Department ✳ *Between Queen's University and the Ulster Museum, Stranmillis* ✳ *Parking outside* ✳ *Refreshments: facilities in the Ulster Museum* ✳ *Toilet facilities* ✳ *Suitable for wheelchairs* ✳ *Dogs on lead* ✳ *Open daily, 7.30am to dusk. Palm House and Tropical Ravine, summer, weekdays, 10am – 5pm, weekends, 2 – 5pm, winter, weekdays, 10am – 4pm, weekends, 2 – 4pm. Guided tours and group visits at any time by arrangement* ✳ *Entrance: free*

Established in 1827, this became a public park in 1895. Today it has lots of vulgar bedding for general admiration; it is well done but not to everyone's taste. There are two reasons to visit this otherwise unexceptional park – the curvilinear iron and glass conservatory (1839 – 1852), one of the finest Victorian glasshouses (Richard Turner built only the wings; the dome is by Young of Edinburgh). It was restored in the 1970s and contains a small collection of tropical plants with massed displays of 'pot mums' and the like in season (again well-grown and finely displayed, but not everyone's favourite). The Tropical Ravine House is the greater delight, and also recently restored. This is 'High Victoriana', with ferns, bananas, lush tropical vines and tree ferns, and goldfish in the Amazon lily pond, and a waterfall worked with a chain-pull! Marvellous, evocative of by-gone crinoline days.

BROOK HALL   10
65 Culmore Road, Londonderry, Northern Ireland. Tel: (0504) 351297

Mr D. Gilliland ✳ *N of Londonderry about ¹/₂m from roundabout on west side of Foyle Bridge* ✳ *Partly suitable for wheelchairs* ✳ *Open by appointment* ✳ *Entrance: by donation*

This mature arboretum on the shores of Loch Foyle contains a good collection of trees and shrubs (including rhododendrons). Fortunately the planting was never cramped so fine specimens are seen to good advantage. *Azara microphylla* is a robust tree here, showing again that the north coast of Ireland has a remarkably temperate climate. The trees and shrubs are labelled and a catalogue has been prepared.

BUTTERSTREAM ★★   11
Trim, Co Meath, Republic of Ireland.

Jim Reynolds ✳ *Best season: summer* ✳ *Suitable for wheelchairs* ✳ *Open May to Sept, daily except Mon, 2 – 6pm* ✳ *Entrance: IR£3*

Like all the best gardens, this is a single-handed work of art. A series of compartments contains different arrangements of plants, ranging from a formal box-hedged garden of old roses and lilies, to an informal gold garden carpeted with ferns and hostas. In the main garden a selection of choice herbaceous perennials in an island bed encircled by wide borders processes through the summer from whites and blues to yellows and reds – phlox, kniphofia, lobelia, macleaya, allium are only a few of the genera represented. A formal pool, replete with water lilies and carp, has a distinct Roman feel, and the large tennis lawn has a restrained gallery of clematis, deep purple hedges and a rustic summerhouse.

CASTLEWELLAN NATIONAL ARBORETUM ★★   12
Castlewellan, Co Down, Northern Ireland.

Forest Service, Dept of Agriculture (Northern Ireland) ✳ *In Castlewellan town, 25m from Belfast, 4m from Newcastle* ✳ *Parking inc. disabled* ✳ *Refreshments: summer only* ✳ *Toilet facilities* ✳ *Partly suitable for wheelchairs* ✳ *Dogs on lead* ✳ *Open all year* ✳ *Entrance: fee for car park £2*

The walled garden, now called the Annesley Garden, contains an outstanding collection of mature trees and shrubs, many planted before the turn of the century by Lord Annesley. Original specimens of some of Castlewellan's cultivars thrive here, in fine condition. In the spring and summer there are many rhododendrons in bloom, and scarlet Chilean fire-bushes (*Embothrium coccineum*). In early autumn, the snow-carpet is the fallen petals of the unequalled collection of eucryphia. The arboretum has a formal axis, with two fountain pools and steps. An herbaceous border runs along part of this. Beyond the walls is a new garden, planted with heathers, dwarf conifers and limes, and with flowering trees (malus, prunus, etc.). Walks lead into the forest and beside the lough. A caravan and camping ground within the forest park provides a wonderful base for exploring this part of Ireland and for visiting the other County Down gardens. Castlewellan is well known to everyone for the bilious golden Leyland cypress that came from here – don't be dismayed – the arboretum contains many more wonderful plants, some unique, all in their prime. You will not see decrepit trees here – the maintenance is exceptionally good.

CITY OF BELFAST INTERNATIONAL ROSE GARDEN   13
Sir Thomas and Lady Dixon Park, Upper Malone Road, Belfast, Northern Ireland.

Belfast Parks Department ✳ *S of Belfast city centre, on Upper Malone Road* ✳ *Best seasons: spring/summer* ✳ *Parking* ✳ *Refreshments: in Stables Tea House* ✳ *Toilet facilities* ✳ *Suitable for wheelchairs* ✳ *Dogs on lead* ✳ *Open all year; walled garden, Mon – Fri, 8am – 4pm, Sat and Sun, 2 – 4pm* ✳ *Entrance: free*

This 130-acre estate was presented to the Corporation in 1959 when plans were made for a rose trial garden. In the late 1980s, it was decided to redevelop the rose garden area, covering 11 acres, and replace it with a display garden tracing the history of the rose, surrounded by alder and oak trees for shelter. The way the roses are paraded, like regiments of foot soldiers on a battlefield in lines and squares and circles, supported by the unhappy massed lines of dwarf rhododendrons, will not appeal to those who like planting to be imaginative. As for the roses, the new ones being trialled are well-nourished if rather similar. Fine old cultivars are conspicuous by their absence, or, when present, often wrongly labelled. Elsewhere, Dixon Park has excellent trees, a walled garden (containing the International Camellia Trials), and an ice house. It is restful to walk on the signposted trails through the groves and the picnic areas near the car park are popular.

CREAGH 14
Skibbereen, Co Cork, Republic of Ireland. Tel: (028) 21267

Mr Peter Harold Barry ✳ *4m from Skibbereen on road to Baltimore – on right through white-painted iron gate* ✳ *Parking at house. Small coaches only* ✳ *Suitable for wheelchairs* ✳ *Dogs on lead* ✳ *Open April to Sept, daily, 10am – 6pm* ✳ *Entrance: IR£1, children free*

Definitely a garden for those who seek solitude and silence, far from traffic. Paths lead through woodland underplanted with rhododendron species and cultivars, and down to the sea. A serpentine mill-pond is now fringed with gunnera, cordyline and hydrangea, the bold effect inspired by the paintings of 'Le Douanier' Rousseau. There are some fine tender species, including *Telopea truncata*, *Rhododendron* 'Sesterianum', a magnificent *Vitex agnus-castus*, and feathery *Azara microphylla* 'Variegata'. A valiant garden lovingly maintained by the elderly owner, wherein one feels the wilderness is slowly winning, creating a truly wild, Irish pleasaunce.

DERREEN ★ 15
Lauragh, Killarney, Co Kerry, Republic of Ireland

The Hon. David Bigham ✳ *15m from Kenmare on road along S side of Kenmare Bay, towards the Healy Pass* ✳ *Best season: April/May* ✳ *Parking* ✳ *Toilet facilities* ✳ *Open April to Oct, daily, 11am – 6pm* ✳ *Entrance: IR£1.50*

The broad sweep of plush lawn and the bald outcroppings of rock by the house do not prepare visitors for the lushness of the walks which weave through native woodlands and palisades of jade-stemmed bamboo. The evocatively-named King's Oozy – a path that has a hankering to be a river – leads to a grove of tall, archaic tree-ferns (*Dicksonia antarctica*) with socks of filmy ferns. Wellies are the plantsmen's only requirement to enjoy the rhododendrons that shelter among clipped entanglements of *Gaultheria shallon*. Probably one of the wettest places in Britain and Ireland, a fact you're reminded of by the lushness (and midges in season!)

DOWNHILL CASTLE 16
Co Derry, Northern Ireland.

The National Trust ✳ *5m W of Coleraine on A2 coast road, 1m W of Castlerock*

Parking at Bishop's Gate and at Lion Gate ✳ Suitable for wheelchairs ✳ Dogs on lead ✳ Mussenden Temple open ✳ Grounds always open ✳ Entrance: free

For the architectural historian this is a must – the Mussenden Temple, sited on the clifftop with spectacular views along the coast of Northern Ireland, must be one of the most extraordinary libraries (that was its original purpose) in the world. The walk there is rough, through thistles and sheep droppings. The ruins of Downhill House, the Earl-Bishop's palace, are gaunt, and from the rear towards the Bishop's Gate Miss Jan Eccles has created a garden memorable for the miniature water-meadow full of candelabra primroses (yellow and pink) with startling clumps of dark *Iris kaempferi*. Dressed stones from tumbledown buildings and armless statues are enveloped with happy plantings, bergenia and fuchsia, roses spilling from a rickety pergola, and the sprightly Miss Eccles will be delighted to chat. A gem of a garden to which The National Trust could devote more attention.

FERNHILL ★   17
Sandyford, Co Dublin, Republic of Ireland. Tel: (01) 956000

Mrs Sally Walker ✳ On main Dublin – Enniskerry road, 8m from central Dublin ✳ Parking ✳ Toilet facilities ✳ Partly suitable for wheelchairs ✳ Plants for sale ✳ Open March to Nov, Tues – Sat, 11am – 5pm, Sun, 2 – 6pm ✳ Entrance: IR£2.50, OAP IR£1.50, children IR£1

The plantings of rhododendron species and cultivars provide spectacles of colour from early spring into mid-summer; many of the more tender rhododendrons flourish here. The garden is situated on the eastern slope of the Dublin Mountains and has a laurel lawn, some fine nineteenth-century plantings and an excellent flowering specimen of *Michelia doltsopa*. The walkways through the wooded areas wind steeply past many other shrubs, principally those that thrive on acid soil – pieris and camellia are also outstanding. There is a small rock garden and a water garden near the house, and drifts of daffodils in the spring. A sculpture exhibition has become an annual feature.

FLORENCE COURT   18
Florence Court, Co Fermanagh, Northern Ireland. Tel: (036582) 249

The National Trust ✳ 8m SW of Enniskillen, via A4 Sligo road or A32 Swanlinbar road, 4m from Marble Arch Caves ✳ Parking ✳ Refreshments: teas and lunches in North Pavilion ✳ Toilet facilities, inc disabled ✳ Suitable for wheelchairs ✳ Dogs on lead ✳ Shop ✳ House open different times ✳ Estate open all year, 10am – 1 hour before dusk. Closed 25th Dec. Parties by arrangement ✳ Entrance: Forest Park and Pleasure Gardens £1 per car (house and gardens £2.10, children £1.10) (1991 prices)

The original, the mother of all Irish yews (*Taxus baccata* 'Fastigiata') still grows in the laurel-infested woodland about a quarter of a mile from the splendid mansion at Florence Court. Well worth the walk; the path allows glimpses of the mountains and the fine 'Brownian' park in front of the house. Some fine weeping beeches and old rhododendrons grow near the house, and work is in progress on revitalizing the walled garden. Strong shoes essential (especially in rainy season!) if you wish to pay respects to the venerable, 250-year-old tree. Ice-house and saw mill. The nearby caves (open to public) are worth visiting too, making a rewarding day out, with some fine views.

FOTA ARBORETUM ★   19
Fota Trust, Carrigtwohill, Co Cork, Republic of Ireland. Tel: (021) 812728

Fota Trust   ✳   9m E of Cork city, on road to Cobh   ✳   Parking beside arboretum (also serving Fota Wildlife Park). IR£1.50 per car   ✳   Refreshments at Wildlife Park   ✳   Toilet facilities in car park   ✳   Suitable for wheelchairs   ✳   Dogs on lead   ✳   Shop in Wildlife Park   ✳   Arboretum open April to Sept, daily, 10am – 6pm, Sun, 11am – 6pm, Oct, Sat and Sun, 11am – 6pm   ✳   Entrance: free for arboretum. Plant catalogue available IR£2

Many of the superb specimen trees in this garden are undoubtedly among the best examples in Ireland and Britain. By the house is a cedar of Lebanon, undercarpeted with cyclamen; a handkerchief tree (*Davidia involucrata*), exquisite pieris, contorted tree-ferns, *Magnolia campbellii* and much, much more. A banana palm lingers in the border with fuchsia and watsonia cultivars. The Italian garden is, however, a mere shadow, and the orangery derelict, its sentinel *Phoenix dactylifera* patiently waiting the outcome of present uncertainties. At the time of writing the whole island is under a sale-option which may lead to large-scale development altering its unique character. Meanwhile the arboretum slumbers, needful of a clear guiding spirit, but still a delight for those who enjoy trees and shrubs.

GLENVEAGH CASTLE ★★   20
Glenveagh National Park, Churchill, Letterkenny, Co Donegal, Republic of Ireland. Tel: (074) 37088/37090/37262

Office of Public Works   ✳   15m NW of Letterkenny   ✳   Parking at Visitor Centre. Access to garden and castle by official minicoaches only   ✳   Refreshments and meals   ✳   Toilet facilities   ✳   Castle open, IR£1   ✳   Garden open Easter to last Mon in Oct, daily, 10.30am – 6.30pm (open to 7.30pm on Sun June to Aug). Other times by arrangement   ✳   Entrance: IR£1.50, OAP and groups per person IR£1, students and children IR60p

The centre-piece of the Glenveagh National Park is the garden around Glenveagh Castle. The castle is set beside a mountain lough encircled with high, peat-blanketed mountains, in the middle of windswept moorlands, a most unpromising site. But, as in so many Irish gardens, surprises are countless. The lower lawn garden has fringing shrubberies, and, beyond, steep pathways wind through oak woods in which are planted scented, white-flowered rhododendrons, and numerous other tender shrubs from southern lands. Terraced enclosures with terracotta pots of plants and sculpture are encountered unexpectedly. The jardin potager at the castle has rank on rank of ornamental

vegetables and flowering herbs. This is a paradise for p
keen on seeing fine specimens of unusual aspec
Fascicularia pitcairniifolia, and many more. Sadly, Glenv
the mountain is closed to the public, and there bee.
off parts of this wonderland. Linger, and walk the moun
bus back to the remarkable heather-roofed Visitor Cent
landscaping (except the appallingly trained rowans!)

GUY L. WILSON DAFFODIL GARDEN ★   21
University of Ulster, Coleraine, Co Londonderry, Northern Ireland. Tel: (0265) 44141

*University of Ulster * On Cromore road, about 1m N of Coleraine town on road to Portstewart * Best season: spring * Parking * Dogs on lead * Open daily * Entrance: free*

The daffodils in this garden represent one of the National collections (established under the patronage of the National Council for the Conservation of Plants and Gardens although it was commenced long before the NCCPG scheme). It is principally based on Irish-bred cultivars particularly those of Guy Wilson; however, among the 1000 plus cultivars represented are daffodils from New Zealand and the USA, as well as Britain, and there are both old and modern cultivars. The daffodils are interplanted with shrubs in island beds. The setting is attractive, but the garden now shows signs of diminished care and attention due to cut-backs by the university. Vandalism clearly is a problem – flowers wantonly damaged and picked daffodils strewn on paths were seen on a recent visit. The labels have all been removed (to prevent theft) which makes a nonsense of the collection as an educational facility. The purpose of such a collection is to allow people to look and learn – we must sympathise with the problems faced by the university and hope that some imaginative scheme can be devised to allow visitors to discover the names of the host of daffodils.

HEYWOOD GARDEN   22
Salesian House, Ballinakill, Co Laois, Republic of Ireland. Tel: (0502) 3334

*Outside Ballinakill village. 3m from Abbeyleix (turn E in town following sign to Ballinakill) * Parking * Partly suitable for wheelchairs * Dogs on lead * Open April to Sept, 11am – 6pm by appointment * Entrance: IR£2, students and children IR£1*

Edwin Lutyens' walled garden with pergola and lawns is acknowledged as his finest small-scale work in Ireland. It is a gem, now restored close to its original state as far as the walls and ornaments are concerned. The planting is being restored, in the style of Gertrude Jekyll with the advice of Graham Stuart Thomas. On the driveway leading towards the school buildings is an eighteenth-century folly. There is a long way to go before the garden is again sparkling, but it is still well worth visiting.

ILNACULLIN (commonly known as Garinish Island) ★★   23
Glengarriff, Co Cork, Republic of Ireland. Tel: (027) 63040

*National Parks and Monuments Service, Office of Public Works * On an island*

* Toilet facilities * Open March and Oct, daily, 10am – 4.30pm, * *pm, April to June and Sept, daily, 10am – 6.30pm, Sun 1 – 6pm, July * *ug, daily, 9.30am – 6.30pm, Sun, 11am – 7pm * Entrance: IR£1.50, *dents and children IR60p, groups of 20 or more £1 per person. Travel is by boat, charge for which is IR£4 return fare (1991 prices)*

The boat trip across the sheltered inlets of Bantry Bay, past sun-bathing seals, with views of the Caha Mountains, is doubly rewarding; landing at the slipway you gain entrance to one of Ireland's gardening jewels begun in the early 1900s. Most visitors cluster around the Casita and reflecting pool, designed by Harold Peto, to enjoy (on clear days) spectacular scenery, and some quite indifferent annual bedding. But walk beyond, to the Temple of the Winds, through shrubberies filled with plants usually confined indoors – tree ferns, Southern Hemisphere conifers, rhododendron species and cultivars. A flight of stone steps leads to the Martello tower, and thence the path returns to the walled garden and Italianate garden. Plant enthusiasts can spend many happy hours with such delights as *Lyonothamnus floribundus* var. *aspleniifolius* and a myriad of manuka (*Leptospermum scoparium*, the New Zealand tea tree); take a picnic and linger; if wet, bring boots or strong shoes and an umbrella. Wonderful.

JAPANESE GARDEN ★   24
Irish National Stud, Tully, Kildare, Co Kildare, Republic of Ireland. Tel: (045) 21617

*Irish National Stud * 1m outside Kildare town, 25m SW of Dublin * Parking * Refreshments * Toilet facilities * Plants for sale * Shop * The Irish National Stud and Horse Museum open * Open Easter Sunday to Oct, daily 10am – 5pm, Sat, 10am – 5.30pm, Sun, 2 – 5.30pm. Guided tours on request * Entrance: IR£2, OAP and students IR£1.50, children IR£1. Groups of 20 or more welcome*

Created between the years 1906-1910. Devised by Colonel William Hall-Walker (later Lord Wavertree), a wealthy Scotsman of a famous brewery family and laid out by the Japanese Eida and his son Minory, the gardens, symbolising the 'Life of Man', are acclaimed as the finest Japanese gardens in Europe. This is not a plantsman's garden, for few of the plants are Japanese; to be sure there are some excellent old maples, but many of the trees and shrubs are clipped and shaped beyond reason. The overshadowing Scots pines are exquisite. A pathway meanders through artificial caves, into a watery stream, past the tranquil ponds and on to the weeping trees of the grave. Beautiful stone lanterns grace the garden which is in the style of a Japanese 'tea garden'. On a misty day with smoke from a distant fire billowing across, this visitor recalls it as mysterious, beautiful.

JOHN F. KENNEDY ARBORETUM ★   25
New Ross, Co Wexford, Republic of Ireland. Tel: (051) 88171

*Office of Public Works * 8m S of New Ross * Parking * Refreshments: café May to Sept, April weekends only. Picnic area * Toilet facilities * Suitable for wheelchairs * Dogs on lead * Visitor Centre with Kennedy memorial and video*

* *Open daily, May to Aug, 10am – 8pm, April and Sept, 10am – 6.30pm, Oct to March, 10am – 5pm* * *Entrance: IR£1, family IR£3, season ticket IR£10, coach IR£10, minibus IR£5*

A modern spacious arboretum laid out in botanical sequence with rides; from the summit of a nearby hill is a superb panorama of the park and Co Wexford. Best to begin at the viewpoint – turn left just beyond the main entrance and drive to summit car park to see the layout. At the arboretum be prepared for a long walk – fortunately those not keen on gardening tend to linger near the café so that the distant reaches are quiet and empty. Planting began in the 1960s and now 4500 different trees and shrubs are growing, ranging from conifers to flowering shrubs. Most species are represented by several specimens, and keen plantsmen can linger long examining the groups. Good labelling. A colourful planting of dwarf conifers is on the western side, a small lake on the east. While primarily a scientific collection, the arboretum now has an established elegance.

KILLRUDDERY   26
Bray, Co Wicklow, Republic of Ireland. Tel: (01) 2863405

Earl and Countess of Meath * *1m S of Bray on road to Greystones* * *Parking* * *Toilet facilities* * *Partly suitable for wheelchairs* * *House open with conducted tours at extra charge* * *Open May, June, Sept, daily, 1 – 5pm* * *Entrance: IR£1, OAP, students and children over 12 IR50p, under 12 free (house and gardens £IR2.50, OAP, students and children over 12 IR£1.50, children under 12 not admitted. All children must be accompanied)*

The joy of Killruddery, a seventeenth-century garden with nineteenth-century embellishments, is the formal hedges, known as 'The Angles' set beside the formal canals which lead to a ride into the distant hills. There is a collection of nineteenth-century French cast statuary, a sylvan theatre created in beech, and a fountain pool enclosed in a beech hedge too. The excellent conservatory (nineteenth-century), alas, has a perspex dome. The landscape features are unique, and Killruddery deserves to be better known, but it is not a garden for keen plantsmen without designer tastes.

LISMORE CASTLE GARDENS   27
Lismore, Co Waterford, Republic of Ireland. Tel: (058) 54424

Duke and Duchess of Devonshire * *Entrance in Lismore town* * *Parking* * *Open 11th May to 11th Sept, daily except Sat, 1.45 – 4.45pm* * *Entrance: IR£1.80, children under 16 IR90p. Reduced rates for parties of 20 or more during normal working hours.*

Do not come to Ireland just to see Lismore Castle gardens, but the situation of the castle overlooking the River Blackwater is stunning. Entering through the gatehouse, there are two gardens, the upper reached by a stairway in the gatehouse and terraced with patches of vegetables; and the reduced glasshouse by Joseph Paxton (an interesting ridge-furrow house). The view from the main axis to the church spire is fine. In the lower garden are a few meritricious plants, but the principal feature, an ancient yew-walk carpeted softly with the dropped leaves, is wonderful. For that only can this be regarded as a garden of note – the rest is mundane. Yet Edmund Spenser is said to have written *The Fairie Queene* here, and it is the Irish home of the Duke of Devonshire who has only Chatsworth (see entry) to console him in England.

MOUNT CONGREVE ★★   28
Kilmeaden, Co Waterford, Republic of Ireland. Tel: (051) 841 03 or (051) 841 15

Mr Ambrose Congreve ✳ Best season: spring ✳ Partly suitable for wheelchairs ✳ Open strictly by appointment ✳ Entrance: IR£15, reduced for parties of 13 or more

In emulation of Exbury, Ambrose Congreve has amassed an unequalled collection of rhododendron, camellia and magnolia species and cultivars, with many other trees as 'icing on the cake'. It is a staggering collection which cannot be appreciated in a single short visit. Indeed any visit to this garden is a formidable prospect: over 100 acres of shrubs, mass upon mass, for every cultivar is planted in groups of about a dozen (a dismal scene when the evergreens are not in bloom). Colours clash, for it cannot be said that this garden is 'designed' from the basic skeleton; it is an eccentric congregation. Yet highlights are memorable. In early March a forest of *Magnolia campbellii* offers pink to white goblets to the rooks. A languid walled garden, dominated by an ancient gingko, provides a more mundane space with a fine late eighteenth-century vinery and summer-flowering borders. There is enough here to satiate the most avid rhododendron and camellia passion. Too much for most, but at least others can wonder at the whims of one collector, including his diminutive pagoda.

MOUNT STEWART HOUSE, GARDEN AND TEMPLE OF THE WINDS ★★   29
Greyabbey, Newtownards, Co Down, Northern Ireland. Tel: (024774) 387

The National Trust ✳ On Ards Peninsula, 5m from Newtownards on road (A20) to Portaferry, 15m E of Belfast ✳ Parking 300 yards ✳ Refreshments: light refreshments and teas same time as house. ✳ Toilet facilities ✳ Partly suitable for wheelchairs ✳ House open at different times ✳ Garden open April to Aug, daily, 12 noon – 6pm. Sept and Oct, Sat and Sun only, 12 noon – 6pm ✳ Entrance: IR£2.70, children IR£1.35

Of all Ireland's gardens this is The One not to miss. Any adjective that evokes beauty can be applied to it, and it's fun too. In the gardens in front of the house is a collection of statuary, satirising British political and public figures – dodos, monkeys and boars. The planting here is formal, with rectangular beds of 'hot' and 'cool' colours. Beyond in the informal gardens are mature trees and shrubs, a botanical collection with few equals, planted with great panache and maintained with outstanding attention to detail. Spires of giant lilies (cardiocrinum), aspiring eucalyptus, banks of rhododendrons, ferns and blue poppies, rivers of candelabra primulas – and much more. Walk along the

lakeside path to the hill that affords a view over t...
tender shrubs such as *Metrosideros umbellata* flouris...
family cemetery. Leading from it is the Jubilee Avenu...
stag. Mount Stewart is a whole day for those keen on...
seen several times during the year truly to savour its rich...
water, buildings and trees. The Temple of the Win...
Stuart's banqueting hall of 1785, is also memorable.

MOUNT USHER ★ 30
Ashford, Co Wicklow, Republic of Ireland. Tel: (0404) 40116/ 40205

Mrs Madelaine Jay ✳ *At Ashford, on main Dublin – Wexford road, 30m S of Dublin* ✳ *Parking* ✳ *Refreshments: tea rooms, no picnics* ✳ *Toilet facilities* ✳ *Partly suitable for wheelchairs* ✳ *Shopping courtyard* ✳ *Open 17th March to 3rd Nov, Mon – Sat, 10.30am – 6pm, Sun, 11am – 6pm* ✳ *Entrance: IR£2.20, OAP, students and children IR£1.50. Special group rates for groups of 20 or more*

The Vartry river babbles through this exquisite garden over gentle weirs and under bridges which allow visitors to meander through the collections. Mount Usher is a plant-lovers' paradise. *Pinus montezumae* is always first port-of-call, a shimmering tree, magnificent when the bluebells are in flower. The philosophy of Mount Usher eschews chemicals of all kinds, and the lawns are cut in a cycle which allows the bulbs and wildflowers in them to seed naturally. Throughout there are drifts of rhododendrons, fine trees and shrubs including many that are difficult to cultivate outdoors in other parts of Britain and Ireland. The grove of eucalyptus at the lower end of the valley is memorable; a kiwi-fruit vine (*Actinidia chinensis*) cloaks the piers of a bridge, and beside the tennis court is the gigantic original *Eucryphia* x *nymansensis* 'Mount Usher'. In spring, bulbs and magnolias, in summer a procession of rhododendrons, in autumn russet and crimson leaves falling from maples – a garden for all seasons.

MUCKROSS HOUSE AND GARDENS ★ 31
Killarney National Park, Killarney, Co Kerry, Republic of Ireland. Tel· (064) 31947/31440

National Parks and Monument Service; Office of Public Works ✳ *4m from centre of Killarney, on road to Kenmare* ✳ *Parking* ✳ *Restaurant* ✳ *Toilet facilities* ✳ *Suitable for wheelchairs* ✳ *Dogs on lead* ✳ *Craft shop* ✳ *Open for pedestrians all year, with car access, 8am – 5pm (July and Aug, 8am – 7pm)* ✳ *Entrance: free*

The garden around Muckross House is almost incidental to the spectacle of the lakes and mountains of Killarney. It is principally renowned as a viewing area for the wild grandeur of the mountains. The lawns sweep to clumps of old rhododendrons and Scots pines, and there is a huge natural rock garden which is plagued with noisy children in high season. There is no peace here except on wet winter days. But leave the garden and take the lough-side trails, and enjoy the wildwoods with their unique assemblages of plants – *Sorbus anglica* (English whitebeam), yew and, above all, the almost eternal strawberry tree (*Arbutus unedo*). There is a mystical yew woodland carpeted with mosses. Throughout

Park the cursed *Rhododendron ponticum* is being slowly and
fully eliminated. Would that the jarveys could go too; don't be tempted
by for their extravagant transport from the town – the car park is free and
beside the house!

NATIONAL BOTANIC GARDENS, GLASNEVIN ★★ 32
Glasnevin, Dublin 9, Republic of Ireland. Tel: (01) 377596/ 374388

*Department of Agriculture and Food ✻ 1m N of central Dublin ✻ Parking very
limited in summer and at weekends ✻ Refreshments: arrangements for groups only
may be made in advance by writing to the Director ✻ Toilet facilities ✻ Suitable
for wheelchairs except for main Palm House ✻ Shop ✻ Open daily except 25th
Dec, summer, 9am – 6pm, winter, 9am – 4.30pm. Opening times for glasshouses
are posted at entrance ✻ Entrance: free*

A fine garden which still retains its Victorian exactitude with close-cut lawns
and succulent carpet-bedding (in summer only!), but with an air of decrepi-
tude, and the visitor facilities are parsimonious. The plant collection generally
is fine, but in places the shrubs and trees are past their best. In the winter, the
glasshouses are worth visiting; by spring there are daffodil-crowded lawns and
flowering cherries; the summer highlight is the double, curving herbaceous
border, and in autumn the fruit-laden trees and russet foliage can be magical.
The Turner conservatory (1843 – 1869), the finest in Ireland, is being restored.
Glasnevin is undoubtedly worth visiting, especially by gardeners with a strong
interest in shrubs and perennials; soil conditions preclude large-scale
rhododendron planting, and anyone passionate about alpines will be very
disappointed. Highlights are hard to enumerate, but a few outstanding plants
may be mentioned: *Zelkova carpinifolia* (especially in winter a marvellous
'architectural' tree) the Chain tent (*c.* 1836) with ancient wisteria; *Picea omorika*
(at pond); *Fascicularia pitcairniifolia* and *Ochagavia carnea* (at Cactus house);
cycads in Palm House; *Parrotia persica* (near entrance, wonderful in February
and October); and of course 'The Last Rose of Summer'!

NATIONAL WAR MEMORIAL 33
Dublin, Republic of Ireland.

*Trustees of the National War Memorial ✻ In Kilmainham ✻ Parking ✻
Suitable for wheelchairs ✻ Open during daylight hours ✻ Entrance: free*

Sir Edwin Lutyens' Irish gardens (see also Heywood, Co Laois) are not nearly
as well-known as his English ones. This memorial garden (1936, dedicated
1940), recently restored and planted anew, is typical of his reserved, calm style
with sunken rose gardens, a simple altar stone, colonnades and formal plantings
of trees. In the Book-room are volumes with the names of Irish men and women
who died in World War I.

POWERSCOURT ★ 34
Enniskerry, Co Wicklow, Republic of Ireland. Tel: (01) 2867676

Slazenger family ✻ 11m S of Dublin, just outside village of Enniskerry ✻

Parking ∗ *Refreshments: licensed restaurant* ∗ *Toilet facilities* ∗ *Partly suitable for wheelchairs* ∗ *Dogs on lead* ∗ *Plants for sale* ∗ *Shop* ∗ *House a ruin after a fire in 1974. Occasional exhibitions and children's play area* ∗ *Guided tours available* ∗ *Open March to Oct, 9.30am – 5.30pm* ∗ *Entrance: IR£2.50, children IR£1.50. Separate charge for waterfall*

Powerscourt is a 'grand garden', a massive statement of the triumph of Art over the Natural Landscape. In its present form, with an amphitheatre of terraces and great central axis (mid-nineteenth century), the garden is largely the design of the inimitable Daniel Robertson. The elaborate High Victorian parterre, garishly bedded-out, has been eliminated and the well-maintained lawns are now peacefully embellished. In some ways Powerscourt is beyond compare – the axis formed by the ceremonious stairway leading down to the Triton Pond and jet, and stretching beyond to the Great Sugarloaf Mountain, is justly famous – it can however be glimpsed in a few minutes (and that is what many tourists do). In other ways Powerscourt is over-rated. The herbaceous border is incongruously sited and mediocre. The Japanese garden is merely a miscellany of red-painted bridges and stone lanterns. When you visit Powerscourt give those features a miss, and walk along the terrace towards the Pepperpot, through the mature conifers which Lord Powerscourt collected – a big cone pine (*Pinus coulteri*), the tallest in Ireland and Britain, is here. Wander on, to the edge of the pond, and look up, along the stairway, past the monumental terraces to the facade of the burnt-out house. That's the view of Powerscourt that is breath-taking – a man-made amphitheatre guarded by winged horses. Statuary and the famous perspective gate; an avenue of monkey puzzles and a beech wood along the avenue; these add to Powerscourt's glory.

ROWALLANE ★★   35
Saintfield, Co Down, Northern Ireland. Tel: (0238) 510131

The National Trust ∗ *¹/₂m S of Saintfield on A7, Belfast – Downpatrick road* ∗ *Parking* ∗ *Refreshments: tea rooms with light refreshments, April to Sept, 2 – 6pm* ∗ *Toilet facilities* ∗ *Partly suitable for wheelchairs* ∗ *Dogs on lead* ∗ *Trust shop* ∗ *Open March, daily, Mon – Fri, 10.30am – 5pm. April to Oct, weekdays, 10.30am – 6pm, weekends, 2 – 6pm. Nov to March 1993, Mon – Fri, 9am – 5pm. Closed 25th, 26th Dec and 1st Jan* ∗ *Entrance: March to Oct, £2.30, Nov to Feb, £1.20. Parties outside normal hours extra charge by appointment only*

While famous as a 50-acre rhododendron garden, and certainly excellent in this regard, Rowallane has much more to interest keen gardeners. In summer, the walled garden blossoms in lemon and blue, while, around, hoheria cast white petals in the wind. In secluded places, a handkerchief tree blows; there is a pale-yellow-leaved pieris, a restored Victorian bandstand (music-filled on summer weekends) and orchid meadows. Rock garden with primulas, meconopsis, heathers etc. and several areas of natural wild flowers. Any season will be interesting, and for the real enthusiast there are rhododendron species and cultivars in bloom from October to August. The original plant of *Viburnum plicatum* 'Rowallane' is in the walled garden as is the original *Chaenomeles* x *superba* 'Rowallane'; a feature is made of *Hypericum* 'Rowallane' at the entrance to the walled garden.

45 SANDFORD ROAD ★★   36
Ranelagh, Dublin 6, Republic of Ireland.

Helen Dillon ✳ *Best season: spring – late autumn* ✳ *Parking in street* ✳ *Toilet facilities* ✳ *Limited access for wheelchairs* ✳ *Plants for sale according to season* ✳ *Open mid-March to mid-Oct, Sun, 2 – 5pm. Groups at any time by arrangement* ✳ *Entrance: IR£3, OAP IR£2*

Within a walled rectangular garden, typical of Dublin's Georgian town houses, Helen Dillon has created one of the best designed and planted gardens in Ireland. As a central foil there is an immaculate lawn which enhances the colourful embroidery of the borders which on exploration turn into a necklace of secret rooms with raised beds for rarities, such as lady's slipper orchids, or double-flowered *Trillium grandiflorum*. On the terrace, terracotta pots sprout more rare plants: *Trochocarpa thymifolia* and the blue sweet pea (*Lathyrus nervosus*). Clumps of *Dierama pulcherrimum* arch over the sphinxes, and a small alpine house and conservatory shelter the choicest – *Clematis florida* 'Sieboldii', *Lapageria rosea*, prize-winning ferns, alpines and bulbs. The mixed borders of shrubs and herbaceous perennials are changeful, each season revealing unusual plants and exciting colour combinations. A listing of the plants in Mrs Dillon's garden would not shame a large botanical garden. Each plant has its proper place, all is ordered with no forbidding sense of contrivance. The exuberance overwhelms the formality, and the garden is both a finely-designed pleasaunce and a plantsman's veritable nirvana.

TALBOT BOTANIC GARDEN ★   37
Malahide Castle, Malahide, Co Dublin, Republic of Ireland.
Tel: (01) 450940

Dublin County Council ✳ *Outside Malahide, 10m N of Dublin* ✳ *Parking* ✳ *Refreshments: lunches and teas in castle* ✳ *Suitable for wheelchairs* ✳ *Dogs on lead* ✳ *Shop in castle* ✳ *House open* ✳ *Garden open May to Sept, daily, 2 – 4.30pm. Conducted tour of walled garden, Wed, 2pm* ✳ *Entrance: IR50p, children free if accompanied (1991 prices)*

Malahide Castle was the home of the Talbot family for many centuries; following the death of Lord Talbot de Malahide it was acquired by Dublin County Council. The garden consists of three parts – the outer demesne (now occupied by playing fields, well-kept lawns and shrubberies, pathways); the main shrubberies (open to the public as above) and the walled garden (open only by special arrangement and on Wednesdays for guided tours). The main shrubberies planted by Lord Talbot contain a varied mixture of trees and shrubs, some of which are outstanding and rare. However, the finest part of the collection is in the walled garden – here Lord Talbot planted such exotics as *Telopea truncata, Bomarea caldasii, Garrya* x *issaquahensis*, and numerous others. Olearia was a favourite genus and is well represented here. Australasian genera are also represented (e.g. pittosporum, grevillea, cyathodes, acacia); *Berberis valdiviana* and *Pseudopanax ferox* lurk in an out-of-the-way corner. By the castle is a large cedar of Lebanon with cyclamen below, and a spacious lawn. The garden is worth visiting; the pity is that so many of the shrubs are still clipped into uncomfortable shapes, and that very few of the plants are fully labelled.

TOLLYMORE 38
Newcastle, Co Down, Northern Ireland.

Forest Service, Department of Agriculture (N.I.) * *2m from Newcastle, in foothills of Mourne Mountains* * *Parking* * *Refreshments* * *Toilet facilities* * *Partly suitable for wheelchairs* * *Dogs* * *Shop* * *Open all year, 8am – sunset* * *Entrance: fee for car park £2*

A fine conifer forest, now a forest park, with walks, treks and rivers on the northern flank of the Mourne Mountains. A small arboretum is adjacent to the main car park and contains some fine trees – *Aesculus indica* and the original *Picea abies* 'Clanbrassilliana'. Of interest perhaps only to the more dedicated dendrophiles, but a fine park for the family outing.

TRINITY COLLEGE BOTANIC GARDEN 39
Palmerston Park, Dublin 6, Republic of Ireland. Tel: (01) 972070

School of Botany, Trinity College, Dublin * *Adjacent to Palmerston Park, near Ranelagh, South Dublin* * *Parking in street* * *Suitable for wheelchairs* * *Open Mon-Fri, 9am – 5pm. Appointment preferred* * *Entrance: free*

This is essentially a research garden, but there is a small arboretum, order (family) beds and a collection of Irish native plants, as well as some glasshouses; a fragment of *Todea barbara* from a plant donated in 1892 grows in one glasshouse. Also a collection of *Saxifraga* sp. and the rare Mauritius blue-bell (*Nesocodon mauritianus*). *Melianthus major* flowers well every year, and there are good specimens of *Salix hibernica* and *Sorbus hibernica*. For the botanically curious only.

TULLYNALLY CASTLE 40
Castlepollard, Co Westmeath, Republic of Ireland. Tel: (044 61159

Thomas Pakenham * *1m NW of Castlepollard on road to Granard* * *Parking* * *Castle open 15th July to 15th Aug, 2.30 – 6pm* * *Grounds open May to Oct, 10.30am – 6pm* * *Entrance: IR£1, children IR50p*

The long, rough entrance drive passses between mature oaks. At the castle there are terraces with views across the demesne which is endowed with some fine mature trees. A winding path leads towards a canal into a small walled garden with a grotesque Victorian pond and fountain. This is not an inspiring place, but it is of note to garden historians. A few trees of exceptional size are present.

WHAT THE FAIRIES SAW 41
Sneem, Co Kerry, Republic of Ireland.

In village of Sneem, on 'Ring of Kerry' between Kenmare and Waterville * *Parking nearby* * *Open permanently* * *Entrance: free*

This village is the sculpture 'capital' of Ireland with a series of monumental works commemorating the late President of Ireland Cearbhail O Dállaigh. A white marble panda sits on a rock, and a gleaming stainless steel 'Tree of Life' shimmers in North Square. Beside the Roman Catholic Parish Church, on rocky ground by the sea, is the most extraordinary sculpture garden, a series of pyramidal stone structures titled 'What the Fairies Saw'. Coloured glass lights set into dry-stone walls illuminate the interiors of several. Together they form a 'garden' unique in these islands.

SCOTLAND

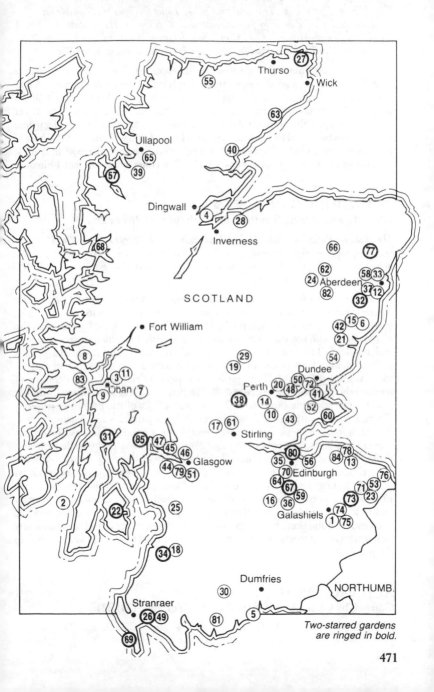

Two-starred gardens
are ringed in bold.

471

ABBOTSFORD 1
Melrose, Roxburghshire, Borders. Tel: (0896) 2043

Mrs P. Maxwell-Scott ✱ *3m W of Melrose on A6091, turn SW on to B6360. Just S of A72* ✱ *Parking* ✱ *Teas and picnics* ✱ *Toilet facilities* ✱ *Suitable for wheelchairs. Disabled enter by private entrance* ✱ *Shop* ✱ *House open* ✱ *Garden open mid-March to Oct, Mon – Sat, 10am – 5pm, Sun, 2 – 5pm* ✱ *Entrance: £2, children £1, rates for parties: £1.60 per person, children 80p*

Sir Walter Scott's magnificent house, built beteen 1817 and 1821 to satisfy his yearning to become a laird, has a garden that is rich in Scottish allusions. A yew hedge to the south of the house has medallions from an old cross inset, and a fountain in the same formal garden came from the same cross. The River Tweed flows past the house and there are fine views across a stretch of garden. Herbaceous beds lead to a gothic-type fern house filled with other plants beside ferns, such as orchids. However, the dedicated Scott scholar will find most interest in the house, amongst historical relics collected by the laird himself.

ACHAMORE GARDENS ★ 2
Isle of Gigha, Argyll, Strathclyde. Tel: (05835) 267 or 268

Mr Malcolm Potier ✱ *Take A83 to Tayinloan then by ferry to Gigha* ✱ *Best season: spring* ✱ *Refreshments at hotel* ✱ *Toilet facilities* ✱ *Partly suitable for wheelchairs* ✱ *Dogs on lead* ✱ *Open daily all year round* ✱ *Entrance: £2, OAP and children £1, collecting box*

An amazing idea to create such a superb garden on the Isle of Gigha. The journey there is via most beautiful countryside finishing up with the ferry trip, surrounded by squawking sea birds. In 1944 Sir James Horlick purchased the whole island with the sole purpose to create a garden in which to grow the rare and unusual. This was accomplished with the advice of James Russell. A delightful woodland landscape was planted with a vast collection of rarities from around the world. The garden is especially rich in fine specimens of tender rhododendrons such as *R. lindleyii*, *R. fragrantissimum*, and *R. macabeanum* to name but a few. The overall effect of the garden is tropical. There are many varieties of camellias, cordylines, primulas and Asiatic exotica. A great number of genera are represented by very good specimens, thriving in Gigha's mildness. There is a very fine *Pinus montezumae* in the walled garden; drifts of Asiatic primulas feature around the especially pretty woodland pond. The rhododendrons are unsurpassed in variety, quality and sheer visual magnitude. Gigha is a must, a Mecca for the keen plantsman and avid gardener. Few gardens outside the National botanic collections can claim such diversity and rarity. Although it is true that in recent years the number of gardeners has been reduced and there has been a slight air of neglect, the island now has a new owner who is said to wish to preserve the character of Gigha and keep it open to the public.

ACHNACLOICH 3
Connel, by Oban, Argyll, Strathclyde. Tel: (063171) 221

Mrs T.E. Nelson ✱ *3m E of Connel off A85* ✱ *Best season: April to June* ✱

*Parking * Partly suitable for wheelchairs * Dogs on lead * Plants for sale *
Open 4th April to 27th June and 2nd Aug to Oct, daily, 10am – 6pm * Entrance:
£1, OAP 50p, children free*

A castellated Scottish baronial house beautifully situated above the loch on a
rocky cliff. A curved drive sweeps past massed bulbs in spring, and later there
are azaleas and fine Japanese maples. Natural woodland with interlinked glades
is beutiful in spring with bluebells, primroses and wood anemones. Other gaps
are planted with primulas, magnolias and rare rhododendrons. Fine views to
Loch Etive and surrounding mountains. Garden walks recently extended.

ALLANGRANGE   4
**Munlochy, Black Isle, Ross and Cromarty, Highlands.
Tel: (046381) 249**

*Major and Mrs A. Cameron * Signposted from A9, 5m N of Inverness * Best
season: May to July * Teas * Toilet facilities in house * Suitable for
wheelchairs * Dogs on lead * Plants for sale * Open 10th May, 7th June, 5th
July for charity, 2 – 5.30pm and at other times by appointment * Entrance: £1,
children 20p*

A very attractive garden which spills down the hillside in a series of descending
terraces merging naturally with the rolling agricultural landscape of the Black
Isle. The formal part of the garden incorporates white and mauve gardens, a
pair of camomile lawns, many old and shrub roses, tree peonies and a small
corner for plants of variegated foliage. In July climbing Himalayan roses,
including *Rosa filipes* 'Kiftsgate' make a spectacular display. There is also a
small pool garden, and to the rear of the house a developing woodland garden
with unusual rhododendrons, primulas, meconopsis and *Cardiocrinum giganteum*. The hand of an accomplished flower painter, Elizabeth Cameron, shows
itself in the garden design, the choice of plants and in the colour combinations
in the garden. Well worth the detour from the A9

ARBIGLAND   5
Kirkbean, Dumfries and Galloway. Tel: (038788) 283

*Captain and Mrs J.B. Blackett * From New Abbey, signposted on A710 Solway
coast road * Best season: May to mid-June, Sept * Parking free * Teas, picnics
on beach * Toilet facilities * Dogs on lead * Secluded private sandy beach
which can be used by visitors * House open 22nd to 31st May * Garden open
May to Sept, Tues to Sun and Bank Holiday Mons, 2 – 6pm * Entrance: £2,
children 50p, under 5 free*

The ancient 'broadwalk', lined with fine specimen trees, leads down towards
the sea and the woodland garden. One area, called 'Japan' takes its name from
the Japanese maples and azaleas which have been arranged around a small
burn. Nearby is a large pool, especially attractive in the autumn when it reflects
the colours of the trees that surround it; the border around the lawn is full of
unusual and interesting plants. The formal sunken garden has been created on
the foundations of the original house. The old walled garden, at present

disused, dates from the original eighteenth-century house and contains one of the finest *Pieris japonica* in Scotland, over 20 ft high.

ARBUTHNOTT HOUSE   6
Laurencekirk, Grampian.

*The Viscount of Arbuthnott * 8m from Laurencekirk, 3m from Inverbervie on B967 between A92 and A94 * Parking * Refreshments: tea and biscuits * Toilet facilities * Plants for sale * House open * Garden open for charity on specified days * Entrance: £1, children 50p (1991 prices)*

The policies and the enclosed garden all date from the late seventeenth-century and are contained within the valley of the Bervie Water. The entrance drive is flanked by rhododendrons and the verges full of primroses and celandines in spring. The road crosses a fine bridge topped by imposing urns before reaching the house set high on a promontory with most of the garden sloping very steeply to the river. This garden is unusual in that it has always been treated as an extension of the house, rather than being laid out at some distance. The sloping part has four grassed terraces and this pattern is dissected by diagonal grassed walks radiating out in a manner reminiscent of the Union Jack. This fixed structure creates long garden 'rooms' and vistas as the garden is explored. The garden plan is very old but much of today's mature planting was done by a Lady Arbuthnott in the 1920s and this is continued by the present Lady Arbuthnott. Herbaceous borders, old roses together with shrub roses and ramblers, shrubs underplanted with hostas, meconopsis and lilies, lilacs and viburnums provide colour throughout the summer. A metal stag for target practice stands at the bottom of the slope by the lake.

ARDANAISEIG GARDEN AND HOTEL   7
Kilchrenan, Argyll, Strathclyde. Tel: (08663) 333

*4m E from Kilchrenan on route B845 * Best seasons: April, May, July, Oct * Parking * Refreshments at hotel, no children under 8 * Dogs on lead * Plants for sale * Hotel open, formerly Scottish baronial house * Garden open April to Oct, 10am – 8pm * Entrance: by collection box at car park £1, children free*

A picturesque 10-mile drive from Taynauilt down the peninsular makes a fitting introduction to this traditional Argyll garden. Attractive slate paths guide the visitor round 20 acres of well-planted woodland set behind an 1834 baronial house, now a very comfortable hotel, with lovely views across Loch Awe. The species and hybrid rhododendrons are particularly fine. Note the unusual curved walls of the walled garden which has a particularly good herbaceous border for this part of the world.

ARDTORNISH   8
Lochaline, Morvern, Highlands. Tel: (096784) 288 (Estate office)

*Mrs John Raven * 30m from Corran. From Corran ferry, S of Fort William, cross*

to Morvern and take route left on A861 towards Lochaline, then left on A884.
Gardens 2m before Lochaline on left ✳ *Best seasons: April, May and Oct* ✳
Parking ✳ *Dogs on lead* ✳ *Plants for sale in kitchen garden* ✳ *12 units*
available for self-catering accommodation, 5 of them in the house ✳ *Open April to*
Oct, 10am – 5pm ✳ *Entrance: £1, children free. Collecting box*

A plantsman's garden with a particularly fine and extensive collection of
unusual shrubs, deciduous trees and rhododendrons set against a background
of conifers, a loch and outstanding highland scenery. The gardens have
developed over the past 100 years or more following the first house on the site,
established by a distiller from London in the 1850s. They are on a steeply
sloping site and rainfall is heavy. Mrs Raven's late husband wrote a book about
their other garden, Docwra's in Hertfordshire (see entry), and he assisted his
wife in following her parents' footsteps in trying to establish a plantsman's
paradise here. Apart from the area around the house, there is a pleasing air of
informality about the gardens which include a boggy primula garden, Bob's
Glen with *Rhododendron thomsonii* and *prattii* and a larger glen with still more
species and hybrid rhododendrons. There is an alpine meadow and a
flourishing kitchen garden.

ARDUAINE GARDENS ★   9
by Oban, Argyll, Strathclyde.

Mr E. and Mr H. Wright ✳ *On the A816, 18m S of Oban, 9m N of Kilmartin.*
Joint entrance with Loch Melfort Hotel ✳ *Parking, refreshments and toilet facilities*
at the hotel ✳ *Dogs on lead* ✳ *Open April to June, daily except Thurs and Fri,*
10am – 6pm. Garden may be open for longer in 1992, check with Argyll tourist
associations ✳ *Entrance: £1.50, children under 14 free*

Although not included in many guide books, Arduaine (pronounced Ardoony if
you are asking the way) is a very special place. Visitors are gently welcomed and
guided round a maze of intertwining pathways which run up and down hills and
amongst lawns and a series of interlocking ponds. The romance of the setting
overlooking the lovely Asknish Bay is equal to the romance of the gardens'
history. Created in the 1900s by J.A. Campbell they were much neglected after
1945 but were tended by a faithful nanny until they were sold in 1971 to the
Wright brothers. Here is one of the best collections of rhododendrons in
Scotland, as well as many other interesting trees, shrubs and herbaceous plants,
all planted in harmony with a great understanding of colour and texture.

THE BANK HOUSE   10
Glenfarg, Perth and Kinross, Tayside. Tel: (05773) 275

Mr and Mrs C.B. Lascelles ✳ *In Glenfarg village, 50 yards along Ladeside, by*
Glenfarg Hotel ✳ *Best season: spring to late summer* ✳ *Parking on road* ✳
Partly suitable for wheelchairs ✳ *Plants for sale* ✳ *Open by appointment* ✳
Entrance: £2

The principal garden is approached through a paved area with additional
planting above low retaining walls. An apple and clematis tunnel leads the

visitor onwards to large curved beds set into lawns on a gently-sloping site. A horseshoe-shaped yew hedge underplanted with yellow archangel and star of Bethlehem is a fine spring feature. Bulbs and early-flowering herbaceous plants carry the display to summer. The owners have built up an eclectic collection of rare and unusual plants of much garden merit and these are grown to perfection using organic gardening techniques. The careful planting, with great regard to colour and form, makes for a very instructive visit. A smaller garden, across the street with a 'flowform cascade' water feature and a 'yin and yang' design circular bed may be visited at any time.

BARGUILLEAN 11
Taynuilt, Argyll, Strathclyde. Tel: (08662) 375

Mr Sam S. MacDonald ✳ *3m from Taynuilt. Minor road to Kilmore off A85* ✳ *Best season: April to June* ✳ *Parking* ✳ *Dogs on lead* ✳ *Open daily, March to Oct, 8am – 9pm* ✳ *Entrance: £1, children free*

Nine-acre woodland garden with areas of established rhododendrons, azaleas and conifers and some rare trees and shrubs on a highland hillside overlooking a lochan with views to Ben Cruachan. Much new planting with modern rhododendron hybrids, from the NW of the United States, among native birch and oak woodland makes for interesting comparisons with established rhododendron gardens of the West Coast and is excellent for the evaluation of these cultivars for Scottish gardens. A very peaceful garden, achieving much in a difficult situation. Good nursery adjacent. Abundant wildlife.

BEECHGROVE GARDEN ★ 12
Beechgrove Terrace, Aberdeen, Grampian. Tel: (0224) 625233

BBC Scotland ✳ *1¹/₂m from city centre* ✳ *Refreshments: tea and biscuits on charity day* ✳ *Suitable for wheelchairs* ✳ *Open daily except Fri, 9am – dusk and for charity 2nd Aug, 11am – 5pm* ✳ *Entrance: free except on charity day when £1, OAP and children 50p*

This garden was begun in 1978 for use in conjunction with BBC Scotland's gardening programme of the same name. During 1990 the garden was cleared except for one area, now referred to as the 'established garden' and new gardens begun. These include two terrace gardens, a housing estate garden suitable for a family, a suburban garden for the more knowledgeable gardener and a 'clay corner' to demonstrate the possibilities for difficult soils. There is a conservatory and some small glasshouses. Examples of paving, fencing, vegetables, fruit, a children's play area, a small pool, troughs, etc, complete the garden. It is a very interesting and instructive garden for the aspiring beginner but has less to offer the dedicated plantsman.

BELHAVEN HOUSE ★ 13
Belhaven, Dunbar, East Lothian, Borders. Tel: (0368) 62392

Sir George Taylor ✳ *On the outskirts of Dunbar, route A1087 – Belhaven* ✳

Parking ✳ *Dogs* ✳ *Open by appointment* ✳ *Entrance: 60p (1991 price)*

Sir George Taylor's associations with Royal Botanic Garden, Edinburgh and as Director of Kew Gardens has brought about the development of a small, but fascinating garden, filled with a great many treasured trees, shrubs and herbaceous plants. The peat garden is very good, but it is the trough garden that excels. Some 20 troughs are heavily planted with very choice alpines and rockery plants of great variety. It is a good garden for the keen plantsperson. There is a heavy emphasis on the genus *Primula* on which Sir George is a great authority. The plants from the Past garden and nursery is nearby (see entry).

BELL'S CHERRYBANK GARDENS   14
Cherrybank, Perth, Tayside. Tel: (0738) 27330

United Distillers UK ✳ *On A9 into Perth city centre. Gardens located S of main road* ✳ *Parking* ✳ *Refreshments: light teas* ✳ *Toilet facilities* ✳ *Suitable for wheelchairs* ✳ *Guide dogs only* ✳ *Open May to Oct, daily, 9am – 5pm* ✳ *Entrance: free*

This is a modern garden surrounding the commercial offices of Arthur Bell and Sons Ltd, whisky distillers. It is in fact two gardens, the first laid out in the early 1970s, plus the Scottish National heather collection begun in 1983. Their aim is to have the world's largest collection of heathers. Apart from the heathers, the plant collections are not outstanding, but they are well-maintained and beautifully designed. Interest is sustained throughout the total of 18 acres by water features, modern sculptures, pleasant vistas, a tiny putting green, tubular bells and an aviary. The children's play area includes a roundabout for wheelchair-bound children. A remarkable sundial designed by Ian Hamilton-Finlay, the sculptor, is here (see entry for Little Sparta).

BENT   15
Laurencekirk, Kincardineshire, Grampian.

Mr and Mrs James Mackie ✳ *2¹/₂m from Laurencekirk on B9120 to Fettercairn* ✳ *Parking* ✳ *Refreshments* ✳ *Toilet facilities* ✳ *Suitable for wheelchairs* ✳ *Plants for sale* ✳ *Open for charity 5th July, 2 – 5pm* ✳ *Entrance: £1, children 50p*

A plantsman's garden in an open windy situation set into rich agricultural landscape. Old roses, hardy geraniums and grey-leaved plants are grouped in the shelter of the farmhouse walls. A collection of stone troughs is arranged on the paved terrace. A wide lawn leads to mixed borders of shrubs, hardy perennials, irises and lilies protected by sandstone walls. There is a small white garden edged with box. Fine old roses, including some rescued from derelict gardens in the surrounding area, are planted throughout this garden.

BIGGAR PARK ★   16
Biggar, Lanarkshire, Strathclyde. Tel: (0899) 20185

Capt and Mrs David Barnes ✳ *S end of Biggar on A702, 30m SW of Edinburgh*

* *Parking* * *Refreshments* * *Toilet facilities* * *Suitable for wheelchairs* *
Dogs on lead * *Plants for sale* * *Open 7th June, 1.30 – 5.30pm and 12th July,
2 – 6pm. Visitors welcome at other times by appointment* * *Entrance: £1*

A Japanese garden of tranquillity welcomes one to this well-planned 10-acre plantsman's garden. Sue Barnes' efficient labelling adds greatly to the enjoyment when walking through the woodland, the small arboretum and admiring the well-planted ornamental pond which have all been designed carefully to give year-round interest. This starts with a stunning display of daffodils which are followed by glades of meconopsis, rhododendrons and azaleas in early summer before the huge herbaceous borders burst into colour. The centrepiece, however, must be the outstanding walled garden reached through a fine rockery bank beside the eighteenth-century mansion house. The view through the wrought-iron gate stretches the length of a 50 yard double herbaceous border attractively backed by swags of thick ornamental rope hanging from rose 'pillars', whilst either side is divided into intensively planted sections divided by pleasing grass paths.

BLAIRHOYLE ★   17
Port of Menteith, by Stirling, Central.

Lt Colonel and Mrs J.D. Pattullo * *2m E of Lake of Menteith, 3m W of
Thornhill on A8733* * *Parking* * *Toilet facilities* * *Partly suitable for
wheelchairs* * *Dogs on lead* * *Open April to Oct, Wed, 1 – 5pm and by
appointment* * *Entrance: £1 for charity*

One of the choicest of the 'private' gardens in Scotland, it and the arboretum were originally laid out by George Crabbie (of ginger wine fame) at the beginning of this century. It is a plantsman's garden of 16 acres with magnificent views across to the Fintry Hills. The renowned arboretum leads down to an ornamental lake and the walled garden bursts with herbaceous plants, roses, fruit and vegetables. Even more attractive are the sweeping lawns which surround and lead into a large, but easily assimilated variety of mature shrubs, trees, rhododendrons, azaleas, primulas, ground-cover plants and heathers.

BLAIRQUHAN   18
Maybole, Ayrshire, Strathclyde. Tel: (06557) 239

James Hunter Blair * *7m SE of Maybole on B7045. Signposted* * *Parking* *
Refreshments * *Toilet facilities* * *Sutaible for wheelchairs* * *Dogs on lead* *
Plants for sale * *Shop* * *House open* * *Garden open mid-July to mid-Aug,
daily except Mon, 2 – 5pm* * *Entrance: £2.50 (house and garden)*

Approached by a three-mile drive along the River Girvan giving good opportunities to admire the 1860 pinetum and the extensive wood and parkland. The three-acre walled garden with original glasshouses is traditionally planted and currently being restocked. Visitors should allow time to see the house which was built in 1820 by William Burn for Sir David Hunter Blair, 3rd Baronet, and contains all the furniture especially made at the time but which has been decorated and arranged with great style by the present owner.

BOLFRACKS 19
Aberfeldy, Perthshire, Tayside. Tel: (0887) 20207

Mr J.D. Hutchison ✳ *2m W of Aberfeldy on A827 towards Loch Tay* ✳ *Parking limited* ✳ *Plants for sale* ✳ *Open mid-April to mid-Oct, daily, 10am – 6pm* ✳ *Entrance: £1, children free. Honesty box at gate*

There has been a garden on this site for 200 years, but the present garden was started by the owner's parents in the 1920s and reshaped by the owner over the last 20 years. Three acres of walled plantsman's garden, well laid out and planned to demonstrate the potential of an exposed hillside with a northerly aspect. Astounding views over the Tay Valley are matched by the garden's own interesting features. Gentians do well on this soil. Fine masses of bulbs in spring and good autumn colour. Peat walls and stream garden. A small wild garden is presently being laid out.

BRANKLYN GARDEN 20
Dundee Road, Perth, Tayside. Tel: (0738) 25535

The National Trust for Scotland ✳ *¹/₂m from Queen's Bridge on A85* ✳ *Best season: early summer* ✳ *Parking ¹/₄m from entrance. Coaches and disabled parking at gate* ✳ *Toilet facilities* ✳ *Some paths too narrow for wheelchairs* ✳ *Plants for sale* ✳ *NTS sales table* ✳ *Open March to Oct, daily, 9.30am to sunset* ✳ *Entrance: £1.50, OAP and children 80p. Parties £1.20 (60p) per person*

John and Dorothy Renton created this garden nearly in sight of the centre of Perth and certainly within sound. Work commenced in 1922 and in 1955 Dorothy was awarded the Veitch Memorial Medal by the Royal Horticultural Society. Branklyn extends to about three acres with the main interest being in alpine and ericaceous plants in its magnificent scree rock garden on the side of the tennis court. There is a splendid collection of dwarf rhododendrons. The National Trust took over the garden in 1968, following the death of Dorothy Renton in 1966 and of her husband the following year, and a substantial restructuring and improvement programme is taking place. Essential work is restoring Branklyn to its rightful position as an outstanding plantsman's garden with its main feature which has been described as 'a true rock-gardener's paradise'. It is impossible to describe all the splendid things to be found here, from the fine trees to the comprehensive collection of dwarf and smaller rhododendrons, the meconopsis to the cyprepediums, and the garden will repay many visits.

BRECHIN CASTLE ★ 21
Brechin, Tayside. Tel: (03562) 4566 (Estate office)

The Earl and Countess of Dalhousie ✳ *1m from Brechin, route A94* ✳ *Best season: late May, early June* ✳ *Parking* ✳ *Teas in garden* ✳ *Open 31st May, 28th June for charity, 2 – 6pm* ✳ *Entrance: £1, children 50p*

The main axis of the walled garden is punctuated by a series of individual features. At the first one of these, four Lawson cypresses, a view down steps to the pond garden below is obtained. Subsequent events include a laburnum grove, a birch grove and a cherry grove, all flanked by castellated clipped yew hedges. Arguably one of the best walled gardens in Scotland. The eighteenth-century castle itself is half a mile away, approached by more recent plantings of azaleas and situated on a rocky cliff overlooking the River South Esk.

BRODICK CASTLE ★★ 22
Isle of Arran, Strathclyde. Tel: (0770) 2202

The National Trust for Scotland and Cunninghame District Council ✻ On Isle of Arran, 2m from Brodick. Ferry from Ardrossan or Kintyre ✻ Best season: late April/early May (woodland garden), May to Aug (formal garden) ✻ Parking free ✻ Restaurant dates as castle ✻ Toilet facilities ✻ Partly suitable for wheelchairs ✻ Dogs on lead ✻ Shop ✻ Castle open 17th April to Sept, daily, 1 – 5pm. From 1st to 17th April and 3rd to 24th Oct, open Mon, Wed and Sat, 1 – 5pm (last admission 4.30pm) ✻ Gardens and country park open all year, 10am – dusk ✻ Entrance: £2, children £1 (castle and gardens £3, children £1.50). Party rates for booked parties of 20 or more £2.50 per adult, £1 per child

High above the shores of the Firth of Clyde and guarding three approaches to Western Scotland is this red-brick castle, a sign that Arran has been the scene of many territorial disputes over the centuries. Its garden was an overgrown jungle of rhododendrons until the Duchess of Montrose arrived after World War I; she was much helped after 1930 when her daughter married John Boscawen of Tresco Abbey (see entry). Many of the trees and plants here came by boat from Tresco in the Scillies. Others came from subscriptions to the second generation of great plant-hunters like Kingdon-Ward and, in particular, George Forrest, one of the greatest of all collectors. Plants from the Himalayas, Burma and China, normally considered tender, flourish in the Gulf Stream climate. A good display of primulas in bog garden. The walled formal garden to the east of the castle is over 250 years old and has recently been restored as a Victorian garden with herbaceous plants, annuals and roses. It is impossible to list all the treasures of the woodland garden, but perhaps the most surprising is the huge size of the specimens in the lower rhododendron walk where *R. sinogrande* are found, larger than a normal tree with blooms up to two feet long. Memorable views over Brodick Bay.

BUGHTRIG 23
Leitholm, Nr Coldstream, Berwickshire, Borders.

Major General and The Hon. Mrs Charles Ramsay ✻ ¹/₄m E of Leitholm on B6461 ✻ Parking ✻ Refreshments ✻ Toilet facilities ✻ Suitable for wheelchairs ✻ Dogs on lead ✻ Plants for sale ✻ Open 28th June or 12th July, 2.30 – 5.30pm for charity ✻ Entrance: £1, children free

This traditional garden with an 'English' flavour was created by the owner's mother as a more attractive interpretation of the original six-acre walled garden. The immaculately-maintained borders are a lesson to all and the box edgings look as if they have been clipped with nail scissors. There is a pleasing display of herbaceous plants, shrubs, vegetables and young trees. Glasshouses within the walled garden are well-stocked, and there are good specimen trees and quality plantings throughout.

CANDACRAIG   24
Strathdon, Grampian. Tel: (09756) 51226

*Mrs E.M. Young * On A97 Huntly – Dinnet road then A944 (formerly B973) Strathdon – Tomintoul road * Best season: July to Aug * Parking * Light refreshments in tearoom * Toilet facilities * Suitable for wheelchairs * Plants for sale * Shop * Open strictly by appointment in 1992 while garden is closed for redevelopment*

At an altitude of 1000 feet this old walled garden dates from 1820 and covers a three-acre sheltered site in upper Deeside. The garden is now being systematically restored by the present owner and features herbaceous borders, old roses, cottage garden flowers and a wild garden area. There is a Victorian summerhouse in Gothic style.

CARNELL   25
Hurlford, Ayrshire, Strathclyde. Tel: (056384) 236

*Mr and Mrs J.R. Findlay and Mrs J.B. Findlay (The Garden House) * 4m from Kilmarnock, 6m from Mauchline on A719, 1¹/₂m on Ayrshire side of A76 * Parking free * Refreshments on day of opening * Dogs on lead * Plants for sale. Also flowers and home-bakes * Sixteenth-century peel tower * Garden open 26th July, 2 – 6pm * Entrance: £1.50, children under 12 free*

Exquisite example of 100 yards of linear herbaceous borders facing a rectangular pool with informal planting as a contrast on the opposite bank. Also interesting rock garden, lilies. Walled garden. Burmese and Japanese features. Garden adjacent to house currently being developed. All plants and vegetables grown with organic compost produced *in situ*.

CASTLE KENNEDY AND LOCHINCH
GARDENS ★★   26
Stranraer, Wigtownshire, Dumfries and Galloway. Tel: (0776) 2024

*The Earl and Countess of Stair * 5m from Stranraer on A75 * Best season: April/May * Parking * Teas * Toilet facilities * Partly suitable for wheelchairs * Dogs on lead * Plants for sale * Shop * Open Easter to Sept, daily, 10am – 5pm * Entrance: £1.50, OAP £1, children 50p (1991 prices). Party rates on application*

One of Scotland's most famous gardens set on a peninsular between two lochs and well worth a visit for its sheer 67-acre magnificence and spectacular spring colour. The gardens were originally laid out in 1730 around the ruins of his castle home by Field Marshal the 2nd Earl of Stair who used his unoccupied dragoons to effect a major remoulding of the landscape, combining large formal swathes of mown grassland with massive formal gardens, criss-crossed with avenues and allées of large specimen trees. The garden is internationally famous for its pinetum, currently being replanted, for its good variety of tender trees and for its species rhododendrons including many of Sir Joseph Hooker's original introductions from his Himalayan expeditions. The monkey puzzle avenue, now sadly a little tattered, was once the finest in the world and there is also one of noble firs and another of hollies underplanted with embothriums and eucryphias. An impressive 2-acre circular lily pond puts everyone else's in their proper place and a good walk from this brings you to the ruined castle and its walled garden, well planted with theme borders. The small plant sales area, personally supervised by Lady Stair, is recommended for inexpensive home-grown and unusual plants.

CASTLE OF MEY ★★ 27
Caithness, Highlands.

H.M. Queen Elizabeth the Queen Mother ✳ *1¹/₂m from Mey* ✳ *Parking* ✳ *Teas* ✳ *Toilet facilities* ✳ *Suitable for wheelchairs* ✳ *Dogs on lead* ✳ *Open for 3 days a year for charity* ✳ *Entrance: 70p, OAP and children under 12, 40p (1991 prices)*

The Castle originates from the late sixteenth century and was renovated by The Queen Mother in 1955. Gardening would not be possible in such an exposed position without the protection of the 'Great Wall of Mey'. Within the walled garden, The Queen Mother has collected her favourite flowers; many were gifts and have special meaning. The personal private feeling pervades the whole garden which is especially well-planted and maintained. The colour schemes are very good, blending the garden with the vast natural panorama within which it is situated. The mild sea-climate allows many unusual plants to be grown so far north.

CAWDOR CASTLE ★ 28
Cawdor, Nairn, Highlands. Tel: (06677) 615

The Earl of Cawdor ✳ *Between Inverness and Nairn on the B9090 off the A96* ✳ *Best season: summer* ✳ *Parking* ✳ *Refreshments: restaurant, teas. Picnic area* ✳ *Toilet facilities* ✳ *Partly suitable for wheelchairs* ✳ *Shop* ✳ *House open* ✳ *Garden open May to Sept, daily, 10am – 5.30pm* ✳ *Entrance: £3.50, OAP £2.80, children £1.90. Family ticket £10. Parties of 20 or more on application*

Frequently referred to as one of the Highland's most romantic castles and steeped in history, Cawdor Castle is a fourteenth-century keep with seven-teenth- and nineteenth-century additions. The surrounding parkland is handsome and well-kept, though not in the grand tradition of classic landscapes. To the side of the castle is the formal garden where recently-added wrought-iron arches frame extensive herbaceous borders, a peony border, a very old hedge of mixed varieties of *Rosa pimpinellifolia*, the Scots or Burnet rose, a rose tunnel, old apple trees with climbing roses, interesting shrubs and lilies. An abundance of lavender and pinks complete a rather Edwardian atmosphere. The castle wall shelters *Exochorda*, *Abutilon vitifolium*, *Carpenteria californica* and *Rosa banksiae*. Pillar-box red seats create a jarring note in an otherwise splendidly flowery garden. The walled garden below the castle is being developed with a holly maze, a thistle garden and a white garden. There are fine views everywhere of the castle, the park and the surrounding countryside which one can enjoy more actively by walking one of the five nature trails. These vary in length from half to five miles and are an ideal way to admire the magnificent mature woodland.

CLUNY HOUSE 29
by Aberfeldy, Perthshire, Tayside. Tel: (0887) 20795

*Mr J. and Mrs W. Mattingley * 32m NW of Perth. N of Aberfeldy, over the Wade's Bridge, take the Weem – Strathtay Road. Cluny House is signposted about 3m along this road * Best seasons: spring, early summer or late autumn * Limited parking * Plants for sale and plant and seed list available on request * Open March to Oct, 10am – 6pm * Entrance: £1.50, children free*

Unlike most other gardens this is as truly wild as one can find – friendly weeds grow unchecked for fear of disturbing the NCCPG collection of Asiatic primulas. Sheltered slopes create a moist micro-climate where all the plants flourish abundantly, including a Wellingtonia with the British near record girth of 35½ft. Superb woodland garden where many of the plants were grown from seed collected by Mrs Mattingley's father during the Ludlow/Sherriff expedition to Bhutan in 1948. Special treats are the carpets of bulbs, trilliums and meconopsis, a fine selection of Japanese acers, *Prunus serrula*, 500 different rhododendrons, *Cardiocrinum giganteum*, 6ft lysichitum and many fine specimen trees. The view over the Tay makes a fitting finale only a few yards from the car parks.

CORSOCK HOUSE 30
Corsock, Castle Douglas, Dumfries and Galloway.

*Mr and Mrs M.L. Ingall * 10m N of Castle Douglas on A712. Also signposted from A75 onto B794 * Best season: May * Parking * Refreshments for May opening date * Toilet facilities * Dogs on lead * Open 24th May for charity and by arrangement * Entrance: £1, children 50p*

A most attractive 20-acre woodland garden with exceptionally fine plantings both of trees (*Fagus sylvatica*, Wellingtonia, oak, Douglas fir, cercidiphyllum, acer) and of rhododendrons (*thomsonii, lacteum, loderi, prattii, sutchuenense*). The knowledgeable owner has contributed most imaginatively to the layout of the gardens over the last 20 years, creating glades, planting vistas of azaleas and personally building a temple and *trompe l'oeil* bridge which give the gardens a classical atmosphere. An impressive highlight is the large water garden, again cleverly laid out and with the water-edge plantings set off by a background of mature trees with good autumn colour.

CRARAE GLEN GARDEN ★★ 31
Minard, by Inverary, Argyll, Strathclyde. Tel: (0546) 86614

*Crarae Gardens Charitable Trust * 1m from Minard on A83 * Best season:*

spring and autumn ✳ *Parking* ✳ *Refreshments: teas and coffee* ✳ *Toilet facilities* ✳ *Suitable for wheelchairs* ✳ *Dogs on short lead* ✳ *Plants for sale* ✳ *Shop* ✳ *Open daily: summer, 9am – 6pm and winter during daylight hours* ✳ *Entrance: £1.70, children 70p. Wheelchair users free*

The gardens were originally started by the present owner's grandmother, Grace Campbell, in the early part of this century. Inspired by her great nephew, Reginald Farrer, a famous traveller and plant collector, she and subsequently her son George Campbell (1894-1967), spent many years creating this superb 'Himalayan ravine' set in a Highland glen. Using surplus seed from the great plant expeditions, numerous gifts from knowledgeable friends and the shared expertise of a network of famous horticulturalists, they planted a variety of rare trees which were Sir George's first love, exotic shrubs and species rhododendrons which now form great canopies above the winding paths. These, together with many other plants from the temperate world make a magnificent spectacle of colour and differing perspectives, the whole enlivened by splendid torrents and waterfalls. The autumn colouring of sorbus, acers, liriodendrons, prunus, cotoneasters and berberis is one of the great features of the garden.

CRATHES CASTLE GARDEN ★★ 32
Crathes Castle, Banchory, Grampian. Tel: (033044) 525

The National Trust for Scotland ✳ *3m E of Banchory and 15m W of Aberdeen on A93* ✳ *Parking 200 yards from gardens, signposted* ✳ *Refreshments: licensed restaurant* ✳ *Toilet facilities* ✳ *Suitable for wheelchairs* ✳ *No dogs in garden, but nature/dog trail in grounds* ✳ *Plants for sale* ✳ *National Trust shop* ✳ *Castle open Easter to Oct, daily, 11am – 6pm* ✳ *Garden open daily, 9.30am – dusk* ✳ *Entrance: £2.50, OAP and children £1.30 (house and garden £3.50, children £1.70)*

The first view of Crathes is breath-taking – a romantic castle set in flowing lawns. The building looks much as it did in the mid-sixteenth century but there is no record of how the garden then looked, although the yew topiary of 1702 survives. Sir James Burnett, who came here in 1926, was a keen collector and his wife was an inspired herbaceous planter, and the garden today is their achievement. In all there are eight gardens each reflecting a different theme. Rare shrubs reflect Burnett's interest in the Far East where he served in the army. Splendid wide herbaceous borders with clever plant associations are Lady Burnett's heritage, most famous of which is the white border. There are many specialist areas such as the trough garden and a collection of grasses; the large greenhouses contain a unique collection of carnations. Extensive wild gardens and grounds with picnic areas, with 15 miles of marked trails. Often compared to Hidcote but with evident inspiration from Jekyll, Crathes has wonders for the plantsperson, the designer and the ordinary visitor.

CRUICKSHANK BOTANIC GARDEN 33
St Machar Drive, Old Aberdeen, Grampian. Tel: (0224) 272704

The Cruickshank Trust and University of Aberdeen ✳ *1¹/₂m N from city centre in Old Aberdeen on A978. Public entry by gate in the Chanonry* ✳ *Best season: May to Aug ✳ Suitable for wheelchairs ✳ Dogs on lead ✳ Open all year, Mon – Fri, 9am – 4.30pm, May to Sept, Sat and Sun, 2 – 5pm ✳ Entrance: free. Children must be accompanied by an adult*

Endowed by Miss Anne H. Cruickshank in 1898 to cater for teaching and research in botany at the University of Aberdeen and for the public good, the original six acres were designed by George Nicholson of Kew. That layout disappeared with World War I tree and shrub plantings. The long wall, herbaceous border and sunken garden date from 1920 but much reverted to vegetable cultivation during World War II. In 1970, the garden was extended and a new rock garden made. A terrace garden was added by the long wall in 1980, a new rose garden in 1986 and the peat walls restored in 1988. The rock garden with a series of connecting pools has interesting alpines, bulbs and dwarf shrubs. A small woodland area is rich in meconopsis, primulas, rhododendrons and hellebores. Proximity to the North Sea does not permit good growth of large conifers with the exception of dawn redwood and *Pinus radiata*. There are fine species lilacs, witch hazels and the long wall shelters more tender exotics. The total area of the present garden is 11 acres, of which 4 acres are planted as an arboretum – this is reached by a path from the summit of the rock gardens.

CULZEAN CASTLE AND COUNTRY PARK ★ ★   34
Maybole, Ayrshire, Strathclyde.

The National Trust for Scotland ✳ 14m S of Ayr on A719 ✳ Parking ✳ Refreshments ✳ Toilet facilities ✳ Suitable for wheelchairs ✳ Dogs under control ✳ Plants for sale ✳ Shop ✳ Castle open ✳ Country park and gardens open April to 25th Oct, 10.30am – 5.30pm ✳ Entrance: Country park: car £5, motor cycles £1.10, additional charges for coaches. Castle: £3, OAP and children £1.50

350,000 people a year visit Culzean, thought of by many as the flagship of The National Trust for Scotland. The castle was originally a medieval fortified house atop the Ayrshire cliffs, but was extensively restructured by Robert Adam from 1771 in what has become known as his 'Culzean' style. This is reflected in the many fine architectural features scattered throughout the grounds and in particular the handsome Home Farm Courtyard, now a visitor centre. The country park landscape covers 563 acres with a network of woodland and cliff-top paths, and the gardens themselves cover a spacious 30 acres and include all the traditional elements of a grand garden at the turn of the century, the main elements being a fine fountained pleasure garden and a vast walled garden with herbaceous and vegetable plantings. Charming camellia house of 1818.

DALMENY PARK   35
Mons Hill, South Queensferry, West Lothian. Tel: (031) 331 4804

The Earl of Rosebery ✳ 7m W of Edinburgh city centre off A90 ✳ Parking ✳ Mons Hill is open for charity one or possibly two Suns at end of Feb/beginning of March depending on the snowdrops. Admission charge.

Mons Hill is a partly wooded hill of semi-natural hardwoods with several acres of wild snowdrops, and outstanding views towards the Pentland Hills,

Edinburgh and the Firth of Forth, weather permitting. The snowdrops are over a quarter of a mile uphill from the car park and must be seen to be believed. However, wellington boots are recommended. There is no possibility of taking wheelchairs or vehicles up the hill.

DALMENY HOUSE
South Queensferry, West Lothian. Tel: (031) 331 4804

The grounds around Dalmeny House are open when the house is open May to Sept, Sun - Thurs, 2 – 5.30pm ✳ Teas ✳ Entrance: grounds free but car parking charge being considered. House (with collection) £3, children 10 – 16 £1.50, under 10 free

Some one and a half miles from Mons Hill is the Garden Valley and other ornamental areas close to Dalmeny House. These feature rhododendrons, also azaleas and specimen trees. Both house and Garden Valley are suitable for wheelchairs.

DAWYCK BOTANIC GARDEN 36
Stobo, Peebleshire, Borders. Tel: (07216) 254

Royal Botanic Garden, Edinburgh ✳ 8m SW of Peebles, 28m from Edinburgh on B712 ✳ Best seasons: spring and autumn ✳ Parking ✳ Partly suitable for wheelchairs ✳ Guide dogs only ✳ Open 15th March to 22nd Oct, 10am – 6pm and at other times by arrangement ✳ Entrance: £1, concessions and childrens 50p. Special discounts for groups. Season tickets covering Dawyck, Logan and Younger available – telephone Royal Botanic Garden (031) 552 7171

This is a specialist garden of the Royal Botanic Garden, Edinburgh, the home of the famous Dawyck beech; the garden has a large variety of interesting mature trees. Landscaped burnside walks take the visitor through mature woodland clothing the steep slopes of the tributary of the River Tweed, a setting that abounds in wildlife.

DRUM CASTLE 37
Drumoak, by Banchory, Kincardine and Deeside, Grampian. Tel: (03308) 204

The National Trust for Scotland ✳ Off A93, 3m W of Peterculter, 10m W of Aberdeen ✳ Parking ✳ Refreshments ✳ Toilet facilities ✳ Shop ✳ House open May to Sept, daily, 2 – 6pm, Oct, Sat and Sun, 2 – 5pm. £3, OAP and children £1.50 ✳ Garden open May to Oct, daily, 10am – 6pm ✳ Entrance: grounds and garden free but donations welcome

Within the old walled garden adjacent to the castle, The National Trust for Scotland has established a 'garden of historic roses' which was officially opened in June 1991 as part of the Diamond Jubilee celebrations of the Trust. The four quadrants of the garden are designed and planted with roses and herbaceous plants appropriate to the seventeenth, eighteenth, nineteenth and twentieth centuries. The central feature is a copy of the gazebo at Tyninghame, East Lothian, and a small garden house in one corner, now restored, acts as an interpretive centre.

DRUMMOND CASTLE ★★ 38
Muthill, Nr Crieff, Perthshire, Tayside. Tel: (076481) 321

Grimsthorpe and Drummond Castle Trust Ltd ✳ 2m S of Crieff on A822 ✳ Best season: June and July ✳ Parking 300 yards past main entrance ✳ Toilet facilities ✳ Partly suitable for wheelchairs ✳ Open May to Aug, daily and Sept, Wed and Sun, 2 – 6pm (last admission 5pm) ✳ Entrance: £1.50, OAP and children 75p

The gardens to this fine castle were first laid out in 1630 by John Drummond, 2nd Earl of Perth. Next to the castle, across a courtyard, is the house and below both is the great parterre garden with, at its centre, the famous sundial made by the master mason to Charles I. When the garden was revived by Lewis Kennedy, who worked at Drummond from 1818 to 1860, he achieved what the *Oxford Companion* calls 'effectively the re-creation of an idea of the seventeenth-century Scottish garden'. The long St Andrew's cross design has Italian, French and Dutch influences. Beautiful white marble Italian statuary is set in arbours along the southern borders, giving an overall sense of tranquillity and order. The *Oxford Companion* believes that the old arrangement of filling the 'compartments' of the cross with shrubs and herbaceous plants was more effective than today's style in which some may feel the structure is too prominent. The fruit and vegetable gardens and glasshouses should also be visited.

DUNDONNELL 39
By Garve, Ross-shire, Highlands. Tel: (085483) 206

Mr A.S. Roger and Mr N. Roger ✳ 24m from Ullapool, 31m from Garve off A832 between Braemore Toll and Gruinard Bay ✳ Parking ✳ Teas ✳ Toilet facilities ✳ Partly suitable for wheelchairs ✳ Plants for sale ✳ Open 4th, 10th June, 9th, 15th July, 2 – 5.30pm ✳ Entrance: £1.50, children 50p

Unlike many of the gardens of Scotland's west coast Dundonnell does not rely on rhododendrons for its effect. It is a very individual garden of grassed walks, box-edged paths, enclosures made by borders of varying sizes all within a garden walled on three sides with the fourth side bounded by the river. Very old yew and holly trees are striking, and there are also many exotic trees and shrubs – *Stewartia* species, *Acer palmatum* 'Senkaki', *Quercus pontica*, species hydrangeas, *Decaisnea fargesii* and the bamboo *Chusquea*. The laburnum tunnel is as unexpected as the extensive collection of bonsai, many of considerable size, grown in a slatted house. This is a very tranquil garden to be appreciated at a leisurely pace – even the heavy rainfall will not detract from its charm.

DUNROBIN GARDENS ★ 40
Golspie, Sutherland, Highlands. Tel: (0408) 633177/633268

The Sutherland Trust ✳ 1m N of Golspie on A9 ✳ Parking ✳ Refreshments:

Tea Rooms ✳ *Toilet facilities* ✳ *Shop* ✳ *House open* ✳ *Garden open May, Mon – Thurs, 10.30am – 12.30pm, and June to Sept, Mon – Sat, 10.30am – 5.30pm, Sun, 1 – 5.30pm* ✳ *Entrance: £3, OAP £2, children £1.50, family £7.50 (Groups £2.80 per person, children £1.40)*

These Victorian formal gardens were designed in the grand French style to echo the architecture of Dunrobin Castle which rises high above them and looks out over the Moray Firth. They were laid out by the architect Charles Barry in 1850, when there was a staff of 40 gardeners (there is a staff of only four now). Descending the stone terraces, one can see the round garden (evocative of the Scottish shield, the head gardener suggests), rose beds, grove, parterre and herbaceous borders laid out beneath. The round ponds, some with fountains, are a particular feature, together with the wrought-iron Westminster gates. The garden is under development – a rhododendron and fern bank has been planted, and other features are planned, within the limitations of a south-east facing site on sandy soil. An eighteenth-century summerhouse which was converted into a museum in the nineteenth century is now also open to the public. In the policies (estate lands) there are many woodland walks.

EARLSHALL CASTLE ★   41
Leuchars, Fife. Tel: (0334 839) 205

Major and Mrs D.R. Baxter, Baron and Baroness of Earlshall ✳ *Follow signs from centre of Leuchars, A919* ✳ *Parking* ✳ *Refreshments* ✳ *Suitable for wheelchairs in garden* ✳ *Guide dogs only* ✳ *Plants for sale occasionally* ✳ *Shop* ✳ *House open as gardens* ✳ *Gardens open Suns in April, 17th to 20th April and then May to Sept, daily, all 2 – 6pm. Booked parties any time by prior arrangement* ✳ *Entrance: £2.80, OAP £2.30, children £1. Parties £2.30 per person*

A walled garden situated beside the restored sixteenth-century castle divided by yew hedges into a series of external 'rooms'. The most significant of these contains topiary 'chessmen' (although some visitors maintain that they are 'abstracts'), and there is also a secret garden, orchard garden, herbaceous border and 'bowling green' with rose terrace, and an attractively laid-out kitchen garden. Interesting garden architecture includes a gardener's cottage, dowry house, summerhouse and arbour, all bearing the stamp of Sir Robert Lorimer's eye for detail. Lorimer, famous for Kellie Castle (see entry) believed in gardens as a place of repose and solitude, formal near the house but becoming 'less trim as it gets further... and then naturally marries with the demesne that lies beyond'. Altogether, a most delightful retreat from the world outside.

EDZELL CASTLE ★   42
Edzell, Nr Brechin, Angus, Tayside. Tel: (0356) 648631

Historic Scotland ✳ *4m N of Brechin. Take A94 and after 2m fork left on B966* ✳ *Parking* ✳ *Picnic area* ✳ *Toilet facilities* ✳ *Suitable for wheelchairs* ✳ *Dogs* ✳ *Ruins* ✳ *Garden open April to Sept, Mon – Sat, 9.30am – 6pm, Sun, 2 – 6pm, Oct to March, Mon – Sat, 9.30am – 4pm, Sun, 2 – 4pm* ✳ *Entrance: £1.20, OAP and children 6 to 16 60p, under 6 free. 10% reduction for parties*

In 1604 Sir David Lindsay made a remarkable small walled garden at his fortress at Edzell; it remains today probably the oldest complete and unaltered garden in the country. By the time they came into the custody of H.M. Office of Works in 1932, the garden and castle had lain in ruins for over 150 years. Although the plantings are new, dating from the 1930s, they are elaborate examples in the manner of the period of the early seventeenth century. Meticulously-kept parterres of box, lawn, and bedding are contained within walls of unique and curious design. There are 43 panels of alternating chequered niches and sculptured symbolic figures. There are large recesses below for bee skeps. The whole is laid out to be viewed from a corner garden-house and the windows of the now-ruined castle. The village of Edzel is quite small and a charming example of an ordered Victorian Scottish highland village. There are shops, a tea room and a small hotel. A must for lovers of the historical and romantic. The pleasaunce is probably unique in its historical context, but the modern plantings make it a disappointing experience in some respects.

FALKLAND PALACE GARDEN 43
Falkland, Fife. Tel: (0337) 57397

The National Trust for Scotland ＊ *11m N of Kirkcaldy via A912* ＊ *Parking 100 yards from palace* ＊ *Refreshments in village* ＊ *Toilet facilities* ＊ *Suitable for wheelchairs* ＊ *National Trust shop* ＊ *House open as garden (last tour of palace 5pm)* ＊ *Garden open April to Oct, Mon – Sat, 10am – 6pm, Sun, 2 – 6pm* ＊ *Entrance: £2, children £1 (palace and garden, £3, children £1.50)*

This was originally the kitchen garden for the sixteenth-century palace where Mary Queen of Scots played as a girl. In World War II it became a forest nursery but was remodelled soon afterwards. The Palace itself lends a gracious and dignified atmosphere to this seven-acre garden as the visitor strolls round the rose garden and admires the herbaceous borders. The shrub island borders are now fully mature and provide a good illustration of how to break up large areas of lawn if that is what you want. In addition, visitors may gain admission from the garden to the royal tennis court (i.e. real tennis) where occasional competitions of this old game are still staged. Features include an outdoor chequers game in the herb garden. Interesting village houses nearby.

FINLAYSTONE 44
Langbank, Renfrewshire, Strathclyde. Tel: (047554) 285

Mr George Gordon Macmillan of Macmillan ＊ *On A8 20m from Glasgow, follow large signpost W of Langbank* ＊ *Best season: spring and autumn* ＊ *Parking* ＊ *Refreshments: tea room in walled garden* ＊ *Toilet facilities* ＊ *Suitable for wheelchairs* ＊ *Dogs on lead (off lead in woodland)* ＊ *Shop open at weekends* ＊ *House open, April to Aug, Sun, 2.30 – 4.30pm* ＊ *Garden open all year, daily, 11am – 5pm* ＊ *Entrance: £1.20, children 80p*

Designed, enhanced and tended over the last 50 years by the late Lady Macmillan, much respected doyenne of Scottish gardens, and her family, this spacious garden is imaginatively laid out over 10 acres with a further 70 acres of mature woodland walks. Large, elegant lawns framed by long herbaceous borders, interesting shrubberies and mature copper beech look down over the River Clyde. John Knox's tree, a Celtic paving 'maze' laid out by Lady Macmillan's daughter-in-law Jane, a paved fragrant garden with the handicapped in mind and a new bog garden are all added attractions.

GEILSTON HOUSE 45
Nr Cardross, Dunbartonshire, Strathclyde. Tel: (0389) 841467

*Miss M.E. Bell * 1m W of Cardross on A814 * Best season: May, Oct *
Parking * Teas on open day * Suitable for wheelchairs * Plants for sale *
Open by appointment and for charity on 23rd May, 2.30 – 5.30pm * Entrance:
75p, children 25p*

A well-maintained walled garden with herbaceous borders and a heather garden which contains about ninety different varieties. Adjoining this garden is a small woodland 'glen garden' where rare and unusual shrubs, trees, rhododendrons and azaleas flourish on the banks of a small burn in picturesque surroundings. The autumn colour is also worth experiencing.

GLASGOW BOTANIC GARDENS 46
Great Western Road, Glasgow, Strathclyde. Tel: (041) 3342422

*Glasgow Corporation * Near the centre of Glasgow, corner of Great Western Road
and Queen Margaret Drive * Parking outside * Toilet facilities * Suitable for
wheelchairs * Dogs on lead * Gardens open daily, 7am – dusk. Kibble Palace
Glasshouse open 10am – 4.45pm (4.15pm in winter). Main Range open 1 –
4.45pm (from 12 noon on Sun and to 4.15pm in winter) * Entrance: free*

A pleasant afternoon's walk with well-maintained herbaceous, shrub and annual borders. Unimaginative landscaping completely obscures an otherwise attractive water feature with large shrubs, and it is difficult to believe that the 60 odd underplanted plots known confusingly as the 'Systematic Garden' can be of much value to the modern student or average visitor. That said, the chief attraction, and well worth visiting, is the rusting old Kibble Palace glasshouse of 1873 where naked statues keep warm in a temperate zone climate. In the series of inter-connecting neighbouring glasshouses are much-improved displays of orchids,begonias, cacti and tropical plants – all meticulously maintained.

GLENARN 47
Rhu, Dunbartonshire, Strathclyde. Tel: (0436820) 493

*Michael and Sue Thornley * On A814 between Helensburgh and Garelochhead.
Go up Pier Road to Glenarn Road * Parking * Refreshments on special open
days only * Toilet facilities * Dogs on lead * A few plants for sale * Open
21st March to 21st June, dawn to dusk * Entrance: £1*

Established in the 1930s in a Victorian garden by the Gibson family and fed by the famous plant expeditions of that decade, this is a very special woodland garden. Well-kept paths meander round a 10-acre sheltered bowl, sometimes tunnelling under superb giant species rhododendrons (including a *falconeri* grown from Hooker's original seed in 1849), sometimes allowing a glorious vista across the garden to the Clyde estuary, and sometimes stopping the visitor short to gaze with unstinted admiration at 40 foot magnolias, pieris, olearias, eucryphias and hoherias. Michael and Sue Thornley, both professional architects, acquired Glenarn some years ago and with almost no help are successfully replanting and restoring where necessary, whilst still retaining the special atmosphere created by such magnificent growth. An especially pleasing finale is provided by winding down through a nook-and-cranny, granny garden – sadly and inappropriately not suitable for those who find walking difficult.

GLENDOICK GARDENS LTD 48
Glencarse, By Perth, Tayside. Tel: Nursery (073886) 205; Garden centre (073886) 260

Mr and Mrs Peter Cox ✳ *8m from Perth, 14m from Dundee on A85* ✳ *Parking in grounds* ✳ *Toilet facilities* ✳ *Partly suitable for wheelchairs* ✳ *Garden centre open all year at the main road* ✳ *Open May, Suns, 2 – 5pm and parties by appointment during May* ✳ *Entrance: £1.50*

One of the world's most comprehensive collections of rhododendrons is contained within the grounds of this fine Georgian mansion which has an association with Bonnie Prince Charlie who is reputed to have visited the Laird of Glendoick one dark night in 1745. The plant collection was assembled by the late Euan H.M. Cox and added to and continued by the present owners.

GLENWHAN GARDEN ★ 49
Dunragit, by Stranraer, Wigtownshire, Dumfries and Galloway. Tel: (05814) 222

Mr and Mrs Knott ✳ *7m E of Stranraer, 1m off A75 at Dunragit. Signposted* ✳ *Parking* ✳ *Refreshments* ✳ *Toilet facilities* ✳ *Partly suitable for wheelchairs* ✳ *Guide dogs only* ✳ *Plants for sale* ✳ *Shop* ✳ *Garden open Easter to Sept, daily, 10am – 5pm* ✳ *Entrance: 1.50, children 50p*

This very exciting garden has a commanding view over Luce Bay and the Mull of Galloway, and is set in an area of natural beauty, with rocky outcrops and Whinnie Knowes. Difficult to believe that it was only started 11 years ago and is run by the owners and one man. Because of the Gulf Stream and consequent mild climate exotic plants thrive amongst the huge collections of trees, shrubs and plants. Seats and walkways abound in this maze of hilly plantings mostly overlooking the central lochans and bog gardens. Collections whether of genera or reminders of friends or particular themes of interest are to be seen everywhere. Expanding and progressing at a steady rate, the creator of this private garden, Tessa Knott, has worked hard, illustrating and inspiring proof that the making of a large garden can be possible. She has had no formal horticultural training and began as a complete amateur in the plant world.

GOWRANES ★ 50
Kinnaird by Inchture, Perthshire, Tayside. Tel: (0828) 86752

Professor and Mrs Park ✳ 11m from Perth and Dundee, 3m from Inchture. Follow signs for Kinnaird turn off A85 Perth – Dundee road ✳ Best seasons: spring and early summer ✳ Parking ✳ ☆Refreshments: by request ✳ Toilet facilities ✳ Plants for sale ✳ Open 14th June, 2 – 6pm and by appointment ✳ Entrance: £2 (inc. tea and home-baked biscuits), children free

A garden full of surprises, lovingly carved out of a difficult sloping rocky site with magnificent views over the Carse of Gowrie. The house is partly surrounded by stone-flagged terraces overflowing with plants. Lower-level lawns are planted with specimen trees such as *Abies koreana* and *Prunus serrula*. From here maze-like paths lead you up and down through cool, intensive plantings of shade-loving plants, rhododendrons, camellias, azaleas, ferns, meconopsis and many others. At the bottom of the slope there is a rushing burn that has been formed into a series of pools and waterfalls. This marks the western boundary. Great masses of primulas have seeded themselves here amongst the gunneras, hostas and *Lysichiton americanus*. The site was originally a pig farm and much to the horror of the present owners, many 'bodies' were found during the garden construction but, as they say, they probably contributed to the healthy and lush-looking plants.

GREENBANK GARDEN ★ 51
Nr Clarkston Toll, Glasgow, Strathclyde. Tel: (041639) 3281

The National Trust for Scotland ✳ Take A726 to Clarkston, turn off opposite railway station, follow signs ✳ Best seasons: spring and summer ✳ Parking ✳ Refreshments ✳ Toilet facilities ✳ Suitable for wheelchairs ✳ Dogs on lead, but not in walled garden ✳ Plants for sale ✳ Shop ✳ Garden open all year, daily except 25th, 26th Dec, 1st, 2nd Jan 1993, 9.30am – sunset ✳ Entrance: £1.40, children 70p (1991 prices)

Large old walled garden of eighteenth-century house divided into many sections, all of which are imaginatively planted. The colour combinations are especially good. All the plants are in very good condition and admirably labelled. An old hard tennis court in the corner has been converted into a spacious and pleasant area for the disabled, with raised beds and a waist-high running water pond. Wheelchair access to the glasshouse and potting shed allows disabled people to attend classes and work here. Woodland walks are filled with spring bulbs and shrubs and usually Highland cattle in the paddock.

HILL OF TARVIT MANSION HOUSE 52
Cupar, Fife. Tel: (0334) 53127

The National Trust for Scotland ✳ 2¹/₂m S of Cupar off A916 ✳ Parking ✳ Picnic area ✳ Toilet facilities ✳ Partly suitable for wheelchairs ✳ Shop in house ✳ House open April, Sat and Sun, 2 – 6pm, May to Oct, daily, 2 – 6pm ✳ Garden open daily, 10am – sunset ✳ Entrance: £1, children 50p

The garden surrounds the charming Edwardian mansion designed in 1906 for a jute magnate by Sir Robert Lorimer who also laid out the grounds. There is a lovely rose garden and delightful woodland walk to a toposcope. Good size borders are filled with an attractive variety of perennials, annuals and heaths, and the grounds as a whole contain many unusual ornamental trees and shrubs now reaching maturity. The views over Fife are particularly fine. The garden is maintained by the National Trust which regularly upgrades the plantings to include newer and unusual specimens. A good garden for amateurs and keen plantspersons alike.

THE HIRSEL 53
Coldstream, Berwickshire, Borders. Tel: 0890) 2834

Lord Home of the Hirsel. KT ✳ *50m from Edinburgh, 60m from Newcastle, W of Coldstream on A697* ✳ *Parking* ✳ *Refreshments: café in main season* ✳ *Toilet facilities* ✳ *Suitable for wheelchairs* ✳ *Dogs on lead* ✳ *Craft workshops* ✳ *Grounds open daily during daylight hours* ✳ *Entrance: small adult charge*

Hirsel House is not open but at all seasons of the year the grounds have much of interest and enjoyment for the visitor who values the peace and ever-changing beauty of the countryside. There is something for the ornithologist, botanist, forester, zoologist, historian and archaeologist. In spring, snowdrops and aconites and then acres of daffodils herald the coming summer. The birds, resident and migrant, of which 169 have been definitely identified within the estate boundaries, start busying themselves around their nesting sites. From mid/late-May to mid-June the rhododendron wood, Dundock, is justly famous for its kaleidoscopic colouring and breath taking scents. In October and November, the leaves turning on trees and shrubs provide attractive autumn colouring, and hundreds of duck, geese and gulls make the lake their nightly home. In winter the same trees are stark but magnificent in their skeletal forms against storm clouds and sunsets.

HOUSE OF PITMUIES ✳ 54
Guthrie, by Forfar, Tayside. Tel: (02412) 245

Mrs Farquhar Ogilvie ✳ *1¹/₂m from Friockheim, route A932* ✳ *Best season: May to July* ✳ *Parking* ✳ *Refreshments: off A932 ¹/₂m W at Trumpeton Forge Tea-room open daily, except Tues, 12 noon – 5pm* ✳ *Toilet facilities* ✳ *Partly suitable for wheelchairs* ✳ *Dogs on lead* ✳ *Home-grown plants and soft fruit for sale in season* ✳ *House open for parties and teas by appointment* ✳ *Garden open daily, April to Oct, 10am – 5pm and at other times by appointment* ✳ *Entrance: £1.50 by collection box*

In the grounds of an attractive eighteenth-century house and courtyard, these beautiful walled gardens lead down towards a small river with an informal riverside walk and two unusual buildings, a turreted dovecote and a Gothic wash-house. There are rhododendron glades with other unusual trees and shrubs, but pride of place must go to the spectacular semi-formal gardens behind the house. Exquisite old-fashioned roses and a series of long borders containing a dramatic palette of massed delphiniums and other herbaceous 'perennials in July constitute one of the most memorable displays of its type to be found in Scotland.

HOUSE OF TONGUE ★   55
Tongue, by Lairg, Sutherland, Highlands. Tel: (084755) 209

Countess of Sutherland ✳ *1m N of Tongue off A838* ✳ *Parking* ✳ *Open by appointment and 1st Aug for charity* ✳ *Entrance: £1, children 50p*

Sheltered from wind and salt by tall trees, this walled garden is a haven in an otherwise exposed environment. Adjoining the seventeenth-century house, it is laid-out after the traditional Scottish acre with gravel and grass walks between herbaceous beds and hedged vegetable plots and orchard. A stepped beech-hedged walk leads up to a high terrace which commands a fine view over the Kyle of Tongue. The centrepiece of the garden is Lord Reay's sundial (1714) – a sculpted obelisk of unusual design.

INVERESK LODGE AND VILLAGE GARDENS   56
Nr Musselburgh, East Lothian, Lothian. Tel: (031) 2265922

Various owners inc. The National Trust for Scotland (Lodge) ✳ *6m E of Edinburgh, S of Musselburgh via A6124* ✳ *Best season: summer* ✳ *Parking* ✳ *Lodge open as gardens* ✳ *Lodge open all year, Mon – Fri, 10am – 4.30pm, Sun 2 – 5pm. Privately owned gardens in the village open one day only for charity* ✳ *Entrance: £1, children 50p, honesty box*

This large seventeenth-century house in the village of Inveresk, now owned by The National Trust for Scotland, is situated on a steeply sloping site. The high stone retaining walls are well-planted with a wide range of climbers. There are numerous flower beds; a particularly good border is devoted to shrub roses. A peat bed permits a greater diversity of planting. The garden has been completely remade since it came under the ownership of The Trust. No attempt has been made to recreate a period style. The garden is 'modern' in most respects, semi-formal, well planted, very well-maintained and offers a wide selection of plants flowering from spring through autumn. The village itself is a unique, unspoilt example of eighteenth-century villa development with houses dating from the late seventeenth and early eighteenth centuries. All have well laid-out gardens enclosed by high walls and containing a wide range of shrubs and trees as well as some unusual plants. Open one day for charity by admission ticket to cover all gardens. Plant stalls and teas.

INVEREWE GARDEN ★★   57
Poolewe, Ross and Cromarty, Highlands. Tel: (044586) 229

The National Trust for Scotland ✳ *6m NE of Gairloch on A832* ✳ *Parking* ✳ *Restaurant April to 18th Oct* ✳ *Toilet facilities* ✳ *Partly suitable for wheelchairs* ✳ *Plants for sale* ✳ *Shop and Visitor Centre* ✳ *Open all year, daily, 9.30am – sunset* ✳ *Entrance: £2.80, children £1.40, adult parties £2.40 per person, schools £1.20*

This garden is spectacular. Created in 1865 on the shores of the sea loch, Loch Ewe, it covers the entire Am Ploc Ard peninsular. Planned as a wild garden around one dwarf willow on peat and sandstone, it has been developed as a series of walks through herbaceous and rock gardens, a wet valley, a rhododendron walk and a curved vegetable garden and orchard. This is a plantsman's garden (labelling is discreet) containing many sub-tropical species from Australia, New Zealand, China and the Americas, sheltered by mature beech, oak and pine trees. New Zealand alpines include the National collection of the genus *Ourisia*. The garden is well-tended and way-marked. Note: midge repellent is essential and on sale at main desk.

JOHNSTON GARDENS 58
Viewfield Gardens, Aberdeen, Grampian. Tel: (0224) 276276

Aberdeen City Council * *In Aberdeen, 1/4m S of Queens Road (A944 to Alford), 1/4m W of junction with ring road* * *Best seasons: spring and summer* * *Parking* * *Toilet facilities* * *Partly suitable for wheelchairs* * *Open daily, 8am – dusk* * *Entrance: free*

When Johnston House was demolished and the grounds sold for redevelopment, it was impossible to utilise the deepest area of the ravine. This was converted into a water and rock garden by the City of Aberdeen Parks and Recreation Department. The result is a very congenial oasis of trees, shrubs and mature rhododendrons surrounding a small lake complete with an island, rustic bridges and resident waterfowl. The rock and scree gardens have some interesting plants, and primulas and astilbes edge the outlet from the lake in summer.

KAILZIE GARDENS 59
Peebles, Peebleshire, Borders. Tel. (0721) 20007

Mrs M.A. Richard * *2 1/2m from Peebles on B7062* * *Parking* * *Tea room and restaurant* * *Toilet facilities* * *Suitable for wheelchairs* * *Dogs on lead* * *Plants for sale when available* * *Shop* * *Open April to Oct, 11am – 5.30pm* * *Entrance: £1, children 50p (1991 prices)*

'A Pleasure Garden' is the description in one of the advertisements for Kailzie (pronounced Kailie) and very apt it is too. The gardens of 17 acres are situated in a particularly attractive area of the beautiful Tweed Valley and are surrounded by breath-taking views. The Old Mansion Home was pulled down in 1962 and the vast walled garden, which still houses the magnificent greenhouse, was transformed by Angela Richard from vegetables to a garden of meandering lawns and island beds. Full of interesting shrubs and plants for drying, there are many surprises including a herb garden, choice flower area, secret gardens, loving seats invitingly placed under garlanded arbours and several pieces of statuary which have been thoughtfully placed. A magnificent fountain at the end of the herbaceous borders leads on to woods and huge stately trees, and from here you may stroll down the Major's walk which is lined with laburnum and underplanted with rhododendrons, azaleas, blue poppies and primulas. From here you can go to the small waterfowl lake.

KELLIE CASTLE 60
Pittenweem, Fife. Tel: (03338) 271

The National Trust for Scotland ✻ *3m NNW of Pittenweem on B9171* ✻ *Best season: summer* ✻ *Parking 100 yards, closer parking for disabled* ✻ *Refreshments in castle* ✻ *Toilet facilities, not for disabled* ✻ *Partly suitable for wheelchairs* ✻ *Shop* ✻ *House open 29th March to 1st April, 2 – 6pm, 6th to 28th April, Sat and Sun, 2 – 6pm, May to Oct, daily, 2 – 6pm (last tour 5.30pm)* ✻ *Garden and grounds open all year, daily, 10am – sunset* ✻ *Entrance: £1, children 50p (castle and garden £2.80, OAP and children £1.40)*

The garden has no particular relationship to the sixteenth-century house, having been restored by Professor James Lorimer in early Victorian times. Entered by a door in a high wall, the garden is small (one acre) and inspires dreams within every gardener's reach. Simple borders, such as one of catmint only, capture the imagination as hundreds of bees and butterflies work the flowers. Areas of lawn are edged with box hedges, borders, arches and trellises. In one corner, behind a trellis, is a small romantic garden within a garden. A large, white-painted commemorative seat designed by Huw Lorimer provides outstanding focal interest at the end of one of the main walks. The recently-appointed head gardener is establishing a collection of old and unusual vegetable varieties and employing only organic gardening methods, putting heart back into the soil through liberal use of compost. Roses on trellis and on arches abound.

KILBRYDE CASTLE 61
Dunblane, Perthshire, Central. Tel: (0786) 823104

Sir Colin Campbell ✻ *Off A820 Dunblane – Doune road* ✻ *Best season: April to July* ✻ *Parking* ✻ *Partly suitable for wheelchairs* ✻ *Open 29th March, 19th April, 10th May, 7th June, 5th, 26th July, 16th Aug, 13th Sept, 2 – 6pm for charity and also by appointment* ✻ *Entrance: £1.50*

A good example of a partly-mature 20-acre garden created over the last 10 years by the enthusiastic owner and his highly knowledgeable helper, who are constantly introducing new features and plant content. Imaginatively-placed borders filled with constant colour on wide lawns sloping down to a woodland water garden.

KILDRUMMY CASTLE GARDENS ★ 62
Nr Alford, Aberdeen, Grampian. Tel: (09755) 71264 and 71277

Kildrummy Castle Garden Trust ✻ *2m from Mossat, 10m from Alford, 17m from Huntly. Take A944 from Alford, following signs to Kildrummy, left on A97* ✻ *Parking: car park free inside hotel main entrance. Coaches park up hotel delivery entrance* ✻ *Toilet facilities* ✻ *Suitable for wheelchairs* ✻ *Dogs on lead* ✻ *Plants for sale* ✻ *Kildrummy Castle Hotel open, 09755 71288 for reservations* ✻ *Visitor centre and video room* ✻ *Woodland walks, children's play area* ✻ *Open April to Oct, daily, 10am – 5pm* ✻ *Entrance: £1.50, children 9 – 16 50p, 3 – 8 20p*

The gardens are set in a deep valley between the ruins of a thirteenth-century castle and a Tudor-style house, now a hotel. The rock garden, by Backhouse of

York (1904), occupies the site of the quarry which provided the stone for the castle. The narrowest part of the ravine is traversed by a copy of the fourteenth-century Auld Brig O'Balgownie, Old Aberdeen built by Col. Ogston in 1900. This provides both an excellent viewpoint and also a focus for the water garden commissioned from a firm of Japanese landscape gardeners at the same period. The reflections in the still water of the larger pools increase the impact of the luxurious plantings of *Lysichiton americanus*, primulas, a notable *Schizophragma hydrangeoides*; there are fine maples, rhododendron species and hybrids, oaks and conifers. Although a severe frost pocket, the garden can grow embothriums, dieramas and other choice plants. A garden for all seasons, but especially beautiful in autumn.

LANGWELL 63
Berriedale, Caithness, Highlands. Tel: (05935) 278

Lady Anne Bentinck ✳ *2m from Berriedale on the A9 Helmsdale to Wick road* ✳ *Best season: July to Aug* ✳ *Parking* ✳ *Teas on charity open days* ✳ *Partly suitable for wheelchairs* ✳ *Open 9th, 16th Aug, 2 – 5.30pm* ✳ *Entrance: £1 (1991 price)*

The bare landscape of Caithness does not support too many gardens of interest, but here in the shelter of the Langwell Water is one of the happy exceptions. Reached by a two-mile drive through mature woodland this old walled garden provides the shelter necessary to grow a good range of plants. A map of 1877 already shows a formal plan but the present-day cruciform layout, centred on a sundial, dates from 1916 when it was made by John Murray. An old yew arch dates perhaps from the early 1800s. Murray's hedges of thuya have had to be removed recently but new hedges have been planted. The main area is kept in the old tradition of a mixture of flower borders, fruit and vegetables and there is a small rockery area. At the bottom end is a formal pool surrounded by yew hedging and hidden to one side a small pool filled with water soldiers, *Stratiotes aloides*.

LAWHEAD CROFT 64
Tarbrax, Lanarkshire, Lothian. Tel: (050185) 274

Sue and Hector Riddell ✳ *12m from Balerno, 6m from Carnwath on A70* ✳ *Best season: summer* ✳ *Parking* ✳ *Refreshments on open days* ✳ *Toilet facilities* ✳ *Mostly suitable for wheelchairs* ✳ *Dogs on lead* ✳ *Open for parties by appointment only* ✳ *Entrance: £1.50*

Nearly 1000ft up in the midst of the bleak Lanarkshire moors, Sue and Hector Riddell have planted shelter belts and laboriously carved out a luxuriant garden. Grass walks lead from one interesting border to another, all full of unusual plants. Colour associations and leaf contrasts are carefully thought out. There is an enchanting series of garden rooms all with a different theme. A garden of great ideas including an excellent bonsai collection. Recently most of the vegetable garden has been swept away and replanted in a great sweep of curved, tiered and circular beds of spectacular and original design.

LECKMELM SHRUBBERY AND ARBORETUM 65
Little Leckmelm House, Lochbroom, by Garve, Ross-shire, Highlands. Tel: (0854) 612377

Sir Charles and Lady Troughton ✳ *4m E of Ullapool on A835* ✳ *Best season: April/Sept* ✳ *Parking in walled garden* ✳ *Open daily, 10am – 5pm* ✳ *Entrance: £1, OAP and children 50p*

Planted in about 1870, this was derelict for 50 years until reclamation started in 1984 by the present owners. A 10-acre woodland garden with many fine examples of species rhododendron. There are many different pine and cypress trees, now mature, a huge eucalyptus and a magnificent weeping beech. It remains a simple quiet woodland garden, well worth a visit.

LEITH HALL ★ 66
Kennethmont, by Huntly, Aberdeen, Grampian. Tel: (04643) 216

The National Trust for Scotland ✳ *1m W of Kennethmont on B9002 and 34m NW of Aberdeen* ✳ *Parking* ✳ *Refreshments: picnic area and teas on charity open days* ✳ *Toilet facilities* ✳ *Dogs* ✳ *Stalls on charity open days* ✳ *House open inc. exhibition: May to Sept, 2 – 6pm (last tour 5.15pm), Oct, weekends, 2 – 5pm. £3, children £1.50, parties £1.60, schools 80p* ✳ *Garden open all year, daily, 9.30am – sunset* ✳ *Entrance: by donation*

Since it came into the care of The National Trust for Scotland, the gardens of Leith Hall have been expanded and upgraded. But it is the old garden, remote from the house, that offers the greatest pleasure to the garden enthusiast. This comprises large borders and a large, well-stocked rock garden. The design is simple, romantic and allows a tremendous display of flowers during the whole of summer and early autumn. Especially fine is the magenta *Geranium psilostemon* and a border of solid catmint running from top to bottom of the garden. There are no lawns or open courtyards and no dominating architecture, just massive plantings of perennials and the odd rarity amongst the rocks. The extensive policies offer woodland walks, views and excellent opportunities for birdwatching around the lake.

LITTLE SPARTA ★★ 67
Dunsyre, Nr Lanark, Lanarkshire, Strathclyde.

Mr Ian Hamilton-Finlay ✳ *Turn off A721 at Newbigging for Dunsyre. 1m W of Dunsyre is an unmarked very rough farm track up to Little Sparta, marked at the foot by a sign saying 'Stonypath, Little Sparta'* ✳ *Best season: June* ✳ *Parking* ✳ *Guide dogs for the blind only* ✳ *Open by appointment in writing (SAE please)* ✳ *Entrance: free*

A clue as to what is hidden in Ian Hamilton-Finlay's totally unexpected garden is given on arrival at the gate to the property, where a beautifully-carved quotation from Heraclitus greets you. Hamilton-Finlay believes that a garden should appeal to all the senses and particularly should provoke thought, both serious and trivial, and he has therefore revived the art of emblematic gardening which died out in Britain in the seventeenth century. He achieved an international reputation in the process. It is impossible to describe Little Sparta briefly, except to say that he has transformed a sizeable hill farmstead (starting in 1966 with the idea of establishing a testing-ground for his sculptures) into a garden full of images, allusions and symbols. Not all are easily understood or interpreted, which doesn't matter as this is a garden not a crossword puzzle. However, before visiting Littla Sparta it may help to read one of the many articles about it – for example in the King and Rose book *Gardening with Style*.

LOCHALSH WOODLAND GARDEN
(Balmacara Estate) ★   68
Balmacara, Highlands. Tel: (059986) 207

The National Trust for Scotland ✳ 1m E of Kyle of Lochalsh off A87 ✳ Best season: spring ✳ Parking (¹/₂m walk to garden) ✳ Partly suitable for wheelchairs ✳ Open all year, daily, 9am – sunset. Kiosk and Coach House open from May ✳ Entrance: £1, children 50p (1991 prices)

The garden is approached down the wooded road to the village of Glaick on the lochside and from there, across the water, rise the magnificent mountains of Skye. Woodland planting on this steep-sided, six and a half-acre site was begun in 1887 around Lochalsh House, and the canopy of beeches, larches, oaks and pines is now outstanding. Garden planting was started in 1979 with rhododendrons and shrubs from Tasmania, New Zealand, the Himalayas, China and Japan. Paths created through the woods give a choice of walks, both in terms of gradient and length. Beside these and in glades, fallen branches have been used to build curved, raised beds for the new plantings, which include many primulas and ferns, all of which are labelled. The Coach House Visitor Centre contains interpretive displays on rural industry, geology, and shore, woodland and moorland wildlife.

LOGAN BOTANIC GARDEN
AND LOGAN HOUSE ★★   69
Port Logan, by Stranraer, Dumfries and Galloway. Tel: (077686) 231

Royal Botanic Garden, Edinburgh/Sir Ninian Buchan-Hepburn, Bt. ✳ On B7065 ¹/₂m S of junction with A716 ✳ Best seasons: spring and summer ✳ Parking ✳ Teas ✳ Toilet facilities ✳ Suitable for wheelchairs ✳ Open 15th March to Oct, daily, 10am – 6pm and at other times by arrangement ✳ Entrance: £1.50, concessions £1, children 50p. Season tickets covering Dawyck, Logan and Younger available – telephone Royal Botanic Garden (031) 552 7171

Logan is a fascinating sub-tropical garden situated on the southernmost tip of Scotland – the Rhinns of Galloway. The exceptionally mild climate allowed the creation of a formal garden in the Mediterranean style. The garden was originally started in 1860 by Mrs James McDouall, a great aunt of the present owner, and continued by her two sons, Kenneth and Douglas. It was through their plant collecting abroad and dedication to beauty that this unique garden was created. In 1970 the garden was divided and the walled section was named Logan Botanic Garden, as an annexe to the Royal Botanic Garden in Edinburgh. The old original and greater part of the garden belongs to Logan House. Now, under the care of The Royal Botanic Garden Edinburgh, Logan is a fascinating collection of rare and unusual sub-tropical plants. Chusan palms (*Trachycarpus fortunei*), tree ferns (*Dicksonia antarctica*), cabbage palms (*Cordyline australis*), and a large number of Australian and New Zealand plants are mixed with hardier temperate plants to give a unique air to this superb garden. Ancient magnolias and meconopsis (Himalayan blue poppies) make a magnificent spring show. Throughout the summer season there are endless banks of flowers appearing along meandering walks that eventually lead to a formal pool filled with various water lilies – surrounded by tree ferns and vast cabbage palms. This garden is a must for the keen plantsman as many of Britain's finest specimens can be found here. The *Gunnera manicata* by the entrance attains a leaf size greater than anywhere else in Britain. Logan is certainly one of Great Britain's finest and most unusual gardens. Logan House garden is open for one day for charity. The fine Queen Anne house has a garden with rare exotic tropical plants and shrubs.

MALLENY HOUSE GARDENS   70
Balerno, Midlothian, Lothian. Tel: (031449) 2283

*The National Trust for Scotland * In Balerno village, on A70 Edinburgh – Lanark road * Best seasons: summer and autumn * Parking * Suitable for wheelchairs * Open all year, 10am – dusk * Entrance: £1, OAP 50p (honesty box)*

Aptly described as The National Trust for Scotland's secret garden, Malleny seems an old and valued friend soon after meeting and reflects the thoughtful planning by the head gardener. An impressive Atlantic cedar reigns over this relatively small garden assisted by a square of early seventeenth-century clipped yews and yew hedges. As well as containing the NCCPG collection of nineteenth-century shrub roses and a permanent display from the Scottish Bonsai Association, Malleny's 12ft wide herbaceous borders are superb as is the large glasshouse containing a continual display of flowering plants. Don't forget the attractively laid-out herb and ornamental vegetable garden.

MANDERSTON ★   71
Duns, Borders. Tel: (0361) 83450

*The Lord Palmer * 2m E of Duns on A6105 * Best season: early Aug, woodland garden May and June * Parking * Refreshments: tea room in grounds * Toilet facilities * Partly suitable for wheelchairs * Dogs on lead * Plants for sale * Shop * House open as for gardens * Gardens open early May to Sept, Sun and Thurs, end May and Aug Bank Holiday Mons or parties by appointment * Entrance: £3.30 (house and garden) (1991 price)*

One of the last great classic houses to be built in Britain, Manderston was modelled on Robert Adams' Kedleston Hall in Derbyshire (see entry). It was described in 1905 as a 'charming mansion inexhaustible in its attractions' and this might equally well apply to the gardens which remain an impressive example of gardening on the grand scale. Four magnificently formal terraces planted in Edwardian style overlook a narrow serpentine lake and a chinoiserie bridging dam tempts one over to the woodland garden on the far side, thus elegantly effecting the transition from formal to informal. No expense was spared creating the gardens and this air of opulence and good quality is much evident in the formal walled gardens to the north of the house. They are a lasting tribute to the very best of the Edwardian era when 100 gardeners were employed to do what two now do to the same immaculately high standard. Gilded gates open on to a panorama of colourful planting on different levels, with fountains, statuary and a charming rose pergola all complementing each other. Even the greenhouses were given lavish treatment with the walls created from lumps of limestone to resemble an exotic planted grotto.

MEGGINCH CASTLE 72
Errol, by Perth, Tayside.

Lady Strange ✳ 8m E of Perth off A85 Perth – Dundee road ✳ Best season: Aug ✳ Suitable for wheelchairs ✳ Dogs on lead ✳ Open every Wed, 2 – 5pm, and daily, 2 – 5pm in Aug ✳ Entrance: £1.50, children 50p

Originally a fifteenth-century tower house, Megginch meaning Beautiful Island, was considerably restructured by Robert Adam in 1790 and also by successive generations and this gives the gardens and the gothic courtyard of 1806 a timeless atmosphere. A small fountain parterre to the side of the house is of particular interest for its yew and variegated holly topiary, including an unusual topiary yew crown planted to commemorate Queen Victoria's Jubilee. A few yards away is a thousand year-old yew, at 72 feet the highest in Scotland. Try and visit Megginch during August when a stunning 120-yard double border – the length of the eighteenth century walled garden is a glorious blaze of annual plantings. So many dahlias can rarely have been displayed. An adjacent walled garden of the same period contains an interesting astrological garden with relevant plants pertaining to each sign of the zodiac.

MELLERSTAIN ✳ ✳ 73
Gordon, Etterick, Borders. Tel: (057381) 292

The Earl of Haddington ✳ Halfway betwen Galashiels and Coldstream. Turn S in Gordon on A6089 and turn W after 2m or turn off B6397 2m N of Smailholm ✳ Parking ✳ Teas ✳ Toilet facilities ✳ Suitable for wheelchairs ✳ Charity gift shop and craft gallery ✳ House open. Extra charge ✳ Garden open May to Sept, daily except Sat, 12.30 – 5pm ✳ Entrance: £1.50, children free

A bastion of formal garden layout with dignified terraces overlooking an 'arranged' landscape. The house of Mellerstain is a unique example of the work of the Adam family; both William and son, Robert, worked on the building. The garden is formal, comprised of very dignified terraces, ballustraded and 'lightly' planted with climbers and simple topiary. The great glory of the garden is the landscape complete with lake and woodlands in the style of Brown and Repton, but designed early this century by Sir Reginald Blomfield. The view of the Cheviot Hills from the terraces is one of the finest to be found in this lovely area of the Scottish Borders. Mellerstain is a must for lovers of the formal landscape.

MERTOUN 74
St Boswells, Roxburghshire, Borders. Tel: (0835) 23236

The Duke of Sutherland ✻ *2m NE of St Boswells on B6404* ✻ *Best season: spring and summer* ✻ *Parking* ✻ *Toilet facilities* ✻ *Suitable for wheelchairs* ✻ *Open April to Sept, Sat and Sun, 2 – 6pm. Also open Bank Holiday Mons* ✻ *Entrance: £1, OAP and children 50p*

Overlooking the Tweed and with Mertoun House in the background, this is a lovely garden to wander round and admire the mature specimen trees, azaleas, daffodils and a most attractive ornamental pond flanked by a good herbaceous border. The focal point is the immaculate three-acre walled garden which is everything a proper kitchen garden should be. Walking up from a 1567 dovecote, thought to be the oldest in the county, through a healthy orchard, the visitor reaches the traditional box hedges, raised beds and glasshouses of the main area. Neat rows of vegetables, herbs and bright flowers for the house vie for attention with the pruning of the figs and peaches in the well-stocked glasshouses.

MONTEVIOT 75
Nr Jedburgh, Borders. Tel: (08353) 380

Earl and Countess of Ancram ✻ *Turn off A68 on B6400 to Nisbet. Entrance second turning on right* ✻ *Best season: July and August* ✻ *Parking free* ✻ *Refreshments in Woodland centre, 1/2m from house* ✻ *Toilet facilities* ✻ *Partly suitable for wheelchairs* ✻ *Dogs on lead* ✻ *Plants for sale* ✻ *Open 19th July, 2 – 5pm* ✻ *Entrance: £1, OAP 50p, children under 14 free*

The river garden designed by Percy Cane in 1960s which runs down to the River Teviot is currently being restored with herbaceous perennials and shrubs. Beside it, the semi-enclosed terraced rose gardens overlooking the river below have a large collection of hybrid teas, floribundas and shrubs. Beside the house is an attractive formal herb garden. The pinetum is full of unusual trees reaching great heights, and nearby a water garden has recently been created, planted with unusual rhododendrons and azaleas. A circular route around the gardens is also planned. Fine views.

NETHERBYRES 76
Eyemouth, Berwickshire, Borders. Tel: (08907) 50337

Lieut-Col S.J. Furness ✻ *1/4m from Eyemouth on A1107* ✻ *Parking by house* ✻ *Suitable for wheelchairs* ✻ *Open twice yearly in April and July for charity and April to Sept for small parties by appointment* ✻ *Entrance: £1, children 50p*

Having lost its Victorian conservatory and vinery, the garden has perhaps mislaid a little of its charm, but is worth seeing for the unique elliptical wall and for the traditional mix of flowers, fruit and vegetables grown there.

PITMEDDEN GARDEN ★★ 77
Pitmedden, Ellon, Grampian. Tel: (06513) 2352

The National Trust for Scotland ✻ *1m W of Pitmedden village on A920 and 1m N of Udny. 14m N of Aberdeen* ✻ *Parking* ✻ *Refreshments: tea room. Picnic* *area * Toilet facilities inc. disabled * Suitable for wheelchairs and wheelchairs supplied * Museum of Farming Life * Gardens, museum, etc, open May to Sept, daily, 10am – 6pm * Entrance: £2.40, concessions and children £1.20*

Like Edzell Castle, the great garden of Pitmedden exhibits the taste of seventeenth-century garden makers and their love of patterns made to be viewed from above. The rectangular garden is enclosed by high terraces on three sides and by a wall on the fourth. Very ornamental patterns are cut in box on a grand scale, infilled with rather garish annuals. The overall impact is striking when viewed from either of two period stone gazebos with ogee roofs or when walking along the terraces. Simple topiary and box hedging are abundant. There is a rather curious contemporary fountain made from fragments preserved at Pitmedden and others from the Cross Fountain at Linlithgow. There is a small herb garden near the tea room. Fine borders of herbaceous plants outline the parterre garden to the south and west. When The Trust received Pitmedden in 1952 all that survived was the masonry. Since nothing remained of the original plans, contemporary plans for Holyroodhouse Palace gardens were used in recreating what is seen today. A garden well worth visiting at any time of the year.

PLANTS FROM THE PAST 78
The Old House, 1 North Street, Belhaven, Dunbar, East Lothian, Borders. Tel: (0368) 63223

*Dr David Stuart and Mr James Sutherland * 1m W of Dunbar. From A1 take A1087 towards Dunbar, through West Barns. Turn left at crossroads after Dunbar town sign, turn first right then first left into North Street * John Muir car park two minutes' walk away and signposted from gates * Partly suitable for wheelchairs * Plants 'from the past' for sale in adjacent nursery * Garden open March to Sept, daily except Tues, 1 – 5pm * Entrance: by collecting box*

Garden historians will delight in this garden which has been renovated during the last five years and planted to an early eighteenth-century design. After the narrow village streets, it is a vivid experience to pass through the gates in the high wall into this gracious parterre. A broad gravel walk directs the eye to the restored eighteenth-century summerhouse, with its terrace and abundantly-filled urns. Viewed from there, the parterre garden appears to consist of a maze-like pattern of flower beds, but take the time to walk the gravel paths between them to appreciate the vibrant colours, subtle textures and evocative, half-remembered scents of the plants. At one side a raised grass walkway leads through to the nursery and sales area in the old kitchen garden where a catalogue of plants is available that includes information on when each species was first grown or introduced into the UK. There is also a cottage garden around the house which has box hedges and old shrub roses but unfortunately this is open only occasionally.

POLLOK HOUSE ★ 79
Glasgow, Strathclyde. Tel: (041) 6320274

*City of Glasgow District Council * 3¹/₂m from city centre, well signposted. A736 in Pollakshaws * Parking * Teas (reservations (041) 6497547 * Toilet facilities * Suitable for wheelchairs * House open and gallery * Garden open all year, weekdays, 10am – 5pm, Sun, 2 – 5pm. Closed 25th Dec and 1st Jan * Entrance: free*

Everyone should visit the Burrell Art Collection, Scotland's gem, and Pollok House and gardens are thrown in free. A visit to Pollok House offers a full day's entertainment. The house itself, an Adam design, features a lovely formal terrace of box parterres, beautifully planted and maintained by Glasgow Parks. There are lovely borders near the water and a nineteenth-century woodland garden on the ridge nearby. Stone gazebos with ogee roofs. The grounds are famous for their bluebells in spring. Pollok House holds the famous Stirling Maxwell collection of European decorative arts. In the grounds is the 1985 Musuem of the Year, the Burrell Collection, one of the world's finest private collections of the decorative arts. The building was designed to encompass the surrounding woodland. The parkland around is beautifully planted and maintained.

ROYAL BOTANIC GARDEN ★★   80
Edinburgh, Lothian. Tel: (031) 5527171

Department of Agriculture and Fisheries for Scotland ✳ *$1^1/2$m N of city centre in Leith Walk above Cannongate* ✳ *Parking* ✳ *Toilet facilities* ✳ *Suitable for wheelchairs* ✳ *Exhibition hall and Inverleigh Visitor Centre open* ✳ *Garden open daily except 25th Dec and 1st Jan, Mon-Sat, 10am – 4pm in winter, 10am – 6pm in spring, and 10am – 7pm in summer. Suns, 11am to same closing times* ✳ *Entrance: free*

Set on a hillside with magnificent panoramic views of the city, the Royal Botanic Garden of Edinburgh is one of the finest botanic gardens in the world; arguably the finest garden, physically, of its type in Britain. The 75 acres of gardens are filled with hundreds of thousands of plants, trees and shrubs from all over the world with a particular emphasis on Himalayan and Chinese species. The rhododendron collection is vast, the rock garden is among the finest in the world, and the heather collection is renowned. The conservatories hold enormous collections of tropical, sub-tropical and xerophytic plants and were among the earliest to be internally landscaped. The home demonstration gardens are very well done. The perennial border is one of the largest in the UK, approaching 600 feet. The many paths meander through numerous areas of specific interest, all beautifully planted and maintained to the very highest degree. The overall standard of horticulture is superb. The specimen trees are amongst the finest in Britain – the birch collection is unexcelled. This is a garden that takes years to know well. It is forever being improved and replanted.

THREAVE SCHOOL OF GARDENING ★   81
Stewartry, Castle Douglas, Dumfries and Galloway. Tel: (0556) 2575

The National Trust for Scotland ✳ *1m W of Castle Douglas off A75* ✳ *Parking* ✳ *Refreshments: restaurant April to Oct, daily, 10am – 5pm* ✳ *Toilet facilities* ✳ *Suitable for wheelchairs* ✳ *Shop* ✳ *Visitor Centre. Exhibition April to Oct, daily, 9am – 5.30pm* ✳ *Garden open all year, daily, 9am – sunset* ✳ *Entrance: £2.80, children £1.40, party rates: £2.20, OAP and children £1.10*

Nearly 1500 acres of policies (estates), woodland and gardens used as a school since 1960 and catering for young aspiring gardeners. Numerous perennials, annuals, trees and shrubs are used in innovative ways and maintained to a high standard by the resident students of gardening. For the visitor the main interest is a modern design relying heavily on island beds, which can be compared and contrasted with other layouts. Threave is famous for its collection of daffodils and is lovely in spring when these are complemented by the rhododendrons and flowering trees and shrubs. The gardens extend to 65 acres.

TILLYPRONIE 82
Tarland, Grampian. Tel: (03398) 81238

The Hon. Philip Astor ✳ *4¹/₂m from Tarland via A97 Dinnet – Huntly road* ✳ *Parking* ✳ *Teas* ✳ *Toilet facilities* ✳ *Partly suitable for wheelchairs* ✳ *Dogs on leads* ✳ *Open 30th Aug for charity, 2 – 5pm* ✳ *Entrance: £1, children 40p*

Set on the south-facing slope of a hill at over 1000 feet above sea level this is a cold garden, but shelter belts dating from the mid-1800s ensure that a wide range of plants can be grown. More shelter planting was added in the period 1925-51. The overall layout was completed in the 1920s and was the work of George Dillistone of Tunbridge Wells. The terraces below the house date from the same period and support narrow herbaceous borders. The house walls provide shelter for less hardy climbers and trained *Buddleia davidii* cultivars make a good display in August. Curved stone steps lead between extensive heather gardens onto lawns which sweep down to the ponds which have colourful plantings of astilbes, filipendulas, lysichitons, primulas and ferns. There are fine specimens of *Picea breweriana* and many other conifers and an area devoted to dwarf varieties. Spectacular views over rich farmland and nearby hills end with the Gramplans on the horizon. The small pinetum set in pine and birch forest was planted by the late Lord Astor.

TOROSAY CASTLE AND GARDENS 83
Craignure, Isle of Mull, Argyll, Strathclyde. Tel: (06802) 421

Mr Christopher James ✳ *1¹/₂m from Craignure. Steamer 6 times daily from Oban to Craignure. Motor boat during high season. Miniature steam railway from Craignure ferry. Lochuline to Fishnish, then 7m S on A849* ✳ *Best season: May* ✳ *Teas* ✳ *Toilet facilities* ✳ *Partly suitable for wheelchairs* ✳ *Dogs on lead* ✳ *Shop* ✳ *Castle open, mid–April to mid–Oct, 10.30am – 5.30pm. Admission extra* ✳ *Garden open all year, daily, sunrise – sunset* ✳ *Entrance: £1.50, OAP, students, children £1*

House in baronial castle style by Bryce (1858). Main garden formal Italian based on a series of descending terraces with unusual statue walk. This features one of the richest collections of Italian rococo statuary in Britain and alone justifies the crossing from Oban to Mull. Vaguely reminiscent of Powis Castle (see entry), this is a dramatic contrast with the rugged island scenery. The peripheral gardens are also a contrast – an informal water garden and Japanese garden looking out over Duart Bay; also a small rock garden. Rhododendrons and azaleas are a feature but less important than in other west-coast gardens. Collection of Australian and New Zealand trees and shrubs.

TYNINGHAME HOUSE ★   84
Tyninghame, Nr East Linton, Lothian. Tel: (0620) 860491

Tyninghame Gardens Ltd ✳ *25m E of Edinburgh between Haddington and Dunbar. N of A1, 2m E of A198* ✳ *Parking* ✳ *Suitable for wheelchairs* ✳ *Open two days for charity, probably May and July. Phone for details*

Tyninghame is renowned for the gardens created by the Dowager Lady Haddington from 1947 onwards, which have been described as of 'ravishing beauty'. They consist of a formal rose garden, terraces, a secret garden, an Italian garden and an area of woodland. When her husband died in 1986, her son reluctantly sold the house, but those who worried about the garden's future need not to have feared, as the conversion and addition of two houses was handled by Kit Martin with great sensitivity. Tyninghame is close to the sea, with fine views in all directions, and those who are able to visit it on the open days will have a rare opportunity of seeing how the unique character of the garden has been maintained, perhaps enhanced, by the architectural changes around it.

YOUNGER BOTANIC GARDEN ★★   85
Benmore, Dunoon, Strathclyde. Tel: (0369) 6261
Royal Botanic Gardens Edinburgh

Dunoon, Argyll. 1m from junction of A885 and A815 ✳ *Best season: May to June* ✳ *Teas at main entrance* ✳ *Toilet facilities* ✳ *Suitable for wheelchairs* ✳ *Open daily, 15th March to Oct, 10am – 6pm and at other times by arrangement* ✳ *Entrance: £1.50, concessions £1, children 50p. Special discounts for groups. Season tickets covering Dawyck, Logan and Younger available – telephone Royal Botanic Garden (031) 552 7171*

Benmore's 100 acres of woodland gardens have been under development since 1820. The gardens are approached along Britain's finest Wellingtonia (*Sequoiadendron giganteum*) avenue. The tallest is more than 150 feet. Numerous other fine specimen conifers are to be found throughout the gardens. There are exceptionally fine monkey puzzles (*Araucaria araucana*) that retain their lower branches. But Benmore is most famous for its extensive rhododendron and magnolia collections on the hillside beside the River Eachaig in one of Britain's most breath-taking natural settings; the Highlands at their best. A myriad of paths take the visitor along the mountainside through vast plantations of rare shrubs and trees. Marvellous vistas open from time to time. The only obviously man-made feature is a great rectangular lawn enclosed on three sides by walls but open to the mountains on the fourth. This garden is bisected by borders filled with a collection of dwarf conifers. A handsome pavilion overlooks it all. There are other informal beds filled with Australian and New Zealand shrubs and herbaceous plants; a large collection of heathers. Benmore is well worth a visit both for its natural beauty and its vast specimen plant collections. Be prepared for a full day's outing, a great deal of walking, and rain.

WALES

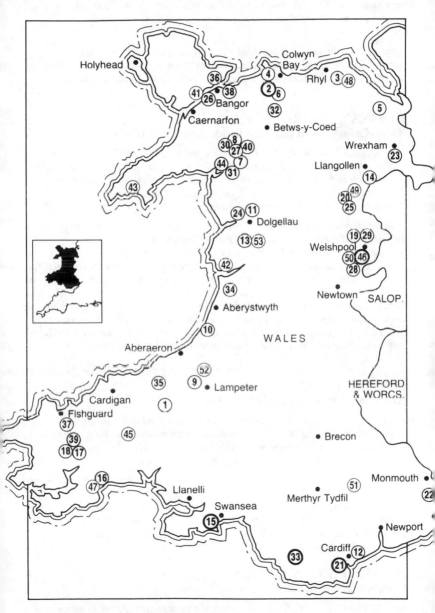

Two-starred gardens are ringed in bold.

BLAENGWRFACH ISAF 1
Bancyffordd, Dyfed. Tel: (055936) 2604

Mrs Gail Farmer ✳ 2m W of Llandyssul on Newcastle Emlyn road. First left by Halfmoon pub, 1¹/₂m until farm track on right ✳ Best season: spring ✳ Parking very limited ✳ Teas 1m away in village ✳ Plants for sale ✳ Shop, adjacent craft workshops ✳ Garden open April to June by appointment, 10am – 5pm ✳ Entrance: 75p

Created over the last 15 years from a green field site, this is essentially a cottage garden, but recent plantings of trees and shrubs to attract wildlife and plants suitable for pressed flowers give great diversity. Good autumn colour.

BODNANT GARDEN ★★ 2
Tal-y-Cafn, Colwyn Bay, Gwynedd. Tel: (0492) 650460

The National Trust ✳ 7m S of Llandudno, just off A470 ✳ Best season: April to Oct ✳ Official car park 50 yards from garden nursery ✳ Lunches, teas and light refreshments in Pavilion Restaurant, picnic area in car park ✳ Toilet facilities ✳ Partly suitable for wheelchairs ✳ Plants for sale in adjacent nursery ✳ Open 14th March to Oct, daily, 10am – 5pm (last admission 4.30pm) ✳ Entrance: £2.80

Bodnant is one of the finest gardens in the country, not only for the magnificent collections of rhododendrons, camellias and magnolias but also for its beautiful setting above the River Conway and the extensive views of the Snowdonia range. The gardens, which cover 80 acres, have several interesting features, the most well known being the laburnum arch which is an overwhelming mass of bloom in early June. Others include the lily terrace, curved and stepped pergola, canal terrace, Pin Mill and dell garden. The whole effect was created by the Aberconway family (who bought Bodnant in 1874) over successive generations, aided by the garden staff, including three generations of Puddles, and by the background of large native trees planted in the 1790s.

BODRHYDDAN 3
Rhuddlan, Clwyd. Tel: (0745) 590414

Lord Langford ✳ Take A5151 Rhuddlan – Dyserth road and turn left. Signposted ✳ Parking ✳ Teas ✳ Suitable for wheelchairs (garden and ground floor of house) ✳ House open ✳ Garden open June to Sept, Tues and Thurs, 2 – 5.30pm ✳ Entrance: £1.50, children 75p (house and garden)

The main feature of the garden is a box-edged parterre designed by William Nesfield. Other points of interest are clipped yew informal walks, three pools, one with rainbow trout, new plantings and ancient specimens of oak. There is also a 1612 pavilion by Inigo Jones which houses St Mary's Well, revered since pagan times and said to have been used for clandestine marriages.

BODYSGALLEN HALL ★ 4
Llandudno, Gwynedd. Tel: (0492) 584466

Historic House Hotel ✳ Take A55 (North Wales Expressway) from Bangor and at the intersection turn onto A470 towards LLandudno. Hotel and garden are 1m on right ✷ *Parking* ✷ *☆Refreshments* ✷ *Open all year, daily* ✷ *Entrance: free to guests and visitors to the hotel*

The owners have restored both house and gardens of this seventeenth-century country house to a high standard. The naturally-occurring limestone outcrops provide an interesting array of rockeries and terraces. One of the major features is a knot garden sympathetically planted with herbs, another is a formal walled rose garden. A number of well-established and interesting trees and shrubs can be seen, including medlar and mulberry. A woodland walk adds a further dimension.

BRYN DERWEN   5
Wrexham Road, Mold, Clwyd. Tel: (0352) 756662

Roger and Janet Williams ✷ *¹/₂m from Mold Cross on old Mold – Wrexham road (B5444), opposite Alun School and Sports Centre* ✷ *Plants for sale when available* ✷ *Open by appointment only* ✷ *Entrance: £1, children 25p*

A small town garden planted with a wide variety of interesting plants including alliums, cistus, euphorbias, ferns, hostas and grasses to give colour all year round. The planting is intensive and imaginative, and the garden has been featured on BBC Radio Wales *Garddio*.

BRYN MEIFOD   6
Graig, Glan Conwy, Conway Bay, Clwyd. Tel: (0492) 580875

Dr and Mrs K. Lever ✷ *Just off A470, 1¹/₂m S of Glan Conwy. Follow signs for Aberconwy Nursery* ✷ *Parking* ✷ *Toilet facilities* ✷ *Plants for sale in adjacent nursery open all year, Tues – Sun, 9am – 5pm* ✷ *Garden open June and Aug, Sun, 2 – 5pm; May and Sept, Thurs, 2 – 5pm* ✷ *Entrance: by collecting box for charity*

The garden, situated next to the Lever's nursery renowned for the quality of plants sold, is being extended and modified. In effect a new garden is being created within the framework of an existing established one, a process of interest in itself. The planting is imaginative and includes some unusual plants in skilfully designed settings which set them off to best effect. There is a lack of artificiality in what is currently a lovely garden with the promise of even more to come, for example a scree area being planted with alpines.

BRYNMELYN   7
Cymerau Isaf, Ffestiniog, Gwynedd. Tel: (076676) 2684

Mr and Mrs A.S. Taylor ✷ *2m SW of Ffestiniog on A496* ✷ *Best season: spring to autumn* ✷ *Parking in lay-by opposite junction to Manod (¹/₄m to garden along path at lower gate bearing right after garage)* ✷ *Open May to Sept, 10am – 1pm, 2 – 5pm. Telephone first before 10am or after 9pm* ✷ *Entrance: collecting box*

An interesting garden, not only for its range of plant material, but also for its wild mountainside-setting. Divided into smaller gardens each with its own theme and character, it lends itself well to the overall informal style and its nature reserve and woodland setting.

BRYN-Y-BONT 8
Nantmor, Nr Beddgelert, Gwynedd. Tel: (076686) 448

The Misses M. Davis and J. Entwisle ✳ *2¹/₂m S of Beddgelert, turn left over the Aberglaslyn Bridge onto A4085. After 500 yards turn left up hill marked Nantmor. Bryn-y-Bont is second house on right* ✳ *Parking* ✳ *Plants for sale* ✳ *Open 24th, 25th May, 20th, 21st June, 11am – 5pm and April to Sept by appointment. Small parties welcome* ✳ *Entrance: 75p, children free*

This is a well-designed garden taking full advantage of the view over the Glaslyn Vale. Mixed borders and rhododendron beds give way to a woodland area where a variety of trees are being introduced. Featured in Radio Wales *Get Gardening* in 1990.

CAE HIR ★ 9
Cribyn, Lampeter, Dyfed. Tel: (0570) 470839

Mr W. Akkermans ✳ *From Lampeter take A482 towards Aberaeron. After 5m at Temple Bar take B4337 signed Llanybydder. Cae Hir is 2m further on left* ✳ *Best season: summer* ✳ *Parking* ✳ *Refreshments* ✳ *Plants for sale* ✳ *Shop* ✳ *Open daily except Mon, 1 – 6pm* ✳ *Entrance: £1.50, OAP £1.25, children 50p*

A six-acre hillside garden, created by the owner since 1985. At its best in early summer when the full effect of the various coloured areas can be seen: a formal blue garden, a circular red garden and an informal yellow garden. Plenty of seating for enjoying the views on the other side of the valley. Be sure to find the bonsai corner tucked behind the hedge. In the lower part of the garden is a small nursery; a water garden is being developed nearby.

CARROG ★ 10
Llanddeiniol, Llanon, Nr Aberystwyth, Dyfed. Tel: (0974) 202369

Mr and Mrs Geoffrey Williams ✳ *6m S of Aberystwyth on private road off A487* ✳ *Best seasons: spring and summer* ✳ *Parking* ✳ *Toilet facilities* ✳ *Suitable for wheelchairs* ✳ *Dogs on lead* ✳ *Open by appointment and for charity 28th June, 2 – 6pm* ✳ *Entrance: £1, children 25p*

From the flowers of varied spring bulbs to the autumn colours of rare maples and birches, this garden is alive with interest for the plant lover. Grass paths wend amongst collections of sorbus, eucalyptus and sweetly scented old-fashioned roses, with rhododendrons flowering well into summer. The walled garden is home for many treasures, such as fremontodendron, rare lilac species and *Abutilon megapotamicum*.

CEFN BERE 11
Cae Deintur, Dolgellau, Gwynedd. Tel: (0341) 422768

Mr and Mrs Maldwyn Thomas ✳ *N of Bala – Barmouth road (not by-pass) near*

Dolgellau, turn at top of the main bridge, turn right within 200 yards, then 2nd right behind school and up hill ✳ *Parking at roadside* ✳ *Refreshments in Dolgellau* ✳ *Toilet facilities* ✳ *Open spring and summer months by appointment only* ✳ *Entrance: collecting box*

This relatively small garden has a very diverse plant collection amassed over the last 35 years. Planted informally but within a formal framework, it is a delight to amateur and professional gardeners alike. The alpine house, bulb and peat frames are well worth seeing; so too are the old-fashioned roses.

CEFN ONN PARK ★ 12
Cardiff, South Glamorgan.

Cardiff City Council ✳ *From Cardiff centre take A469 under M4. Turn first right then left opposite Lisvane Station. From elsewhere, at M4 junction 32, turn S of A470. Take first left to T-junction, turn right, turn left at church, turn left at T pass under M4, first right then left opposite Lisvane Station* ✳ *Best season: spring and early summer* ✳ *Parking* ✳ *Toilet facilities* ✳ *Suitable for wheelchairs* ✳ *Dogs on lead* ✳ *Open all year during daylight hours* ✳ *Entrance: free*

Cefn Onn Park is something out of the ordinary for a city. It retains a little of the formality common in such areas, with straight gravelled paths running through the centre, but from there on the similarity ends. No large areas of bedding plants, rather, large areas of informally-planted azaleas and rhododendrons. Layer upon layer of colour and perfume reaching up into the upper storey of trees, which can only be appreciated by standing on the bank opposite in order to see them at all. The camellias and magnolias here have also become trees, rather than bushes, and the visitor may have to guard against a cricked neck trying to see everything. Small streams and pools could be quite attractive, but were suffering from the usual park problem of those few visitors who find it impossible to take their rubbish home. It may also be a little dull during the summer months once the rhododendrons are over.

CENTRE FOR ALTERNATIVE TECHNOLOGY 13
Machynlleth, Powys. Tel: (0654) 702400

2¹/₂m N of Machynlleth on A487 ✳ *Parking inc. coaches at base of site, but for elderly and disabled at top of steep drive. Also access by water-balanced cliff railway* ✳ *Self-service vegetarian restaurant (Easter – Oct)* ✳ *Toilet facilities* ✳ *Partly suitable for wheelchairs* ✳ *Guide dogs only* ✳ *Plants for sale* ✳ *Shop* ✳ *Open March to 5th Jan, daily, 10am – 5pm* ✳ *Entrance: admission to whole of Centre £3.50, students and OAP £2, children £1.20, family ticket £7.50 (1991 prices)*

High in the heart of a former slate quarry, and at the heart of the environmentally-friendly community there, is the most exciting garden. Compactly laid out, using natural and recycled materials to form harmoniously-shaped raised beds, ponds and walks, the garden is vibrant (in June) with colour and insect life drawn to the organically-grown flowers and companion-planted vegetables. There are suggestions, too, for urban gardeners and displays of land reclamation, wildlife gardening, composting and solar-powered fountains. Wind turbines in different sizes and designs could be considered unusual (but highly functional) garden sculptures of the future.

CHIRK CASTLE ★ 14
Chirk, Clwyd. Tel: (0691) 777701

The National Trust ✳ *¹/₂m W of Chirk village off A5, up private drive of 1¹/₂m* ✳ *Best season: spring* ✳ *Parking 200 yards from garden* ✳ *Refreshments: light lunches and teas, picnic area in car park* ✳ *Toilet facilities* ✳ *Partly suitable for wheelchairs* ✳ *Shop* ✳ *Castle open as gardens 12 noon – 5pm (last admission 4.30pm)* ✳ *Gardens open April to 28th Sept, daily except Mon and Sat (but open Bank Holiday Mons), 3rd Oct to 1st Nov, Sat and Sun only, 12 noon to 6pm (last admission 4.30pm)* ✳ *Entrance: £3.40, children £1.70 (castle and garden)*

A six-acre garden of trees and flowering shrubs including rhododendrons and azaleas. Interesting formal gardens with some excellent nineteenth-century topiary in yew. Also a rockery garden. Herbaceous borders, ha-ha and folly. The castle dates from 1300 but is set in an eighteenth-century landscaped park.

CLYNE GARDENS ★★ 15
Black Pill, Swansea, West Glamorgan. Tel: (0792) 401737

Swansea City Council ✳ *From Swansea take Mumbles road, turn right at Woodman Roast Inn* ✳ *Best season: spring* ✳ *Parking* ✳ *Refreshments at Woodman Roast Inn* ✳ *Toilet facilities* ✳ *Suitable for wheelchairs* ✳ *Dogs on lead* ✳ *Open all year, 8am – dusk* ✳ *Entrance: free*

A large (50 acres) well-kept garden to interest everyone from the beginner to the more knowledgeable. There is a stream running through the bog area, fed by a lake via a waterfall and spanned by a Japanese bridge. A tower, built by Admiral Algernon Vivian,the last private owner of the garden, from which to view his rhododendrons, is now dwarfed by them.

COLBY WOODLAND GARDEN 16
Colby Lodge, Amroth, Narberth, Dyfed. Tel: (0558) 822800

The National Trust ✳ *Adjoining Amroth beside Carmarthen Bay* ✳ *Best season: April and May* ✳ *Parking 50 yards from garden. Disabled may park closer* ✳ *Refreshments* ✳ *Toilet facilities* ✳ *Partly suitable for wheelchairs* ✳ *Shop* ✳ *Garden open 30th March to Oct, daily, 10am – 5pm. Also open in winter during daylight hours* ✳ *Entrance: £2, children 70p*

This early nineteenth-century estate garden round a Nash-style house is now mainly woodland with some formal gardens. The walled garden is planted informally for ornamental effect. The woodland garden is planted extensively with rhododendrons and contains some interesting tree species.

CWM-PIBAU 17
**New Moat, Clarbeston Road, Haverfordwest, Dyfed.
Tel: (0437 532) 454**

Mrs Drew ✳ *From Haverfordwest take A40 through Roberston Wathen. Turn left on B4313. Follow signs to New Moat. 3m from Clarbeston Road on outskirts of New Moat, there is a concealed drive on left. Continue up ¹/₂m drive, keeping left* ✳ *Parking* ✳ *Refreshments on charity days* ✳ *Toilet facilities* ✳ *Dogs on lead* ✳ *Open all year by appointment* ✳ *Entrance: £1 for charity*

Created by Mrs Drew since 1978 and therefore still very young. It has as a background some mature woodland once belonging to a nearby manor house, and the driveway to the house is very long and rather uneven. Parking is at the start of the drive and visitors should be aware that it is quite a long, uphill walk back (although on charity days it is possible to get a lift back to the car). A good many rhododendrons have been planted along the side of the drive which leads to lawns and herbaceous plantings near the house. Paths are then signposted to take the visitor down through shrub plantings and along a stream planted with moisture-lovers. This area is still very young, but leads on to more woodland with embothriums and rhododendrons.

THE DINGLE ★ 18
Crundale, Haverfordwest, Dyfed. Tel: (0437) 764370

Mrs A.J. Jones ✳ *3m NW of Haverfordwest* ✳ *Best season: spring to autumn* ✳ *Parking* ✳ *Teas* ✳ *Toilet facilities* ✳ *Suitable for wheelchairs* ✳ *Plants for sale in small nursery adjoining* ✳ *Shop* ✳ *Open daily except Tues, March to Oct, 10am – 6pm* ✳ *Entrance: £1, children 50p, season ticket £4*

A plantsman's secluded garden where foliage and plant structure play an important part in the layout and design. A collection of many rare and unusual plants, including over 150 different old-fashioned and species roses. Formal beds, scree beds, herbaceous borders, water garden and woodland walks all blend within an informal framework.

THE DINGLE ★ 19
Welshpool, Powys. Tel: (0938) 555145

Mr and Mrs Roy Joseph ✳ *3m N of Welshpool. Take A490 to Llanfyllin for 1m and then turn left for Groespluan. After 1³/₄m fork left* ✳ *Best seasons: early June and mid-Oct* ✳ *Parking* ✳ *Toilet facilities* ✳ *Partly suitable for wheelchairs* ✳ *Plants for sale* ✳ *Open daily except Tues, 9am – 5pm* ✳ *Entrance: 75p, children free*

Four acres of south-facing, very steep garden, planted with many evergreens for year-round interest. Beds have been created with colour schemes in mind and plants have been carefully chosen to harmonise. A large pool at the bottom gives another dimension to the garden and a breathing space before climbing back to the house.

DOLWEN ★ 20
Cefn Coch, Llanrhaeadr-ym-Mochnant, Powys. Tel: (069189) 411

Mrs Frances Denby ✳ *On B4580 Oswestry – Llanrhaedr road. Turn sharp right in village at Three Tuns Inn* ✳ *Parking* ✳ *Refreshments* ✳ *Toilet facilities* ✳ *Plants for sale* ✳ *Shop* ✳ *Open May to Sept, Fri and last Sun in months May to Aug, 2 – 4.30pm* ✳ *Entrance: £1*

A woodland and water garden situated high in the hills with very good views. The owner has used the land to good advantage. The whole area is very rocky, and large boulders have been used imaginatively to create pools and support bridges across a stream. There is an interesting collection of waterside plants.

DYFFRYN BOTANIC GARDEN ★★ 21
St Nicholas, Cardiff, South Glamorgan. Tel: (0222) 593328

South & Mid Glamorgan Council ✳ *4m W of Cardiff on A4232 turn S on A4050 and then W to Dyffryn* ✳ *Parking* ✳ *Refreshments and picnics* ✳ *Toilet facilities* ✳ *Suitable for wheelchairs* ✳ *Dogs on lead* ✳ *Plants for sale* ✳ *Shop* ✳ *House now a conference centre run by Mid Glamorgan and South Glamorgan County Councils. Open air theatre in garden. Butterfly house attached to shop. Extra charge* ✳ *Open March to Oct, daily, 9am – dusk* ✳ *Entrance: £1.50, OAP and children 75p*

Dyffryn has been described as The Garden of Wales and one of Wales' best-kept secrets. An Edwardian garden, created out of a Victorian original between 1906 and 1914, it was designed by Thomas Mawson, a leading landscape architect rather overshadowed by his contemporary Lutyens. When the owner died, the garden (and Mawson's services) were retained by his son, Reginald Cory, a distinguished horticulturalist whose special interest was Eastern plants such as those brought here by E.H. Wilson. To the south of the fine house is a large open lawn with ornamental lily pond and, to the west, a series of 'rooms' each enclosed by yew. These are the Roman garden, the paved court, the swimming pool garden and the round garden. Beyond these is the west garden with large beds and borders and fine trees and shrubs. There is also a Japanese garden and a begonia garden. There is a vine walk, particularly splendid in its autumn colours. This is also the time to visit the arboretum which contains some of the finest *Acer griseum* (paperbark maple) in the country. Large greenhouse and a cacti collection in the special house in the rose garden. A full description of Dyffryn together with a note on the trees was given in the RHS journal Vol III Pt 4 (April 1986).

EDGE HILL 22
Cwmcarvan, Trelleck, Monmouth, Gwent. Tel: (0600) 860473

Mr and Mrs Tony Shearston ✳ *Telephone for directions* ✳ *Best seasons: spring and summer* ✳ *Limited parking* ✳ *Open by appointment* ✳ *Entrance: £1*

Directions are needed from the owners to discover this exceptionally lovely garden hidden down narrow lanes lush with bracken, wild flowers and ferns. The house, neatly tucked into a hillside, supports a well-behaved company of climbers including unusual species clematis scrambling to the eaves. The garden extends alongside in a series of three well-planned enclosures, separated by steps and paths, the whole reflecting 20 years of the owners' consuming love for this garden, a triumph of immaculate maintenance and creative planting. From every vantage point there are stunning views across the wide, fertile Usk valley to the Black Mountains. Inviting seats are well-placed, the impact of the surrounding wilder beauties heightened by the viewer's own position in this cultivated space with its soft velvet grass and artful planting. Contrasts of colour and form are confident and plants are happy, rarities jostling with old favourites. Summer tubs and planters overflow with marguerites, and an overall strong design is accented by fine specimen trees and conifers. Odd calls from ornamental birds break the silence.

ERDDIG ★   23
Wrexham, Clwyd. Tel: (0978) 355314

*The National Trust * 2m S of Wrexham off A525 * Best season: spring * Parking 200 yards from garden * Refreshments: licensed restaurant, also light teas and lunches, picnic area in car park * Toilet facilities inc. disabled * Suitable for wheelchairs (wheelchairs provided but house difficult) * Dogs on lead in grounds * Plants for sale * Joiner's shop manufacturing quality garden furniture * House open (last admission 4pm) * Garden open April to Sept, daily except Thurs and Fri (but open Good Fri), 11am – 6pm * Entrance: £4.50, children £2.25, groups £3.60 per person (house and garden)*

Erddig's gardens, a rare example of early eighteenth-century formal design, were almost lost along with the house. They have been carefully restored. The large walled garden contains varieties of fruit trees known to have been grown there during that period and there is a canal garden and fish pool. South of the canal walk is a Victorian flower garden. Later Victorian additions include the parterre and walk. National ivy collection here; also a narcissus collection. Parties may have conducted tours with the head gardener by prior arrangement.

FARCHYNYS COTTAGE   24
Bontddu, Gwynedd. Tel: (034149) 245

*Mrs G. Townshend * On A496 Dolgellau – Barmouth road, after Bontddu on right. Signposted * Best season: spring * Parking * Teas * Plants for sale when available * Open April to Nov, daily except Sat, 11.30am – 6pm (Wed, 2.30 – 6pm) * Entrance: by collecting box 50p*

This woodland garden overlooking the Mawddach estuary is set in natural oak and conifer woodland which adds to its attraction. There is much new planting, but azaleas, rhododendrons and magnolias are well established and would repay a spring visit when a system of pools and a stream, now being completed, should be in operation.

FOUR WINDS   25
Llanrhaedr Y.M., Nr Oswestry, Shropshire. Tel: (069189) 423

*Mr and Mrs Douglas Job * From Shrewsbury take A5 towards Llangollen, turn*

WALES

left at Knockin and keep on B4396, crossing over A483 ✷ *Best season: end June/ July* ✷ *Parking in lane* ✷ *Refreshments: tea, coffee and cakes* ✷ *Toilet facilities* ✷ *Plants for sale* ✷ *Open June to Sept, Fri, 10am – 6pm and by appointment* ✷ *Entrance: 50p, children free*

This small garden is for lovers of roses (of which there are 150 including shrub), pelargoniums and house plants. Gesneriads are a speciality, and there are African violets including Chinese types, episcias, hoyas, streptocarpus, eccremocarpus, abutilons, plumbagos, clivias and many fuchsias and chrysanthemums.

FOXBRUSH 26
Aber Pwll, Port Dinorwic, Gwynedd. Tel: (0248) 670463

Mr and Mrs B.S. Osborne ✷ *3m from Bangor on Caernarvon road, approach to Port Dinorwic on left opposite W Lodge to Vaynol Estate* ✷ *Parking in layby opposite for cars and coaches* ✷ *Refreshments* ✷ *Toilet facilities* ✷ *Suitable for wheelchairs* ✷ *Plants for sale* ✷ *Craft shop* ✷ *Garden open 19th April, 17th May, 21st June, 19th July, 11am – 5pm* ✷ *Entrance: £1*

The present owners have created this garden since they bought the site of an old mill in 1968. It is a very difficult site to garden as it is subject to extensive flooding by the stream running through its entire length. The garden is part-walled with extensive planting of this feature, and the current three acres of varied planting are also being extended each year. Many wheelbarrows are planted as small landscapes, just the right height for wheelchairs.

FRONHEULOG ★ 27
LLanfrothen, Penrhyndeudraeth, Gwynedd. Tel: (0766) 770558

Mr and Mrs J. Baily Gibson ✷ *From Llanfrothen via B4410 Rhyd road after ¹/₂m turn left, after 200 yards turn left again; opposite Hen Ysgoldy* ✷ *Limited parking* ✷ *Open mid-April to mid-Sept by appointment only* ✷ *Entrance: by collecting box*

A beautifully-kept garden where the natural contours and exposed rocks have been cleverly exploited. A rich variety of heathers and conifers give colour and interest at all times. New and surprising areas continually open up during the visit. A fascinating and imaginative example of cultivating a natural hillside to the best advantage. Dramatic views.

GLAN SEVERN 28
Berriew, Welshpool, Powys. Tel: (0686) 640200

Mr and Mrs N. Thomas ✷ *From Welshpool take A483 S. After 5m the entrance is on left by bridge over River Rhiew* ✷ *Parking* ✷ *Toilet facilities* ✷ *Suitable for wheelchairs* ✷ *Plants for sale* ✷ *Open by appointment only all year, 2 – 6pm* ✷ *Entrance: £1, children 10p*

Large mature garden reclaimed by new owners. A three-acre lake with islands where ducks and moorhens breed. The stream which feeds the lake is newly planted along the banks with moisture-loving plants. A large area of lawn contains mature trees, herbaceous borders and a water feature. A grotto which has been carefully restored is now being replanted.

GLEBE HOUSE ★ 29
Guilsfield, Welshpool, Powys. Tel: (0938) 553602

Mrs Jenkins and Mrs Habberley ✳ 3m N of Welshpool off A490 (Llanfyllin) ✳ Parking ✳ Toilet facilities ✳ Suitable for wheelchairs ✳ Open by appointment ✳ Entrance: £1

This is a real cottage garden. A series of small gardens lead off from each other, with a mixture of shrubs, herbaceous plants, roses, herbs and fruit. Backing everything and climbing up the walls and trees is a large collection of clematis, said to total 130 varieties.

HAFOD GARREGOG 30
Nantmor, Caernarfon, Gwynedd. Tel: (076686) 282

Hugh and Angela Mason ✳ 5m N of Penrhyndeudraeth ✳ Parking ✳ Partly suitable for wheelchairs ✳ Dogs on lead ✳ Open 10th May, 11am – 5pm and April to Sept by appointment ✳ Entrance: 75p, children free

A small garden created by the owners since 1971 in a woodland setting with fine mountain views above the River Hafod. The garden is essentially rhododendrons and azaleas, with a lot of other colour, especially foliage colour provided by shrubs. There is a vegetable garden and water garden.

HEN YSGOLDY 31
Llanfrothen, Penrhyndeudraeth, Gwynedd. Tel: (0766) 771231

Mr and Mrs Michael Jenkins ✳ From Llanfrothen via B4410 to Rhyd, after ¹/₂m turn left. Garden is first on right opposite drive to Fronheulog ✳ Limited parking ✳ Open April to Sept by appointment ✳ Entrance: by charity collecting box

The site provides great opportunities with two streams, several different levels within the two acres, a natural sloping rock face turned into a heather garden and a naturally-formed rockery. Rich alluvial soil and an extremely mild and sheltered position afford maximum and varied growing conditions. All these advantages have been fully exploited by the garden's creator and the present owners. The result is a garden of continually unfolding aspects of establishing trees and shrubs, including magnolias, rhododendrons, azaleas and embothriums which have been supplemented by a rich and varied collection of herbaceous plants; hostas, crocosmias, ligularias and ferns provide colour and interest through to autumn.

MAENAN HALL 32
Nr Llanrwst, Gwynedd. Tel: (0492) 640441

The Hon Christopher McLaren ✳ 2m N of Llanrwst on E side of A470, ¹/₄m S of

Maenan Abbey Hotel ✳ *Parking* ✳ *Teas* ✳ *Suitable for wheelchairs* ✳ *Plants for sale* ✳ *Open 17th May, 30th Aug, 11am – 5pm (dates not finalised at time of going to press)* ✳ *Entrance: £1.40, children 50p*

Created in 1956 by the late Christabel Lady Aberconway, formal gardens surround the Elizabethan and Queen Anne house. These develop to less formal gardens and 10 acres of mature woodland. The present owners have extended the planting of ornamental trees and shrubs in both formal and informal settings. Azaleas, rhododendrons and camellias, the latter situated in a dell at the base of a cliff, will make a spring visit rewarding, whilst a large number of eucryphias will be spectacular in late summer. There are many distinctive aspects of the garden including a fine collection of roses. Not far from Bodnant (see entry).

NEWCASTLE HOUSE ★★ 33
West Road, Bridgend, Mid-Glamorgan. Tel: (0656) 766880

Mr Fraser-Jenkins ✳ *From Bridgend town centre go 400 yards up Park Street, turn right to St Leonards Road and right into West Road* ✳ *Parking* ✳ *Toilet facilities* ✳ *Open by appointment* ✳ *Entrance: £1*

This brings new meaning to the term 'plantsman's garden' for here is indeed a creation by an unusually knowledgeable plantsman. It is a relatively small town garden, made up of several smaller, interconnected gardens totally surrounded by walls. The lush planting within means each area is self-contained and yet leads on to the next, giving the visitor a feeling of being many miles from civilisation rather than a short distance from a busy town. Unusual trees abound here, and the sympathetic walls are hosts to a variety of shrubs and climbers, some well-known like roses and clematis, others rarely heard of and even more rarely seen. Rhododendrons, camellias, pieris and other lime haters defy the rules and flourish in a garden overlying limestone. The fern lovers can see the NCCPG collection of *Dryopteris*; go in June and you will see a huge specimen of *Buddleia colvillei* dripping with its unusual flowers. Cold greenhouses shelter plants too tender for even this favoured garden. Many plants have been raised by the owner who is always ready to share his knowledge with the visitor.

7, NEW STREET 34
Talybont, Aberystwyth, Dyfed. Tel: 097086) 529

Miss M. Henry ✳ *6m NE of Aberystwyth on A487 in Talybont* ✳ *Parking on main road opposite Shell garage* ✳ *Refreshments in village* ✳ *Plants for sale* ✳ *Open all year by appointment* ✳ *Entrance: collecting box for charity*

A very good example of what can be achieved in a tiny space. Although only 5 yards wide and 25 yards long, the owner has managed to give the impression of a much larger garden. Design has played an important part in the arrangement: small paths and steps, changes in levels, several areas in which to sit and plants used as screens have made this a garden to walk round rather than see at a glance. Pots and home-made troughs make ideal homes for small plants, many of which spill out and seed themselves to give an informal touch. By no means all the plants are naturally small – some quite large shrubs and trees are kept to scale by very clever and careful pruning.

PANT-YR-HOLIAD ★   35
Rhydlewis, Llandysul, Dyfed. Tel: (023975) 493

Mr and Mrs G. Taylor ＊ From Cardigan take coast road to Brynhoffnant. Take B4334 towards Rhydlewis for 1m, turn left and garden second left ＊ Best season: spring ＊ Parking ＊ Teas by appointment ＊ Toilet facilities ＊ Partly suitable for wheelchairs ＊ Plants for sale ＊ Open Easter to Sept, Wed, Fri and Sun, 2 – 5pm ＊ Entrance: £1, children 50p

This five-acre woodland garden, created by the owners since 1971, was started in an area of natural woodland backing on to the farmhouse. Over the years since then, hundreds of rhododendrons (species and hybrids) have been planted along the banks. Acers, eucalyptus, eucryphias and many other rare and unusual trees are now reaching maturity, and the paths wander in and around to give something to please the eye wherever the visitor may care to look. A stream runs through the middle of the garden creating a boggy area which is home for iris and primulas as well as the numerous species of ferns which abound here and also giving a congenial home to a *Rhododendron macabeanum*. A fairly recent addition to the garden is a summer walk along which slate-edged beds are filled with herbaceous plants. A small pergola has a seat, surrounded by roses, from which the lovely view over the valley may be enjoyed, and the remainder of the walk is beneath more arches of climbing roses. Nearer the house are a herb garden and alpine beds. Between the house and car park are a series of pools for ornamental waterfowl.

PENCARREG ★   36
Glan Y Menai Drive, Glyn Garth, Nr Menai Bridge, Gwynedd. Tel: (0248) 713545

Miss G. Jones ＊ 1¹/₂m NE of A545 Menai Bridge towards Beaumaris, Glan Y Menai drive is a turning on the right, Pencarreg is 100 yards down on right ＊ Parking in layby on main road, limited parking on the courtyard for small cars and disabled ＊ Suitable for wheelchairs ＊ Open all year by appointment only ＊ Entrance: by collecting box for charity

This beautiful garden, with a wealth of species planted for all year interest, has colour which has been achieved by the use of common and unusual shrubs. A small stream creates another delightful and sympathetically-exploited feature. The garden terminates at the cliff edge and this, too has been skilfully planted. The views to the Menai Straits and the Carneddi Mountains in the distance make it obvious why this garden has featured in two television programmes.

PENLAN-UCHAF FARM GARDENS   37
Gwaun Valley, Nr Fishguard, Dyfed. Tel: (0348) 881388

Mr and Mrs Vaughan ＊ 7m from Fishguard take B4313. 3¹/₂m from Newport take A487 to Cwm Gwaun. Situated next to Sychpant Forest car park ✻ *Parking* ✻ *Refreshments* ✻ *Toilet facilities* ✻ *Partly suitable for wheelchairs* ✻ *Dogs on lead* ✻ *Open Easter to Nov, daily, 10am – dusk* ✻ *Entrance: £1, OAP and children 50p, children under 3 free*

A medium-sized garden on a hillside near the top of the Gwaun Valley. The drive is very steep, but the view from the tea room is worth the effort. A very young garden but the owners have realised that its position will make many trees and shrubs an impossibility so they have chosen alpines and summer bedding. Some 12,000 spring bulbs, and fuchsias, geraniums and annuals give plenty of colour later. A raised herb garden, suitable for wheelchairs and the blind, is being developed.

PENRHYN CASTLE ★   38
Bangor, Gwynedd. Tel: (0248) 353084

The National Trust ✻ *1m E of Bangor on A5122* ✻ *Best season: spring and summer* ✻ *Parking* ✻ *Refreshments: hot meals and teas, picnic in grounds* ✻ *Toilet facilities inc. mother and baby facilities and disabled* ✻ *Suitable for wheelchairs, golf buggy available for garden and park* ✻ *Dogs on lead in grounds only* ✻ *Shop* ✻ *Castle open as for gardens, 12 noon – 5pm, July to Aug opens 11am (last audio tour 4pm, last admission 4.30pm)* ✻ *Garden open April to Nov, daily except Tues, 11am – 6pm* ✻ *Entrance: £2, children £1 (castle and garden £3.80)*

Large garden covering 40 acres with some fine specimen trees, shrubs and a Victorian walled garden in terraces with pools, lawns and a wild garden. Although the site of the house dates from the eighteenth century, the gardens are very much early Victorian, dating from the building of the present castle by Thomas Hopper.

PICTON CASTLE ★   39
The Rhos, Haverfordwest, Dyfed. Tel: (0437) 751379

Hon. R.H. Phillipps and Lady Marion Phillipps ✻ *2m E of Haverfordwest on A40. Signposted* ✻ *Best season: spring* ✻ *Parking* ✻ *Refreshments* ✻ *Toilet facilities* ✻ *Suitable for wheelchairs* ✻ *Dogs on lead* ✻ *Plants for sale* ✻ *Shop* ✻ *House open mid-July to mid-Sept, also Easter Sunday and Bank Holidays. Conducted tours Sun and Thurs* ✻ *Garden open Easter Sun and Mon and following Bank Holidays. Grounds open: Easter Sat to Sept, daily except Mon, 10.30am – 5pm* ✻ *Entrance: £2, children £1 (1991 prices)*

Picton Castle gardens have a history going back many hundreds of years, but it is only since 1954 that the gardens in their present form have come into being. Fortunate in having wind shelter planted many years ago, the garden flourishes and has an air of maturity although it is described by the owners as being young. Some of the shrubs are also quite ancient; a rhododendron 'Old Port' on the edge of the lawn is believed to be a few hundred years old, but the majority are much more recent. It follows that there are many labels on the rhododendrons as a great number are hybrids bred by the present head gardener and un-named. The walled garden is being reclaimed and at present contains a variety of herbs and some herbaceous plants, but needs filling up with more interesting plantings. Round this are escallonia hedges and climbing roses, including one 'Lion's Eye' raised by the gardener.

PLAS BRONDANW GARDENS   40
Llanfrothen, Gwynedd.

5m NE of Porthmadog between Llanfrothen and Croesor ∗ Parking ∗ Refreshments for groups by prior arrangement and in summer only ∗ Partly suitable for wheelchairs ∗ Open throughout the year ∗ Entrance: £1, children 25p

This garden, in the grounds of the house given to Sir Clough Williams-Ellis by his father, is quite separate from the village of Portmeirion, and was created by the architect over a period of 70 years. His main objective was to provide a series of dramatic and romantic prospects inspired by the great gardens of Italy. It includes architectural features, such as the orangery; visitors should walk up the avenue that leads past a dramatic chasm to the folly, from which there is a fine view of Snowdon.

PLAS NEWYDD   41
Llanfairpwll, Anglesey, Gwynedd. Tel: (0248) 714795

The National Trust/The Marquess of Anglesey ∗ 1m SW of Llanfairpwll ∗ Best season: spring ∗ Parking ¹/₄m from house and garden ∗ Refreshments: light lunches and teas ∗ Toilet facilities inc. disabled ∗ Suitable for wheelchairs ∗ Plants for sale in adjacent nursery (not NT) ∗ Shop ∗ House open inc. military museum ∗ Garden open April to 27th Sept, daily except Sat, 12 noon – 5pm, 2nd Oct to 1st Nov, Fri and Sun only, 12 noon – 5pm. In July and Aug gardens open at 11am (last admission 4.30pm) ∗ Entrance: £3.30 (house and garden)

An eighteenth-century house by James Wyatt, also an attraction because it contains Rex Whistler's largest wall painting. Humphry Repton's suggestion of 'plantations... to soften a bleak country and shelter the ground from violent winds' has resulted in an informal open-plan garden, with shrub plantings in the lawns and parkland, which slopes down to the Menai Straits and frame the view of the Snowdonia peaks. There is a formal Italian-style rose garden to the front of the house. The influence of the Gulf Stream enables the successful cultivation of many frost-tender shrubs and a special rhododendron garden is open in the spring when the gardens are at their best, although they are expertly tended throughout the year.

PLAS PENHELIG ★   42
Aberdovey, Gwynedd. Tel: (065472) 676

Mr and Mrs A.C. Richardson ∗ At Aberdovey, between the two railway bridges ∗ Best season: spring ∗ Parking ∗ Teas ∗ Toilet facilities ∗ Plants for sale ∗ Open 31st March to Oct, Wed – Sun, 2.30 – 5.30pm ∗ Entrance: collecting box in hotel reception

A traditional Edwardian estate garden of seven acres reclaimed over the past 10 years. An informal garden with lawns, terraces, pools, fountains, orchard, rock garden and herbaceous borders. Spring bulbs, azaleas, rhododendrons, magnolias, euphorbias, roses and some mature tree heathers of immense size. The jewel is the half-acre walled kitchen garden, including 900 square feet of glass with vines and peaches.

PLAS-YN-RHIW 43
Pwllheli, Gwynedd. Tel: (0758) 88219

The National Trust ✳ 12m from Pwllheli on S coast road to Aberdaron ✳ Best season: spring ✳ Parking 80 yards from house and garden. No coaches ✳ Toilet facilities inc. disabled ✳ Shop ✳ House open but to limited numbers ✳ Garden open April to 27th Sept, daily except Sat, 12 noon – 5pm, 4th Oct to 1st Nov, 12 noon – 4pm (last admissions ¹/₂hr before closing) ✳ Entrance: £2, children £1, family £5

Essentially a cottage garden around a partly medieval manor house, on west shore of Hell's Mouth Bay. Flowering trees and shrubs, rhododendrons, camellias and magnolias, divided by formal box hedges and grass paths extending to three quarters of an acre. The Trust has recently extended Plas-yn-Rhiw to include 150 acres of woodland, purchased from the Forestry Commission. Snowdrop wood on high ground above garden.

PORTMEIRION ★ 44
Penrhyndeudraeth, Gwynedd. Tel: (0766) 770 228 (Hotel manager)

2m SE of Portmadoc near A487 ✳ Parking at top of village ✳ Self-service restaurant open 10am – 5pm. Ice Cream Parlour ✳ Toilet facilities ✳ Partly suitable for wheelchairs but steep in places ✳ Shops ✳ Village open to hotel non-residents daily, 9.30am – 5.30pm. Guided tours by the head gardener by arrangement ✳ Entrance: £2.70, OAP £2.20, children £1.25, under 5 free. Reduced prices Nov to March

Architect Clough Williams-Ellis' wild essay into the picturesque is a triumph of eclecticism with Gothic, Renaissance and Victorian-styled buildings arranged as an Italianate village around a harbour and set in 70 acres of subtropical woodlands crisscrossed by paths. This 'light opera' is played out against the backdrop of the Cambrian mountains and the vast empty sweep of estuary sands. The gentle humour of the architecture extends to the plantings in both horizontal and vertical planes – in formal gardens and in the wild luxuriance which clings to rocky crags. One visitor was overheard to remark that 'only the plastic geckos were missing'. Portmeirion provides one of Britain's most stimulating objects for an excursion, and during the period of the June festival in nearby Criccieth there are nine other good gardens open in the district. Write (with SAE) to Criccieth Festival Office, PO Box 3, 52 High Street, Criccieth, Gwynedd LL52 0BW for details.

POST HOUSE GARDENS ★ 45
Cwmbach, Whitland, Dyfed. Tel: (09948) 213

Mrs Jo Kenaghan ✳ From Carmarthen W on A40, take B4298 through Meidrim.

*Leave by centre lane signposted Llanboidy, turn right at crossroads signposted Blaenwaun then right at next crossroads to Cwmbach * Best seasons: spring and early summer * Parking in official car park * Refreshments * Toilet facilities * Partly suitable for wheelchairs * Plants for sale * Shop * Open all year during daylight hours * Entrance: £1, OAP 75p, children 50p*

Some five acres of woodland valley garden, begun in 1978, wind along the bank of the River Sien. Paths lead through shrubberies to a large pool with golden orfe and grass carp, then by a bridge across the river and back by stepping stones to a bog garden (also reached by path). Steps lead up to paths at higher levels which meander between shrubberies housing many species and hybrid rhododendrons and on through a rose garden planted with old roses. Above the pond a summerhouse provides seating from which to see *Rosa filipes* 'Kiftsgate' and 'Himalayan Musk Rose' now rampant through and over adjacent trees; several other seats give views of different areas. Near the entrance to the garden a glasshouse (built over an old mill) and a conservatory extend the range of well-known and unusual plants, which together with the wild flowers and wooded background make up this interesting garden.

POWIS CASTLE ★★ 46
Welshpool, Powys. Tel: (0938) 4336

*The National Trust * ³/₄m from Welshpool on A483, well signposted * Parking * Refreshments: Teas and light lunches * Toilet facilities * Partly suitable for wheelchairs (but not castle) * Plants for sale * Shop * Castle open * Garden open April to June, and Sept to 1st Nov, daily except Mon and Tues. In July and Aug, daily except Mon but open Bank Holiday Mon, 11am – 6pm. 'Meet the gardener' tours by special arrangement * Entrance: £3.20, children £1.60 (garden and museum), £5.40, children £2.70 (castle, garden and museum)*

This is a garden originally laid out in 1720 based on even earlier designs. Its most notable features are broad hanging terraces interestingly planted with huge clipped yews. On the second terrace, brick alcoves opposite fine lead urns and figures above the orangery below. Some fruit trees remain on the terraces where in the nineteenth century advantage was taken of the micro-climate to grow fruit and vegetables until a kitchen garden was established. The latter is now a flower garden. Unusual and tender plants and climbers prosper in the shelter of walls and hedges. This garden is not for the faint-hearted because it is very steep, but it's well worth the effort to relish the views which are as fine as any, anywhere. A good collection of old roses. Excellent guide book available with lists of plants.

SAUNDERSFOOT BAY LEISURE PARK 47
Broadfield, Saundersfoot, Dyfed.

*Mr Ian Shuttleworth * On B4316 ³/₄m from centre of Saundersfoot * Parking * Toilet facilities * Suitable for wheelchairs * Dogs on lead * Plants for sale * Open 30th March to 28th Sept, daily, 10am – 5pm * Entrance: 50p*

An unusual garden as it has been designed around a 20-acre holiday caravan park. Different and interesting shrubs have been used as hedges round the caravans; there are large herbaceous borders, and unusual trees and shrubs surround the whole park. The central area of lawns is framed by mixed herbaceous and shrub borders, and leading past a colourful planting of conifers to a laburnum walk is a large water feature. The Park also holds the National collection of *Potentilla fruticosa*.

TREM-AR-FOR 48
125 Cwm Road, Dyserth, Clwyd. Tel: (0745) 570349

Mr and Mrs L. Whittaker ∗ Take A5151 Dyserth – Rhuddlan road. Turn left at crossroads signed Cwm, fork left and at traffic derestriction sign house on left ∗ Best season: spring ∗ Parking ∗ Plants for sale when available ∗ Open by appointment only ∗ Entrance: by collecting box

This small three-quarter-acre garden offers dramatic views of Snowdon and Anglesey and is of great interest to the enthusiastic gardener. Its steep limestone terraces are filled with many rare and interesting plants with special emphasis on alpines.

TYNANT 49
Moelfre, Clwyd. Tel: (069170) 381

Mr and Mrs D.J. Williams ∗ 8m W of Oswestry take B4580 to Llansilin, thence follow signs to Moelfre. Signposted ∗ Parking ∗ Suitable for wheelchairs ∗ Plants for sale when available ∗ Open by appointment all year ∗ Entrance: £1, OAP and children 50p

Well-stocked and imaginatively-planted areas around the house, from damp-loving riverside plants to a scree bed. A wild woodland walk along the mill stream. The most bold undertaking was the planting of two acres of steep hillside with many and varied shrubs and trees, (often grown from seed), with interesting use of ground-cover plants and interplanting of shrub roses. Not many would have undertaken the planting of such a steep site nor been so successful in its outcome.

VAYNOR PARK 50
Berriew, Welshpool, Powys. Tel: (0686) 640406

Mr and Mrs W. Corbett-Winder ∗ 1m from Berriew off B4385 Welshpool – Newtown Road ∗ Best season: May to Oct ∗ Parking ∗ Refreshments and toilet facilities in Berriew ∗ Open May, daily, 10am – 6pm and June to Oct by appointment ∗ Entrance: donations to charity

Mature parkland garden with fine old trees. Old climbing roses, herbaceous borders, rose garden and fine views of surrounding countryside.

WALES NATIONAL GARDEN FESTIVAL 51

The National Garden Festival for 1992 is being held on an island site in the valley town of Ebbw Vale, Gwent. It opens on 1st May and closes on 4th Oct. This festival will restore a site of classic industrial dereliction and provide jobs in an area where unemployment has now reached 45 per cent.

This is the fifth and probably the last of the series of National garden festivals which began in 1984 and, like the others, is designed to improve a site previously spoiled, in this case by mining and steel works. But at Ebbw vale the site, in the bottom and climbing high up one flank of a steep-sided valley, is by far the most spectacular. And with so much time available for planning the structural planting of thousands of trees and shrubs was already well established by 1990; they are now satisfactorily mature. High on the valley side is a large area of natural woodland which has existed for many years, and here a woodland walk gives splendid views over the whole vale. Another outstanding area of the festival is the large lake with its Chinese tea house. Thanks to the marvels of modern landscape engineering the lake is located 23 metres above the River Ebbw which flows in pipes below. Further particulars from Garden Festival Wales, Festival House, Victoria, Ebbw Vale, Gwent or telephone (0495) 350198.

WINLLAN 52
Talsarn, Lampeter, Dyfed. Tel: (0570) 470612

Mr and Mrs Ian Callan ＊ 8m NNW of Lampeter on B4342 ＊ Best season: May to mid-July ＊ Parking ＊ Home-made teas on charity open day ＊ Partly suitable for wheelchairs ＊ Dogs on lead but not on charity open day ＊ Plants and crafts for sale on charity open day ＊ Small shop ＊ Open 21st June, 2 – 5.30pm and May and June, daily except Fri, and July and Aug, Mon – Fri, 12 noon- 6pm. Coaches by appointment ＊ Entrance: £1, children 50p, under 12 free

This six-acre garden has been created by the owners solely as a haven for the wildlife which is disappearing so rapidly countrywide. Starting from the barren patch of riverbank, the soil from the first area was scraped away and deposited in the second field. A few years on now, this first area is home to over 200 wild flowers and more appear all the time; these in turn attract the butterflies which thrive in the rich meadow. Where the soil was deposited, a small area of woodland was planted and again this has its attendant wild flowers and birds. Beyond the wood is a hay meadow, and along the length of the garden is the river creating another habitat. Although there is a small area of conventional garden, rather unimaginatively planted, the emphasis is on the wild inhabitants – a small pond is a very lively habitat, with frogs, toads and dragonflies.

YNYSHIR HALL 53
Eglwsfach, Machynlleth, Powys. Tel: (0654) 781209

Mr and Mrs R. Reen ＊ On A487 Aberystwyth to Machynlleth road in village of Eglwysfach ＊ Best season: May/June ＊ Parking ＊ ☆Refreshments ＊ Toilet facilities ＊ Dogs on lead ＊ Open all year ＊ Entrance: £1

Although the house was once owned by Queen Victoria, the 12 acres of gardens were not really developed and extensively planted until in the hands of William Mappin who owned the Hall from 1930-70. During this time many unusual trees were planted and the grounds were landscaped. Water played an important part in the garden, and the present owners have discovered pools and a water course which are being cleared and replanted. The trees are now nearing maturity and are very fine specimens which create a noble background for a variety of rhododendrons, azaleas, camellias and other shrubs. Early visitors can see massed plantings of daffodils and fritillaries, moving on to magnolias and other later-flowering shrubs, finishing the season with autumn colour from the maples. There is a famous 'Ironstone tree' dating from the period when Queen Victoria visited the Hall. The 500 acres of woodland round the house were given to the RSPB by Mappin. The Hall itself is now a hotel, with the Victorian walled garden used to grow produce for guests.

Biographies of the Great Gardeners

SIR CHARLES BARRY (1795-1860) A highly successful architect (Houses of Parliament etc), he popularised the formal Italian style of gardening in the mid-nineteenth century creating impressive designs incorporating terraces, flights of steps, balustrading, urns, fountains and loggias. His most notable gardens were at Trentham Park (Staffordshire), Dunrobin Castle (Highlands), Cliveden (Buckinghamshire) and Shrubland Hall (Suffolk).

CHARLES BRIDGEMAN (– 1738) Famous for the way in which he exploited the outstanding features of the sites for which he designed gardens, Bridgeman provides the link between the rigid formality of much of seventeenth-century garden design and the apparent freedom of the landscape movement pioneered by William Kent and 'Capability' Brown. While retaining features such as geometric parterres close to the house and straight alleys, he also incorporated wilderness and meadow areas linked by meandering paths. By introducing the ha-ha wall he made vistas of the surrounding landscape part of his designs. Apart from work for Royal patrons such as Kensington Gardens (where he was responsible for the Round Pond and the Serpentine) Bridgeman carried out important works at Blenheim (Oxfordshire), Claremont (Surrey), Rousham (Oxfordshire) and Stowe (Buckinghamshire).

LANCELOT 'CAPABILITY' BROWN (1716 – 1783) Having worked as head gardener and clerk of works at Stowe early in his career, Brown became familiar with the work of Bridgeman and Vanbrugh and helped to execute the designs of William Kent and James Gibbs. Their influence was particularly noticeable in the buildings he designed for his later schemes. However, he was much more radical than any of them, discarding formality when creating very natural-looking landscapes for his clients. Banishing all flowering plants and vegetables he confined them in walled gardens well away from the house and by using ha-ha walls to prevent the ingress of cattle he made the surrounding meadow land appear to run right up to the house walls. Making lakes by excavation and damming streams, he used the excavated soil to create slopes elsewhere which he clad with distinctive clumps of often quite large specimens of native trees to provide the type of park which seemed to flow naturally into the countryside and suited the hunting requirements of the sporting eighteenth-century squirearchy. To many people it seems that Brown strove to bring the rolling landscapes of his native North Northumberland to his clients' parks in the flatter midlands and South.

PERCY CANE (1881 – 1976) A great admirer of Harold Peto, he was editor and owner of *My Garden Illustrated* and *Garden Design* before World War II. He designed many large gardens in Britain and overseas, in which he resolved the conflict between the formal and naturalistic approach to design by arranging formal features such as terraces close to the house and allowing the treatment to become more and more relaxed as the boundaries of the garden were approached. Some of his best work in England was done at Dartington Hall in Devon.

MARGERY FISH (1888 – 1969) An informed plantswoman and influential lecturer and author who was a great partisan of the nineteenth century designer William Robinson's naturalistic approach to gardening. This she applied on a cottage scale in her own garden at East Lambrook Manor in Somerset, now being preserved very much as it was during her lifetime.

CHARLES HAMILTON (1704 – 86) Under the influence of William Kent between 1738 and 1773, when he was obliged to sell the estate at Painshill Park in Surrey to pay his debts, Hamilton created one of Britain's most picturesque landscape gardens which is now in process of being restored. As well as being a talented designer, he was an exemplary plantsman incorporating many exotics in his schemes, particularly those from North America. He also designed a cascade and grotto at Bowood in Wiltshire and advised on work at Holland Park in London and Stourhead in Wiltshire.

HENRY HOARE II (1705 – 85) He was the scholarly member of the banking family and greatly influenced the design of the great landscape garden at Stourhead in Wiltshire. A friend of Charles Hamilton, Lord Burlington and William Kent, he shared their naturalistic approach towards landscaping.

GERTRUDE JEKYLL (1843 – 1932) By both her writings and the example of her work (much of it accomplished in partnership with the architect Sir Edwin Lutyens) during the last years of the last century and the first quarter of this, she has probably had as much influence on the appearance of British gardens as any other designer. As someone trained initially as a painter and an embroiderer, her great strength was in carefully considered and subtle use of plant colour. Finding inspiration in the happy informality of cottage gardens, she created large interwoven swathes of plants rather than confining them to precise, 'spotty' patterns and in so doing she changed our attitude towards the way in which borders should be planted. One of the best examples of Gertrude Jekyll's work in partnership with Edwin Lutyens has recently been restored at Hestercombe Court (Somerset). [Note: Her name rhymes with Treacle].

SIR GEOFFREY JELLICOE (1900 –) Shortly after becoming an architect, Jellicoe made an extensive study of Italian gardens with J.C. Shepherd which led to their producing in 1925 what has become a classic book *Italian Gardens of the Renaissance*. The publication of *Gardens and Design* in 1927 confirmed his understanding of basic principles and helped to bring him interesting commissions such as the design of a very large formal garden at Ditchley Park in Oxfordshire. After World War II he was given much public work, including the large water garden in Hemel Hempstead town centre, the Cathedral Close in Exeter, the Kennedy memorial at Runnymede and a large theme park at Galveston in Texas. Among his work for private clients, the gardens at Sutton Place in Surrey and at Shute House in Dorset are notable. His witty designs have a strong architectural quality and he tends to leave the planting to other people. In the past his late wife Susan suggested the planting for many of his schemes and she shared the authorship of the very authoritative *The Landscape of Man* published in 1975 which discusses very fully the history and art of landscape design. He is now working on a vast scheme in the United States.

LAWRENCE JOHNSTON (1871 – 1948) One of the most outstandingly stylish twentieth-century gardeners, Johnston was an American who spent much of his youth in Paris and built two great gardens in Europe and influenced the design of a great many others, such as that of Harold Nicolson and Vita Sackville-West at Sissinghurst in Kent. He began to make the garden at Hidcote Manor in Gloucestershire in 1905 and in Britain pioneered the idea of creating a series of sheltered and interconnected garden 'rooms' each of which surprised by its different contents and treatment. Close to Menton in Southern France, at a property called La Serre de la Madone, Johnston could include in his planting schemes many Southern Hemisphere plants which were not hardy enough to survive at Hidcote and allow his formal schemes to be softened by the terracotta, orange tree, and bougainvillea, of the Mediterranean.

INIGO JONES (1573 – 1652) Best known as a prolific architect, Jones brought formal Palladian ideas acquired on two visits to Italy to garden design at Arundel House in Sussex, Wilton House in Wiltshire and Lincoln's Inn in London. Apart from his own work, he strongly influenced William Kent (see below) who edited a book of his designs.

WILLIAM KENT (1685 – 1748) This former apprentice coach painter from Hull twice made the Grand Tour of Italy with his most influential patron, Lord Burlington. Heavily influenced by the paintings of Claude and Salvator Rosa, he later tried to introduce the type of romantic landscape encountered in their canvases into his gardens, freeing them from much of the formality which had dominated previous British gardening. His work at Rousham (Oxfordshire), Holkham Hall (Norfolk), Chiswick House (London), Claremont (Surrey) and Stowe (Buckinghamshire) had a great influence on Lancelot Brown, Charles Hamilton of Painshill Park and Henry Hoare of Stourhead.

BATTY LANGLEY (1696 – 1751) A landscaper and architect who was an early partisan of the transitional garden in which a formal layout was allied to a slightly freer and more natural planting. While by no means advocating the totally natural approach to landscaping adopted by 'Capability' Brown later in the century, his book *New Principles of Gardening* which was published in 1728 was probably responsible for changing attitudes. As an architect he remained attached to the idea that landscaped parks should contain temples, pavilions and folly ruins.

JOHN CLAUDIUS LOUDON (1783 – 1843) A prolific author who founded the very successful *Gardener's Magazine* and published a popular and comprehensive *Encyclopedia of Gardening* (first published in 1822 and regularly updated), he was a considerable influence on the design of the middle- and small-sized villa gardens being made in their thousands by the burgeoning middle class. Initially a partisan of picturesque designs, he later favoured more formal arrangements and latterly advocated the adoption of the so-called gardenesque style in which each plant was isolated and displayed to its best advantage – an approach still favoured in the beds of many of our parks. Much of his design work has been lost, but there is a good surviving example in Derby Arboretum.

SIR EDWIN LUTYENS (1869 – 1944) A fine architect who between 1893 and 1912 created approximately 70 gardens in partnership with Gertrude Jekyll. Her subtle planting always softened and complemented the strong architectural nature of his garden designs. And they in their turn splendidly integrated the house in the garden and its site. A fine example of the work of the partnership at Hestercombe in Somerset is in process of being restored. There Lutyens' genius for using classical masonry forms in a highly imaginative and individual way is wonderfully displayed. [Note: His name is pronounced to rhyme with escutcheons.]

WILLIAM NESFIELD (1793 – 1881) In a long and adventurous life he was a soldier and talented watercolour painter specialising in the depiction of cascades in Europe and America before becoming a landscaper when he was over 40. He was persuaded by his brother-in-law, the famous architect Anthony Salvin, to use his talent for making pictures to help him design gardens. While his work was eclectic and the style he chose for his gardens usually reflected that of the houses which they surrounded, he was responsible for a reintroduction of the parterre as a garden feature in the nineteenth century. One of the best can still be seen at Holkam Hall in Norfolk. At the Royal Botanic Gardens at Kew as well as a parterre he made a pond and created the vistas from the Palm House.

SIR HAROLD NICOLSON (1886 – 1968) *see* Vita Sackville-West

RUSSELL PAGE (1906 – 1985) Trained as a painter, he quickly became absorbed by garden design and between 1935 and 1939 worked in association with Sir Geoffrey Jellicoe. After the war he gained an international reputation and worked on many projects in Europe and America, including the garden at the Frick Gallery in New York and the Battersea Festival Gardens in London. He encapsulated many of his ideas about garden design in *The Education of a Gardener*, first published in 1962.

JAMES PAINE (1716 – 1789) Distinguished designer of garden buildings, including the bridge at Chatsworth in Derbyshire, Gibside Chapel in Tyne and Wear and the Temple of Diana at Weston Park in Shropshire.

SIR JOSEPH PAXTON (1803 – 1865) Gardened at Chatsworth in Derbyshire for 32 years from 1826 where he made the great fountain and the great conservatory in which he pioneered ideas later used in the design of the Crystal Palace. One of the early designers of public parks including that at Birkenhead and Halifax, he was also influential as a writer and was one of the founders of *The Gardener's Chronicle*.

HAROLD PETO (1854 – 1933) A talented architect who worked for the partnership which later employed the young Edwin Lutyens and who undoubtedly influenced his style. A lover of Italianate formal gardens, one of Peto's best works was his own garden at Iford Manor in Wiltshire, but his canal garden at Buscot Park in Oxfordshire and the garden on Garinish Island, County Cork, are other notable achievements which can still be enjoyed.

HUMPHRY REPTON (1752 – 1818) The most influential eighteenth-century landscaper after the death of Lancelot Brown, he was a great protagonist of Brown's ideas but he did tend to favour thicker planting than Brown, and the buildings he used to draw the eye into the landscape were rustic rather than classical. However, he restored formality to gardens in the form of terracing with flights of steps and balustrading near the house. His success in selling his ideas to clients was due to the production of excellent 'before and after' pictures of their parks, demonstrating the effects to be obtained if his schemes were adopted. These pictures with an explanatory text were bound into books which later became known as Repton's 'Red Books' because red was the colour of their binding. Repton was notable for his energy, producing over 400 Red Books and working on such fine estates as Holkham Hall in Norfolk, Sheffield Park in Sussex, Cobham Hall in Surrey, Woburn Abbey in Bedfordshire and Sheringham Park in Norfolk which is his best-preserved work.

WILLIAM ROBINSON (1838 – 1935) An Irishman who settled in England and became one of the most prolific writers and influential designers of his epoch. By his teaching and his example he liberated gardeners from the prim rigidity which had begun to dominate garden design in the mid-nineteenth century. Instead of the tightly-patterned bedding displays which the Victorians had adopted in order to show off the host of annual bedding plants which the explorers were sending home, he advocated a very free and natural attitude towards the creation of herbaceous and mixed beds. It was Robinson's attitudes towards planting which early inspired Gertrude Jekyll. Gravetye Manor in West Sussex was his most famous garden and it is still preserved at the hotel on the site.

VITA SACKVILLE-WEST (1892 – 1962) With her husband, Sir Harold Nicolson, she made two notable gardens. The first at Long Barn, Sevenoaks Weald, Kent was based on a Nicolson design which she planted during and after World War I. The second and most famous, at Sissinghurst Castle, was begun in 1932 and developed during the rest of her life. The Nicolsons were friendly with Laurence Johnston, and their attitude to gardening was certainly influenced by the ideas which he exploited at Hidcote.

WILLIAM SHENSTONE (1714 – 1763) An early partisan of picturesque gardening who bankrupted himself making a fine landscape garden of his own, Shenstone wrote an essay entitled *Unconnected thoughts on gardening* which analysed picturesque gardening and contained advice from which hundreds of landscapers have subsequently benefitted.

SIR JOHN VANBRUGH (1644 – 1726) A considerable dramatist and spectacular architect of palaces like Blenheim in Oxfordshire and Castle Howard in Yorkshire. Although he did not design landscapes himself, he ensured that his houses were magnificently sited and often created buildings for their gardens, such as the bridge at Blenheim. He also adorned landscapes made by other designers of great gardens such as Stowe in Buckinghamshire, and Claremont in Surrey.

HENRY WISE (1653 – 1738) Gardener to Queen Anne and taken into partnership by George London who ran the large Brompton Park nurseries in Kensington. The partners planted many of the last of the great formal gardens in the late-seventeenth century tradition at Chelsea Hospital, Longleat House in Wiltshire, Hampton Court, Bushey Park and Kensington Palace.

Specialist Gardens

ARBORETA

Many of the gardens in the *Guide* are extensively treed, and this list concentrates on mature arboreta, in which the trees are labelled.

Avon *Claverton Manor*
Bedfordshire *Luton Hoo*
Cambridgeshire *Elton Hall*
Cheshire *Cholmondeley Castle Gardens, Jodrell Bank Arboretum, Tatton Park*
Cumbria and the Isle of Man *Holker Hall, Muncaster Castle*
Derbyshire *Chatsworth House*
Devon *Bicton College of Agriculture*
Dorset *Forde Abbey, Minterne Gardens*
Essex *Cracknells, Saling Hall*
Gloucestershire *Batsford Arboretum, Westonbirt Arboretum*
Hampshire and Isle of Wight *The Sir Harold Hillier Gardens and Arboretum*
Hereford and Worcester *Eastnor Castle, Hergest Croft*
Hertfordshire *The Beale Arboretum*
Kent *Bedgebury National Pinetum, Belmont, Emmetts Garden, Ladham House, Riverhill Gardens*
Leicestershire *Wartnaby Gardens, Whatton House*
Lincolnshire *Grimsthorpe Castle*
London (Greater) *Royal Botanic Gardens, Kew*
Manchester, Greater *Haigh Hall Gardens*
Merseyside *Ness Gardens*
Midlands (West) *University of Birmingham Botanic Garden*
Norfolk *Holkham Hall*
Oxfordshire *University Arboretum*
Shropshire *Hodnet Hall*
Suffolk *The Rookery*

Surrey *Coverwood Lakes and Garden, London University Botanic Gardens, Royal Horticultural Society's Garden, Tilgates, Winkworth Arboretum*
Sussex, East *Sheffield Park Garden*
Sussex, West *High Beeches, Leonardslee Gardens, Nymans, Wakehurst Place, West Dean Gardens*
Warwickshire *Arbury Hall*
Wiltshire *Bowood, Broadleas, Corsham Court*
Yorkshire (North) *Castle Howard, Thorp Perrow Arboretum*
Yorkshire (South and West) *The Northern College Gardens, Temple Newsam*
Ireland *Brook Hall, Castlewellan National Arboretum, Fota Arboretum, John F. Kennedy Arboretum*
Scotland *Blairhoyle, Castle Kennedy and Lochinch Gardens, Cruickshank Botanic Garden, Leckmelm Shrubbery and Arboretum, Monteviot*
Wales *Dyffryn Botanic Garden*

HERB GARDENS

Many gardeners now grow herbs for the kitchen, and this listing is mainly devoted to those who make an ornamental feature of necessity.

Avon *Claverton Manor*
Bedfordshire *Toddington Manor*
Cambridgeshire *Emmanuel College, Cambridge, The Herb Garden*
Cheshire *Arley Hall, Little Moreton Hall, Norton Priory Museum and Gardens*
Cornwall *Mary Newman's Cottage*
Cumbria and the Isle of Man *Acorn Bank Garden, Levens Hall*
Derbyshire *Haddon Hall, Hardwick Hall, The Herb Garden*

Dorset *Cranborne Manor, Sandford Orcas Manor*
Essex *Fanners Green, Tye Farm*
Gloucestershire *Alderley Grange, Barnsley House, Painswick Rococo Gardens (being restored), Sudeley Castle*
Hampshire and Isle of Wight *The Gilbert White Museum, Hollington Herb Garden, Petersfield Physic Garden, Queen Eleanor's Garden*
Hereford and Worcester *Staunton Park*
Hertfordshire *Hatfield House, Knebworth House*
Kent *Iden Croft Herbs, Long Barn, Marle Place, Scotney Castle, Sissinghurst Castle*
Lancashire *Leighton Hall, Sellet Hall Gardens*
Lincolnshire *Doddington Hall, Gunby Hall*
London (Greater) *Chelsea Physic Garden, Hall Place, Lambeth Palace Gardens, Museum of Garden History, 7 St George's Road*
Norfolk *Besthorpe Hall, Congham Hall Hotel, Norfolk Lavender Ltd*
Northamptonshire *Hill Farm Herbs, Holdenby House Gardens, Sulgrave Manor*
Northumberland *Bradley Gardens Nursery, Herterton House, Hexham Herbs*
Nottinghamshire *Rufford Country Park*
Somerset *Combe Sydenham Hall, Gaulden Manor, R.T. Herbs and Garden*
Suffolk *Helmingham Hall, Netherfield Herbs*
Surrey *Royal Horticultural Society's Garden*
Sussex, East *Bateman's, Clinton Lodge, Crown House, Michelham Priory, Offham House*
Sussex, West *Fitzhall, Mill House, Parham House and Gardens*
Tyne and Wear *Bede Monastery Museum*

Wiltshire *Broadleas*
Yorkshire (North) *Harlow Carr Botanical Gardens*
Scotland *Earlshall Castle, Falkland Palace Garden, Kailzie Garden, Malleny House, Monteviot*
Wales *Bodysgallen Hall, Pant-yr-Holiad, Penlan-Uchaf Farm Gardens*

ROSE GARDENS

Most of the entries are for rose gardens, though some may be included because they have a number of unusual varieties although not a rose garden as such. It is hoped that owners of listed gardens have labelled their rose varieties. Many beautiful roses will of course be found in other gardens not listed.

Bedfordshire *Luton Hoo*
Berkshire *Stratfield Saye*
Buckinghamshire *Chicheley Hall*
Cambridgeshire *Elton Hall, The Rectory, St John's College, Cambridge*
Cheshire *Arley Hall, Bridgemere Garden World, Cholmondeley Castle Gardens, Dorfold Hall, Tatton Park, Tirley Garth*
Cumbria and the Isle of Man *Dalemain, Holker Hall, Hutton-in-the-Forest, Levens Hall*
Derbyshire *Haddon Hall, Kedleston Hall, Melbourne Hall*
Devon *Bickleigh Castle, Docton Mill, Powderham Castle, Rosemoor Garden*
Dorset *Cranborne Manor, The Manor House, Parnham*
Durham *Raby Castle Gardens*
Essex *Hyde Hall Garden, Panfield Hall, Saling Hall*
Gloucestershire *Abbotswood, Barnsley House, Hunts Court, Kiftsgate Court, Misarden Park Gardens, Painswick Rococo Garden, Stancombe Park, Sudeley Castle*
Hampshire and Isle of Wight *Barton Manor, Broadhatch House, Exbury*

Gardens, Fairfield House, The Gilbert White Museum, Jenkyn Place, Mottisfont Abbey, Northcourt, Nunwell House, Rotherfield Park, Stansted House, Ventnor Botanic Garden

Hereford and Worcester Eastnor Castle, Hergest Croft, How Caple Court, Spetchley Park

Hertfordshire Benington Lordship, Gardens of the Rose

Humberside Sledmere House

Kent Chartwell, Emmetts Garden, Godinton Park, Goodnerstone Park, Hever Castle, Leeds Castle, Mount Ephraim, Scotney Castle, Sissinghurst Castle, West Farleigh

Leicestershire Arthingworth Manor, Ashwell Lodge, Belvoir Castle, Whatton House

Lincolnshire Burghley House, Doddington Hall, Grimsthorpe Castle, Hall Farm and Nursery, Manor House

London (Greater) Cannizaro Park, Capel Manor, Fenton House, Gunnersbury Park, Hall Place, Hampton Court Palace, Lambeth Palace Gardens, Priory Gardens, Queen Mary's Rose Garden, Royal Botanic Gardens, Syon Park

Manchester (Greater) Heaton Hall

Merseyside Ness Gardens, Speke Hall

Midlands (West) Birmingham Botanic Gardens and Glasshouses, University of Birmingham Botanic Garden

Norfolk Glavenside, Norfolk Lavender Ltd, Mannington Hall, Rainthorpe Hall

Northamptonshire Holdenby House, Kelmarsh Hall, Rockingham Castle, Sulgrave Manor

Northumberland Belsay Hall, Chillingham Castle, Hexham Herbs

Nottinghamshire Holme Pierrepont Hall

Oxfordshire Blenheim Palace, Greys Court, Kingston Lisle Park, Oxford Botanic Garden, Stonor Park, Wroxton Abbey

Shropshire Benthall Hall, David Austin Roses, Hodnet Hall, Weston Park

Somerset The Bishops Palace, Brympton d'Evercy, Clapton Court, Combe Sydenham, Gaulden Manor, Water Meadows, Wootton House

Staffordshire Eccleshall Castle Gardens, Little Onn Hall, Shugborough, Trentham Park Gardens, Wolseley Garden Park

Suffolk Euston Hall, Helmingham Hall, Somerleyton Hall

Surrey Albury Park Mansion, Bradstone Brook, Loseley Park, Polesden Lacey, Royal Horticultural Society's Garden, The Walled Garden

Sussex, East Bateman's, Beeches Farm, Crown House, Great Dixter, Duckyls

Sussex, West Apuldram Roses, Berri Court, Hammerwood House Garden, Nymans, Parham House, Upper House

Tyne and Wear Seaton Delaval Hall

Warwickshire Arbury Hall, Farnborough Hall, Ilmington Manor, Ragley Hall, Ryton Gardens, Warwick Castle

Wiltshire Avebury Manor, Bowood House, Broadleas, Corsham Court, Heale House, Ifford Manor, Lackham College, Longleat House, Manor Farm, Pound Hill House, Wilton House

Yorkshire (North) Castle Howard, Copt Hewick Hall, Newby Hall, Norton Conyers

Yorkshire (South and West) Bramham Park, Harewood House, Lotherton Hall, Nostell Priory, Temple Newsam

Ireland City of Belfast International Rose Garden

Scotland Arbigland, Blairquhan, Cawdor, Drum Castle, Dunrobin Castle, Earlshall Castle, Hill of Tarvit, The Hirsel, Malleny House, Manderston, Mellerstain, Monteviot, Tyninghame House

Wales *Bodysgallen Hall, The Dingle (Haverfordwest), Four Winds, Vaynor Park*

WATER AND BOG GARDENS

Most of these entries are for water gardens or features; bog gardens are also included.

Avon *Goldney Hall*
Berkshire *Scotlands*
Buckinghamshire *Manor House (Lyde Garden), Stowe*
Cambridgeshire *Duxford Mill, Island Hall*
Cheshire *Arley Hall, Cholmondeley Castle Gardens, Dorfold Hall*
Cornwall *Penberth, Pencarrow (under development), Trebah, Trevarno*
Derbyshire *Chatsworth*
Devon *Coleton Fishacre Garden, Docton Mill, Ugbrooke Park*
Dorset *Charlton Cottage, Compton Acres, Forde Abbey, Mapperton House, The Old Mill, Shute House, Stour House*
Essex *The Beth Chatto Gardens, Feeringbury Manor, Glen Chantry, The Magnolias, Saling Hall, Volpaia*
Gloucestershire *Abbotswood, Bell House, Frampton Court, Lydney Park Gardens, Ryelands House, Sezincote, Westbury Court Garden*
Hampshire and Isle of Wight *Barton Manor, Exbury Gardens, Greatham Mill, Longstock Park Gardens, Merdon Manor, Spinners*
Hereford and Worcester *Burford House Gardens, Hergest Croft, How Caple Court*
Humberside *Burnby Hall, Burton Constable Hall*
Kent *Godinton Park, Ladham House, Mount Ephraim*
Lancashire *Linden Hall*
Leicestershire *Wartnaby Gardens, Whatton House*
London (Greater) *Golders Hill Park, Hampton Court Palace, Kensington Palace Gardens, 338 Liverpool Road, Walpole Park, The Water Gardens*
Manchester (Greater) *Fletcher Moss Botanical Gardens and Parsonage Gardens*
Norfolk *Glavenside, Goodnerstone Water Gardens, How Hill Garden, Lake House, Mannington Hall*
Northumberland *Chillingham Castle*
Nottinghamshire *Newstead Abbey, Pureland Japanese Garden*
Oxfordshire *Buscot Park, Cornwell Manor*
Shropshire *Brownhill House, Hodnet Hall*
Somerset *Ambleside Aviaries and Gardens, Bittescombe Manor, Clapton Court Gardens, Gaulden Manor, Water Meadows*
Staffordshire *Wolseley Garden Park*
Suffolk *Haughley Park*
Surrey *Coverwood Lakes, Hascombe Court, Pinewood House, Vann, Virginia Water Lake*
Sussex, East *Kidbrook Park, Sheffield Park Garden*
Sussex, West *Mill House, Upper House, West Dean Gardens*
Wiltshire *Bowood House, Great Chalfield Manor, Heal House, Stourhead, Wilton House*
Yorkshire (North) *Constable Burton, Newby Hall and Gardens, Studley Royal and Fountains Abbey*
Yorkshire (South and West) *Harewood House, Roundhay Park*
Ireland *Creagh, Fernhill, Japanese Garden*
Scotland *Ardtornish, Corsock House, Crarae Glen Garden, Kilbryde Castle, Kildrummy Castle Gardens, Monteviot, Torosay Castle*
Wales *Bodrhyddan, Cae Hir, The Dingle (Haverfordwest), The Dingle (Welshpool), Dolwen, Foxbrush, Glan Severn, Hafod Garregog*

WILD GARDENS AND WILDERNESSES

The term wild garden/wilderness

includes a range of types of garden, including wildlife gardens, which have been specifically designed to avoid the formal, cultivated garden. In general, the wild garden forms only a part of the total area.

Cambridgeshire *Docwra's Manor, St John's College, Cambridge*
Cheshire *Adlington Hall, Arley Hall, Dorfold Hall*
Cumbria and the Isle of Man *Corby Castle, Hutton-in-the-Forest, Levens Hall, Muncaster Castle*
Derbyshire *Chatsworth*
Devon *Arlington Court, Greenway House, Powderham Castle*
Dorset *Athelhampton, Charlton Cottage, Dean's Court, Edmondsham House, Kesworth, Mapperton, Parnham*
Essex *Olivers*
Gloucestershire *Jasmine House, Painswick Rococo Garden, Stancombe Park*
Hampshire and Isle of Wight *The Manor House*
Hereford and Worcester *How Caple Court*
Hertfordshire *Hatfield House, Knebworth House*
Humberside *The Cottages*
Kent *Godinton Park, Hole Park, Marle Place, Penshurst Place, Riverhill House, West Farleigh Hall*
Lancashire *Sellet Hall*
Leicestershire *Belvoir Castle, Whatton House*
Lincolnshire *Doddington Hall, Fulbeck Hall, Grimsthorpe Castle*
London (Greater) *Camley Street Natural Park, Hampton Court Palace, Isabella Plantation, Syon Park, Trinity Hospice*

Midlands (West) *Castle Bromwich Hall*
Norfolk *How Hill Farm, Mannington Hall, The Old Rectory*
Northamptonshire *Cottesbrooke Hall, Rockingham Castle Gardens*
Northumberland *Belsay Hall, Chillingham Castle, Hexham Herbs*
Oxfordshire *Christchurch Meadow, Oxford*
Shropshire *Limeburners*
Somerset *Combe Sydenham, Hadspen House*
Staffordshire *Eccleshall Castle*
Suffolk *Helmingham Hall, Otley Hall, Shrubland Hall*
Surrey *Hatchlands, Pyrford Court, The Royal Horticultural Society's Garden*
Sussex, East *Bateman's, Michelham Priory*

Sussex, West
Duckyls, Hammerwood House Garden, High Beeches Garden, Nymans, Stonehurst, West Dean Gardens
Warwickshire *Charlecote Park, Ryton Gardens, Warwick Castle*
Wiltshire *Corsham Court, The Courts, Stourton House Garden*
Yorkshire (North) *Constable Burton Hall, Norton Conyers*
Yorkshire (South and West) *Bramham Park*
Ireland *Annes Grove, The Burren, Downhill Castle*
Scotland *Ardtornish, Candacraig, Cawdor Castle, Crarae Glen, Mellerstain House*
Wales *Penrhyn Castle, Post House Gardens, Winllan*

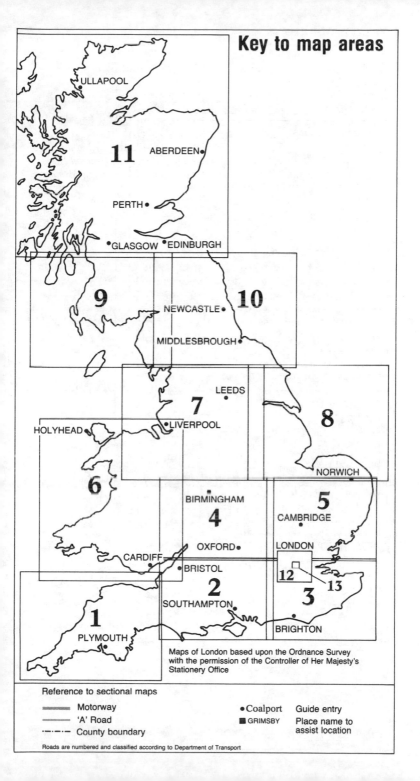

Key to map areas

ULLAPOOL

11

ABERDEEN

PERTH

•GLASGOW •EDINBURGH

9   NEWCASTLE   **10**

MIDDLESBROUGH

LEEDS

HOLYHEAD   **7**   •LIVERPOOL   **8**

6   NORWICH

BIRMINGHAM

4   CAMBRIDGE   **5**

OXFORD•

CARDIFF   •   LONDON

BRISTOL   **2**   **12** □   **13**

SOUTHAMPTON   **3**

1

PLYMOUTH   BRIGHTON

Maps of London based upon the Ordnance Survey
with the permission of the Controller of Her Majesty's
Stationery Office

Reference to sectional maps

~~~~~~ Motorway

~~~~~~ 'A' Road

–·–·– County boundary

• Coalport   Guide entry

■ GRIMSBY   Place name to
                         assist location

Roads are numbered and classified according to Department of Transport

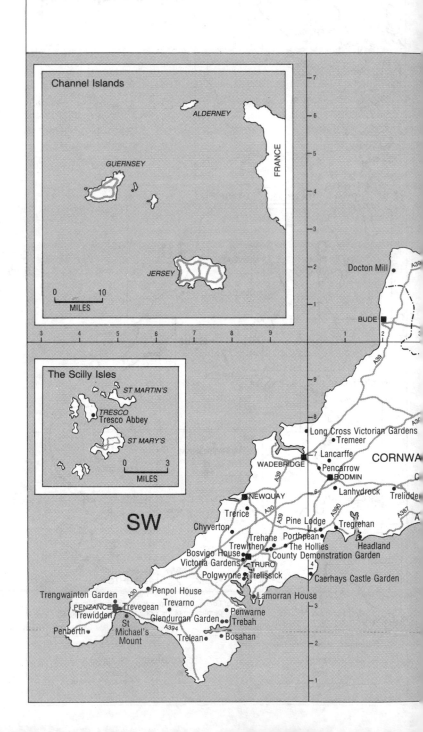

Channel Islands

ALDERNEY

GUERNSEY

FRANCE

JERSEY

0   10
MILES

The Scilly Isles

ST MARTIN'S

TRESCO
Tresco Abbey

ST MARY'S

0   3
MILES

Docton Mill •

BUDE

Long Cross Victorian Gardens
• Tremeer

Lancarffe   **CORNWA**

WADEBRIDGE   • Pencarrow
                   BODMIN

NEWQUAY   • Lanhydrock   Trelidde

Trerice   A387

Chyverton   Pine Lodge
                 Trehane   • The Hollies   Tregrehan

SW   Trewithen County Demonstration Garden   Headland

Bosvigo House   Polgwynne TRURO
Victoria Gardens   Trelissick

Trengwainton Garden   Penpol House   Lamorran House

PENZANCE   • Trevegean   Trevarno   Caerhays Castle Garden
Trewidden   Penwarne

Penberth •   St   Glendurgan Garden   • Trebah
             Michael's
             Mount   Trelean •   • Bosahan

1

The Manor House •

SS

ST

AVON

WESTON
SUPER
MARE

M5

A38

Ambleside Aviaries and Gardens •

2

Greencombe •

Seithe •

Woodborough •

Somerset College
of Agriculture

Marwood
Hill •

Arlington Court •

Dunster Castle •

Combe Sydenham Hall •

Woodside •
BARNSTAPLE ■

Barford Park •

Gaulden Manor •

Hestercombe House
Gardens •

Tapeley
Park •

A361

A39

Bittescombe Manor •

A396

TAUNTON ■

SOMERSET

Rosemoore
Garden •

A377

Parnham
House

DEVON

Middle
Hill •

Knightshayes •

A361

M5

Lower Severalls •
Wayford Manor •
Water Meadows ■

Clapton Court Gardens •
Forde Abbey • The Old
Rectory

park •

The Bungalow •

University
of Exeter •

Killerton •

A30

Croftdene •

Burrow Farm
Gardens •

Langmoor
Manor

The Glebe House •

The Old Vicarage •

The Moorings •

Andrew's
Corner •

EXETER ■

A30

Vicar's
Mead •

Castle Drogo •

Mardon •

Bicton College of Agriculture •
Bicton Park •

Higher Knowle •

Powderham
Castle •

Lee Ford •

sleigh
ouse

Ughbrooke Park •

A38

A381

R. Dart

The Garden House •

Bickham
House

Bickleigh Castle •

Dartington
Hall •

Castle Tor •

SY

ary Newman's Cottage

Saltram • Fardel Manor •

Paignton Zoo and Botanical Garden •

House

Avenue Cottage Gardens •

The Old
Rectory •

Greenway House •

Coleton Fishacre Garden •

A379

nbc
e

PLYMOUTH
udor Rose Garden
1 Beaumont Road

Overbecks
Museum and Garden •

SX

0   10   20
MILES

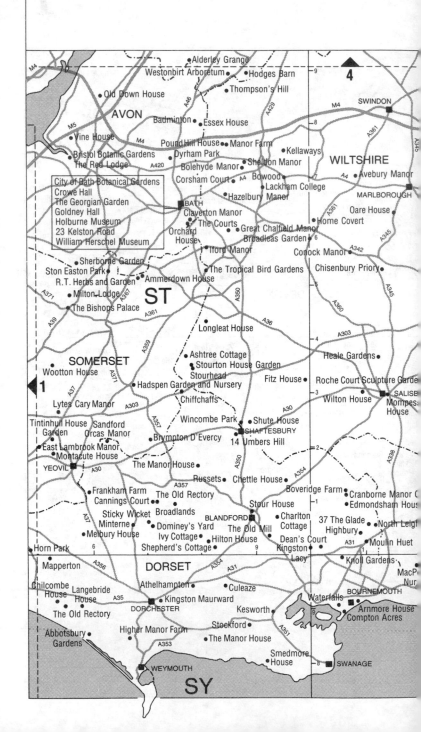

Alderley Grange
Westonbirt Arboretum • • Hodges Barn
Thompson's Hill
Old Down House

4

M4   SWINDON

AVON
Badminton • Essex House
M5
Vine House
M4   Pound Hill House • Manor Farm   Kellaways
Bristol Botanic Gardens   Dyrham Park
The Red Lodge   A420   Bolehyde Manor   Sheldon Manor   WILTSHIRE
Corsham Court   A4 Bowood   Avebury Manor
City of Bath Botanical Gardens   Lackham College
Crowe Hall   Hazelbury Manor   MARLBOROUGH
The Georgian Garden   Oare House
Goldney Hall   BATH   Home Covert
Holburne Museum   Claverton Manor
23 Kelston Road   The Courts   Great Chalfield Manor
William Herschel Museum   Orchard   Broadleas Garden   Conock Manor
                          House
Sherborne Garden   Iford Manor   Chisenbury Priory
Ston Easton Park   The Tropical Bird Gardens
R.T. Herbs and Garden   Ammerdown House
Milton Lodge
ST   A360
The Bishops Palace
A361   A303
Longleat House   Heale Gardens
A359
SOMERSET   Ashtree Cottage
Wootton House   Stourton House Garden   Roche Court Sculpture Garde
1   Stourhead   Fitz House   SALISE
Hadspen Garden and Nursery   Wilton House   Mompes
Lytes Cary Manor   A303   Chiffchaffs   House
Tintinhull House Sandford   Wincombe Park   Shute House
Garden   Orcas Manor   SHAFTESBURY
East Lambrook Manor   Brympton D'Evercy   14 Umbers Hill
Montacute House
YEOVIL   A30   The Manor House
Russets • Chettle House
Frankham Farm   The Old Rectory   Boveridge Farm Cranborne Manor (
Cannings Court   Edmondsham Hous
Sticky Wicket Broadlands   Stour House   37 The Glade North Leigh
Minterne   Dominey's Yard   BLANDFORD   Charlton   Highbury
Melbury House   Ivy Cottage The Old Mill Cottage   Dean's Court Moulin Huet
Horn Park   Shepherd's Cottage Hilton House   Kingston   Knoll Gardens
Lacy
Mapperton   A356   DORSET   MacP
Chilcombe Langebride   Athelhampton   Culeaze   BOURNEMOUTH
House   House   A35   Waterfalls   Arnmore House
The Old Rectory   Kingston Maurward   Compton Acres
DORCHESTER   Kesworth
Abbotsbury   Higher Manor Farm   Stockford
Gardens   A353   The Manor House   Smedmore
House   SWANAGE
WEYMOUTH
SY

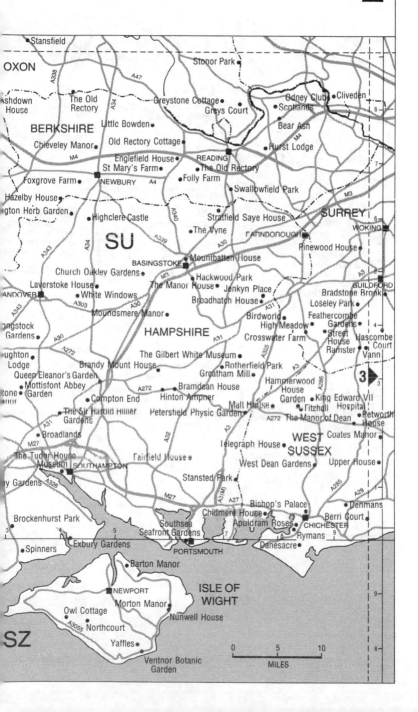

Stansfield

OXON

shdown
House

The Old
Rectory

BERKSHIRE

Chieveley Manor

Foxgrove Farm

Hazelby House

gton Herb Garden

Little Bowden

Old Rectory Cottage

Englefield House

St Mary's Farm

NEWBURY

Highclere Castle

SU

Church Oakley Gardens

Laverstoke House

ANDOVER

White Windows

Moundsmere Manor

HAMPSHIRE

ngstock
Gardens

ughton
Lodge

Queen Eleanor's Garden

Mottisfont Abbey
Garden

tone
nor

Compton End

The Sir Harold Hillier
Gardens

Broadlands

The Tudor House
Museum

SOUTHAMPTON

y Gardens

Brockenhurst Park

Spinners

Exbury Gardens

Greystone Cottage

Greys Court

READING

The Old Rectory

Folly Farm

Swallowfield Park

Stratfield Saye House

The Vyne

FARNBOROUGH

BASINGSTOKE

Mountbatten House

Hackwood Park

The Manor House

Jenkyn Place

Broadhatch House

Birdworld

High Meadow

Crosswater Farm

The Gilbert White Museum

Brandy Mount House

Rotherfield Park

Greatham Mill

Bramdean House

Hinton Ampner

Petersfield Physic Garden

Mall House

Telegraph House

Fairfield House

Stansted Park

Southsea
Seafront Gardens

PORTSMOUTH

Barton Manor

NEWPORT

Morton Manor

Owl Cottage

Northcourt

Nunwell House

Yaffles

Ventnor Botanic
Garden

Odney Club

Scotlands

Cliveden

Bear Ash

Hurst Lodge

SURREY

WOKING

Pinewood House

GUILDFORD

Bradstone Brook

Loseley Park

Feathercombe
Gardens

Street
House

Nascombe
Court

Ramster

Vann

King Edward VII
Hospital

Hammerwood
House
Garden

Fitzhall

The Manor of Dean

Petworth
House

Coates Manor

WEST
SUSSEX

West Dean Gardens

Upper House

Bishop's Palace

Chidmere House

Apuldram Roses

CHICHESTER

Rymans

Danesacre

Berri Court

Denmans

ISLE OF
WIGHT

SZ

0   5   10

MILES

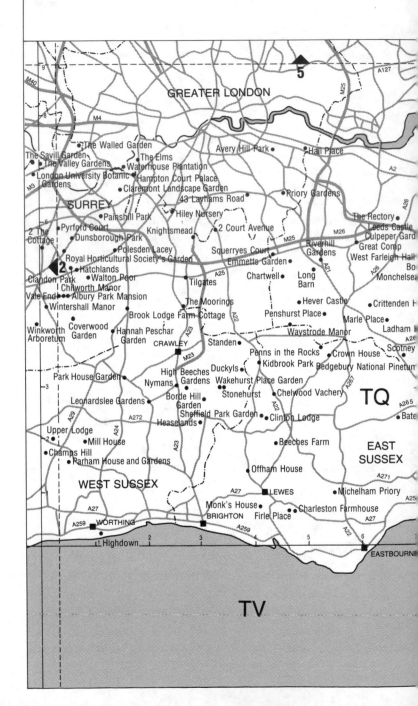

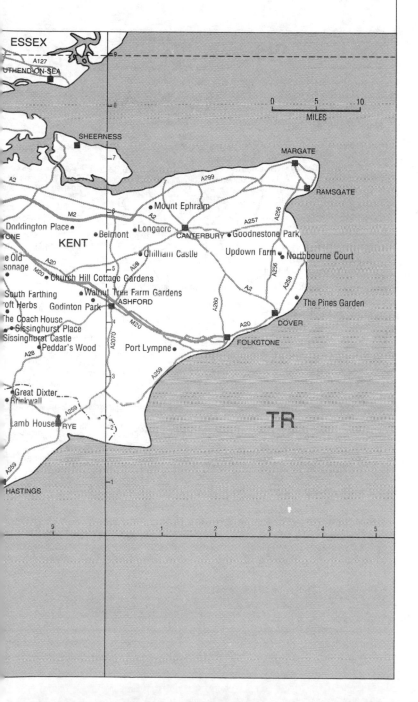

3

ESSEX

A127

UTHEND-ON-SEA

0   5   10
MILES

SHEERNESS

MARGATE

A299

RAMSGATE

A2

M2

Mount Ephraim

A2

A256

Doddington Place

Belmont

Longacre

CANTERBURY

Goodnestone Park

A257

TONE

KENT

The Old

A20

Chilham Castle

Updown Farm

Northbourne Court

sonage

M20

Church Hill Cottage Gardens

A28

A2

A256

A258

South Farthing

Walnut Tree Farm Gardens

oft Herbs

Godinton Park

ASHFORD

The Pines Garden

The Coach House

M20

A260

DOVER

Sissinghurst Place

A2070

A20

Sissinghurst Castle

FOLKSTONE

Peddar's Wood

Port Lympne

A28

A259

Great Dixter

Brickwall

A259

TR

Lamb House

RYE

A259

HASTINGS

9   1   2   3   4   5

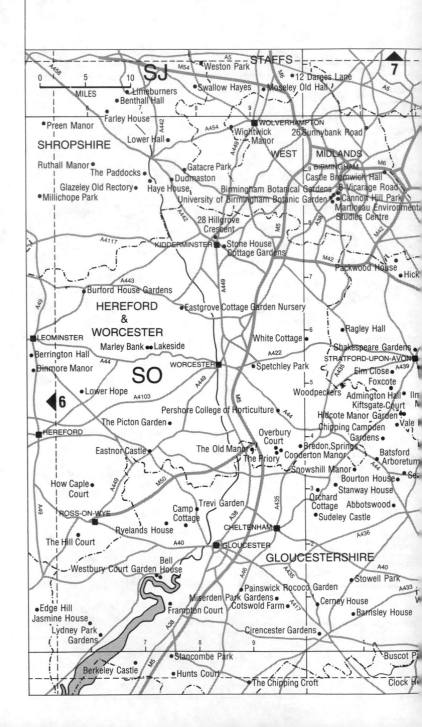

SJ

STAFFS

Weston Park

12 Darges Lane

A5

A5

A458

0   5   10
MILES

M54

M6

Limeburners

Swallow Hayes

Moseley Old Hall

Benthall Hall

Farley House

A442

A454

WOLVERHAMPTON

Preen Manor

Lower Hall

Wightwick Manor

26 Sunnybank Road

SHROPSHIRE

A449

WEST

MIDLANDS

Ruthall Manor

The Paddocks

Gatacre Park

BIRMINGHAM

M6

Castle Bromwich Hall

Glazeley Old Rectory

Dudmaston

Haye House

Birmingham Botanical Gardens

8 Vicarage Road

Millichope Park

University of Birmingham Botanic Garden

Cannon Hill Park

Martineau Environmental
Studies Centre

A4117

A442

28 Hillgrove
Crescent

M5

A38

M42

KIDDERMINSTER

Stone House
Cottage Gardens

A42

A442

A443

Packwood House

Hick

A449

Burford House Gardens

7

A49

HEREFORD
&
WORCESTER

Eastgrove Cottage Garden Nursery

6

Ragley Hall

LEOMINSTER

Marley Bank

Lakeside

White Cottage

Shakespeare Gardens

A44

A422

STRATFORD-UPON-AVON

Berrington Hall

WORCESTER

A435

Elm Close

A439

Dinmore Manor

SO

A449

Spetchley Park

Foxcote

5

Admington Hall

Ilm

6

Lower Hope

A4103

M5

Woodpeckers

Kiftsgate Court

Pershore College of Horticulture

A44

Hidcote Manor Garden

Vale

The Picton Garden

Chipping Campden
Gardens

HEREFORD

Overbury
Court

Batsford
Arboretum

Eastnor Castle

The Old Manor

Bredon Springs

Conderton Manor

A44

The Priory

Snowshill Manor

Se

How Caple
Court

A449

M50

Bourton House

Stanway House

A49

ROSS-ON-WYE

Camp
Cottage

Trevi Garden

A38

A435

3

Orchard
Cottage

Abbotswood

Ryelands House

CHELTENHAM

Sudeley Castle

The Hill Court

A40

GLOUCESTER

2

A436

Bell
House

GLOUCESTERSHIRE

Westbury Court Garden

A46

A435

A40

Painswick Rococo Garden

Stowell Park

A433

Edge Hill

Jasmine House

Miserden Park Gardens

Cerney House

W

Lydney Park
Gardens

Frampton Court

Cotswold Farm

A417

Barnsley House

A38

Cirencester Gardens

7

8

9

Stancombe Park

Buscot P

M5

Hunts Court

Berkeley Castle

The Chipping Croft

Clock F

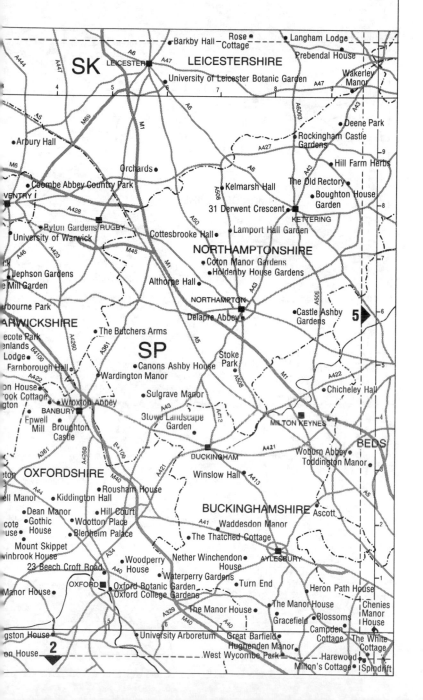

4

SK

LEICESTERSHIRE

Barkby Hall • Rose Cottage • Langham Lodge
Prebendal House
LEICESTER •
University of Leicester Botanic Garden
Wakerley Manor

• Arbury Hall

Orchards •

• Coombe Abbey Country Park

COVENTRY

Deene Park •
Rockingham Castle Gardens
Hill Farm Herbs •
The Old Rectory •
Kelmarsh Hall •
Boughton House Garden •

31 Derwent Crescent •
KETTERING
Rylton Gardens RUGBY
University of Warwick
Cottesbrooke Hall •
Lamport Hall Garden •

NORTHAMPTONSHIRE
Coton Manor Gardens •
Holdenby House Gardens •
Althorpe Hall •
NORTHAMPTON
Jephson Gardens
The Mill Garden
Harbourne Park

WARWICKSHIRE
• The Butchers Arms
Delapre Abbey •
Castle Ashby Gardens •

5

SP

Stoke Park
ecote Park
enlands
Lodge •
Farnborough Hall •
Canons Ashby House •
Wardington Manor
on House •
rook Cottage
gton
BANBURY •
Epwell Mill
Broughton Castle
Sulgrave Manor •
Stowe Landscape Garden
Chicheley Hall •

MILTON KEYNES

Woburn Abbey •
Toddington Manor •
BEDS

DUCKINGHAM
Winslow Hall •

OXFORDSHIRE
Rousham House •
Kiddington Hall •
ell Manor
Dean Manor •
Gothic House
cote
Wootton Place •
use
Hill Court •
Blenheim Palace •
Mount Skippet
winbrook House
23 Beech Croft Road
Manor House •
OXFORD •

BUCKINGHAMSHIRE
Ascott
Waddesdon Manor •
The Thatched Cottage •
AYLESBURY

Woodperry House •
Nether Winchendon House •
Waterperry Gardens •
Oxford Botanic Garden
Oxford College Gardens
The Manor House •
Turn End •
Heron Path House •

The Manor House •
Gracefield •
Blossoms
Campden Cottage
Chenies Manor House

gston House
on House

2

University Arboretum
Great Barfield
Hughenden Manor •
West Wycombe Park •

Harewood •
Milton's Cottage •
The White Cottage
Splndrift

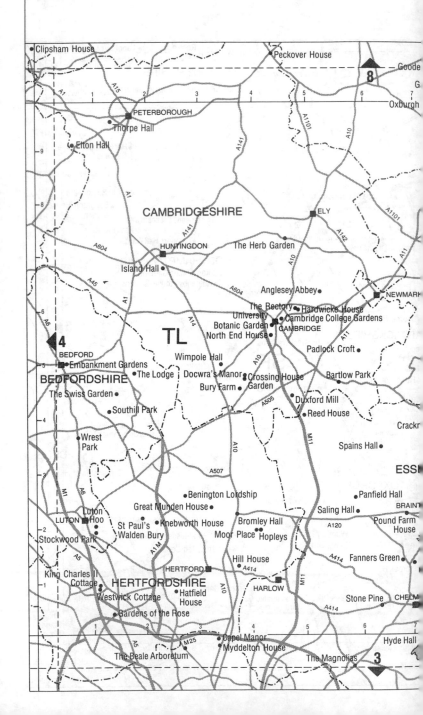

Clipsham House

Peckover House

Goode

8

G.

Oxburgh

A1 1 A15 2 3 4 5 6 7

A1101

A10

PETERBOROUGH

Thorpe Hall

Elton Hall

9

A141

A1

8

CAMBRIDGESHIRE

ELY

A1101

A604

A142

A11

7

HUNTINGDON

The Herb Garden

A10

A45

Island Hall

A604

Anglesey Abbey

NEWMARKET

A1

A14

The Rectory

Hardwicke House

6

A6

University

Cambridge College Gardens

Botanic Garden

CAMBRIDGE

4

North End House

A11

BEDFORD

TL

BEDFORDSHIRE

Embankment Gardens

Wimpole Hall

Padlock Croft

5

The Lodge

Docwra's Manor

Crossing House

The Swiss Garden

Bury Farm

Garden

Bartlow Park

A10

Southill Park

Duxford Mill

A505

Reed House

4

Wrest

Park

Crackn

A10

Spains Hall

M11

3

A507

Benington Lordship

Panfield Hall

ESSI

Great Munden House

Saling Hall

BRAINT

M1

A6

Luton

Knebworth House

Bromley Hall

A120

Pound Farm

House

LUTON

Hoo

St Paul's

Moor Place

Hopleys

2

Stockwood Park

Walden Bury

A1M

A414

Fanners Green

A5

Hill House

King Charles II

HERTFORD

A414

Cottage

A10

HARLOW

M11

Stone Pine

CHELM

1

Westwick Cottage

HERTFORDSHIRE

Hatfield

House

Gardens of the Rose

A414

1 2 3 4 5 6 7

A5

Capel Manor

Hyde Hall

The Beale Arboretum

M25

Myddelton House

The Magnolias

3

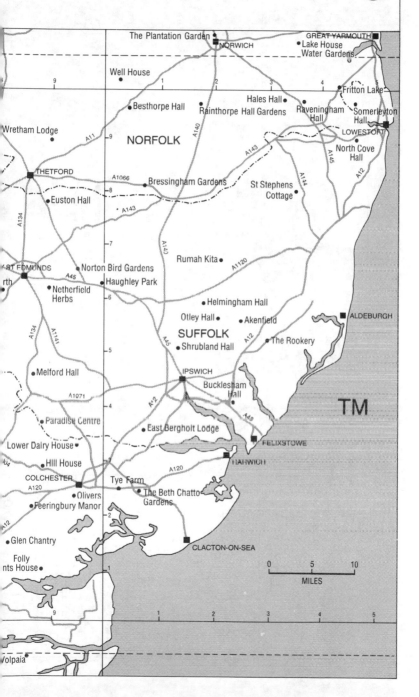

The Plantation Garden • NORWICH
GREAT YARMOUTH ■
• Lake House
Water Gardens

Well House •

Besthorpe Hall •
Rainthorpe Hall Gardens •
Hales Hall •
Raveningham Hall
• Fritton Lake
Somerleyton Hall

Wretham Lodge •

NORFOLK

LOWESTOFT

THETFORD ■
A1066
Bressingham Gardens •
St Stephens Cottage •
North Cove Hall
A143

• Euston Hall

A143

Rumah Kita •
A1120

ST EDMUNDS
• Norton Bird Gardens
A45
• Haughley Park
• Netherfield Herbs
Helmingham Hall •
Otley Hall • • Akenfield
SUFFOLK
• Shrubland Hall
• The Rookery
ALDEBURGH ■

• Melford Hall
A1071
IPSWICH ■
Bucklesham Hall
TM

• Paradise Centre
• East Bergholt Lodge

Lower Dairy House •
FELIXSTOWE
• Hill House
HARWICH

COLCHESTER ■
A120
Tye Farm •
• The Beth Chatto Gardens
• Olivers
• Feeringbury Manor

• Glen Chantry

Folly
nts House •

CLACTON-ON-SEA ■

0   5   10
MILES

Volpaia

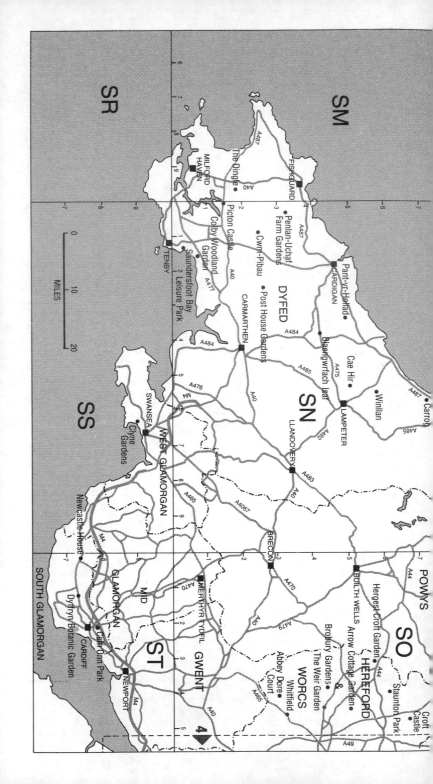

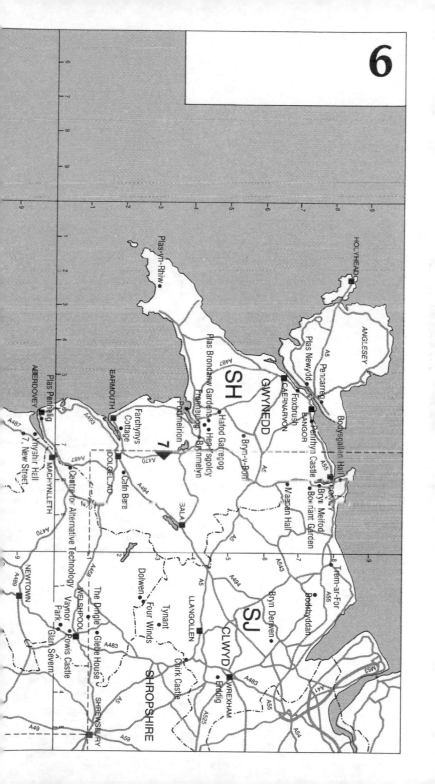

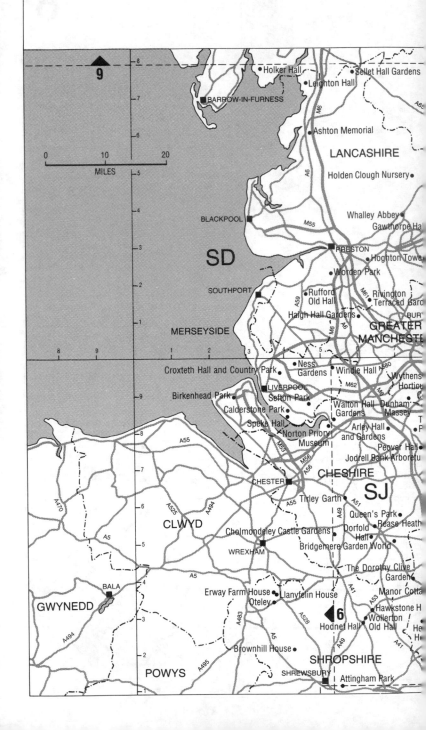

9

8

7

6

LANCASHIRE

0   10   20
MILES

5

4

3

2

1

Holker Hall
Leighton Hall
Sellet Hall Gardens

BARROW-IN-FURNESS

Ashton Memorial

Holden Clough Nursery

Whalley Abbey
Gawthorpe Ha

BLACKPOOL

SD

PRESTON
Hoghton Towe
Worden Park

M55

Rufford
Old Hall
SOUTHPORT
MERSEYSIDE

Rivington
Terraced Gard

Haigh Hall Gardens
GREATER
MANCHESTE

BUR'

8   9   1   2   3   4   5

Croxteth Hall and Country Park
Ness Gardens
Windle Hall
Wythens
Hortic

Birkenhead Park
LIVERPOOL
Sefton Park
Calderstone Park
Speke Hall
Norton Priory
Museum

Walton Hall
Gardens
Dunham
Massey

Arley Hall
and Gardens

Peover Hall
Jodrell Bank Arboretu

CHESTER
CHESHIRE

SJ

Tirley Garth

Queen's Park
Rease Heath

CLWYD
Cholmondeley Castle Gardens
WREXHAM

Dorfold
Hall
Bridgemere Garden World

The Dorothy Clive
Garden

BALA
GWYNEDD

Erway Farm House
Oteley
Llanyfelin House

Manor Cotta

Hawkstone H
Wollerton
Old Hall

6

Hodnet Hall
He
He

Brownhill House

SHROPSHIRE
POWYS
SHREWSBURY
Attingham Park

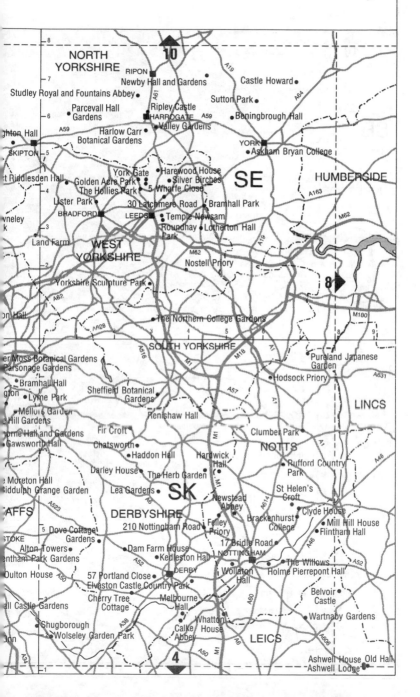

8

NORTH YORKSHIRE

▲
10

RIPON
Newby Hall and Gardens

Castle Howard •

7

Studley Royal and Fountains Abbey •

Sutton Park •

A19

Parcevall Hall
Gardens

Ripley Castle
HARROGATE   A59

• Beningbrough Hall

A64

6

ghton Hall

A59

Harlow Carr
Botanical Gardens

Valley Gardens

YORK
• Askham Bryan College

SKIPTON   5

York Gate

Harewood House
• Silver Birches

SE

A163

HUMBERSIDE

t Riddlesden Hall

Golden Acre Park •
The Hollies Park

5 Wharfe Close

M62

4

Lister Park •

30 Latchmere Road

• Bramhall Park

BRADFORD   LEEDS

• Temple Newsam

wneley
k

3

Land Farm •

**WEST
YORKSHIRE**

Roundhay
Park

• Lotherton Hall

A19

2

Nostell Priory

M62

A62

• Yorkshire Sculpture Park •

8 ▶

on Hall

M180

• The Northern College Gardens

A628

3

4

5

8

8

9

SOUTH YORKSHIRE

A616

M1

M18

A1

er Moss Botanical Gardens
Parsonage Gardens

• Pureland Japanese
Garden

A631

• Bramhall Hall
gton   • Lyme Park

Sheffield Botanical
Gardens

A57

• Hodsock Priory

LINCS

• Mellors Garden
Hill Gardens

Renishaw Hall

A1

rne Hall and Gardens
• Gawsworth Hall

Fir Croft

Chatsworth •

• Clumber Park •

NOTTS

A1

A46

Moreton Hall
ddulph Grange Garden

• Haddon Hall

Darley House •

The Herb Garden

Hardwick
Hall

• Rufford Country
Park

Lea Gardens

SK

M1

St Helen's
Croft

A523

DERBYSHIRE

Newstead
Abbey

A614

AFFS

5

Dove Cottage
Gardens •

210 Nottingham Road •

Felley
Priory

Brackenhurst
College

• Clyde House

• Mill Hill House
• Flintham Hall

STOKE
ntham Park Gardens

Alton Towers •

• Dam Farm House

17 Bridle Road •

A46

A52

oulton House

A50

• Kedleston Hall

NOTTINGHAM

• The Willows

57 Portland Close
Elvaston Castle Country Park

DERBY

Wollaton
Hall

Holme Pierrepont Hall

ll Castle Gardens

3

Cherry Tree
Cottage

Melbourne
Hall

A60

Belvoir
Castle

• Shugborough
• Wolseley Garden Park

A38

Whatton
Calke House
Abbey

A6

• Wartnaby Gardens

A606

on

A34

A50   M1

LEICS

▼
4

Ashwell House Old Hall
Ashwell Lodge

1

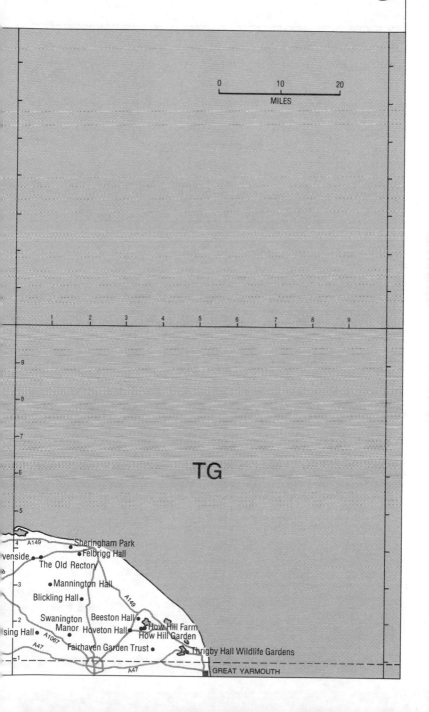

0   10   20
MILES

1   2   3   4   5   6   7   8   9

9

8

7

TG

6

5

4   A149   ●Sheringham Park
venside ●   ●Felbrigg Hall
     The Old Rectory
3   ●Mannington Hall
Blickling Hall ●
      A149
2   Swanington   ●Beeston Hall
    Manor   Hoveton Hall ● ●How Hill Farm
sing Hall ●   A1067   How Hill Garden
   A47   ●Fairhaven Garden Trust ●   🐾 Thrigby Hall Wildlife Gardens
1
      A47   GREAT YARMOUTH

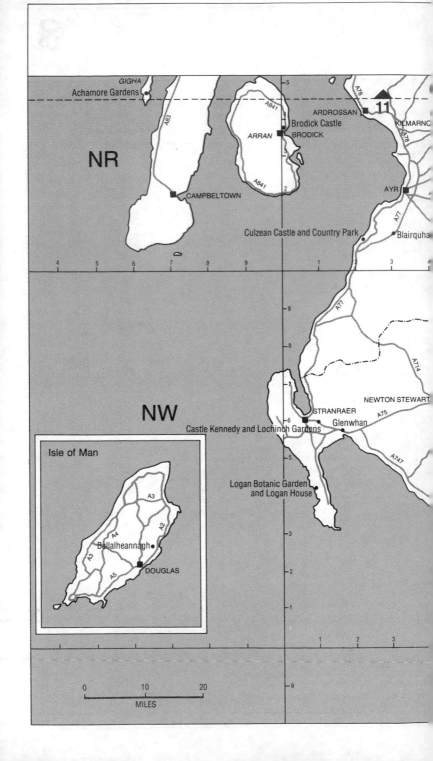

GIGHA
Achamore Gardens

A83

NR

ARRAN

A841

A841

CAMPBELTOWN

5

Brodick Castle
BRODICK

A841

2

Culzean Castle and Country Park

A78

11

ARDROSSAN

KILMARNC

A78

AYR

A77

Blairquha

4   5   6   7   8   9   1   2   3

9

A77

8

A714

NEWTON STEWART

NW

7

6

STRANRAER

A75

Glenwhan

Castle Kennedy and Lochinch Gardens

5

A747

Logan Botanic Garden
and Logan House

3

Isle of Man

A3

A4   A2

Ballalheannagh

A3

A5   DOUGLAS

2

1

1   2   3

9

0   10   20

MILES

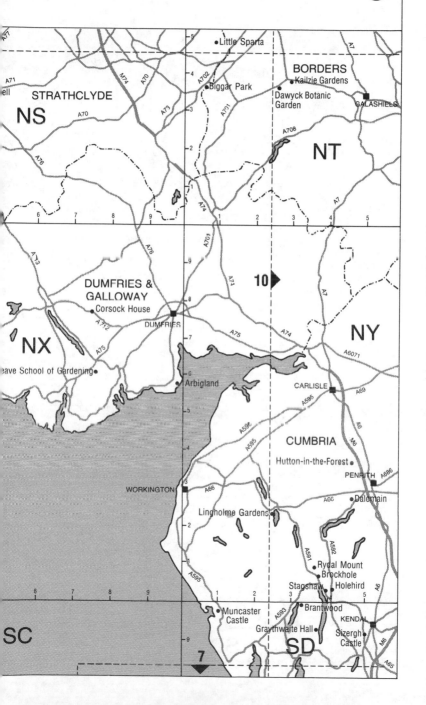

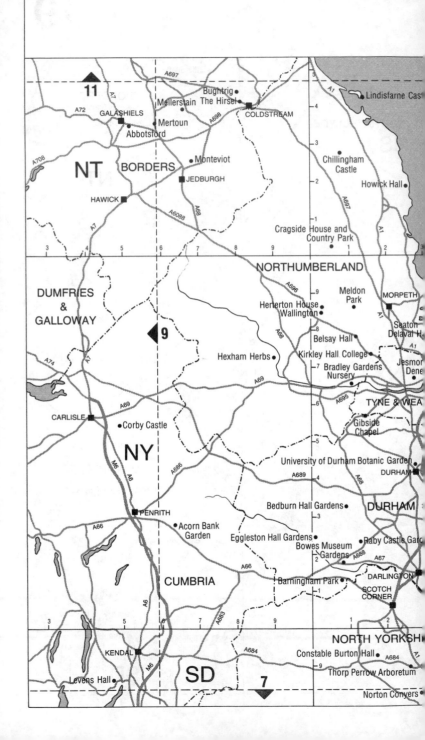

11

A697

A7

Mellerstain

Bughtrig
The Hirsel

Lindisfarne Cast

GALASHIELS

A72

Mertoun

A698

COLDSTREAM

A1

Abbotsford

A708

NT

BORDERS

Monteviot

Chillingham
Castle

JEDBURGH

Howick Hall

HAWICK

A7

A6088

A68

Cragside House and
Country Park

A697

A1

3   4   5   6   7   8   9   1   2

NORTHUMBERLAND

DUMFRIES
&
GALLOWAY

A696

Meldon
Park

9

MORPETH

Herterton House
Wallington

9

A1

Seaton
Delaval H.

A1

A74

A7

A68

Belsay Hall

Kirkley Hall College

8

Hexham Herbs

Bradley Gardens
Nursery

7

A695

Jesmor
Dene

A69

TYNE & WEA

CARLISLE

Corby Castle

6

Gibside
Chapel

NY

A686

5

M6

A6

University of Durham Botanic Garden

A689

4

A68

DURHAM

Bedburn Hall Gardens

3

DURHAM

PENRITH

Acorn Bank
Garden

Raby Castle Gard

A66

Eggleston Hall Gardens

Bowes Museum
Gardens

A688

A67

2

DARLINGTON

CUMBRIA

A66

Barningham Park

1

SCOTCH
CORNER

A683

A6

3   4   5   6   7   8   9   1   2

NORTH YORKSH

KENDAL

M6

A684

Constable Burton Hall

A684

A1

9

SD

7

Thorp Perrow Arboretum

Levens Hall

Norton Conyers

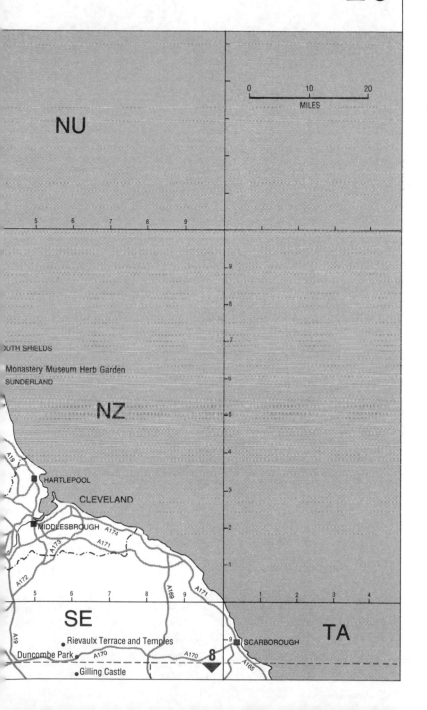

10

NU

0   10   20
MILES

5   6   7   8   9

9

8

7

OUTH SHIELDS

Monastery Museum Herb Garden

SUNDERLAND

6

NZ

5

4

A19

3

HARTLEPOOL

CLEVELAND

MIDDLESBROUGH A174

2

A173

A171

A172

1

5   6   7   8   A169 9 A171

1   2   3   4

SE

A19

Rievaulx Terrace and Temples

Duncombe Park A170   A170 8 A165

Gilling Castle

9 SCARBOROUGH

TA

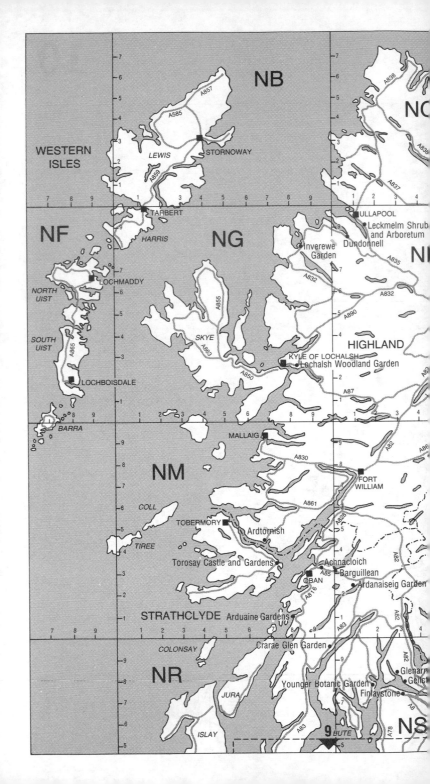

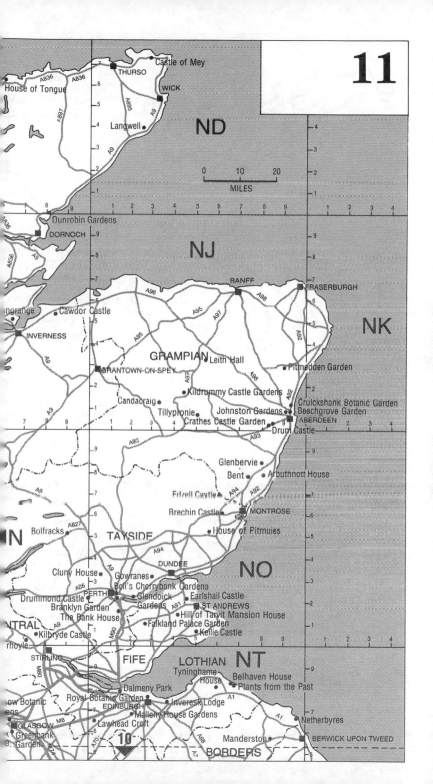

11

House of Tongue

A836 A836
THURSO
Castle of Mey
WICK
A895
A9
Langwell
ND

0   10   20
MILES

8   9   1   2   3   4   5   6   7   8   9   1   2   3   4

Dunrobin Gardens
DORNOCH

NJ

BANFF
FRASERBURGH
A96   A98

ngrange   Cawdor Castle
INVERNESS
A95   A97
A92   NK
A9
A95
GRAMPIAN   Leith Hall
GRANTOWN-ON-SPEY
Pitmedden Garden
A96
A9
Kildrummy Castle Gardens
A92
Candacraig   Cruickshank Botanic Garden
Tillyphonie   Johnston Gardens   Beechgrove Garden
Crathes Castle Garden   ABERDEEN
Drum Castle
A93   A93

Glenbervie
Bent   Arbuthnott House
Edzell Castle   A94   A92
Brechin Castle   MONTROSE
Bolfracks   A827   TAYSIDE
House of Pitmuies

N
Cluny House   A94
DUNDEE
Gowranes   NO
Boll's Cherrybank Gardens
A9
Drummond Castle   PERTH   Glendoick   Earlshall Castle
Branklyn Garden   Gardens   ST ANDREWS
The Bank House   Hill of Tarvit Mansion House
Kilbryde Castle   Falkland Palace Garden   Kellie Castle
NTRAL   A9
M90
hoyle
STIRLING   FIFE
M80   LOTHIAN   NT
Tyninghame   Belhaven House
House   Plants from the Past
Dalmeny Park
ow Botanic   Royal Botanic Garden   Inveresk Lodge
ens   EDINBURGH   A1
Malleny House Gardens
GLASGOW   M8   Lawhead Croft   Netherbyres
Greenbank   A70   A68
Garden   10   Manderston   BERWICK UPON TWEED
A1
BORDERS

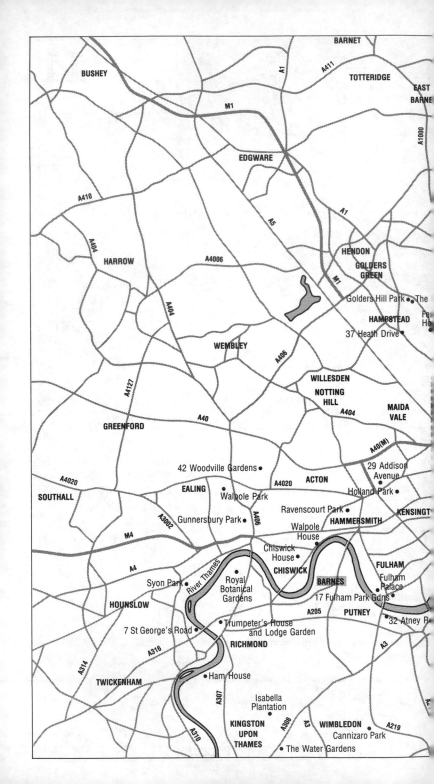

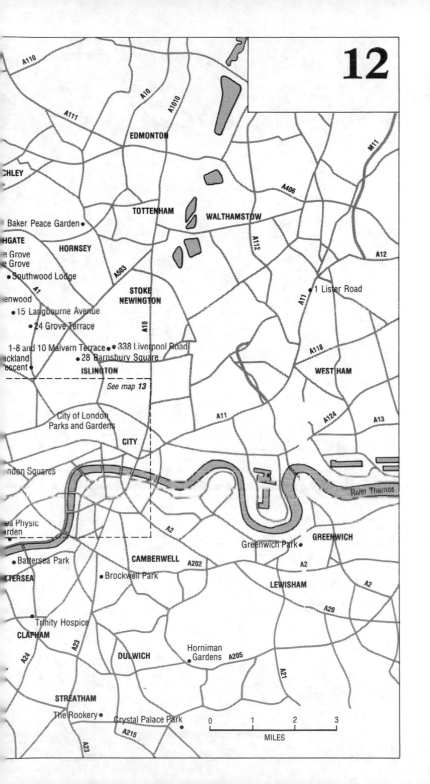

12

A110

A111

A10

A1010

EDMONTON

CHLEY

A406

M11

TOTTENHAM

WALTHAMSTOW

Baker Peace Garden ●

HORNSEY

A112

A12

HGATE

e Grove
e Grove

A503

● Southwood Lodge

A1

STOKE
NEWINGTON

A11

● 1 Lister Road

enwood

● 15 Langbourne Avenue

A10

● 24 Grove Terrace

A118

1-8 and 10 Malvern Terrace ● ● 338 Liverpool Road
ckland   ● 28 Barnsbury Square
escent ●   WEST HAM

ISLINGTON

See map 13

City of London
Parks and Gardens

A11

A124

A13

CITY

ndon Squares

River Thames

ea Physic
rden

A2

GREENWICH

Greenwich Park ●

● Battersea Park

CAMBERWELL

A202

A2

● Brockwell Park

LEWISHAM

A2

TERSEA

A20

● Trinity Hospice

CLAPHAM

A23

Horniman
Gardens

A205

A24

DULWICH

A21

STREATHAM

The Rookery ●   Crystal Palace Park ●

0   1   2   3

A215

MILES

A23

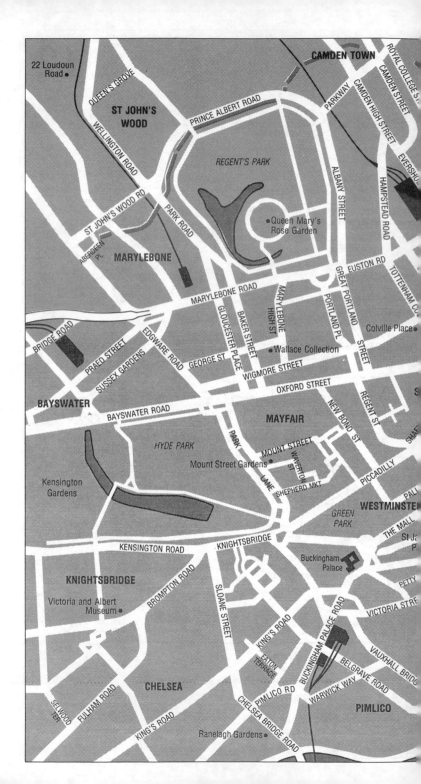

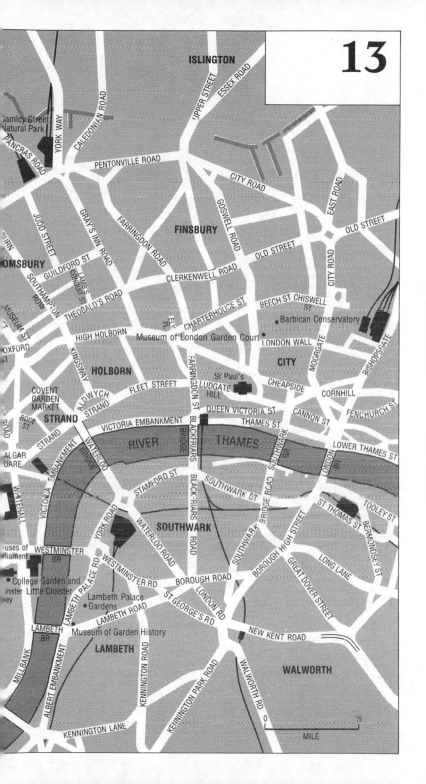

ISLINGTON

romley Street
Natural Park

PANCRAS ROAD

YORK WAY

CALEDONIAN ROAD

UPPER STREET

ESSEX ROAD

PENTONVILLE ROAD

CITY ROAD

EAST ROAD

OLD STREET

JUDD STREET

GRAY'S INN ROAD

FARRINGDON ROAD

GOSWELL ROAD

FINSBURY

OLD STREET

CITY ROAD

3URN

OMSBURY

GUILDFORD ST

SOUTHAMPTON ROW

LAMB'S CONDUIT ST

THEOBALD'S ROAD

CLERKENWELL ROAD

CHARTERHOUSE ST

BEECH ST CHISWELL
ST

MUSEUM ST

HIGH HOLBORN

ELY PL

Barbican Conservatory

Museum of London Garden Court

LONDON WALL

MOORGATE

BISHOPSGATE

OXFORD
St

KINGSWAY

HOLBORN

ALDWYCH

FLEET STREET

FARRINGDON ST

St Paul's
LUDGATE
HILL

CITY

CHEAPSIDE

CORNHILL

FENCHURCH ST

COVENT
GARDEN
MARKET

ROSE
ST

STRAND

STRAND

VICTORIA EMBANKMENT

Queen Victoria St

CANNON ST

THAMES ST

LOWER THAMES ST

ALGAR
UARE

STRAND

WATERLOO BRIDGE

VICTORIA EMBANKMENT

BLACKFRIARS BRIDGE

RIVER   THAMES

SOUTHWARK BR

LONDON BR

STAMFORD ST

BLACKFRIARS ROAD

SOUTHWARK ST

ST THOMAS ST

TOOLEY ST

WHITEHALL

VICTORIA EMBANKMENT

WATERLOO BRIDGE

YORK ROAD

WATERLOO ROAD

SOUTHWARK

SOUTHWARK BRIDGE ROAD

BOROUGH HIGH STREET

GREAT DOVER STREET

BERMONDSEY ST

LONG LANE

uses of
Parliament

WESTMINSTER
BR

WESTMINSTER RD

BOROUGH ROAD

LONDON RD

College Garden and
inster Little Cloister
ey

LAMBETH PALACE RD

Lambeth Palace
Gardens

LAMBETH ROAD

ST GEORGE'S RD

NEW KENT ROAD

LAMBETH
BR

Museum of Garden History

LAMBETH

MILLBANK

ALBERT EMBANKMENT

KENNINGTON ROAD

ST GEORGE'S RD

KENNINGTON PARK ROAD

WALWORTH RD

WALWORTH

KENNINGTON LANE

0   ½

MILE

INDEX

Glossary of Garden Terms

Bath house A rectangular sunken pool for cold water bathing, with seating approached by steps.

Belvedere A high point on a building, or a summerhouse, which commands a beautiful view.

Bosket A block of very closely planted trees.

Claire-voyée A gap in a wall or hedge which extends the view by allowing a glimpse of the surrounding countryside.

Exedra An area of turf within a semi-circular hedge which is usually used to display ornaments or locate a semi-circular seat; or the seat itself.

Finial An ornament such as an urn or a pointed sculptural form used to cap features like gateposts, the tops of spires, the top corners of buildings, etc.

Folly A decorative building with no serious function except perhaps to lure attention along a vista or to improve the composition of the garden 'picture'.

Gazebo Dog latin for 'I will gaze', used to describe a building usually sited on a high terrace from which the surrounding landscape can be enjoyed.

Ha-ha A deep ditch separating the garden from the landscape beyond. It allows the unscreened view to be enjoyed from the house but is profiled in such a way that livestock cannot enter the garden.

Knot garden Geometric patterns of low growing hedge plants such as box or shrubby germander which are made to appear as though they intertwine like knotted cord. The areas between the hedges are filled with plants or decorative gravels.

Mount An artificial hill usually surmounted by an arbour from which landscapes both inside and beyond the garden can be enjoyed from a different perspective.

Palisade A tall hedge of deciduous trees or shrubs with interlaced branches.

Parterre An intricately patterned formal garden which usually includes other features such as statuary, water basins and fountains, much larger than a knot garden.

Patte d'oie Literally 'goose foot'; a series of usually three formal paths or grand avenues leading fan-wise from a single point through densely planted trees.

Pleaching Training the branches of a line of trees horizontally by pruning and attaching them to canes and wires, so that the remainder can be intertwined as they grow to form a screen of foliage.

Ribbon bed A very narrow band of bedding plants which the Victorians were fond of using to border their lawns.

Rustic work Garden features such as garden houses, fences or seats made from unbarked tree branches frequently embellished with such decoration as patterns made from sectioned pine cones.

Stilt hedge Clipped trees, such as limes, which have all branches removed for several feet above the ground to reveal a line of bare trunks like stilts.

Tapis vert A long strip of lawn between paths or canals.

Théâtre de verdure Similar to ... usually more spacious than an exedr... turf 'stage' with a back cloth of trim... hedge and sometimes other hedge... posed like the wings of a theatre.

Treillage Architectural features suc... as arbours, obelisks or ambitious screens made out of trellis.

Trompe l'oeil A feature designed to deceive the eye, such as a path which narrows as it recedes from a viewpoint to exaggerate the perspective and make the garden seem larger.

Report Form

The next edition of the *Guide* will be improved if readers will write to tell us

(i) if gardens are not included which you think should be
(ii) if you visit a garden in the guide and want to confirm its merits or propose an up-grading
(iii) if you visit a garden and believe its merits are overestimated by our inspector.

The form at the end of the guide can be used for this purpose, or you may just send your comments on a sheet of paper. Handwriting is not always distinct, so if possible please print difficult words or Latin names for plants. Also please print your name clearly. All those who write will help to improve the standards of garden visiting by making good gardens open to the public known to a wider circle. The great thing is to enjoy your garden visiting, just as our inspectors have done. Happy visiting in 1992.

Send your comments to **The Good Gardens Guide**
Vermilion
Random Century House
20 Vauxhall Bridge Road
London SW1V 2SA

Good Gardens Guide Report Form

To the Editors of the Good Gardens Guide:
From my own experience the following garden should/should not be included in the *Guide*

I GARDEN NAME

    Address line 1

    Address line 2

        etc

    Telephone:

    Name of owner(s):

II DESCRIPTION

    1. Location:

    2. Opening times:

    3. Best season:

    4. Entrance charge:

    5. Plants for sale:

    6. House open / times:

    7. Type of garden:

    8. Features / condition:

    9. Brief details of its main characteristics.